Great Dishes
of the World
in Color

GALAHAD BOOKS · NEW YORK

Illustrations by *John Scott-Martin*

Photography by
Eric Carter
Christian Délu
Irwin Horowitz
Arne Krüger
John Lee
John Miller

Edited by Jennifer Feller

Published by
Galahad Books
a division of A & W Promotional Book Corporation
95 Madison Avenue, New York, NY 10016
Library of Congress Catalog Card Number: 76–11593
ISBN: 0–88365–369–9
© Copyright The Hamlyn Publishing Group Limited 1976

Some material in this book has already been published
in *The World of Food* series:
Provincial France (First printing 1972)
Italy (First printing 1973)
China (First printing 1973)
Published by
The World Publishing Company, New York
Published simultaneously in Canada by
Nelson, Foster & Scott Ltd.

Printed in England by Jarrold and Sons Limited, Norwich

CONTENTS

INTRODUCTION

Today people have broadened their horizons through travel and this has had an immense influence over their food habits. It is not surprising, therefore, that in kitchens and on tables everywhere exotic foods and foreign dishes are making their appearance where two or three decades ago they would have been unknown and unthought of. As horizons narrow, all the world becomes one's heritage.

The shapes and colors of the four corners of the earth are being fed into our senses through the media almost every hour of the day. But it is only in the kitchen that we have the complete freedom to experiment and concoct and bring home the flavors of distant lands. For the adventurous and the romantically inclined, these experiments and experiences are ones which can hardly be denied. It can give great pleasure and satisfaction to dine off dishes normally served in hot desert lands or cooked by the lagoons of the Pacific islands. Or to prepare Soochow Melon Chicken or Peking Duck for a special celebration. The long winter months are ideally suited to provide the time and opportunity to enliven our existence by creating the flavors and foods of places and holidays we have known, and preparing for places we intend to go to and the holidays we dream about. Dreams, after all, give life its silver lining. Although we cannot go everywhere, we can cook the food of many countries.

In this book, the food and cooking of many regions of the world are brought between two covers, an unrivaled culinary 'package tour' of famous and fabled areas with all their intriguing color, history, geography and traditions.

In the dishes of Scandinavia one can feel the North Sea swelling off the rocky shores of Norway and see the Baltic lapping against that inimitable seafront at Copenhagen and the countless islands which cluster around the approaches to Stockholm, where the fish and seafoods hauled in from the shallows are as fresh as they are sweet. The British Isles have many traditional dishes, uninfluenced by French and other continental practices, which are genuinely reflective of the taste of Elizabethan times and the spacious days of the Victorian and Edwardian eras. In the classical and regional dishes of France, one cannot help but feel a sense of history – that flavor of the Grand Siècle – which reflects the grandeur of Europe's recent past. The same applies to the more robust German dishes – which must beckon continually to all with healthy appetites – culled from the many picturesque regions of Germany. Equally, the Spanish, Italian, Jewish dishes and those from the Eastern Mediterranean are steeped in the history and geography of all those famous and colorful countries.

In China one has an entirely different continent, with a distinct culinary history and tradition of its own, which perhaps because of its extensive range, unique refinement and unparalleled vigor, has engendered a momentum which is only now being felt throughout the five continents of the world. In the Far Eastern dishes one becomes aware of the immensity of the Pacific and the lifestyles of its many peoples. Not least of all are the food and cooking of the United States, in which one can sense this vast territory, spreading from 'sea to shining sea' across the grain-laden plains of the Middle West, and feel the vitality of the teeming cities, from New York to New Orleans, from Philadelphia to San Francisco.

Kenneth H. C. Lo

AMERICAN

Ann Seranne

Photography by Irwin Horowitz

The United States is a land of many moods and many cultures. Within its fifty states reside first and second generation ethnic groups from almost all the other countries of the world. Since the first Pilgrim ships arrived with their cargo of religious and political refugees from England, the United States has become a melting pot of immigrants. All these groups – and the original settlers, the American Indians – have contributed to American cooking to make it nutritious, varied and interesting.

Once the problems of survival were solved, and after the horrendous 'Starving Times' of Jamestown and Plymouth, American women fed their families remarkably well. They dealt ingeniously with native food products, and made the best of whatever was available from land, forest, lake or sea, until permanent settlements were established and the soil was cultivated to produce truly American crops such as maize or Indian corn. It was corn that sustained the Pilgrims and nourished those adventuresome frontiersmen who crossed the plains and moved west in covered wagons to conquer new territories. Beans and peas, pumpkins and many varieties of vegetable marrow, watermelon and other types of melons, sweet potatoes and cranberries are other native foods which have played an important role, not only in the cooking of America but in the cooking of the world.

The Pilgrims learned from the Indians how to use these crops and today some favorite dishes are still based on those original recipes, most of which have been improved over the years and modified to meet the demands of more sophisticated palates.

Generally speaking, a cook in any part of the United States can duplicate the typical dishes of any area in her home kitchen; dishes such as Louisiana gumbo, Boston baked beans, Texas barbecued beef, California Crab Louis salad or Minnesota wild rice casserole. She has at her fingertips not only a bewildering assortment of American food products, but the best from almost every country in the world.

The American cook is quick to embrace new combinations of flavors and to experiment with different herbs and spices, exotic fruits and vegetables. She has learned to be creative with fish and the inexpensive cuts of meat, and has become proficient in the preparation of many so-called 'gourmet' dishes. Classic methods of food preparation have been simplified by the use of electric appliances designed to take the work out of cooking. Imaginative substitutions are used for obscure ingredients. Such prepared foods as soy sauce, canned water chestnuts and bean sprouts have become staples in many American kitchens, taking their place beside the many convenience foods such as canned broths, gravies, tomato products, dried cereals and pastas.

American cooking has come a long way from the 'meat and potato' era, to a knowledgeable age of curiosity in cooking, resulting in an enormous variety of dishes. Despite American food manufacturers who spend billions of dollars on new products devised to 'keep the cook out of the kitchen', American women and a surprising number of men live to cook rather than cook to live, and it is they who have been instrumental in raising the standard of cooking in the United States to an all-time high. The recipes in this section represent the best to be found in American homes across the nation.

SPARE RIBS WITH MONTANA SAUCE

Serves 4

4–4½ lb spare ribs	1 teaspoon sugar
for the sauce:	1½ teaspoons salt
1 small onion	2 teaspoons chili powder
1 clove garlic	¼ teaspoon cayenne pepper
½ cup butter	2 teaspoons Worcestershire sauce
1 cup water	¼ teaspoon Tabasco sauce
¼ cup vinegar	1 teaspoon black pepper
1 teaspoon dry mustard	1 teaspoon paprika

To precook the spare ribs and make them moist and juicy, spread the spare ribs in a large roasting pan, cover tightly with aluminum foil and bake the ribs in a preheated moderate oven (350°) for 1½ hours. Meanwhile, prepare the sauce. Peel and finely chop the onion and garlic. Place in a saucepan with the butter, water and vinegar. Add the mustard, sugar, salt, chili powder, cayenne pepper, Worcestershire sauce, Tabasco sauce, black pepper and paprika. Bring to a boil and simmer for 30 minutes.

When the spare ribs have cooked for the required time, remove the foil and baste the ribs with the sauce. Continue cooking for a further 30 minutes, turning the spare ribs from time to time in the sauce.

Note: This sauce may be used to baste steaks, chops or chicken while roasting or barbecuing.

OYSTERS ROCKEFELLER

Serves 4

1 stalk celery	2 tablespoons Pernod or anisette
6 scallions	1 tablespoon Worcestershire sauce
1 small clove garlic	salt
1 cup butter	freshly ground black pepper
¼ cup chopped parsley	cayenne pepper
2 cups chopped cooked spinach	rock salt (see recipe)
¼ teaspoon anise seed	24 freshly shucked oysters on
⅓ cup toast crumbs	half shell

Chop the celery very finely, chop the scallions and peel and crush the garlic. Melt the butter in a skillet and sauté the celery, scallions, garlic and parsley for about 4 minutes, or until the vegetables are softened. Transfer the mixture to a blender and add the spinach, anise seed, toast crumbs, Pernod and Worcestershire sauce. Add salt, pepper and cayenne pepper to taste. Blend until the sauce is thoroughly puréed. If a blender is not available, rub the ingredients through a sieve or pound in a mortar until reduced to a pulp.

Spread a thick layer of rock salt on each of 4 individual gratin dishes. Arrange 6 oysters on each dish. Spread 1 tablespoon of the sauce over each oyster, spreading it to the edge of the shell. Place the dishes in a preheated very hot oven (450°) and bake for 5 minutes, or until the sauce bubbles.

7

ISLAND SHRIMP

Serves 4

1 lb raw shrimp	½ cup lime juice or
3 cloves garlic	¾ cup lemon juice
3 fresh or dried chilies	1 teaspoon salt

Put the shrimp into a saucepan with salted water to cover. Bring to a boil and simmer gently for 5 minutes. Drain and put the shrimp immediately into iced water. Peel and remove the dark vein running down the back of each shrimp. Peel and finely chop the garlic and finely chop the chilies.

Put the shrimp into a glass bowl and sprinkle with the garlic, chilies, lime juice and salt. Marinate the shrimp in the refrigerator for several hours before serving. Impale each shrimp on a cocktail stick and serve very cold as an appetizer.

OLYMPIA OYSTER COCKTAIL

Serves about 10

1 quart freshly shucked Olympia oysters	2 tablespoons lemon juice
4 stalks celery	2 teaspoons Worcestershire sauce
½ cup chili sauce	¼ teaspoon Tabasco sauce

Rinse the oysters well. Pick out any little bits of shell. Finely chop the celery and combine with the chili sauce, lemon juice, Worcestershire sauce and Tabasco sauce. Stir in the oysters. Spoon the mixture into individual glasses and chill well before serving.

GUACAMOLE

Makes about 1¼ cups

1 large avocado	2 teaspoons finely chopped onion
1 small clove garlic	¼ teaspoon salt
1 tablespoon olive oil	¼ teaspoon freshly ground pepper
1 tablespoon lemon juice	Tabasco sauce to taste

Peel the avocado, remove the pit and set it aside. Place the flesh in a bowl. Peel and crush the garlic. Mash the avocado coarsely with a silver fork to prevent discoloration and mix in the garlic, olive oil, lemon juice, onion, salt and pepper. Season the mixture generously with Tabasco sauce to taste. Place the pit in the mixture until ready to serve to prevent discoloration. Cover the bowl and place in the refrigerator until chilled. Discard the pit and serve the avocado as a dip with crisp raw vegetables or small savory crackers.

Island shrimp

FLORIDA FROGS' LEGS

Serves 2–3

12 pairs frogs' legs	¼ cup butter
½ cup all-purpose flour	1 small clove garlic
½ teaspoon salt	2 tablespoons lemon juice
¼ teaspoon pepper	watercress
bacon drippings	radish roses

Soak the frogs' legs in lightly salted water for 2 hours. Combine the flour, salt and pepper. Drain the legs, dry on absorbent paper and then roll in the seasoned flour. Sauté the legs in hot bacon drippings in a skillet for about 7 minutes, turning frequently. Arrange on a heated serving dish.

Pour off all the bacon drippings and add the butter to the skillet. Peel and finely chop the garlic and sauté in the butter over moderate heat. As soon as the butter bubbles and begins to turn brown, stir in the lemon juice. Pour the sauce immediately over the frogs' legs and garnish with watercress and radish roses. (To make radish roses see Danish Blue Cheese and Radish open sandwich, page 80.)

DAKOTA CORNED BEEF SAUERKRAUT BALLS

Makes 50 balls

1 (1-lb) can sauerkraut	¾ cup milk
1½ cups water	½ cup dry breadcrumbs
1 small onion	2 eggs
1 (12-oz) can corned beef	flour (see recipe)
¼ cup butter	fine dry breadcrumbs for
¼ cup all-purpose flour	coating
¼ teaspoon dry mustard	oil for deep-frying
1 teaspoon grated fresh	
horseradish root	

Empty the sauerkraut into a saucepan and add the water. Bring to a boil and simmer for 15 minutes. Peel and quarter the onion. Drain the sauerkraut thoroughly and put through the medium blade of a food shredder or chop with a sharp knife, along with the corned beef and the onion.

Melt the butter in a saucepan. Stir in the flour, mustard and horseradish. Gradually stir in the milk and cook, stirring constantly, until the sauce is smooth and very thick. Add the sauerkraut mixture and cook over low heat for 10 minutes, stirring occasionally. Stir in the breadcrumbs and cook for a few minutes longer. Chill for several hours or overnight.

Beat the eggs. Form the sauerkraut mixture into 1-inch balls. Roll the balls in flour, dip in the beaten egg then roll in breadcrumbs. Heat the oil in a deep saucepan to 365° and fry the balls for 3–4 minutes, or until crisp and golden brown. Drain on absorbent paper. Serve as an appetizer.

Note: These may be made before required and refrigerated or frozen. Reheat in a moderately hot oven (400°) for 10 minutes before serving.

COLD CREAM OF CUCUMBER SOUP

Serves 6

3 cucumbers
1 medium-sized onion
1 cup water
½ teaspoon dried dill weed or mint
½ teaspoon salt
dash white pepper
3 tablespoons all-purpose flour
2 cups chicken stock
1 cup heavy cream
2 drops green food coloring

for the garnish:

1 thin cucumber
6 tablespoons cultured sour cream
fresh dill or mint

Peel and slice the cucumbers. Peel and dice the onion. Place the cucumbers and onion in a large saucepan and add the water, dill weed or mint, salt and pepper. Bring to a boil and simmer for 20 minutes, or until the cucumbers and onion are tender. Blend the flour with a little of the chicken stock to make a thin paste and stir into the cucumbers with the remaining chicken stock. Bring to a boil and simmer for 30 minutes. Press through a sieve or blend, half at a time, in a blender to make a purée. Cool and chill. Before serving, stir in the cream and food coloring and correct the seasoning with salt and pepper.

Serve in individual soup plates garnished with unpeeled, thinly sliced raw cucumber, 1 tablespoon of sour cream for each serving and a sprinkling of chopped dill or mint.

CORN CHOWDER

Serves 4

1 large onion
4 large potatoes
2 slices salt pork
3 cups water
6 soda crackers
1 cup rich milk (half cream, half milk)
8 oz fresh or frozen corn kernels
salt and pepper
paprika

Peel and chop the onion. Peel and dice the potatoes. Cut the pork into small cubes and sauté in a large saucepan until crisp and golden brown. Add the onion and cook until soft and transparent. Add the potatoes and water. Bring to a boil and simmer for 20 minutes, or until the potatoes are tender.

Meanwhile, crumble the soda crackers into the rich milk and set aside to soften. When the potatoes are tender, add the softened crackers and the corn. Season with salt and pepper to taste and cook over low heat for 5–10 minutes without boiling. Serve each portion with a sprinkling of paprika on top.

Note: The first corn chowder was made in Massachusetts. Now, in some parts of the country, chopped green sweet pepper is added; in other parts bits of tomato are added for flavor and color.

Corn chowder

NEW ENGLAND CLAM CHOWDER

Serves 6

1 quart fresh chowder clams or quahogs, or 2 (8-oz) cans minced clams (see note)	3 medium-sized potatoes
	2 slices salt pork
	1 small onion
1 stalk celery with leaves	1 stalk celery
1 medium-sized onion	salt and pepper
1 small bay leaf	2 cups light cream
dash thyme	2 tablespoons butter
6 cups cold water	paprika

Scrub the clams and place in a large saucepan. Chop the celery coarsely, peel and dice the onion. Place in the pan with the clams and add the bay leaf, thyme and water. Bring to a boil, cover the pan tightly and cook for 10 minutes, or until the shells open. Remove the clams and discard the shells. Strain the clam liquid into a large saucepan through a sieve lined with cheesecloth. Discard the strained vegetables and the bay leaf. Peel and cube the potatoes and simmer in the clam liquid for 20 minutes, or until tender.

Meanwhile, peel back the tough outer sheath from the soft belly of each clam and cut away the connecting cord. Dice the bellies and mince the tough outer sheaths. Cover with a little of the hot clam liquid and set aside.

Chop the salt pork and fry in a large saucepan until crisp and golden brown. Chop the onion and thinly slice the celery, add to the salt pork and cook over low heat for 10 minutes, or until the vegetables are tender. Add the clam liquid and potatoes, then simmer for 5–10 minutes longer. Season with salt and pepper to taste. Heat the cream. Just before serving, stir in the clams, butter and hot cream. Heat, but do not boil. Serve immediately in large heated soup bowls, sprinkling each serving with paprika. Serve with oyster crackers.

Note: To make a chowder with canned minced clams, drain the liquid from the clams into the saucepan, reserving the clams, and follow the recipe, adding a little water for additional liquid to cover the potatoes as they cook.

PHILADELPHIA PEPPERPOT SOUP WITH DUMPLINGS

Serves 8

for the soup:	salt and pepper
2 lb dressed honeycomb tripe	generous dash cayenne pepper
1 veal hock with meat	**for the dumplings:**
1 large onion	2 cups all-purpose flour
1 carrot	½ teaspoon salt
4 medium-sized potatoes	1 cup chopped beef suet
1 bay leaf	about ⅔ cup water
few sprigs parsley	1 tablespoon finely chopped
½ teaspoon thyme	parsley
½ teaspoon crushed red chili	

The preparation of this dish should be commenced the day before it is required. Ask your butcher how much longer the tripe needs to be cooked. Put it into a heavy saucepan with 6 pints of water and bring to a boil. Reduce the heat, cover and barely simmer for the required length of time, or until the tripe is tender. Let the tripe cool in the stock. When cool enough to handle, remove the tripe and cut into small pieces. Strain and reserve the stock, which should measure about 4 pints.

While the tripe is cooking, wash the veal hock and put it into another heavy saucepan with water to cover. Bring the water to a boil and remove any scum that rises to the surface. Reduce the heat and simmer for 3 hours. Cool, then remove the meat from the veal bone and cut into small pieces. Add the veal meat to the tripe. Strain the veal stock into the tripe stock. Place the meat and stock in the refrigerator overnight.

Next day, remove any solidified fat from the surface of the stock and return the stock to the saucepan. Peel and dice the onion and carrot and add to the stock. Bring to a boil and simmer for 1 hour. Peel and dice the potatoes. Add the tripe and veal, potatoes, bay leaf, parsley, thyme, crushed chili, salt and pepper to taste and cayenne pepper. The soup should be quite peppery. Continue to simmer for 45 minutes.

While the soup simmers, make the dumplings. Sift the flour and salt into a bowl. Add the suet and mix with a pastry blender or 2 knives or rub in with the fingertips until evenly mixed. Stir in just enough water to make a soft dough that can be rolled with floured fingers into nuggets the size of walnuts. Drop the dumplings into the simmering soup, cover the pan tightly and simmer for 10 minutes. Pour into a heated soup tureen, sprinkle with chopped parsley and serve.

BRUNSWICK STEW

Serves 8

1 chicken, about 5 lb	12 oz fresh okra or
salt and pepper	2 (10-oz) packages frozen okra
4 quarts water	1 lb fresh or frozen corn kernels
2 medium-sized onions	2 teaspoons salt
1 lb potatoes	½ teaspoon pepper
1½ lb tomatoes	1 tablespoon sugar
1½ lb shelled lima beans	

Cut the chicken into eight portions and season well. Place in a large saucepan, add the water and bring to a boil. Simmer the chicken for 1½ hours, or until the flesh is easily removed from the bones. Remove the chicken with a perforated spoon and when cool enough to handle, discard the bones and cut the meat into bite-sized pieces. Set aside.

Peel and slice the onions, peel and dice the potatoes and peel and chop the tomatoes. Add to the broth remaining in the pan with the lima beans and okra. Bring to a boil and cook over low heat until the vegetables are tender, stirring occasionally. Pour in a little hot water if necessary, to make a total of at least 4 pints of liquid. Add the reserved chicken meat, the corn, salt, pepper and sugar. Simmer for 15 minutes. Serve hot.

LOBSTER STEW

Serves 3

3 quarts water	½ cup butter
3 tablespoons salt	1 quart hot rich milk (half milk,
1 live lobster, about 1½ lb	half cream)

Bring the water and salt to a rapid boil in a large saucepan. Plunge the live lobster head first into the water. Cover and cook for 8 minutes. Remove from the water and set aside to cool. When the lobster has cooled sufficiently to handle easily, split the body in half lengthwise and crack the claws. Remove the meat, discarding the gills, the intestinal vein that runs down the tail and the sac lying in the back of the head. Cut the meat into good-sized chunks. Save the green liver and the pink coral, if any.

Melt the butter in a heavy saucepan and simmer the liver and coral for 6 minutes. Add the lobster pieces and cook over very low heat for 5–10 minutes. Remove the pan from the heat and cool slightly. Slowly trickle in the milk, stirring constantly. Stirring is the most important part of this recipe, since curdling can take place unless the stew is stirred while adding the milk. Continue to stir until the stew becomes an attractive pink. Remove from the heat, cool, cover and refrigerate for 5–6 hours before reheating and serving.

GRAND CENTRAL STATION OYSTER BAR STEW

Serves 4–6

2 cups light cream	2 tablespoons butter
2 cups milk	salt and pepper
1 quart freshly shucked	celery salt
oysters with their liquid	paprika

Heat the cream and milk together in a saucepan but do not boil. Heat the oysters and their liquid with the butter in another saucepan until the oysters plump and the edges begin to curl. Remove from the heat immediately. Combine the hot cream mixture with the hot oysters and liquid. Season with salt, pepper and celery salt to taste. Pour into heated soup bowls and sprinkle with paprika. Serve with oyster crackers.

Note: The Oyster Bar in Grand Central Station opened in 1912. It is still a favorite stopping-off place for commuters who enjoy this dish made according to the original recipe.

Lobster stew

ALASKAN SALMON SUPPER LOAF

Serves 6–8

2 (1-lb) cans salmon	¼ teaspoon pepper
1 large onion	3 tablespoons chopped parsley
4 stalks celery	4 teaspoons grated lemon rind
¼ cup butter or margarine	¼ cup lemon juice
8 oz mushrooms	2 eggs
2 cups fine fresh breadcrumbs	½ cup milk
½ teaspoon salt	1½ lb potatoes

Flake the salmon, reserving the liquid. Peel and chop the onion and chop the celery. Heat the butter in a skillet and sauté the celery and onion in the butter for 10 minutes, or until tender. Peel and coarsely chop the mushrooms and sauté for 5 minutes with the celery and onion, stirring frequently. Combine the cooked vegetables with the breadcrumbs in a mixing bowl. Add the salmon, the reserved salmon liquid, salt and pepper, parsley, lemon rind and lemon juice. Lightly beat the eggs and add to the salmon mixture with the milk.

Grease a large loaf pan or line the base with waxed paper. Fill with the salmon mixture. Bake in a preheated moderately hot oven (375°) for 50 minutes.

Meanwhile, peel the potatoes and boil in salted water to cover until tender. Drain and cream with a little milk and butter. Keep warm until required.

Turn out the salmon loaf on to a heated serving platter. Remove the paper (if used) and garnish the top with creamed potato. Broil under moderate heat for about 3 minutes, or until the potato topping is tinged with brown.

SHRIMP CREOLE

Serves 6

1 large onion	dash cayenne pepper
2 cloves garlic	1 bay leaf, crushed
⅓ cup cooking oil	1 large green sweet pepper
1½ tablespoons all-purpose flour	¼ cup finely chopped parsley
⅓ cup tomato paste	3 tablespoons chopped scallion
1 (1-lb 12-oz) can tomatoes	tops
1 teaspoon salt	2 lb fresh or frozen raw shrimp,
¼ teaspoon pepper	shelled and deveined

Peel and very finely chop the onion and garlic. Heat the oil in a heavy saucepan and sauté the onion and garlic for about 5 minutes until transparent but not brown. Mix in the flour and cook, stirring constantly, until the mixture becomes lightly browned. Add the tomato paste, the tomatoes with their liquid, salt, pepper, cayenne pepper and the bay leaf. Bring to a boil, cover and simmer for 20 minutes. Halve the sweet pepper, remove the seeds and finely chop the flesh. Place in the pan with the parsley, scallion tops and shrimp. Cover and simmer for 15 minutes longer. Serve over cooked rice with a tossed green salad.

13

LOBSTER NEWBURG

Serves 2–3

2 tablespoons butter	cayenne pepper
12 oz cooked lobster meat in large chunks	1 cup heavy cream
	½ cup sherry or Madeira
salt	3 egg yolks

Heat the butter in a heavy saucepan and sauté the lobster meat for several minutes, or until heated through. Sprinkle with salt and cayenne pepper to taste. Add the cream and sherry and bring the liquid to simmering point. Lightly beat the egg yolks and combine with a little of the hot liquid, then stir into the lobster mixture. Cook over very low heat for about 2 minutes, stirring constantly, but do not boil. Serve on hot buttered toast or with cooked rice.

FILLETS OF SOLE MARGUERY

Serves 6

for the fish:

6 fillets of sole or flounder	12 fresh shrimp, shelled and deveined
salt and white pepper	**for the sauce:**
3 tablespoons melted butter	6 tablespoons butter
½ cup clam juice or fish stock	2 tablespoons all-purpose flour
1 cup dry white wine	1 cup milk
2 tablespoons lemon juice	¼ cup heavy cream
for the garnish:	salt
12 freshly shucked oysters with their liquid	2 egg yolks

Arrange the fillets side by side in a buttered skillet and sprinkle with salt, pepper and the melted butter. Pour the clam juice, wine and lemon juice around the fillets. Cover and poach over low heat for 10 minutes, basting occasionally. With a broad spatula carefully transfer the cooked fillets to a heated ovenproof serving dish; cover and keep warm. Bring the poaching liquid to a boil and boil until the liquid is reduced to about ½ cup.

Meanwhile, in a separate pan poach the oysters in their own liquid, just until they plump and the edges curl. Drain the oyster liquid into the skillet and boil again to reduce the volume of liquid. Arrange the oysters on top of the fillets. Poach the shrimp in water to cover for 5 minutes, drain and arrange around the fillets.

Melt one-third of the butter for the sauce in a heavy saucepan. Stir in the flour. Gradually stir in the milk and cook, stirring, until the sauce is smooth and thickened. Stir in the cream and add the reduced liquid. Cook over low heat for 5 minutes, stirring occasionally. Correct the seasoning with salt to taste. Combine the egg yolks with a little of the hot cream sauce, then stir into the remaining sauce. Stir over low heat while adding the remaining butter, little by little. Do not let the sauce boil. Pour the sauce over the fillets and put under the broiler for 2–3 minutes, or until the sauce becomes tinged with brown.

BAKED RED SNAPPER

Serves 4

1 red snapper, about 3 lb	1 large onion
salt and pepper	1½ lb tomatoes
½ teaspoon dry mustard	2 tablespoons finely chopped parsley
¼ cup bacon drippings	
1 tablespoon all-purpose flour	1 teaspoon sugar

Clean, wash and thoroughly dry the red snapper. Rub the fish inside and out with salt, pepper and mustard. Place in a greased roasting pan and brush with 1 teaspoon of the bacon drippings. Sprinkle with the flour. Bake in a preheated moderately hot oven (375°) for 15 minutes, then reduce the heat to moderate (350°).

Meanwhile, peel and finely chop the onion and sauté in the remaining bacon drippings in a skillet until transparent. Peel and chop the tomatoes and add with the parsley and sugar to the skillet. Bring to a boil and simmer for 5 minutes. Season the tomato mixture quite highly with salt and pepper and pour over the fish. Continue to bake for 40 minutes, basting occasionally with the sauce in the pan and adding a little boiling water, if necessary, if the sauce reduces too much. Transfer the fish to a heated serving dish and pour over the sauce.

PLANKED LAKE SUPERIOR WHITEFISH

Serves 4

1 whitefish, about 3½–4 lb	1 egg yolk
salt and pepper	**for the sauce:**
¼ cup butter	½ cup melted butter
2 tablespoons water	2 tablespoons lemon juice
1 tablespoon lemon juice	3 tablespoons finely chopped parsley
2 lb potatoes	

Oil a hardwood plank, about 2 inches thick, or a large ovenproof plate and put it into a preheated hot oven (450°) for 10–15 minutes. Meanwhile, fillet the whitefish (see note). Place the fish fillets, skin side down, on the hot plank and sprinkle generously with salt and pepper. Dot with half the butter. Melt the remaining butter and stir in the water and lemon juice. Bake the fish in the hot oven for about 25 minutes, basting several times with the melted butter mixture.

Meanwhile, peel the potatoes and boil in salted water to cover until tender. Drain and cream with a little milk and butter.

Remove the plank from the oven and make a ring of potatoes around the fish, or pipe the creamed potatoes in swirls. Beat the egg yolk with 1 tablespoon water and brush over the potatoes. Return the plank to the oven for 5 minutes, or until the potatoes are lightly browned.

To make the sauce, combine the melted butter, lemon juice and parsley and pour into a sauceboat. Serve the fish from the plank and serve the sauce separately.

Note: Clean the fish and cut off the head. Cut along the backbone from head to tail. Insert the blade of the knife at a slight angle to the backbone. Keeping the sharp edge toward the tail, ease the flesh gently away from the bone with slicing movements. When the whole fillet is freed, open out the fish and cut off the fillet at the tail. Using the tip of the knife, ease off the backbone from the other fillet and cut off the tail. Cut the fillets into serving-size portions.

POACHED HALIBUT WITH EGG SAUCE

Serves 6

4 pints water
1 medium-sized onion
1 medium-sized carrot
2 stalks celery with leaves
few sprigs parsley
2 tablespoons lemon juice or vinegar
1 bay leaf
4 cloves
½ teaspoon peppercorns

2 teaspoons salt
3 lb fresh halibut steaks
for the sauce:
¼ cup butter
¼ cup all-purpose flour
2 cups hot rich milk (half milk, half cream)
salt and pepper
3 hard-cooked eggs

Pour the water into a saucepan large enough to hold the halibut. Peel and coarsely chop the onion, carrot and celery and place in the pan with the parsley. Add the lemon juice, bay leaf, cloves, peppercorns and the salt. Bring to a boil and simmer for 20 minutes.

Carefully lower the fish into the simmering water. Bring the water to simmering point' again, lower the heat and poach the fish until cooked. Allow 5 minutes per pound. Do not let the water boil.

When cooked, set aside the fish in the liquid and make the sauce. Melt the butter in a saucepan, add the flour and cook for a few moments, stirring constantly. Remove the pan from the heat. Add the milk all at once. Return the pan to the heat and cook, whisking or stirring rapidly, until the sauce is smooth and thickened. Add salt and pepper to taste. Cook over low heat for 5 minutes, stirring occasionally. Shell and chop the eggs and stir into the sauce. Remove the fish from the pan, place on a heated serving platter and pour the egg sauce over the fish.

Planked Lake Superior whitefish

15

Oregon celery vinaigrette

CRAB LOUIS SALAD

Serves 2

1 head lettuce	1 tablespoon chili sauce
1 lb fresh crab meat	1 teaspoon lemon juice
1 small green sweet pepper	dash salt
3 scallions	**for the garnish:**
6 green olives	2 tomatoes, quartered
1 cup mayonnaise	2 hard-cooked eggs, sliced
¼ cup heavy cream	

Wash and shred the lettuce and arrange on 2 individual plates. Divide the crab meat between the 2 plates. Place in the refrigerator to chill. Halve the green pepper, remove the seeds and very finely chop the flesh. Finely chop the scallions and olives. Combine with the mayonnaise, cream, chili sauce, lemon juice and salt.

Pour the dressing over the chilled crab meat and garnish with the tomato quarters and egg slices.

OREGON CELERY VINAIGRETTE

Serves 4

4 large celery hearts	1 tablespoon chopped green sweet
2 tablespoons vinegar	pepper
⅓ cup salad oil	1 tablespoon chopped canned
¼ teaspoon paprika	pimiento
1 teaspoon salt	

Split the celery hearts lengthwise. Trim and wash thoroughly under cold running water. Place in a large saucepan and barely cover with lightly salted water. Simmer for 30–40 minutes, or until tender but still firm. Drain and cool.

Combine the vinegar, salad oil, paprika, salt, green sweet pepper and pimiento. Pour the dressing over the cooked celery. Chill for at least 30 minutes before serving.

CAESAR SALAD

Serves 6–8

1 clove garlic	2 eggs
¾ cup olive oil	¼ cup lemon juice
2 cups diced stale French bread	8 anchovy fillets
2 large heads Romaine	½ cup grated fresh Parmesan
freshly ground black pepper	cheese
½ teaspoon salt	

Peel and crush the garlic and add to the olive oil. Let stand overnight. The next day, heat a third of the garlic-flavored oil in a small skillet and sauté the bread cubes until golden. Drain on absorbent paper and set aside. Strain the remaining oil to remove the garlic.

Wash the lettuces and tear the leaves into a salad bowl. Sprinkle the black pepper and salt over the leaves. Add the remaining oil and toss until each leaf is glossy with the oil. Lower the eggs into a small saucepan of boiling water and boil for 1 minute. Remove the eggs and break them into the middle of the salad. Squeeze the lemon juice over the eggs and toss again until the lettuce leaves look creamy. Add the anchovy fillets and correct the seasoning of the salad with salt and lemon juice. Sprinkle with the Parmesan cheese, add the bread cubes and toss again lightly before serving.

NEW ENGLAND BOILED DINNER

Serves 8

4 lb corned beef or brisket	2 lb potatoes
1 large bay leaf	3 lb small onions
1 teaspoon peppercorns	8 small beets
1 lb carrots	1 large head cabbage

Wash the beef well and place in a large heavy saucepan with cold water to cover. Add the bay leaf and peppercorns. Bring to a boil, partially cover and simmer for 2½ hours, adding water if necessary to keep the meat covered all the time.

Peel and halve the carrots and peel the potatoes; add to the pan and simmer for 30 minutes. Peel the onions, add to the pan and simmer for a further 30 minutes. Meanwhile, steam or boil the beets in their skins for 45 minutes, or until tender. Peel and keep hot.

Transfer the beef from the pan to the center of a large serving platter and keep hot. Discard the coarse outer leaves of the cabbage and cut away the hard center core. Cut the head into 8 wedges. Add the wedges to the pan with the liquid and vegetables and simmer for 15 minutes.

Drain the vegetables and arrange around the beef. Alternatively, slice the meat across the grain into thin slices. Place a wedge of cabbage in the center of each individual plate and cover with several slices of meat. Surround with the vegetables. Serve with mustard and creamed horseradish and, if liked, a sauceboat of melted butter with chopped parsley.

POT ROAST WITH SOUR CREAM

Serves 8

6 lb beef chuck roast	1 cup cultured sour cream
1 teaspoon salt	1 bay leaf
freshly ground black pepper	1 tablespoon light brown sugar
3 tablespoons all-purpose flour	½ cup tomato paste
2 small onions	4 cups water
¼ cup bacon drippings or fat	cornstarch (see recipe)

Rub the roast with the salt and pepper, then sprinkle with the flour. Peel and chop the onions. Heat the bacon drippings or fat in a large flameproof casserole or Dutch oven and brown all sides of the beef evenly over moderate heat. Add the onions, sour cream, bay leaf, brown sugar, tomato paste and water. Cover tightly and roast in a preheated moderate oven (350°) for 3 hours, or until the meat is very tender.

Discard the bay leaf and transfer the meat to a heated serving platter. Allow 1½ teaspoons of cornstarch per 1¼ cups liquid in the casserole. Blend the cornstarch with cold water and stir into the casserole juices. Bring to a boil and cook, stirring constantly, until the gravy has thickened. Pour into a gravy boat and serve with the meat.

New England boiled dinner

TAMALE CASSEROLE

Serves 6

8 oz hot sausage (*chorizos* or
  pepperoni)
1 large onion
2 cloves garlic
2 medium-sized green sweet
  peppers
8 oz lean beef, ground
4 oz fresh or frozen corn kernels

½ cup sliced ripe olives
1 tablespoon olive liquid from a
  can or jar of olives
½ teaspoon salt
1 tablespoon chili powder
1 cup grated Cheddar cheese
2 (15-oz) cans *tamales* in
  chili gravy

Brown the sausage in a large skillet. Meanwhile, peel and chop the onion and garlic very finely. Halve the green pepper, remove the seeds and dice the flesh. Remove the sausage from the skillet and place on absorbent paper to drain. Pour off all but ¼ cup of the sausage drippings in the skillet. Sauté the onion, garlic and the green pepper in the skillet until tender and the onion is golden brown. Stir in the ground beef and cook, stirring frequently, until the meat loses all red color. Break or crumble the sausage and add to the beef with the corn, olives, olive liquid, salt and chili powder. Mix well and simmer for 15 minutes. Spoon the mixture into a large shallow baking dish.

Remove and discard the corn husks from the *tamales* and arrange them on top of the meat mixture in the baking dish. Pour over any extra gravy from the cans of *Tamales*. Bake uncovered in a preheated moderate oven (350°) for 20 minutes. Sprinkle with the cheese and return the dish to the oven for a further 15 minutes, or until the cheese has melted and the sauce is bubbling. Serve immediately.

ROAST LEG OF LAMB WITH APRICOTS

Serves 8–10

1 tablespoon salt
2 teaspoons dry mustard
1 tablespoon all-purpose flour
¼ teaspoon pepper
1 leg of lamb, about 6 lb

1 (1-lb 12-oz) can apricot halves
  in syrup
stick cinnamon, about 2 inches
mint jelly (see recipe)
mint leaves (optional)

Combine salt, mustard, flour and pepper in a small bowl. Wipe the lamb with a damp cloth and arrange it meaty side up on a rack in an open roasting pan. Sprinkle with the mixed seasonings and roast in a preheated very hot oven (475°) for 30 minutes. Reduce the temperature to moderate (350°) and continue to roast for an additional 1 hour for medium rare, or 1½ hours for well done.

Meanwhile, place the apricot halves and syrup in a saucepan. Add the cinnamon stick, bring to a boil and simmer for 3 minutes.

Remove the roast from the pan and place on a heated serving plate. Surround with the apricot halves cut side up. Place 1 teaspoon mint jelly in each apricot half. If fresh mint leaves are available, garnish each half with a mint leaf in addition to the jelly.

SMITHFIELD HAM COOKED WITH APPLES

Serves a party

1 Smithfield or country-cured
  ham, about 14 lb
1½ lb baking apples
2¼ cups light brown sugar
1 pint cider vinegar

for the glaze:
⅔ cup light brown sugar
⅓ cup French mustard
2 tablespoons dry sherry
whole cloves (see recipe)

Soak the ham for up to 24 hours, changing the water at least 3 times to remove the salt. Wash in cold running water and scrub with a stiff brush. Put the ham in a large saucepan, cover with water and bring to simmering point. Peel and quarter the apples and add to the pan with the brown sugar and the vinegar. Partially cover the pan and simmer for 18 minutes per pound, or until the small bone at the shank end can be easily removed. The ham should be completely covered with water throughout the cooking time.

When the ham is cooked take it out of the pan, discard the liquid and when the ham is cool enough to handle, remove the skin and trim off the excess fat. Score the remaining fat deeply into diamonds.

For the glaze, mix the brown sugar, mustard and sherry to a paste. Spread the mixture evenly over the fatty surface of the ham. Stud each diamond with a whole clove and bake in a preheated moderate oven (350°) for about 40 minutes, or until the crust is well browned, basting occasionally with the juices. Cool and serve very thinly sliced.

OREGON HAM SLICE WITH FRUIT

Serves 4

1 large slice cooked ham, about
  1 inch thick
1 teaspoon butter or margarine
8 oz crushed strawberries,
  with juice
2 tablespoons water

few cloves
½ cup sugar
2 tablespoons lemon juice
2 canned pineapple rings
4 whole strawberries

Cut the ham into quarters. Melt the butter in a heavy skillet, brown the ham lightly on both sides then transfer to a shallow baking dish. Add 3 tablespoons of the strawberry juice and the water to the juices remaining in the skillet. Swirl the skillet over moderate heat until the liquid simmers, then pour the liquid over the ham. Cover the baking dish with aluminum foil and bake in a preheated moderately hot oven (375°) for 45 minutes. Remove the ham from the oven and stud the fatty parts with cloves.

Meanwhile, combine the crushed strawberries, sugar and lemon juice in a saucepan and bring to a boil. Pour the hot fruit over the ham and return to the oven, uncovered, to bake for 20 minutes longer. Baste occasionally with the juices. Broil the pineapple rings under moderate heat for 2–3 minutes. Transfer the ham and sauce to a heated serving platter and garnish with halved pineapple rings. Place a whole strawberry in the groove of each pineapple half.

Crown roast with corn stuffing

CROWN PORK ROAST WITH CORN STUFFING

Serves 8

6–7 lb crown pork roast (12–14 ribs)	6 oz fresh or frozen corn kernels
salt and pepper	1 (11-oz) can cream style corn
for the stuffing:	1 cup fine fresh breadcrumbs
1 egg	1½ teaspoons salt
1 medium-sized onion	dash pepper
1 small green sweet pepper	preserved kumquats (see recipe)

Have the butcher prepare the crown roast, forming the rib chops into a neat ring. Sprinkle with salt and pepper and place in a shallow roasting pan. Wrap pieces of aluminum foil around the bone ends to keep them from charring. Roast in a preheated moderate oven (325°) for 1½ hours.

Meanwhile, prepare the corn stuffing. Lightly beat the egg. Peel and very finely chop the onion. Halve the green pepper, remove the seeds and finely chop the flesh. Combine the egg, onion and green pepper with the whole kernel corn, cream style corn, breadcrumbs, salt and pepper. Mix well.

Remove the roast from the oven and fill the center of the ring with the stuffing, piling it up high in the center. Return to the oven and roast for a further 1½ hours, or until the meat is well cooked. Transfer to a heated serving platter. Remove the foil from the bone tips, and either place paper frills over the tips before serving or place a preserved kumquat over each bone tip.

PUERTO RICAN PORK LOIN ROAST

Serves 8

6 lb pork loin roast	½ cup olive oil
2 large cloves garlic	½ cup unsweetened orange juice or lime juice
2 teaspoons oregano	
½ teaspoon coarsely ground black pepper	2 cups hot water
	¼ cup all-purpose flour
2 teaspoons salt	dash cayenne pepper

Make deep cuts between the ribs of the loin. Peel and finely chop the garlic and mix with the oregano, pepper, salt and olive oil. Thoroughly rub the mixture into the cuts and all over the surface of the meat. Place the meat in the refrigerator overnight. Put the loin, meat side up, on a rack in a shallow open roasting pan and roast in a preheated moderate oven (350°) for about 3 hours. Baste with the orange juice and the hot water, a little at a time, during roasting. When the meat is brown and well roasted, remove from the oven and transfer to a heated serving platter. Pour the juices from the pan into a large measuring cup and allow the fat to rise to the surface.

Return ¼ cup of the fat to the roasting pan and discard the rest of the fat. The remaining liquid should measure 1½ pints. If not, add hot water to make up this amount. Place the roasting pan over direct heat and stir in the flour. Cook, stirring, until the mixture bubbles. Gradually stir in the hot liquid, stirring constantly while scraping the bottom and sides of the pan with a wooden spoon to loosen all the brown particles. When smooth and thickened, add a dash of cayenne pepper and correct the seasoning with salt. Strain into a gravy boat and serve with the roast.

CHICKEN OKRA GUMBO

Serves 6

1 chicken, about 4–5 lb	3 tablespoons all-purpose flour
6 tablespoons margarine or shortening	1½ lb fresh okra
	4 quarts water
1 large onion	2 bay leaves
12 oz tomatoes	½ teaspoon dried thyme
1 clove garlic	salt and pepper
2 stalks celery	cayenne pepper

Cut the chicken into serving portions. Heat the margarine in a large heavy saucepan and sauté the chicken until browned on all sides. Meanwhile, peel and chop the onion and tomatoes. Finely chop the garlic and chop the celery. Drain the chicken pieces and set aside. Stir the flour into the hot fat remaining in the pan. Cook over moderate heat, stirring constantly, until the mixture becomes golden brown. Add the onion, garlic and celery to the flour mixture. Cover and cook over low heat for about 10 minutes, or until the vegetables are tender.

Slice the okra and add to the pan. Cook for about 10 minutes or until the ingredients are well blended. Add the chicken pieces, water, bay leaves, thyme and the salt, pepper and cayenne pepper to taste. Bring to a boil and simmer for about 1½ hours, or until the chicken is tender. Serve with cooked rice.

MARYLAND FRIED CHICKEN WITH CREAM GRAVY

Serves 4

for the chicken:	1 cup water
1 frying chicken, about 3 lb	**for the gravy:**
½ cup all-purpose flour	¼ cup all-purpose flour
1 teaspoon salt	2 cups light cream
¼ teaspoon pepper	salt and pepper
½ cup butter	

Cut the chicken into quarters. Wash and dry each portion thoroughly. Combine the flour, salt and pepper in a paper bag and shake the chicken portions in the seasoned flour until well coated. Melt the butter in a heavy skillet and brown the chicken quickly on all sides. Reduce the heat to low, add the water, cover and cook for 30 minutes. Remove the lid and continue to cook for 20–30 minutes, or until the chicken is very tender and crisp. Transfer to a serving dish and keep warm.

To make the gravy, stir the flour into the drippings remaining in the skillet. Gradually stir in the cream. Add salt and pepper to taste. Cook over moderate heat, stirring constantly, until the gravy is smooth and thickened. Simmer for 3 minutes then pour into a heated sauceboat.

Garnish the chicken pieces with fried bananas and bacon rolls and serve with the cream sauce and Dutch Welshkorn oysters (see page 28).

20

CREAMED CHICKEN

Serves 4

1 chicken, about 3½ lb	1 fresh or dried chili
1 medium-sized onion	1 bay leaf
3 stalks celery with leaves	½ teaspoon dried thyme
½ lemon	2 egg yolks
2 teaspoons salt	¼ cup lemon juice
½ teaspoon peppercorns	2 tablespoons butter
1 large clove garlic	2 tablespoons all-purpose flour

Place the chicken, breast down, in a large heavy saucepan. Add enough water to come about three-fourths of the way up the sides of chicken. Peel and slice the onion, coarsely chop the celery and slice the lemon. Add the onion, celery, lemon, salt, peppercorns, garlic, chili, bay leaf and thyme to the pan. Place the pan over high heat and bring the liquid to simmering point, lower the heat, partially cover and simmer for 1½ hours, or until the chicken is very tender. Add

Maryland fried chicken with cream gravy

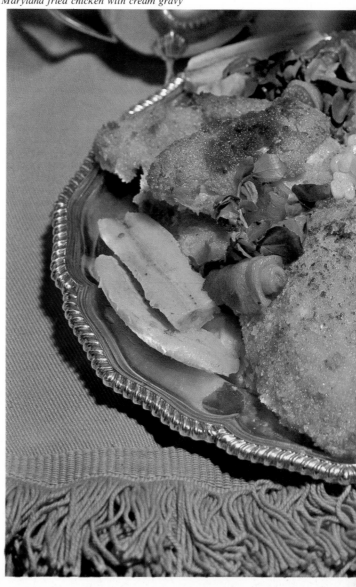

additional salt to the broth to taste, seasoning it rather highly.

Beat the egg yolks and lemon juice in a cup or small bowl. Set aside. Melt the butter in a heavy saucepan. Stir in the flour and cook, stirring, until the mixture bubbles. Remove from the heat. Remove the chicken from the broth and keep warm. Strain the broth through a sieve into a bowl and reserve 2 pints. Discard the vegetables and spices. Any excess broth may be used in another recipe or for soup. Add the reserved broth to the butter mixture, return to the heat and stir constantly until the sauce is smooth and slightly thickened. Add a little of the hot sauce to the egg yolk mixture and stir the egg yolk mixture into the hot sauce. Cook, stirring, for 1 minute, being careful not to allow the sauce to boil. Remove immediately from the heat.

Slice the chicken breast and thigh meat on to a heated serving plate and coat generously with the sauce. Serve with cooked rice.

CHICKEN JAMBALAYA

Serves 4

1 frying chicken, about 4 lb	1 bay leaf
1 large onion	few drops Tabasco sauce
2 cloves garlic	dash powdered saffron
6 scallions	2½ pints water
1 green sweet pepper	2 cups long-grain rice
½ cup olive oil	1 canned pimiento
1 (1-lb) can tomatoes	8 oz canned or frozen *petits pois*
1 tablespoon salt	

Cut the chicken into four portions. Peel and finely chop the onion and garlic. Trim and chop the scallions. Halve the green pepper, remove the seeds and slice the flesh. Heat the olive oil in a large flameproof casserole or Dutch oven and sauté the chicken until well browned. Remove the chicken and set aside.

Add the onion, garlic, scallions and the green pepper to the hot oil remaining in the casserole. Sauté for about 5 minutes, or until lightly browned, adding a little more oil if necessary. Drain the tomatoes and reserve the liquid. Add the salt, bay leaf, Tabasco sauce, powdered saffron and drained tomatoes to the casserole. Cook over low heat for 6–7 minutes. Add the browned chicken, tomato liquid, water and rice. Stir to mix and bring the liquid to a rapid boil. Remove from the heat, cover tightly and bake in a preheated moderately hot oven (400°) for about 45–50 minutes, or until the rice is tender and most of the liquid has been absorbed.

Cut the pimiento into thin strips. Heat the peas, drain and sprinkle over the rice. Garnish with strips of pimiento.

POLYNESIAN CHICKEN

Serves 4

2 cups grated fresh coconut	½ teaspoon turmeric
1¼ cups boiling water	1 teaspoon ground coriander
1 small onion	1 chicken, about 3–4 lb
2 cloves garlic	1 tablespoon sugar
2 tablespoons peanut oil	1 tablespoon vinegar
1 teaspoon salt	1 cup coconut milk (see recipe)

To make the coconut milk, pour the boiling water over the grated coconut and let stand for 20 minutes. Strain through a fine sieve or cheesecloth, pressing out as much 'milk' from the coconut as possible. Reserve the amount required for the recipe.

Meanwhile, peel and finely chop the onion and garlic. Heat the peanut oil in a large saucepan and sauté the onion with the garlic until the onion is tender but not brown. Stir in the salt, turmeric and coriander. Cut the chicken into four portions and sauté in the spice mixture about 5 minutes on each side, or until the chicken is lightly browned. Add the sugar, vinegar and coconut milk. Simmer very gently over low heat for 20 minutes.

Before serving, remove the chicken from the sauce and either broil or barbecue over glowing coals until brown and tender, basting frequently with the remaining sauce. Serve with cooked rice.

ROAST GOOSE WITH FRUIT STUFFINGS

Serves 8

1 goose, about 10–12 lb
1 teaspoon salt
1 orange
3 tablespoons lemon juice
for the apricot stuffing:
4 oz dried apricots
1 stalk celery
1 tablespoon finely chopped
  parsley
1 cup dry breadcrumbs
¼ cup soda cracker crumbs
¾ teaspoon salt
¼ teaspoon paprika

2 tablespoons melted butter or
  melted goose fat
**for the wild rice and chestnut
stuffing:**
8 oz chestnuts
1 cup wild rice
1½ pints water
1 teaspoon salt
½ small onion
½ cup melted butter or melted
  goose fat
¼ teaspoon pepper

Wipe the goose with a damp cloth and sprinkle inside and out with salt. Grate the orange rind and squeeze the orange. Mix together the orange rind and juice and lemon juice.

To make the apricot stuffing, cover the apricots with water and bring to a boil. Simmer for 20 minutes, or until plump and tender. Drain the apricots and reserve the liquid. Chop the celery. Chop the apricots and combine with the celery, parsley, breadcrumbs, soda cracker crumbs, salt, paprika and melted butter. Moisten with the apricot liquid. Set aside.

To make the wild rice and chestnut stuffing, slit the skins of the chestnuts, place in a saucepan, cover with water and bring to a boil. Simmer gently for 30 minutes, or until the chestnuts are tender. Set the chestnuts aside to cool, then remove the skins. Wash the rice well and put into a saucepan with the water and salt. Bring to a boil and simmer for 40 minutes, or until tender. Drain. Peel and chop the onion very finely. Combine the rice, chestnuts, onion, melted butter and pepper. Mix well and set aside.

Lightly fill the neck cavity of the goose with apricot stuffing and the body cavity with wild rice and chestnut stuffing. Sew up or skewer together the openings and truss the goose. Prick the skin generously with a fork, paying particular attention to the fatty areas around the legs and wings. Place the goose, breast down, on a rack in a shallow roasting pan and roast in a preheated moderate oven (325°) for 3 hours, removing the fat from the pan as it accumulates. Turn the goose breast up and pour the orange juice mixture over it. Continue to roast for 2 hours longer for a 10-lb goose, or 3 hours longer for a 12-lb goose. For a smaller goose roast for a total of 30 minutes per pound. Baste occasionally with the pan juices during the rest of the roasting period. Remove the trussing strings or skewers before serving.

Roast goose with fruit stuffings

ROAST TURKEY WITH YAQUINA OYSTER STUFFING

Serves 14–16

for the stuffing:
8 oz turkey fat, chopped
1 large onion
4 stalks celery
10–12 cups dry breadcrumbs
3½ teaspoons salt
1 teaspoon pepper
1 teaspoon dried sage

24 freshly shucked oysters with
   their liquid
for the turkey:
1 turkey, about 10–12 lb
salt
1 cup butter
¼ cup all-purpose flour
½ cup boiling water

For the stuffing, heat the turkey fat in a skillet until the fat is rendered and the bits of tissue are crispy. Peel and chop the onion. Chop the celery. Add the onion and the celery to the skillet and sauté for about 10 minutes, or until tender but not brown. Combine the onion and celery in a mixing bowl with the breadcrumbs, salt, pepper and sage. Fold in the oysters and their liquid.

Loosely stuff the filling into the turkey cavity and neck area allowing enough space for expansion. Sew up or skewer together the openings and truss the turkey. Place the turkey on its side on a rack in a large open roasting pan and sprinkle with salt. Cream half the butter with the flour and spread the breast, legs and wings with this mixture.

Roast in a preheated hot oven (450°) for 30 minutes, then reduce the oven temperature to moderate (350°). Roast for 3 hours longer. Melt the remaining butter in the boiling water and pour a little over the roasting turkey at half-hour intervals. After 1 hour, turn the turkey to the other side. After 2 hours, turn the bird breast side up for the remainder of the roasting time. If the turkey browns too quickly, cover the breast and thighs with aluminum foil or a buttered cloth. Remove the trussing strings or skewers before serving.

MINNESOTA WILD RICE CASSEROLE

Serves 6

2 cups wild rice
2 teaspoons salt
1 green sweet pepper

2 small onions
8 stalks celery
½ cup butter

Wash the rice thoroughly in several changes of water, then soak in cold water for 2 hours. Drain, place in a saucepan and cover generously with boiling water. Add the salt, bring to a boil and cook, uncovered, for 30 minutes. Drain thoroughly and set aside.

Halve the green pepper and remove the seeds. Peel the onions. Finely chop the pepper, onions and the celery. Melt the butter in a skillet and sauté the vegetables for about 10 minutes, or until partially soft but not brown. Stir the vegetables and butter into the rice. Transfer to a buttered 4-pint casserole or baking dish. Cover and bake in a preheated moderate oven (350°) for 1 hour. Serve hot in the casserole.

SUCCOTASH

Serves 6

8–10 oz frozen baby lima beans	½ teaspoon salt
¾ cup water	freshly ground black pepper
8 oz fresh or frozen corn kernels	½ cup light cream
2 tablespoons butter	3 tablespoons chopped parsley

Place the frozen lima beans and water in a saucepan. Bring to a boil and simmer until the beans are easily separated with a fork. Cover and cook over low heat for 3 minutes. Drain and retain the beans in the pan. Add the corn kernels, butter, salt and pepper to taste and then the cream. Cook over low heat for 20–30 minutes, but do not allow the cream to boil. Transfer to a heated dish, garnish with the chopped parsley and serve.

LOUISIANA RED BEANS

Serves 8

1 lb dried red kidney beans	¼ green sweet pepper
1 ham bone with a generous amount of meat	1 large bay leaf
	1 tablespoon sugar
1 teaspoon salt	dash cayenne pepper
1 large onion	3 tablespoons chopped parsley
1 clove garlic	cooked rice (see recipe)
1 stalk celery	

Wash and pick over the beans. Place in a bowl, cover with cold water and soak overnight.

Place the beans and the water in which they were soaked in a saucepan, add the ham bone and salt and bring to a boil. Cook over low heat for 1½ hours, adding a little boiling water from time to time if the beans become too dry. Peel and finely chop the onion and garlic. Chop the celery and the green pepper. Crush the bay leaf. Add the onion, garlic, celery, green pepper, bay leaf, sugar, cayenne pepper and parsley to the pan and continue cooking for 30 minutes – 1 hour, or until the beans are very tender and moist. Serve over mounds of cooked rice.

BOSTON BAKED BEANS

Serves 6

1 lb pea or navy beans	1 teaspoon dry mustard
8 oz salt pork	1 teaspoon pepper
1 medium-sized onion	½ cup molasses
1½ teaspoons salt	

Pick over the beans and soak overnight in plenty of cold water. Drain, place in a saucepan and cover with fresh water. Bring slowly to a boil and simmer gently for 1¼ hours, or until tender but not overcooked. Add boiling water, if necessary, to keep the beans covered with liquid.

Soak the salt pork in boiling water for 10 minutes. Drain and cut off two thin slices. Put one slice on the bottom of a 4-pint casserole and slice the other into slivers. Score the remaining salt pork deeply at frequent intervals, but without cutting all the way through. Set aside.

Using a perforated spoon, transfer the beans from their cooking liquid to the casserole. Stir in the slivered salt pork. Peel the onion and bury it in the center of the beans. Combine the salt, mustard, pepper and molasses with 1¼ cups of the bean liquid and pour over the beans. Add enough additional bean liquid or boiling water to just cover. Push the scored piece of salt pork into the center of the beans. Cover and bake in a preheated very cool oven (250°) for 6 hours. Uncover during the last half hour to brown the beans on top and add more liquid from time to time, if needed, to keep them moist.

LOUISIANA CANDIED SWEET POTATOES

Serves 4

4 medium-sized sweet potatoes, about 2½ lb	½ teaspoon freshly grated nutmeg
	6 tablespoons butter
¾ cup light brown sugar	4 paper-thin slices lemon
¼ cup granulated sugar	¼ cup water
¼ teaspoon salt	

Peel the sweet potatoes and cut into strips similar in size to French fries or ½ inch wide by 2 inches in length. Place in an 8- by 12-inch ovenproof dish. Sprinkle with the sugars, salt and nutmeg, then dot with butter. Place the lemon slices on top and add the water to the dish. Bake in a preheated moderately hot oven (400°) for 1 hour, or until the sweet potatoes are tender and the sugar and butter have become the consistency of thick syrup. During baking, baste occasionally with the syrup in the dish.

DEEP-FRIED OKRA

Serves 4

1 lb young fresh or frozen okra	1 tablespoon cold water
2 cups water	dash salt
¼ teaspoon salt	dash cayenne pepper
2 tablespoons lemon juice	cracker crumbs (see recipe)
1 egg	shortening for deep-frying

If using fresh okra, wash and trim the stems. Do not cut into the pods or the juice will be lost. Place the water, salt and lemon juice in a saucepan and bring to a boil. Drop in the pods and simmer for 10 minutes. Drain well.

Beat the egg with the cold water and add the salt and cayenne pepper. Dip each okra into this mixture and roll in the cracker crumbs. Deep-fry until golden brown in shortening heated to 365°. Drain on absorbent paper and serve hot.

Succotash

BAKED BANANAS

Serves 6

6 large bananas, not too ripe
¼ cup melted butter

¼ cup light brown sugar
¼ cup rum

Peel and split the bananas lengthwise and arrange them in a buttered shallow ovenproof dish. Sprinkle the melted butter, brown sugar and rum over the bananas. Bake in a preheated moderate oven (350°) for 20 minutes. Serve hot or flambé with rum for special occasions.

SPICED PEACHES

Makes 4 lb

6 lb fresh clingstone peaches
7 cups sugar
1 pint water
stick cinnamon, about 4 inches

12 cloves
1 small ginger root
1 pint vinegar

Drop the peaches into rapidly boiling water for 1 minute, remove and strip off the skins. Put half the sugar with the water in a saucepan. Bring to a boil and boil rapidly for 5 minutes. Lower the heat, drop the peeled peaches into the syrup and simmer for 5 minutes. Take the pan off the heat and let the peaches stand in the syrup for 2–3 hours.

Remove the peaches. Tie the cinnamon, cloves and ginger in a cheesecloth bag and add to the syrup. Add the vinegar and remaining sugar. Bring to a boil and boil rapidly for 10–15 minutes. Return the peaches to the pan and simmer for about 20 minutes, or until the peaches are tender and the syrup is thick.

Remove the pan from the heat and let the peaches stand in the syrup overnight. Discard the spice bag and pack the peaches into sterilized jars. Bring the syrup to a boil and pour over the peaches to fill the jars. If preferred, a stick of cinnamon and a few cloves may be added to each jar. Seal the jars and store. This is an excellent preserve to serve with roast meats or poultry.

Baked bananas

FROZEN RUM CREAM

Serves 6–8

4 egg yolks
¼ cup sugar
3 egg whites
1½ cups heavy cream
½ cup dark rum

Beat the egg yolks and sugar in a mixing bowl until thick and pale in color. Beat the egg whites in another bowl until stiff and glossy and fold into the egg yolk mixture. Whip the cream and fold into the mixture. Stir in the rum. Turn into a refrigerator tray and freeze for 8 hours before serving.

BURNT CREAM

Serves 6

¼ cup sugar
1 tablespoon cornstarch
6 egg yolks
3 cups heavy cream
2 teaspoons vanilla extract
1 cup light brown sugar

Gradually beat the sugar and cornstarch into the egg yolks and continue to beat for 2–3 minutes, or until the mixture is thick and pale in color. Heat the cream to simmering point and gradually pour it into the egg yolk mixture, stirring constantly.

Strain the mixture into a saucepan and cook over gentle heat, stirring rapidly and constantly with a wooden spoon, reaching all over the bottom and sides of the pan, until the cream thickens enough to coat the spoon. Be careful not to let it boil. Remove from the heat and continue to stir rapidly for 2 minutes to cool the cream. Stir in the vanilla extract and pour the cream into a heat-resistant serving dish. Chill for several hours or overnight.

Put the bowl in a shallow pan containing cracked ice. Sprinkle the brown sugar evenly over the top of the cream. Broil for 4–5 minutes, or until the sugar melts and caramelizes. Be careful not to let the sugar burn. Serve immediately or chill again for several hours before serving.

LEMON CHEESECAKE

Serves 6

for the crust:
16 graham cracker squares
½ cup sugar
½ teaspoon grated nutmeg
¼ cup melted butter

for the filling:
1 lb cream cheese
2 eggs
1 tablespoon lemon juice
1½ cups cultured sour cream
½ cup sugar
2 tablespoons melted butter

To make the crust, crush the graham crackers and mix with the sugar, nutmeg and melted butter. Line a buttered 9-inch pie plate with the crumb mixture.

To make the filling, allow the cream cheese to soften at room temperature. Beat the eggs lightly with the lemon juice in a mixing bowl. Stir in the sour cream and the sugar. Gradually beat in the cream cheese to make a smooth mixture. Stir in the melted butter. Pour the mixture into the lined pie plate and bake in a preheated moderate oven (325°)

for 30–40 minutes, or until set in the center. The filling will be very soft but will become firmer as the cake cools. Chill thoroughly before serving.

KEY LIME PIE

Makes 1 8-inch pie

for the crust:
1½ cups graham cracker crumbs
¼ cup sugar
½ cup melted butter or margarine
for the filling:
1 envelope gelatin
½ cup lime juice
2 eggs
1 tablespoon sugar
1⅓ cups sweetened condensed milk (1 large can)
½ teaspoon grated lime rind

To make the crust, combine the crumbs and the sugar. Mix in the melted butter. Press the mixture into a buttered 8-inch pie plate. The crust may be well chilled or, if preferred, baked in a preheated moderately hot oven (400°) for 10 minutes before the filling is added.

To make the filling, soak the gelatin in the lime juice in a double boiler for 5 minutes, then stir over simmering water until the gelatin is completely dissolved. Separate the eggs. Beat the yolks until pale in color. Beat the egg whites until fluffy, add the sugar slowly and continue to beat to make a stiff, glossy meringue. Stir the lime mixture and egg yolks into the condensed milk and beat thoroughly. Fold the meringue carefully into the lime mixture and pour into the prepared pie shell. Allow to set and sprinkle with grated rind before serving.

LEMON CHEESE PIE

Makes 1 9-inch pie

for the pastry:
1 cup all-purpose flour
1 egg yolk
1 tablespoon water
¼ teaspoon salt
½ cup cold butter
for the filling:
½ cup butter
1½ cups sugar
3 eggs
½ cup lemon juice
1 cup heavy cream
1 teaspoon grated lemon rind

Prepare the pastry as for Southern Pecan Pie, see following page.

On a lightly floured board, roll out the pastry to about ⅛ inch thick and about 1½ inches larger than the diameter of a 9-inch pie plate. Line the pie plate with the pastry and flute the edge.

For the filling, cream the butter and sugar until fluffy. Add the eggs one at a time, beating well after each addition. Stir in the lemon juice. Pour into the uncooked pie shell and bake in a preheated moderate oven (350°) for 35–40 minutes. Remove from the oven and set aside to cool.

When the pie is cool, whip the cream and pipe in a decorative border around the edge of the filling. Sprinkle with the grated lemon rind.

SOUTHERN PECAN PIE

Makes 1 9-inch pie

for the pastry:

1 cup all-purpose flour
1 egg yolk
1 tablespoon water
¼ teaspoon salt
½ cup cold butter (see recipe)

for the filling:

2 tablespoons soft butter
1 cup sugar
3 large eggs
1 cup dark corn syrup
1 teaspoon vanilla extract
¼ teaspoon salt
1 cup halved pecan nuts

To make the pastry, put the flour into a mixing bowl and make a well in the center. Put the egg yolk, water and salt into the well. Cut in the butter, which should be firm and cold but not directly out of the refrigerator or freezer. Begin working the ingredients in the center to a smooth paste, then gradually work in the flour until all the ingredients can be gathered into a rough dough. A few drops of water may be necessary, depending upon the size of the egg yolk. If the pastry is too soft to roll out easily, chill in the refrigerator for 30 minutes.

On a lightly floured board, roll out the pastry to about ⅛ inch thick and about 1½ inches larger than the diameter of a 9-inch pie plate. Line the pie plate with the pastry, flute the edge and bake blind in a preheated moderately hot oven (400°) (see note).

Cream the butter and sugar together thoroughly. Beat the eggs and add to the creamed mixture with the corn syrup, vanilla extract and salt. Beat well. Sprinkle the halved pecan nuts in the cooked pie shell. Pour the mixture over the pecan nuts. Bake in a preheated hot oven (450°) for 10 minutes. Reduce the oven temperature to moderate (350°) and bake for 30–35 minutes longer. Cool and serve with whipped cream.

Note: To bake a pie shell, line it with foil or waxed paper and weigh down with dried beans or rice. Bake in the center of the oven for 15 minutes.

CREAM WAFFLES

Makes 4 waffles

1 cup all-purpose flour
3 teaspoons baking powder
¼ teaspoon salt

3 eggs
1 cup heavy cream

Sift the flour, baking powder and salt into a mixing bowl. Separate the eggs. Beat the egg yolks vigorously and gradually beat in the cream. Stir the egg yolk mixture into the flour mixture, and beat with a rotary whisk, electric mixer or fork until the batter is smooth. Beat the egg whites until stiff and fold into the batter. Chill the batter for 30 minutes.

Lightly grease and heat a waffle iron. Pour a little of the batter into the heated waffle iron, cook for 3–4 minutes then turn out and keep warm. Repeat with the rest of the mixture.

DUTCH WELSHKORN OYSTERS (CORN FRITTERS)

Serves 4

4 eggs
8 oz fresh or frozen corn kernels
4 tablespoons all-purpose flour

1 teaspoon salt
¼ teaspoon black pepper
¼ teaspoon cayenne pepper

Separate the eggs. Combine the corn kernels and egg yolks in a mixing bowl, and beat well. Sift in the flour, salt and the peppers, and mix to a batter. Beat the egg whites until stiff but not dry and fold into the corn mixture. Drop by spoonfuls (the size of oysters) on to a well-greased hot griddle or skillet and fry until golden brown on both sides. Serve hot.

Note: In inland regions of the Middle Atlantic states, fresh oysters were not always available. This dish, looking very much like batter-fried oysters, was devised to 'fool the eye' and please the palate.

CORN BISCUITS

Makes 24 biscuits

¾ cup milk
¼ cup yellow corn meal
1½ cups all-purpose flour
4 teaspoons baking powder

1 teaspoon salt
¼ cup melted butter
soft butter (see recipe)

Scald the milk in a saucepan. Remove from the heat and stir in the corn meal. Set aside. Combine the flour, baking powder and salt in a mixing bowl. Stir in the melted butter and the corn meal mixture. Turn out on to a well floured board and knead gently with floured fingers until the dough holds together. Knead in a little more flour, if necessary. Roll out ¼ inch thick on a lightly floured board and cut with a 2-inch floured biscuit cutter. Score the biscuits slightly off center with the back of a knife and brush each with soft butter. Fold over each biscuit envelope-style and arrange on a baking sheet. Bake in a preheated hot oven (425°) for 15 minutes.

WHEAT GERM MUFFINS

Makes 12 medium-sized muffins

2 cups all-purpose flour
3 teaspoons baking powder
1 teaspoon salt
2 tablespoons sugar

½ cup wheat germ
1 egg
1 cup milk
¼ cup melted butter

Combine the flour, baking powder, salt, sugar and wheat germ in a mixing bowl. Beat the egg into the milk and add to the mixing bowl. Mix lightly until all the dry ingredients are moistened, then stir in the melted butter. Grease the muffin tins and fill the cups two-thirds full of batter. Bake in a preheated moderately hot oven (400°) for 20–25 minutes. Remove the muffins and serve warm.

CHEESE BISCUITS

Makes 16 2-inch biscuits

2 cups all-purpose flour
2½ teaspoons baking powder
½ teaspoon salt
⅔ cup margarine or shortening
⅔ cup milk
1 cup grated Cheddar cheese
½ cup butter

Combine the flour, baking powder and salt in a mixing bowl. Cut in the margarine with a pastry blender or two knives, or rub in with the fingertips until evenly mixed. Add the milk and stir gently with a fork until the dough holds together. Gather the dough into a ball, turn it on to a lightly floured board and knead gently with floured fingers, about 12 kneading strokes.

Roll the dough out ½ inch thick on a lightly floured board and cut with a 2-inch floured plain cutter. Melt the cheese and butter in a double boiler until the mixture is smooth, stirring occasionally. Dip the top of each biscuit into the butter and cheese mixture and place on a baking sheet 1 inch apart with the cheese side up. Alternatively, place the biscuits in a baking pan and spoon the cheese sauce on top of each one. Bake in a preheated hot oven (425°) for 12–15 minutes. Serve hot. These biscuits are excellent with baked ham for lunch.

SPOON BREAD

Serves 4

2 cups milk
1 cup yellow corn meal
1 teaspoon salt
¼ cup melted butter
4 eggs

Heat the milk to simmering point in a saucepan. Gradually stir in the corn meal and cook, stirring constantly, until the mixture is smooth and thick. Stir in the salt and melted butter. Set aside to cool.

Separate the eggs. Beat the egg yolks and stir into the corn meal mixture. Beat the egg whites until stiff and fold in. Pour into a buttered 4-pint casserole and bake in a preheated moderately hot oven (375°) for 35–40 minutes, or until lightly brown. Serve hot and spoon the bread from the casserole at the table.

Spoon bread

BOSTON BROWN BREAD

Makes 3 small loaves or 2 large loaves

1 cup yellow corn meal	¾ cup molasses
1 cup graham flour	1 tablespoon sugar
1 cup rye flour	2 cups sour milk or buttermilk
1 teaspoon baking soda	¾ cup seedless raisins
1 teaspoon salt	

Combine the corn meal, graham flour, rye flour, baking soda and salt in a mixing bowl. Stir in the molasses, sugar, sour milk or buttermilk and raisins and stir until well mixed. Place rounds of waxed paper in the bottom of 3 1-lb coffee cans or 2 large pudding molds. Grease the cans or molds and fill two-thirds full of mixture. Cover with aluminum foil tied tightly over the tops.

Place the cans upright on a rack in a large saucepan and add water to reach halfway up the sides. Cover the pan and bring the water to a boil. Boil gently for 2 hours or until the bread is firm and dry on top, adding more boiling water from time to time if needed. Remove from the pan and cool slightly before turning the bread out on to a wire rack. Let stand until cold.

ANADAMA BREAD

Makes 2 loaves

½ cup white or yellow corn meal	2 cakes compressed yeast or
2 tablespoons butter or shortening	2 packages active dry yeast
½ cup molasses	⅓ cup warm water
2 teaspoons salt	6–8 cups all-purpose flour
2 cups boiling water	

Measure the corn meal, butter, molasses and salt into a large mixing bowl. Pour in the boiling water and stir until the butter is melted. Let stand until lukewarm. Blend the yeast with the warm water and stir it into the corn meal mixture. Beat in two-thirds of the flour, a little at a time, then work in enough additional flour to make a soft dough. Grease the surface of the dough, cover lightly with a tea towel and let stand in a warm place for 1 hour, or until the dough has doubled in bulk. In cold weather, or if the kitchen is cool, rising time might take a little longer.

Punch down the dough, turn it out on to a floured board and knead until smooth. Form into a long thick roll and cut in half crosswise. Put each half into a greased loaf pan, cover with a tea towel and set aside to rise for 1 hour, or until the dough is well rounded over the edge of the pan. Bake in a preheated hot oven (375°) for 55 minutes–1 hour. Remove the loaves from the oven, turn out and cool on wire racks. To obtain a shiny crust, brush the tops of the loaves with melted butter while still hot.

SALLY LUNN BREAD

Makes 2 loaves

1 cup milk	6 tablespoons lukewarm water
½ cup butter	about 7 cups all-purpose flour
2 tablespoons sugar	3 eggs
2 teaspoons salt	1 tablespoon soft butter
1 cake compressed yeast or	
1 package active dry yeast	

Put the milk and butter into a small saucepan. Heat until the butter melts and the mixture simmers, then pour into a large mixing bowl to cool. Stir in the sugar and the salt. Soften the yeast in the lukewarm water.

When the milk mixture is lukewarm, beat in about one-third of the flour, then the yeast mixture. Lightly beat the eggs and stir them into the mixture. Gradually beat in another third of the flour to make a smooth elastic dough. Finally, knead in enough of the remaining flour to make a dough that is quite soft but not sticky. Cover lightly with a tea towel and let rise in a warm place for 1½ hours, or until the dough has doubled in bulk.

Punch down the dough and turn out on to a lightly floured board. Knead until smooth and elastic, form into a ball and cut in half. Shape each half into a long narrow loaf and put into 2 greased or oiled loaf pans. Brush the surface of the dough lightly with the soft butter, cover with a tea towel and set aside to rise for about 1 hour, or until the dough is well rounded above the top of each pan. Bake in a preheated hot oven (425°) for 30–40 minutes, or until golden brown. Remove from the pans and cool on a wire rack. Serve with butter and jam. Sally Lunn bread is delicious toasted.

PINEAPPLE BREAD

Makes 2 loaves

4 cups all-purpose flour	6 tablespoons butter
4 teaspoons baking powder	1½ cups light brown sugar
½ teaspoon baking soda	2 eggs
½ teaspoon salt	2 cups canned crushed
1½ cups coarsely chopped	pineapple, including juice
macadamia nuts, pecan nuts or	
walnuts	

Combine the flour, baking powder, baking soda and salt in a mixing bowl. Stir in the nuts. Cream the butter and brown sugar together in another mixing bowl. Beat in the eggs, one at a time, and continue beating until the mixture is smooth. Stir in half the flour mixture, the crushed pineapple with its juice, then the remaining flour mixture. Divide the mixture between 2 large well-oiled loaf pans. Bake in a preheated moderate oven (350°) for 50 minutes–1 hour, or until a skewer inserted in the center comes out clean. Cool for 5 minutes, then turn out on a wire rack to cool completely before slicing. Serve thinly sliced with butter.

Boston brown bread

31

HONOLULU BARS

Makes 25 bars

⅔ cup melted butter or margarine
2 cups light brown sugar
3 eggs
2¾ cups all-purpose flour
2½ teaspoons baking powder

½ teaspoon salt
1 cup coarsely chopped
    macadamia nuts, pecan nuts or
    walnuts
6 oz semi-sweet chocolate pieces

Cream the melted butter and brown sugar in a mixing bowl. Add the eggs, one at a time, beating well after each addition. Sift together the flour, baking powder and salt into another bowl. Stir the chocolate and nuts into the flour mixture. Add the ingredients to the egg mixture and mix until smooth. Spread the mixture in a large greased oblong baking pan. Bake in a preheated moderate oven (350°) for 30–35 minutes. Cool and cut into bars before serving.

PHILADELPHIA STICKY BUNS

Makes 12

1 cake compressed yeast or
    1 package active dry yeast
¼ cup lukewarm water
1 cup milk
4½ cups all-purpose flour
6 tablespoons melted butter
6 tablespoons sugar

2 egg yolks
1 teaspoon salt
2 teaspoons grated lemon rind
1 teaspoon cinnamon
½ cup currants
¼ cup butter
¾ cup light brown sugar

Sprinkle or crumble the yeast into the lukewarm water to soften. Scald the milk, empty it into a large mixing bowl and cool to lukewarm. Stir in 1½ cups of the flour, add the yeast mixture and beat until the mixture is smooth. Cover lightly and let stand in a warm place until bubbles form on the surface. Stir in two-thirds of the melted butter and two-thirds of the sugar. Beat the egg yolks and add with the salt and the grated lemon rind.

Stir in the remaining flour, then knead until the dough is smooth and springy, adding a little more flour if necessary. Cover and set aside to rise in a warm place for about 1 hour, or until doubled in bulk.

Punch down the dough and turn out on to a floured surface. Roll out into a long rectangle about ¾ inch thick. Brush the surface with the remaining melted butter and sprinkle with the remaining sugar mixed with the cinnamon. Sprinkle with the currants. Roll lengthwise into a long roll and cut into 1-inch slices. Place a heavy 9- or 10-inch baking pan over direct heat and in it melt the ¼ cup butter. Remove the pan from the heat and sprinkle the bottom with the brown sugar. Place slices of dough, cut side down, on top of the sugar, cover and let rise again in a warm place until puffy and about doubled in bulk. Bake in a preheated moderate oven (350°) for 25–30 minutes, or until nicely browned on top. Turn the buns out to cool.

LOUISIANA PECAN PRALINES

Makes about 40 pralines

2 cups light brown sugar
1 cup granulated sugar
1 cup water

1 cup light cream
3 cups halved pecan nuts

Combine the brown sugar, granulated sugar, water and cream in a saucepan. Bring to a boil and cook to the soft ball stage (238° on a candy thermometer). Remove from the heat and beat the mixture until creamy. Stir in the nuts. Drop by spoonfuls on to a greased baking sheet and let stand until cool.

LADY BALTIMORE CAKE

Makes 1 8-inch cake

for the cake:
1 cup butter
2 cups sugar
3 cups cake flour
6 teaspoons baking powder
½ teaspoon salt
1 cup milk
7 egg whites
½ teaspoon rose water flavoring

for the frosting and filling:
3 cups sugar
¾ cup water
¼ teaspoon cream of tartar
4 egg whites
⅓ cup chopped seedless raisins
3 dried figs, chopped
1 cup chopped nuts
½ cup chopped candied cherries
½ cup chopped candied pineapple

In a large mixing bowl, cream the butter and sugar together thoroughly until the mixture is fluffy. Combine the flour, baking powder and salt and stir into the creamed mixture alternately with the milk. Beat the egg whites until stiff enough to hold a peak and fold gently into the mixture. Fold in the rose water flavoring. Divide the mixture between 3 7-inch round cake pans lined with waxed paper. Bake in a preheated moderate oven (350°) for 30–35 minutes, or until an inserted skewer comes out clean. Leave in the pans for 5 minutes, then turn out on to wire racks to cool.

For the frosting and filling, combine the sugar, water and cream of tartar in a heavy saucepan. Bring to a boil and boil rapidly until the syrup spins a short thread (236° on a candy thermometer). Beat the egg whites until they stand in stiff peaks. Gradually add the syrup, beating constantly until the frosting is thick and shiny. Fold the chopped raisins and figs into the frosting with the nuts, cherries and pineapple. Sandwich the cakes together with part of the frosting and cover the top and sides of the cake with the remaining frosting.

Lady Baltimore cake

33

BRITISH

Marguerite Patten

Photography by John Miller

The variable climate of Britain, with its comparatively mild winters and ample rainfall, is ideal for the growing of a wide variety of fruits and vegetables and the raising of cattle. The dairy produce is excellent, with numerous local cheeses, Cheddar, Stilton, Cheshire, Leicester and Sage Derby being only a few of the best known. British meat is of exceptional quality—tender lamb from the South Downs, Wiltshire, Suffolk and York hams and, of course, beef, the most highly prized being Scotch. Roast beef with roast potatoes, Yorkshire pudding and creamed horseradish must be to many the supreme classical English dish.

Fish and shellfish are plentiful—lobster and mackerel from the West Country, the famous sole from Dover, oysters from Whitstable and the Welsh coast, salmon from Scotland and Ireland and the many varieties of North Sea fish such as cod, haddock and herring. The countries and counties of Britain all offer their own specialties to enrich the national cuisine. Kent and the Vale of Evesham in Worcestershire vie with each other for the title of 'the garden of England'. Their orchards of cherries, apples and pears present a wonderful picture in the spring. Norfolk is renowned for its fine turkeys, much in demand for the traditional Christmas dinner. In the north of England where high tea, a combination of tea and supper, is a main meal of the day, baking comes into its own, giving the British cuisine excellent recipes for teacakes, breads and cakes.

Some of the most fertile and productive farming land in Britain is to be found in the Lowlands of Scotland. It is particularly suitable for the growing of oats and barley, both of which appear frequently in Scottish cooking, and for soft fruits—jams and jellies are a national specialty which perfectly complement the many varieties of bread, rolls and oatcakes served for breakfast and tea.

Scotland is perhaps particularly noted for the excellence and variety of its fish, two of the most well-known being herring and salmon, and for its beef. Scotch beef is expensive and a great deal of mutton is therefore used in traditional dishes—sheep are reared for both wool and meat throughout Scotland. There is a wide variety of game in the remote Highlands. The season for deer lasts from June to January, but probably the most prominent date in the shooting calendar is August 12, the traditional start of the grouse season.

The cuisine of Wales is plain and wholesome rather than exotic. The staple meat is mutton, for the hill country is ideally suited to sheep farming. Potatoes, root vegetables and, of course, leeks, the national emblem, are the most common accompaniments. Griddle baking is a specialty, and Welsh cakes, the round fruited girdle scones, are a real treat eaten freshly baked and lavishly buttered. As in all parts of Britain, fish and shellfish are excellent, one specialty of the Gower coast being oyster soup, and the hill streams and rivers abound in salmon and trout. Wales has its own cheeses, the most famous being Caerphilly, a mild, white cheese.

Traditional food in Ireland also has simplicity as its keynote. The climate and soil of Ireland is ideal for the potato which is the staple food, often combined with pork, bacon or ham, the most popular meat. The Irish are also great bread makers. The seafood is excellent and salmon, eel and trout are also plentiful, forming the basis for some of Ireland's best recipes.

POTTED SHRIMP

Serves 4

2–2½ lb fresh shrimp, unshelled	dash black pepper
½ cup butter	½ head lettuce
grated nutmeg (see recipe)	2 lemons, sliced

If using freshly caught shrimp, boil them until pink in color and shell while still warm. If buying cooked shrimp, put into hot water, let stand for 1 minute and then drain and shell them.

Put half the butter into a saucepan and heat until melted but not brown. Add the shrimp with a generous dash of nutmeg and the pepper. Heat gently, shaking the pan frequently, until the shrimp are warm. Prolonged heating will make them tough. Spoon into 4 small pots and let stand until the butter cools and sets. Melt the remaining butter, pour over the shrimp and let stand until the butter is quite firm. Cover and store in a cool place or freeze until required.

Loosen the layer of butter on the surface of each pot, using the top of a knife, and unmold the shrimp on to serving plates. Garnish with lettuce leaves and lemon slices and serve with thinly sliced brown bread and butter.

SCALLOPED CRABS

Serves 4

2 cooked crabs, about 1½–2 lb each	2 teaspoons distilled or pure malt vinegar
few drops olive oil	½–1 teaspoon cayenne pepper
1 (2-oz) can anchovy fillets	1 lemon, cut into wedges
6 tablespoons butter	few sprigs parsley
1 cup fine fresh breadcrumbs	

Remove the legs and claws of the crabs by twisting gently in a circular motion. Place each crab on its back with the tail flap toward you. With the fingers of both hands on the shell and both thumbs under the tail flap, push upward until the body breaks away from the shell. Discard the grayish-white stomach bag, which lies behind the head in the shell, and the gray feathery 'dead men's fingers' from each body. Crack the legs and claws and remove all the white meat. Reserve the small claws. Tap sharply along the false line on the underside of each shell and it should come away quite neatly. Scrub the shells, dry them well and rub lightly with the olive oil to make them shiny.

Drain the anchovy fillets, chop half of them and reserve the remainder. Heat the butter in a skillet, add the breadcrumbs and sauté until pale golden brown. Mix both the white and dark meat of the crabs together in a bowl with the chopped anchovy fillets, one-third of the breadcrumbs and the vinegar. Season to taste with the cayenne pepper, adding it sparingly since it is very hot. Press the crab meat mixture back into the shells (see note). Sprinkle with the remainder of the sautéed breadcrumbs and heat in a preheated hot oven (425°) for about 10–12 minutes, or brown under the broiler. Top the crabs with a lattice of the remaining whole anchovy fillets. Garnish with the lemon, parsley and small crab claws.

Note: If there is too much mixture for the crab shells, put the surplus into scallop shells and arrange round the crabs.

POTTED CHEESE

Serves 4

12 oz cheese, white Cheshire,
    Lancashire or Cheddar
⅔ cup butter
2 teaspoons dry mustard

2 tablespoons dry sherry
⅔ cup finely chopped walnuts (see
    note)

Finely grate the cheese. Soften it by pounding in a mortar with a pestle, rubbing through a sieve or beating with a wooden spoon until it is the consistency of butter. Cream half the butter until very soft and fluffy. Add the cheese to the butter and cream again. Blend the mustard with the sherry and gradually stir into the cheese mixture. Beat in the walnuts. Put the mixture into 4 small pots. Melt the remaining butter, cool and then spoon over the top of each pot of cheese. Cover and keep in a cool place or in the refrigerator. Slice and serve with crackers, bread or fresh fruit.

Note: Fresh, dried or pickled walnuts may be used. The brown skins on fresh walnuts should be removed by blanching. Fresh walnuts enhance while preserving the original color and flavor of the cheese, but many people enjoy the distinctive 'bite' of the black pickled walnuts.

COCK-A-LEEKIE

Serves 4–6

12 prunes
1¼ cups water
1 stewing chicken
4 pints chicken stock or water

salt and pepper
1½ lb leeks
few sprigs fresh parsley, chopped

Soak the prunes overnight in the water. Drain before using.

Wash the chicken and put into a very large saucepan with the stock. Add the giblets but omit the liver since it darkens the stock. Bring the liquid to a boil and skim the surface. Lower the heat, add salt and pepper to taste, cover tightly and simmer gently for 2½ hours, or until the chicken is very tender. Remove the chicken from the pan, discard the giblets and set the chicken aside. Strain the stock, return it to the pan and boil rapidly until reduced by half. Skim the fat from the surface of the liquid and discard (see note).

Remove the meat from the chicken breasts and dice finely. Reserve the remainder of the chicken flesh for another dish. Trim the leeks and rinse thoroughly under cold running water. Cut into very small rings and add to the chicken stock along with the prunes. Simmer over moderate heat for 40 minutes. Add the chicken flesh and heat for a few minutes. Taste, and adjust the seasoning. Pour into a heated soup tureen and garnish with the parsley. Alternatively, a little grated cheese sprinkled in at the last minute adds extra flavor.

Note: The stock may be cooled and refrigerated until the fat hardens. The fat can then be lifted away from the surface of the stock.

Cock-a-leekie

OYSTER SOUP

Serves 4

12 oz scrag end of mutton	pepper
3 medium-sized onions	¼ cup butter
1 lb mutton bones	½ cup all-purpose flour
4 pints water	24 small oysters (see note)
1 blade mace or ¼ teaspoon	1 leek or 2 tablespoons chopped
ground mace	fresh parsley

Cut the mutton into pieces. Peel and slice the onions. Place the mutton and onions in a saucepan with the bones, water, mace and pepper. Do not add salt since the oysters are salty. Bring to a boil over high heat. Skim the surface of the liquid, cover the pan and simmer for about 1½ hours. Strain the stock carefully through a cheesecloth until clear. Discard the bones, meat and vegetables. Return the stock to the pan and boil until it is reduced by half.

Heat the butter in a saucepan over moderate heat. Stir in the flour and cook gently, stirring constantly, until pale golden brown. Add the stock gradually, mixing well after each addition. Bring to a boil, stirring constantly until the mixture becomes smooth and thickened. Trim the leek and discard the coarse outer leaves. Rinse thoroughly under cold running water and then slice thinly. Remove the oysters from their shells and add any oyster liquid to the soup. Put the oysters into heated soup bowls. Check the seasoning of the soup and then pour over the oysters. (A generous dash of cayenne pepper and a little lemon juice may also be added before serving for more flavor.) Garnish with the parsley or thinly sliced leek and serve.

Note: This soup may also be made substituting sliced scallops, mussels or clams.

WINDSOR SOUP

Serves 6-8

8 oz beef chuck or round	salt and pepper
3 lb beef bones	⅔–1¼ cups Madeira or sweet
1 calf's foot	red wine
4 pints water	1 tablespoon chopped fresh
bouquet garni (see recipe)	parsley

Cut the beef into ½-inch cubes and place in a large saucepan. Rinse the beef bones and calf's foot thoroughly under cold running water. Add to the pan with the water, *bouquet garni* (3 bay leaves, 3 sprigs parsley, 1 sprig thyme, tied together) and salt and pepper to taste. Bring to a boil and skim the surface. Lower the heat, cover the pan and simmer gently for 2½ hours.

Discard the bones, beef and *bouquet garni*. Strain the soup, add the wine, reheat and adjust the seasoning. Pour into heated soup bowls and garnish with the parsley or a more elaborate garnish such as tiny pieces of lobster or chopped anchovy fillets.

Note: The flavor of shellfish blended into this soup is very pleasant and may be achieved by adding small pieces of flaked lobster when reheating the soup.

COD STEAKS AND BACON

Serves 4

4 cod steaks, about 8 oz each	1 teaspoon grated lemon rind
salt and pepper	1 tablespoon chopped fresh
2 tablespoons lemon juice	parsley
4 slices bacon	salt and pepper
3 tablespoons butter	1 egg
for the stuffing:	2 tablespoons lemon juice
1½ cups fine fresh breadcrumbs	**for the garnish:**
⅓ cup chopped beef suet or	few sprigs fresh parsley
¼ cup melted butter	8 tomatoes

Rinse the fish under cold running water and dry well. Sprinkle each side with salt and pepper to taste and the lemon juice. Remove any rind from the bacon. Grease the bottom of a shallow ovenproof dish with half the butter.

To make the stuffing, mix together the breadcrumbs, suet, lemon rind, parsley and salt and pepper to taste. Lightly beat the egg and stir into the mixture along with the lemon juice to make a moist stuffing. Divide the stuffing into 4 equal portions and press one portion on top of each piece of fish. Wrap the bacon around the fish and lift carefully into the dish. (The cod steaks may be placed on buttered foil for stuffing and then lifted on to the dish.) Melt the remaining butter and brush over each piece of stuffed fish. Bake in a preheated moderately hot oven (375°) for approximately 20 minutes, or until the fish is tender. Do not overcook. Transfer the fish to a heated serving dish and garnish with parsley and baked or broiled tomatoes.

SALMON PATTIES

Serves 4

8 oz salmon, cooked	**for the batter:**
8 oz potatoes, cooked and	1 cup all-purpose flour
mashed	dash salt
½ teaspoon grated lemon rind	1 egg
2 teaspoons lemon juice	⅔ cup milk
1 teaspoon chopped chives or	⅓ cup light cream
grated onion	oil for deep-frying
2 teaspoons chopped fresh parsley	1 lemon, sliced
(or use half parsley and half	
fresh tarragon)	
salt and pepper	
1 egg	

Flake the salmon and place in a mixing bowl with the mashed potatoes, lemon rind, lemon juice, chives, parsley and salt and pepper to taste. Lightly beat the egg and add to the mixture. Mix thoroughly to a stiff consistency. Turn out on to a lightly floured board and shape the salmon mixture into 8 small round flat cakes. Set aside in a cool place or in the refrigerator while making the batter.

To make the batter, sift the flour and salt into a mixing bowl and make a well in the center. Beat together the egg, milk and cream. Pour the egg mixture into the well and beat with a wooden spoon to form a smooth batter.

Dip the salmon cakes into the batter, drain off the surplus and deep-fry in hot oil until crisp and golden brown. Drain on absorbent paper and arrange on a heated serving plate. Garnish with the lemon slices and serve hot.

MACKEREL WITH GOOSEBERRY SAUCE

Serves 4

4 mackerel	⅓ cup sugar
1 sprig fennel	⅔ cup water
6 tablespoons butter	2 tablespoons butter
salt and pepper	1 tablespoon chopped fresh
for the sauce:	parsley (optional)
1 lb gooseberries	few sprigs fennel or parsley

Clean the mackerel, discard the heads and rinse the fish under cold running water. Remove the backbones, taking care to maintain the shape of the fish. Finely chop the fennel. Spread the insides of the fish with half the butter, season well with salt and pepper to taste and sprinkle with half the fennel. Fold the fish back into shape. Melt the remaining butter in a small saucepan. Brush the melted butter over the fish and sprinkle with the remaining fennel. Broil the fish under moderate heat, turning over once, until the flesh is tender.

Meanwhile, wash the gooseberries without removing the stems. Place in a large saucepan with the sugar and water. Simmer over moderate heat until the fruit is reduced to a pulp. Rub the fruit and juice through a sieve to make a purée and discard the seeds and skins. Return the purée to the pan, add the butter with the chopped parsley and reheat. Arrange the fish on a heated dish and garnish with sprigs of fennel or parsley. Serve with the hot gooseberry sauce and new potatoes.

DOVER SOLE WITH ORANGE OR LEMON BUTTER

Serves 2

2 Dover or lemon sole,	salt and pepper
about 8–12 oz each	2 teaspoons grated orange or
1¼ cups water	lemon rind
1 bay leaf	¼ cup butter
⅔ cup fish stock (see recipe)	1 orange or lemon, cut into
⅔ cup white wine	wedges

To make the fish stock, remove the skins of each fish and reserve. Leave the fish whole. Put the skin into a saucepan with the water and the bay leaf and simmer gently for 15 minutes. Strain the stock into a clean saucepan and then reboil until reduced to ⅔ cup. Put the fish stock, whole fish and wine into a large saucepan. Season lightly with salt and pepper. Poach the fish gently for 10 minutes, spooning the liquid over the fish once or twice.

Meanwhile, blend the orange or lemon rind with the butter. Remove the fish from the liquid and place on a buttered heated flameproof dish. Spread the flavored butter over the fish and cook for 5–6 minutes under a hot broiler. Garnish with the orange or lemon wedges and serve.

FINNAN HADDIE IN CREAM SAUCE

Serves 4

2 lb smoked haddock
about 2 cups milk
1 bay leaf
pepper
¼ cup butter

¼ cup all-purpose flour
2 teaspoons dry mustard
1¼ cups light cream
dash cayenne pepper
1 lemon, sliced

Cut off the tail and fins of the smoked haddock and cut the fish into 4 portions. Place in a large shallow saucepan or skillet and cover completely with the milk. Add the bay leaf and a little pepper. Bring just to a boil, then lower the heat and simmer until the fish is cooked but not broken. Carefully remove the fish from the liquid, drain thoroughly and place on a heated serving dish. Cover with buttered paper or foil and keep hot.

Strain the milk and, if necessary, add more milk to make 1½ cups. Heat the butter in a saucepan, stir in the flour and mustard and cook for 2–3 minutes. Remove from the heat and add the flavored milk and the cream, a little at a time, mixing well after each addition. Bring to a boil over moderate heat, stirring constantly until the mixture thickens. Pour some of the sauce over the fish and serve the remainder in a sauceboat. Sprinkle the fish with cayenne pepper and garnish with the lemon. Finnan haddock prepared in this way is particularly good accompanied by young carrots and new potatoes.

Dover sole with lemon butter

Cheese pudding

STEAK AND KIDNEY PIE

Serves 4–5

for the filling:

1½ lb beef chuck or round

4 oz beef kidney

¼ cup all-purpose flour

½ teaspoon salt

dash pepper

¼ cup lard or beef drippings

2½ cups water

1 large onion (optional)

4 oz button mushrooms (optional)

8 oysters (optional)

for the flaky pastry:

2 cups all-purpose flour

dash salt

¾ cup butter or ½ cup butter and ¼ cup shortening

about ⅔ cup cold water

for glazing:

1 egg

1 tablespoon water

Cut the beef into 1-inch cubes and discard any excess fat. Discard any membrane and fat from the kidney and cut into pieces the same size as the beef. Blend the flour with the salt and pepper on a plate. Coat the meat thoroughly in the seasoned flour. Melt the lard in a saucepan, add the meat and fry over moderate heat for 5 minutes. (If using the onion, mushrooms or oysters, see note.) Gradually blend in the water and bring to a boil, stirring constantly until thickened. Lower the heat, cover the pan and simmer gently for about 2 hours, or until the beef is tender. Taste, and adjust the seasoning.

Meanwhile, prepare the flaky pastry. Sift the flour and salt together into a mixing bowl. Soften the butter on a plate, reshape it into a rectangle and divide it into 3 equal portions. Add one portion of the butter to the flour mixture. Rub the mixture lightly between the fingertips, allowing it to fall back into the bowl. When evenly mixed, add the lemon juice and

enough water to make a smooth, elastic dough.

Turn the dough out on to a floured board, knead lightly and roll out to a rectangle. Cut the second portion of the butter into small pieces and dot over the top two-thirds of the rectangle. Fold the lower third of the rectangle up over the center third and the top third down to enclose the butter completely between the layers. Give the dough a quarter-turn to the right so that an open end is toward you. Seal both ends by pressing down firmly with a rolling pin, then 'rib' the pastry by pressing the dough with a rolling pin at regular intervals.

Roll the dough out carefully to a rectangle again and repeat the above process using the remaining portion of butter. Turn, seal the ends and 'rib' the pastry. Let the pastry stand in a cool place or in the refrigerator for several hours before the final rolling.

Roll out the pastry to about 1 inch larger all around than a 9-inch pie dish. Grease the rim of the pie dish and place on it a narrow strip cut from the pastry. Spoon the hot meat mixture into the dish. Reserve most of the gravy. Moisten the top of the pastry strip with a little water and cover the pie with the pastry lid. Press the edges firmly together to seal, cut off any surplus pastry with a sharp knife and make horizontal cuts along the edge. Make a slit in the lid to allow the steam to escape during cooking. Cut any leftover pastry into decorative shapes such as leaves, a rose or a tassel and arrange on the pastry. Beat the egg and water together and brush over the pastry. Bake in a preheated hot oven (450°) for 25 minutes, then lower the heat to 375° for a further 10–12 minutes. Reheat the reserved gravy and serve separately in a gravy boat with the pie.

Note: If using the onion, mushrooms or oysters, add as follows. Slice the onion thickly and sauté with the meat in the saucepan. Add the mushrooms to the saucepan during the last 5 minutes cooking time. Blend the oysters with the cooked meat before spooning the meat mixture into the pie dish.

CHEESE PUDDING

Serves 4

1 cup fine fresh breadcrumbs	⅔ cup cream (see note)
1½ cups grated Cheddar cheese	dash dry mustard
1¼ cups milk	salt and pepper
3 tablespoons butter	3 eggs

Put the breadcrumbs into a bowl with the cheese. Heat the milk in a saucepan with three-fourths of the butter, the cream, mustard and salt and pepper to taste. Do not allow to boil. Beat the eggs lightly. Beat the hot milk into the beaten eggs. Strain the mixture over the breadcrumbs and cheese and set aside for 15–20 minutes to allow the breadcrumbs to absorb the liquid. Grease a 1-quart pie dish or soufflé dish with the remaining butter. Pour the cheese mixture into the dish and bake in a preheated moderately hot oven (375°) for about 45 minutes, or until well risen and golden brown. Serve at once with a crisp green salad.

Note: For a less rich pudding, substitute milk for the cream.

ROAST BEEF WITH ROAST POTATOES

Serves 6–8

1 rolled rib roast, about 3 lb	salt and pepper
¼ cup beef drippings (see recipe)	6 large potatoes

Place the beef in a large roasting pan. If the beef is very lean, spread the drippings over the top and sides. Sprinkle lightly with salt and pepper. Roast in a preheated hot oven (425°) for 15 minutes per pound plus an additional 15 minutes. At the end of this time the beef will be slightly underdone and red in the center. For a well done roast, allow 20 minutes per pound plus an additional 20 minutes.

Peel and rinse the potatoes. Dry thoroughly with absorbent paper, cut into halves and sprinkle very lightly with salt. Place in the pan with the beef about 1 hour before the end of the roasting time. Baste the potatoes with the fat in the pan and turn them several times so they become crisp and evenly browned on the outside but soft in the center.

Remove the potatoes and drain well. Place the meat in the center of a large heated meat dish and arrange the potatoes around the sides. Serve immediately with Yorkshire pudding and creamed horseradish (see below). Traditionally, the beef is carved at the table.

Note: Other vegetables such as parsnips or onions may be roasted and served with beef in the same way as the potatoes. Allow 1¼–1½ hours roasting time for onions. Parsnips should be boiled for 20–25 minutes, well drained and then roasted for 35–40 minutes.

YORKSHIRE PUDDING

Serves 4–6

1 cup all-purpose flour	⅔ cup milk
dash salt	2 tablespoons shortening or
1 egg	meat drippings
⅔ cup water	

Sift the flour and salt into a mixing bowl. Using a wooden spoon, beat in the egg and gradually beat in about one-third of the liquid, or just enough to make a thick batter. Beat vigorously until the batter is smooth, then gradually add the remaining liquid. Set aside in a cool place until required.

About 30–40 minutes before the end of the roasting time for the meat, heat the shortening or meat drippings in a Yorkshire pudding pan or roasting pan about 7 by 5 inches. Pour in the batter. Place the pan on the top shelf of a preheated hot oven (425°) and bake for about 30–40 minutes, or until well risen and golden brown.

Note: To cook a Yorkshire pudding in the traditional way, lift the meat from the roasting pan about 45 minutes before the end of the roasting time for the meat. Pour off nearly all the meat drippings, reserving 1–2 tablespoons in the pan. Pour in the batter and replace the pan in the oven. Place the meat on a trivet over the roasting pan or on a shelf above the pan so the juices from the meat will drip on to the Yorkshire pudding during cooking.

CREAMED HORSERADISH

Serves 4–6

¼ teaspoon dry mustard	3 tablespoons grated fresh
¼ teaspoon salt	horseradish root
dash pepper	1 tablespoon white vinegar or
dash sugar	lemon juice
⅔ cup heavy cream	

Mix together the mustard, salt, pepper, sugar and cream. Add the grated horseradish, then very gradually beat in the vinegar. Serve as an accompaniment to roast beef.

Melton Mowbray pie

WILTSHIRE HAM IN CIDER

Serves 4–6

1 cooked ham, about 4 lb
about 3¾ cups apple cider
12 small onions
4 cloves

bouquet garni (see recipe)
pepper
½ cup fine dry breadcrumbs

If the ham is well salted, cover with cold water and soak overnight. The next day, discard the water and place the ham in a large saucepan. Add enough cider to cover. Bring to a boil over moderate heat, skimming the surface occasionally. Lower the heat and simmer for 1 hour. Peel the onions and add them whole to the ham with the cloves, *bouquet garni* (3 bay leaves, 3 sprigs parsley, 1 sprig thyme, tied together) and pepper to taste. Continue simmering for a further 40 minutes, or until the onions are tender but unbroken.

When the ham and onions are tender, carefully remove them from the pan.

Strip off and discard the rind from the ham and sprinkle the fatty surface with the breadcrumbs. Serve the ham with the onions, lima beans, young carrots and mashed potatoes. The cider in which the ham was cooked may be served separately as an unthickened sauce.

MELTON MOWBRAY PIE

Serves 5–6

for the filling:
1½ lb lean boneless pork, cut from
　the leg
8 oz pork shoulder
6–8 anchovy fillets or 1 teaspoon
　anchovy paste
dash pepper
¼ cup chicken or veal stock
for the hot water crust pastry:
3 cups all-purpose flour

dash salt
⅔ cup water
½ cup lard or shortening
1 egg
1 tablespoon water
for the jelly:
¾ cup chicken or veal stock
1 teaspoon gelatin

The following recipe gives two methods of preparing the pie mold. See note for the alternative method.

Cut the pork into ½-inch cubes and chop the anchovies. Mix the pork and anchovies together in a mixing bowl and add the pepper and the stock. Do not add any salt. If using anchovy paste instead of anchovies, blend it with the pepper and stock and add to the pork mixture. Set the mixture aside until required.

Sift the flour and salt into a mixing bowl. Make a well in the center. Place the water and lard in a saucepan and heat until the lard melts and the water boils. Remove from the heat and immediately pour the hot liquid into the flour. Blend the mixture with a knife to make a rough dough. Turn out on to a floured board and knead lightly while the dough is still warm.

Divide the pastry into thirds. Cover one-third of the dough and set aside in a warm place until required. Roll out one-third of the dough to a 7-inch circle and place in the bottom of a lightly greased 7-inch deep spring-form pan. Roll out the remaining third of the pastry into a rectangle the depth of the pan being used and long enough to go around the circumference of the pan. Line the inside of the pan, pressing the seams firmly together. If necessary, brush with a little water to make sure the joins are firmly sealed. Turn the rim of the pastry down slightly to make a firm base for the pastry lid. Pack the reserved pork and anchovy filling into the pie shell.

Roll out the reserved one-third of the pastry into a circle to fit the top of the pie. Put the pastry lid over the filling, trim off the surplus and seal the edges firmly. Make a hole or slit in the pastry lid. Make leaves or a rose with the surplus pastry, moisten the decorations with a little water and press on to the pastry. Beat the egg with the water and brush over the pie surface and decoration to glaze. Bake in a preheated moderate oven (350°) for about 2½ hours. Lower the heat to 325° after 1½ hours if the pastry becomes too brown. Remove the pie from the oven and cool completely.

For the jelly, measure the stock into a saucepan, sprinkle in the gelatin and allow to soak for a few moments. Stir over low heat until dissolved. Remove from the heat and cool until almost setting. Pour the mixture into the pie through the hole or steam vent in the pastry lid. Set aside in a cool place for several hours until the jelly sets. Serve the pie with a green salad.

Note: An alternative method of preparing a 'raised' pie is to raise or mold the pastry by hand around a 7-inch deep spring-form pan which has been greased and floured. Roll two-thirds of the pastry into a large circle. Place the pan in the center of the pastry and mold the warm dough firmly around it. Wrap a double layer of waxed paper around the pastry for additional support. Let stand until cool then remove the waxed paper and the pan. Proceed as above, reducing the baking time by 15 minutes.

SALTED BEEF

Makes 4–6 lb

5 quarts water
2 cups salt
¾ cup light brown sugar

2 teaspoons saltpeter
4–6 lb heel of round or boned
　beef brisket

Place the water, salt, sugar and saltpeter in a very large saucepan. Stir over low heat until the sugar is dissolved, then add the beef. Bring to a boil, lower the heat then simmer steadily for 5 minutes. Remove the beef, skim the surface of the liquid, strain into a very large enameled bowl or earthenware jar and let stand until cold. Wipe the beef carefully, trim away any excess fat and put into the brine. Cover and let stand in a cold place for a minimum of 7 days to obtain mildly salted beef, or about 10 days for a stronger flavor. Turn the beef in the brine each day. Use as required.

FAGGOTS

Serves 4–6

1 large onion	dash chopped fresh thyme or
12 oz–1 lb pork liver or	dried thyme
1 pork heart, about 8 oz	⅔ cup fine fresh breadcrumbs
4 oz pork shoulder	or oatmeal
salt and pepper	1 egg
dash ginger	about ½ cup stock
dash chopped fresh sage or dried	1 pork caul (optional)
sage	

Peel and slice the onion. Rinse the liver and pork under cold running water. Discard any tough fibrous parts. Place the onion, liver and pork in a saucepan, cover with cold water and season with salt and pepper. Place over high heat and bring to a boil. Lower the heat and simmer for 45–50 minutes, or until the meat is tender. Drain off and reserve the stock.

Finely grind the liver and pork and mix in the ginger, sage, thyme, breadcrumbs and egg. Add enough of the reserved stock to form a moist mixture and add salt and pepper to taste. Form the mixture into 2- to 3-inch balls and wrap each ball in a piece of the caul. Place the balls fairly close together in a lightly greased pan. Alternatively, spread the mixture into a greased 8-inch square pan, mark into squares and cover with a sheet of greased cooking foil. Cook in a preheated moderately hot oven (400°) for about 1 hour. Serve the faggots hot with brown gravy and pease pudding (see page 52) or mashed potatoes.

HAM IN WHISKEY AND CREAM

Serves 4

2 large potatoes	2 medium-sized baking apples
salt and pepper	1 tablespoon light brown sugar
1 egg yolk	¼ cup butter or bacon drippings
2 tablespoons butter	⅔ cup beef stock
¼ cup all-purpose flour	⅔ cup Irish whiskey
4 slices smoked ham, about	⅓ cup heavy cream
8 oz each	

Peel the potatoes and cut into quarters. Cook in salted water to cover until tender. Drain, mash and season well with salt and pepper to taste. Beat the egg yolk and butter into the mashed potato and set aside in a warm place until required.

Meanwhile, mix the flour with a little pepper. Remove any rind from the ham slices and coat the ham on both sides with the seasoned flour. Peel, core and thinly slice the apples, then sprinkle with the sugar. Heat the butter in a large skillet over moderate heat and fry the ham slices for 2–3 minutes on each side, or until tender. Place the slices on a heated serving dish and keep hot.

Pour the stock and whiskey into the skillet and bring to a boil. Put the apples into the hot liquid and simmer gently for 5 minutes. Lower the heat and stir in the cream. Return the ham to the skillet and heat gently for 2–3 minutes, but do not boil.

Using a large star tip in a pastry bag, pipe the mashed potato mixture in a border around the edge of a large ovenproof serving plate and place under a hot broiler until lightly brown. Arrange the ham in the center of the plate and carefully spoon the sauce over the slices. Serve immediately.

ROAST LAMB AND ACCOMPANIMENTS

Serves 4

leg or square cut shoulder of	3 tablespoons distilled or pure
lamb, about 4 lb (see note)	malt vinegar
salt and pepper	**for the cucumber sauce:**
for the mint sauce:	2 cucumbers
¼ cup chopped fresh mint	salt and pepper
1 tablespoon sugar	¼ cup butter
2 teaspoons boiling water	1¼ cups white stock or water
(optional)	⅔ cup heavy cream

Place the lamb in a roasting pan and season lightly with salt and pepper. Unless the lamb is very lean, there is no need to add any fat. Roast, uncovered, in a preheated hot oven (425°), allowing 20 minutes per pound plus an additional 20 minutes. If the joint is wrapped in aluminum foil or a covered roasting pan is used, then allow an additional 15–20 minutes cooking time.

To make the mint sauce, rinse the mint under cold running water, dry well and strip the leaves from the stems. Finely chop the leaves on a board with the sugar. Place the mixture in a bowl and stir in the water and vinegar. Alternatively, put the water and vinegar into a blender, then add the sugar and the mint leaves. Blend for a few moments until finely chopped.

To make the cucumber sauce, peel the cucumbers. If a little of the skin is left on the cucumbers it will give a pale green color to the sauce. Cut the cucumbers into ½-inch pieces, then cut each piece into fine strips. Season lightly with salt and pepper to taste. Set aside for about 30 minutes to draw out the excess water. Melt the butter in a saucepan, add the cucumber strips and sauté for several minutes. Add the white stock and simmer until tender. Rub the mixture through a sieve or use a blender to make a purée. Return the purée to the pan and stir in the cream. Reheat gently but do not allow to boil. Taste and adjust the seasoning.

Serve the hot roast lamb with the sauces, peas and new potatoes.

Note: A crown roast may also be served with these sauces. The center of the crown may be stuffed before roasting, or filled with young vegetables just before serving. Protect the ends of the bones with aluminum foil to prevent burning. Garnish each bone with a paper frill, olive or candied cherry.

Roast lamb and accompaniments

JUGGED HARE

Serves 4–6

1 (3-lb) hare, with the blood, if
  possible
1 tablespoon vinegar
3¾ cups water or hare stock
  (see recipe)
salt and pepper
½ cup all-purpose flour
2 medium-sized onions
3 medium-sized carrots (optional)
6 tablespoons shortening
bouquet garni (see recipe)
1 lemon (optional)
¼ cup redcurrant jelly
⅔ cup port or claret

for the forcemeat balls:
2 cups fine fresh breadcrumbs
2 tablespoons chopped fresh
  parsley
salt and pepper
½ teaspoon finely grated lemon
  rind
2 teaspoons lemon juice
dash mixed dried herbs
½ cup chopped beef suet or
  ¼ cup melted butter
1 egg

The blood of the hare gives a rich flavor to the sauce. Cut the
hare into pieces, place in a large saucepan, cover with water
and add the vinegar. Soak the pieces of hare for 1 hour to
whiten the flesh.

Meanwhile, to make the hare stock, put the liver and head
of the hare into a second large saucepan with water to cover
and salt and pepper to taste. Cover tightly and simmer for a
minimum of 30 minutes. Strain the stock and add water to
make 3¾ cups. Reserve the liver.

Mix the flour with ½ teaspoon salt and a dash of pepper.
Drain and dry the hare pieces and coat with the seasoned
flour. Peel and slice the onions and carrots, if used. Carrots
give a sweeter flavor to the sauce. Melt the shortening in a
saucepan over moderate heat and sauté the hare pieces for 5
minutes. Remove the hare and set aside until required.

Add the onions and carrots to the hot fat in the pan and
sauté for 3–4 minutes. Add the stock gradually, stirring well
after each addition, and bring to a boil, stirring constantly
until thickened and boiling. Place the hare pieces and the
liver in the sauce with the blood and *bouquet garni* (3 bay
leaves, 3 sprigs parsley, 1 sprig thyme, tied together). Halve
the lemon, remove the seeds and add the lemon halves to the
pan. Lemon flavor gives bite to the sauce. Cover the pan and
simmer the hare for 2 hours.

Remove the hare pieces and keep hot. Discard the lemon
and *bouquet garni*. Rub the vegetables and liquid from the
pan through a sieve, or use a blender to make a purée and
return to the pan. Add the redcurrant jelly and wine and heat
gently until the jelly dissolves. Taste and adjust the
seasoning. Return the hare to the sauce, cover the pan and
simmer for a further 1 hour. Alternatively, the hare and
sauce may be put into a casserole, covered and cooked in a
preheated moderate oven (325°) for 1¼–1½ hours.

To make the forcemeat balls, mix together the breadcrumbs, parsley, salt, pepper, lemon rind, lemon juice, dried
herbs, suet and the egg. Shape into 12 small balls and bake
on a greased baking sheet near the top of a preheated
moderate oven (325°) for 20–30 minutes. Serve the jugged
hare with the forcemeat balls. Garnish with fried bread
croutons or candied cherries and serve redcurrant jelly
separately.

Jugged hare

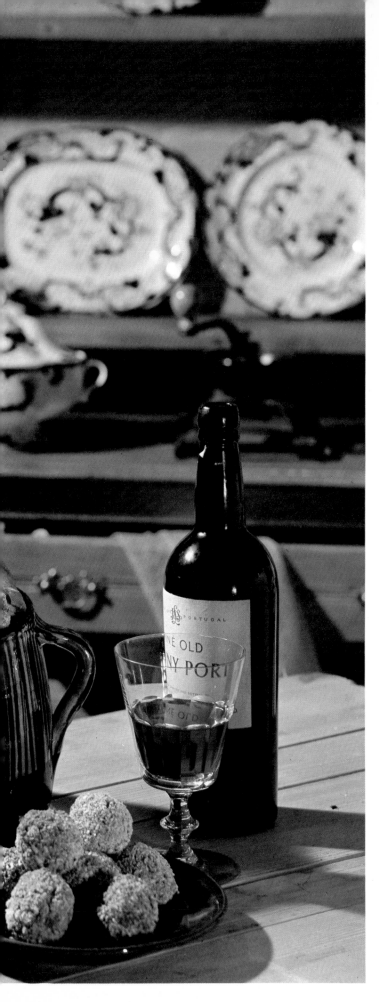

CASSEROLE OF PORK

Serves 4

1 head cabbage, about 1 lb	½ teaspoon chopped fresh sage
3 large onions	2 teaspoons chopped fresh parsley
¼ cup butter	dash grated nutmeg
salt and pepper	**for the garnish:**
4 large pork loin chops, about 8 oz each	2 medium-sized baking apples
	2 tablespoons butter
1¼ cups sweet cider or apple juice	2 tablespoons light brown sugar

Discard the coarse outer leaves of the cabbage, reserving just the heart. Cut in quarters lengthwise, cut away the hard center core and finely shred. Peel and thinly slice the onions. Melt the butter in a saucepan and sauté the cabbage and onions for 2–3 minutes. Season well with salt and pepper and place in a large, shallow casserole. Arrange the pork chops over the cabbage mixture, pour the cider over the chops and sprinkle with the sage, parsley and nutmeg. Cover the casserole tightly and cook in a preheated moderate oven (350°) for about 1–1½ hours, or until the meat is very tender.

Meanwhile, prepare the garnish. Peel, core and cut the apples into thin rings. Melt the butter in a heavy skillet, add the apple rings and sauté until just tender. Sprinkle with the sugar and arrange the apple rings around the edge of the pork chops in the casserole before serving.

CORNISH PASTIES

Serves 4

for the filling:	**for the basic pie dough:**
12 oz beef round	3 cups all-purpose flour
2 medium-sized potatoes	dash salt
2 medium-sized onions	½–¾ cup butter or shortening
small piece swede or turnip (optional)	(see recipe)
	about ¼ cup water
salt and pepper	**for glazing:**
1 tablespoon water or beef bouillon	1 egg
	1 tablespoon water

To make the filling, cut the beef into ½-inch cubes and place in a mixing bowl. Peel and finely dice the potatoes, onions and swede, and add to the beef. Season well with salt and pepper to taste and blend with the water.

Prepare the pastry as for Mince Pies, page 53. Use the smaller quantity of butter if a less rich pastry is desired. Roll out to ¼ inch thick and cut into 4 circles, about 7 inches in diameter. (In Cornwall, if the pasty is to be served hot for a family meal, one large pasty is traditionally made instead of several small ones.)

Place the circles on a baking sheet. Place the filling across the center of the pastry, moisten the edges of the pastry with water and bring the opposite edges together to enclose the filling completely. Press the pastry edges firmly together to seal in the filling and flute them. Lightly beat the egg with the water. Brush the pastry with the egg mixture. Bake in a preheated moderately hot oven (400°) for 20 minutes, then lower the heat to 325° and bake for a further 25–30 minutes for small pasties, or a further 45 minutes for a large pasty. Serve hot or cold.

Note: For a sweet filling use apples, sugar and seedless white raisins.

MUTTON PIES

Serves 4

for the filling:	for the hot water crust pastry:
12 oz boneless mutton, cut from the shoulder or loin	3 cups all-purpose flour
	dash salt
salt and pepper	½ cup shortening or margarine
1 cup currants or raisins	¾ cup water
⅓ cup light brown sugar	1 egg

To make the filling, coarsely grind the meat. Season well with salt and pepper and set aside until required. Wash the currants, soak in boiling water for a few minutes, drain and dry. Mix the currants and brown sugar together.

Prepare the pastry as for Melton Mowbray Pie, page 43. Roll out to ⅛ inch thick on a lightly floured board while still warm. Cut out 8 small circles and press into lightly greased deep patty pans. Cut the remaining dough into slightly smaller circles for the lids. Place the lids in a warm place until ready to use so the pastry remains pliable.

Put the mutton and raisins in alternate layers in the lined patty pans, starting and finishing with the mutton. Press down lightly, as the filling should be fairly compact. Brush the edges of the pastry with water and cover each pie with a pastry lid. Make a slit in the center of each pie and decorate with pastry roses and leaves made from the pastry trimmings. Lightly beat the egg and brush over the surface of each pie. Bake in a preheated moderately hot oven (400°) for 20 minutes, then lower the heat to 375° and bake for a further 15 minutes, or until the pastry is golden brown and the meat is tender. Serve the pies hot, with salad or cooked leeks.

KENTISH CHICKEN PUDDING

Serves 5–6

for the suet pastry:	2 cups water
2½ cups all-purpose flour sifted with 2½ teaspoons baking powder	3 medium-sized onions
	6 medium-sized carrots
dash salt	2 tablespoons all-purpose flour
1 cup chopped beef suet	salt and pepper
about ⅔ cup water	
for the filling:	
1 stewing chicken with giblets, about 4½ lb	

To make the suet pastry, sift the flour and salt together in a large mixing bowl. Add the suet. Stir in enough of the water to form a soft dough. Turn the dough on to a floured board and knead lightly. Roll into a large circle, cut out one fourth of the circle in a wedge shape and set aside for making the pastry lid. Lower the remaining three-fourths of the circle into a greased 2-quart heat-resistant bowl or pudding mold. Bring the cut edges of the dough together and press on to the sides and bottom of the bowl, sealing the edges together. Trim any surplus dough from the top. By lining the bowl in this way you avoid any uneven pleats in the dough. Wipe the chicken. Put the giblets into a saucepan with the water and simmer for a minimum of 30 minutes to make a good stock. The heart may be diced when partially cooked and added to the filling.

Discard the skin from the chicken. Joint the chicken, remove the flesh from the bones and cut into large pieces. Peel and slice the onions and carrots and mix with the chicken flesh and heart. Sprinkle with the flour and salt and pepper to taste. Place the prepared chicken mixture in the bowl or pudding mold. Add enough of the giblet stock to half cover the filling. Reserve any remaining stock.

Roll the reserved dough into a circle the same size as the top of the bowl. Brush the rim of the pastry with water and press the lid into position. Traditionally, a linen pudding cloth is used to cover a steamed pudding. It is first dipped into boiling water, then into flour, so it becomes moisture-proof. To cover the pudding, make a fold down the center of the cloth to allow the pudding to rise as it steams, place it over the pudding and tie securely with string around the edge of the bowl. Then bring up the four corners and tie them neatly together over the pudding. Make a handle with the string. Alternatively, lightly greased waxed paper or aluminum foil may be used, in which case simply trim away the spare paper or foil below the string and make a handle as before. Place the pudding in a steamer over boiling water (see note). Steam for at least 3½–4 hours. Keep the water boiling constantly throughout the cooking time and replenish with additional boiling water when necessary.

When the pudding is cooked, remove the bowl from the steamer with the string handle or with tongs and remove the covering. Dry the outside of the bowl. Fold a napkin lengthwise, so that it is as wide as the bowl is high. Wrap the napkin around the bowl and secure the ends with a small safety pin or tuck them into the fold of the napkin. To serve, remove the first slice of pudding and pour in the reserved stock which has been reheated.

Note: When a steamer is not available, the pudding may be put into a large saucepan with boiling water reaching halfway up the sides of the bowl. Cover the pan and boil steadily throughout the cooking time. Replenish with boiling water when necessary.

LANCASHIRE HOT-POT

Serves 4

1½ lb rolled lamb shoulder or lamb rib roast	1 small turnip
	1 large onion or 2 leeks
salt and pepper	about 2 cups water
2 large potatoes	meat drippings (see recipe)
2 carrots	

Season the lamb with salt and pepper to taste. Peel and thickly slice the potatoes, carrots, turnip and onion. If using leeks instead of onion, trim, rinse thoroughly under cold running water and cut into 1-inch pieces. Place the lamb, potatoes, carrots, turnip and onion in layers in a deep casserole, adding additional salt and pepper to taste. End with an overlapping layer of potatoes. Add enough of the water to reach about one-third of the way up the casserole. Place small pats of meat drippings on top of the potatoes. Cover the casserole and cook in a preheated cool oven (300°) for 2½–3 hours. Remove the cover about 30 minutes before the end of cooking and increase the temperature to 400° to brown the top layer of potatoes. Serve with pickled red cabbage.

HAGGIS

Serves 10–12

1 sheep's pluck (liver, heart and lungs)
salt and pepper
1¼ cups stock (see recipe)
2 medium-sized onions
2⅔ cups oatmeal
1⅓ cups chopped beef suet
dash cayenne pepper

Rinse the pluck thoroughly under cold running water. Open the heart and cut away the gristle and vessels. Put the pluck into a saucepan and cover with cold water. Season lightly with salt and pepper and simmer over moderate heat for 1¼ hours. Remove the pluck from the pan and reserve 1¼ cups of the stock. Discard the remainder. Grind the pluck. Peel and grate the onions. Mix together the reserved stock, pluck, onions, oatmeal and suet. Season well with salt and pepper and the cayenne pepper. Put the mixture into a greased heat-resistant bowl or pudding mold. Do not fill more than three-fourths full since there must be room for the haggis to swell during cooking. Cover the bowl with greased waxed paper or aluminum foil. Place in a steamer over boiling water, and steam for at least 4 hours. Keep the water boiling constantly throughout the cooking time and replenish with additional boiling water when necessary. (If no steamer is available, see Kentish Chicken Pudding, preceding page, for an alternative method of steaming.)

Remove the haggis from the bowl and serve at once with mashed neeps (turnips). Scotch whisky is generally served with haggis, and a little whisky is sometimes poured over it.

Note: The true haggis is difficult to make at home as the various ingredients must be put into a sheep's stomach bag. Apart from the problem of obtaining this, there is the rather unpleasant and lengthy task of cleaning the bag. Modern Scottish cooks, however, often make haggis in a bowl, and while it may not look the same, the flavor is excellent.

ROAST VENISON

Serves 6

2 medium-sized onions
1¼ cups red wine
bouquet garni (see recipe)
dash salt
8 peppercorns
2 teaspoons prepared mustard
2 tablespoons olive oil
4½–5 lb haunch of venison
1 cup lard or shortening
for the game chips:
3 medium-sized potatoes
oil for deep-frying
¾ cup fried breadcrumbs

To make the marinade, peel and thickly slice the onions and place in a large bowl with the wine, *bouquet garni* (3 bay leaves, 3 sprigs parsley, 1 sprig thyme, tied together) and salt. Add the peppercorns, mustard and olive oil. Rinse the venison under cold running water and dry thoroughly with absorbent paper. Place the venison in the marinade. Cover and set aside in a cool place for 2–3 days. Turn the meat once or twice a day so the marinade soaks into the meat.

When ready to cook, remove the venison from the marinade and place in a roasting pan with the lard. Roast in a preheated moderately hot oven (400°), allowing 20 minutes per pound plus an additional 20 minutes. Baste frequently with the fat in the pan.

At the end of the cooking time, strain the marinade and reserve for making the game sauce (see page 52) or gravy.

To make the game chips, peel the potatoes, cut into wafer-thin slices and dry well. In a deep-fat fryer, heat the oil to 365°. Put the potato slices into a frying basket and fry for 1–2 minutes. Lift out and drain on absorbent paper. Reheat the oil, fry the chips for a further 30 seconds and drain again. Game chips should be very crisp.

Serve the venison with the fried crumbs, game chips, watercress, redcurrant jelly and either game sauce (see page 52) or gravy.

Roast venison

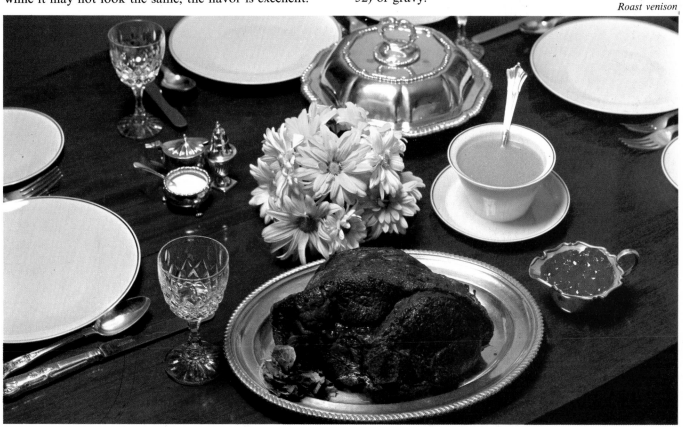

ROAST TURKEY WITH CHESTNUT STUFFING

Serves 12–14

1 turkey, about 12–16 lb
turkey giblets
½ cup melted butter or
    14 slices bacon
2 lb pork sausages
14 slices bacon for bacon rolls

for the stuffing:
1½ lb chestnuts or 1 (1-lb) can
    unsweetened chestnut purée
giblet stock or salted water
    (see recipe)
1 lb pork sausage meat
1 cup finely chopped walnuts
salt and pepper

Wipe the turkey inside and out with a damp cloth or absorbent paper. Place the heart, gizzard and neck in a small saucepan, cover with water and simmer for 1–2 hours. Add the liver for the last 10–15 minutes of the cooking time. Strain and reserve the giblet stock.

If using fresh chestnuts, make a cut in the flat end of each chestnut with the point of a sharp knife, place the chestnuts in a large saucepan, cover with water and simmer for 10 minutes. Drain, and remove the skins while the chestnuts are still warm. Replace the nuts in the pan and cover with the giblet stock or salted water. Bring to a boil and simmer for a further 20 minutes, or until tender. Drain the chestnuts well and rub through a sieve to make a purée.

Mix the puréed chestnuts or the canned chestnut purée with the sausage meat and walnuts. Season well with salt and pepper. Lightly press a little of the stuffing into the neck cavity of the turkey. Pull the neck skin over the stuffing and secure at the back with a skewer. Twist the wings under the bird so they lie flat with the tips together. Stuff the body cavity with the remainder of the stuffing, but do not pack tightly to allow for expansion. Tie the drumsticks together with string or secure under the band of skin next to the tail.

Brush the turkey well with the melted butter, or cover with the bacon slices, particularly over the breast. Alternatively, cover tightly with aluminum foil. To calculate the cooking time for a turkey weighing up to 12 lb, allow 15 minutes per pound and an additional 15 minutes at the end of the cooking time. For a turkey over 12 lb, allow 12 minutes per pound and an additional 12 minutes at the end of the cooking time. Place the turkey on a rack in a shallow roasting pan. Roast in a preheated moderately hot oven (375°) for the calculated time. If using bacon, remove for the last 12–30 minutes to brown the bird. If cooking the turkey in aluminum foil, allow about 30 minutes extra time. The foil should be removed for the last 30–40 minutes to brown the turkey.

Place the sausages in the pan with the turkey for the last 30–40 minutes of the cooking time. Roll up the bacon fairly tightly and thread on to metal skewers. Place in a separate pan and cook in the oven with the turkey for about 15 minutes.

Serve the turkey garnished with sausages and bacon rolls and accompanied by Brussels sprouts, chestnuts, roast potatoes and bread sauce (see page 52).

Note: If using canned chestnut purée, the texture and taste of the stuffing will differ slightly.

ROAST DUCKLING WITH SAGE AND ONION STUFFING AND APPLE SAUCE

Serves 4

2 small ducklings, about 3 lb each
salt and pepper
for the stuffing:
2 large onions
1¼ cups water
salt and pepper
2 teaspoons chopped fresh sage or
    1 teaspoon dried sage

2 tablespoons melted butter or
    ¼ cup chopped beef suet
⅔ cup fine fresh breadcrumbs
1 egg (optional)
for the sauce:
1 lb baking apples
⅔ cup water
about ¼ cup sugar
2 tablespoons butter (optional)

Place the ducklings in a roasting pan and season the skin very lightly with salt and pepper.

To make the stuffing, peel and coarsely chop the onions and simmer in the water with a dash of salt for 10 minutes. Drain and reserve the liquid. Chop the onions more finely, place in a mixing bowl and add pepper to taste. Add the sage, butter and breadcrumbs and mix well. Adjust the seasoning.

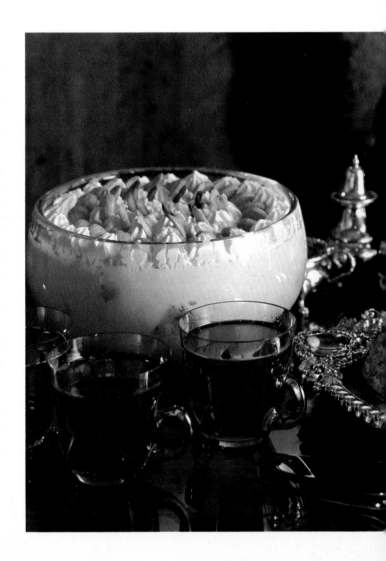

Either use the egg and a little onion liquid, or use only the reserved liquid to make a moist stuffing. Put the stuffing into a lightly greased ovenproof dish and cover with foil.

Place the ducklings and the stuffing in a preheated moderately hot oven (400°). Roast the ducklings for 15 minutes per pound plus an additional 15 minutes. If the birds are unequal in weight, adjust the roasting time for each one accordingly. For an older duck, roast at the same temperature as for the ducklings, allowing 20 minutes per pound plus an additional 20 minutes. Prick the skin of each duckling very lightly with a fine skewer after the first 30 minutes, so the excess fat is released and the skin becomes crisp.

To make the sauce, peel and slice the apples. Simmer in a small heavy saucepan with the water and sugar until very soft. Rub the apples through a sieve, or use a blender to make a purée. Beat a little butter into the sauce, if desired. Pour into a heated sauceboat. Serve the ducklings with new potatoes, peas seasoned with a small sprig of mint and the apple sauce.

Note: To give extra crispness to the skin, cook the ducklings as above until the last 15 minutes of the cooking time. Then pour off the fat from the pan. Blend 3 tablespoons of honey with 1 tablespoon hot water, brush over the ducklings and continue cooking.

Roast game birds with game chips; trifle (see page 56)

DEVILED POULTRY OR GAME

Serves 4

4 pieces cooked chicken, turkey or game	3 drops Worcestershire sauce
¾ cup butter	dash cayenne pepper
2 teaspoons prepared mustard	dash salt
1–2 teaspoons curry powder	3 tablespoons sweet chutney

Make several cuts in the chicken to enable the deviled mixture to penetrate the flesh. Cream the butter with the mustard, curry powder, Worcestershire sauce, cayenne pepper, salt and chutney (see note). Spread the mixture evenly over the chicken and place on a rack in a broiler pan. Broil under moderate heat for 10–15 minutes on each side. The deviled mixture which drips into the broiler pan may be used to baste the chicken. Serve with boiled rice and a crisp green salad.

Note: The addition of ⅔ cup fine fresh breadcrumbs blended with the butter gives an interesting texture to the deviled mixture.

ROAST GROUSE

Serves 4

2 young grouse (see note)	giblets of the grouse
¼ cup butter (see note)	4 slices white bread
salt and pepper	1 cup fried breadcrumbs
4–8 slices bacon or 6 tablespoons butter	watercress

Wash the grouse and dry well. Put half the butter inside each bird (this helps to keep the flesh moist). Season the grouse with salt and pepper and cover with the bacon slices or butter to prevent the flesh from excessive drying. Set aside until required.

Place the giblets in a small saucepan, cover with water and simmer until tender. Strain and reserve the stock for the port wine gravy (see page 52). Mash and season the liver from the giblets. Trim and discard the crusts from the bread slices. Toast the bread and spread with the mashed liver. Place in a roasting pan and put the grouse on top. Place the pan in a preheated moderately hot oven (400°) and roast for 15 minutes per pound plus an additional 15 minutes at the end of the cooking time. Rinse the watercress under cold water and set aside until required.

To serve the grouse, cut each bird in half and place the halves on the slices of toast. Garnish with game chips (see Roast Venison, page 49), fried crumbs and watercress. Serve with redcurrant jelly or bread sauce, and port wine gravy (see page 52).

Note: This recipe may be used for other game birds, provided they are young and tender. If roasting pheasant, allow 20 minutes per pound plus an additional 20 minutes at the end of the cooking time.

REDCURRANT JELLY

Makes about 3 lb

2 lb redcurrants   sugar (see recipe)
2½ cups water

Wash the redcurrants, place in a large saucepan with the water and simmer slowly to obtain a thick pulp. Strain through a jelly bag or several thicknesses of cheesecloth.

Measure the liquid into a saucepan and add 2 cups sugar to each 2½ cups liquid. Stir over low heat until the sugar dissolves then boil rapidly without stirring until a few drops, placed on a cold plate, set and crinkle when pushed with the finger.

Skim the surface and pour the jelly into hot clean jars to within ½ inch of the top. Tap the jars lightly to remove any air bubbles. Cover the surface of the jelly immediately with waxed paper discs. When cold, cover securely with a lid or saran wrap and store in a cool dry place away from strong light.

PORT WINE GRAVY

Serves 4

1¼ cups giblet stock   salt and pepper
¼ cup clarified game drippings   dash light brown sugar
  or butter   ⅔ cup port
¼ cup all-purpose flour

Strain the stock through a layer of cheesecloth. Heat the drippings or butter in a saucepan. Stir in the flour and cook gently for several minutes, or until the flour begins to turn golden brown but does not burn. Stir in the stock and bring to a boil, stirring constantly until thickened. Add salt and pepper to taste, the brown sugar, port and any sediment from the roasting pan. Heat the gravy and strain it through a sieve before pouring into a gravy boat. Serve with roast grouse (see page 51) or any other roasted game.

GAME SAUCE

Serves 4–6

1 medium-sized onion   salt and pepper
1 large tomato   3 tablespoons dry sherry
2 medium-sized mushrooms   ⅔ cup red wine or Madeira
¼ cup butter or drippings   1 tablespoon malt vinegar
¼ cup all-purpose flour   about 3 tablespoons sugar
1¼ cups meat stock (see note)   about ¾ cup redcurrant jelly

Peel and chop the onion and tomato. Rinse and chop the mushrooms. Heat the butter in a saucepan over moderate heat. Add the onion, tomato and mushrooms and sauté for a few minutes. Stir in the flour and cook over low heat for 1–2 minutes, stirring frequently. Gradually add the meat stock and bring to a boil, stirring constantly until thickened.

Strain the mixture and season with salt and pepper to taste. Return the mixture to the pan and add the sherry, wine, vinegar, sugar and redcurrant jelly. Heat gently until the jelly melts. Taste, and adjust the seasoning if necessary. Serve the sauce hot as an accompaniment to roast game

birds or roast venison (see page 49).

Note: If preferred, a little brown ale may be substituted for part of the meat stock.

BREAD SAUCE

Serves 6–8

1 large onion   3 tablespoons butter or margarine
3 cloves   salt and pepper
2 cups fine fresh breadcrumbs   ⅓ cup light cream
2 cups milk

Peel the onion and stick with the cloves. Put the onion and breadcrumbs into a saucepan. Add the milk, butter and salt and pepper to taste and bring to a boil. Remove from the heat and let stand in a warm place for 20–30 minutes to allow the onion flavor to penetrate the sauce.

Just before serving, remove the onion, stir in the cream and reheat without boiling. This sauce should be the consistency of a thick cream and should be well seasoned. Serve as an accompaniment to roast turkey (see page 50).

PEASE PUDDING

Serves 8–10

1 lb dried yellow split peas   ¼ cup butter
1 ham bone, about 2 lb   salt and pepper
1 large onion   1 egg (optional)

Soak the peas overnight in plenty of cold water. Put the ham bone in a large saucepan, cover with cold water and soak overnight.

Drain the peas and the ham bone. Place the ham bone in a large saucepan and cover with fresh cold water. Simmer gently over moderate heat for about 1 hour. Discard the bone and reserve the stock. Finely chop the onion. Place the peas and onion in a second saucepan and cover with the reserved ham stock. Simmer gently over moderate heat for about 2 hours, or until the peas are very tender. The peas should absorb all the liquid. Add the butter. Taste, and season with salt and pepper. Beat the egg and add to the peas.

Put the mixture into a heat-resistant bowl or pudding mold and cover with buttered aluminum foil or waxed paper. Place the bowl in a steamer over rapidly boiling water and steam for about 45 minutes. Keep the water boiling constantly throughout the cooking time and replenish with additional boiling water when necessary. (If no steamer is available, see Kentish Chicken Pudding, page 48, for an alternative method of steaming.) Turn the pudding out of the bowl on to a heated serving dish and serve hot with faggots (see page 44) or with pork. To reheat pease pudding, either resteam or cut into slices and heat gently in bacon drippings.

Note: A little chopped or dried sage may also be added to flavor the pudding.

Mincemeat: Many of the original recipes for mincemeat contained minced (ground) beef with the fruits and spices, which is the reason for the rather odd name of this traditional sweet filling for Christmas pies. Mince pies were originally oval in shape, not round, to represent the manger, and Christmas fare is not complete without them. They are easy to freeze. Leave on the baking sheets in the quick-freeze compartment until frozen firm. Pack carefully in rigid containers with foil between the layers. Overwrap, seal and label. Store in the freezer until required.

MINCEMEAT

Makes about 2½ lb

1 baking apple
2⅔ cups mixed dried fruit
(currants, candied orange and lemon peel and seedless white raisins)
¾ cup chopped beef suet or ½ cup melted butter or margarine
½ cup light brown sugar
1 cup chopped mixed candied peel

1 cup blanched chopped almonds
1 teaspoon finely grated lemon rind
½ teaspoon cinnamon
1 teaspoon mixed spice (cinnamon, nutmeg and allspice)
½ teaspoon grated nutmeg
¼ cup lemon juice
⅓ cup brandy, whiskey or rum

Peel, core and grate the apple. Place in a large mixing bowl with the remaining ingredients. Mix thoroughly until all the ingredients are evenly distributed. Pack the mixture into clean, dry jars. Cover and seal. Store in a cool, dry place until required. The mincemeat can be used at once but the flavor improves if left to mature for at least 1 month.

MINCE PIES

Makes 12 pies

for the basic pie dough:
2 cups all-purpose flour
dash salt
½ cup butter
about ⅓ cup cold water

for the filling:
about 1 cup mincemeat (see above)
2 tablespoons sugar

To make the basic pie dough, sift the flour and salt into a mixing bowl. Cut the butter into pieces and add. Rub the mixture lightly between the fingertips, allowing it to fall back into the bowl. When the butter is evenly distributed and the mixture is like fine breadcrumbs, add the water and mix to a dough. Turn out on to a lightly floured board and knead until smooth.

Roll out the pastry to about ¼ inch thick and cut into 2½-inch circles using a floured round cutter. Place half of the circles on a greased baking sheet. Place 1 teaspoon of the mincemeat in the center of each circle. Moisten the edges of the pastry circles with cold water. Cover each one with a pastry lid and press the edges firmly together to seal. Cut two small slits in each lid to allow the steam to escape during baking. This helps to keep the pastry crisp. Bake in a preheated moderately hot oven (400°) for 20 minutes. Sprinkle with sugar and serve hot or cold.

Note: Flaky pastry may also be used for mince pies. Prepare the pastry as for Steak and Kidney Pie, page 40, and make up the mince pies as above. Bake in a preheated hot oven (425°) for 15 minutes, then reduce the heat to 400° and bake for 5 minutes. Sprinkle with sugar and serve hot or cold.

CHERRY COBBLER

Serves 4

1½ lb Bing cherries or 2 (1-lb) cans
¼ cup water
⅓ cup sugar
for the cobbler:
1½ cups all-purpose flour sifted
  with 1½ teaspoons baking powder

3 tablespoons butter or
  margarine
6 tablespoons sugar
4–5 tablespoons milk (see recipe)

If using fresh cherries, wash them and remove the stems but do not pit them. If using canned cherries, drain the juice from the cans and reserve 3–4 tablespoons. Place the cherries in a 9-inch pie dish and add the water and sugar or, for the canned cherries, the juice, substituting this for the sugar and water in the recipe. If using fresh cherries, put a piece of aluminum foil or waxed paper over the fruit and bake in a preheated moderately hot oven (375°) for 15 minutes.

Meanwhile, prepare the cobbler. Sift the flour into a mixing bowl. Cut the butter into pieces and add to the flour. Rub the mixture lightly between the fingertips, allowing it to fall back into the bowl. When the butter is evenly distributed, stir in two-thirds of the sugar. Add enough milk to form a soft dough. Turn the dough out on to a lightly floured board and roll until ½ inch thick. Cut the dough into 2-inch circles using a floured round cutter. Brush the circles with the remaining milk and sprinkle with the remaining sugar.

Arrange the circles on top of the hot cherries. Raise the oven heat to 425° and bake for a further 15–20 minutes, or until the cobbler is well risen and golden brown. Serve hot with cream.

CHRISTMAS PUDDING

Makes 4 small or 2 large puddings

¼ cup candied cherries
⅔ cup dried apricots
8 prunes
1 cup blanched almonds
1 medium-sized carrot
1 large baking apple
1 cup all-purpose flour
½ teaspoon cinnamon
½ teaspoon nutmeg
½ teaspoon mace
½ teaspoon allspice
2⅔ cups fine fresh white
  breadcrumbs
1 cup dark brown sugar
1¼ cups chopped beef suet or
  ¾ cup melted butter

1 cup currants
2 cups seedless white raisins
4 cups seedless raisins
1½ cups chopped mixed candied
  peel
1 teaspoon grated lemon rind
2 teaspoons grated orange rind
4 eggs
3 tablespoons corn syrup
3 tablespoons lemon juice (see
  note)
6 tablespoons orange juice (see
  note)
3 tablespoons sweet sherry
1 cup dark beer (see note)

Coarsely chop the candied cherries, dried apricots, prunes and blanched almonds. Peel and grate the carrot. Peel, core and grate the apple.

Sift the flour, cinnamon, nutmeg, mace and allspice into a large mixing bowl. Add the breadcrumbs, brown sugar, suet, currants, seedless white raisins, seedless raisins, mixed candied peel and the lemon and orange rind. Add the prepared cherries, apricots, prunes, blanched almonds, carrot and apple. Mix the ingredients thoroughly and make a well in the center. Lightly beat the eggs and pour into the

well with the corn syrup, lemon and orange juice if used, sherry and beer. Stir well until the ingredients are thoroughly moistened. Cover with a cloth and set aside overnight to mature in flavor.

Grease and lightly flour 4 small or 2 large heat-resistant bowls or pudding molds, and divide the mixture equally among them. Press firmly into the bowls, filling each one to within 1 inch of the top. To make a light crumbly pudding, pack the mixture less tightly. Cover with waxed paper, buttered on each side, then aluminum foil or another piece of waxed paper.

Steam the larger puddings for 6–7 hours or the smaller ones for 4–5 hours, or allow 1–2 hours in a pressure cooker at 15 lb pressure. (If no steamer is available, see Kentish Chicken Pudding, page 48, for an alternative method of steaming.) When the puddings are cooked, remove them from the water, uncover and set aside until cold. Cover each with a clean dry cloth or waxed paper, tie securely and store in a cool dry place. Allow the puddings to mature for at least 3 weeks before using.

When required for use, cover the pudding with fresh greased waxed paper and resteam for 2–3 hours. Turn the pudding out of the bowl and serve hot with Cumberland rum butter (see below).

Note: To make a very moist pudding, include the lemon and orange juice. For a drier pudding omit the lemon and orange juice or use half the quantity of beer.

CUMBERLAND RUM BUTTER

Makes approximately 1¼ lb

1 cup unsalted butter
1½–2 cups light brown sugar
dash cinnamon

dash grated nutmeg
about 3 tablespoons rum

Cream the butter until very soft and light. Gradually beat in the sugar. The amount of sugar added depends upon how sweet a butter is desired. Beat in the cinnamon and nutmeg and gradually add the rum, beating thoroughly after each addition to prevent the mixture from curdling.

Put into attractive serving pots, seal tightly and store in a cool place. Serve as an accompaniment to Christmas pudding (see above) or on bread or toast.

SNOWDON PUDDING

Serves 4–6

3 tablespoons butter
1 cup seedless raisins
¾ cup chopped beef suet
2 cups fine fresh breadcrumbs
¼ cup cornstarch or rice flour
dash salt
1 teaspoon grated lemon rind

⅓ cup orange marmalade
for the sauce:
1 large lemon
1 cup water
2 tablespoons cornstarch
1¼ cups sweet red wine
½ cup sugar

Butter a 1½-quart heat-resistant bowl or pudding mold with 2 tablespoons of the butter. Press half the raisins against the bottom and sides of the bowl. Place the remaining raisins in a mixing bowl and add the suet, breadcrumbs, cornstarch, salt, lemon rind and marmalade. Mix to a stiff consistency, then spoon the mixture into the bowl and press down firmly. Butter a sheet of waxed paper or aluminum foil, using the remaining butter. Cover the bowl and secure with string. Place the bowl in a steamer over rapidly boiling water and steam for 1½–1¾ hours. Replenish with boiling water when necessary. (If no steamer is available, see Kentish Chicken Pudding, page 48, for an alternative method of steaming.)

To make the sauce, thinly pare the rind from the lemon and put into a saucepan with the water. Simmer for 15 minutes to extract the lemon flavor. Strain, discard the lemon rind and return the liquid to the pan. Squeeze the lemon and add the juice to the pan. Blend the cornstarch with the wine and stir into the lemon liquid. Add the sugar, place the pan over low heat and bring to a boil, stirring constantly until thickened and smooth.

When the pudding is cooked, remove the paper and turn out of the bowl on to a heated serving plate. Serve immediately with the hot sauce.

SWEET FANTASY

Serves 4

3 egg yolks	1¾ cups heavy cream
½ cup sugar	⅓ cup lemon juice
1 teaspoon grated lemon rind	

Beat the egg yolks in a mixing bowl with the sugar and lemon rind. Gradually add the cream. Place the bowl over a saucepan of hot, but not boiling water and whip until the mixture begins to thicken.

Divide the lemon juice between 4 small glass dishes and spoon the cream mixture carefully on top. Serve immediately.

ORANGE CUSTARDS

Serves 4

2 Seville oranges (see note)	1¼ cups light cream
⅔ cup water	1¼ cups milk
¼ cup sugar	few blanched pistachio nuts or
4 eggs	blanched almonds

Thinly pare the rind from the oranges, taking care not to include any white inner skin which will give a bitter taste to the custard. Put the rind with the water and sugar into a saucepan, cover tightly and simmer for 10 minutes. Strain the orange flavored liquid into a small bowl and set aside to cool slightly. Add the eggs and beat well.

Meanwhile, warm the cream and milk together in a saucepan. Stir the cream mixture into the egg mixture. Taste and add a little sugar if necessary. Strain the custard into 4 individual molds and place them in a pan or ovenproof dish with cold water to come halfway up the sides of the molds. Place the pan in a preheated moderate oven (325°) and bake for about 1 hour. Decorate with the pistachio nuts and serve hot or cold.

Note: When bitter Seville oranges are out of season, the custard may be made with sweet oranges, but the amount of sugar should then be slightly decreased.

Orange custards

TRIFLE

Serves 6–8

for the custard:

4 eggs

1 egg yolk

¼ cup sugar

⅔ cup light cream

2½ cups milk

1 lemon

for the base:

1 baked sponge cake

¼ cup raspberry jam or
redcurrant jelly

24 ratafias

⅔ cup sweet sherry

3 tablespoons Drambuie or
brandy

½ cup blanched almonds

for the decoration:

1¼ cups heavy cream

1 egg white (optional)

½ cup blanched almonds

8 small pieces candied
fruits or candied cherries

12 ratafias

¼ cup blanched pistachio nuts

To make the custard, beat the eggs and egg yolk with the sugar in a mixing bowl. Stir in the cream and the milk. Pour the mixture into the top of a double boiler or stand the bowl over a saucepan of hot, but not boiling water. Thinly pare the rind from the lemon and add a few strips of the rind to the custard mixture. Cook over low heat, stirring constantly, until the mixture is thick enough to coat the back of a spoon. Remove from the heat, discard the lemon rind and let stand until cool. Stir the custard frequently to prevent a skin from forming on the surface.

For the base, split the prepared sponge cake in half, spread with the jam and cut into pieces. Arrange in a shallow glass serving bowl with the ratafias. Blend the sherry with the Drambuie and spoon it over the cake and ratafias to soak them. For a moister texture, extra sherry may be used or the sherry and liqueur diluted with a little fruit juice. Sprinkle the almonds over the sponge cake. Pour the custard over the sponge cake and almonds to cover completely and let stand until the custard sets.

To make the decoration, whip the cream until it just holds its shape. If desired, beat the egg white until very stiff and fold into the whipped cream for a lighter and less rich topping. Pile the whipped cream on top or around the edge of the custard. Alternatively, pipe the cream over the top, using a star tip in a pastry bag. Decorate with the almonds, candied fruits, ratafias and pistachio nuts.

SUMMER PUDDING

Serves 4–5

about 6–8 thin slices white bread

1 lb raspberries

8 oz redcurrants

8 oz blackcurrants

3 tablespoons water

½ cup sugar

1¼ cups heavy cream

Cut off the bread crusts. Lightly butter a 1½-quart bowl or pudding mold. Line the bowl with the bread slices covering the bottom and sides of the bowl completely. Reserve a few slices for the top of the pudding.

Place the raspberries, redcurrants and blackcurrants in a large saucepan and add the water and sugar. Simmer over moderate heat until the fruit is soft. If desired, the seeds may be removed by sieving the cooked fruit at this stage. Spoon the fruit into the bread-lined bowl and cover with a layer of the remaining bread slices. Place a square of waxed paper over

the top of the pudding, then a small saucer or plate and finally a weight to compress the contents of the bowl. Set aside overnight in a cool place.

Next day, remove the weight, saucer and the paper, loosen the pudding in the bowl with a spatula and turn out on to a deep plate. Whip half the cream and pile on top of the pudding or, with a star tip in a pastry bag, pipe the cream in a decorative pattern. Serve the remaining cream separately.

RATAFIAS

Makes about 36 cookies

¾ cup finely ground almonds

1 egg white

3 drops ratafia or almond extract

6 tablespoons sugar

Loosen any lumps in the ground almonds. Beat the egg white until frothy but not stiff. Add the ratafia or almond extract, the sugar and two-thirds of the almonds. Stir gently until well blended, adding the remaining ground almonds as necessary to form a soft and slightly sticky mixture. Form the mixture into balls about ½ inch in diameter. Place on to very lightly buttered baking sheets. Bake in a preheated moderately hot oven (375°) for about 6–7 minutes.

Cool for several minutes, then lift the ratafias from the sheets with a spatula. Ratafias may be stored in a tightly covered container.

BAKEWELL TART

Serves 4–6

for the basic pie dough:

2 cups all-purpose flour

dash salt

½ cup butter

about ⅔ cup cold water

for the filling:

6 tablespoons butter

6 tablespoons sugar

1 egg

¼ cup all-purpose flour

¾ cup finely ground almonds

¼ cup chopped mixed candied
peel (optional)

½ cup soft cake crumbs

3 tablespoons milk

¼ cup raspberry jam

sifted confectioners' sugar for
dusting

Prepare the pastry as for Mince Pies, page 53. Roll out the pastry to ¼ inch thick and line an 8-inch pie pan or shallow sponge cake pan.

To make the filling, cream the butter and sugar together in a mixing bowl until very soft and fluffy. Beat in the egg. Sift the flour and fold into the creamed mixture with the almonds, candied peel, cake crumbs and milk. Spread the jam over the bottom of the pastry shell. Spoon the filling over the top of the jam and spread evenly with a knife. Bake in a preheated moderately hot oven (375°) for 40–50 minutes. Cool slightly, remove from the pie pan or sponge cake pan and dust lightly with the confectioners' sugar.

Apple cake

APPLE CAKE

Serves 6–8

3 cups all-purpose flour sifted
   with 3 teaspoons baking
   powder
⅔ cup butter
¾ cup granulated sugar
2 medium-sized baking apples
1 egg

2 tablespoons light brown sugar
¼ teaspoon cinnamon
1 tablespoon milk
for the topping:
2 tablespoons granulated sugar
dash cinnamon

Measure the flour into a mixing bowl. Cut the butter into pieces and add. Rub the mixture lightly between the fingertips, allowing it to fall back into the bowl, until the butter is evenly distributed. Stir in the granulated sugar. Peel, core and dice the apples. Beat the egg. Blend the brown sugar with the cinnamon and coat the apples with this mixture. Stir the apples into the flour mixture. Add the egg and milk and mix to a soft sticky dough which should be stiff enough to stand in peaks. Line an 8-inch round spring-form pan or 9-inch tube pan with greased and lightly floured waxed paper. Spoon the dough into the pan, smooth flat on top and sprinkle with the sugar and cinnamon. Bake in a preheated moderate oven (350°) for about 1¼ hours, or until the cake is firm and golden brown. Lower the heat to 300° after 50 minutes if the cake becomes too brown. Remove from the oven, cool slightly and turn out on to a wire rack. Serve while still warm with a hard cheese, such as Cheddar, or a pat of butter.

EVE'S PUDDING

Serves 4

1½ lb baking apples
⅔ cup water
¼ cup sugar
for the topping:
¼ cup butter

½ cup all-purpose flour
1½ cups milk
2–3 drops vanilla extract
3 eggs
2 tablespoons sugar

Peel and slice the apples. Place in a saucepan, add the water and sugar and simmer gently until the apples are soft. Remove from the heat and put the apples into a 1½-quart lightly greased pie dish.

For the topping, heat the butter in a large saucepan, stir in the flour and cook for 2 minutes. Stir in the milk with the vanilla extract and bring to a boil. Cook, stirring constantly, until thickened, and remove from the heat. Separate the eggs. Stir the sugar and egg yolks into the hot sauce and beat well. Beat the egg whites until very stiff and fold into the sauce. Spoon the sauce over the apples and spread evenly. Bake in a preheated moderately hot oven (375°) for about 40 minutes. Serve immediately.

Flummery

QUEEN OF PUDDINGS

Serves 4–6

⅓ cup raspberry jam	¾ cup chopped candied lemon
1⅓ cups fine fresh breadcrumbs	peel
2½ cups milk	**for the meringue:**
2 tablespoons butter	3 egg whites
3 egg yolks	6 tablespoons sugar
2 tablespoons sugar	4 candied cherries
1 teaspoon grated lemon rind	small piece angelica

Spread half the jam on the bottom of a 1½-quart pie dish. Put the breadcrumbs into a mixing bowl. Heat the milk and butter together in a saucepan until hot, but not boiling. Beat the egg yolks with the sugar and stir in the hot milk. Strain the mixture into the breadcrumbs and stir in the grated lemon rind and candied lemon peel. Let stand for 10–15 minutes. Pour the thickened mixture into the pie dish and bake in a preheated moderate oven (325°) for 45 minutes–1 hour, or until just firm to the touch. Spread the remaining jam on top of the pudding.

To make the meringue, beat the egg whites until very stiff and beat in half the sugar. Fold in the remaining sugar very gently using a metal spoon. Spread the meringue over the pudding and decorate with the cherries and angelica. Replace in the oven for 15–20 minutes, or until the meringue is golden on the peaks. Serve hot.

LEMON SORBET

Serves 4

2 large or 3 medium-sized lemons	1 teaspoon gelatin
1¼ cups water	2 egg whites
1 cup sugar	

Thinly pare the rind from the lemons, without including any of the white inner skin. Put the lemon rind and water into a saucepan, cover tightly and simmer gently for about 8 minutes. Remove from the heat and add the sugar and gelatin while the liquid is still hot. Stir until both have dissolved. Meanwhile, squeeze the lemons and pour the juice into a mixing bowl. Strain the gelatin mixture on to the lemon juice. Stir to blend, then pour into a freezing tray or other container and freeze until slightly thickened. Beat the egg whites until very stiff, then fold into the partially frozen lemon mixture. Taste and add a little extra sugar if too sour. Freeze until firm and store until required.

Serve the sorbet in stemmed glasses with frosted rims. To prepare the frosting, lightly beat 1 egg white with a fork – the mixture should not be frothy. Pour into a saucer or shallow plate. Dip the rim of each glass first into the egg white then into sugar. Chill the glasses. Remove the sorbet from the freezer, let stand for a few minutes then spoon into the glasses.

Note: If freezing sorbets in a home freezer, the mixture may be put into the empty lemon cases and frozen in these, then wrapped in plastic bags for storage. If freezing more slowly in an ordinary domestic refrigerator, the lemon case hinders freezing and therefore there is a tendency for the egg whites to separate. It is better to freeze the mixture in ice trays and pack into the lemon cases when frozen if you wish to serve the sorbet in this way.

FLUMMERY

Serves 6

1¼ cups light cream
stick cinnamon, about 2 inches
2 teaspoons orange flower water
   or 2 teaspoons grated orange
   rind
½ cup sugar (see recipe)

1 cup finely chopped
   blanched almonds
2 teaspoons gelatin
3 tablespoons brandy
⅔ cup medium-sweet white wine
1¼ cups heavy cream
½ cup whole blanched almonds

Put the light cream, cinnamon stick and orange flower water into a saucepan and heat almost to the boiling point. Stir in half the sugar and the chopped almonds. Remove the pan from the heat.

Mix the gelatin with the brandy in a small heat-resistant bowl and place in a pan of very hot water until the gelatin dissolves. Gradually stir the gelatin into the cream mixture. Strain the mixture through a fine sieve, then add the remaining sugar and the wine. Flummery should have a sharp flavor; therefore the quantity of sugar may be reduced, if desired. Allow the cream mixture to cool until just beginning to thicken. Whip the heavy cream until stiff enough to stand in peaks and fold into the cream mixture. Pile into individual glasses or a shallow glass bowl. Decorate with the whole blanched almonds which may be lightly toasted, if preferred.

GINGER CAKE

Makes 1 8-inch cake

2 cups all-purpose flour
1 teaspoon ginger
½ teaspoon baking powder
½ cup butter
½ cup sugar

1 egg yolk
¼ cup sieved apricot jam
for the meringue:
2 egg whites
½ cup sugar

Sift the flour, ginger and baking powder into a mixing bowl. Cut the butter into pieces and add. Rub the mixture lightly between the fingertips, allowing it to fall back into the bowl. When the butter is evenly distributed and the mixture is like fine breadcrumbs, stir in the sugar. Add the egg yolk and knead to a stiff dough. Press the dough into an 8-inch round shallow cake pan or pie pan. Alternatively, shape into a circle directly on a baking sheet. Prick the surface with a fine skewer to prevent the mixture from rising. Bake in a preheated moderately hot oven (400°) for about 20 minutes, or until golden brown. Cool slightly, then spread with the jam.

Beat the egg whites until very stiff. Gradually beat in half the sugar. Fold in the remaining sugar, using a metal spoon. Pile the meringue over the cake base or pipe it, using a star tip in a pastry bag. Return the cake to a very cool oven (250°) for 1 hour, or until the meringue is crisp and golden brown. Cool and serve.

JUNKET

Serves 3–4

2½ cups milk
1 tablespoon sugar
2 teaspoons rennet

1 cup heavy cream
grated nutmeg

Pour the milk into a saucepan and place over moderate heat until barely lukewarm. Remove from the heat and stir in the sugar and rennet. Pour into individual serving dishes or into one large serving dish, and let stand at room temperature for several hours. Do not disturb the junket or put into the refrigerator until it has set. Top with whipped cream and grated nutmeg or serve with fresh fruit.

ECCLES CAKES

Makes 12–15

for the flaky pastry:
2 cups all-purpose flour
dash salt
¾ cup butter or ½ cup butter and
   ¼ cup shortening
about ⅔ cup cold water
for the filling:
6 tablespoons butter
6 tablespoons granulated or light
   brown sugar

½ cup seedless white raisins
½ cup currants
¾ cup chopped mixed candied peel
¼ cup lemon juice
1 teaspoon grated lemon rind
¼ teaspoon mixed spice
   (cinnamon, nutmeg and
   allspice)
for glazing:
3 tablespoons milk
2 tablespoons sugar

Prepare the flaky pastry as for Steak and Kidney Pie, page 40. It is important to allow the pastry to rest between rollings, particularly after the final rolling, since for Eccles cakes the pastry is thinly rolled.

To make the filling, cream the butter and sugar together in a mixing bowl. Add the raisins, currants, candied peel, lemon juice, lemon rind and mixed spice and mix thoroughly.

Roll out the pastry to ⅛ inch thick. Cut into 3½-inch circles. Place a little of the filling in the center of each circle. Brush the edge of the pastry with water, gather the outside edge over the filling and press together at the top to seal firmly. Turn each cake over so the sealed edge is underneath. Roll gently on top with a rolling pin to flatten and form a circle about 3 inches in diameter. Make 2 or 3 splits on top of each cake and lift on to a baking sheet. Brush with milk and sprinkle very lightly with the sugar. Bake in a preheated hot oven (425°) for about 20 minutes, or until the pastry is well risen and golden brown. Lower the heat for the final 5–8 minutes, if the cakes are becoming too brown. Serve cold with tea or coffee.

Note: In Shropshire, similar cakes are filled with butter blended with sugar, currants, chopped mixed candied peel and fresh mint. Banbury cakes contain finely crushed cookie crumbs flavored with a little rum and are generally made in an oval shape.

GINGERBREAD

Makes 1 9-inch cake

3 cups all-purpose flour	¾ cup butter
1½ teaspoons baking soda	⅔ cup molasses
1 teaspoon mixed spice	¼ cup corn syrup
(cinnamon, nutmeg and	⅔ cup water
allspice)	2 eggs
2 teaspoons ground ginger	¼ cup milk
6 tablespoons granulated or light	
brown sugar	

Sift the flour, baking soda, mixed spice and ginger into a mixing bowl. Add the sugar and make a well in the center. Melt the butter with the molasses and corn syrup in a heavy saucepan over moderate heat. Cool slightly, pour into the dry ingredients and beat well. Pour the water into the same pan, bring to a boil and stir to loosen any molasses left in the pan.

Add the eggs and milk to the mixture and beat well. Then add the hot water from the pan and beat again. Pour the mixture into a greased and lined 9-inch spring-form pan or 9-inch square pan. Bake in a preheated cool oven (300°) for about 1–1¼ hours. Do not open the oven door until the last 5 minutes as the gingerbread will sink in the middle if subjected to a sudden draught.

Press gently in the center of the gingerbread and if no impression remains the gingerbread is done. Place the pan on a wire rack and let stand until almost cool, since gingerbread breaks easily when warm. Turn out and remove the paper lining immediately. When cold, wrap in waxed paper or foil and store in a tightly covered container for at least 1 week before eating.

WELSH CAKES

Makes about 16 cakes

2 cups all-purpose flour	⅔ cup currants
2 teaspoons baking powder	1 egg
dash salt	about 2 teaspoons milk
½ cup butter or margarine	sugar for dusting
6 tablespoons sugar	

Sift the flour and salt into a mixing bowl. Cut the butter into pieces and add. Rub the mixture lightly between the fingertips, allowing it to fall back into the bowl. When the butter is evenly distributed and the mixture is like fine breadcrumbs, stir in the sugar and currants. Add the egg and enough milk to make a soft dough. Turn the dough out on to a floured board, knead lightly and roll out to ¼ inch thick. Cut the dough into small triangles or into 2½-inch circles using a floured round cutter.

Lightly grease a griddle or a heavy skillet with shortening and heat very slowly for about 20 minutes before using. Test the temperature of the griddle by sprinkling a little flour on the surface. If the flour turns golden brown in 1 minute the griddle is the correct temperature; if it takes more than 1 minute, allow the griddle to heat a little longer. If the flour browns very quickly, lower the heat and allow the griddle to cool before cooking the cakes. Cook the cakes for about 3 minutes on each side, or until firm and golden brown. Place on a wire rack, sprinkle with sugar and set aside to cool

slightly. Serve freshly baked.

Note: Welsh cakes should be crisp and sugary on the outside and light inside. They should be eaten freshly baked, but if any are left over they may be reheated for a few moments in the oven or on the griddle. They will become crisp and fresh-tasting again.

OATCAKES

Makes 8–12 oatcakes

¼ cup all-purpose flour	2 cups rolled oats
dash salt	2 tablespoons melted clarified
dash baking soda	drippings or butter
dash cream of tartar	about ⅔ cup milk (see recipe)

Sift the flour, salt, baking soda and cream of tartar into a mixing bowl. Add the rolled oats and make a well in the center. Slightly cool the melted clarified drippings or butter and pour into the well with enough of the milk to form a soft mixture. Sprinkle the pastry board with a few extra oats. Divide the dough into two or three portions and knead thoroughly on the board. Roll each portion into a large circle about ¼ inch thick. Cut each circle into quarters and place on lightly greased baking sheets. Bake in a preheated moderate oven (325°) for about 20–30 minutes, or until the edges are crisp and beginning to curl. Cool on the baking sheets, remove and store in an airtight container. Serve with butter and cheese or butter and jam.

SCOTCH PANCAKES

Makes 12–18 pancakes

1 cup all-purpose flour	2 tablespoons sugar
2 teaspoons baking powder	1 egg
1 teaspoon cream of tartar	⅔ cup milk
dash salt	2 tablespoons butter

Sift the flour, baking powder, cream of tartar and salt into a mixing bowl. Add the sugar and make a well in the center. Beat the egg and milk together, pour into the well and mix to a smooth batter with a wooden spoon. Melt the butter and stir in the batter. The butter is not essential but helps to keep the pancakes moist. Grease and heat a griddle or a large, heavy skillet. To test if the correct temperature has been reached, drop a teaspoonful of the batter on the hot surface. The underside should turn golden brown within 1 minute. Drop tablespoonfuls of the batter on to the hot griddle. Cook until the surface of the pancakes is covered with bubbles, then turn over and cook for a half a minute, or until brown.

When the first batch is ready, remove the pancakes from the griddle or skillet and wrap them in a clean tea towel to prevent them from drying and curling at the edges as they cool. Continue until all the pancakes are cooked and serve spread with butter and jam or honey.

Oatcakes; Scotch pancakes

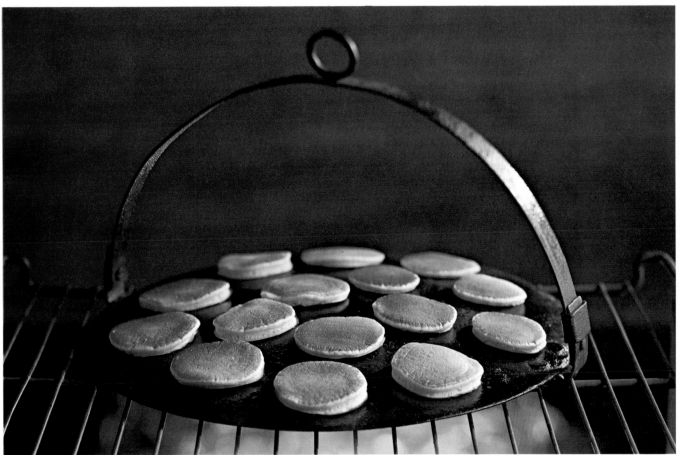

SCANDINAVIAN

Lennart Thölén and Ejler Jørgensen

Photography by John Lee

As is inevitable with two countries so similar in culture, climate and geography, there is little difference between Norwegian and Swedish cooking. Many of the national dishes are claimed by both countries to be their own. In Norway, the cold table – koldt bord – is a culinary institution of the same kind and of the same importance as the Swedish smörgåsbord.

The Norwegian housewife has always been proud of her stockpot; full-bodied, nourishing soups are something of a mainstay in Norwegian home economy. The main feature of Norwegian cooking, however, is fish in all its forms. Norway's long Atlantic seaboard, deep fjords, rivers and mountain streams, ensure abundant supplies of fish and shellfish. If one particular fish is to be singled out as typical of the Norwegian cuisine it is the cod. Nowhere in the world is it so delicious and prepared so devotedly as in Norway. Notable too are the country's fish puddings and mousses, which literally melt in the mouth. Fish balls, one of the earliest of all fish products to be prepared commercially, are of Norwegian origin and continue to be one of the country's favorite dishes.

Husmanskost, country fare, is the everyday cooking of Sweden and the foundation of the Swedish cuisine. Swedish dishes are suited to a relatively severe climate and are usually substantial, sustaining and nutritious. The Sunday roast is veal, though pork has a time-honored place in Swedish cooking, often being prepared with prunes and apples.

As in all the Scandinavian countries, fish plays an important role in catering. Special mention should perhaps be made of the herring, the most popular and the most abundant fish, served from south to north in a great number of guises. Game is plentiful in the vast forests of Sweden, and the traditional recipes are ancient and rich in variations.

Among the herbs and spices used, dill is preeminent. It is perhaps the most characteristically Swedish of all seasonings and may be traced as a green thread woven through the fabric of the Swedish cuisine, enhancing the flavor of meat, fish, sauces and stews.

Denmark, although a small country, retains a distinctive character which sets it apart from the rest of Scandinavia. Until a century ago, Denmark had a very unproductive agriculture. A poor soil which was unsuitable for growing cereal crops made the Danes turn to livestock so that now Denmark is a major exporter of meat and dairy produce. It is only natural that Danish cooking should make great use of cream and butter to enrich sauces, soups and desserts.

Another important source of food is the sea and Danish fish dishes are unusual and delicious. Smoked, fresh and pickled herring and mackerel always appear in some guise on the cold table. There are also excellent freshwater fish such as pike and salmon which are often cooked in cream or served with a rich butter sauce.

The Danish cuisine is renowned for its smørrebrød, or open sandwiches, but it is probably in the area of baking that the Danes excel. Above all others, the pastries most associated with Denmark are undoubtedly the wienerbrød, known throughout the rest of the world simply as Danish pastries. Ideal for serving when friends drop in, these delicate, buttery pastries represent the best of Denmark's renowned hospitality and cooking.

HERRING SALAD MOLD

Serves 6

1 salted herring	pickled beet juice (see recipe)
4 medium-sized potatoes	freshly ground white pepper
4 medium-sized pickled beets	**for the garnish:**
1 dill pickle	2 hard-cooked eggs
1 large baking apple	1 small pickled beet
3 tablespoons finely chopped	**for the dressing:**
onion	¾ cup heavy cream
8 oz cooked meat, finely	1 teaspoon dry mustard
chopped	pickled beet juice (see recipe)

Clean the herring and rinse under cold running water. Fillet the fish, discarding the skin and bones. (See Planked Lake Superior Whitefish, page 14.) Soak overnight in plenty of cold water to remove the excess salt. Drain well. Peel the potatoes and boil until tender. Drain and set aside until cold. Dice the herring, potatoes, beets and dill pickle and place in a large bowl. Peel, core and dice the apple. Add the apple, onion and meat to the bowl. Mix thoroughly. Sprinkle with pickled beet juice and pepper to taste. Pack the salad into a mold and place in the refrigerator, or in a cold place, for several hours.

To prepare the garnish, finely chop the egg yolks and whites separately. Finely chop the beet. Unmold the salad on to the center of a serving plate and garnish with concentric circles of chopped beet and egg.

To make the dressing, lightly whip the cream and then stir in the mustard. Add pickled beet juice to taste. Serve with the salad.

DANISH LIVER PÂTÉ

Serves 6

8 oz chicken livers	1 egg
8 oz pork liver	**for the sauce:**
8 oz fat back or bacon fat	2 tablespoons butter
6 anchovy fillets	¼ cup all-purpose flour
1 teaspoon finely ground black	2 cups milk
pepper	⅔ cup port or Madeira
¼ teaspoon nutmeg	

Finely grind the chicken livers, pork liver and fat back. Add the anchovies, pepper, nutmeg and egg. Mix thoroughly.

To make the sauce, melt the butter in a small saucepan. Remove from the heat and stir in the flour. Add the milk gradually, mixing thoroughly after each addition. Bring to a boil over moderate heat, stirring constantly until the mixture thickens. Remove from the heat and stir in the port or Madeira.

Stir the sauce into the liver mixture and blend thoroughly. Pour into a loaf pan or mold about 9 by 5 inches. Bake in a preheated moderate oven (350°) for 1½–2 hours, or until set.

When cooked, remove from the oven and set aside to cool. Turn out of the pan and cut into thick slices. Serve with toast.

SUNNY EYE

Serves 1

1 egg yolk	1 tablespoon chopped onion
5 anchovy fillets	1 tablespoon chopped pickled
1 tablespoon capers	beet

Place the yolk in an eggcup. Lay a small plate on top and invert both the eggcup and the plate carefully so none of the yolk escapes. Leave the eggcup in place.

Chop the anchovy fillets and arrange with the capers, onion and beet in concentric circles around the rim of the eggcup. (The beet should form the outer ring.) Remove the eggcup just before serving. Mix the egg yolk with the other ingredients at the table. Serve as an appetizer.

JANSSON'S TEMPTATION

Serves 4

8 Swedish anchovies or	1 oz butter
1 (2-oz) can anchovy fillets	freshly ground white pepper
2 medium-sized onions	1¼ cups light cream
3 large potatoes	

If using Swedish anchovies, clean and fillet them and discard the bones. If using canned anchovy fillets, soak them in milk or water for 10–15 minutes to remove the excess salt and then drain. Peel and slice the onions. Peel the potatoes and cut into ¼- by 2-inch strips. Melt half the butter in a skillet over moderate heat. Add the onions and sauté until soft but not browned.

Arrange the anchovy fillets, potatoes and onions in layers in a well-buttered casserole, beginning and ending with a layer of potatoes. Season each layer with pepper. Pour half the cream on top. Cover the casserole tightly with the lid, or aluminum foil, and bake in a preheated moderately hot oven (400°) for about 30 minutes. Remove the lid or foil. Pour the remaining cream over the top and dot the surface with the remaining butter. Bake for 25 minutes, or until the potatoes are tender. Serve hot from the casserole.

CUCUMBER SALAD

Serves 4

1 large cucumber	3 tablespoons sugar
2 teaspoons salt	white pepper
½ cup distilled white vinegar	1 tablespoon chopped parsley

The cucumber may be peeled or not, according to taste. If not, simply rinse under cold running water and pat dry. Slice the cucumber very thinly into a shallow dish. Sprinkle with the salt and lightly press by covering with a plate and placing a weight on top. Set aside for 1 hour, then pour away all the juices that have collected.

Mix together the vinegar, sugar and white pepper to taste. Pour over the pressed cucumber slices and allow to stand for 1 hour. Sprinkle with chopped parsley and serve.

GLASSBLOWER'S HERRING

Serves 8

2 salted herring	1 medium-sized carrot
6 tablespoons distilled white	3 thin slices fresh horseradish root
vinegar	2 thin slices fresh ginger root
⅔ cup water	2 teaspoons mustard seeds
¾ cup sugar	2 bay leaves
1 medium-sized onion	

Clean the fish but leave the skins and backbones intact. Soak in water overnight to remove the excess salt.

Place the vinegar, water and sugar in a saucepan and bring slowly to a boil. Remove from the heat and set aside until cold. Meanwhile, rinse the fish under cold running water and pat dry with a cheesecloth or absorbent paper. Cut the fish into 1-inch pieces. Peel and thinly slice the onion and carrot.

Arrange layers of the fish, onion, carrot, horseradish, ginger, mustard seeds and bay leaves in a glass jar and add the vinegar solution. Place the jar in the refrigerator, or in a cold place, for several days. Serve directly from the jar as an appetizer, or include on the *smörgåsbord*.

MARINATED HERRING

Serves 4

4 fresh herring	8 cloves
1 tablespoon salt	2 bay leaves
2½ cups distilled white vinegar	1 teaspoon saltpeter
4 shallots	2 tablespoons sugar
½ teaspoon whole allspice	onion rings for garnish
½ teaspoon white peppercorns	

Clean the herring. Discard the heads and remove the backbones. Rinse the fish thoroughly under cold running water and pat dry with a cloth or absorbent paper. Place in a shallow dish and sprinkle lightly with the salt. Cover with half the vinegar and set aside to marinate overnight.

Peel and finely chop the shallots. Drain the vinegar from the herring and pat dry. Place the fish in layers in an earthenware container and sprinkle each layer with the chopped shallots and the allspice, peppercorns, cloves, bay leaves, saltpeter and sugar. Cover the herring with the remaining vinegar and set aside for 2–3 hours.

Before serving, drain the herring, cut into strips 1 inch wide and garnish with onion rings.

It can undoubtedly be a stimulating experience to be confronted by the magnificence of a large *smörgåsbord*, the Swedish word for the famous Scandinavian cold table. It developed at a time when people liked to eat copiously and well, and to take their time about it. Now it is revived in all its splendor only at Christmas time and during the tourist season in large hotels and restaurants, but on a modified scale it is a very enjoyable way of entertaining.

Accompaniments for the *smörgåsbord* may be set out on the main table or on a side table. Have as many varieties of bread as possible, both crisp and fresh. The fresh should be sliced but covered up until the last minute to prevent it drying out. Make sure there is plenty of butter placed around the table and, to be very Danish, homemade drippings made from pork, goose or duck, or a mixture of the three. There should be a good selection of pickles and pickled vegetables as well as jams and jellies for those who prefer sweet accompaniments with strong cheese. The final extras are salt and pepper, preferably in mills, mustards, oil and vinegar and mayonnaise. The drinks normally served with a *smörgåsbord* are ice-cold *schnapps* and cold beer, but a light wine, red, white or rosé, is equally appropriate.

Start with fish dishes, how many varieties depending on the number of guests. A typical table would include two or three different marinated herring dishes, smoked fish, shrimp and a selection of canned fish with small dishes of garnishes such as capers, chopped onions and onion rings. Follow with cold, sliced meats, colorfully garnished, liver pâté, egg dishes and various salads, some with mayonnaise and others with oil and vinegar. Finally, bring in the cheeses. Four or five varieties would be a suitable number, a mild one, a strong one and two or three cream cheeses. Serve with various breads and a selection of fresh fruit.

from left to right:
top row: *Sunny eye; herring salad mold (see page 63)*
second row: *Swedish steak and onions; dill-cured salmon; country-cured ham; glassblower's herring*
third row: *Swedish meat balls (see page 72); Jansson's temptation; vanilla cream (see page 82); cucumber salad*
bottom row: *Danish liver pâté (see page 63); marinated herring*

DILL-CURED SALMON

Serves 8

1 middle cut of salmon, about 2¼ lb	10 white peppercorns, crushed
¼ cup salt	**for the garnish:**
¼ cup sugar	2 lemons, cut in wedges
large bunch dill	4 sprigs dill

Scale the salmon but do not rinse. Place the salmon on end and cut in half vertically through the backbone. Remove and discard the backbone and all the small bones, but leave the skin on. Mix together the salt and sugar and rub the fleshy sides with the mixture.

Place one half of the salmon on a plate skin-side down. Sprinkle with half the dill and all the peppercorns. Place the other half of the salmon on top, skin-side up, with the thick part lying on top of the thin part of the other half. Cover with the remaining dill. Put a weighted plate or heavy chopping board on top. Place in the refrigerator, or in a dark cold place, for 24 hours.

When ready to serve, discard the dill and peppercorns from the salmon and slice the flesh thinly, discarding the skin. If using as a *smörgåsbord* dish, arrange the slices in rolls and garnish with the lemon wedges and dill. Alternatively, the slices may be arranged on a serving dish and the salmon served accompanied by boiled potatoes and dill mayonnaise (see page 76).

MEADOW SOUP

Serves 4

1 medium-sized carrot	2¼ cups water
1 parsnip	1 teaspoon salt
1 leek	1 tablespoon all-purpose flour
1 small cauliflower	2¼ cups milk
1 small piece celeriac	salt and white pepper
(celery root)	1 tablespoon chopped parsley

Peel the carrot and parsnip and cut into thin strips. Trim and thoroughly wash the leek and slice thinly. Break the cauliflower into florets and rinse under cold running water. Cut the celeriac into strips. Place the water and salt in a large saucepan and bring to a boil. Add the carrot, parsnip, cauliflower and celeriac. Simmer over moderate heat for 10–12 minutes. Add the leek and continue simmering until all the vegetables are tender.

Blend the flour with a little of the milk and stir into the soup. Bring to a boil and simmer for 3–4 minutes, stirring constantly. Add the remaining milk and reheat the soup until boiling. Season with salt and pepper to taste. Pour into a heated soup tureen and sprinkle with the parsley. Serve with buttered crisp rye bread topped with slices of cheese.

TRONDHEIM SWEET SOUP

Serves 6

4½ cups water	1 tablespoon lemon juice
½ cup barley	1 tablespoon all-purpose flour
1 cup raspberry juice	⅔ cup milk
½ cup raisins	6 tablespoons cultured sour cream
½ cup pitted cooked prunes	6 tablespoons heavy cream
2 tablespoons sugar	

Bring the water and barley to a boil in a large saucepan over moderate heat. Lower the heat, cover the pan tightly and simmer for 2 hours. Add the raspberry juice, raisins, prunes, sugar and lemon juice. Blend the flour with the milk and beat into the soup. Simmer for 10 minutes.

Beat the sour cream and pour into a soup tureen. Add the soup, stirring vigorously. Whip the heavy cream until stiff. Serve the soup hot or cold with the whipped cream as an accompaniment.

Meadow soup

66

YELLOW PEA SOUP
WITH PORK

Serves 4

2 cups yellow split peas
  (see note)

for soaking:
4½ pints water
3 tablespoons salt

for cooking:
4½ pints water
1 medium-sized onion
1 lb smoked picnic shoulder
  of pork
1 teaspoon dried marjoram
¼ teaspoon ground ginger

Place the peas in a large bowl with the water and the salt and soak overnight. Drain the peas and place in a large saucepan. Add the fresh water for cooking and bring to a boil over high heat (see note).

Peel the onion, leaving it whole. Add the onion, pork, marjoram and ginger to the saucepan. Cover the pan, lower the heat and simmer the soup for 1–2 hours, or until the peas are tender. Remove and discard the onion. Lift out the pork, carve it into thin slices and keep hot. Serve the soup first and then serve the pork with mustard as a second course.

Note: In Denmark whole yellow peas are normally used. If these are used, remove the skins with a perforated spoon as they float to the surface when the peas are first brought to a boil.

WHITE CABBAGE SOUP
WITH MEAT BALLS

Serves 4

for the soup:
1 head white cabbage, about 1¾ lb
2 tablespoons butter
2 teaspoons corn syrup or sugar
6½ cups beef or ham stock
5 whole allspice
5 white peppercorns
salt

for the meat balls:
3 tablespoons dry white
  breadcrumbs
¾ cup water
8 oz lean veal, ground
8 oz lean pork, ground
2 egg yolks
1 teaspoon salt
¼ teaspoon white pepper

To make the soup, remove and discard the coarse outer leaves and center core of the cabbage and shred coarsely. Melt the butter in a large saucepan over high heat. Add the cabbage and syrup and sauté until the cabbage is golden brown, stirring constantly. Add the stock, allspice and peppercorns. Cover tightly and simmer for about 30 minutes, or until the cabbage is tender. Season with salt to taste.

To make the meat balls, place the breadcrumbs in a bowl with the water and soak for 2–3 minutes. Add the veal, pork, egg yolks, salt and pepper. Work the mixture until it is smooth, then shape into walnut-sized balls. Place these in the soup toward the end of the cooking time and simmer for 5 minutes. Transfer to a heated soup tureen and serve.

ELDERBERRY SOUP

Serves 8–10

2¼ lb elderberries
4 stalks rhubarb (optional)
2 teaspoons grated lemon rind
½ cup lemon juice

6½ pints water
4 baking apples
sugar (see recipe)
⅓ cup cornstarch

Holding the thick portion of each elderberry stem, strip the berries off with the tines of a fork. Rinse them thoroughly under cold running water. Trim and rinse the rhubarb and cut into small pieces. Place the elderberries, rhubarb, lemon rind, lemon juice and water in a large saucepan. Bring to a boil over moderate heat then lower the heat and simmer for 25–30 minutes. Strain through a sieve, reserving the liquid but discarding the fruit.

Peel, core and quarter the apples and place in a second saucepan. Pour in enough water to cover partially and add sugar to taste. Simmer over moderate heat until tender but still whole. Drain the apples (reserving the juice) and place in a soup tureen. Keep hot.

Pour the reserved apple juice and elderberry liquid into a large saucepan and bring to a boil over moderate heat. Blend the cornstarch with enough cold water to make a smooth thin paste. Pour into the hot soup, stirring vigorously. Continue stirring until the soup comes to a boil. Pour the soup over the apples in the soup tureen and serve immediately. Alternatively, in the summer this soup is delicious served cold with a spoonful of heavy cream for each serving.

CHERVIL SOUP

Serves 6

12 new carrots
5½ pints beef stock
½ cup unsalted butter
¾ cup all-purpose flour

6 eggs
salt and pepper
6 tablespoons finely chopped fresh
  chervil

Scrape the carrots, rinse under cold running water and slice. Pour about one-fourth of the stock into a saucepan and bring to a boil over moderate heat. Add the carrots. Lower the heat and simmer for 25–30 minutes.

Meanwhile, melt the butter in a large saucepan and stir in the flour. Remove the pan from the heat and add the remaining stock gradually, mixing thoroughly after each addition. Bring to a boil over moderate heat, stirring constantly until the mixture thickens. Add the carrots with the stock in which they were cooked. Simmer for 25–30 minutes. Meanwhile, poach the eggs.

Season the soup with salt and pepper to taste and add the chervil. Place an egg in each soup bowl and add the soup. Serve immediately.

GRILLED SALMON WITH BÉARNAISE SAUCE

Serves 6

1 middle cut of salmon, about
   2¼ lb
1 teaspoon coarse salt
1 tablespoon olive oil
2 lb fresh asparagus
1 lb fresh spinach
¼ cup unsalted butter
1 red sweet pepper
1 tablespoon chopped parsley
3 lemons, cut in half
for the sauce:
1 teaspoon finely chopped shallot

2 teaspoons chopped fresh
   tarragon
2 teaspoons chopped fresh chervil
1 sprig thyme
1 bay leaf
salt and pepper
3 tablespoons white wine vinegar
3 tablespoons dry white wine
3 egg yolks
1 teaspoon cold water
1 cup melted butter
1 teaspoon lemon juice

Rinse the salmon under cold running water. Dry well with a cloth. Rub the salmon inside and out with coarse salt. Cut into 6 cutlets. Brush both sides of each cutlet with olive oil.

Cut off the woody fibrous base from each asparagus spear and lightly scrape any coarse skin from the lower half of the stem. Rinse the asparagus under cold running water. Cook in lightly salted boiling water until tender. Drain well.

Meanwhile, to make the sauce, place the shallot, half the tarragon and chervil, the thyme, bay leaf, salt and pepper to taste, vinegar and wine in a small heavy saucepan. Bring to a boil, then simmer until reduced by half. Mix the egg yolks with the water and add to the reduced mixture. Beat constantly over very low heat until the mixture begins to thicken. Pour in the butter a little at a time, beating constantly until the mixture becomes very thick. Beat in the lemon juice. Remove from the heat and strain through cheesecloth. Stir in the remaining tarragon and chervil. Keep hot in a double boiler, or in a bowl over a saucepan of boiling water.

Broil the salmon cutlets under moderate heat for 5–6 minutes on each side. Meanwhile, remove the stems and rinse the spinach thoroughly under cold running water. Melt the butter in a skillet, add the spinach, cover and cook over low heat for 5–10 minutes, stirring frequently.

Remove the seeds from the red pepper and slice the flesh very thinly.

Transfer the cooked fish to a heated serving dish and garnish with the asparagus, sautéed spinach, red pepper, parsley and lemon halves. Serve with the *béarnaise* sauce and French bread. A dry white wine or champagne is excellent with this dish.

HERRING BALLS WITH CURRANT SAUCE

Serves 4

1 large salted herring
3 medium-sized potatoes
1 medium-sized onion
6 oz leftover cooked meat
1 egg
1 teaspoon potato flour
¼ teaspoon white pepper
3 tablespoons water
¼ cup fine toasted
   breadcrumbs
2 tablespoons butter

for the sauce:
3 tablespoons currants
1¼ cups water
3 tablespoons butter
3 tablespoons all-purpose flour
6 tablespoons vegetable stock
1 tablespoon corn syrup or sugar
1 tablespoon white wine vinegar
salt

Clean the herring and rinse under cold running water. Fillet the fish, discarding the skin and bones. (See Planked Lake Superior Whitefish, page 14.) Soak overnight in plenty of cold water to remove the excess salt. Peel the potatoes and boil until tender. Peel the onion. Grind the fish with the potatoes, onion and meat. Add the egg, potato flour and pepper. Mix well, then stir in the water.

Shape the mixture into 1½-inch balls and flatten these slightly. Coat with the breadcrumbs. Heat the butter in a skillet over moderate heat. Add the herring balls and sauté for 2–3 minutes on each side, or until golden brown. Remove from the skillet and keep hot in a serving dish.

To make the sauce, clean and rinse the currants. Place in a saucepan with the water and simmer over moderate heat for 8–10 minutes, or until tender. Strain off the cooking liquid and reserve. Melt two-thirds of the butter in a small saucepan and stir in the flour. Gradually add the cooking liquid and the stock. Bring to a boil, stirring constantly until the mixture thickens. Simmer the sauce for 10 minutes. Add the syrup, vinegar and salt to taste. Bring the sauce back to a boil. Add the currants and stir in the remaining butter. Serve hot with the herring balls.

Grilled salmon with béarnaise sauce

FRIED HERRING WITH BROWN BUTTER SAUCE

Serves 4

4 large herring	**for the sauce:**
seasoned flour for coating	½ cup unsalted butter
1 beaten egg	3 tablespoons distilled white
fine fresh breadcrumbs for coating	vinegar
¼ cup unsalted butter	1 lemon, quartered

Scrape the fish carefully to remove the scales. Discard the heads, tails and fins. Clean the herring and rinse under cold running water. Dry inside and out with a clean cloth or absorbent paper. Coat each fish with the flour, egg and breadcrumbs. Alternatively, coat with flour only.

Melt the butter in a heavy skillet over moderate heat. Fry the herring for 4–5 minutes on each side. Hold the fish closed by pressing them lightly with a spatula during the first few minutes of frying, otherwise they tend to open up. Remove the fish from the skillet, drain on absorbent paper and keep hot in a serving dish.

To make the sauce, cook the butter in a heavy saucepan over moderate heat until the frothing stops and it is well browned. Remove the pan from the heat immediately and stir in the vinegar. Pour the hot sauce over the fish. Garnish with the lemon and serve immediately.

FAEROESE COD BALLS WITH CURRY SAUCE

Serves 6

2 lb cod fillets	1 small banana
1 medium-sized onion	1 lb baking apples
¼ cup melted butter	¼ cup butter
½ cup all-purpose flour	¼ cup curry powder
2 egg yolks	1 tablespoon lemon juice
4 egg whites	dash Tabasco sauce
salt and pepper	⅔ cup heavy cream
for the curry sauce:	3 tablespoons tomato paste
3–4 shallots	1 teaspoon mango chutney
1–2 cloves garlic	salt and pepper

Discard the skin and any bones from the fish and rinse the fish under cold water. Grind the flesh or blend in a blender. Peel and finely chop the onion and add to the fish with the butter, flour, egg yolks and egg whites. Season with salt and pepper. Mix thoroughly and shape into 12 large balls about the size of small dessert apples. Simmer in lightly salted boiling water for 10–12 minutes. When the cod balls are cooked they will rise to the surface. Remove from the pan with a perforated spoon and place in a heated serving dish.

To make the curry sauce, peel and finely chop the shallots and garlic. Sieve the banana. Peel, core and quarter the apples and cover with cold water until required. Melt the butter in a saucepan over moderate heat. Add the shallots, garlic and curry powder. Fry gently for 10 minutes. Drain the apple slices and add to the curry mixture. Add the mashed banana. Cook for 10–15 minutes over low heat until the apples are reduced to a pulp. Add a little water if the mixture begins to stick to the pan. Stir in the lemon juice,

Tabasco sauce, cream, tomato paste and chutney. Add salt and pepper to taste and continue cooking until the mixture is reduced by about one-fifth. The sauce should be fairly thick. Serve hot with the cod balls. Boiled potatoes should accompany this dish.

CRAB SANDWICH

Serves 4

4 thin slices white bread	¼ cup mayonnaise
¼ cup butter	1 tablespoon chopped fresh dill
8 oz canned crab meat	or 2 teaspoons dried dill weed
1 egg	

Cut off the crusts from the bread. Spread each slice of bread with butter. Discarding any hard membrane, spread the crab meat on the buttered slices. Separate the egg yolk from the white. Mix the yolk with the mayonnaise and dill. Beat the white until stiff peaks are formed, then fold into the mayonnaise mixture. Spread the egg mixture over the crab. Place the slices on a baking sheet and bake in a preheated hot oven (450°) for 10 minutes. Serve as an appetizer, or with a green salad as a light supper dish.

BORNHOLM HERRING OMELET

Serves 6

6 smoked herring fillets	2 teaspoons all-purpose flour
4 large tomatoes	½ cup butter
1 large onion	salt and pepper
6 eggs	2 teaspoons chopped fresh chives
6 tablespoons milk	

Cut the fish into small pieces. Slice the tomatoes. Peel and chop the onion. Beat together the eggs, milk and flour.

Heat the butter in a large skillet over moderate heat. Pour in the egg mixture. When the egg is partly set, sprinkle with the pieces of fish and the onion. Place the tomato slices on top and sprinkle with salt and pepper to taste. Continue cooking until the egg is almost set. Sprinkle with the chopped chives and serve immediately from the skillet.

Fried herring with brown butter sauce;
Bornholm herring omelet

BAKED PIKE WITH MOREL SAUCE

Serves 4

1 pike, about 2¼ lb
1 tablespoon salt
1 beaten egg
3 tablespoons coarse toasted breadcrumbs
1 tablespoon butter
⅔ cup water
⅔ cup heavy cream
for the sauce:
1 cup dried morels or dried mushrooms, soaked and drained

2 tablespoons butter
1 tablespoon all-purpose flour
1¾ cups heavy cream
salt and white pepper
1 tablespoon medium dry sherry
for the garnish:
1 lemon, thinly sliced
4–5 sprigs parsley

Scale and clean the fish. Leave the head on but remove the fins. Rinse thoroughly under cold running water and dry with a cheesecloth or absorbent paper. Rub the fish with the salt and place it, spine-side upward, in a well-buttered casserole. Brush with the egg and sprinkle with the breadcrumbs. Dot with pats of the butter.

Bake in a preheated hot oven (425°) for 10 minutes. Add the water, pouring it along the side of the dish and not directly over the fish. Bake for 40 minutes, or until the fish is almost tender. Add the cream and bake for 5 minutes.

Meanwhile, to make the sauce, place the morels in a saucepan and add enough water to cover them completely. Bring to a boil over high heat. Lower the heat and simmer for 2–3 minutes. Remove the pan from the heat and discard the water. Coarsely chop the morels. Melt the butter in a skillet over moderate heat. Add the morels and sauté for 2–3 minutes. Sprinkle in the flour, then slowly add the cream, stirring constantly. Lower the heat and simmer the sauce gently for 20 minutes. Season with salt and pepper to taste and add the sherry.

Garnish the pike with slices of lemon and parsley. Serve with the morel sauce and boiled potatoes.

HARE WITH JUNIPER BERRIES

Serves 5

1 hare, drawn and skinned
1 medium-sized onion
2 medium-sized carrots
generous ½ cup butter
1¼ cups beef stock
¾ cup dry red wine

¼ cup lemon juice
5 juniper berries, crushed
few sprigs parsley
½ bay leaf
3 tablespoons all-purpose flour
salt and white pepper

Joint the hare into 10 equal-sized pieces. Rinse thoroughly under cold running water, then dry with a cloth or absorbent paper. Peel and chop the onion and carrots. Heat half the butter in a heavy saucepan over moderate heat until pale golden brown. Add the hare and sauté with the onion and carrots until well browned. Add the stock, wine, lemon juice, juniper berries, parsley and bay leaf. Bring to a boil, then lower the heat and cover the pan tightly. Simmer for 1½–2 hours, or until tender.

Blend the remaining butter and flour to form a soft paste.

Stir into the pan juices and simmer for 3–4 minutes. Season with salt and pepper to taste. Transfer to a heated serving dish and serve the hare with boiled potatoes and rowanberry or redcurrant jelly.

SWEDISH MEAT BALLS

Serves 4

½ cup fine toasted breadcrumbs
¾ cup water
½ medium-sized onion
¼ cup butter
8 oz lean beef, ground
4 oz lean veal, ground

4 oz lean pork, ground
1 egg
salt and freshly ground black pepper
1 tablespoon all-purpose flour
¾ cup beef stock

Soak the breadcrumbs in the water for a few minutes. Drain and place in a bowl. Peel and finely chop the onion. Melt one-fourth of the butter in a skillet over moderate heat and sauté the onion until lightly browned. Add the onion, beef, veal, pork and egg to the breadcrumbs. Beat the mixture vigorously with a wooden spoon until smooth. Season with salt and pepper. Moisten the fingertips slightly and shape the mixture into walnut-sized balls. Place on a dampened chopping board.

Heat the remaining butter in a skillet over low heat. Add the meat balls and fry slowly for about 10 minutes, shaking the skillet occasionally so they maintain their round shape and are evenly browned. Sprinkle them with the flour, then pour the stock over. Cover the skillet and simmer for 4–5 minutes. Serve with boiled or mashed potatoes, cranberry sauce and cucumber slices sprinkled with salt.

MOCK CHICKEN

Serves 6

6 veal escalopes, about 8 oz each
salt and pepper
6 slices bacon
¼ cup chopped parsley
¼ cup butter
6 tablespoons tomato paste
2 cups water

for the gravy:
2 tablespoons butter
¼ cup all-purpose flour
veal stock (see recipe)
⅔ cup light cream
salt and pepper
gravy coloring (optional)

Pound each veal escalope with a meat mallet until about ¼ inch thick. Sprinkle with salt and pepper. Flatten the bacon slices with a spatula and place one slice on each escalope. Sprinkle with chopped parsley and roll up, completely enclosing the bacon and parsley. Secure each roll with a toothpick or fine string.

Cook the butter in a heavy saucepan over moderate heat until the frothing stops and it is pale golden brown. Add the veal rolls and fry until lightly browned. Add the tomato paste and the water blended together. This should completely cover the veal. If necessary, add more water. Simmer for 25–30 minutes, or until the meat is tender.

Draw the pan off the heat and remove the rolls. Transfer to a heated serving dish and carefully remove the toothpicks or string. Reserve the stock for the gravy.

To make the gravy, melt the butter in a small saucepan over moderate heat. Remove from the heat and stir in the flour. Add the reserved stock gradually, mixing well after each addition. Return to low heat and bring slowly to the simmering point, stirring constantly until the mixture thickens. Stir in the cream. Reheat, but do not boil. Season to taste with salt and pepper and add a little gravy coloring, if wished. Strain the gravy and serve with the mock chicken, accompanied by boiled potatoes and cucumber salad (see page 64.

CHICKEN IN HORSERADISH SAUCE

Serves 6

1 boiling chicken, about 4½ lb	½ cup all-purpose flour
2 teaspoons salt	2¼ cups light cream
8 oz celeriac (celery root)	¼ cup grated fresh horseradish
2 medium-sized carrots	root
2 medium-sized onions	sugar and salt to taste
2 leeks	1 tablespoon finely chopped
for the sauce:	parsley
¼ cup butter	

Place the chicken in a large saucepan and cover with water. Add the salt. Peel and thickly slice the celeriac, carrots and onions. Trim the leeks and rinse thoroughly under cold running water. Place the prepared vegetables in the pan with the chicken and bring to a boil over moderate heat. Lower the heat and simmer the chicken for about 2 hours, or until tender. Remove the chicken from the pan and cut into large pieces, discarding any skin and bone. Keep hot in a serving dish.

Meanwhile, melt the butter in a saucepan over moderate heat. Stir in the flour and cook the mixture for about 1 minute. Remove from the heat and add the cream a little at a time, mixing thoroughly after each addition. Stir in the grated horseradish and return to moderate heat. Stir constantly over low heat until the mixture thickens. Do not boil. Remove from the heat and add sugar and salt to taste. Pour the hot sauce over the chicken, sprinkle with the chopped parsley and serve immediately with puff pastry triangles.

Chicken in horseradish sauce

MARINATED POT ROAST

Serves 6

3½ lb rolled rump roast of beef	5 juniper berries, crushed
for the marinade:	2 bay leaves
4½ cups beer	**for cooking:**
6 tablespoons distilled malt	4 oz fat back
vinegar	1 tablespoon salt
½ cup sugar	2 tablespoons butter
1 medium-sized onion	1½ cups beef stock
1 medium-sized carrot	**for the sauce:**
5 white peppercorns	¾ cup marinade (see recipe)
5 whole allspice	3 tablespoons all-purpose flour
5 whole cloves	6 tablespoons heavy cream
	salt and white pepper

Wipe the beef with a damp cloth or absorbent paper. Pour the beer and vinegar into a large stoneware crock or china bowl. Add the sugar and stir. Peel and slice the onion and carrot. Add the onion, carrot, peppercorns, allspice, cloves, juniper berries and bay leaves to the crock. Put the beef into the marinade, making sure it is well covered by the liquid. Set the crock aside for 5–6 days in a cold place, turning the meat occasionally.

Remove the meat, rinse quickly under cold running water and dry thoroughly. Reserve the marinade. Cut the fat back into narrow strips. Lard the beef with the fat back, using a larding needle; alternatively, pierce the meat with a sharp knife and insert the strips of fat. Rub the salt into the meat. Melt the butter in a heavy saucepan. Add the meat and sauté until thoroughly browned. Heat the stock separately and add to the meat. Cover the pan tightly and bring to a boil over moderate heat. Lower the heat and simmer for about 2 hours, or until the beef is tender.

Take the pan off the heat. Remove the beef and keep hot. Pour ¾ cup of the reserved marinade into the meat juices in the pan. Blend the flour with the cream and add to the pan. Place over moderate heat and bring to a boil, stirring constantly until the mixture thickens. Simmer for 2–3 minutes. Season with salt and pepper to taste. Serve the beef with the sauce, mashed potatoes, lingonberry preserve or cranberry sauce and dill pickles.

STUFFED PORK TENDERLOINS

Serves 4–6

2 pork tenderloins, about 1 lb	3 tablespoons butter
each	1¼ cups water
1–2 baking apples	3 tablespoons tomato paste
8 prunes, soaked overnight	⅔ cup light cream
salt and pepper	

Trim the pork tenderloins and remove any skin or sinew. Using a sharp knife, cut each tenderloin lengthwise but only halfway through. Open out and beat gently with a rolling pin to flatten them slightly. Peel, core and slice the apples and pit the prunes. Arrange the apple slices and prunes down the center of each piece of meat. Season with salt and pepper. Close the pork tenderloins again and tie tightly with fine string to hold the shape.

Melt the butter in a heavy skillet. Add the meat and brown it thoroughly. Pour in the water and tomato paste and bring just to a boil. Cover and simmer gently for 20–30 minutes. Add the cream. Season with salt and pepper and simmer gently for a further 10–15 minutes, or until the meat is tender.

Lift the tenderloins from the skillet, slice crosswise and arrange neatly on a serving dish. Pour the sauce from the skillet into a hot sauceboat. Serve the meat with the sauce, boiled potatoes and sweet red cabbage (see page 76).

WILD DUCK IN CREAM SAUCE

Serves 6

3 wild ducks	juice of 1 lemon
milk (see recipe)	salt and pepper
1½ cups butter	**for the garnish:**
6½ cups heavy cream	3 dessert apples
¼ cup redcurrant jelly	¼ cup rowanberry or cranberry
2 teaspoons crumbled Roquefort	jelly
or Danish blue cheese	

Clean the wild ducks and rinse them thoroughly under cold running water. Place in a large bowl and cover with milk. Set aside for 12 hours. (This minimizes the fishy taste.) Remove the ducks from the milk and dry thoroughly.

Heat the butter in a large heavy skillet and sauté the ducks until well browned. Place the ducks in a casserole and add the cream and the redcurrant jelly. Cover and cook in a preheated moderate oven (325°) for 1–1½ hours, or until the ducks are tender. To test the ducks, pinch the drumsticks; if the flesh feels soft this indicates that it is cooked sufficiently. It is important that each drumstick is tested.

Lift the ducks out of the casserole. Cut each one in half and place on a heated serving dish. Cover and keep hot while completing the sauce.

Skim the fat from the sauce in which the ducks were cooked. Pour the sauce into a saucepan, place over moderate heat and reduce by about half.

While the sauce is reducing, peel, core and halve the apples. Simmer in water to cover for about 5 minutes, or until tender but still whole. Drain well and place a spoonful of rowanberry jelly on each half.

Stir the cheese and lemon juice into the sauce. Season to taste with salt and pepper. Pour some of the sauce over the ducks and serve the remainder in a sauceboat. Garnish the ducks with the halved apples and serve immediately with caramelized potatoes (see page 76).

Stuffed pork tenderloins

FRICASSEE OF VEAL WITH DILL SAUCE

Serves 4

2–2½ lb rolled leg of veal
2 teaspoons salt for each
   4½ cups water
1 small onion
5 white peppercorns
½ bay leaf
for the sauce:
2 tablespoons butter
3 tablespoons all-purpose flour

1¾ cups veal stock (see recipe)
3 tablespoons chopped fresh dill
   or 1 tablespoon dried dill weed
1 tablespoon white wine vinegar
2 teaspoons sugar
¼ teaspoon salt
1 egg yolk
few sprigs dill

Trim the veal and wipe with a cloth or absorbent paper. Place in a saucepan with enough water to cover the meat completely. Add the salt. Bring to a boil over high heat and then skim. Peel and slice the onion and add to the veal with the peppercorns and bay leaf. Simmer for 1¼–1½ hours, or until the veal is tender.

Remove the veal from the pan and cut into 1½-inch cubes. Place on a heated serving dish and keep hot. Reserve the stock for the sauce.

To make the dill sauce, melt the butter in a small saucepan over moderate heat. Stir in the flour, then gradually stir in the reserved stock. Bring to a boil, stirring constantly until the mixture thickens. Add the chopped dill, vinegar, sugar and salt. Remove the pan from the heat and beat in the egg yolk. Pour the sauce into a sauceboat. Garnish the veal with the sprigs of dill and serve with the sauce and boiled potatoes or boiled rice.

BAKED BACON PANCAKE

Serves 4

2 eggs
2½ cups milk
1½ cups all-purpose flour
½ teaspoon salt

12 oz Canadian-style bacon,
   in 1 piece
1 tablespoon vegetable oil

Beat the eggs with one-fourth of the milk. Place the flour and salt in a bowl. Stir in the eggs and remaining milk and beat until smooth. Set the batter aside for 10 minutes.

Cut the bacon into ¼-inch cubes. Heat the oil in a 9- by 7-inch roasting pan and fry the bacon until crisp. Pour the batter over the bacon and bake in a preheated hot oven (425°) for 30–40 minutes, or until browned. Cut into portions and serve with cranberry sauce and a green salad.

DANISH HASH

Serves 6

1 lb leftover cooked meat	1 teaspoon curry powder
4 large onions	(optional)
8 medium-sized potatoes	1 tablespoon paprika
salt and pepper	1 tablespoon turmeric
1 cup butter	6 eggs

Cut the meat into very small cubes of uniform size. Peel and coarsely chop the onions. Peel the potatoes, cut into small cubes and sprinkle with salt. Divide the butter into 3 portions and heat one portion in a heavy skillet over moderate heat. Add the meat and fry for about 10 minutes, or until golden brown. Season to taste with salt and pepper. Remove and keep hot.

Add the second portion of butter to the skillet. Fry the onions with the curry powder, paprika, turmeric and salt and pepper to taste for 10–15 minutes, or until soft and golden brown. Remove and add to the meat.

Add the remaining butter to the skillet. Fry the potatoes until golden brown. Add the meat and onions to the potatoes in the skillet, mix well and season with salt and pepper to taste. Arrange on a large warm serving dish.

Fry the eggs and place on top of the hash. Serve immediately.

CARAMELIZED POTATOES

Serves 4

1½ lb even-sized new	¾ cup sugar
potatoes	6 tablespoons butter

Cook the potatoes in their skins in boiling salted water for 10–15 minutes, or until tender. Drain and peel the potatoes, then rinse in cold water.

Place the sugar in a skillet over low heat. Stir occasionally until the sugar has melted and turned to a golden caramel. Add the butter to the skillet. When melted, add the potatoes. Continue to fry, shaking the skillet gently until the potatoes are completely coated with the caramel and are golden brown. Serve immediately. Caramelized potatoes are particularly suitable for serving with roast pork, roast duck and roast goose.

SWEET RED CABBAGE

Serves 6

1 head red cabbage, about 2 lb	1 cup redcurrant juice or
¼ cup butter	¼ cup redcurrant jelly
3 tablespoons sugar	dissolved in ¾ cup hot water
6 tablespoons vinegar	salt

Discard the coarse outer leaves of the cabbage. Quarter it and cut away the hard center core. Finely shred the cabbage and place in a large saucepan with the butter, sugar, vinegar, redcurrant juice and salt to taste. Bring to the simmering point over moderate heat, then lower the heat and cover the pan with a tight-fitting lid. Cook the cabbage for about

1 hour, or until tender. During the last 15 minutes, stir the cabbage constantly. Add more vinegar, sugar or salt to taste. Serve hot.

DILL MAYONNAISE

Serves 8

1 tablespoon French mustard	3 tablespoons white wine vinegar
1 tablespoon Swedish or sweet	¾ cup vegetable oil
mustard	salt and white pepper
1 tablespoon sugar	⅓ cup finely chopped dill

Mix the mustards together in a small bowl. Add the sugar and vinegar and stir to form a paste. Add the oil drop by drop, beating well after each addition. Season with salt and pepper to taste and stir in the dill. Serve as an accompaniment to dill-cured salmon (see page 65).

NORRLAND POTATO DUMPLINGS

Serves 6

6 large potatoes	1 medium-sized onion
¾ cup barley meal	1¼ lb cooked lean salt pork
1¼ cups all-purpose flour	

Peel, rinse and coarsely grate the potatoes. Twist the grated potato in a cloth to squeeze out the water. Place in a bowl with the barley meal and the flour and stir to form a soft mixture. Peel and finely chop the onion. Finely chop the pork. Mix the onion and pork together.

Shape the potato mixture into dumplings about the size of an apple and make a hollow in each one with the thumb. Press a little of the pork mixture into each hollow and seal the opening so the filling is completely enclosed. Place the dumplings in a large saucepan half filled with lightly salted boiling water. Simmer gently for 30–35 minutes, or until they float to the surface. Remove with a perforated spoon. Drain well and serve with melted butter and lingonberry preserve or cranberry sauce.

Danish hash

76

Denmark's national specialty is *smørrebrød*, colorful, appetizing open sandwiches. They are invariably eaten for lunch, but their attractive appearance and the ease and speed with which they can be prepared make them an excellent and unusual choice for an informal supper party.

Two or three open sandwiches are sufficient for each person. Arrange them on large trays or wooden boards and allow guests to help themselves using a broad server rather like a cake slice. In Denmark it is customary to serve the open sandwiches made with fish first, and then the meat, poultry and cheese varieties. Supply each guest with a knife and fork with which to eat the sandwiches and serve tiny glasses of ice-cold Danish *schnapps* with the fish, followed by tall, cool glasses of Danish lager with the remainder of the meal.

A small version of an open sandwich is called a *snitter*. They are triangles of bread garnished in the same way as the open sandwich and are often served in the evenings with tea or beer, either for home entertainment or at a restaurant after the theatre.

The bread chosen for open sandwiches should be fresh with a good crust, and close-textured to take the weight of the toppings. Brown bread goes well with ham, liver pâté or egg, whereas white bread makes a suitable base for shrimp, chicken or beef. When strong-flavored toppings are used, such as salami, marinated herring or Danish blue cheese, the traditional Danish rye bread should be used.

Danish Open Sandwiches
top: *Liver pâté with mushrooms and bacon; ham with Italian salad; egg and tomato*
center: *Liver pâté with cucumber and pickled beet; Danish blue cheese and radish; marinated herring and onion; caviar with egg; shrimp and lemon*
bottom: *Ham with scrambled egg; salami and onion*

ITALIAN SALAD

Serves 4

1 large beet, cooked	**for the mayonnaise:**
1 large potato, cooked	2 egg yolks
2 medium-sized carrots, cooked	salt and pepper
2 thick slices celeriac (celery	1 cup olive oil
root), cooked	2 tablespoons distilled vinegar
1 dessert apple	2 teaspoons tarragon vinegar
1 dill pickle	

Using a whisk, or a small wooden spoon, mix the egg yolks with salt and pepper to taste in a small bowl. Add the oil a drop at a time, beating thoroughly after each addition. Continue until all the oil has been added and the mixture has become thick and smooth. Stir in the vinegars.

Dice the beet, potato, carrots, celeriac, apple and dill pickle and place in a serving dish. Coat the diced vegetables very thickly with the mayonnaise.

GRATED CARROT AND APPLE SALAD

Serves 4

1 lb carrots
1 lb dessert apples

juice of 1–2 lemons
sugar to taste

Scrape or peel the carrots as necessary. Peel the apples. Grate the apples and carrots finely and mix with the lemon juice. Add sugar to taste. Serve in a glass bowl.

LIVER PÂTÉ WITH MUSHROOMS AND BACON

2–3 slices Danish liver pâté
 (see page 63)
buttered bread
few slices mushrooms, sautéed in
 butter

1 slice bacon, crisply fried
1 small lettuce leaf

Cut the liver pâté into thick slices and arrange these overlapping on the buttered bread. Heap a few slices of sautéed mushrooms in the center. Arrange the slice of fried bacon across the top and tuck the lettuce leaf into one side.

HAM WITH ITALIAN SALAD

2–3 thin slices cooked ham
buttered bread
1 crisp lettuce leaf

1 tablespoon Italian salad
 (see preceding page)
1 wedge tomato

Fold each slice of ham loosely in half and arrange slightly overlapping on the buttered bread. Place the lettuce leaf in the center and spoon in the Italian salad. Place the tomato wedge on top.

EGG AND TOMATO

4 slices tomato
4 slices hard-cooked egg
buttered bread

mustard and cress or chopped
 chives

Arrange the slices of egg and tomato alternately in 2 rows of 4 on the buttered bread. Garnish with mustard and cress or chopped chives in the center.

SCRAMBLED EGG FOR OPEN SANDWICHES

4 eggs
1¼ cups milk

1 teaspoon salt
dash white pepper

Break the eggs into a bowl and add the milk and seasoning. Beat lightly to mix the ingredients. Pour into a greased 1-quart baking dish and place the dish in a larger baking or roasting pan filled to a depth of 1 inch with cold water. Bake in a preheated cool oven (300°) for about 1 hour, or until the mixture is set firm. Remove from the heat and allow to cool, preferably overnight. Cut into strips and use as required.

LIVER PÂTÉ WITH CUCUMBER AND PICKLED BEET

1½ oz Danish liver pâté
 (see page 63)
buttered bread

1 slice fresh cucumber
1 slice pickled beet
1 small lettuce leaf

Spread the liver pâté generously on the buttered bread. Make a cut from the edge to the center of the cucumber and beet slices. Place them together and bend each half in opposite directions to make a twist. Arrange on top of the pâté, off center, and tuck the lettuce leaf into one side.

MARINATED HERRING AND ONION

1 marinated herring fillet
 (see page 64)

buttered rye bread
3–4 onion rings

Cut the herring fillet into 1-inch pieces. Arrange neatly on the buttered bread and top with overlapping rings of onion.

DANISH BLUE CHEESE AND RADISH

2 slices Danish blue cheese
buttered rye bread

1 radish

Cut the cheese slices about ¼ inch thick and arrange overlapping on the buttered rye bread. Garnish with the washed radish cut in thin slices or with a radish rose. To make the rose, cut the radish in sections down from the top, leaving a part uncut at the stem end to hold the radish together. Place in iced water until the radish opens out like a rose. Drain and use as a garnish.

CAVIAR WITH EGG

1 oz Danish caviar
buttered bread

1 raw egg yolk

Spread the caviar generously over the buttered bread. Make a slight hollow in the center and gently tip in the egg yolk.

HAM WITH SCRAMBLED EGG

2–3 thin slices cooked ham
buttered bread
1 strip scrambled egg (see above)

1 teaspoon chopped chives
1 wedge tomato

Fold each slice of ham to give height to the sandwich and arrange attractively over the buttered bread. Place the strip of scrambled egg across the top and sprinkle with the chives. Garnish with the tomato wedge on one side.

SHRIMP AND LEMON

1 crisp lettuce leaf
buttered bread

2 oz shelled shrimp
1 slice lemon

Press the lettuce leaf on to the well-buttered bread. Neatly pile the shrimp on to the lettuce leaf. Cut the lemon slice halfway through, bend the ends in opposite directions to make a twist, and place on top.

SALAMI AND ONION

3 thin slices Danish salami
buttered rye bread

4 raw onion rings
sprig parsley

Arrange the slices of salami overlapping each other on the buttered bread. Snip 3 of the onion rings with scissors and arrange them over the salami, linking them through each other into the unbroken ring of onion. Garnish with a sprig of parsley.

YEOMAN'S SNUFF

Serves 4

2 tablespoons butter
1 cup fine fresh wholemeal
  breadcrumbs
1¼ cups heavy cream

1 teaspoon vanilla sugar
  (see note)
2½ oz semi-sweet chocolate
6 tablespoons strawberry jam

Melt the butter in a heavy skillet over moderate heat. Add the breadcrumbs and sauté until crisp and browned. Remove from the skillet and set aside until cool.

Whip the cream with the vanilla sugar until stiff. Grate the chocolate. Arrange layers of breadcrumbs, jam, chocolate and cream in a glass bowl. Finish with a layer of cream and sprinkle a little grated chocolate on top.

Note: Vanilla sugar may be bought from continental delicatessens or alternatively prepared by placing a vanilla bean in a jar of sugar until the flavor is absorbed.

EGG CHEESE

Serves 6

6½ pints milk
6 eggs
2 teaspoons acetic acid or vinegar

¼ teaspoon salt
¼ cup sugar

Pour three-fourths of the milk into a saucepan. Beat the eggs with the remaining milk, the acetic acid and the salt. Add to the milk in the pan. Stir constantly over very low heat until the mixture curdles. (It should not be allowed to boil.) Remove the pan from the heat, cover tightly and set aside for about 10 minutes until the curds separate from the whey.

Remove the curds with a perforated spoon and place in layers in an egg-cheese mold (a special pan with small holes in it). Alternatively, spoon the curds into a sieve lined with cheesecloth and placed over a bowl. Sprinkle a little of the sugar on each layer.

Put the egg cheese in the refrigerator, or in a cold place, for several hours. When all the whey has drained off, unmold the egg cheese and serve with raspberry jam.

Yeoman's snuff

VANILLA CREAM

Serves 6

4 envelopes gelatin
⅔ cup water
4 egg yolks
6 tablespoons sugar

2½ cups milk
½ teaspoon vanilla extract
1¼ cups heavy cream

Blend the gelatin with the water in a small bowl. Stand the bowl in hot water until the gelatin has completely dissolved.

Beat the egg yolks with the sugar in a large bowl. Bring the milk to a boil. Remove from the heat and add to the egg mixture, beating vigorously. Return to the saucepan and bring almost to a boil, beating constantly. Remove from the heat and stir in the dissolved gelatin. Add the vanilla extract. Set aside until cold, stirring frequently.

Whip the cream until thick and stir into the cold egg mixture. Pour into a 1½-quart mold and leave in a cool place to set. Turn out and serve when required.

COUNTRY GIRLS IN VEILS

Serves 4

9 tablespoons butter
5 cups rye breadcrumbs
generous ½ cup sugar
2¼ cups applesauce

about ½ cup strawberry jam or
   redcurrant jelly
1¼ cups heavy cream

Melt the butter in a large heavy saucepan over moderate heat until the frothing stops. Add the breadcrumbs and the sugar and cook gently for 5–10 minutes, stirring frequently. The crumbs will absorb all the butter and become crisp. Spread half the crumbs in the bottom of a glass serving dish. Cover with the applesauce and a layer of jam. Cover with the remaining crumbs. Whip the cream until thick and spread over the top layer of crumbs. Decorate with the remaining jam and serve cold.

RICE AND ALMOND MOLD

Serves 8

6½ cups milk
1 cup short-grain rice
1 teaspoon salt
⅔ cup sugar
1 vanilla bean
2 envelopes gelatin
1 tablespoon confectioners' sugar,
   sifted

3 cups heavy cream
1¼ cups blanched almonds,
   flaked
for the raspberry purée:
1¼ cups sugar
2½ cups water
3¼ cups raspberries
3 tablespoons kirsch

Heat the milk in a saucepan until boiling and add the rice, salt, sugar and vanilla bean. Pour into a casserole and cover tightly. Cook in a preheated moderately hot oven (400°) for 30–40 minutes, or until the rice is tender. Remove the vanilla bean.

Meanwhile, dissolve the gelatin in ¼ cup hot water. Rinse a 3-quart mold with cold water and dust lightly with the confectioners' sugar. Stir the dissolved gelatin into the rice and allow the mixture to cool. Lightly whip the cream and

fold into the rice with the almonds. Pour into the prepared mold and set aside in a cold place until set.

Meanwhile, to prepare the raspberry purée, dissolve the sugar in the water over low heat. Add the raspberries and simmer gently for a few minutes, or until the raspberries are reduced to a purée. Sieve the purée to remove the pips. Pour into a bowl and set aside to cool, then stir in the kirsch and chill until ready to serve.

Serve the rice and almond mold with the raspberry purée, both well chilled.

Note: This dessert is served on Christmas Eve if the traditional rice pudding has not been served as a first course. A bowl of it is always put aside for the *nisse* – a mischievous elf who is part of the Christmas festivities.

NORWEGIAN RHUBARB COMPOTE

Serves 4–6

1½ lb rhubarb
6 tablespoons water
1 cup sugar
1 tablespoon potato flour
for the custard:
2 eggs
2 tablespoons sugar

1 cup milk
2 teaspoons vanilla sugar (see
   Yeoman's Snuff, preceding
   page)
for the decoration:
10 cooked prunes
10 blanched almonds

Trim and rinse the rhubarb. Cut it into 2-inch pieces. Bring the water and sugar to a boil over moderate heat. Add the rhubarb. Lower the heat and simmer for about 5 minutes, or until the rhubarb is still whole and barely tender. Remove it with a perforated spoon and place in a serving dish. Leave the syrup in the pan, but remove from the heat. Blend the potato flour with a little water and stir into the syrup. Return the pan to the heat. Bring to a boil and simmer for 3 minutes, or until thickened, stirring constantly. Pour the syrup over the rhubarb and mix well. Set aside to cool.

To make the custard, beat the eggs and sugar together in a bowl until the mixture thickens and becomes pale yellow in color. Scald the milk and beat it vigorously into the egg mixture. Pour the custard into a saucepan and stir constantly over low heat until it thickens. Remove the pan from the heat and add the vanilla sugar. Stir until the custard is cold and pour it over the rhubarb. Pit the prunes and place an almond inside each one. Decorate the rhubarb custard with the stuffed prunes. Serve cold.

Strawberry gateau

STRAWBERRY GATEAU

Makes 1 10-inch gateau

for the sponge layers:

3 eggs

6 tablespoons sugar

¾ cup all-purpose flour

¼ cup melted butter

for the custard filling:

⅔ cup milk

1 egg

2 teaspoons sugar

2 teaspoons cornstarch

few drops vanilla extract

for the fruit filling:

1⅔ cups strawberries

2 macaroons, crushed

3 tablespoons sherry

for the decoration:

1¼ cups heavy cream

3 walnuts, finely chopped or

    whole strawberries (see recipe)

First prepare the cake layers. Beat the eggs and sugar together until light and foamy. Carefully fold in half the flour, then the melted butter and lastly the remaining flour. Divide the mixture equally between 2 greased 10-inch layer cake pans. Bake in the center of a preheated moderately hot oven (400°) for 20–25 minutes, or until the sponge layers are evenly risen and golden brown. Remove and cool on a wire rack. When completely cold, cut each sponge across in half to make 4 sponge layers altogether.

For the custard filling, bring the milk to a boil in a saucepan. Meanwhile, mix the egg, sugar, cornstarch and vanilla extract together in a bowl. Gradually beat the boiling milk into the egg mixture. Blend well and return the custard to the saucepan. Replace over the heat and bring back to a boil, stirring all the time. Simmer for 2 minutes, then draw off the heat and set aside to cool.

To make the fruit filling, hull and wipe the strawberries. Place the first sponge layer on a serving plate. Sprinkle with

the macaroons and then with the sherry. Cover with half the strawberries. Place the second sponge layer on top and spread with the cooled custard. Place the third layer on top and cover with the remaining strawberries. Finally, top the cake with the last sponge layer.

To decorate, lightly whip the cream and spread over the top and sides of the gateau. Sprinkle with the chopped walnuts or decorate with the whole strawberries. Chill before serving.

SMÅLÄNDSK CHEESECAKE

Serves 4–5

6½ pints milk

¼ cup all-purpose flour

2 teaspoons prepared rennet

2 eggs

1 cup heavy cream

¼ cup blanched almonds,

    chopped

3 tablespoons sugar

Heat the milk to 95°. Pour into a large bowl and beat in the flour and rennet. Stir until the mixture thickens, then set aside until it separates into curds and whey. Stir a few times so the whey rises to the surface. Strain the mixture and discard the whey.

Pour the curds into a bowl. Lightly beat the eggs. Add to the curds with the cream, almonds and sugar. Pour into a buttered mold or ovenproof dish and place in a pan half-filled with water. Bake in a preheated moderate oven (350°) for 1 hour. Allow the cheesecake to cool in the mold. Turn out and serve with whipped cream and strawberry jam.

DANISH FRUIT DESSERT

Serves 6

2¼ lb redcurrants and raspberries (see note)
4½ cups water
2¼ cups sugar
⅓ cup sago flour or
2½ tablespoons cornstarch
1 vanilla bean
sugar (see recipe)
3 tablespoons chopped almonds

Prepare the fruit according to kind and place in a large saucepan with the water. Simmer over moderate heat for 15–20 minutes, or until the fruit is very soft. Press through a sieve and return to the pan. Add the sugar and stir until dissolved. Blend the sago flour or cornstarch with a little water to make a smooth, thin paste. Stir this into the fruit purée. Bring to a boil over moderate heat, stirring constantly until the mixture thickens. Remove from the heat and add the vanilla bean. Cool, remove the vanilla bean and pour into large glass dishes. Sprinkle with sugar (to prevent a skin forming) and chopped almonds. Serve with ice-cold heavy cream.

Note: Other fruit combinations which are equally good are: redcurrants and blackcurrants; redcurrants and cherries; redcurrants, raspberries, strawberries and blackcurrants.

CREAM PUDDING

Serves 4

¼ cup water
2 envelopes gelatin
3 eggs
¼ cup sugar
2¼ cups milk or light cream
½ vanilla bean
⅔ cup heavy cream
for the caramel sauce:
⅓ cup sugar
⅓ cup water
⅔ cup heavy cream

Measure the water into a small saucepan and sprinkle in the gelatin. Stir over low heat until the gelatin has dissolved (but do not allow to boil). Draw off the heat. Separate the eggs, placing the yolks together in one bowl and the whites in a second larger bowl. Add the sugar to the yolks and beat together until thick and light in color. Pour the milk or cream into a saucepan. Add the vanilla bean and bring to a boil. Draw off the heat and remove the vanilla bean, then beat the hot milk into the egg yolks and sugar. Blend well and return the mixture to the pan. Heat gently, stirring constantly until the custard begins to thicken, but do not allow to boil. Draw off the heat, stir in the dissolved gelatin and set aside until the. mixture is cool and beginning to set.

Lightly whip the cream and stiffly beat the egg whites. Fold both into the mixture and pour into a 1½-quart ring mold previously rinsed out with cold water. Set aside in a cool place until set firm:

For the caramel sauce, heat the sugar gently in a dry saucepan stirring occasionally, until the sugar has melted and turned to a caramel. Add the water (take care at this stage as the mixture will boil furiously with the addition of the cold liquid). Continue to stir over the heat until the mixture has formed a smooth, thin, caramel liquid. Draw off the heat and set aside until quite cold. Lightly whip the cream and fold into the caramel liquid.

Unmold the cream pudding, pour over the caramel sauce and serve.

PANCAKE GATEAU

Serves 4

for the pancakes:
2 eggs
2½ cups milk
1½ cups all-purpose flour
1 teaspoon sugar
¼ teaspoon salt
3 tablespoons melted butter
butter for frying
for the filling:
sugar-coated berries or jam or applesauce
for the meringue:
3 egg whites
¼ cup sugar

Beat the eggs with half the milk. Beat in the flour, sugar and salt, and finally, the remaining milk. Stir in the melted butter just before cooking the pancakes.

Heat a pancake pan, or a small skillet, and add a pat of butter. Pour in a little batter and tilt the pan so the batter spreads to cover the bottom. Fry until golden brown on one side, then very carefully turn the pancake over and fry until golden brown on the other side. Turn the pancake out, and repeat the procedure until all the batter is used. The mixture will make 10–12 thin pancakes. Stack the pancakes on a round, heated, ovenproof serving dish, spreading a little of the chosen filling between the layers.

To make the meringue, beat the egg whites until stiff. Continue beating for a little longer, then carefully fold in the sugar. Spread the meringue over the top and sides of the pancake gateau. Bake in a preheated moderate oven (350°) for about 10 minutes, or until the meringue is slightly crisp and golden brown. Serve with whipped cream.

CREAM CONES

Makes 16 cones

3 tablespoons sugar
1 egg
⅓ cup all-purpose flour
½ teaspoon vanilla extract
1 teaspoon water
for the filling:
⅔ cup heavy cream
redcurrant jelly or raspberry jam (see recipe)

Beat the sugar and egg in a bowl until light and creamy. Gently fold in the flour, vanilla extract and water. Blend well.

Grease several baking sheets and flour lightly. Using a tablespoon, spread the mixture thinly on the baking sheets in oval shapes about 4 by 2½ inches. Spread only 3 or 4 portions of the mixture on each sheet at a time. If necessary bake them in batches. Bake in a preheated hot oven (425°) for about 5 minutes, or until lightly browned. Keeping the remainder warm, remove one baked oval from the sheet using a spatula. Shape into a cone using the palms of the hands and place in a clean bottle neck or narrow tumbler so it keeps its shape. Remove when cool and firm. Repeat until all the ovals have been made into cones.

Just before serving, whip the cream until stiff and spoon or pipe into the cones. Decorate each one with a teaspoon of jam or jelly. Arrange attractively side by side on a plate, or stand up in a bowl filled with sugar to hold them steady.

Unfilled cones may be stored for several weeks in an airtight container.

Cream cones

POPPY SEED ROLLS

Makes about 12 rolls

2 cups all-purpose flour
½ teaspoon salt
1 teaspoon sugar
generous ¾ cup butter
2 eggs

1 cake compressed yeast or
  1 envelope active dry yeast
¼ cup milk
poppy seeds for coating

Sift the flour and salt into a large bowl. Add the sugar. Cut ½ cup of the butter into small pieces and rub into the dry ingredients. Make a well in the center and crack into it one of the eggs.

Blend the compressed yeast with the cold milk. If using dry yeast, warm the milk, sprinkle in the dry yeast and set aside for 10 minutes until frothy. Add the yeast mixture to the center of the flour and mix all the ingredients together to make a dough. Knead the dough well and set aside to rest in a cool place for 10 minutes.

On a lightly-floured working surface, roll the dough out to a rectangle about 8 inches wide and 24 inches long. Brush the surface of the dough with cold water and cover with the remaining butter, thinly sliced. Fold the dough in three from left to right to make one strip of dough about 24 inches long and 2½ inches wide. Turn this around so the longest side is horizontal. Cut into 2-inch wide strips. Arrange on a baking sheet, place in a lightly oiled plastic bag and leave to rise in a warm place for about 30 minutes.

Beat the remaining egg. Brush the surface of each roll with beaten egg and sprinkle lavishly with poppy seeds. Bake in a preheated hot oven (425°) for 12–15 minutes. Slice through and spread with butter. Serve warm.

HAAKON COOKIES

Makes about 80

2¼ cups all-purpose flour
generous ¾ cup butter
¾ cup confectioners' sugar, sifted

1 vanilla bean
sugar for coating

Sift the flour into a large mixing bowl. Cut the butter into pieces and rub lightly into the flour using the fingertips. Add the sugar and the seeds from the vanilla bean. Gather the mixture together to make a dough and turn out on a lightly floured working surface. Knead lightly. Divide the mixture in half and roll each piece into a sausage about 1½ inches thick and about 10 inches long. Roll each sausage in sugar and place in the refrigerator or a cold place for about 1–2 hours, or until firm. Cut each portion of dough into thin slices about ¼ inch thick and place on a greased baking sheet. Bake in a preheated moderately hot oven (400°) for 10–15 minutes. Cool on a wire rack and store in an airtight container.

DANISH PASTRY DOUGH

Makes 2 lb dough

1 cake compressed yeast or	1½ cups butter
1 envelope active dry yeast	1 egg
2 tablespoons sugar	pinch ground cardamom
½ teaspoon salt	3 cups all-purpose flour
⅔ cup cold milk	

Dissolve the yeast, sugar and salt in the milk in a large bowl. If using dry yeast the milk should be hand hot and the mixture should be set aside for 15 minutes until it becomes frothy. Soften about one-eighth of the butter and beat it with the egg and cardamom. Add to the yeast mixture and blend well. Add the flour and mix thoroughly to a fairly soft dough. Knead the dough for 1–2 minutes on a lightly floured surface. Cover and set aside to rest for 10 minutes.

Soften the remaining butter and reshape into a slab about 4 by 8 inches. Roll the rested dough into a square about 10 by 10 inches. Place the slab of butter lengthwise in the center of the dough. Fold the uncovered sides of the dough over the butter, overlapping a little down the center. Press the edges of the dough lightly together, completely enclosing the butter. Roll out carefully into a rectangle about 18 by 6 inches. Fold the bottom third of the dough up and the top third down, making a square about 6 by 6 inches. Give the pastry a half turn to the right and roll again into a rectangle. The dough should be rolled and folded 3 times in this way. If the dough becomes sticky or elastic, cover and set aside to rest in a cool place for 15–20 minutes between each rolling and folding.

Before using the dough, it should be covered and rested for at least 30 minutes.

Using the Danish pastry dough

In most cases two or more variations of Danish pastries are prepared at one baking. The fillings and toppings in each of the following recipes are sufficient for 1 lb Danish pastry which is half the basic quantity of dough. With the prepared basic recipe for 2 lb of Danish pastry, any two of the following variations can be prepared.

ENVELOPES

Makes 18–24

1 lb Danish pastry dough	**for baking:**
for the filling:	1 beaten egg
6 tablespoons butter	½ cup almonds, chopped
6 tablespoons sugar	**for the decoration:**
vanilla extract (see recipe)	2 teaspoons hot water
	1 cup confectioners' sugar
	¼ cup raspberry jam

Make the dough following the instructions above, and use half the dough to make this recipe.

To make the filling, cream the butter and sugar together until soft and fluffy. Beat in vanilla extract to taste.

Roll the dough into an oblong about ⅛ inch thick. Cut the dough into squares 3 by 3 inches. Place 1 level teaspoonful of the filling in the center of each square. Draw the 4 corners of the dough together and press firmly on to the filling so the

join will not open during the baking. Place the envelopes on a baking sheet and set aside in a warm place to rise for 15–20 minutes. Brush with the beaten egg and sprinkle with the chopped almonds. Bake in a preheated hot oven (450°) for 15 minutes.

Meanwhile, add the hot water to the confectioners' sugar and blend to a smooth, fairly thick glacé frosting. When the pastries are baked, decorate when still warm with a teaspoonful of jam in the center of each and spread with a little frosting. Then remove from the baking sheet and cool on a wire rack.

CREAM BALLS

Makes about 12

1 lb Danish pastry dough	2 egg yolks
for the pastry cream:	1–2 tablespoons sugar
⅔ cup light cream	**for the decoration:**
2 tablespoons sugar	melted butter and vanilla sugar
¼ vanilla bean	(see recipe)
2 tablespoons cornstarch	

Make the dough following the instructions above, and use half the dough to make this recipe.

To make the pastry cream, pour the cream into a small heavy saucepan. Add half the sugar and the vanilla bean. Place over moderate heat until hot, but not boiling. Remove from the heat. Meanwhile, mix the cornstarch with the remaining sugar in a small bowl. Stir in the egg yolks and 6 tablespoons of the hot cream. Pour this mixture into the remaining hot cream and bring to a boil over moderate heat, stirring constantly until the mixture thickens. Remove the vanilla bean. Pour the pastry cream into a bowl and sprinkle with sugar to prevent a skin forming. Set aside until cold.

Roll the dough into an oblong about ⅛ inch thick. Cut the dough into squares 4 by 4 inches. Place 2 tablespoonfuls of the pastry cream in the center of each square and draw the edges of the dough together to enclose the filling completely. Arrange on a baking sheet with the joins underneath and set aside in a warm place to rise for 15–20 minutes. Bake in a preheated hot oven (450°) for 10 minutes.

To decorate the cream balls, brush with melted butter and then dip into vanilla sugar while still hot. Cool on a wire rack.

Danish pastries – envelopes and combs

86

SNAILS

Makes 18–24

1 lb Danish pastry dough

for the filling:

¼ cup butter

¼ cup sugar

vanilla extract (see recipe)

for baking:

½ cup chopped mixed candied peel

¼ cup cinnamon

1 beaten egg

½ cup almonds, blanched and
   slivered

for the frosting:

2 teaspoons hot water

1 cup confectioners' sugar

Make the dough following the instructions on the preceding page, and use half the dough to make this recipe.

To make the filling, cream the butter and sugar together until soft and fluffy. Beat in vanilla extract to taste.

Roll the dough into an oblong about ⅛ inch thick. Spread the filling over the dough and sprinkle with the candied peel and the cinnamon. Roll the dough into a sausage shape and cut into slices ½–¾ inch thick. Place well spaced out on a baking sheet, pressing each one down quite firmly in the center. Set aside in a warm place to rise for 15–20 minutes. Brush with the beaten egg and sprinkle with the almonds. Bake in a preheated hot oven (450°) for 10 minutes.

Meanwhile, add the hot water to the confectioners' sugar and blend to a smooth, fairly thick, glacé frosting. When the pastries are baked, spread each with a little frosting while still hot. Then remove from the baking sheet and cool on a wire rack.

COMBS

Makes 18–24

1 lb Danish pastry dough

for the almond paste:

½ cup finely ground almonds

2 tablespoons sugar

¼ cup confectioners' sugar, sifted

2 teaspoons lightly beaten egg

1 drop almond extract

6 tablespoons butter

vanilla extract (see recipe)

for baking:

1 beaten egg

¼ cup vanilla sugar (see
   Yeoman's Snuff, page 81)

Make the dough following the instructions on the preceding page, and use half the dough to make this recipe.

To make the almond paste, place the almonds, sugar and confectioners' sugar in a bowl. Stir and then add the 2 teaspoons of egg and the almond extract. Mix to a smooth paste. If the mixture is dry and crumbly, add a little more egg. Blend the butter with the almond mixture to make a soft paste. Add vanilla extract to taste.

Roll the dough into an oblong about ⅛ inch thick. Cut into long strips about 3 inches wide. Spread each strip thinly with the almond paste.

Fold the strips lengthwise and cut into 3-inch pieces. Make 5 cuts, ½ inch long and about ½ inch apart, on the folded edge on each piece to produce a comb shape. Place on a baking sheet and set aside in a warm place to rise for 15–20 minutes. Brush with the egg and sprinkle with the vanilla sugar. Bake in a preheated hot oven (450°) for 10 minutes.

Remove from the baking sheet while still hot and cool on a wire rack.

GERMAN

Arne Krüger

Photography by Arne Krüger and John Miller

Two distinct phases can be seen in the German cuisine. Before the Napoleonic wars in the early nineteenth century, German cooking was mainly determined by the seasonal availability of fruit, vegetables and meat, which were prepared according to local customs. The ingenuity of the people, who had to provide nourishing meals from the coarser cuts of meat and the more common vegetables, combined with the culinary skill exercised in the palaces of ruling princes and on the great estates, helped to develop a great variety of regional dishes, based on such foods as were readily available in the area. Where the country was covered by extensive forests and game was plentiful, game dishes were a prominent feature on menus. In regions dominated by lakes and rivers, or in those bordering on the sea, an endless variety of fish dishes could be found. And in the more luxuriant areas, where cattle breeding and agriculture were the main means of support, the food showed a tendency to be excessively rich with cream being used in the preparation of most dishes.

When Napoleon's armies marched over Europe, terms and methods derived from the French cuisine were gradually assimilated by the Germans. However, new trends were not always accepted without resistance and it often took a long time for a 'foreign' dish to be incorporated into the local menus. Eventually, many of the new dishes became adjusted to such an extent that they barely resembled the original version.

New developments came about by the end of the last century, when modern means of transport and of storing and preserving food opened up new possibilities. New varieties of fruit and vegetables became generally available, with the result that German cooking was tremendously enriched and began to make a name for itself.

The German cuisine is strongly regional in character. In recent years there has been a revival of interest in traditional cooking, as can be seen by the many restaurants specializing in country fare which have appeared in the larger towns.

Delicious seafood comes from the coast of northern Germany–mussels, eels, sole, herring–providing heartwarming stews and soups. Westphalia is renowned for its pumpernickel, the dark rye bread which is so delicious with the smoked hams and cheeses and strongly flavored sausages from the same areas. Freshwater fish, in particular carp, pike and trout, come from the rivers and lakes of Franconia, the region of the Main, Neckar and Rhine rivers. Carp is traditionally served for Christmas Eve dinner in Germany, and many recipes for its preparation have been handed down over the generations.

Dumplings and sausages are popular everywhere and each region has its own special way of making them, varying the seasoning according to the herbs available. A favorite dish in Thuringia, sweet and sour lentils with blood sausage, incorporates another national culinary feature, the mixing of sweet flavors with sour ones. Perhaps the most well-known of these dishes is *sauerbraten*–marinated beef in white raisin sauce.

Finally, mention must also be made of the superb cakes and rich pies, filled with fruit, nuts and chocolate, for which Germany is justly renowned.

BLACK FOREST HUNTER'S BREAKFAST

Serves 4

6 medium-sized potatoes	⅓ cup oil
4 oz button mushrooms	salt and pepper
8 oz leftover cooked game, such as venison	4 eggs

Bake the potatoes in their jackets in a preheated moderately hot oven (400°) for 1 hour, or until tender. Set aside to cool. Peel the potatoes and cut into slices. Wash and slice the mushrooms. Cut the game into small cubes.

Heat the oil in a large skillet over moderate heat. Add the potatoes, mushrooms and game. Cover the skillet and allow the mixture to heat through. Season with salt and pepper. Beat the eggs and pour over the potato mixture. Cook very gently until the eggs are just set. Cut the omelet into portions and serve with a lettuce salad.

ONION TART

Serves 4–6

for the pastry:	for the filling:
1 cake compressed yeast or 1 package active dry yeast	2 lb onions
⅓–½ cup lukewarm milk (see recipe)	3 tablespoons butter
dash sugar	3–4 eggs
2 cups all-purpose flour	½ cup cultured sour cream
¼ cup melted butter	6 tablespoons all-purpose flour
1 egg yolk	½ teaspoon salt
½ teaspoon salt	1 teaspoon caraway seeds
	5 slices bacon

To make the dough, crumble the yeast into the lukewarm milk, add the sugar and stir until dissolved. If using dry yeast, stir the sugar into the lukewarm milk and sprinkle in the dry yeast. Let the mixture stand for 10 minutes, until it is frothy. Mix 3–4 tablespoons of the flour into the yeast mixture. Cover and set aside in a warm place for 15 minutes.

Sift the remaining flour into a bowl and add the yeast mixture, cooled melted butter, egg yolk and salt. Beat with a wooden spoon until the dough is bubbly and, if necessary, add a little more milk. Knead well with floured hands until the dough leaves the hands and the side of the bowl clean. Cover the bowl with a damp cloth, making sure the cloth does not touch the dough, and put in a warm place until the dough has doubled in bulk.

To make the filling, peel and finely slice the onions. Melt the butter in a large skillet and sauté the onions over low heat until soft. Remove the skillet from the heat. Mix together the eggs, sour cream and flour until smooth. Stir this mixture into the onions. Add the salt and caraway seeds. Roll out the dough and line a 9-inch pie pan. Pour in the filling and smooth the top with a spatula. Cut the bacon into small pieces and sprinkle over the top. Bake the tart in a preheated moderately hot oven (400°) for 30–45 minutes until set and golden brown. Serve hot from the oven, warm or cooled, but never straight from the refrigerator.

VINEYARD SNAILS

Serves 4

24 canned snails, with shells
1 medium-sized onion
1 clove garlic
2 slices bacon
¼ cup butter
⅓ cup chopped fresh parsley

3 tablespoons chopped fresh chives
½ teaspoon sugar
salt
3 tablespoons fine fresh breadcrumbs

Drain the snails and reserve the liquid. Wash and dry the shells. Peel and finely chop the onion and garlic. Chop the bacon finely. Soften the butter in a small saucepan for a few moments over moderate heat. Remove the pan from the heat and stir in the onion, garlic, bacon, parsley, chives, sugar, salt and breadcrumbs. Mix until creamy.

Place 1 snail in each shell. Add 1 teaspoon of the reserved juice and sufficient amount of the butter mixture to fill the opening. Place the snails in snail plates or, if these are not available, sprinkle a thick layer of coarse salt, about 3 inches deep, in the bottom of an ovenproof dish and arrange the snails, open end upward, on the salt. Place the snail plate or dish in the center of a preheated cool oven (300°) and cook for 15–20 minutes. Serve hot, with crusty white bread and a dry white wine.

POTATO SOUP WITH SMOKED MEAT

Serves 4

4 medium-sized potatoes
bunch flavoring vegetables (fresh parsley, celery leaves and leek)
4¼ cups beef stock
½ teaspoon salt
¼ teaspoon pepper
4 oz bacon, in 1 piece
4 medium-sized onions

6 oz *Hamburger Rauchfleisch* (smoked meat) or smoked cooked ham
⅓ cup chopped fresh parsley
⅓ cup chopped fresh chives
3 tablespoons chopped fresh chervil

Peel the potatoes and cut into cubes. Wash and chop the parsley and celery leaves. Trim the leek, wash thoroughly and chop. Place the vegetables in a saucepan and add the stock. Bring to a boil over high heat, then reduce the heat and simmer, partially covered, for 15–20 minutes, or until the potatoes are cooked. Remove the pan from the heat and press the liquid and vegetables through a sieve. Season with the salt and pepper and keep hot.

Removing any rind, cut the bacon into small cubes. Peel and chop the onions and cut the smoked meat or ham into small strips. Lightly sauté the bacon in a large skillet for 4–5 minutes. Add the onions and sauté for a few minutes. Add the smoked meat or ham and continue cooking, stirring frequently, until the mixture becomes lightly browned. Spoon the sautéed ingredients on top of the hot soup, garnish with the chopped herbs and serve immediately.

BROTH WITH LIVER DUMPLINGS

Serves 4

4 oz beef liver
1 medium-sized onion
1 clove garlic (optional)
½ cup all-purpose flour
2 eggs
¾ cup milk

salt and pepper
2–3 sprigs parsley
2 teaspoons grated lemon rind
dash dried marjoram
4¼ cups clear, strong broth

Grind or finely chop the liver. Peel and chop the onion and garlic. Beat together the flour, eggs and milk in a bowl. Season with salt and pepper. Chop the parsley. Add the liver, onion, garlic, parsley, lemon rind and marjoram to the egg mixture, and thoroughly mix the ingredients. Drop half teaspoonfuls of the mixture into a saucepan of rapidly boiling salted water. Add only a few at a time to maintain a rolling boil. Remove the floating dumplings with a perforated spoon as soon as they rise to the surface. Keep them hot in a heated soup tureen. Heat the broth. Pour it over the dumplings and serve immediately.

MEAT AND VEGETABLE SOUP WITH SPÄTZLE

Serves 3–4

1¼ lb beef, chuck or round
4 pints water
1 teaspoon salt
2 large carrots
¼ celeriac (celery root)
2 medium-sized onions
1 leek
4 medium-sized potatoes

1 teaspoon mixed pickling spice
1 teaspoon salt
¼ teaspoon pepper
¼ teaspoon grated nutmeg
8 oz *Spätzle* (see page 107)
2 tablespoons butter
7–8 sprigs parsley

Cut the meat into large cubes and place in a large saucepan with the water and salt. Bring to a boil over high heat, then lower the heat and simmer for 40 minutes. Meanwhile, peel and chop the carrots, celeriac and one of the onions. Trim, wash and chop the leek. Peel and dice the potatoes. Add the chopped vegetables to the meat in the pan, with the pickling spices, salt, pepper and nutmeg, and cook with the meat for the last 15 minutes.

Using half quantities of the ingredients, prepare the *Spätzle* according to the recipe on page 107 and put them into a pan filled with plenty of boiling salted water. Simmer for 12 minutes, then drain in a sieve and keep hot. Peel and finely chop the remaining onion. Melt the butter in a saucepan, add the onion and sauté until golden brown. Add the *Spätzle* and mix thoroughly. Chop the parsley. Arrange the meat and vegetables on a heated serving plate, top with the *Spätzle* mixture and sprinkle with the parsley. Serve immediately.

Vineyard snails

Württemberg soup with pancake strips

PALATINE ONION SOUP

Serves 4

3 small onions	4¼ cups beef stock
2 tablespoons butter	1 egg yolk (optional)
1 teaspoon tomato paste	3 tablespoons heavy cream
¼ teaspoon paprika	(optional)
1 tablespoon all-purpose flour	

Peel and slice the onions. Melt the butter in a saucepan and sauté the onions until golden brown. Stir in the tomato paste and paprika and simmer over low heat for 3–4 minutes. Stir in the flour and add the stock gradually, stirring to blend the ingredients. Bring to a boil, stirring constantly, then lower the heat and simmer gently for 15–20 minutes. Remove from the heat. The soup may be thickened with an egg yolk and cream, in which case blend the yolk and cream in a small mixing bowl, add a few tablespoons of the hot soup to the egg mixture and blend well. Slowly pour the mixture into the soup, stirring constantly. Serve immediately with fried croutons.

WÜRTTEMBERG SOUP WITH PANCAKE STRIPS

Serves 4

1 egg	small bunch fresh chives
dash salt	2 tablespoons butter
dash grated nutmeg	4¼ cups clear, strong beef
½ cup all-purpose flour	broth
½ cup water	

Blend the egg, salt and nutmeg together in a bowl. Using a wooden spoon, stir in the flour and water alternately. Mix thoroughly after each addition to make a thin batter. Chop the chives and add half to the batter. Melt a little of the butter over moderate heat in a large, heavy skillet. Pour about half the batter into the center of the skillet, then tilt it in all directions until the batter covers the bottom, making an almost transparent pancake. Cook, turning the pancake once, until it is a deep golden color on both sides. Keep the pancake hot and repeat the process, making 2 large pancakes. Cut the pancakes into very thin strips. Heat the broth, add the pancake strips and the remaining chives and serve.

PIKE WITH LEMON AND SOUR CREAM SAUCE

Serves 6

1 pike, about 2½–3½ lb	2 cups cultured sour cream
1 teaspoon salt	1 tablespoon lemon juice
½ teaspoon pepper	1 teaspoon grated lemon rind
10 slices bacon	1 teaspoon sugar
½ cup shortening	salt and pepper
3 tablespoons all-purpose flour	1 tablespoon coarsely chopped
1 cup cold water	lemon balm (optional)

Clean the pike, leaving the fish whole. Wash inside and out and remove all membranes and traces of blood. Remove the scales with the back of a knife or a special scaling knife and then rinse under cold water and dry with absorbent paper. Mix together the salt and pepper and rub the inside of the pike with this seasoning. Cut the bacon into thin strips and, using a larding needle, thread the strips through the flesh of the pike at right angles to the backbone. Melt the shortening in a roasting pan. Put the fish into the hot fat, spine-side upward, place the pan in the center of a preheated moderately hot oven (400°) and cook for about 40 minutes. Baste the fish during the cooking. The fish is cooked when the fins on the back come away easily.

Lift the pike carefully from the pan, place on a heated serving dish, spine-side upward, and keep hot. Add the flour to the residue in the roasting pan and mix over low heat to a smooth paste. Add the cold water and mix until well blended. Add the sour cream, lemon juice, grated lemon rind and sugar. Heat, stirring constantly, until the sauce has thickened. Adjust the seasoning with salt and pepper to taste. Add the lemon balm and serve the sauce separately in a sauceboat. Serve the fish with potatoes boiled in their skins and a fresh green salad.

FRISIAN MUSSEL STEW

Serves 5–6

2½ quarts fresh mussels	¾ cup white wine
2 leeks	½ teaspoon salt
1 medium-sized onion	¼ teaspoon white pepper
1 green sweet pepper	1 teaspoon grated lemon rind
½ cup butter	

Mussels must be alive before cooking. Discard any that are not tightly closed or do not close when sharply tapped. Scrub the shells in plenty of cold water, using a hard brush. Remove the beards, rinse the mussels under cold running water and set aside while preparing the other ingredients.

Discard the coarse outer leaves of the leeks and cut the leeks in half lengthwise. Wash thoroughly and shred finely. Peel and chop the onion. Remove the seeds from the sweet pepper and chop the flesh. Melt the butter in a large saucepan over moderate heat. Add the leeks and sauté lightly

for 3–4 minutes. Add the wine, onion, sweet pepper, salt, pepper and lemon rind. Put the mussels into the pan, cover with a tightly fitting lid and raise the heat. Cook for 7–8 minutes, during which time the mussels will open. Discard any that have not opened. Pour the stew into a heated tureen or into 5 or 6 heated plates. Serve with dark rye bread and butter.

CARP IN SOUR CREAM SAUCE

Serves 4

1 carp, about 4 lb	⅓ cup fine fresh breadcrumbs
salt and pepper	¼ cup firm butter
1 medium-sized onion	¼ cup melted butter
¼ cup lemon juice	few sprigs parsley
½ cup cultured sour cream	1 tablespoon capers (optional)

Clean and scale the carp. Wash thoroughly, inside and out, removing all the dark membrane and traces of blood. Sprinkle with salt and pepper. Peel and finely chop the onion and sprinkle over the bottom of a buttered casserole. Place the carp on the bed of onion. Sprinkle with the lemon juice, pour over the sour cream and sprinkle with the bread-crumbs. Cut the butter into cubes and dot over the top. Pour over the melted butter. Bake in the center of a preheated moderately hot oven (375°) for 30 minutes. Meanwhile, chop the parsley. Serve the fish hot, garnished with the parsley, and capers if used, and accompanied by creamed potatoes.

FRIED PLAICE WITH ANCHOVY SAUCE

Serves 4

4 plaice or gray sole, about	3 tablespoons shortening
8–12 oz each	2 tablespoons butter
½ teaspoon salt	½ teaspoon anchovy paste
2 tablespoons lemon juice	1 lemon
½ cup all-purpose flour	3 tablespoons chopped fresh
rind of a smoked ham or	parsley
2 tablespoons bacon drippings	

Trim and clean the fish, but leave whole. Rinse under cold running water and dry thoroughly. Rub the fish with the salt and lemon juice, then coat with the flour and set aside for about 20–30 minutes, so the flour forms a fairly hard crust.

Scrape the fat off the back of the ham rind. Melt this or the bacon drippings in a skillet with the shortening – this gives the fish its typical smoky taste. When the fat is very hot, put the fish into the skillet one at a time, with the dark skin downward. Lower the heat slightly and fry the fish for 4–5 minutes on each side. Remove the fish from the skillet, drain on absorbent paper and keep hot on a serving dish. After the last fish has been fried, stir the butter and anchovy paste into the residue in the skillet to make a thin sauce. Meanwhile, slice the lemon. Pour the sauce over the fish, garnish with the parsley and the lemon slices and serve with potato salad.

STEWED EEL IN DILL SAUCE

Serves 4

1 large eel or 2 small eels, about 2–2¼ lb	½ cup vinegar
salt (see recipe)	**for the sauce:**
bunch flavoring vegetables (carrot, celery and leek)	2 leeks
	¼ cup butter
4¼ cups water	3 tablespoons all-purpose flour
1 bay leaf	2 cups eel stock (see recipe)
6 whole allspice	bunch fresh dill
6 white peppercorns	½ teaspoon salt
1 teaspoon salt	¼ teaspoon pepper
2 slices lemon	¼ cup light cream

Clean the eel and discard the head. Rub the skin liberally with salt to remove the slippery surface and wash well under cold running water. Drain, chop into 1-inch pieces and place in a saucepan. Peel and dice the carrot. Wash and chop the celery. Wash and chop the leek, discarding the coarse outer leaves. Place the vegetables in a second saucepan. Add the water, bay leaf, allspice, peppercorns, salt and lemon slices. Place over high heat and bring to a boil, then lower the heat and simmer for 10–15 minutes. Heat the vinegar until hot but not boiling. Pour over the eel and let stand for 10 minutes. Strain the liquid from the vegetables over the eel and vinegar, discarding the vegetables. Place the pan over moderate heat and bring just to the simmering point. Simmer for 2 minutes, then strain off the stock and reserve. Place the eel in a covered dish and keep hot.

To make the dill sauce, wash and chop only the white parts of the leeks, discarding the outer leaves. Melt the butter in a saucepan and sauté the leeks until tender. Remove from the heat and stir in the flour. Add the reserved stock gradually, stirring well after each addition. Chop half the dill and reserve the remainder. Season the sauce with the salt and pepper and stir in the chopped dill. Return to the heat and bring to a boil, stirring constantly until the mixture thickens. Stir in the cream. Pour the sauce over the eel and garnish with the reserved dill.

PICKLED HERRING WITH BEANS

Serves 4

1½ lb fresh green beans	2 oz bacon or pork fat
1 medium-sized onion	8 pickled herring fillets, about 1 lb
⅓ cup water	
¼ cup butter	⅓ cup chopped fresh parsley
sprig fresh savory	1 tomato, quartered
1 tablespoon flour	

Rinse the beans and break into 1-inch pieces. Peel and finely chop the onion. Place the beans and onion in a saucepan with the water, butter and savory. Bring to a boil over moderate heat then lower the heat and simmer, uncovered, for 15 minutes. Sprinkle the flour evenly over the beans, using a small sieve or sprinkling by hand. Mix well and simmer the beans for a further 10 minutes. Remove and discard the savory.

Cut the bacon or pork fat into very small cubes or chop finely. Place in a heavy saucepan and sauté over moderate heat until the fat runs. Pour into a heated sauceboat.

Meanwhile, rinse the herring fillets under cold water and dry well. Serve the herring chilled, or on crushed ice, garnished with the parsley and tomato. Serve the beans and the bacon sauce separately.

Potatoes, boiled in their jackets, make a good accompaniment, with *schnapps* or light beer to drink.

Pickled herring with beans

STEWED VEAL WITH PRUNES

Serves 4–6

1–1¼ lb lean veal or veal tenderloin	1 tablespoon all-purpose flour
1 medium-sized onion	1 cup white wine
3–4 tablespoons butter	1 cup water
water (see recipe)	4 oz tenderized prunes (see note)
¼ teaspoon salt	1 teaspoon lemon juice
dash pepper	¼ teaspoon sugar

Cut the veal into large cubes. Peel and chop the onion. Melt the butter in a large saucepan, add the onion and the veal cubes and sauté over low heat until golden brown. Simmer until the juices from the onion and meat have been absorbed. Then add 6–7 tablespoons of water and continue simmer until the water has been absorbed. Repeat this procedure once or twice more until the onions are very soft but not burned. Add the salt, pepper and flour. Stir until well blended. Add the wine and the water, stirring constantly, and bring to a boil. Lower the heat and simmer for 30 minutes.

Meanwhile, wash the prunes and remove the pits. Add the prunes to the saucepan and cook for a further 10 minutes. Adjust the seasoning, if necessary. Add the lemon juice and sugar. Serve with boiled potatoes or noodles and a green salad.

Note: If tenderized prunes are not available, substitute ordinary prunes which have been soaked for 2–3 hours or overnight.

DÜSSELDORF CHOPS

Serves 4

4 veal rib chops	dash pepper
4 shallots	1 tablespoon melted butter
6 mushrooms	1 egg yolk
4 oz fat back	1 cup fine fresh breadcrumbs
2 truffles (optional)	¼ cup butter
few sprigs parsley	4 slices lemon
½ teaspoon salt	

Bone the chops and remove any sinews from the meat. Peel the shallots and cook in boiling salted water for 5–10 minutes until tender, then drain. Wash and dry the mushrooms. Finely chop or grind the veal, shallots, mushrooms, fat back, truffles, if used, and parsley. Mix the ingredients together thoroughly. Shape the mixture into 4 chops. Sprinkle with salt and pepper, cover and set aside for 1 hour.

About 30 minutes before serving the chops, mix the melted butter with the egg yolk. Coat each chop first with the egg mixture and then with the breadcrumbs. Melt the ¼ cup of butter in a heavy flat skillet. Add the chops and sauté slowly until golden brown on both sides. Arrange the chops on a heated serving dish and garnish with the lemon slices. Serve with cauliflower and creamed potatoes.

SAUTÉED VEAL

Serves 4

1 lb rolled leg of veal	¼ teaspoon salt
2 tomatoes	dash paprika (optional)
¼ cup butter	½ cup yogurt
1 tablespoon all-purpose flour	dash sugar
½ cup hot water	

Cut the veal into very thin slices. Peel and chop the tomatoes. Heat the butter in a large skillet over high heat and sauté the meat until golden brown, stirring constantly. Lower the heat to moderate and sprinkle the flour over the meat. Stir in the tomatoes, hot water, salt, paprika, yogurt and sugar. Bring to a boil, stirring constantly, and cook for 3–4 minutes. Pour into a heated serving dish and serve immediately with rice, bread or mashed potatoes, and a green salad.

LEG OF VEAL WITH SOUR CREAM SAUCE

Serves 4

2 lb leg of veal	1 medium-sized onion
1 cup vinegar	1 medium-sized carrot
1 cup water	salt and pepper
1 bay leaf	1¼ cups cultured sour cream
2 cloves	1 tablespoon all-purpose flour
4 whole peppercorns	1 teaspoon sugar
3 slices bacon	

Wipe the meat with a damp cloth. Prepare the marinade by mixing together the vinegar, water, bay leaf, cloves and peppercorns. Place the meat in a china or earthenware bowl and pour the marinade over. Cover and leave to pickle in the mixture for 2–3 days, turning frequently. Lift the meat out of the marinade and dry well. Reserve the marinade.

Cut the bacon into thin strips and lard the meat with it, using a larding needle, or push the bacon strips into small slits in the meat with a sharp knife. Peel and slice the onion and carrot and place with the meat in a roasting pan.

Sprinkle with salt and pepper and pour in half the marinade. Place the pan in the center of a preheated moderately hot oven (400°) and roast for 1–1½ hours. Spoon over a little of the sour cream, at about 15-minute intervals, during the roasting. Remove the meat from the oven and keep hot in a covered dish. Strain the liquid from the roasting pan through a sieve into a small saucepan. Blend the flour and sugar with a little water to form a smooth paste and stir into the strained liquid. Add the remaining sour cream. Place the pan over moderate heat and bring slowly to the simmering point, stirring constantly until the mixture thickens. Slice the meat and serve on a heated plate. Serve the sauce separately.

VEAL AND MUSHROOM SOUFFLÉ

Serves 4

1 medium-sized cauliflower	⅔ cup cauliflower stock
3 cups water	(see recipe)
1 teaspoon salt	2 eggs
8 oz button mushrooms	few sprigs parsley
1 lb leftover roast veal	½ cup milk or cultured sour cream
¼ cup butter	dash pepper
¼ cup all-purpose flour	½ cup grated hard cheese

Break the cauliflower into florets and wash thoroughly. Discard the leaves and stem. Put the water and salt into a saucepan and bring to a boil. Add the cauliflower and cook until almost tender. Drain well and reserve ⅔ cup of the stock. Wash and slice the mushrooms. Cut the cooked veal into small cubes.

Melt three-fourths of the butter in a saucepan, add the mushrooms and sauté over moderate heat until soft. Stir in the flour and then add the reserved cauliflower stock gradually, mixing thoroughly after each addition. Stir until the mixture thickens, then remove from the heat and cool slightly. Butter a 2-quart soufflé dish and place the cauliflower and meat in the bottom. Separate the eggs and chop the parsley. Stir the milk or sour cream, egg yolks, pepper and parsley into the cooled mushroom sauce. Beat the egg whites until stiff and fold into the mushroom mixture. Pour into the prepared soufflé dish. Sprinkle with the grated cheese and top with the remaining butter, cut into small pieces. Bake in the center of a preheated moderately hot oven (375°) for 30 minutes. Reduce the heat to 350° and bake for a further 20–30 minutes, or until the soufflé is well risen and lightly browned. When baked, the center should still be slightly creamy. Serve immediately.

BEEF TONGUE WITH WHITE RAISIN SAUCE

Serves 4

1 fresh beef tongue, about 4½ lb	3 tablespoons butter
bunch flavoring vegetables	3 tablespoons all-purpose flour
(carrot, celery and leek)	2–3 cups stock from the
1 medium-sized onion	tongue (see recipe)
2 cups salt	3 tablespoons wine vinegar
6 peppercorns	¼ cup tomato paste
for the sauce:	1 tablespoon sugar
1 cup seedless white raisins	salt and pepper

Rinse the tongue under cold running water and place in a large saucepan. Peel and chop the carrot. Wash and chop the celery. Wash and chop the leek, discarding the coarse outer leaves. Peel and chop the onion. Add the carrot, celery, leek, onion, salt and peppercorns to the tongue. Add cold water to cover, place the pan over high heat and bring to a boil. Lower the heat and simmer gently, partially covered, for 4½–5 hours. If necessary, add more water during the cooking to keep the tongue covered. When cooked, remove the tongue from the pan and rinse under cold water. Peel off the skin and remove the bones and gristle from the back of the tongue. Set aside until required. Strain the stock and reserve the amount required for the sauce. Discard the vegetables.

To make the sauce, soak the raisins in cold water for 3–4 hours. Drain and place in a saucepan. Add just enough fresh water to cover. Bring to a boiling point over moderate heat and simmer for 10–15 minutes, or until the raisins are tender. Melt the butter in another saucepan, stir in the flour and cook over moderately high heat, stirring constantly until the mixture browns. Remove from the heat. Add the reserved stock gradually, mixing well after each addition. Return the pan to moderate heat and bring to a boil, stirring constantly until the mixture thickens. Add the raisins, vinegar, tomato paste, sugar and salt and pepper to taste and cook for a further 3–4 minutes. Slice the tongue thinly and heat the slices in the sauce for about 3–4 minutes. Transfer to a heated dish and serve immediately.

CURLY KALE WITH SAUSAGE

Serves 4

2½–3 lb curly kale	1 large onion
4 oz bacon, in 1 piece	1 large potato
¼ cup cooking oil	salt and pepper
4 pints water	dash grated nutmeg
1¼ lb cooking *Mettwurst* (see note)	1 beef bouillon cube

Strip the leaves of the curly kale from the stems and wash thoroughly in cold water. Place in a saucepan of boiling salted water. Bring back to a boil, then drain and rinse with cold water. Dice the bacon. Heat the oil in a large saucepan, add the bacon and sauté lightly until golden brown. Add the kale and water. Place the saucepan over moderate heat and bring to a boil. Lower the heat, cover the pan and simmer for 1½ hours.

Place the *Mettwurst* on top of the kale. Add a little more water, if necessary, but there must not be too much liquid. Simmer for 20 minutes. Peel and grate the onion and potato. Lift out the sausage and keep hot. Stir the kale well and add the onion, potato, salt and pepper to taste, nutmeg and the bouillon cube. Simmer for 10 minutes. Drain off any excess liquid and arrange the kale and the sausage on a heated shallow serving dish. Serve accompanied by roast potatoes.

Note: Mettwurst is a coarse sausage which is made in several varieties. It may be mild or strong, soft or fairly firm, smoked or unsmoked. Available in most continental delicatessen shops.

Curly kale with sausage

SPICED PORK CHOPS

Serves 4

4 pork rib chops	3–4 peppercorns
1 tablespoon caraway seeds	3–4 juniper berries
1 medium-sized onion	salt and pepper
3–4 tablespoons water	1 tablespoon all-purpose flour

Lightly beat the pork chops with a mallet to flatten them and rub with the caraway seeds. Peel and finely chop the onion. Heat the water in a skillet. Add the chops, onion, peppercorns and juniper berries. Sprinkle with salt and pepper and simmer the chops, partially covered, over moderate heat for 20–30 minutes, or until tender. Remove the skillet from the heat. Arrange the chops on a heated plate, cover and keep hot.

Add 3–4 extra tablespoons water to the juices in the skillet and bring to a boil. Blend the flour to a smooth paste with a little cold water. Stir the paste into the juices in the skillet and mix well. Place over moderate heat and bring to a boil, stirring constantly. Adjust the seasoning and pour the sauce over the chops. Serve with cooked shredded white cabbage sprinkled with melted pork drippings.

BAVARIAN PORK OR VEAL FORESHANKS

Serves 4

2 large pork or veal foreshanks	1 medium-sized carrot
1 teaspoon salt	1 cup light ale or beer
1 teaspoon paprika	1 bay leaf
¼ teaspoon pepper	½ teaspoon caraway seeds
¼ cup shortening	1 cup water
2 medium-sized onions	1 tablespoon cornstarch

Wash the foreshanks and dry them with a cloth. Rub the meat all over with the salt, paprika and pepper. Heat the shortening in a heavy roasting pan or flameproof casserole over moderate heat and brown the foreshanks for 15 minutes, turning frequently. It is important that they should be browned evenly all over, but not burned.

Peel and chop the onions and carrot and add to the roasting pan or casserole with the meat. Add all but 3 or 4 tablespoons of the light ale, the bay leaf and the caraway seeds. Place the pan in a preheated moderately hot oven (400°) and cook for 45–50 minutes. After 10 minutes, baste with the pan juices.

Transfer the foreshanks to a broiler pan. Place the pan under moderate heat and baste with the remaining ale until the skin on the foreshanks becomes crisp and tender.

To make the sauce, blend the water with the cornstarch and stir into the remaining juices in the roasting pan. Cook over moderate heat, stirring constantly, until the sauce thickens. If necessary, adjust the seasoning. Strain through a sieve into a heated sauceboat. Make incisions in the foreshanks before serving, loosening the sinews so the meat can easily be removed from the bone. Serve with the sauce, boiled potatoes, a mixed salad and beer.

Sweet and sour lentils with blood sausage

SAUERKRAUT WITH PORK

Serves 4

2 tablespoons lard or goose fat	1 lb bacon, in 1 piece,
1 onion	soaked overnight
1¼ lb sauerkraut	4 pork rib chops
⅔ cup dry white wine	8 medium-sized potatoes
1 baking apple, peeled and sliced	¼ cup kirsch
10 juniper berries, crushed	8 frankfurters
3 cups chicken stock	

Use a flameproof casserole or a large heavy saucepan. Melt the lard or goose fat in the casserole. Peel and chop the onion, add it to the fat and brown it. Stir in the sauerkraut over high heat and add the white wine, apple and juniper berries. Stir in the stock, cover and cook very slowly for 3 hours.

Add the soaked bacon and the pork chops. Cover and cook for 30 minutes. Meanwhile, wash and scrub the potatoes, but do not peel them. Cook for 15–20 minutes in boiling water. Add the kirsch to the sauerkraut and cook for a further 10 minutes. Prick the frankfurters with a fork, so they do not burst, and put them into a saucepan of boiling water. Keep the heat low and warm the frankfurters through. Remove the bacon from the casserole and slice it. Spoon the sauerkraut into the middle of a large, heated serving dish. Lay the pork chops, bacon and frankfurters on top and surround with the potatoes. Serve with a well cooled white wine.

SWEET AND SOUR LENTILS WITH BLOOD SAUSAGE

Serves 4

8 oz brown lentils	3 tablespoons all-purpose flour
bunch flavoring vegetables	¼ cup wine vinegar
(celery, carrot, onion and leek)	½ teaspoon salt
4 oz fat back or salt pork	dash pepper
2 medium-sized onions	1 lb *Blutwurst* (blood sausage)

Pick over the lentils. Wash well and soak overnight in plenty of cold water. The next day bring them to a boil very slowly in the water in which they were soaked. Wash the celery, peel the carrot and onion and wash the leek, discarding the coarse outer leaves. Chop the vegetables, add to the lentils and continue to simmer over low heat for about 1½ hours.

Cut the fat back or salt pork into cubes and sauté briefly in a separate saucepan. Peel and slice the onions, add to the pan and sauté quickly, until lightly browned. Stir in the flour and continue cooking until the mixture is well browned. Stir in the vinegar, salt and pepper. Mix thoroughly and add to the lentils. Cook for 5–10 minutes, or until well blended. Add the blood sausage and simmer, very slowly to prevent the sausage from bursting, for a further 10–15 minutes. Remove the sausage, split it open and scoop out the filling on to a heated serving plate. Pour the lentil mixture into a heated serving dish. Serve immediately.

BAYREUTH STUFFED CABBAGE

Serves 4

1 head white cabbage, about 1 lb	2–3 cloves
3 medium-sized onions	1 cup cultured sour cream
⅓ cup oil	1 lb cooked beef and pork,
1 teaspoon salt	ground
dash pepper	3 slices bacon or fat back
small piece bay leaf	

Wash the cabbage. Remove the center core with a sharp knife and discard it. Peel off the large outer leaves. Blanch these in hot water, rinse in cold water and set aside. Finely shred the remaining cabbage. Peel and chop the onions. Heat the oil in a skillet and sauté the onions until soft. Add the shredded cabbage, salt, pepper, bay leaf and cloves and simmer over low heat for 10 minutes. Remove the skillet from the heat and mix the cabbage mixture with the sour cream and ground meat. Adjust the seasoning if necessary.

Butter a casserole and line it with 2 of the blanched cabbage leaves. Arrange the meat and cabbage mixture on top. Cover with the remaining cabbage leaves. Arrange the bacon slices on top and bake in a preheated moderately hot oven (375°) for 30–35 minutes. Serve hot.

HUNTER'S MEAT LOAF

Serves 4–6

2 hard-cooked eggs	1 large onion
2 stale crusty bread rolls	2–3 sprigs parsley
8–12 oz lean stewing beef	5 slices bacon
8–12 oz pork tenderloin	¼ cup all-purpose flour
1 egg	(see recipe)
½ teaspoon salt	¼ cup shortening
dash pepper	½ cup water
2 teaspoons grated lemon rind	½ cup yogurt
dash dried marjoram	

Shell the hard-cooked eggs. Soak the rolls in a little cold water for 2–3 minutes, then squeeze out the excess water. Grind together the beef and pork. Beat the egg. Mix the soaked bread with the ground meat and add the beaten egg, salt, pepper, lemon rind and marjoram. Peel and finely chop the onion. Chop the parsley. Dice the bacon and sauté lightly in a skillet for 2–3 minutes. Add the onion and parsley and sauté for a further 2–3 minutes. Remove from the heat, add to the meat mixture and mix well. Shape the meat mixture into a large loaf, placing the hard-cooked eggs in the center. The eggs should be completely enclosed. Dust the meat loaf lightly with half the flour and set aside for about 30 minutes.

Melt the shortening in a wide saucepan or flameproof casserole over moderate heat. Place the meat loaf in the hot fat and sauté until brown on all sides. Add the remaining flour to the hot fat and stir in the water. Cover the pan and simmer gently over low heat. If using a casserole, cover it and place in the center of a preheated moderate oven (350°). Cook the meat loaf for 45 minutes – 1 hour. Add a little more water during the cooking, if necessary. Lift the meat loaf from the liquid and place on a heated serving plate. Add the yogurt to the liquid remaining in the pan and stir until the sauce is well blended and hot. Pour the sauce into a sauceboat and serve with the meat loaf.

SILESIAN HEAVEN

Serves 4

8 oz dried apples	2 tablespoons all-purpose flour
8 oz dried pears	dash salt (optional)
8 oz dried prunes	1 tablespoon lemon juice
1¼ lb bacon, in 1 piece	1 tablespoon sugar
¼ cup water	

Soak the dried apples and pears overnight, then drain. Soak the prunes in cold water to cover for about 1 hour. Place the bacon in a saucepan and barely cover with cold water. Bring to a boil over moderate heat, cover the pan, reduce the heat and simmer for 1 hour. Add the drained apples and pears, the prunes and the water in which the prunes were soaked. Simmer for a further 30 minutes. Mix the water and flour to form a smooth paste and stir into the liquid in the pan. Continue stirring until the liquid thickens. Taste and add salt if necessary (the dish will have absorbed some salt from the bacon). Stir in the lemon juice and sugar. Serve with Silesian potato dumplings (see page 105).

WESTPHALIAN STEW

Serves 4

1 lb bacon, in 1 piece	4 medium-sized potatoes
8 oz shelled fresh fava or lima	2–3 pears
beans	2 medium-sized baking apples
1½ lb fresh green beans	salt and pepper
4 medium-sized carrots	

Place the bacon in a saucepan and cover with cold water. Bring to a boil and simmer gently for about 30 minutes, or until the bacon is tender. Place the fava beans in a second saucepan and just cover with cold water. Bring to a boil and simmer for 10–15 minutes, or until just tender.

Meanwhile, lift the cooked bacon from the liquid and keep hot. Reserve the bacon liquid. When the beans are almost cooked, strain off the water and replace it with the reserved bacon liquid.

Clean and slice the green beans. Peel and dice the carrots and potatoes. Peel and slice the pears and apples. Add the green beans, carrots and potatoes to the fava beans and simmer gently without stirring until the vegetables are tender. Add the pears and apples and simmer for a further 15 minutes, or until the fruit is just tender. If necessary, the stew may be thickened with 1 tablespoon of flour blended with a little cold water. Stir in gently and bring to a boil. Season with salt and pepper to taste. Cut the bacon into cubes and add to the stew. Heat the stew through and serve in a heated dish.

Bayreuth stuffed cabbage

HEAVEN AND EARTH

Serves 6–8

2 lb large potatoes
2 teaspoons salt
2 lb baking apples
½ cup sugar
2 large onions

5 slices Canadian-style bacon
pepper
1 lb *Blutwurst* (blood sausage)
2 tablespoons butter

Peel the potatoes, cut into thick slices and place in a large saucepan. Add the salt and cover the potatoes with water. Cook over moderate heat for 15–20 minutes, or until the potatoes are tender. Meanwhile, peel, core and quarter the apples. Place in a second saucepan, add the sugar and cover with water. Simmer very gently until the apples are tender.

When the potatoes are tender, drain off and discard one-third of the water, leaving the remaining water and the potatoes in the pan. Mash the cooked potatoes very thoroughly, then beat with a rotary beater or hand whisk until very smooth. Add the apples, including the liquid in which they were cooked, and stir well. Place the pan over low heat and simmer gently.

Peel and finely slice the onions and dice the bacon. Sauté both together in a saucepan until browned. Add to the potatoes and apples and season to taste. Cut the blood sausage into 2 or 3 pieces and cut each piece in half lengthwise. Melt the butter in a skillet, place the sausage, cut side down, in the butter and fry quickly. Serve the apple and potato mixture in a heated tureen garnished with the fried blood sausage.

OXTAIL WITH HORSERADISH SAUCE

Serves 4

1¼ lb oxtail joints
2 medium-sized carrots
½ small celeriac (celery root)
1 leek
1 teaspoon salt
4 pints water
5 medium-sized potatoes

for the horseradish sauce:

3 slices white bread
⅓ cup milk
⅓ cup heavy cream
⅓ cup grated horseradish
dash salt
½ teaspoon sugar
2 teaspoons lemon juice

Rinse the oxtail joints thoroughly in cold water. Peel and coarsely chop the carrots and celeriac. Trim, wash and slice the leek. Put the meat into a large saucepan with the water. Place over high heat and bring to a boil, removing the scum with a metal spoon as it rises to the surface. Reduce the heat, add the salt, carrots, celeriac and leek, and simmer, partially covered, for 1½ hours. After about 1 hour, peel the potatoes and cut into cubes. Add the potatoes to the meat for the remainder of the cooking time.

To make the sauce, trim the crusts from the bread and discard. Cut the bread into small cubes. Heat the milk and cream in a saucepan until just simmering. Remove the pan from the heat, add the bread, horseradish, salt, sugar and lemon juice and beat until fairly smooth. Pour the sauce into a heated sauceboat. Serve the meat in a heated dish with the vegetable broth and horseradish sauce separately.

BEEF IN BEER SAUCE

Serves 4

1 medium-sized onion	12 white peppercorns
1 medium-sized carrot	1 teaspoon sugar
1 cup dark sweet malt beer or stout	1¼ lb beef brisket
1 teaspoon salt	2 tablespoons butter
1 bay leaf	1 tablespoon all-purpose flour

Peel and slice the onion and carrot and place in a saucepan with the beef, salt, bay leaf, peppercorns and sugar, and sufficient water to cover the meat to be cooked. Place the pan over high heat and bring to a boil. Add the meat, reduce the heat and simmer, partially covered, for about 2 hours, or until the meat is tender. Turn the meat over from time to time during the cooking.

Lift the beef from the pan and keep hot. Strain the cooking liquid and reserve. Discard the vegetables. Melt the butter in a saucepan. Stir in the flour and cook gently until the mixture is golden brown. Add the reserved liquid, a little at a time, stirring well after each addition. Place the pan over moderate heat and bring to a boil, stirring constantly until the mixture thickens. Adjust the seasoning, if necessary.

Carve the meat into slices and arrange on a large heated serving dish. Pour half the beer sauce over the beef and serve the remaining sauce separately. Serve with pickled beets and boiled potatoes accompanied by malt beer or a mixture of equal quantities of malt beer and a sparkling white wine.

SAUERBRATEN (MARINATED BEEF)

Serves 4

2 oz bacon or fat back	**for cooking the beef:**
2 lb lean beef pot roast	salt and pepper
for the marinade:	¼ cup shortening
1 large onion	½ cup water
1–2 carrots	1 tablespoon all-purpose flour or cornstarch
1 celeriac (celery root)	
½ beef bouillon cube	1 tablespoon blanched chopped almonds
2 cups water	
1 cup wine vinegar	¼ cup seedless white raisins
1 bay leaf	salt and pepper
3–4 juniper berries	little dry white wine
3–4 cloves	dash sugar
3–4 peppercorns	¼ cup cultured sour cream
	lemon juice (see recipe)

Cut the bacon into thin strips and lard the beef with it, using a larding needle. Alternatively, make cuts in the meat with a sharp knife and insert the strips into the cuts. To prepare the marinade, peel and chop the onion, carrot and celeriac. Place the vegetables in a saucepan with the ½ bouillon cube, water, vinegar, bay leaf, juniper berries, cloves and peppercorns and bring to a boil. Simmer gently for 3–4 minutes, then set aside to cool. Place the meat in a stone crock, cover with the marinade and marinate for 3 days, during which time the meat must be turned occasionally.

Remove the meat and reserve the marinade. Dry the meat with a cloth or absorbent paper and rub with salt and pepper. Melt the shortening in a heavy saucepan, add the meat and brown on all sides. Add the water and an equal quantity of the marinade, cover the pan and simmer over low heat for 1¼ hours. Lift out the meat and keep hot. Add 4–5 tablespoons cold water to the liquid remaining in the pan and bring to a boil. Blend the flour or cornstarch with a little cold water to a smooth paste and stir into the boiling liquid. Add the almonds and raisins and season with salt and pepper to taste. Add white wine to taste, the sugar and sour cream. Taste the sauce, and if preferred add a few drops of lemon juice. Pour into a hot sauceboat. Serve the meat in one piece and carve at the table. Serve the sauce separately.

BOILED BEEF WITH FRANKFURT GREEN SAUCE

Serves 4

1½ lb beef brisket	1 cup cultured sour cream
bunch flavoring vegetables (onion, carrot, leek, celery stalk and leaves and parsley sprigs)	3 tablespoons wine vinegar
	½ teaspoon salt
	dash pepper
2 lb potatoes	½ teaspoon sugar
1 teaspoon salt	1 cup chopped fresh herbs (parsley, chives, chervil, sorrel, tarragon, borage and dill)
for the sauce:	
4 eggs	
¼ cup oil	dash dry mustard (optional)

Rinse the beef under cold running water and place in a large saucepan. Cover with cold water, place the pan over high heat and bring to a boil. Reduce the heat and simmer, partially covered, for 1 hour. Peel and chop the onion and carrot. Wash and chop the leek, celery stalk and leaves and the parsley sprigs. Peel the potatoes and cut into large pieces. Add these vegetables with the salt to the meat in the pan and simmer for 20–30 minutes, or until the potatoes are well done.

Meanwhile, prepare the sauce. Boil the eggs for 5–7 minutes; they should be slightly soft in the center. Cool in cold water and shell. Separate the yolks from the whites and chop the whites finely. Mash the yolks in a bowl, using a wooden spoon. Add the oil, a drop at a time, beating until the mixture is smooth and thick. Stir in the sour cream, vinegar, salt, pepper, sugar, chopped herbs and egg whites. A dash of dry mustard may also be added. Cover the bowl and set aside for 30 minutes or until required. Lift the meat from the pan, carve into slices and arrange on a heated serving plate. Serve the vegetables separately with some of the strained cooking liquid. Serve the sauce in a sauceboat.

Sauerbraten (marinated beef)

JELLIED GOOSE

Serves 4

½ goose, about 3–5 lb	1½ teaspoons salt
3 medium-sized carrots	3–4 peppercorns
1 large onion	1 bay leaf
½ celeriac (celery root)	2 tablespoons powdered gelatin
1 leek	1 tablespoon sugar
1 parsley root or bunch parsley	3 tablespoons vinegar
stems	salt and pepper
4 pints water	

Wash and dry the meat and chop into small pieces. Peel and chop the carrots, onion and celeriac. Trim, wash and chop the leek. Scrape and chop the parsley root (if using parsley stems, wash and chop). Put the water and salt into a large saucepan, place over high heat and bring to a boil. Add the pieces of goose, with the carrots, onion, celeriac, leek, parsley root or stems, peppercorns and bay leaf. Lower the heat, cover and simmer for 1 hour, or until the meat is cooked. Remove from the heat and set aside to cool.

When lukewarm, remove the pieces of goose and place in a glass dish. Strain the liquid and reserve. Discard the vegetables. Mix the gelatin and sugar with a little of the liquid in a small saucepan. Stir over low heat until the gelatin is dissolved and add the mixture, with the vinegar, to the remaining reserved liquid. Adjust the seasoning, if necessary, with salt and pepper to taste. Set aside until cold and beginning to set, then pour over the goose pieces and chill until set into a firm jelly. Serve with fried potatoes.

HARE IN YOGURT AND SOUR CREAM

Serves 4

saddle and hind legs of 1 hare	*bouquet garni* (see recipe)
5 slices bacon	½ cup red wine
salt and pepper	½ cup yogurt
1 medium-sized onion	½ cup cultured sour cream
1 medium-sized carrot	½ cup stock or water
¼ cup butter	

Remove all sinews and skin from the hare, as they tend to harden during cooking. Rinse and dry the pieces thoroughly. Cut the bacon into thin strips. Using a larding needle, insert the strips in the flesh of the hare, or make small slits with the point of a knife and insert the strips. Sprinkle the pieces with salt and pepper. Peel and slice the onion and carrot. Melt the butter in a roasting pan and add the hare, onion, carrot, *bouquet garni* (1 bay leaf, 3 sprigs parsley and 1 sprig thyme, tied together) and wine. Pour over the yogurt and sour cream. Place the pan in the center of a preheated moderately hot oven (375°) and roast for 1½–2 hours, basting frequently. Lift the hare from the pan and cut into slices. Keep hot in a covered dish while preparing the sauce.

To make the sauce, add the stock or water to the liquid remaining in the roasting pan and bring to a boil. Stir until well blended. Strain the sauce over the hare and serve with Thuringian potato dumplings (see page 106) and cranberry sauce.

CALF LIVER WITH APPLE RINGS

Serves 4

2 lb potatoes	½ cup butter
1 lb calf liver	2 baking apples
3 tablespoons all-purpose flour	2 medium-sized onions
½ teaspoon salt	¾ cup water
¼ teaspoon white pepper	

Peel the potatoes and cook in boiling salted water until tender. Mash and keep warm. Meanwhile, cut the liver into 8 slices. Season the flour with the salt and pepper and coat the liver. Melt half the butter in a large heavy skillet and sauté the liver for about 5 minutes, turning the slices frequently; the inside should still be pink. Spoon the mashed potato on to a heated serving dish. Remove the liver from the skillet and place on the bed of mashed potato. Cover the dish and keep hot.

Peel and core the apples and cut into thick rings. Heat the remaining butter in a second skillet and gently sauté the apple rings for about 2–3 minutes on each side, or until tender and golden brown. Remove from the skillet, place on top of the liver and keep hot.

Meanwhile, peel the onions and slice into rings. Add to the butter remaining in the skillet and sauté until pale golden brown. Drain and arrange the onions on top of the liver with the apples. Add half the water to the residue in each of the skillets, heat until boiling and then blend the contents of the two skillets together to make a gravy. Strain the gravy over the dish and serve immediately.

WHITE CABBAGE SALAD

Serves 4

1 small firm white cabbage	dash pepper
1 teaspoon salt	1–2 tablespoons cultured sour
¼ cup oil	cream or yogurt (optional)
3 tablespoons vinegar	

Wash the cabbage. Remove the center core with a sharp knife and discard. Grate the cabbage very finely. If the cabbage is old or tough, pour boiling water over it and let stand for 2 minutes, then drain and rinse with cold water. Sprinkle with half the salt and pound with a mallet or a rolling pin until the cabbage is limp and slightly soft. The salt will make the juices run.

Prepare a salad dressing with the oil, vinegar, remaining salt and the pepper. Shake or stir vigorously. Mix the dressing into the cabbage and add the sour cream or yogurt, if liked. Mix again and let the salad stand, covered, for 1–2 hours before serving with roast pork, sausages or veal foreshanks (see page 98).

BAKED NOODLES WITH HAM AND CHEESE

Serves 4

8 oz noodles, macaroni or spaghetti	½ teaspoon salt
6 oz cooked ham, in 1 piece	1 cup cultured sour cream or yogurt
small bunch chives	2 tablespoons butter
1 cup grated hard cheese	1 tablespoon fine dry breadcrumbs
2 eggs	

Cook the noodles in plenty of salted water for 10–12 minutes, or until just tender. Drain well in a colander. Cut the ham into small cubes. Chop the chives. Butter a 1½-quart casserole. Put a third of the noodles in the bottom of the casserole. Sprinkle with half the ham, half the chives and a third of the grated cheese. Add another layer of noodles. Top with the remaining ham and chives and a third of the grated cheese and finish with a layer of noodles.

Beat together the eggs, salt and sour cream or yogurt and pour the mixture evenly over the noodles. Sprinkle the remaining cheese over the top.

Cut the butter into small pieces and dot over the cheese. Sprinkle with the breadcrumbs. Bake in a preheated moderately hot oven (375°) for 40 minutes. Serve with a fresh green salad.

SILESIAN POTATO DUMPLINGS

Serves 4

2 lb potatoes	dash grated nutmeg
¼ cup all-purpose flour	4 oz white bread
¼ cup semolina flour	¼ cup butter
½ teaspoon salt	

If possible, cook the potatoes the day before. Scrub, but do not peel, the potatoes and place them in a saucepan of boiling water. Simmer gently for 15–25 minutes until just soft. Drain and let stand overnight.

Peel the potatoes and mash or grate them. Place in a bowl and mix in the flour, semolina flour, salt and nutmeg to form a smooth dough. With floured fingers, shape the mixture into 8 large dumplings and set aside on a floured surface.

Cut the bread into cubes. Melt the butter in a heavy saucepan and gently sauté the cubes until pale golden brown. Drain. Ease the dumplings open and press about 4 sautéed cubes into the center of each dumpling. Seal up the opening, completely enclosing the cubes. Fill a large saucepan three-fourths full with salted water. Bring the water to a boil, add the dumplings, then reduce the heat and simmer for 20 minutes. Remove the dumplings with a perforated spoon and drain on a plate before serving. Serve hot with Silesian Heaven (see page 100) or with a casserole such as *Sauerbraten* (see page 102).

Silesian potato dumplings

THURINGIAN POTATO DUMPLINGS

Serves 4

9 medium-sized potatoes   ¼ cup butter
2 slices rye bread

Peel the potatoes and grate two-thirds of them. Place the grated potatoes in a linen bag or a sieve and squeeze out as much moisture as possible, so they are quite dry. Reserve the liquid. Place the grated potato in a large bowl, spreading out the shreds by hand. Let the liquid stand for a little while, pour off the water very carefully and add the residue at the bottom of the bowl (the potato starch) to the grated potatoes.

Meanwhile, cook the remaining potatoes in boiling salted water until tender. Drain, leaving 4–6 tablespoons of water in the pan. Mash the potatoes and cook over moderate heat, stirring constantly, until the mixture is fairly thick. Take care when the mixture comes to a boil since it may splash. Pour the boiling potatoes quickly over the grated raw potatoes and mix together to form a smooth dumpling paste.

Cut the bread into small cubes. Melt the butter in a skillet, add the bread cubes and sauté until browned. Drain. With hands rinsed in cold water, shape the potato mixture into 8 dumplings. Press 3 or 4 bread cubes into the center of each dumpling and seal the opening.

Bring plenty of well-salted water to a boil and drop the dumplings in. Lower the heat, half cover the saucepan and let the dumplings poach. When they rise to the surface they are ready. Lift the dumplings out with a perforated spoon and serve at once with a stew or casserole.

DRESDEN DUMPLINGS

Serves 4

¼ cup butter   ¾ cup all-purpose flour
½ cup stock or milk   2 eggs
dash salt, pepper and nutmeg   **to cook the dumplings:**
  (see recipe)   4 pints broth or stock

Heat the butter and stock or milk in a saucepan. If milk is used, add salt, pepper and nutmeg. Remove the pan from the heat. Cool a little of the stock and stir into the flour. Stir the paste into the hot stock. Return the pan to the heat and cook, stirring constantly, until the mixture leaves the sides of the pan clean. Remove from the heat and cool slightly. Add the eggs, one at a time, mixing well after each addition, until the mixture is shiny and fairly stiff. Cover the pan and set aside until cold.

To cook the dumplings, boil the broth or stock. Drop teaspoonfuls of the dumpling mixture into the boiling broth. Cover the pan and let the dumplings poach over moderate heat until they rise to the surface. Serve the dumplings with the soup or, drained, with roast meat.

Cheese noodles

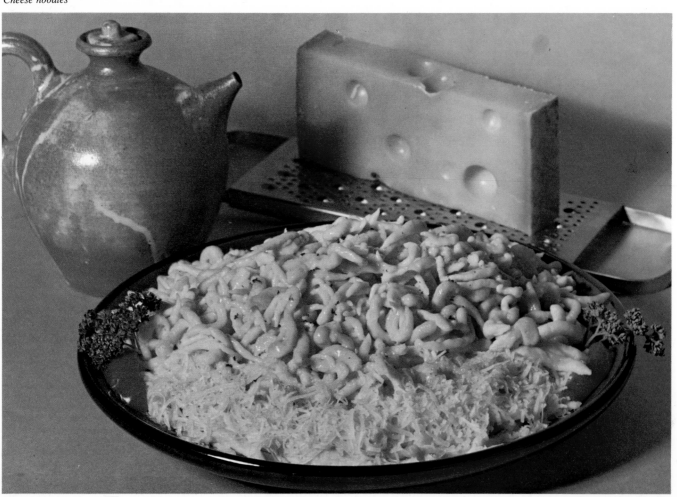

FRANCONIAN DUMPLINGS

Serves 4

4 stale crusty bread rolls	3 eggs
¼ cup butter	2 teaspoons salt
4 cups all-purpose flour	1 cup water or milk

Cut the rolls into large cubes. Heat the butter in a skillet and sauté the bread cubes until lightly browned. Mix the flour with the eggs, salt and water or milk in a bowl to form a soft dough. Stir the bread cubes into the dough and let stand for 1 hour. With wet hands, form the mixture into 8 dumplings.

Drop the dumplings into a large saucepan of boiling salted water. Bring to a boil, keeping the lid on the pan. Lower the heat and simmer, partially covered, for 20–25 minutes. Serve hot with a meat stew or with roast meat.

CARAWAY SEED DUMPLINGS

Serves 4

8 stale crusty bread rolls	½ teaspoon salt
1 teaspoon caraway seeds	1 cup lukewarm milk
1 medium-sized onion	2 eggs
2 tablespoons butter	

Cut the rolls into thick slices and place in a mixing bowl. Crush the caraway seeds and peel and slice the onion. Heat the butter in a skillet, add the onion and sauté lightly until soft. Cover the sliced bread with the onion, sprinkle with the salt and add the lukewarm milk. Cover the bowl with a plate and let stand for 5 minutes until the milk has been completely absorbed and the rolls are soft. Add the crushed caraway seeds and the eggs and mix thoroughly.

Using a wet tablespoon, scoop out a portion of the mixture and lower the spoon with the dumpling into a saucepan of boiling salted water. Once the dumpling is in the boiling water, it will slip off the spoon. Continue until all the mixture is used, making about 16 dumplings. Lower the heat and simmer the dumplings gently for 15–20 minutes. Remove from the water with a perforated spoon and drain on a plate before serving with a roast or casserole.

CHEESE NOODLES

Serves 4

3½ cups all-purpose flour	1 cup grated hard cheese
½ teaspoon salt	¼ cup melted butter
3 eggs	¼ cup hot beef stock
½ cup water	

Sift the flour and salt into a bowl and make a well in the center. Add the eggs and water and beat with a wooden spoon until all the liquid has been absorbed. Knead the dough in a bowl until smooth. Roll out on a floured board to ⅛ inch thick and cut into fine strips to make noodles. Drop the noodles, a few at a time, into boiling salted water. When they rise to the surface, remove them from the water with a perforated spoon.

Place a layer of noodles in a heated serving dish and sprinkle with a little of the grated cheese. Repeat until all the noodles have been used up. Finish with a layer of noodles. Pour the melted butter and the beef stock over the noodles just before serving. Garnish with any remaining cheese. Serve with a green salad or tomato salad.

SPÄTZLE

Serves 4–6

4 cups all-purpose flour	2 eggs
1 teaspoon salt	1 cup water

Sift the flour and salt into a bowl and make a well in the center. Add the eggs and mix together. Stir in the water gradually, beating well after each addition. Beat the mixture to make a well-aerated, soft dough. Dip a pastry board in cold water. Spread a spoonful of dough on it and then hold the board at a slant over a pan of lightly salted boiling water. Using a spatula, scrape thin strips, about ¼ inch wide, into the water. When the noodles rise to the surface, remove with a perforated spoon. Dip briefly into hot water to remove the excess starch. Drain the *Spätzle* in a sieve and keep warm in a covered dish until all the dough has been used.

POTATO NOODLES

Serves 6

8 medium-sized potatoes	2½ cups all-purpose flour
1 egg	¼ cup butter
1 teaspoon salt	3 tablespoons dry breadcrumbs
dash grated nutmeg	

Scrub the potatoes but do not peel them. Place in a large saucepan and cover with cold salted water. Bring to a boil and cook for 20–25 minutes, or until tender. Drain, skin and mash the potatoes. Add the egg, salt, nutmeg and flour, and mix together to make a fairly firm dough. If necessary, add a little more flour.

Lightly flour a pastry board. Divide the dough into 4 portions and make up long rolls of the mixture, about ½ inch thick. Cut into 1-inch pieces. Shape each piece into a thin roll, about 2 inches long. Drop the noodles into lightly boiling water in a wide, but not too shallow, saucepan. Simmer gently until they rise to the surface, then remove with a perforated spoon and drain in a sieve. Melt the butter in a skillet, fry the breadcrumbs until golden brown and sprinkle over the noodles. Serve with sauerkraut.

COTTAGE CHEESE FINGERS

Serves 4–6

6 medium-sized potatoes	⅔ cup currants
1 egg	all-purpose flour (see recipe)
1 cup cottage cheese	oil or shortening for deep-frying
dash salt	1 teaspoon sugar
dash grated nutmeg	¼ teaspoon cinnamon
2 teaspoons grated lemon rind	

If possible, cook the potatoes the day before. Scrub, but do not peel, the potatoes. Put into a saucepan of boiling salted water and cook over moderate heat for about 20 minutes, or until just soft. Drain and let stand overnight.

Peel the potatoes and grate or press through a sieve into a bowl. Beat the egg and add with the cottage cheese, salt, nutmeg, lemon rind and currants to the grated potatoes. Mix thoroughly, working in as much flour as the mixture will absorb. With well-floured hands roll into small finger or croquette shapes. Deep-fry in hot oil or shortening until golden brown. Drain on absorbent paper. Mix the sugar with the cinnamon, sprinkle over the cheese fingers and serve hot with a fruit sauce, such as plum (see below).

PLUM SAUCE

Makes about 2¼ cups

1 lb plums	1 tablespoon butter
¼ cup sugar	1 tablespoon cornstarch
dash cinnamon	½ cup water

Remove and discard the pits from the plums, using a sharp knife, and put the fruit into a saucepan. Add the sugar and cinnamon and enough water to barely cover the fruit. Bring to a boil over high heat, then lower the heat and simmer for 10–15 minutes, or until the fruit is tender. Remove from the heat and stir in the butter. Blend the cornstarch with the water and stir into the cooked fruit. Return to the heat and bring to a boil, stirring constantly. Serve the sauce hot.

DIPLOMAT PUDDING

Serves 4–6

6 stale crusty bread rolls	few drops rum extract
1½ cups milk	⅓ cup currants
1½ cups blanched almonds	⅓ cup seedless white raisins
4 eggs	3 tablespoons cornstarch
⅔ cup butter	3 tablespoons fine fresh white
⅔ cup sugar	breadcrumbs
vanilla extract or grated lemon rind	

Cut the rolls into cubes and place in a bowl. Bring the milk to a boil and pour over the rolls. Cover and let stand for 30 minutes. Chop the almonds and separate the eggs. Cream the butter with the sugar and egg yolks until the mixture is soft. Stir in the vanilla extract or grated lemon rind to taste and the rum extract. Beat the softened bread until smooth and

add the almonds, currants, white raisins and cornstarch. Add the fruit mixture to the butter mixture and beat thoroughly. Beat the egg whites until stiff and fold into the mixture.

Grease a 2-quart heat-resistant bowl or pudding mold and sprinkle the inside with the breadcrumbs. Spoon the mixture into the bowl and cover with a cloth or waxed paper. Place the bowl in a saucepan, pour in boiling water to reach halfway up the sides of the bowl, cover the pan and steam for about 1½ hours. Replenish with boiling water when necessary. Serve hot with vanilla sauce (see below).

VANILLA SAUCE

Serves 4–6

2 cups milk	1 tablespoon vanilla sugar
¼ cup granulated sugar	(see note)
3 tablespoons cornstarch	2 egg yolks
3 tablespoons cold water	3 tablespoons advocat liqueur

Bring the milk to a boil over low heat. Add the granulated sugar, stir to dissolve and remove the saucepan from the heat. Measure the cornstarch into a bowl and blend with the water. Stir in the vanilla sugar or the additional sugar and vanilla extract. Stir the cornstarch mixture into the hot milk and return the pan to the heat. Bring to a boil again, stirring constantly, and remove from the heat.

Place the egg yolks in a bowl. Stir the liqueur into the yolks, with ¼ cup of the hot sauce. Blend well and then stir into the hot sauce. Beat thoroughly, set aside to cool and chill in the refrigerator before serving.

Note: If vanilla sugar is not available, substitute granulated sugar to which has been added a few drops of vanilla extract.

RED FRUIT DESSERT

Serves 6

10 oz redcurrants	3 tablespoons cornstarch
10 oz fresh or frozen raspberries	⅓ cup water
1 cup water	1 cup heavy cream (optional)
about 1 cup sugar	

Wash the redcurrants and remove the stems. Pick over the raspberries or defrost them if frozen. Place the redcurrants and raspberries in a large heavy saucepan and add the water. Bring to the simmering point over low heat and cook for 10 minutes. Press the fruit through a sieve into a second pan. Add the sugar, bring to a boil and remove from the heat.

Blend the cornstarch with the water and stir into the hot fruit mixture. Return to the heat and bring to a boil, stirring constantly. Remove the pan from the heat and set aside to cool. Pour into serving glasses. Chill thoroughly and serve with fresh cream. If preferred, the dessert may be decorated with whipped cream.

Red fruit dessert

BAVARIAN CREAM STRUDEL

Serves 4

for the pastry:
2 cups all-purpose flour
dash salt
½ cup lukewarm water
2 tablespoons melted butter
1 egg
for the filling:
3 tablespoons butter

⅓ cup fine fresh breadcrumbs
½–1 cup cultured sour cream
½ cup seedless white raisins
1 cup milk
1 tablespoon sugar
sifted confectioners' sugar
  (see recipe)

To make the pastry, sift the flour and salt on to a pastry board and make a small well in the center. Gradually add the lukewarm water, melted butter and egg. Drawing the flour from around the sides, work the ingredients to a smooth, close-textured dough. Knead the dough thoroughly until small air bubbles appear on the surface. Set aside, cover with a warm cloth and let stand for 30 minutes.

Divide the dough into 3 equal portions. Prepare each portion of the dough in turn. Roll out the pieces of dough on a cloth lightly dusted with flour, until they are the thickness of the back of a knife. Then, using your fingertips and working from the edges, pull out the dough until it is transparent. You should be able to see through it but the dough should not tear. To make the filling, melt two-thirds of the butter in a skillet over moderate heat, add the breadcrumbs and sauté until crisp and golden brown. Spread the sour cream evenly over each piece of dough. Sprinkle with the raisins and sautéed breadcrumbs. Lift the cloth under each strudel in front and roll up, completely enclosing the filling. Bring the milk to a boil, add the sugar and the remaining butter. Pour the milk mixture into a large roasting pan or ovenproof dish and arrange the strudels in the pan, side by side. Place the pan in the center of a preheated moderately hot oven (400°) for about 40 minutes, until the milk has been absorbed and the strudels are pale golden brown. Transfer the strudels to a dish and serve at once, dusted with confectioners' sugar.

RICE DUMPLINGS IN WHITE WINE SAUCE

Serves 4

for the dumplings:
⅔ cup short-grain rice
2 cups milk
¼ cup butter
dash salt
little grated lemon rind
  or vanilla extract
⅓ cup candied lemon peel
6 tablespoons sugar

4 eggs
⅔ cup seedless white raisins
¼ cup all-purpose flour
¼ cup fine dry breadcrumbs
oil or shortening for deep-frying
for the sauce:
2 cups white wine
2 tablespoons sugar
small strip lemon rind

Wash the rice several times in lukewarm water. Cook the rice slowly in the milk with the butter, salt and grated lemon rind or vanilla extract for about 15 minutes, or until tender. Finely shred the candied lemon peel. Separate 1 of the eggs. Mix together in a bowl, the sugar and 2 whole eggs plus 1 egg yolk.

When cooked, drain the rice and add to the bowl with the candied lemon peel, raisins and flour. Mix well and form the mixture into small dumplings. Beat together the remaining egg and the egg white. Dip the dumplings first into the egg mixture, then into the breadcrumbs. Deep-fry in hot oil until pale golden brown and drain thoroughly on absorbent paper. Place the dumplings in a heated dish and keep hot. To make the sauce, heat the wine with the sugar and the strip of lemon rind until hot but not boiling. Strain and pour over the dumplings. Serve immediately.

GOOSEBERRY PIE

Serves 6–8

for the pastry:
⅔ cup butter
2–3 tablespoons ground hazelnuts
  or toasted breadcrumbs
2 cups all-purpose flour
1 teaspoon baking powder
dash salt
½ cup sugar
dash cinnamon

1 tablespoon milk or water
2 egg yolks
for the filling:
1–1½ lb firm gooseberries
½ cup water
1 cup sugar
1 tablespoon dry breadcrumbs
2 egg whites

To make the pastry, cut the butter into small cubes and place in the refrigerator or a cold place for 10 minutes. Butter a 9- or 10-inch pie pan or spring-form pan and sprinkle with the hazelnuts or breadcrumbs. Sift the flour, baking powder and salt on to a pastry board and make a well in the center. Place the sugar, cinnamon, milk or water and egg yolks in the well and distribute the cubes of butter evenly over the flour. First mix together the sugar, cinnamon, milk and egg yolks, then gradually draw in the butter and flour from around the sides. Mix to a smooth dough and let stand in the refrigerator or cold place for 5 minutes. Roll out the pastry and line the prepared pie pan, pressing the pastry carefully over the bottom and around the sides up to the height of 1 inch. Bake in a preheated moderately hot oven (400°) for 20–25 minutes, or until the pastry is golden brown. Set aside to cool.

Meanwhile, prepare the filling. Stem and head the gooseberries, wash thoroughly and place in a heavy saucepan. Add the water and half the sugar. Bring to a boil over moderate heat. Lower the heat and simmer very gently for 5–10 minutes, until the fruit is just tender but still whole. Drain the berries in a sieve and reserve the juice (see note). Sprinkle the breadcrumbs into the cooled pastry shell and arrange the gooseberries on top. Beat the egg whites in a bowl until stiff. Slowly beat in half of the remaining sugar until the mixture stands up in peaks. Using a metal spoon, fold in the remaining sugar. Put the meringue into a pastry bag with a large tip and pipe in a crisscross pattern over the gooseberries. Bake the pie in a preheated hot oven (425°) for 3–4 minutes until the meringue is very lightly browned. Serve warm or cold.

Note: The reserved gooseberry juice may be thickened with 1 teaspoon arrowroot or 2½ teaspoons cornstarch for each 1 cup of juice, and poured over the fruit.

Plum pie with almonds

PEARS IN BATTER

Serves 4

2 lb very ripe pears
2 cups water
1 tablespoon sugar
¼ cup lemon juice
2 oz margarine
for the batter:
2 cups all-purpose flour

1 teaspoon baking powder
½ cup granulated sugar
1 teaspoon vanilla sugar or few
    drops vanilla extract
2 eggs
1¼ cups milk

Peel, halve and core the pears. Rinse under cold running water and place in a heavy saucepan. Add the water, sugar and lemon juice. Bring to a boil over moderate heat, lower the heat and simmer gently for 10 minutes. Drain the pears in a sieve. The juice may be reserved for a sauce (see note).

Grease a 1½-quart baking dish with the margarine. Arrange the pears close together in the dish, rounded side up. Set aside while preparing the batter.

To make the batter, sift together the flour, baking powder, sugar and vanilla sugar into a mixing bowl. Add the eggs and milk. Beat until the mixture is smooth, making a fairly thick batter. Pour the batter over the pears and smooth the top with a knife. Place the dish in the center of a preheated moderate oven (350°) and bake for 1–1¼ hours until the batter is firm, golden brown and well risen. Serve hot or cold as a dessert.

Note: The reserved pear juice may be thickened with 1 teaspoon cornstarch blended with 2–3 teaspoons cold water. The sauce should be served separately, warm or chilled.

PLUM PIE WITH ALMONDS

Serves 6

¾ cup butter
2 cups all-purpose flour
1 teaspoon baking powder
½ cup sugar
dash salt
2 teaspoons grated lemon rind
1 egg or 2 egg yolks

for the filling:
¼ cup cookie crumbs
2 lb firm purple plums
¼ cup sugar
1 teaspoon cinnamon
1 cup flaked blanched almonds

To make the pastry, cut the butter into small cubes and place in the refrigerator for 10 minutes. Butter a 9- or 10-inch pie pan. Sift the flour and baking powder on to a pastry board and make a well in the center. Place the sugar, salt, grated lemon rind and egg or egg yolks in the well. Distribute the cubes of butter evenly over the flour. First mix together the sugar, salt, lemon rind and egg, then gradually draw in the butter and flour from around the sides. Mix to a smooth dough and let stand in a cool place for at least 30 minutes. Roll out the pastry thinly and line the prepared pie pan. To make the filling, sprinkle the cookie crumbs over the bottom of the pastry shell. Halve and pit the plums. Arrange in circles in the pastry shell and sprinkle with the sugar and cinnamon. Sprinkle the almonds over the plums. Place the pie pan in the top of a preheated moderately hot oven (400°) and bake for 20 minutes. Lower the heat to 350° and bake for a further 15 minutes. Serve hot or cold.

BLACK FOREST CHERRY TORTE

Makes 1 9-inch cake

for the cake:

1 cup all-purpose flour	⅔ cup water
1 cup cornstarch	⅔ cup sugar
1 teaspoon baking powder	½ cup kirsch
3 tablespoons unsweetened cocoa	1 teaspoon powdered gelatin
5 eggs	1¾ cups heavy cream
1 cup sugar	sugar (see recipe)

for the filling:

1½ lb Morello or sour cherries	1 cup chopped blanched almonds
	1 oz semi-sweet chocolate, grated

If possible, make the cake about 24 hours before it is needed. Sift together the flour, cornstarch, baking powder and cocoa. Grease and line a 9-inch spring-form pan. Beat together the eggs and sugar in a mixing bowl over a saucepan of hot water until the mixture is thick and warm. Remove the mixing bowl from the water and continue to beat until the mixture is cold. Gently but thoroughly fold in the sifted dry ingredients, using a metal spoon. Pour the mixture into the prepared pan and bake in a preheated moderately hot oven (375°) for 35–40 minutes. Turn out and cool on a wire rack.

Cut the cake into 3 equal layers. Pit the cherries. Heat together ½ cup of the water and the sugar in a small saucepan over low heat until the sugar has dissolved, then boil until the mixture is thick and syrupy. Remove the pan from the heat and add half the kirsch. While still warm, sprinkle over the cake layers.

To make the filling, dissolve the gelatin in the remaining water in a small bowl over a saucepan of hot water. Set aside until cool but not set. Whip the cream until stiff and gently stir in the remaining kirsch and the cooled, dissolved gelatin. Sprinkle in sugar to taste.

Place one cake layer on a cake plate. Spread with a thin layer of the cream filling and arrange the pitted cherries on top, reserving a few for decorating. Cover with a second layer of cake. Spread this thinly with cream filling and cover with the third layer of cake. Spread most of the remaining cream filling over the top and sides of the cake. Coat the sides of the cake with the chopped almonds. Decorate the cake with the remaining cream filling, using a pastry bag and a fluted tip. Sprinkle with the grated chocolate and top with the remaining cherries.

Store in the refrigerator and serve chilled.

STUTTGART CHERRY CAKE

Makes 1 9-inch cake

5 eggs	1¼ cups dark rye breadcrumbs
⅔ cup sugar	1 tablespoon arak or rum
1 teaspoon grated lemon rind	1 lb pitted Bing cherries
1 teaspoon ground cloves	or canned pitted sweet cherries
1 teaspoon cinnamon	¼ cup sifted confectioners' sugar
1 cup finely ground almonds	

Separate the eggs. Beat together the sugar and egg yolks until foamy. Stir in the lemon rind, cloves, cinnamon and ground almonds. Sprinkle the arak or rum over the crumbs, then add the crumbs to the mixture. Beat the egg whites until stiff and fold carefully into the batter.

Pour the batter into a well-buttered 9-inch spring-form pan. Arrange the cherries on top. Bake in the center of a preheated moderate oven (350°) for about 50 minutes. Set aside until cool, then remove the cake from the pan. Dust with the confectioners' sugar and serve.

Black Forest cherry torte

RUM YEAST CAKE WITH WHITE RAISINS

Makes 1 9-inch cake

1 cake compressed yeast or 1 package active dry yeast	4 eggs
	¾ cup butter
1¼ cups lukewarm milk	1 cup sugar
4 cups all-purpose flour	1 cup seedless white raisins
2 teaspoons grated lemon rind	¾ cup finely ground almonds
¼ cup lemon juice	3 tablespoons rum
dash salt	1 cup sifted confectioners' sugar

Dissolve the compressed yeast in the milk in a large bowl. If using dry yeast, stir the yeast into the milk and set aside for 10 minutes. Add half the flour and the grated lemon rind, lemon juice and salt. Cover the bowl with a cloth and leave to rise in a warm place for 20 minutes.

Place the eggs, in their shells, in warm water for 2–3 minutes. (They will then be warmer and a better cake texture will be achieved.) Cream the butter until soft and gradually beat in the eggs and sugar. Beat the remaining flour into the yeast mixture and combine with the butter mixture. Mix in the raisins, almonds and rum with a wooden spoon and beat until the mixture is well aerated. Butter a 2-quart *Kugelhopf* pan or a 9-inch tube pan and pour in the mixture. The pan must be only half full. Smooth the mixture and sprinkle lightly with flour. Cover the pan with a cloth and leave in a warm place until the mixture has risen to the rim. Bake in a preheated hot oven (400°) for 30 minutes. Reduce the heat to 350° and cook for a further 30–40 minutes. Let the cake cool in the pan for 2 hours and then turn out on to a round plate. Dust with the confectioners' sugar to give a snowy appearance.

REDCURRANT CAKE, COUNTRY STYLE

Serves 8–10

4 cups all-purpose flour	1⅓ cups semolina flour
dash salt	2 teaspoons grated lemon rind
1 cake compressed yeast or 1 package active dry yeast	4¼ cups milk
	1 lb fresh redcurrants, stripped from the stems
1 teaspoon sugar	
1 cup lukewarm milk	**for the topping:**
½ cup melted butter	1½ cups cultured sour cream
2 teaspoons grated lemon rind	2 tablespoons sugar
for the filling:	½ cup all-purpose flour
3 tablespoons granulated sugar	
dash vanilla sugar or 1 drop vanilla extract	

Sift the flour and salt into a bowl and make a well in the center. Mix the yeast with the sugar and milk and pour into the well in the flour. Sprinkle a little of the flour over the yeast mixture and set aside until frothy. Add the melted butter and lemon rind. Mix all the ingredients together to form a soft dough. Knead well on a floured board until the dough becomes smooth and elastic. Place the dough in a bowl, cover with a cloth and leave to rise in a warm place until doubled in bulk.

To make the filling, place the sugar, vanilla sugar or

extract, semolina flour and lemon rind in a large, heavy saucepan. Stir in the milk, half at a time. Place the pan over moderate heat and bring the mixture slowly to a boil, stirring constantly with a wooden spoon until the mixture becomes smooth and fairly thick. Remove the pan from the heat, cover with a piece of waxed paper to prevent a skin from forming on top and set aside to cool.

Punch down the dough and roll out to a rectangle, about 12 by 9 inches. Place the dough on a greased and floured baking sheet, cover with a cloth and let rise for 5–10 minutes only. Spread the filling over the slightly risen dough to within about 1½ inches of the edge. Cover with the redcurrants.

To make the topping, mix the sour cream with the sugar and flour and pour the mixture over the redcurrants. Place the baking sheet in the center of a preheated moderately hot oven (375°) and bake for 35–40 minutes, or until the filling has set and the dough is golden brown. Serve hot or cold.

CHOCOLATE HONEY CAKE

Makes about 36 2-inch squares

¾ cup honey	**for the frosting:**
1 cup sugar	2 oz semi-sweet chocolate
¼ cup butter	2 tablespoons unsweetened cocoa
½ cup beer	1 cup confectioners' sugar
1 egg	about 3 tablespoons hot water
3 teaspoons allspice	2 tablespoons butter
3 cups all-purpose flour	¼ cup apricot jam
2 teaspoons baking powder	¼–½ cup halved blanched almonds
1 tablespoon rum	
1 cup finely ground almonds	

Combine the honey, sugar, butter and beer in a large saucepan. Heat gently, stirring until the mixture is blended, then remove from the heat and set aside to cool. Add the egg and beat into the honey mixture with the allspice. Sift in the flour and baking powder, a little at a time, mixing thoroughly after each addition. Stir in the rum and almonds. Spread the mixture in a lightly greased jelly roll pan, about 15½ by 10½ inches, and smooth the surface with a spatula. Bake in the center of a preheated moderately hot oven (375°) for 25–30 minutes, or until firm. Turn out and frost while the cake is still warm.

To make the frosting, melt the chocolate in a double boiler or in a small bowl over a saucepan of simmering water, then remove from the heat. Sift the cocoa with the confectioners' sugar and stir into the melted chocolate. Gradually stir in the hot water until the frosting is thick enough to coat the back of a spoon. Stir in the butter very gently.

First spread the warm cake with the apricot jam and then cover with the chocolate frosting. Leave to set for 5 minutes, then cut the cake into squares while still slightly warm. Place half an almond in the center of each square. Serve immediately, or allow the cake to cool completely and store in an airtight container until required.

EBERSWALDE FRIED RINGS

Makes about 24 rings

2 cups milk
½ cup butter
¼ cup sugar
1 teaspoon grated lemon rind
dash salt

3½ cups sifted all-purpose flour
8 eggs
oil or shortening for deep-frying
sifted confectioners' sugar
  (see recipe)

Put the milk, butter, sugar, lemon rind and salt into a large saucepan. Bring to a boil and remove the pan from the heat. Add the flour and beat with a wooden spoon until smooth. Return the pan to the heat and beat until the mixture leaves the sides and bottom of the saucepan clean. Remove from the heat again and allow to cool until the pan is only slightly warm to the touch. Stir in the eggs, one at a time, and beat until the mixture is smooth and shiny. Place the mixture in a pastry bag fitted with a large star tip.

Heat the oil or shortening for deep-frying in a wide saucepan, but do not let it get very hot. Cut a circle of waxed paper or aluminum foil, ½ inch smaller than the inside of the pan, and dip this into the warmed oil. Remove the paper at once and lay it on a plate. Pipe the mixture in small rings on to the paper. Heat the oil to 375° and slip the round of paper carefully into the hot oil, holding on to the edge with a pair of kitchen tongs, so the rings slip off the paper. Fry the rings on each side until golden brown. Use the same piece of paper again for the next batch of rings. Drain each batch well and dust with confectioners' sugar. Serve warm.

CHRISTMAS BREAD

Makes 1 large loaf

1¼ cups seedless white raisins
1⅓ cups currants
1⅓ cups sugar
3 tablespoons rum (optional)
4 cakes compressed yeast or
  4 packages active dry yeast
2 cups lukewarm milk
8 cups sifted all-purpose flour
1 teaspoon salt
1⅓ cups butter

dash grated nutmeg
dash ginger
grated rind of 1 lemon and
  1 orange
1 tablespoon all-purpose flour
1¾ cups slivered blanched
  almonds
1 cup chopped candied citron peel
6 tablespoons butter
sifted confectioners' sugar
  (see recipe)

Place the raisins and currants in a bowl. Sprinkle the fruit with 3 tablespoons of the sugar and the rum, if used. Covered the bowl and let stand for 24 hours.

Stir the compressed or dry yeast into the lukewarm milk. Sift the flour and salt into a bowl and make a well in the center. Pour the yeast mixture into the well and stir a little of the surrounding flour into the liquid. Cover with a cloth and let stand in a warm place for about 30 minutes. Measure the butter and let stand at room temperature.

Sprinkle the remaining sugar, the nutmeg, ginger and grated lemon and orange rind over the flour. Mix the dry ingredients into the yeast mixture and beat in the softened, but not melted, butter. Knead the dough well on a floured board until no longer sticky. Place in a bowl, cover with a cloth and let stand in a warm place for several hours until doubled in bulk. Sprinkle the raisins and currants with the 1 tablespoon of flour and knead into the dough on a floured board with the almonds and candied peel. Shape the dough into an oval. Cover with a cloth and let rise on the board, in a warm place, for 30 minutes.

Using a rolling pin, make a deep depression lengthwise along the center of the oval and fold one half down over the other. Place the dough on a warm baking sheet lined with waxed paper. Once more cover the dough with a cloth and let rise for a further 30 minutes. Bake in the center of a preheated moderately hot oven (375°) for 1 hour. Remove from the oven and, while still warm, spread liberally with the butter. Then coat thickly with the confectioners' sugar.

Note: Since Christmas bread matures and improves in flavor on keeping, it is advisable to make it at least 1 month before it is required, and keep in an airtight container or wrap in aluminum foil.

ULM SWEET BREAD

Makes 2 loaves

1¼ cups heavy cream
1¼ cups milk
2 cakes compressed yeast or
  2 packages active dry yeast
1 teaspoon sugar
8 cups all-purpose flour
1 cup chopped candied orange
  peel

1 cup chopped candied lemon peel
⅔ cup sugar
2 teaspoons grated lemon rind
1 tablespoon anise seeds
1 tablespoon cardamom
⅓ cup rose water
2 teaspoons salt
1 egg for glazing

Gently heat together the cream and milk until lukewarm. In a bowl, blend the compressed yeast with the teaspoon of sugar and the warmed liquid. If using dry yeast, stir the yeast and sugar into the milk and set aside for 10 minutes. Beat about a fourth of the flour into the yeast mixture. Cover the bowl with a damp cloth and let the mixture stand in a warm place until frothy. Sift the remaining flour into a large bowl and add the orange and lemon peel, sugar, grated lemon rind, anise seeds, cardamom, rose water and salt. Stir the yeast mixture into the dry ingredients and blend together.

Knead the dough thoroughly on a floured board until the anise seeds begin to fall out of the dough. Divide the dough into 2 pieces. Shape the pieces into oblongs and place on a floured baking sheet. Cover the loaves lightly with a cloth and put in a warm place to rise for 1–2 hours, or until almost doubled in bulk.

Beat the egg and brush over the loaves. With a sharp knife, make several lengthwise cuts along the top of each loaf. Place the baking sheet in the center of a preheated hot oven (425°) and bake for 15 minutes. Reduce the heat to 375° and bake for 20–30 minutes. Cool the loaves on wire racks. Serve, thinly sliced, with tea, coffee or hot chocolate.

Eberswalde fried rings

FRENCH

Monique Guillaume

Photography by Christian Délu

The provinces of France have all jealously guarded their culinary secrets. Their dishes are naturally based on food which is readily available locally.

The salt-meadow sheep and superior cattle of Normandy and Brittany are well known. The region produces excellent butter and cream—many recipes combine the bland taste of cream with the tart taste of the local cider apples. The big fishing fleets provide the rest of France with a delicious variety of seafood. Freshwater fish are also plentiful.

Fish, however, is not the only specialty of the region. Brittany is also the kitchen garden of France. Because of the mild climate the vegetables are ready earlier in the season than similar produce from other regions and are welcomed in Paris and other European capitals. The fruit is of equally good quality, especially the apples and the famous Plougastel strawberries.

The cooking of Normandy and Brittany, although good and wholesome is plain. Rich sauces are to be found in the other provinces, especially in the wine-growing regions such as Dauphine-Savoy, Burgundy, Bordeaux, Alsace-Lorraine, Languedoc, Provence. From Provence come liqueurs perfumed with the herbs which are also used extensively in the local dishes—garlic, rosemary, basil, fennel, wild thyme and even lavender—and another factor common to the cooking of Provence is the fragrant, greenish golden oil pressed from locally grown olives. This is the oil used in the famous garlic mayonnaise, aïoli. Garlic and olive oil are also basic ingredients for the dishes of the Pyrenees, along with sweet red and green peppers.

In Languedoc, however, the olives are usually eaten in their natural state or preserved in salt, and melted ham or goose fat is used in the cooking. Pâtés are a specialty of Languedoc—hare, rabbit, mutton—prepared from recipes dating back a thousand years. Toulouse, Carcassone and Castelnaudary each claim the best recipe for the famous cassoulet.

The Massif Central comprises three regions: Bourbonnais, a pleasant country of gentle hills and valleys, full of fruit and vegetable gardens and lakes well stocked with carp and pike; Limousin, a vast parkland where cattle graze and acres of cherry orchards surround the chateaux; and Auvergne, a mountainous land of swift-flowing rivers and forests where wild boar still roam. With all these natural resources the cooking of the Massif Central is excellent. Picanchâgne is a traditional pear cake from the Bourbonnais region; clafouti, a cherry cake from Limousin; milliard, a cherry pudding from the Auvergne.

It is in the wine-growing province of Burgundy that one finds the famous escargots. One of the best soft fruits of this region is the blackcurrant, from which cassis liqueur is distilled and an excellent ice cream can be made.

In Alsace-Lorraine, the traditions of cooking have been preserved more valiantly than anywhere else in France. Lorraine is particularly noted for its quiche, as Alsace is for its onion tart, and game served with fruit sauce, such as the delicious venison with blueberry sauce, is special to this area.

Not to be forgotten are the various cheeses from all over France. They are world-renowned; Camembert, Brie, Port-Salut, Roquefort, Tome au raisin, Boursin are but a few of the best known.

QUICHE LORRAINE

Serves 4

for the pastry:	for the filling:
1½ cups all-purpose flour	10 slices bacon
½ cup butter (see recipe)	2 whole eggs
⅓ cup cold water	3 egg yolks
dash salt	2 cups heavy cream
	freshly ground pepper

Make the pastry as for Mince Pies, page 53. (In Lorraine, unsalted butter is used. If you use salted butter, do not add salt to the pastry.) Shape the dough into a ball and let stand for 1 hour, covered with a cloth.

Roll out the pastry thinly on a floured board, or on a table covered with a floured cloth, shaping it into a circle. Grease a 9-inch *quiche* or tart mold and line it with pastry. Trim the edges with your fingertips. Then press all around the inside of the rim with the tines of a fork. Prick the bottom of the pie at regular intervals, so that it is dotted with tiny holes. Arrange the bacon slices, trimmed if necessary, over the bottom. Bake in a preheated moderately hot oven (400°) for 10 minutes. Remove from the oven and set aside. Beat the eggs, egg yolks and cream together. It is not necessary to add salt as the bacon is already salty, but add pepper lavishly from a mill. Pour the mixture over the bacon and return the *quiche* to the oven for 30 minutes. Serve hot as a first course at a special dinner or as the main course of a light meal.

Note: This is probably the most famous recipe from Lorraine, but it is also made throughout France.

KIDNEYS IN WHITE WINE

Serves 4

4 oz mushrooms	1 teaspoon French mustard
½ cup butter	¾ cup dry white wine
1 shallot	3 white peppercorns, pounded
1 clove garlic	1 tablespoon all-purpose flour
few sprigs parsley	dash salt
4 lamb kidneys	

Cut off the ends of the mushroom stems. Wash and dry the mushrooms and thinly slice lengthwise. Heat 2 tablespoons of the butter in a small saucepan. Peel and chop the shallot. Peel and crush the garlic. Chop the parsley. Add the parsley, shallot, garlic and mushrooms to the butter in the pan. Sauté for a few moments over high heat, then cover and cook for 5 minutes over moderate heat. Remove the pan from the heat.

Remove the fine skin and cores from the kidneys and slice the kidneys thinly. Heat the remainder of the butter in a skillet and, when hot, add the kidneys. Cook for 3 minutes, turning occasionally.

While the kidneys are cooking, mix the mustard with the white wine and pepper. Sprinkle the kidneys with flour, stir, add the seasoned white wine and then the mushroom mixture. Cook for a further 3 minutes over gentle heat to thicken the sauce. Serve the kidneys in sauce on slices of buttered toast or on bread fried in butter. If you want to serve them as a main dish, use twice the amount of kidneys and surround with rice. Serve accompanied by the same dry white wine as was used to prepare the sauce.

117

CHEESE PASTRY RING

Serves 6

4 oz Gruyère cheese	1 cup sifted all-purpose flour
1 cup milk	dash grated nutmeg
generous dash salt	4 eggs
½ cup butter	

Cut the Gruyère cheese into small, very thin slices and set aside until required. Pour the milk into a saucepan and add the salt and butter. Bring slowly to a boil, stirring constantly. When the liquid boils, immediately add the flour and stir briskly with a wooden spoon. Continue to cook over low heat for a few minutes, beating well until the mixture has thickened. Remove the pan from the heat and beat for a little longer. Then add the nutmeg and 3 of the eggs, one by one, beating constantly after each addition. Add the cheese slices to the mixture. Thoroughly grease and flour a baking sheet. Spoon the dough on to it in the shape of a ring. Beat the remaining egg and glaze the pastry ring. Bake in the center of a preheated moderately hot oven (400°) for about 20 minutes. Cut the baked pastry ring into slices and serve hot as a first course, accompanied by a dry white wine.

POTTED HARE

Serves 8

1 saddle of hare	dash dried thyme
few sprigs parsley	5 juniper berries
8 oz lean veal, ground	about 8 oz fat back
6 oz sausage meat	⅓ cup cognac or gin
salt and pepper	

Bone the hare and chop the flesh. Chop the parsley and mix with the ground veal, the sausage meat and the hare. Sprinkle lightly with salt and pepper. Add the thyme. Pound the juniper berries and add. Mix well. Cut the fat back into 8 strips. Line the bottom and sides of a large earthenware casserole with 6 strips. Place the chopped mixture on top. Press well with the palm of the hand. Sprinkle with cognac or gin and place the 2 remaining strips of fat back on top. Cover the casserole. In order to hermetically seal it, wrap a dampened, floured cloth around the lid. Cook in a preheated cool oven (300°) for 4 hours. Serve very cold with a green salad. The dish should be accompanied by a good red wine such as a burgundy.

Note: If you have to keep the potted hare longer than a few days, cover the surface of the *terrine* with a thick layer of melted lard and store in a cool place.

PIPÉRADE

Serves 2

3 green sweet peppers	¼ cup oil
½ small chili (optional)	4 eggs
1 medium-sized onion	salt
2 cloves garlic	¼ cup goose or bacon fat
few sprigs parsley	4 slices prosciutto or bacon
4 tomatoes	

Trim the peppers and chili and remove the seeds. Slice the flesh into small strips. Peel and chop the onion and garlic. Place all together in a large bowl, chop the parsley and sprinkle it over. Scald the tomatoes in boiling water for 1 minute. Drain, peel and remove the seeds. Chop the flesh and add to the pepper mixture.

Heat the oil in a small saucepan, add the vegetables and sauté gently over low heat for 5 minutes, stirring occasionally. Meanwhile, beat the eggs with a little salt. Heat the goose or bacon fat in a skillet. Pour the beaten eggs into the skillet, as for an omelet. Allow them to just set over high heat, then immediately pour the pepper mixture on top. Lower the heat and stir briskly with a wooden spoon, as if scrambling eggs but more quickly. Cook for less than 1 minute. The eggs must be cooked but still moist. Transfer to a heated dish. Lightly fry the prosciutto or bacon slices, arrange on top of the *pipérade* and serve immediately.

DUCK PÂTÉ

Serves 6–8

1 duckling, about 2½ lb	1½ lb lean pork, ground
2 tablespoons butter	generous dash dried sage
salt and pepper	8 oz smoked ham, sliced
dash nutmeg	¼ cup orange liqueur
about 12 oz fat back	(cointreau or curaçao)
few sprigs parsley	or cognac
1 egg	

Rub the duckling with butter and roast it in a preheated very hot oven (475°) for about 30 minutes. Slice the meat, which should still be rosy. Set aside the *aiguillettes* (the flesh from the breast). Bone, skin and grind the rest. Sprinkle with salt, pepper and nutmeg. Cut the fat back into strips. Chop the parsley and beat the egg. Line the bottom and sides of an earthenware dish or bowl with half of the fat back strips. Add the ground duckling flesh and ground pork, chopped parsley, sage and beaten egg, and then the sliced smoked ham and the *aiguillettes* in alternate layers. Sprinkle with the liqueur or cognac. Cover with the remainder of the fat back strips. Cook in a preheated moderately hot oven (400°) for 15 minutes, then lower the heat to 250° and cook for 3½ hours. Serve the pâté cold in the earthenware dish, accompanied by French bread or coarse wholewheat bread and a full-bodied wine.

Pipérade

119

CRAB FLAMBÉ

Serves 6

1 large crab	salt and pepper
few sprigs parsley	1 cup tomato juice
½ cup dark rum or whiskey	

If you buy a live crab, plunge it into a very large pot of boiling water with some white wine and herbs, such as thyme, bay leaf and parsley. Cook for 10–15 minutes for a 2½-lb crab, or according to size. Let cool before removing the flesh from the shell. Prepare the crab as for Scalloped Crabs, page 35. Chop the parsley.

Warm the crab meat and the rum in a skillet over a low heat. Remove the skillet from the heat and flambé. While the rum burns, shake the skillet gently so that the flames spread all over the contents. When the flames have died down, add salt and pepper, the chopped parsley and the tomato juice. Bring to a boil. Serve at once, with rice if you wish to make it a substantial main dish or just as it is for a first course.

SNAILS IN RED WINE

Serves 4

about 40 canned snails, without shells	3 slices bacon
sprig dried thyme	¼ cup lard
2 cloves garlic	1 tablespoon all-purpose flour
4 shallots	¾ cup red wine
small bunch parsley	4 slices white bread
	salt and pepper

Wash and drain the snails and sprinkle with thyme. Peel the garlic and shallots and chop with the parsley. Dice the bacon. Heat the lard in a skillet and lightly sauté the shallots, garlic and parsley. Add the diced bacon. As soon as the mixture is golden brown, sprinkle with flour and stir briskly. Add the red wine gradually, stirring well, then lower the heat, cover and cook gently. Toast the bread, arrange on a heated serving plate and keep warm. Add the snails to the sauce, stir and season. Cook gently for 3 minutes and pour the snails in sauce over the toast.

COQUILLES SAINT-JACQUES

Serves 6

16 sea scallops	2 tablespoons butter
2 shallots	salt and pepper
few sprigs parsley	¾ cup dry white wine

For this recipe use scallops which have been shelled. Slice the white part of the scallop across into 2 or 3 pieces. Peel and chop the shallots and chop the parsley. Melt the butter in a skillet. Add the shallots and the parsley. Sauté for a few moments and then add the scallops. If using fresh scallops, add the coral. Cook over high heat for a few minutes, turning the pieces over until they are a light golden brown. Season with salt and quite a lot of pepper. Remove the skillet from the heat and spoon the scallops into a warm serving dish.

Pour the wine into the skillet and bring quickly to a boil. Pour over the scallops and serve.

MARSEILLES BOUILLABAISSE

Serves 8

4 lb fresh fish, as varied as possible (red snapper, red mullet, cod, sea bass, mackerel, etc.)	bunch parsley
	few sprigs fresh green fennel
	sprig fresh wild savory (optional)
12 crayfish or 1 lobster	4 tomatoes
4½ pints water	16 slices French bread
3 cloves garlic	**for the sauce:**
1 large onion	1 clove garlic
3 shallots	1 small red chili
¾ cup olive oil	1 slice cooked potato
salt and pepper	livers of 3 fish (from the red mullet, if possible)
1 teaspoon saffron strands	
1 wineglass white wine (optional)	

Cut the biggest fish into large pieces. Leave the little ones whole, but clean them. Set aside the livers of the red mullet for the sauce. Bring the water to a boil in a large saucepan. Toss in the crayfish or the lobster. Cook for 7 minutes, then remove from the water. Reserve this water, covered.

Shell the crayfish, or if using lobster, prepare as for Lobster à l'Américaine, page 124, and cut into pieces. Peel the garlic, onion and shallots and chop roughly. Heat the oil in a large saucepan and add the vegetables with the salt, pepper and saffron strands. Sauté lightly over high heat. Add the liquid in which the shellfish were cooked, the wine if used, the herbs and tomatoes. Remove the tomatoes after 1 minute, rinse in cold water, peel and remove the seeds. Replace the tomatoes in the soup. Cook over very low heat until the liquid boils. Add the shellfish and large pieces of fish to the pan. Cook over high heat for 8 minutes. Add the small fish. Lower the heat and simmer for 7 minutes.

Meanwhile, prepare the sauce. Peel the garlic. Pound the red chili (some cooks prefer to soak it for 6 hours in cold water beforehand) with the garlic, potato and fish livers. Thin down this paste with some of the liquid from the fish soup. Pour the sauce into a heated sauceboat.

Line a soup tureen with slices of bread (according to tradition, these should be dried in the oven, not toasted). Remove the shellfish and fish with a perforated spoon and arrange on a heated dish. Pour the soup liquid on the slices of bread. Both dishes should be eaten together accompanied by the sauce.

Marseilles bouillabaisse

120

BACON SOUP

Serves 6

4½ pints water	1 stalk celery
2 onions	sprig parsley
3 shallots	2 cups dried navy or pea beans
2 leeks	(see recipe)
1 green cabbage	pepper
1 lb smoked pork shoulder butt,	12 slices French bread
in 1 piece, soaked overnight	

Measure the water into a saucepan. Peel the onions and shallots, but leave whole. Trim, wash and chop the leeks. Discarding the outer leaves, cut the cabbage into quarters. Add the bacon to the water in the pan with the prepared vegetables, celery, parsley and dried beans. (If the beans are very dry, soak according to the directions on the package.) Season with pepper, cover and bring to a boil. Lower the heat and simmer gently for 3 hours. Remove the bacon and cut into slices. Keep warm on a heated serving dish. Remove the vegetables and keep warm in a separate dish.

Toast the slices of bread and place them in the bottom of a soup tureen. Strain over the soup liquid. Serve the vegetables and the bacon slices separately.

FISH SOUP WITH AÏOLI

Serves 4

2 lb fresh fish, any variety	3 bay leaves
4 pints water	salt and pepper
1 large onion	1 teaspoon saffron strands or
4 cloves	¼ teaspoon saffron powder
2 cloves garlic	*aïoli* (see page 137)
1 piece dried or fresh orange rind	12 slices French bread
few sprigs thyme	

Wash and clean the fish. Cut the larger ones into pieces. Measure the water into a large saucepan. Peel the onion and stick it with the cloves. Peel the garlic. Add both to the pan with the orange rind, thyme and bay leaves. Bring to a boil and add the salt, pepper and saffron. Simmer for 1 minute. Add the fish and simmer for 12 minutes, without a lid. Pour the *aïoli* into a large bowl and very slowly strain the fish stock over it, stirring well. Arrange the slices of bread in a soup tureen and pour over the soup. Serve the fish separately.

Note: This recipe, like many others, varies according to the place where it is made. Sometimes the bread is left out and the soup is poured over the fish. In this case, select large fish and cut into slices.

FRENCH ONION SOUP

Serves 4

3 large onions	4 pints beef stock (see recipe)
¼ cup butter	12 slices French bread
3 tablespoons all-purpose flour	2 cups grated Gruyère cheese

Peel the onions and either finely chop or grate. Melt the butter in a large saucepan. Add the onions and sauté until soft and transparent, but not brown. Sprinkle with flour and cook over low heat for 1 minute, stirring briskly with a wooden spoon. Gradually pour in the stock—made with a bouillon cube, if necessary—stirring constantly. Bring to a boil, then lower the heat until the soup is just simmering and cook for 30 minutes. Toast the slices of bread and serve with the soup. Serve the grated cheese separately.

POACHED EGGS WITH CHEESE AND WINE

Serve 4

few sprigs parsley	dash pepper
2 tablespoons butter	dash nutmeg
1½ cups grated Gruyère cheese	4 eggs
⅓ cup dry white wine	

Chop the parsley. Melt the butter in a gratin dish or shallow flameproof casserole. Add the Gruyère cheese and the white wine. Heat gently, stirring constantly until the cheese melts. Add the pepper, nutmeg and chopped parsley. Cook for a moment, then gently break the eggs into the dish. When almost cooked, put the gratin dish under the broiler for 1 minute. Serve in the dish, accompanied by a white wine.

CARP WITH WHITE WINE, TOMATOES AND MUSHROOMS

Serves 4

1 carp, about 2 lb	½ bottle dry white wine
¾ cup olive oil	3 tomatoes
salt and pepper	3 large mushrooms
scented fresh herbs, such as thyme, savory, fennel and basil	2 tablespoons cornstarch
	2 tablespoons butter

Skin and clean the carp. Wash under cold running water and pat dry. Place the fish in a shallow baking dish. Sprinkle with olive oil, season with salt and pepper and add the herbs. Put the dish in a preheated cool oven (300°). Allow a carp weighing 2 lb to cook for 45 minutes.

Scald the tomatoes for 1 minute in boiling water, peel, remove the seeds and cut the flesh into pieces. Trim, dry and thinly slice the mushrooms. As soon as the carp begins to turn brown or becomes crisp (after about 20–30 minutes), pour over the white wine and surround the fish with the tomatoes and mushrooms. Continue to cook very slowly. When the fish is cooked, the liquid will have reduced a little. When ready to serve, place the carp on a heated serving dish and pour the liquid into a small saucepan. Blend the cornstarch with the butter to make a *beurre manié*, and add it in pieces to the sauce over low heat. Stir constantly, until the sauce is well blended and thickened. Pour over the carp and serve.

TROUT BAKED IN FOIL

Serves 4

4 small trout	3 tablespoons butter
4 sprigs fresh or dried thyme	4 thin slices prosciutto
juice of 1 lemon	

Clean the trout, wash carefully and pat dry. Place a sprig of thyme inside each one. Sprinkle each trout with a little lemon juice. Grease 4 sheets of foil with the butter. Wrap each trout in a slice of ham. Place each fish in a sheet of the foil, greased side to the inside, and completely enclose the fish. Arrange the foil-wrapped fish in a baking dish and bake in a preheated moderately hot oven (400°) for 10 minutes. Then lower the heat to 350° for a further 10 minutes. Serve the trout in their foil packages – each guest will open his own on his plate.

Poached eggs with cheese and wine

Salade rhodanienne

LOBSTER À L'AMÉRICAINE

Serves 3–4

1 lobster, about 2 lb	1 tablespoon meat stock
⅓ cup oil	⅔ cup fish stock (made by cooking
salt and pepper	the heads and bones of fish with
3 tablespoons cognac	thyme and bay leaf in 2 cups
¾ cup dry white wine	water for 30 minutes, or until the
2 shallots	liquid is reduced)
1 clove garlic	generous dash cayenne pepper
	3 tomatoes
	few sprigs chervil and tarragon
	generous ¾ cup butter
	1 lemon

Drop the live lobster into warm water and bring to a boil. Remove from the heat. Place the lobster on a board, back upward, and using a sharp knife split it in half along its entire length. Press the two halves open and remove the gills, the stomach sac in the head and the dark intestinal vein which runs down the tail. The green creamy liver in the head and the coral of the female lobster should be retained. Cut the lobster up, dividing the tail into 4 pieces and splitting the claws into 2 pieces. Heat the oil in a flameproof casserole and add all the lobster pieces except the head. Season with salt and pepper and cook over high heat until the lobster pieces turn very red. Pour off some of the hot fat. Sprinkle with cognac and white wine. Lower the heat and warm for a moment. Remove the casserole from the stove and flambé. Set aside.

Peel and chop the shallots, peel and crush the garlic, strain the fish stock, and scald, peel and chop the tomatoes, removing the seeds. Place the casserole over the heat once again and add the shallots, garlic, meat stock, fish stock, cayenne pepper and tomatoes. Cover and cook in a preheated moderate oven (350°) for 10–15 minutes. While the lobster is cooking, chop the chervil and tarragon very finely and blend with the butter. Remove the lobster from the oven. Take out the pieces and remove all the meat from the shell (or you can serve the meat in the shell). Place on a heated serving plate. Strain the sauce. Then add the herb butter in small pieces and stir until the butter is melted and the sauce well bound together. Pour the sauce over the lobster and sprinkle with lemon juice.

Note: The dish from Brittany is sometimes called Lobster *à l'amoricaine*. The origin of the name is endlessly disputed.

124

SALADE RHODANIENNE

Serves 4

3 large potatoes	4 oz Gruyère cheese
1 cup dry white wine	4 anchovy fillets in oil
salt and pepper	few sprigs fresh chervil
½ bunch watercress	½ cup pitted green olives
8 oz garlic sausage (*saucisson* or *salami*)	¼ cup olive oil
	1 tablespoon vinegar
8 oz smoked ham	

Peel the potatoes, halve them and place in a saucepan of boiling water. Bring to a boil again, then lower the heat and cook for 10 minutes, or until the potatoes are just tender. Drain, cool a little and cut into thick slices. Place in a salad bowl, sprinkle with the white wine and season with salt and pepper.

Wash and trim the watercress. Dice the sausage, ham and Gruyère cheese. Cut the anchovy fillets into small pieces. Chop the chervil. Add the watercress, sausage, ham, cheese, anchovy fillets and olives to the potatoes in the bowl. Sprinkle with the oil and vinegar and then the chervil, and serve.

SALADE DE MORLAIX

Serves 4

1 small or ½ large cauliflower	¾ cup dry white wine
salt	8 anchovy fillets in oil
white pepper	3 tablespoons capers in vinegar

Cut away the stem from the cauliflower, remove any part which is brown or bruised and divide the cauliflower into florets. Cook in lightly salted boiling water for about 5 minutes or until the cauliflower is just tender but still crisp. Drain and place in a salad bowl. While still warm, add a little pepper and sprinkle with white wine. Cut the anchovy fillets into small pieces and add with the capers. Allow to cool completely before serving.

Note: Nasturtium flowers make a colorful garnish when in season. Not only are they decorative, but they also have a slightly peppery taste which gourmets find very delicate.

SALADE AU ROQUEFORT

Serves 4

½–1 head curly-leaved chicory	½ cup heavy cream
1 clove garlic	juice of 1 lemon
1 cup shelled walnuts	⅓ cup peanut oil
6 oz Roquefort cheese	

Wash the chicory, strip off the leaves by hand, one by one (break large leaves in half) and drain well. Peel the garlic and rub the inside of a salad bowl with it. Chop the walnuts and sprinkle them into the salad bowl, add the Roquefort cheese and blend together. Gradually mix in the cream and the lemon juice. Then add the oil and mix thoroughly with a wooden spoon. Add the chicory and mix until thoroughly coated in the salad dressing.

SALADE NIÇOISE

Serves 4

8 small or 6 large tomatoes	20 ripe olives, pitted
1 green sweet pepper	⅓ cup olive oil
7 oz canned tuna fish, drained	2 tablespoons wine vinegar
8 anchovy fillets in oil	1 teaspoon French mustard
12 red radishes (optional)	pepper

Scald the tomatoes in boiling water for 1 minute, drain and peel. Quarter, remove the seeds and place the quarters in a salad bowl. Trim the pepper and remove the stem and seeds. Slice the flesh into thin strips and broil quickly to improve the flavor. Break the tuna fish into large pieces. Cut the anchovy fillets in half. Wash and peel the radishes, leaving on the small tops. Add the tuna, anchovy fillets, radishes and olives to the tomatoes in the salad bowl. Mix the oil, vinegar, mustard and pepper in a small jar. Shake vigorously and pour the dressing over the salad.

GAME SALAD

Serves 4

2 roasted partridges, cold	juice of 1 lemon
1 shallot	6 anchovy fillets in oil
½ cup olive oil or, ideally, walnut oil	6 sweet dill pickles
	1 tablespoon capers in vinegar
1 tablespoon tarragon vinegar	1 lettuce heart
1 teaspoon French mustard	few sprigs tarragon (optional)
salt and pepper	few sprigs parsley
6 small mushrooms	

Carve the birds, removing the skin and bones. Cut the flesh into fairly large pieces. Peel and finely chop the shallot and mix with the oil, tarragon vinegar, mustard, salt and pepper. Pour the dressing into a salad bowl. Add the meat and stir well so that it is lightly coated with the dressing. Wipe the mushrooms and trim the ends (it is better not to wash them). Sprinkle with the lemon juice and add to the salad bowl. Cut the anchovy fillets into pieces and finely slice the dill pickles. Add these and the capers to the salad. Wash and dry the lettuce – use only the freshest leaves in the center. Place these leaves in a circle on a flat dish. Spoon the salad into the center. Chop the tarragon and parsley and sprinkle over the salad.

BOEUF BOURGUIGNON

Serves 4

2 lb chuck steak	sprig thyme
1 shallot	2 bay leaves
2 tablespoons oil	1 teaspoon sugar
2 tablespoons butter	salt and pepper
½ bottle red wine	few sprigs parsley
(preferably burgundy)	4 oz small mushrooms
1¼ cups beef stock (see recipe)	5 slices fat bacon
1 onion	1 tablespoon cornstarch
2 cloves	2 tablespoons water

Cut the beef into large cubes and remove all the fat. Peel and chop the shallot. Heat the oil and butter in a saucepan and add the pieces of meat and the shallot. Sauté gently. Gradually add the wine and the stock—make this with a bouillon cube, if necessary. Peel the onion and stick it with the cloves. Add the onion, thyme and bay leaves. Stir in the sugar and season with pepper and only a little salt, as the stock is salty. Cover and simmer for 1½ hours over low heat. Chop the parsley. Trim, wash and dry the mushrooms.

Before serving, dice the bacon and sauté it gently in a skillet until the fat runs. Add the chopped parsley and mushrooms to the bacon and cook for a few moments. Add this mixture to the beef in the saucepan. Moisten the cornstarch with the 2 tablespoons water and stir the paste into the saucepan. Bring to a boil, stirring briskly. Serve immediately with boiled potatoes and the same wine as was used to make the sauce.

INDIVIDUALLY COOKED STEAKS

Serves 4

1 onion	1 large veal bone, chopped in half,
3 cloves	or the carcass of a chicken
1 leek	5 peppercorns
1 stalk celery	*bouquet garni* (see recipe)
4 medium-sized carrots	4½ pints water
1 turnip	2 lb beef tenderloin, cut into 4
2 teaspoons salt	thick slices

Peel the onion and stick it with the cloves. Trim, wash and slice the leek. Trim and wash the celery and cut the stalk in half. Peel the carrots and turnip and cut into pieces. To make the stock, place all the vegetables, the salt, veal bone or chicken carcass, peppercorns and *bouquet garni* (3 bay leaves, 3 sprigs parsley, 1 sprig thyme, tied together) in a large saucepan with the water, and bring to a boil. If possible, cook the stock in an earthenware pot with an asbestos mat underneath for protection. As soon as the water boils, skim, lower the heat, cover and cook gently for 1–2 hours. Then strain the stock and reheat to boiling point.

Trim the meat. Tie each piece up like a package and make a long loop of string. Hang the steaks from the handle of a wooden spoon. Place the spoon across the top of the pot so that the steaks are suspended in the boiling stock. For rare beef, simmer for 25 minutes; for well-done beef, 30 minutes or longer. Remove the meat and serve with mustard, pickles, coarse salt in little dishes and baked potatoes.

SIRLOIN STEAKS IN BERCY SAUCE

Serves 4

4 sirloin steaks	2 cups dry white wine
salt and pepper	sprig fresh or dash dried thyme
3 tablespoons butter	1 bay leaf
for the sauce:	salt and pepper
1 medium-sized carrot	1 teaspoon sugar
1 shallot	¼ cup butter

Begin by making the sauce. Scrape the carrot and slice it into thin rounds. Peel and finely chop the shallot. Measure the wine into a small saucepan and add the carrot, shallot, thyme, bay leaf, salt and pepper to taste and sugar. Simmer until the wine is reduced by half. Meanwhile, season the steaks and cook them quickly in hot butter in a skillet, rare or well done, according to taste.

When the wine is reduced, remove the sauce from the heat. Strain it and return to the pan. Cut the butter into small pieces and stir into the sauce with a whisk.

Place the steaks on a heated serving dish, cover with the sauce and serve immediately.

CASSEROLE OF TRIPE WITH CIDER AND CALVADOS

Serves 8

3½ lb dressed tripe	sprig thyme
8 medium-sized carrots	2 bay leaves
4 leeks	1 calf's foot or veal foreshank
4 large onions	salt and pepper
3 cloves	1 cup calvados or applejack
few sprigs parsley	4¼ cups dry cider

Wash the tripe carefully in cold water. Drain and cut into 2-inch strips. Clean and peel the vegetables and cut into thin slices. Save one onion, which should be peeled but left whole and stuck with cloves. Line a large earthenware casserole with the sliced vegetables. Place the strips of tripe on top. Add the herbs, the calf's foot, salt and pepper to taste, the calvados and enough cider to cover. Put on the lid and encase it with a dampened, floured cloth to minimize evaporation. Cook in a preheated very cool oven (250°) for 10 hours. Discard the calf's foot and the onion stuck with cloves and serve with boiled potatoes, macaroni or rice.

Note: This casserole may be cooked in a pressure cooker instead of an earthenware casserole. Reduce the cooking time to 2¾ hours.

Individually cooked steaks

CASSOULET

Serves 8

2 lb small navy or pea beans
1 medium-sized carrot
1 large onion
4 cloves
12 oz breast of salt pork
8 oz fresh pork rind
bouquet garni (see recipe)
¼ cup goose fat, lard or bacon fat
4 cloves garlic

for the meat:
1 lb rolled shoulder of lamb
1 lb boneless pork loin roast
¼ cup goose fat, lard or bacon fat
salt and pepper

1 large onion
3 cloves garlic
5 tomatoes
1 cup stock
bouquet garni (see recipe)

for the garnish:
10 oz Toulouse garlic sausage or
    well seasoned cooked sausage
2 large pieces preserved goose
    (optional)
¾ cup toasted breadcrumbs
6 tablespoons goose fat, lard or
    bacon fat

Soak the beans in a bowl of cold water for 3 hours or overnight. Drain. Put the beans into an earthenware pot separated from the heat by an asbestos mat, or into a large saucepan. Peel the carrot and stick the onion with the cloves. Add the whole breast of salt pork, pork rind, carrot, onion, *bouquet garni* (3 bay leaves, 3 sprigs parsley, 1 sprig thyme, tied together) and the fat. Add water to just cover the beans. Peel the garlic and add it. Cover and bring to a boil. Lower the heat and simmer gently, so the beans do not burst. Cook for 2½ hours, stirring gently from time to time and adding a little more water, if necessary.

Meanwhile, brown the shoulder of lamb and pork loin in the goose fat in a large skillet. Transfer the meat to a large saucepan and set aside the skillet for browning the sausage later. Season the meat with salt and pepper. Chop the onion and peel and crush the garlic. Add both to the pan containing the meat. Scald the tomatoes for 1 minute in boiling water, drain and peel. Remove the seeds, chop the tomatoes and add to the pan. Moisten with stock, using a bouillon cube if necessary. Add a little water and the *bouquet garni* (3 bay leaves, 3 sprigs parsley, 1 sprig thyme, tied together) and simmer for the same length of time as the beans.

Cut the sausage into large slices and brown in the skillet which was set aside. Remove and discard the piece of salt pork and pork rind from the beans. Cut the meat into pieces. Place the meat and the beans in a large, deep casserole in alternate layers. Finish with a layer of the preserved goose (if used) and the sausage slices, pushing them down a little into the beans. Sprinkle with breadcrumbs. Add the remaining fat, cut into small pieces. Place the casserole in a large roasting pan half filled with hot water. Cook in a preheated cool oven (300°) for at least 45 minutes. Serve very hot in the casserole.

Cassoulet

LEG OF LAMB
À LA CASSETTE

Serves 6

1 leg lamb, about 3½–4 lb	1 cup water
4 cloves garlic	salt and pepper
6 oz smoked pork shoulder butt, in 1 piece	1 bay leaf
	sprig parsley
¼ cup butter	sprig thyme
4 large potatoes	

Have the butcher cut the knuckle off the leg, or else fold it back, so that the meat can be placed in a deep casserole.

Make a deep incision in the lamb near the knuckle and slide in the garlic cloves. (Peel them or not, according to whether you want a strong or mild garlic taste.) Cube a small piece of the bacon and slice the remainder thinly. Then make six other incisions all over the leg and insert the bacon cubes. Grease the casserole with a little of the butter. Peel the potatoes and slice thinly. Lay the slices in the bottom of the buttered casserole with the sliced bacon. Pour over the water. Season with salt and pepper and add the bay leaf. Place the lamb on top of the potatoes. Chop the parsley. Sprinkle with a few thyme leaves and the parsley. Dot the rest of the butter over the lamb. Cook uncovered in a preheated moderately hot oven (400°) for 1½ hours; allow 25 minutes per lb for fairly well cooked meat. The water should be completely absorbed by the potatoes, and the lamb and the potatoes should be golden brown.

VEAL SWEETBREADS
WITH MUSHROOMS

Serves 6

3 pairs veal sweetbreads	3 tablespoons all-purpose flour
4 oz small mushrooms	⅔ cup dry white wine
few sprigs parsley	salt and pepper
2 tablespoons butter	½ cup heavy cream

The sweetbreads must be very white with no traces of blood. Soak in an earthenware bowl filled with cold water for 2 hours, changing the water 4 or 5 times. Place the sweetbreads in a saucepan, cover with cold water, bring to a boil and simmer for 2–3 minutes. Plunge into cold water, drain and cool. Dry carefully, remove any membrane and cut into thin slices.

Wash and dry the mushrooms. If small, leave whole; otherwise slice lengthwise. Chop the parsley. Sauté the mushrooms and the parsley lightly in the butter for about 3 minutes. Add the sweetbreads, shaking the pan frequently. Sprinkle with flour, stirring gently, and add the white wine and salt and pepper to taste. Cook for 5 minutes, then add the cream, stirring thoroughly. Bring to a boil and cook for 2 minutes. Serve on a heated plate accompanied by the same white wine as is used in the dish.

Note: In restaurants this dish is often garnished with tiny crescents of puff pastry.

129

POULE-AU-POT HENRI IV

Serves 8

1 chicken, about 4 lb	1 large onion
for the stuffing:	3 cloves
2 tablespoons butter	1 leek
1 chicken liver	1 stalk celery
4½ cups breadcrumbs	4 medium-sized carrots
2 eggs	4 turnips
10 slices prosciutto or bacon	salt
salt and pepper	4 peppercorns
1 clove garlic	sprig thyme
few sprigs parsley	3 bay leaves
¼ cup cognac	4½ cups chicken stock
for the stock pot:	1 cup long-grain rice
5½ pints water	

First prepare the stuffing for the chicken. Melt the butter in a skillet, add the chicken liver and brown it. Place the liver in a mixing bowl and mash with the breadcrumbs. Beat the eggs. Finely chop the prosciutto and add to the bowl with the beaten eggs, salt and pepper. Peel the garlic and chop with the parsley. Add to the mixture. Finally, add the cognac, mix well and stuff the chicken with the mixture. Sew up the opening with strong white thread.

Heat the water in a large earthenware pot, protected from the heat by an asbestos mat. Peel the onion and stick it with the cloves. Trim and wash the leek and the celery. Peel the carrots and turnips. Cut up the vegetables and add to the pot with the salt, peppercorns, thyme and bay leaves. Bring to a boil and add the chicken. Simmer for 1½ hours.

About 20 minutes before cooking time is completed, heat the stock for cooking the rice in a saucepan. When boiling, sprinkle in the rice, washed if necessary, and boil rapidly for 15–20 minutes. Drain the rice and spoon into the center of a large serving dish.

Discard the onion stuck with cloves and the herbs. Place the vegetables from the pot around the rice. Serve the chicken separately. Check the seasoning and serve the soup from the pot in individual bowls at the same time or to start the meal.

Note: The soup, just as it is, is quite greasy. An alternative is to reserve it for another meal. If put into a refrigerator or left in a cool place overnight, the fat will rise to the surface and can then be easily removed.

SAUTÉED CHICKEN WITH COGNAC

Serves 4

2 shallots	1 frying chicken, about 3½ lb,
few sprigs parsley	cut into 8 pieces
1 cup small mushrooms	¾ cup dry white wine
5 slices bacon	⅓ cup cognac
few sprigs chervil and tarragon	¾ cup tomato juice
¼ cup butter	salt and pepper
1 tablespoon oil	

Peel and chop the shallots and chop the parsley. Trim, wash and dry the mushrooms. Dice the bacon. Chop the chervil and tarragon. Heat the butter and oil together in a large,

heavy skillet. Add the parsley and the shallots and sauté gently until golden brown. Add the pieces of chicken and sauté over high heat, turning until slightly browned. Add the white wine, a tablespoon at a time, to prevent the chicken from sticking. Lower the heat and cover. After about 30 minutes, when the chicken is brown and tender, remove the skillet from the heat, warm the cognac, add to the skillet and flambé. When the flames have died down, cover and continue to cook gently for a few minutes. Add the mushrooms and cook quickly for 3 minutes. Add the bacon and tomato juice. Cook over a high heat until the liquid is reduced. Season with pepper. Taste before adding salt. Transfer to a heated serving dish, sprinkle with the chopped chervil and tarragon and serve with boiled potatoes or plain boiled rice and green beans.

CHICKEN EN CROÛTE

Serves 4

1 chicken, about 2 lb	3 tablespoons cognac or brandy
for the stuffing:	salt and pepper
5 slices bacon	**for the basic pie dough:**
few sprigs parsley	1½ cups all-purpose flour
sprig thyme	⅓ cup butter
1 egg	⅓ cup water
2½ cups white breadcrumbs	dash salt
¼ cup milk	1 egg for glazing

Wipe the chicken. Chop the bacon, parsley and thyme. Beat the egg. Soak the breadcrumbs in the milk, beaten egg and brandy. Season with the salt and pepper and stir in the bacon and herbs. Mix well and pack the stuffing inside the bird. Sew up the opening with strong white thread.

Make the pastry as for Mince Pies, page 53. Place on a floured board, or on a floured cloth on a table, and roll out thinly to a circle large enough to completely enclose the chicken.

Place the chicken, on its side, on one half of the pastry, with the breastbone toward the center of the circle. Moisten the edge of the circle. Fold over the second half of the pastry to enclose the chicken. Seal the pastry where it joins along the backbone of the bird. Turn the bird breast side up and seal the ends.

Place on a greased baking sheet and brush the pastry with beaten egg. Bake in a preheated moderately hot oven (400°) for 30 minutes. Lower the heat, cover with foil and cook for a further 30 minutes at 350°. To serve, cut away both leg joints. Then carve the chicken, cutting through both pastry and chicken flesh. Serve with a watercress salad.

Poule-au-pot Henri IV

130

DUCKLING WITH GREEN OLIVE STUFFING

Serves 4

1 young duckling, about 3½ lb	6 tablespoons butter
for the stuffing:	1 duckling liver
½ cup pitted green olives	4 slices white bread
3 Toulouse sausages or other well seasoned cooked sausages	¾ cup dry white wine
5 cloves garlic (or to taste)	salt and pepper

Wipe the duckling and prepare the stuffing. Add the olives to a saucepan of boiling salted water and simmer for 5 minutes to soften them. Then drain. Remove the skins from the sausages and slice the sausages into rounds or cut into pieces. Peel and crush the garlic. Mix the olives, sausage and garlic together. Heat a third of the butter in a skillet, add the duckling liver and brown on both sides. Remove the liver from the skillet, mash and add to the stuffing.

Stuff the duckling with the mixture and sew up the opening with strong white thread. Roast on a spit (an electric rotisserie gives excellent results) or place the duckling on a rack in a lightly greased roasting pan and roast in a preheated moderate oven (350°), basting occasionally. Cook for about 45 minutes on the electric rotisserie, or 1 hour in the oven.

Toward the end of the cooking time, dice the bread. Heat the remaining butter in a skillet and brown the bread, turning occasionally. Lightly season the cooked duckling and cut into portions. Arrange them on the sautéed bread on a hot serving dish, with the stuffing on the top. Pour off the fat from the roasting pan (or pan underneath the spit) but save most of the meat drippings. Add the wine, stir with a fork and pour the mixture into a saucepan. Season with salt and pepper. Bring almost to a boil and pour the sauce over the duckling.

STUFFED PARTRIDGES FLAMBÉ

Serves 2

8 juniper berries	salt and pepper
2 partridges	1 cup marc or gin
8 oz foie gras mousse or pâté	¼ cup butter

Crush the juniper berries. Stuff the partridges with a mixture of foie gras mousse or pâté, crushed juniper berries, a seasoning of salt and pepper and 3 tablespoons of the marc or gin. Roast on a spit for about 20 minutes, basting with the butter. Alternatively, roast in a preheated moderately hot oven (400°) for 20–30 minutes. When ready to serve, place the partridges on a hot serving dish, warm the remaining marc or gin, pour it over the birds and flambé. Serve the birds surrounded by soufflé potatoes (see page 136).

PARTRIDGE PIE

Serves 6

for the puff pastry:	few sprigs chervil
4 cups all-purpose flour	sprig dried thyme
1¾ cups very cold water	2 eggs
generous dash salt	1 lb veal, ground
1¾ cups butter, firm but not too hard	salt and pepper
	dash mixed spices
for the pie filling:	6 tablespoons dry white wine
2 partridges	8 slices bacon
2 tablespoons butter	¼ cup calvados or cognac
few sprigs parsley	1 egg for glazing

To make the pastry, sift the flour in a heap on a floured board or a floured cloth placed on the kitchen table, and make a well in the center. Into this well pour the very cold water and the salt. (The importance of using really cold water cannot be stressed enough—it makes all the difference.) Knead lightly with the fingertips, form the pastry into a ball and let 'rest' for 30 minutes in the refrigerator.

Roll the pastry into a large circle. Scatter small pieces of butter (firm, but not straight from the refrigerator) in the middle of this circle and then fold the pastry to enclose the butter, as if making a parcel. Sprinkle with flour and roll out very lightly into a long, narrow rectangle. The pieces of butter will stick out. Fold the rectangle 3 times. Turn it a quarter of the way around. Roll out again into a long,

Stuffed partridges flambé

narrow rectangle, sprinkle with flour and again fold it 3 times. Let 'rest' for 20 minutes. Do the same thing again; that is, roll the pastry into a long, narrow rectangle and fold it 3 times, twice-running, turning the pastry a quarter of the way around each time after folding. Let rest again for 20 minutes. Begin the process again. This is called giving 6 turns to the pastry; in other words, rolling it twice, 3 times.

Rub the birds with butter. Roast in a preheated moderately hot oven (400°) or on a spit for 25 minutes, basting occasionally. Then joint, bone and skin the birds. Chop the parsley and chervil and crumble the thyme. Beat the 2 eggs. Mix the ground veal with salt and pepper, the parsley, chervil, thyme, spices, beaten eggs and wine.

Roll out the pastry and divide into 2 parts, one larger than the other. Line the bottom of a buttered 9-inch pie pan with the larger piece. Remove the bacon rind and finely dice the bacon. Place half on the pastry. Cover with half the prepared stuffing. Put pieces of boned partridge on top. Cover with the remainder of the stuffing, then the remainder of the bacon. Finally, put on the pastry lid, pressing the edges together with the fingertips. Make a small round hole in the center to allow the steam to escape during cooking. Pour the calvados through this opening. Brush with beaten egg. Cook in a preheated moderately hot oven (400°) for 1 hour. Serve hot.

To serve the pie cold, pour a little melted jellied stock, preferably made with partridge bones, through the opening in the pastry lid.

STUFFED ROAST PHEASANT

Serves 4

3 chicken livers	salt and pepper
¼ cup butter	1 hen pheasant
1 small fresh *petit-suisse* cheese	4 slices white bread
or ¼ cup cream cheese	1½ cups heavy cream
few sprigs chives and parsley,	
chopped	

Brown the chicken livers in half the butter. Then mash and mix with the cheese, the chopped herbs and a seasoning of salt and pepper. Stuff the bird with this mixture. Sew up the opening in the pheasant with strong white thread, dot the bird with butter and season lightly with salt and pepper. Roast in a preheated moderately hot oven (400°) for about 30 minutes.

A few minutes before the pheasant has finished cooking, toast the bread. Remove the bird and turn off the oven. Then carve the pheasant into slices and lay these out on a flat serving dish, with the toast in the middle. Cover the toast with the stuffing. Return the dish to the warm oven. Pour the cream into the roasting pan and season lightly with salt and pepper. Heat quickly, stirring constantly, but do not allow the liquid to boil. Pour over the pheasant and serve immediately.

VENISON WITH BLUEBERRY SAUCE

Serves 4

1½ lb boned loin of venison	6–8 slices bacon
1 bottle dry white wine	3 shallots
10 juniper berries	few sprigs parsley
4 carrots	¼ cup butter
1 onion	1 tablespoon peanut oil
6 cloves	**for the blueberry sauce:**
1 teaspoon sugar	10 oz fresh or frozen blueberries
salt	¾ cup sugar
6 peppercorns	⅓ cup water
2 bay leaves	1 tablespoon cornstarch

The venison should be rolled as for roasting and tied up. It is best to marinate it the day before. Put the meat into a large bowl and pour over the wine. Crush the juniper berries and peel and slice the carrots. Peel the onion and stick it with the cloves. Add the juniper berries, carrots, onion, sugar, a little salt, whole peppercorns and bay leaves to the marinade.

Let stand for at least 2–3 hours, or overnight if possible. Then strain the marinade. Wipe the venison thoroughly and cover with the bacon slices, holding the bacon in place with toothpicks. Peel and chop the shallots and chop the parsley. Melt the butter and oil in a large saucepan, add the onions and parsley and sauté gently for a few minutes. Add the meat and gradually pour over the strained marinade until it half covers the meat. Bring to a boil, then lower the heat, cover and cook gently for 1 hour.

Meanwhile, put the blueberries, sugar and water into a second saucepan. Cook for a few minutes over high heat. Lower the heat, cover and simmer gently for 15 minutes. Watch carefully, but do not stir too much to avoid breaking the fruit.

When ready to serve, put the venison on a heated serving dish and remove the bacon. Strain the blueberries, reserving the juice, and place around the venison. Add the reserved blueberry juice to the juices from the venison, moisten the cornstarch with a little water and stir into the combined juices over moderate heat. Bring to a boil, stirring constantly, and pour into a heated sauceboat.

WILD BOAR WITH RED WINE

Serves 4

2 lb wild boar or pork, in 1 piece	salt and pepper
12 juniper berries	1 lemon
1 bottle red wine	2 tablespoons butter
1 onion	¼ cup oil
4 cloves	4 shallots
1 clove garlic	1 teaspoon sugar
few sprigs parsley	⅓ cup cognac
3 bay leaves	1 slice rye bread
sprig thyme	1 tablespoon vinegar

If you use tender young wild boar, it is not necessary to marinate it the day before: 1 hour is enough. Otherwise,

prepare the meat the day before. Roll up the meat into a roast and tie together if necessary. Crush 3 of the juniper berries and rub the meat with them. Place the meat in a bowl and cover with the wine. Peel the onion and stick it with the cloves. Peel the garlic and add to the bowl with the onion, parsley, bay leaves, thyme, salt and pepper and a little rind from the lemon. Marinate overnight.

Remove the meat from the marinade. Heat the butter and oil in a large saucepan. Chop the shallots and add to the pan, then add the meat. Sauté gently, turning several times. As soon as the meat is lightly golden brown, pour over the unstrained marinade. Add the sugar and remaining juniper berries. Cover and cook very gently for 3 hours. Remove the cooked meat from the pan and strain the liquid. Replace the meat in the pan, warm the cognac and pour over. Flambé, keeping the dish away from the heat. Add the strained liquid, reheat and cook for 10 minutes.

Trim the crusts from the rye bread and cut the bread into small pieces. Sprinkle with vinegar and add to the sauce around the meat. Stir and let the sauce cook for a minute to thicken. Serve the meat coated with a little of the sauce, with the remainder in a heated sauceboat. This dish is often served with a purée of chestnuts, potatoes or lentils, and sometimes with all three. The same wine that was used in making the sauce should be served with it.

RATATOUILLE

Serves 6

1 lb eggplants	few sprigs parsley
1 lb zucchini	⅓ cup olive oil
1½ lb tomatoes	sprig thyme
3 sweet peppers, different colors if possible	1 bay leaf
	1 teaspoon sugar
3 shallots	salt and pepper
2 cloves garlic	

Cut the eggplants into pieces and soak in heavily salted water for 30 minutes. Drain, rinse in cold water and drain again. Cut the zucchini into pieces. Scald the tomatoes in boiling water for 1 minute and drain immediately. Peel, cut in half and remove the seeds. Trim the sweet peppers, remove the seeds and chop the flesh. Peel and chop the shallots and garlic and chop the parsley. Heat the oil in a large heavy saucepan and sauté the shallots, garlic and parsley. Add the thyme, bay leaf, remaining prepared vegetables, sugar and seasoning. Cook over high heat for 5 minutes, cover and lower the heat. Cook for 20 minutes, stirring from time to time and, if necessary, adding enough water to keep the mixture moist. Serve hot or cold.

Note: Ratatouille is equally tasty when prepared in advance and reheated when required.

Ratatouille

Potatoes à la lyonnaise

POTATOES À LA LYONNAISE

Serves 4

4 large potatoes
2 large onions
6 tablespoons butter

1 tablespoon oil
few sprigs parsley
salt and pepper

Wash and scrub the potatoes and bake in a preheated moderately hot oven (400°) for about 30 minutes. They should be tender, but not completely cooked. Peel and cut into thick slices. Peel and finely chop the onions. Heat the butter and oil in a skillet and gently brown the slices of potato and onion. Sprinkle with parsley, season with salt and pepper and serve very hot.

SOUFFLÉ POTATOES

Serves 6

4 large old potatoes
oil for deep-frying

salt and pepper

Peel the potatoes and slice into rounds, about $\frac{1}{8}$ inch thick. Dry well–this is important. Heat the oil in a deep skillet to very hot, 360° on a frying thermometer. (Another guide is to add a small cube of bread to the oil; it should turn golden brown within half a minute.) Add the potatoes, a few at a time, and cook over high heat until golden brown. Remove

from the oil and cool. Reheat the oil to 400° and fry the potatoes a second time until swollen and golden brown. Remove from the oil and drain on absorbent paper. Place the potatoes in a heated serving dish. Season and serve at once.

Note: Soufflé potatoes are usually served with game or broiled meats. If they are to accompany a dish with a sauce, serve them on small plates so they do not get soaked with sauce.

POTATOES À LA DAUPHINOISE

Serves 4

3 large potatoes
1 clove garlic
6 tablespoons butter

salt and nutmeg
1½ cups heavy cream
(see note)

Peel and wash the potatoes. Cut into very thin slices and dry well with a cloth. Peel the clove of garlic and rub it around the inside of a baking dish. Butter the dish well, using a third of the butter, and arrange the potato slices inside in layers, seasoning each layer with salt. Sprinkle the top lightly with nutmeg and pour over the cream. Dot the remaining butter over the surface. Bake in a preheated hot oven (425°) for 10 minutes. Then lower the heat to 350° and cook for 1 hour. This dish is excellent served with a roast.

Note: Potatoes *à la dauphinoise* may also be made with milk in place of the cream, or with half milk and half cream.

AÏOLI (GARLIC MAYONNAISE)

Makes approximately 1¼ cups

2 small garlic bulbs	1 cup olive oil
2 egg yolks	juice of 1 lemon
dash salt	1 teaspoon cold water

Peel the garlic and pound it, if possible in a mortar. Add the egg yolks and mix slowly. Add the salt. Then begin to pour in the olive oil, almost drop by drop, as for mayonnaise. When it thickens, add the oil more quickly. Finish by mixing in the lemon juice and then the water.

To prepare in a blender, place the peeled and roughly chopped garlic in the blender with the egg yolks, salt and lemon juice. Cover and blend at low speed for a few moments. Remove the center cap in the blender lid and slowly pour in the oil. When the mixture has thickened and all the oil is added, add the water and switch off.

ARTICHOKE MOUSSELINE

Serves 4

4 lb (about 8 medium-sized)	¼ cup butter
artichokes	salt and pepper
3 tablespoons heavy cream	

For the purée, you should use only the hearts of the artichokes. Do not discard the remainder: when the heart is removed, keep the tender leaves and boil them in water. Use the strained stock for soups.

Cover the artichoke hearts with boiling water and simmer with the lid on for about 35 minutes. Drain and press through a sieve to make a purée. Beat in the cream, butter and seasoning. Alternatively, blend the hearts to a smooth purée in a blender. Then add the remaining ingredients to make a smooth sauce. Just before serving, reheat in a double boiler or a *bain marie* (a pan placed in a large roasting pan filled with boiling water) or in a heavy saucepan over very low heat. Serve with roast veal, pigeons or chicken.

FRESH PEAS IN CREAM SAUCE

Serves 6

3 cups shelled fresh peas	1 teaspoon sugar
¼ cup butter	dash salt
1 head lettuce	⅓ cup heavy cream
few sprigs parsley	2 egg yolks
⅓ cup water	

Rinse the peas. Melt the butter in a heavy saucepan and add the peas. Sauté over high heat for a few minutes, constantly shaking the pan. Wash the lettuce and cut into quarters. Add the lettuce quarters, the parsley and the water to the pan. To keep the temperature low in the traditional manner, cover the pan with a soup dish filled with cold water. As the water in the soup dish becomes hot, replace it with cold water. Cook the peas very slowly for 1 hour, adding a little extra water if necessary. Add the sugar and salt and continue to simmer gently. Meanwhile, blend the cream and egg yolks together in a bowl. Add to the peas and reheat, stirring all the time, but do not boil. Remove the parsley and serve at once.

Potatoes à la dauphinoise

PEACHES IN BRANDY

Makes about 6 lb

24 ripe peaches
2¼ cups sugar
2 cups water
8 cloves

stick cinnamon, broken into
    small pieces
4¼ cups brandy

Prick the peaches in two or three places with a long needle. Place in a large saucepan of boiling water. Leave for a minute and then remove with a perforated spoon. Rinse the peaches under cold running water. Peel and let dry. Cut the peaches in half and place in sterilized jars, filling the jars not more than three-fourths full.

Dissolve the sugar in the water and bring to a boil. Cook for 3 minutes. Pour the syrup over the peaches and add the cloves and the cinnamon. Let cool completely before covering with the brandy. Seal the jars and leave for 1 month before serving. Delicious after a meal, these peaches can also be used to enhance sweet dishes, ice cream, fruit salads and flans.

STRAWBERRY PIE

Serves 6–8

for the sablé pastry:
1¾ cups all-purpose flour
2 egg yolks
½ cup butter
½ teaspoon salt
3 tablespoons water
½ cup sifted confectioners' sugar
for the pastry cream:
1 cup sifted confectioners' sugar
2 egg yolks

½ cup sifted all-purpose flour
1 cup lukewarm milk
½ vanilla bean or few drops vanilla
    extract
dash salt
2 tablespoons butter
for the filling:
1½ lb strawberries
½ cup redcurrant or raspberry jelly

Remove the butter from the refrigerator 1 hour before you begin. Sift the flour into a bowl and make a well in the center. Add the egg yolks, slightly softened butter, salt, water and sugar. Mix very quickly, rubbing between the fingertips to make a dough. Form the dough into a ball. Let rest in a cool place for 20 minutes. Roll out the pastry on a floured board, or on a table covered with a floured cloth. Line a 9-inch greased tart mold with the pastry. To prevent the center from rising, prick with a fork, line carefully with foil or waxed paper and fill with dried beans. Bake in a preheated moderately hot oven (400°) for 25 minutes. Cool for 10 minutes before removing beans and foil.

In the meantime, prepare the pastry cream. Mix the confectioners' sugar and the egg yolks together in a saucepan. Add the flour and stir thoroughly. Add the milk gradually, stirring constantly. Then add the vanilla bean or vanilla extract and the salt. Place the pan over low heat and bring to a boil, stirring constantly with a wooden spoon until the mixture has thickened. Remove from the heat. Lift out the vanilla bean, if used, and add the butter, stirring vigorously. Let the mixture cool until lukewarm. Pour the cream into the cooked pie shell, smoothing it with a spatula. Then clean the strawberries and arrange on top. Melt the redcurrant jelly in a small saucepan over low heat. Spoon over the strawberries. Serve the strawberry pie cold.

VANILLA CREAM PIE

Serves 6

for the puff pastry:
2 cups all-purpose flour
¾ cup very cold water
dash salt
generous ¾ cup butter, firm but not too hard
milk for glazing
for the pastry cream:
1 cup milk

½ vanilla bean or 2–3 drops vanilla extract
grated rind of 1 orange
½ cup sugar
¼ cup all-purpose flour
3 egg yolks
dash salt
2 tablespoons butter
for the topping:
¼ cup sugar

Make the pastry as for Partridge Pie, page 132. Grease an 8- or 9-inch pie pan and line with puff pastry. Prick the pastry with a fork, so it rises evenly. Brush the edges with milk and bake in a preheated moderately hot oven (400°) for 12 minutes.

Meanwhile, prepare the pastry cream. Heat the milk with the vanilla bean or extract and a little grated orange rind. Mix the sugar and flour together in a saucepan. Add the egg yolks and gradually stir in the hot milk mixture. Cook over low heat for about 5 minutes, stirring constantly with a spoon or a whisk until the mixture thickens. Remove the pan from the heat and take out the vanilla bean, if used. Cut the butter into small pieces and stir it in. Pour this thick cream mixture into the pie shell. Sprinkle with the ¼ cup sugar. Broil quickly until the sugar melts and caramelizes. Serve warm.

APPLE PIE

Serves 6–8

for the pastry:
1¾ cups all-purpose flour
3 tablespoons water
dash salt
½ cup sifted confectioners' sugar
½ cup butter
2 egg yolks

for the filling:
2 lb dessert apples
juice of ½ lemon
¼ cup sugar
dash cinnamon
¾ cup apricot jam
3 tablespoons water

Sift the flour into a bowl and make a well in the center. Place the water, salt, sugar, butter, cut into small pieces, and egg yolks in the well. Mix together thoroughly with the flour, rubbing between the fingertips to make a dough. Form the pastry into a ball. Roll out on a floured board, or on a table covered with a floured cloth. Avoid handling it too much as this pastry is very fragile. Line a greased 10-inch tart mold with it.

Peel, quarter and core the apples. Cut into thin slices and sprinkle with the lemon juice. Arrange them, overlapping, in the pie shell. Sprinkle with the sugar and cinnamon. Bake in a preheated moderately hot oven (400°) for 30 minutes. Remove the pie from the oven. Sieve the apricot jam and combine with the water in a small saucepan. Warm through over low heat, then pour evenly over the surface of the pie to form a glaze.

Peaches in brandy

139

Blackcurrant ice cream

CRÊPES SUZETTE

Serves 4

1 cup all-purpose flour	4 small oranges or tangerines
2 eggs	¼ cup butter
½ cup water	shortening (see recipe)
½ cup light ale or beer	1 cup sifted confectioners' sugar
dash salt	8 teaspoons curaçao or cointreau

for the orange butter:
20 sugar cubes

For the batter, sift the flour into a bowl and make a well in the center. Add the eggs, water, ale and salt. Mix in the center of the bowl, gradually drawing in the flour from the sides. When the ingredients are blended, beat to a smooth batter. (The batter can also be prepared in a blender. In this case, place the eggs, water and salt in the blender. Add the flour and then the ale. Cover and blend for a few seconds at high speed.) Let the batter stand for 30 minutes to make it lighter.

Meanwhile, prepare the orange butter. Rub the sugar cubes over the unpeeled fruit to absorb the oil in the rind. Then crush the cubes thoroughly and mix into the slightly softened butter. Add a little orange juice to taste.

Heat a small pancake pan or skillet and, when hot, lightly grease with a piece of shortening. Pour a little of the batter into the pan. Make a pancake, toss it then discard it, for the first one is never successful. Rub the pan again with shortening, reheat and pour about 2 tablespoons of batter into the pan. Tip the pan so that the batter spreads thinly over the surface. As soon as the edges turn golden brown and bubbles start to burst and form little holes on the surface, turn the pancake over. Cook for a moment. Spread each pancake with a little of the orange butter, fold in half twice and place in a hot flat dish. When all the pancakes are made and filled, dredge them with confectioners' sugar. Warm the curaçao and pour over. Flambé and serve.

BLACKCURRANT ICE CREAM

Serves 6

1 lb blackcurrants	juice of ½ lemon
2 cups sifted confectioners' sugar	1½ cups heavy cream

Crush the blackcurrants in a sieve – preferably a conical sieve – and retain the juice. Blend the juice with the confectioners' sugar and the lemon juice. Whip the cream until thick, then fold into the blackcurrant mixture. Pour the mixture into a large ice tray and freeze for about 2 hours, or until firm. The ice cream is sometimes served with additional fresh cream, whipped up with sugar. Serve with sweet white wine or champagne.

BRETON PANCAKES

Serves 8

4 eggs	¾ cup light ale
dash salt	1¾ cups buckwheat flour
⅓ cup dark rum	1 cup water
2 tablespoons oil	lard or bacon fat

Beat the eggs in a large bowl along with the salt, rum and oil. Gradually add the ale and the flour, stirring constantly with a wooden spoon. Cover with a cloth and let stand in a warm place for at least 1 hour. Then stir in the water.

Heat a small pancake pan or skillet and rub with a piece of lard or bacon fat. Pour a little of the batter in the pan and tip it so that the batter spreads all over the bottom. As soon as the pancake is covered with little golden holes, turn it over. Cook a moment longer, then slide on to a plate. In Brittany, the first pancake is given to the birds for luck.

Grease the pan again and cook a second pancake in the same way. Pile them on top of each other on a heated dish, dusting them lightly with sugar. Breton women often use two pans at once to save time. Serve the pancakes with melted butter, honey or jam.

BING CHERRY PUDDING

Serves 4

1 lb Bing cherries	¼ cup sugar
7 tablespoons butter	dash salt
2¾ cups all-purpose flour	½ cup water
3 eggs	

Pit the cherries. Grease a 12-inch round cake pan or a 9-inch loaf pan, using a third of the butter, and place half the cherries in the bottom. Sift the flour into a bowl and make a well in the center. Place the eggs, sugar, salt and water in the well. Stir, drawing the mixture together, then beat to a smooth batter. Pour the batter into the pan, spread it evenly and cover with the rest of the cherries. Dot the surface with the remaining butter. Bake in a preheated moderately hot oven (400°) for about 30 minutes. Allow the pudding to cool before removing it from the pan.

BAKED CHESTNUT PUDDING

Serves 4

1½ lb fresh chestnuts or	1 cup milk
1 lb canned whole chestnuts	1 cup sugar
salt	4 eggs, separated
½ cup butter	dash salt
½ vanilla bean or 2–3 drops vanilla extract	½ cup sifted confectioners' sugar

If using fresh chestnuts, slash them and cook for 15 minutes in boiling salted water. Strain and remove the shells and skins. Return the chestnuts to the saucepan, cover again with boiling water and simmer for 30 minutes, or until tender. If using canned chestnuts, simply drain and rinse them.

Press the chestnuts through a sieve or food mill to make a purée. Cut the butter into small pieces, add it and mix well. Add the vanilla bean or extract to the milk and bring to a boil in a saucepan. Discard the bean, if used, and pour the hot milk slowly over the chestnut mixture, stirring it in gradually. Mix in the sugar and egg yolks. Beat the egg whites with a dash of salt until stiff. Fold into the mixture.

Thoroughly grease a medium-sized soufflé dish and pour in the mixture. Cook in a preheated moderate oven (350°) for 30 minutes. Chill the pudding completely before unmolding, and then sprinkle with confectioners' sugar. Serve as it is, or cover with vanilla-flavored whipped cream.

ALSACE HONEY COOKIES

Makes about 48

1½ cups all-purpose flour	¾ cup finely ground almonds
½ cup sugar	¼ cup milk
½ teaspoon baking powder	1 teaspoon cinnamon
6 tablespoons softened butter	6 tablespoons thick honey

Sift the flour into a mixing bowl and add the sugar and baking powder. Mix with a wooden spoon. Add the butter and rub it into the mixture, using the fingertips. Add the ground almonds and the milk and knead again until the dough is smooth. Roll out on a floured board and cut into a variety of shapes—hearts, stars, diamonds, etc. Place the cookies on a greased baking sheet. Sprinkle cinnamon on each cookie and put a little honey in the center. Bake in a preheated moderately hot oven (400°) for 12 minutes. Serve with white wine, coffee or kirsch.

MADELEINES

Makes about 24

½ cup sugar	½ cup butter
4 eggs	few drops vanilla extract or
dash salt (see recipe)	1 tablespoon orange flower
1 cup cake flour	water

Put the sugar in a bowl. Separate the eggs and beat the whites with the salt until stiff. (Include salt only if unsalted butter is used in the recipe.) Add the whites to the sugar and mix well. Add the egg yolks and mix again. Then add the flour, a little at a time, stirring constantly. Melt the butter and stir it in, with the vanilla extract or orange flower water. Beat with a fork or whisk until the mixture has thickened. (Alternatively, use an electric mixer at slow speed.)

Grease little shell-shaped pans and pour in the mixture to completely fill them. Bake in a preheated moderately hot oven (400°) for 15–20 minutes, until the cakes are golden brown. Remove the Madeleines from the oven and cool in the pans.

PEAR CAKE

Makes 1 9-inch cake

2 cups all-purpose flour	6–8 small pears
1 cup confectioners' sugar	**for the glaze:**
1 tablespoon baking powder	⅔ cup sugar
⅔ cup peanut or corn oil	2 cups water
⅔ cup sweet white wine	dash cinnamon
3 eggs	2 tablespoons cherry jam
small dash salt	

Grease an 8- or 9-inch spring-form pan and line the sides and bottom with waxed paper.

Sift the flour into a bowl and make a well in the center. Sift the sugar into the well, add the baking powder and then the oil and white wine. Mix everything together with a wooden spoon, drawing in the flour from the sides of the bowl. Separate the eggs. Add the egg yolks to the mixture and mix again until quite smooth. Beat the egg whites with a dash of salt until stiff. Fold into the mixture quickly but thoroughly. The mixture must be creamy. Turn into the prepared pan. Bake in the center of a preheated moderately hot oven (400°) for 15 minutes. Then reduce the heat to 350° and bake for a further 20–25 minutes. The cake is cooked as soon as the warmed blade of a knife, pushed into the center, comes out clean. The surface of the cake must be golden brown. Let cool completely before turning out.

Meanwhile, put the sugar for the glaze into a saucepan with the water and bring to a boil. Add the whole pears, washed but unpeeled. Add a dash of cinnamon and the cherry jam to add color. Cook over medium heat for 15 minutes or until the pears are soft. Let cool and drain on absorbent paper. Set the pears upright on the cake, cutting off their bases so they will stand easily.

HONEY SPICE CAKE

Serves 8–12

1 lb (1½ cups) thick honey	2 eggs
4 cups rye flour	½ teaspoon baking soda
dash salt	**for the frosting:**
dash ginger	1 cup sifted confectioners' sugar
dash cinnamon	1 tablespoon lemon juice or kirsch
4 cloves, crushed	candied fruits for decoration
¼ cup milk	

Warm the honey in a saucepan over very low heat, stirring constantly with a wooden spoon. Measure the flour into an earthenware bowl, and make a well in the center. Add the honey, salt and spices. Mix and knead to a rough dough. Cover the dough with waxed paper or a plastic bag to prevent drying. Let stand at room temperature for 24 hours.

Warm the milk. Meanwhile, lightly beat the eggs. Dissolve the baking soda in the warm milk, then beat in the eggs. Add the mixture to the dough and mix well. Knead thoroughly for at least 10 minutes. The dough should be quite stiff and rough in texture. Spoon the dough into a well greased loaf pan. Bake in a preheated moderate oven (325°) for 1 hour 20 minutes, or until a skewer inserted into the cake comes out clean. Cool before removing from the pan.

Mix the confectioners' sugar with lemon juice or kirsch and stir well. Spread the frosting over the surface of the spice cake with a spatula and decorate with pieces of candied fruit.

RASPBERRY RING CAKE

Serves 6

2 eggs	1 tablespoon baking powder
1 cup sugar	**for the filling:**
grated rind of ¼ orange	8 oz raspberries
¾ cup sweet white wine	½ cup sugar
6 tablespoons peanut oil	1 cup heavy cream
2¼ cups all-purpose flour	

Beat the eggs with the sugar and add the grated orange rind. Beat again until the mixture is frothy. Pour the wine and oil into the egg mixture and mix well. Sift the flour and add. Mix again and finally stir in the baking powder. Grease a tube pan, about 9 inches in diameter, and pour in the mixture. Bake in the center of a preheated moderately hot oven (375°) for 35 minutes, or until the cake is risen and brown. Let the cake cool completely before removing from the pan. Place the raspberries in the center of the cake. Dust with the sugar and cover with the cream – whipped, if desired.

PRUNE CAKE

Serves 6

8 oz tenderized prunes	dash salt
1¾ cups all-purpose flour	dash grated nutmeg
1 cup sugar	¼ cup softened butter
1 teaspoon baking powder	1¼ cups milk

This cake is best made with really fresh tenderized prunes. Otherwise, soak the prunes for a few hours in either cold tea or port wine, then drain well. Remove the pits and cut the prunes into small pieces. Sift the flour into a bowl and add the prunes. Then add the sugar, baking powder, salt and nutmeg. Mix by hand. Turn the pieces of prune over and over until well coated. Add the softened butter and mix again. Heat the milk to lukewarm and stir in, a little at a time. Grease a 9-inch spring-form pan and pour in the mixture. Bake in a preheated moderately hot oven (375°) for about 30 minutes. As soon as the top is golden brown, the cake is cooked. Serve warm or cold.

Honey spice cake

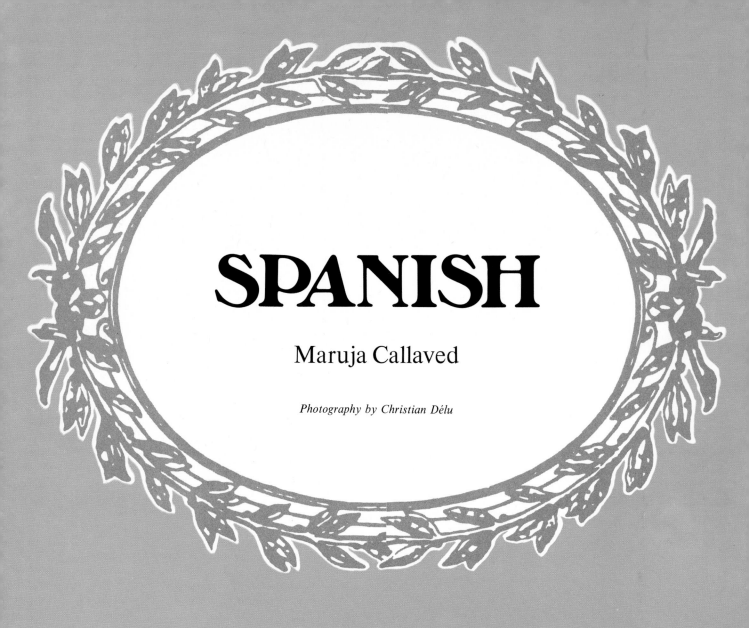

SPANISH

Maruja Callaved

Photography by Christian Délu

Spanish cooking forms an integral part of the history of Spain and was gradually evolved during the successive foreign invasions suffered by the Iberian peninsula.

The Phoenicians brought with them the seeds of the olive trees. The Romans introduced new ingredients to Spanish cooking, among which garlic was the most important. The Arabs brought spices, bitter lemons and oranges and sweet extracts to flavor their confectionery. They taught the Spaniards to make *churros* (batter rings deep-fried in oil), *freixuelos* (honey fritters), sugared and candied almonds, almond paste and nougat. The unification of Spain in 1492 put an end to the long period of foreign occupation.

This amalgam of contributions from other lands and the traditional cooking of the early inhabitants of the Iberian peninsula is the foundation of traditional Spanish cooking.

Fish is a fundamental part of the diet all along the Spanish coastline, although the methods of cooking vary according to the region. In the north, fish is usually prepared with a sauce or garnish, as in such dishes as *marmitako* (fish stew with vegetables), and hake in green sauce, whereas in the south fried fish is more popular. Shellfish is the specialty of Galicia and a few places along the eastern and southern coasts. The inland areas of the north support large herds of cattle and have a large output of agricultural products. Typical local dishes are hashes, stews and beef-steaks. The rivers abound in fresh-water fish and the north is famous for its charcoal-broiled trout.

The eastern coast, on the Mediterranean, not only has abundant fish, but also produces rice, vegetables, fruit and almonds. All these products place the Mediterranean style of cooking among the richest and most varied in Spain. The best-known and probably the finest dish of this region is *paella*.

Southern Spain, with its stretches of tropical vegetation, is the warmest part of the country, where olives, soft fruits, grapes and almonds grow in profusion and where large numbers of cattle and pigs are raised. The dishes of the south are simple and light, and the meals basically consist of fried foods, salads and *gazpacho* (a refreshing, cold vegetable soup).

The central and western parts of the mainland are inland regions which support a large livestock population and produce a high percentage of the country's cereals and wine. Solid, down-to-earth dishes based on these products are typical of these areas.

The gastronomic traditions of Spain are highlighted by a series of carnivals and events held throughout the year. These include the festivals celebrating the grape harvest in September and others that mark the seasons for river fishing and hunting, particularly boar-hunting; the time for sausage-making in winter; the fruit harvest and resultant jam-making in the fall; nougat-making at Christmas, and so on. These are all legacies of a popular and traditional nature and at these times the people keep certain customs in cooking, although the modern way of life is threatening to obliterate them.

Vineyards are cultivated in almost every region of Spain. Many excellent Spanish wines could be mentioned, but the 'king of wines' is sherry, which ranges in color from topaz to mahogany and is a fortified wine with an unequaled bouquet.

OCTOPUS WITH GARLIC AND PAPRIKA DRESSING

Serves 6

2¼ lb octopus or cuttlefish	salt
2 cloves garlic	⅔ cup olive oil
2 teaspoons paprika	

Discard the ink sac, the intestines and the transparent spinal bone from the octopus or cuttlefish. Rinse very thoroughly under cold running water, place on a flat surface and pound with a mallet to tenderize and soften the flesh.

Place the octopus in a large saucepan and add enough water to cover. Bring to a boil, then lower the heat, cover tightly and simmer for 1–1½ hours.

Meanwhile, peel and finely chop the garlic. Combine the garlic, paprika, salt and oil to make the dressing. Drain the fish thoroughly and cut into small pieces. Transfer to a serving dish and sprinkle with the prepared dressing.

SHELLFISH OMELET

Serves 4

for the tomato sauce:	4 fresh or frozen crayfish
1 lb tomatoes	10 fresh mussels
6 tablespoons olive oil	8 eggs
¼ teaspoon salt	3 tablespoons milk
for the omelet:	2 teaspoons salt
20 fresh or frozen scampi or	2–3 tablespoons olive oil
jumbo shrimp	2 teaspoons chopped parsley

To make the tomato sauce, peel and finely chop the tomatoes. Heat the oil in a heavy saucepan and sauté the tomatoes for 10–15 minutes, stirring frequently, until reduced to a pulp. Remove from the heat and press the tomatoes through a sieve to make a fairly thick sauce. Season with salt.

To make the omelet, if using fresh, uncooked scampi and crayfish, rinse thoroughly under cold running water, plunge into lightly salted boiling water and boil for 7 minutes. Drain well and set aside to cool. Scrub the mussels thoroughly under cold running water and remove the beards. Place in a saucepan and add just enough water to cover the bottom of the pan. Cover the pan tightly and steam the mussels over moderate heat for about 5 minutes, or until they open. Discard any that do not open. Remove the mussels from their shells and place in a bowl. Shell and devein the scampi and crayfish, cut into small pieces and place in a bowl with the mussels. Lightly beat together the eggs, milk and salt in a large bowl. Stir in the prepared shellfish.

Heat the oil in a large omelet pan or skillet over moderate heat. Pour in the egg mixture and tilt the pan gently so the egg runs almost to the rim. When the omelet begins to set, lift the edges with a spatula to allow the uncooked egg to run underneath. When the omelet has a high rounded edge but is still slightly soft in the center, place a lightly greased plate over the pan and invert the omelet on to it. Slide it back into the pan so the browned side is on top. Cook for a further 2–3 minutes, shaking the pan gently. Remove from the heat and garnish with the chopped parsley. Cut into portions and serve immediately with the reheated tomato sauce.

145

TUNA FISH OMELET

Serves 4

for the tomato sauce:

1 lb tomatoes
6 tablespoons olive oil
¼ teaspoon salt

for the omelet:

2 medium-sized potatoes, cooked
¼ cup cooked chopped spinach

⅔ cup milk
¼ cup butter
4 oz canned tuna fish
6 eggs
1½ teaspoons salt
1 tablespoon chopped parsley

Prepare the tomato sauce as for Shellfish Omelet on the preceding page. Press the potato and spinach through a sieve to make a purée. Stir in the milk and half the butter and heat gently until hot. Cut the tuna fish into small pieces and add half to the prepared tomato sauce. Heat gently until hot. Beat the eggs and add the salt, parsley and remaining tuna fish.

Heat the remaining butter in an omelet pan or heavy skillet. Add the egg mixture and cook until the omelet is almost set. Place the spinach mixture along the center of the omelet and fold each side toward the middle, completely enclosing the filling. Transfer to a heated serving dish, cover with the tomato sauce and serve immediately.

SCAMPI WITH WHITE RUM

Serves 4

1 small onion
1 tomato
6 tablespoons olive oil
½ teaspoon paprika
2 tablespoons all-purpose flour
2 teaspoons salt

¾ cup water
½–1 cup white rum
20 fresh or frozen scampi or jumbo shrimp, shelled and deveined
¼ cup anisette

Peel and finely chop the onion and tomato. Heat the oil in a skillet and sauté the onion until lightly browned. Add the tomato and paprika and sauté for 1 minute. Stir in the flour and salt. Add the water gradually, stirring well after each addition. Bring to a boil, stirring constantly until the mixture thickens. Stir in the rum and simmer for 2–3 minutes. Add the scampi and simmer for 5 minutes. Add the anisette and simmer for 5–10 minutes. Remove the skillet from the heat and serve.

MARINATED TROUT

Serves 4

4 small trout
6 cloves garlic
6 tablespoons olive oil
3 tablespoons vinegar

2 sprigs parsley
1 teaspoon salt
generous dash white pepper
1 teaspoon paprika

Clean the trout and cut off the fins, tails and heads. Rinse under cold running water and pat dry with absorbent paper. Cut each trout into 3 pieces. Peel and chop the garlic.

Place the trout pieces in a saucepan and add the garlic, olive oil, vinegar, parsley, salt, white pepper and paprika.

Bring to a boil over high heat, then lower the heat and simmer for 10 minutes. Transfer the trout to a heated serving dish and pour over the juices from the pan. Serve immediately as an appetizer or set aside until cold.

BONITO A LA PLANCHA

Serves 6

3½ lb bonito or tuna fish
2 teaspoons salt
4 cloves garlic
3 sprigs parsley

2 tablespoons lemon juice
1 lb small mushrooms
6 tablespoons olive oil

Cut the fish into slices 1½ inches thick. Sprinkle with the salt. Peel 2 cloves of the garlic, place in a mortar with the parsley and pound until smooth. Add the lemon juice. Brush the fish slices with the garlic and lemon mixture.

Traditionally the fish is cooked on a *plancha* (see note), but alternatively it may be cooked in a greased heavy skillet. Cook the slices for 5–6 minutes on each side. Brush with the remaining lemon mixture during the cooking.

Meanwhile, rinse the mushrooms thoroughly under cold running water and simmer in lightly salted boiling water for 5–6 minutes. Drain well. Peel and chop the remaining garlic. Heat the oil in a small saucepan and sauté the garlic for 2–3 minutes. Add the mushrooms and sauté for 5–6 minutes. Drain on absorbent paper.

Arrange the fish slices on a heated serving dish, garnish with the mushrooms and serve as an appetizer.

Note: A *plancha* is a thick iron plate, heated from below, similar to a griddle. Bonito, like tuna fish, is very suitable for cooking *a la plancha* because it contains a high quantity of fat.

RICE AND VEGETABLE MOLD

Serves 4

8 oz Brussels sprouts
2 medium-sized carrots
1½ lb fresh peas
8 oz green beans
2 cloves garlic
6 tablespoons olive oil

2 eggs
2 cups water
1 bay leaf
1 teaspoon salt
1 cup long-grain rice

Discard the coarse outer leaves of the Brussels sprouts and trim the stems. Cut the sprouts into small pieces. Peel and coarsely chop the carrots. Shell the peas. Trim and coarsely chop the beans. Peel the garlic. Cook the Brussels sprouts, carrots, peas and beans separately in lightly salted boiling water until just tender. Drain well.

Heat half the oil in a skillet. Sauté the cloves of garlic for 2–3 minutes, then remove and discard them. Sauté the cooked vegetables in the flavored oil for about 5 minutes. Lightly beat the eggs and stir into the vegetables. Cook for 3–4 minutes, or until the egg sets. Remove from the heat and set aside to cool.

Pour the water into a saucepan and add the remaining oil, the bay leaf and the salt. Bring to a boil. Add the rice, lower

La Mancha soup

the heat and simmer for 12–15 minutes, or until the rice is tender and all the water has been absorbed. Remove from the heat and set aside to cool.

Lightly brush the inside of a 2-quart mold with oil. Place a layer of rice in the bottom followed by a layer of the vegetable mixture. Repeat twice and finish with the layer of rice. Press the top firmly, then turn the mixture out of the mold on to a plate and serve with mayonnaise.

LA MANCHA SOUP

Serves 6

4 cloves garlic	6 tablespoons olive oil
6 slices bread	½ cup all-purpose flour
8 oz Canadian-style bacon, in 1 piece	½ teaspoon paprika
	¼ teaspoon pepper
4 oz *serrano* ham (see note)	2 teaspoons salt
4 oz *chorizo* (see note)	4 pints water

Peel and halve the garlic cloves. Cut the bread, bacon, ham and *chorizo* into ½-inch cubes. Heat the oil in a saucepan and sauté the garlic cloves until they begin to brown. Add the bacon, ham and *chorizo* and sauté for about 5 minutes. Remove with a perforated spoon and drain on absorbent paper. Add the bread cubes and sauté until crisp and golden brown. Remove with a perforated spoon and drain on absorbent paper.

Add the flour, paprika, pepper and salt to the oil remaining in the pan and cook for 5 minutes, stirring constantly. Add the water gradually, stirring well after each addition. Bring to a boil and boil for 15 minutes, stirring constantly. Add the bread cubes, garlic, bacon, ham and *chorizo*. Boil for a further 5 minutes and then serve in deep soup bowls.

Note: Serrano ham is a lightly salted ham for which a mild-cure smoked ham is a good substitute. *Chorizo* is a highly spiced pork sausage containing saffron and garlic.

GAZPACHO

Serves 6

2 cloves garlic	3 thick slices bread
dash cumin	6 tablespoons olive oil
2 lb tomatoes	1 tablespoon salt
2 medium-sized onions	½ cup vinegar
1 cucumber	2½ pints water
2 large green sweet peppers	

Peel the garlic and pound to a paste with the cumin in a mortar. Peel and coarsely chop the tomatoes, onions and cucumber. Remove the seeds from the peppers and chop the flesh. Soak the bread in cold water for about 30 seconds, then squeeze out the excess moisture.

Place three-fourths of the tomatoes, onions, cucumber and peppers in a blender with the garlic paste, bread and oil and reduce to a purée. Pour into a bowl, stir in the salt, vinegar and water and chill thoroughly. (Alternatively, three-fourths of the vegetables may be very finely chopped, then mixed with the bread, garlic paste, oil, salt, vinegar and water and chilled well.) Very finely chop the remaining vegetables and place separately in small bowls as accompaniments to the soup. Serve the *gazpacho*, very cold, in deep soup bowls or cups.

147

COLD RABBIT SOUP

Serves 6

2¼ lb rabbit, with liver

for the marinade:

3 tablespoons olive oil

6 tablespoons vinegar

1 tablespoon salt

1 sprig fresh marjoram or
  ½ teaspoon dried marjoram

for the soup:

1 cup fine fresh breadcrumbs

3 cloves garlic

4 hard-cooked eggs

¾ cup olive oil

1 tablespoon vinegar

4¼ cups water

salt

Rinse the rabbit under cold running water, dry well with absorbent paper and cut into 2-inch pieces. Reserve the liver until required.

To prepare the marinade, pour the oil and vinegar into a bowl and add the salt and marjoram. Mix well and add the rabbit pieces. Turn the pieces over several times until well coated with the marinade. Set aside to marinate for 24 hours.

To make the soup, transfer the rabbit pieces and the marinade to a roasting pan and add the rabbit liver. Roast in a preheated moderate oven (350°) for 30–40 minutes. Remove from the oven and set aside to cool. Reserve the liver. Strip the meat off the bones and set aside until required. Reserve the marinade but discard the bones. Soak the breadcrumbs for 1 minute in cold water. Squeeze to remove the excess moisture and place the crumbs in a mortar. Peel the garlic and place in the mortar. Separate the egg yolks from the whites and use the whites for another recipe if required. Add the egg yolks to the mortar along with the rabbit liver. Pound the breadcrumbs, garlic, egg yolks and liver together until reduced to a paste. Add the olive oil gradually, mixing well after each addition. Pour into a large bowl and stir in the vinegar, water and salt to taste. Add the strips of rabbit meat and the marinade and mix well. Set aside in a cold place until well chilled. Serve in deep soup bowls or cups.

CREAM OF BEAN SOUP

Serves 6

1 lb dried red kidney beans

½ bulb garlic

2 medium-sized carrots

1 medium-sized onion

1 leek

1 bay leaf

4¼ cups milk

¼ cup butter

dash nutmeg

2 hard-cooked eggs or sautéed
  croutons for garnishing

Soak the beans in plenty of cold water for 24 hours. Drain before using. Peel the garlic, carrots and onion. Trim the leek and rinse thoroughly under cold running water.

Place the beans, garlic, carrots, onion, leek and bay leaf in a saucepan. Add enough water to cover. Bring to a boil over high heat, then lower the heat, cover tightly and simmer for 2½–3 hours, or until the beans are very soft. Drain well and discard the liquid. Press the beans through a fine sieve to make a very thick purée, and return the purée to the pan. Add the milk, butter and nutmeg and stir thoroughly until well blended. Chop the eggs if used. Reheat the soup and pour into individual soup bowls. Garnish with the chopped eggs or croutons and serve.

GARLIC SOUP WITH EGGS

Serves 4

5 cloves garlic

8 oz crusty bread

6 tablespoons olive oil

1 teaspoon paprika

2 teaspoons salt

4¼ cups boiling water

4 eggs

Peel 4 cloves of the garlic and slice thinly. Cut the bread into 1-inch cubes. Heat the oil in a skillet and sauté the sliced garlic until well browned. Add the bread cubes and sauté over low heat for 3–5 minutes, or until the garlic and bread are very brown. Remove the skillet from the heat before the garlic burns. Add the paprika and transfer the contents of the skillet to a flameproof casserole. Add the salt and boiling water. Break the eggs into the soup, taking care to keep them whole. Place the casserole over moderate heat and poach the eggs until they are just set. Peel and chop the remaining clove of garlic and sprinkle over the soup. Serve in the casserole.

RICE AND CRAB SOUP

Serves 6

1 lb *centello* (spider crab) or crab
  meat

1 medium-sized onion

8 oz tomatoes

6 tablespoons oil

½ teaspoon paprika

2 teaspoons salt

4 pints boiling water

2 cloves garlic

1 sprig parsley

3 saffron strands

1 cup long-grain rice

Cut the *centello* or crab meat into ½-inch pieces. Peel and finely chop the onion and tomatoes. Heat the oil in a saucepan and sauté the crab meat until lightly browned. Add the onion and sauté for 5 minutes. Add the tomatoes, paprika, salt and water. Cover and simmer for 45 minutes.

Meanwhile, peel the garlic and pound in a mortar with the parsley. Add the saffron and 2 tablespoons of the simmering stock. Add the rice and the garlic mixture to the saucepan and simmer for 20 minutes. Turn off the heat. Adjust the seasoning if necessary and then leave to rest on the hot stove for 3 minutes. Pour into a soup tureen and serve.

Salt cod with chili and tomato sauce

SALT COD WITH CHILI AND TOMATO SAUCE

Serves 6

2¼ lb dried salt cod	6 chilies
1 lb tomatoes	1 tablespoon sugar
2 cloves garlic	¼ cup blanched almonds
all-purpose flour for coating	¾ cup water
¾ cup olive oil	salt

Rinse the dried salt cod under cold running water. Place in a large bowl and cover with water. Set aside for at least 24 hours, changing the water frequently to extract the excess salt.

Peel and chop the tomatoes. Peel the garlic. Drain and rinse the cod. Cut into 2½-inch pieces and coat with flour. Heat the oil in a skillet and sauté the cod pieces until lightly browned. Drain well and place in a shallow ovenproof dish. Sauté the chilies and the garlic for 2–3 minutes in the oil remaining in the skillet, remove with a perforated spoon, drain and set aside. Sauté the tomatoes in the same skillet until reduced to a pulp. Stir in the sugar and remove from the heat. Pound the garlic and almonds to a paste in a mortar. Stir in the water. Add to the tomato pulp with the chilies and salt to taste. Pour the tomato mixture over the fish and bake in a preheated moderate oven (350°) for 20 minutes. Serve in the ovenproof dish.

SALT COD CASSEROLE WITH SWEET PEPPERS

Serves 6

2¼ lb dried salt cod (see note)	2 cloves garlic
8 red sweet peppers	6 tablespoons olive oil
2¼ lb onions	1 teaspoon paprika

Rinse the dried salt cod under cold running water. Place in a bowl and cover with cold water. Set aside for at least 24 hours, changing the water frequently.

Remove the seeds from the peppers and cut the flesh into thin rings. Peel the onions and garlic and cut into thin rings. Drain the cod and place in a large saucepan with enough water to cover. Bring to the simmering point over moderate heat. Remove from the heat, drain, remove the bones and cut the fish into small pieces.

Heat the oil in a skillet and sauté the peppers very gently until soft but not brown. Remove the peppers from the skillet and set aside until required. Add the onions and garlic to the oil remaining in the skillet and sauté until soft but not brown. Remove the skillet from the heat.

Place the cod, peppers and onion and garlic mixture in alternate layers in a casserole. Sprinkle each layer of onion with a little paprika. Cover the casserole and bake in a preheated moderate oven (350°) for about 20 minutes, or until the cod is tender. Serve in the casserole.

Note: Use only the thicker, fleshier portions of the cod.

SEA BREAM IN TOMATO AND WINE SAUCE

Serves 6

1 sea bream or red snapper, about 3½ lb	8 oz tomatoes
2 teaspoons salt	1 medium-sized carrot
1 tablespoon chopped parsley	2 stalks celery
½ cup all-purpose flour	6 tablespoons olive oil
1 large onion	1 tablespoon sugar
2 cloves garlic	6 tablespoons water
	6 tablespoons dry white wine

Clean the fish and cut off the head, tail and fins. Scrape the fish very carefully to remove the scales. Rinse under cold running water and dry with absorbent paper. Cut the fish into slices about 2 inches thick. Sprinkle the slices lightly with salt and chopped parsley and coat with the flour. Peel and finely chop the onion, garlic and tomatoes. Peel and grate the carrot. Finely chop the celery.

Heat the oil in a skillet and fry the fish for 5 minutes on each side. Remove from the skillet and place in a flameproof casserole or saucepan. Sauté the onion, garlic, carrot and celery in the oil remaining in the skillet for 10–15 minutes, or until soft and lightly browned. Add the tomatoes, sugar and water and simmer for about 10 minutes. Press the mixture through a sieve into a bowl. Stir in the wine and pour the sauce over the fish. Simmer for a further 5 minutes.

Transfer the fish to a heated serving plate and pour the sauce over. Serve with boiled potatoes.

HAKE IN GREEN SAUCE

Serves 6

1 hake or cod head	6 tablespoons olive oil
¾ cup water	3 tablespoons chopped parsley
6 hake or cod cutlets, about 6 oz each	6 tablespoons dry white wine
all-purpose flour for coating	1 teaspoon salt
1 medium-sized onion	dash pepper

Place the hake head in a saucepan with the water, bring to a boil and simmer for 10 minutes. Remove and discard the hake head and set the stock aside to cool. Coat the hake cutlets with flour. Peel and chop the onion.

Heat the oil in a flameproof casserole and sauté the onion until it begins to brown. Place the hake cutlets and the parsley in the casserole and sauté gently until the hake is well browned on both sides, turning the casserole constantly in a circular motion (see note). Add the white wine, the reserved fish stock, salt and pepper. Lower the heat and simmer gently for 15–20 minutes, still rotating the casserole at frequent intervals. Serve the hake very hot, preferably in the casserole.

Note: This is a classic Basque dish and the secret of its success lies in the preparation. The casserole must be gently revolved so the hake exudes its gelatin which thickens the sauce.

Sea bream in tomato and wine sauce

150

HAKE WITH STUFFED TOMATOES

Serves 6

¾ cup olive oil
1¾ cups fine fresh breadcrumbs
6 tablespoons milk
2 oz pickled or canned tuna fish
1 teaspoon chopped parsley
1 teaspoon salt
dash pepper

6 large tomatoes
½ cup grated cheese
¼ cup butter
6 slices hake or cod, about
   6 oz each
½ cup all-purpose flour
2 lemons, sliced

Heat 2 tablespoons of the oil in a skillet and sauté the breadcrumbs until crisp and golden brown. Drain on absorbent paper and place in a bowl. Add the milk and set aside for 5 minutes. Add the tuna fish, parsley, salt and pepper and mix well.

Halve the tomatoes and scoop out the pulp and seeds which may be used as required in another dish. Press the breadcrumb mixture into the halved tomatoes. Place in an ovenproof dish, sprinkle with the cheese and place a knob of butter on each tomato half. Bake in a preheated moderately hot oven (375°) for 15–20 minutes.

Meanwhile, coat the hake slices with flour. Heat the remaining oil in a skillet and fry the hake slices for 4–5 minutes on each side, or until the flesh is tender and white and the outside golden brown. Place the fish on a heated serving plate. Arrange 2 tomato halves on each slice. Garnish the fish with the lemon slices and serve hot with sautéed potatoes.

JUGGED HAKE

Serves 4

1 lb hake or cod
1 teaspoon salt
dash pepper
2 cloves garlic
3–4 sprigs parsley
¼ teaspoon paprika
6 tablespoons olive oil

skin of 1 onion
½ cup fine fresh breadcrumbs
6 tablespoons water
¼ cup dry white wine
2 hard-cooked eggs or
   2 canned red pimientos
   for garnishing

Cut the fish into 4 slices and season with the salt and pepper. Finely chop the garlic and parsley. Place the fish in a shallow ovenproof dish and sprinkle with the garlic, parsley and paprika.

Heat the oil in a small saucepan and sauté the onion skin for 3–4 minutes. Discard the onion skin and pour the flavored oil over the fish. Set aside to marinate for about 4 hours. Sprinkle the breadcrumbs over the fish and pour over the water and wine. Bake in a preheated moderately hot oven (375°) for 20 minutes.

To garnish the dish, either very finely chop the hard-cooked eggs and sprinkle them over the surface, or cut the pimientos into thin strips and arrange on the top.

FISH IN ROMESCO SAUCE

Serves 4

2¼ lb halibut or hake
for the romesco sauce:
1 red sweet pepper
1 chili
1 thick slice bread

1 cup olive oil
3 cloves garlic
½ cup finely ground almonds
1 bay leaf, crushed
½ cup water

Cut the fish into 4 pieces. Remove the seeds and chop the red sweet pepper and the chili. Cut off and discard the crusts from the bread. Cut the bread into ½-inch cubes. Heat the oil in a skillet and sauté the red pepper, chili and bread cubes for 5–10 minutes.

Meanwhile, peel the garlic and place in a mortar with the ground almonds and bay leaf. Pound with a pestle until well blended. Add the red pepper, chili and bread cubes and continue pounding until reduced to a paste. Stir in the water.

Heat the oil remaining in the skillet and add the pounded mixture. Cover and simmer for 2 minutes. Add the fish, replace the lid and cook for 15–20 minutes, or until the flesh of the fish is tender and white. Transfer to a heated serving dish and serve.

BASQUE PAELLA

Serves 6

1 lb white-fleshed fish (cod or
   haddock)
1 lb squid
8 oz shelled clams
1 medium-sized onion
4 oz tomatoes
1 clove garlic
1 green or red sweet pepper
1 sprig parsley

few saffron strands
⅔ cup olive oil
12 fresh or frozen scampi or
   jumbo shrimp, shelled and
   deveined
2½ cups water
1½ cups long-grain rice
4 oz fresh or frozen shelled peas
2 teaspoons salt

Clean the fish, wash and cut into pieces. Clean the squid, remove and discard the ink sacs and intestines and cut into pieces. Rinse the clams under cold running water. Peel and finely chop the onion and tomatoes. Peel the garlic. Remove the seeds from the sweet pepper and finely chop the flesh. Pound the garlic, parsley and saffron together in a mortar.

Heat the oil in a *paella* pan, or in a large skillet, and sauté the onion and sweet pepper until lightly browned. Add the tomatoes and sauté for 2 minutes. Add the fish and squid and cook for a further 5 minutes. Add the scampi and clams and cook for a further 5 minutes. Add the garlic, parsley, the saffron mixture and the water and bring to a boil. Add the rice, peas and salt, cover tightly and cook for 5 minutes over high heat. Lower the heat and simmer gently for 15 minutes, or until the rice is just cooked. Remove from the heat and set aside for 5 minutes before serving.

151

SOLE FILLETS WITH MUSHROOM AND SHRIMP SAUCE

Serves 4

2 sole, about 1¼ lb each	2 cups water
¼ cup melted butter	1 medium-sized onion
1 teaspoon salt	2 medium-sized carrots
for the sauce:	4 oz fresh or frozen shrimp,
2½ quarts mussels	shelled and deveined
2⅓ cups small mushrooms	6 tablespoons dry white wine
⅔ cup butter	¼ cup all-purpose flour
1 slice lemon	2 egg yolks
salt	2–3 sprigs parsley

Skin the fish and fillet each one into 4 pieces (see note). Reserve the skin and bones. Brush the fillets well with the melted butter and sprinkle with the salt. Place in a buttered, shallow ovenproof dish and bake in a preheated moderately hot oven (375°) for 20–25 minutes, or until the fish is tender and white.

To prepare the sauce, scrub the mussels under cold running water and remove the beards. Place in a large saucepan and add enough water to cover the bottom of the pan. Cover with a tightly fitting lid, place over moderate heat and steam the mussels for 5–10 minutes, or until the shells open. Discard any that do not open. Take the mussels out of the shells and set aside until required. Discard the shells. Rinse the mushrooms under cold running water, drain and slice thinly. Place in a saucepan with enough water to cover and add half the butter, the lemon slice and a dash of salt. Bring to a boil over moderate heat, then lower the heat and simmer the mushrooms for 5–10 minutes, or until tender. Drain well, discard the lemon slice and set the mushrooms aside until required.

Place the reserved fish skins and bones in a saucepan and add the water. Bring to a boil over moderate heat, then reduce the heat and simmer for 5–10 minutes. Strain the fish stock through a sieve into a clean saucepan and discard the skin and bones. Peel and finely chop the onion and carrots. Add both to the fish stock with the mussels, mushrooms, shrimp, white wine and a dash of salt. Place over moderate heat and bring to a boil. Lower the heat and boil gently for 20 minutes.

Meanwhile, melt the remaining butter in a saucepan and stir in the flour. Cook gently for 2–3 minutes, stirring constantly. Remove from the heat. Blend the egg yolks with a little of the fish stock and gradually add to the flour and butter mixture, stirring thoroughly after each addition. Pour into the fish stock and bring to a boil, stirring constantly until the stock thickens, making a thick sauce. Lower the heat and simmer for 5 minutes. Spoon the sauce over the sole fillets, garnish with the parsley and serve.

Note: To fillet the fish, lay it on a board, dark skin upward, and cut off the fins. Cut down the backbone from head to tail. Then make a semi-circular cut, just below the head, through half the thickness of the fish. With short sharp strokes separate the left fillet from the backbone. Cut away above the tail. Repeat with the right fillet, turn the fish over and remove the fillets on the other side.

Sole fillets with mushroom and shrimp sauce

152

RICE MOLD WITH SQUID

Serves 6

2¼ lb squid	1 tablespoon chopped parsley
1 large onion	**for the rice mold:**
6 tablespoons olive oil	1 small onion
⅔ cup dry white wine	¼ cup olive oil
6 tablespoons water	1 bay leaf
1 tablespoon fine fresh breadcrumbs	2¼ cups long-grain rice
1 tablespoon salt	2 teaspoons salt
	3 cups water

Remove the ink sacs from the squid and set aside until required. Discard the intestines and bones. Cut the squid into thick rings. Peel and chop the onion. Heat the oil in a skillet and sauté the onion until soft and lightly browned. Add the squid and sauté for 5 minutes. Pound the reserved ink sacs in a mortar. Add to the squid with the wine, water, breadcrumbs, salt and parsley. Bring to a boil, then lower the heat and simmer for 10–15 minutes.

To prepare the rice mold, peel and chop the onion. Heat the oil and bay leaf in a saucepan and sauté the onion until lightly browned. Add the rice, salt and water. Bring to a boil, then lower the heat and simmer, uncovered, for 20 minutes. The rice should be dry and fluffy at the end of the cooking time. Press the rice into a buttered 9-inch ring mold. Set aside for 2–3 minutes, then turn out on to a plate. Spoon the squid and the sauce into the center of the rice mold. Serve hot.

STUFFED SQUID

Serves 4

2¼ lb small squid	1 tablespoon chopped parsley
1 medium-sized onion	1 tablespoon tomato paste
1 clove garlic	⅓ cup fine fresh breadcrumbs
3 medium-sized tomatoes	all-purpose flour for coating
2 hard-cooked eggs	6 tablespoons dry white wine
⅔ cup olive oil	

Remove the ink sacs from the squid and set aside until required. Discard the intestines and bones. Cut off the tentacles and chop coarsely. Peel and chop the onion, garlic and tomatoes. Shell and chop the eggs.

Heat one-third of the oil in a skillet and sauté half the onion, the garlic and the parsley for 5 minutes. Add the chopped squid and sauté for a further 5 minutes. Remove from the heat and mix in the chopped egg, tomato paste and breadcrumbs. Stuff the squid with this mixture and close the openings with toothpicks. Coat with flour.

Heat the remaining oil in a skillet and sauté the squid for 15 minutes. Transfer to a casserole. Add the remaining onion and the tomatoes to the hot oil in the skillet and sauté for 5 minutes. Stir in the white wine and pour the mixture over the squid. Bake in a preheated oven (350°) for 30–40 minutes. Strain the ink through a sieve and add to the squid. Bake for a further 5 minutes. Serve hot with fried croutons.

Breaded sardines

SARDINE PIE

Serves 4

for the pastry:

1 cup cornstarch

1½ cups all-purpose flour

⅓ cup lard

1 egg

about 6 tablespoons water

for the filling:

1 lb fresh sardines

¼ cup all-purpose flour

2 medium-sized onions

8 oz tomatoes

4 canned red pimientos

⅓ cup olive oil

1 tablespoon chopped parsley

½ teaspoon salt

for the glaze:

1 egg

To make the pastry, sift the cornstarch and flour into a mixing bowl. Cut the lard into small pieces and add. Using the fingertips, rub the lard into the dry ingredients until evenly distributed. Make a well in the center and add the egg and the water. Mix to a soft dough and knead lightly until smooth. Cover and set aside for 30 minutes.

Meanwhile, make the filling. Clean the sardines, cut off the heads and scrape the fish gently to remove the scales. Rinse under cold running water, dry well with absorbent paper and coat with flour. Peel and chop the onions and tomatoes.

Drain the canned pimientos. Heat half the oil in a skillet and fry the sardines for 2–3 minutes on each side. Drain well on absorbent paper. Heat the remaining oil in the skillet and sauté the onions, tomatoes, pimientos and parsley for about 5–10 minutes, or until the onions are soft but not brown. Remove from the heat and stir in the salt. Mix the sardines with the sautéed mixture and set aside to cool.

Divide the dough in half. Roll out one half into a 9-inch circle and place on a well-buttered baking sheet. Spread the fish mixture over the circle to within 1 inch of the edge. Brush the edge of the pastry with water. Roll out the remaining dough into a circle slightly larger than the base and place over the fish filling. Press the edges of the pie firmly together, completely enclosing the filling. Flute the edges of the pastry and make a small hole in the top to allow the steam to escape during cooking. Beat the egg and brush over the pie to glaze the surface. Bake in a preheated moderately hot oven (400°) for 30–40 minutes, or until golden brown. Serve hot or cold and cut into slices at the table.

BREADED SARDINES

Serves 4

2¼ lb fresh sardines	⅔–1 cup fine fresh breadcrumbs
2 cloves garlic	¼ cup olive oil
1 tablespoon chopped parsley	2 lemons, sliced

Scrape the sardines to remove the scales and then clean them. Cut off the heads and remove the backbones. Peel and chop the garlic. Mix together the garlic, parsley and breadcrumbs.

Brush the sardines with some of the olive oil and then coat with the breadcrumb mixture. Pour the remaining oil into an ovenproof dish and arrange the sardines in the dish. Bake in a preheated moderate oven (350°) for 15–20 minutes, or until the sardines are cooked and the breadcrumbs are crisp. Garnish the sardines with the lemon slices and serve hot.

TUNA FISH WITH TOMATOES

Serves 6

6 fresh tuna steaks, about 6–8 oz each	3 tablespoons chopped parsley
3 medium-sized onions	1 tablespoon salt
2 cloves garlic	1 teaspoon sugar
2¼ lb tomatoes	1 sprig fresh peppermint or ¼ teaspoon dried peppermint

Wipe the tuna steaks with a damp cloth. Peel and chop the onions, garlic and tomatoes.

Heat the oil in a flameproof casserole or a deep skillet and sauté the tuna steaks for about 5 minutes on each side, or until golden brown. Drain on absorbent paper. Sauté the onion and garlic in the oil remaining in the casserole or skillet until lightly browned. Return the tuna steaks to the casserole and reheat for 2 minutes. Add the tomatoes, parsley, salt, sugar and peppermint, cover tightly and cook over very low heat for 20–30 minutes. Draw the pan to the side of the heat and let stand for about 15 minutes before serving.

MARINATED BONITO WITH MIXED VEGETABLES

Serves 6

2 lb bonito or tuna fish	1 cup white wine
1 small onion	2 lb fresh peas
2 medium-sized carrots	1 small cauliflower
2 cloves garlic	all-purpose flour for coating
6 black peppercorns	oil for shallow-frying
3 tablespoons olive oil	6 thick slices bread
3 tablespoons vinegar	6 tablespoons butter
1 lb shallots	

Cut the fish into 6 slices and place in a bowl. Peel and chop the onion, carrots and garlic and sprinkle over the fish. Add the peppercorns, oil and vinegar, and set aside to marinate for 24 hours.

Peel the shallots and place in a saucepan along with the white wine. Bring to a boil over moderate heat, then lower the heat, cover the pan tightly and simmer for 20–25 minutes, or until tender. Shell the peas and cook in lightly salted boiling water for 8–10 minutes, or until tender. Break the cauliflower into florets and rinse well under cold running water. Cook in lightly salted boiling water for about 10 minutes, or until tender.

Meanwhile, remove the slices of fish from the marinade and coat them with flour. Sauté in hot oil for about 4–5 minutes on each side, until cooked and golden brown. Drain on absorbent paper and keep hot. Fry the slices of bread in the same skillet until crisp and golden brown. Drain well and place in the center of a large heated serving dish. Arrange the slices of fish around the bread.

Drain the shallots, peas and cauliflower. Toss the peas in half the butter and the cauliflower in the remainder. Spoon the vegetables over the fried bread and serve.

FISH AND VEGETABLE STEW

Serves 6

2 lb bonito or tuna fish	6 tablespoons olive oil
1 leek	4 oz tomatoes
1 medium-sized carrot	3 tablespoons dried sweet pepper flakes
4 stalks celery	
2 teaspoons salt	2¼ lb potatoes
2½ pints water	2 sprigs mint
1 clove garlic	dash paprika
1 medium-sized onion	6 tablespoons dry white wine
1 green sweet pepper	

Rinse the fish under cold running water. Dry with absorbent paper and cut into 2-inch pieces. Trim the leek and rinse under cold running water. Peel the carrot. Place the leek, carrot and celery in a large saucepan. Add the salt and water and bring to a boil over high heat. Lower the heat, cover and simmer for 15–20 minutes. Strain and reserve the stock, discarding the vegetables.

Meanwhile, peel and chop the garlic and onion. Remove the seeds from the sweet pepper and chop the flesh. Heat half the oil in a skillet and sauté the garlic, onion and sweet pepper for about 10 minutes, or until soft. Remove from the heat and set aside until required. Peel and chop the tomatoes. Heat the remaining oil in a flameproof casserole or a large saucepan and add the tomatoes, pepper flakes and the sautéed vegetables. Sauté gently for 10 minutes, stirring frequently, to make a thick tomato sauce.

Peel the potatoes and cut into thick slices. Place the fish in the casserole, submerging the pieces in the sauce, and cover with the potato slices. Add the mint, paprika, white wine and reserved stock, covering the potatoes completely. Bring to a boil, then lower the heat and simmer for 30 minutes. Serve hot in the casserole.

PEASANT'S SALAD WITH VINEGAR DRESSING

Serves 4

1 red sweet pepper	**for the vinegar dressing:**
2 hard-cooked eggs	3 canned red pimientos
1 medium-sized onion	2 hard-cooked eggs
8 oz tomatoes	3 tablespoons olive oil
8 oz cooked green beans	6 tablespoons vinegar
8 oz canned tuna fish	3 tablespoons finely chopped
½ cup ripe olives	onion
4 cooked artichoke hearts	¼ cup capers
8 oz cooked asparagus	1 tablespoon chopped parsley
	salt

Bake the pepper in a preheated moderately hot oven (400°) for 10–15 minutes, or until the skin is charred. Peel the pepper, remove the seeds and cut into rings. Shell the eggs and cut into slices. Peel and thinly slice the onion and tomatoes. Cut the green beans into 1½-inch lengths. In a large bowl, mix together the pepper, eggs, onion, tomatoes, beans, tuna fish, olives, artichoke hearts and asparagus.

To make the vinegar dressing, finely chop the canned pimientos. Separate the egg whites from the yolks. Chop the egg whites and add to the salad. Pound the yolks to a paste. Mix together the oil and the vinegar and add to the egg yolks very gradually, beating well after each addition, until the mixture thickens slightly. Stir in the pimientos, chopped onion, capers, parsley and salt to taste.

Pour the vinegar dressing over the salad and serve.

SUMMER SALAD

Serves 4

2 large beets	¼ teaspoon freshly ground white
2 large potatoes	pepper
8 oz dried salt cod	3 tablespoons vinegar
4 oz shallots	⅔ cup olive oil
1 clove garlic	6 tablespoons water
2 medium-sized tomatoes	4 hard-cooked eggs
1 tablespoon chopped parsley	¾ cup ripe olives

Rinse the beets and potatoes thoroughly under cold running water. Cook the beets in boiling water for about 1 hour, or until tender. Drain and peel. Cook the potatoes in boiling water for about 20–25 minutes. Drain and peel. Slice the beets and potatoes into rounds about ¼–½ inch thick and place in a deep salad bowl.

Place the cod in a roasting pan and bake in a preheated moderately hot oven (400°) for 15–20 minutes. When the cod is cool enough to handle, remove the bones. Flake the fish and place in a bowl under cold running water to remove the salt.

Meanwhile, peel and finely chop the shallots and garlic. Peel and chop the tomatoes. Mix together the shallots, garlic, tomatoes, parsley, pepper, vinegar, oil and water and beat well. Shell and slice the eggs.

Drain the cod thoroughly, place in the bowl with the beets and potatoes and sprinkle with the tomato mixture. Toss lightly. Garnish the salad with slices of egg and the ripe olives. Serve well chilled.

LAMB PLUCK WITH EGGS

Serves 4

1–2 lamb plucks (liver, heart	2 tablespoons all-purpose flour
and lungs), about 1 lb	1 cup dry white wine
1 medium-sized onion	1 teaspoon salt
3 cloves garlic	dash pepper
⅔ cup olive oil	dash nutmeg
1 sprig parsley	8 eggs
1 bay leaf	

Cut away any gristle and membrane from the lamb plucks and dice finely. Peel and chop the onion and garlic.

Heat the oil in a skillet and sauté the onion, garlic, parsley and bay leaf until the onion is soft but not brown. Remove from the skillet and drain on absorbent paper. Sauté the lamb plucks in the oil remaining in the skillet until lightly browned and tender. Stir in the flour. Add the wine, salt, pepper and nutmeg and simmer for 5 minutes. Stir in the onion, garlic and parsley. Discard the bay leaf. Transfer the mixture to a shallow ovenproof dish. Lightly beat the eggs and pour over the lamb plucks. Bake in a preheated moderately hot oven (375°) for 6–10 minutes, or until the egg has set. Serve immediately.

CASSEROLE OF LAMB TONGUES

Serves 6

6 lamb tongues	1 leek
1 tablespoon salt	1 stalk celery
6 oz summer squash	3 sprigs parsley
1 small onion	1 sprig thyme
2 cloves garlic	6 tablespoons olive oil
1 large carrot	6 tablespoons white wine
2 medium-sized tomatoes	¼ cup melted lard
1 medium-sized potato	⅔ cup fine fresh breadcrumbs

Rinse the lamb tongues thoroughly under cold running water and place in a saucepan. Add 1 teaspoon of the salt and enough water to cover. Bring to a boil over moderate heat, then lower the heat, cover tightly and simmer for about 1½ hours, or until tender.

Meanwhile, peel the squash, onion, garlic, carrot, tomatoes and potato and slice thinly. Trim the leek, rinse thoroughly under cold running water and slice into rings. Chop the celery. Place all the prepared vegetables in a large flameproof casserole or saucepan with the parsley and the remaining salt.

Drain the tongues and, while still warm, remove the skins. Place the tongues on top of the vegetables and sprinkle with the oil. Sauté very gently over moderate heat, stirring the ingredients occasionally, until the tongues are lightly browned on all sides and the vegetables are almost tender. Add the white wine, cover and simmer for 20 minutes.

Remove the tongues from the casserole or saucepan and drain well. Brush with the melted lard and coat with the breadcrumbs. Place in a roasting pan and cook in a preheated very hot oven (425°) for 5 minutes.

Place the tongues in the center of a heated serving dish. Drain the vegetables, place around the edge and serve.

MADRID COCIDO

Serves 6

8 oz chick peas	1 carrot
4½ pints water	1–2 teaspoons salt
1 lb beef brisket	3 medium-sized potatoes
4 oz Canadian-style bacon, in 1 piece	1 large head cabbage, about 2 lb
1 small stewing chicken, about 1–2 lb	6 oz *chorizo* or garlic sausage
1 onion	1 *butifarra* (blood sausage)
1 leek	3 tablespoons olive oil
	8 oz fine egg noodles

Cover the chick peas with cold water and set aside to soak overnight. Drain well. Pour the water into a large saucepan, place over high heat and bring to a boil. Add the chick peas, beef, bacon and chicken. Bring back to a boil and skim the surface.

Meanwhile, peel the onion. Trim the leek and wash thoroughly under cold running water. Peel the carrot and cut into slices. Add the onion, leek, carrot and salt to the pan. Cover tightly, lower the heat and simmer for 3 hours.

While the *cocido* is cooking, peel and cut the potatoes into even-sized pieces. Set aside in cold water to cover. Discard the coarse outer leaves of the cabbage, cut in half and cut away the hard center core. Shred the cabbage and wash well in salted water.

About 20 minutes before the end of the cooking time, add the potatoes to the *cocido*. In a separate saucepan, cook the cabbage, *chorizo* and *butifarra* in boiling salted water for 15 minutes, or until the cabbage is tender. Using a perforated spoon, lift out the sausages and keep hot. Drain the cabbage and return it to the pan with the olive oil. Reheat gently when required.

Draw the cooked *cocido* off the heat, remove the beef, bacon and chicken and, using a perforated spoon, lift out the chick peas and vegetables. Add the fine egg noodles to the hot stock, replace the pan over the heat and simmer for a further 10 minutes. Cut the sausages, beef, bacon and chicken into slices.

Place a mound of the cooked chick peas in the center of a large serving dish. Arrange the sausage, meat and chicken slices around the edge of the dish. Pile the cooked vegetables at each end. Keep hot. Serve the reheated cabbage separately.

Pour the hot stock and noodles into a soup tureen and serve as the first course followed by the dish of meats and vegetables and the cabbage as the main course.

Some ingredients for a typical cocido (boiled dinner)

COUNTRY LAMB STEW

Serves 8–10

4 lb boned lamb, cut from the shoulder or leg	4½ pints water
6 cloves garlic	1 lamb liver
1¼ cups olive oil	⅔ cup fine fresh breadcrumbs
4 teaspoons salt	1 chili
½ teaspoon pepper	6 tablespoons water
	3 tablespoons wine vinegar

Chop the lamb into 2½-inch pieces. Peel and chop the garlic. Heat three-fourths of the oil in a large casserole or saucepan. Add the lamb and garlic and sauté for about 15 minutes, or until golden brown. Sprinkle with the salt and pepper and add the 4½ pints water. Bring to a boil, then lower the heat, cover tightly and simmer the lamb for about 30–40 minutes, or until tender.

Meanwhile, thickly slice the liver. Heat the remaining oil in a skillet and fry the liver until lightly browned but still soft in the center. Remove from the skillet and drain well on absorbent paper. Sauté the breadcrumbs in the oil remaining in the skillet until very lightly browned. Remove from the skillet and drain on absorbent paper.

Remove the seeds from the chili and chop the flesh very finely. Pound the liver, breadcrumbs and chili in a mortar until reduced to a paste. Add the 6 tablespoons water and the wine vinegar and stir the mixture into the simmering lamb about 5–10 minutes before the end of the cooking time. Transfer to a heated serving dish and serve.

CASSEROLED VEAL RIB CHOPS WITH WINE

Serves 6

6 veal rib chops, about 6 oz each	6 tablespoons olive oil
2 teaspoons salt	⅔ cup dry white wine
½ cup all-purpose flour	⅓ cup water
2¼ lb shallots	1 tablespoon chopped parsley
2 large potatoes	

Season the rib chops with salt and coat with flour. Peel the shallots and potatoes. Cut the potatoes into strips similar in size to the shallots. Cover the potatoes with cold water until required.

Heat the oil in a skillet and saute the rib chops for about 5 minutes on each side, or until well browned. Transfer to a casserole and add the white wine and water. Cover and place in a preheated moderately hot oven for 15 minutes.

Meanwhile, drain and dry the potatoes. Sauté the shallots and potatoes in the oil remaining in the skillet for 5–10 minutes or until browned on all sides. Add to the casserole and cook for a further 15–20 minutes, or until the meat, shallots and potatoes are tender.

Sprinkle with the chopped parsley and serve in the casserole.

Veal and ham rolls with orange sauce

VEAL AND HAM ROLLS WITH ORANGE SAUCE

Serves 4

4 veal escalopes, about 4 oz each	2 tablespoons butter
4 slices *serrano* or mild-cure	dash nutmeg
smoked ham, about 2 oz each	thinly pared rind of ½ orange
1 teaspoon salt	**for the sauce:**
¼ teaspoon pepper	1 small onion
1 beaten egg	2 teaspoons cornstarch
½ cup fine dry breadcrumbs	½ cup fresh orange juice
6 tablespoons olive oil	½ teaspoon grated orange rind
2 lb potatoes	6 tablespoons dry sherry
½ cup milk	

If the veal escalopes are too thick to roll up, flatten them with a meat mallet. They should be the same size as the slices of ham. Place one slice of ham on each veal escalope. Roll up with the veal on the outside and secure with toothpicks. Sprinkle with salt and pepper and coat with the beaten egg and the breadcrumbs.

Heat the oil in a skillet and sauté the veal rolls for 10–15 minutes, or until tender and golden brown. Drain on absorbent paper, place in a heated serving dish and keep hot.

Peel the potatoes and cut into small pieces. Cook in lightly salted boiling water until tender. Drain well and mash very thoroughly with the milk, butter and nutmeg.

While the potatoes are cooking, prepare the sauce. Peel and finely chop the onion. Reheat the oil remaining in the skillet and sauté the onion until lightly browned. Stir in the cornstarch and cook for 1 minute. Add the orange juice, grated orange rind and sherry, a little at a time, stirring thoroughly after each addition. Bring to a boil, stirring constantly, and simmer very gently for 5–10 minutes.

Pour the orange sauce over the veal and ham rolls, garnish with the mashed potato and the pared orange rind and serve.

HAM WITH MÁLAGA SAUCE

Serves 4

6 tablespoons butter	4 slices *serrano* or mild-cure
⅔ cup Málaga wine or port	smoked ham, about 4 oz each

Melt the butter in a heavy skillet. Add the wine and simmer gently for 10 minutes. Place the slices of ham in the skillet and simmer for 8–10 minutes, or until the wine has reduced to about a quarter of the original quantity. Transfer to a heated serving dish and serve immediately with sautéed potatoes as an accompaniment.

Note: Málaga wine is strong and sweet, similar to the wine of Oporto. It combines with the ham to make a dish with a unique, sophisticated taste.

The following three recipes may be adapted and varied according to ingredients available. Morcilla may be substituted for butifarra, salt pork for bacon, etc.

ASTURIAN FABADA

Serves 6

1 lb navy beans	2 *morcillas* (see note)
4 oz salt pork, in 1 piece	4 oz Canadian-style bacon, in
generous 3 pints water	1 piece
10 saffron strands or ¼ teaspoon	4 oz *serrano* or mild-cure smoked
ground saffron	ham
1 *chorizo* or garlic sausage	salt

Soak the beans overnight in plenty of cold water. Soak the piece of salt pork separately for about 1 hour in cold water. Drain the beans and pork well before using.

Place the beans and salt pork in a flameproof casserole and add the water to completely cover the beans. Place over moderate heat and bring to a boil. Lower the heat immediately and simmer gently for about 1 hour.

Meanwhile, if using saffron strands, pound them to a powder in a mortar. When the beans have been cooking for 1 hour, add the *chorizo*, *morcillas*, bacon, *serrano* ham and saffron. Do not cover the casserole. Cook very gently for 2–3 hours without stirring. The beans should absorb all the liquid and be tender, but unbroken.

Just before the end of the cooking sprinkle lightly with salt to taste and serve from the casserole.

Note: Morcilla is a pork sausage similar to a blood sausage.

SAUSAGE AND BEAN CASSEROLE

Serves 4

4½ lb fresh fava or lima beans	3–4 sprigs mint
5 slices bacon	2 teaspoons salt
1 medium-sized onion	6 tablespoons dry white wine
3 cloves garlic	4 oz *butifarra* (blood sausage)
1 large tomato	1 tablespoon chopped parsley
2 tablespoons lard	1 bay leaf

Shell the beans. Cut the bacon into small pieces. Peel and chop the onion, garlic and tomato. Heat the lard in a large saucepan and fry the bacon for 3–4 minutes. Add the onion and sauté until lightly browned. Add the tomato, mint sprigs, salt and beans and sauté for 10 minutes, stirring frequently. Add the wine, the whole *butifarra*, garlic, parsley and bay leaf. Cover tightly and simmer for about 15 minutes, or until the beans are tender. Transfer to a heated dish and serve.

Sausage and bean casserole

SIMMERED PORK AND BEANS

Serves 4

1 lb navy beans	4 oz Canadian-style bacon, in
2 medium-sized onions	1 piece
1 bulb garlic	4 oz smoked pork hock
4 oz fresh pork shoulder	2 teaspoons salt
1 pig's foot	3 saffron strands

Soak the beans overnight in plenty of cold water. Drain before using. Peel the onions and cut into quarters. Peel the garlic.

Place the beans in a large saucepan with the onion, garlic, pork shoulder, pig's foot, bacon, smoked pork hock, salt and saffron. Add enough water to completely cover the ingredients. Place over moderate heat and bring to a boil. Lower the heat, cover tightly and simmer for 2½–3 hours, or until the beans are very soft and the liquid has almost completely evaporated. Do not stir during the cooking as this will break the beans. Serve hot.

GROUND PORK PIE

Serves 6

for the pastry:	for the filling:
4 cups all-purpose flour	1 medium-sized onion
1 teaspoon salt	4 oz ham
6 tablespoons olive oil	¼ cup lard
6 tablespoons dry white wine	14 oz lean pork, ground
generous dash cinnamon	2 eggs
6 tablespoons milk	**for the glaze:**
2 tablespoons sugar	1 beaten egg

To make the dough, sift the flour and salt into a mixing bowl and make a well in the center. Mix together the olive oil, wine, cinnamon, milk and sugar and pour into the flour. Mix to a fairly firm dough and knead well until smooth. Cover with a damp cloth and set aside for about 1 hour.

To make the filling, peel and chop the onion. Chop the ham. Melt the lard in a skillet over moderate heat and sauté the onion until soft and lightly brown. Add the ham and the ground pork and sauté gently for about 15–20 minutes, or until tender. Beat the eggs and stir them into the meat mixture. Continue stirring until the egg sets, then remove from the heat immediately.

Divide the dough in half. Roll out one half into a 10-inch circle and place on a well-buttered baking sheet. Spread the prepared meat filling over the circle to within 1 inch of the edge. Brush the edge of the pastry with water. Roll out the remaining dough into a circle slightly larger than the base and place over the meat filling. Press the edges of the pastry firmly together, completely enclosing the filling. Flute the edge of the pie and make a small hole in the top to allow the steam to escape during cooking. Brush well with the beaten egg to glaze the surface. Bake in a preheated moderately hot oven (375°) for 30–40 minutes, or until golden brown. Serve hot or cold, cut into slices.

VALENCIA PAELLA

Serves 6

1 chicken, about 3 lb	4¼ cups water
1 tablespoon salt	1 teaspoon paprika
2 lb fresh peas	3 saffron strands
8 oz green beans	12 cooked snails
1 clove garlic	2¼ cups long-grain rice
1 medium-sized tomato	1 lemon, cut in wedges
6 tablespoons olive oil	

Cut the chicken into 14 or 16 pieces and sprinkle with the salt. Shell the peas. Trim the beans and cut into 2½-inch pieces. Peel and finely chop the garlic and tomato. Heat the oil in a *paella* pan or in a large heavy skillet. Sauté the chicken pieces for 5 minutes, then add the garlic and tomato and sauté for 2 minutes. Add the peas and beans and sauté for 2 minutes. Add the water and paprika and bring to a boil. Add the saffron strands and the snails. Lower the heat and simmer for 20 minutes. Add enough boiling water to replace the amount that has evaporated. Raise the heat until the water is boiling rapidly and then stir in the rice. Boil for 2 minutes, then lower the heat and simmer gently for about 12–15 minutes, or until the rice is tender and dry. Remove from the heat, but leave on the hot stove for 5 minutes. Garnish with the wedges of lemon and serve from the *paella* pan.

SAUTÉED CHICKEN WITH SWEET PEPPERS AND TOMATOES

Serves 6

1 chicken, about 3½ lb	8 oz *serrano* or mild-cure smoked
1 medium-sized onion	ham
2 cloves garlic	¾ cup olive oil
2¼ lb red sweet peppers	1 tablespoon salt
2¼ lb tomatoes	1 sprig parsley

Divide the chicken into 6 portions. Peel and finely chop the onion and garlic. Halve the peppers, remove the seeds and cut each pepper into 4 or 6 pieces. Peel and chop the tomatoes. Chop the ham.

Heat the oil in a flameproof casserole or saucepan. Sauté the chicken portions until well browned. Add the onion and half the garlic. Sauté until the onion is well browned and soft. Add the peppers and ham and sauté for 5 minutes. Add the tomatoes and salt. Cover tightly and cook very gently for 20–25 minutes, or until the chicken is tender.

Pound the remaining garlic with the parsley in a mortar and then mix in 1 tablespoon cold water. Stir this mixture into the casserole 10 minutes before the end of the cooking time.

Transfer to a heated serving dish and serve.

FRIED CHICKEN WITH MELON SALAD

Serves 6

1 chicken, about 3 lb
salt
6 cloves garlic
⅔ cup olive oil

for the salad:
1 lb melon (approximately
  ½ small honeydew)

1 lb dessert apples
1 cup shelled walnut halves
1 teaspoon finely grated lemon
  rind
6 tablespoons olive oil
salt

Divide the chicken into joints and remove the flesh from the bones. Cut the flesh into 1½-inch pieces and sprinkle with salt. Discard the bones. Peel the garlic and cut each clove in half lengthwise.

Heat the oil in a skillet and sauté the chicken for about 5 minutes. Add the garlic and sauté the chicken for a further 5–10 minutes, or until tender and golden brown. Drain well on absorbent paper and set aside to cool.

Meanwhile, peel the melon, remove the seeds and cut into pieces. Place in a deep salad bowl. Peel, core and slice the apples and add to the melon with the walnut halves, lemon rind and olive oil. Season with salt and toss lightly. Chill well. Arrange the chicken on a serving dish and serve with the melon salad.

WILD DUCK WITH FRIED VEGETABLES

Serves 6

1 wild duck, about 3½ lb
2 teaspoons salt
4 oz *serrano* or mild-cure smoked
  ham
¼ cup lard
¼ cup brandy
6 tablespoons dry white wine

for the vegetables:
2 medium-sized eggplants
1 egg
½ cup all-purpose flour
¾ cup olive oil
6 cooked artichoke hearts
2 large potatoes

Wipe the duck with a damp cloth and sprinkle with the salt. Finely chop the ham. Heat the lard in a flameproof casserole or large saucepan and sauté the duck until lightly browned on all sides. Add the ham and sauté until the duck is well browned, then pour in the brandy and simmer for 5 minutes. Add the wine, cover tightly and simmer gently for 1–1¼ hours, or until the duck is tender.

Meanwhile, to prepare the vegetables, wipe the eggplants with a damp cloth and cut into rounds ½–1 inch thick. Beat the egg, stir in the flour and coat the eggplants with the batter. Heat half the oil in a skillet and sauté the eggplants for 3–4 minutes on each side, or until tender and golden brown. Drain and keep hot. Coat the artichoke hearts in the same way and sauté for about 5 minutes, or until golden brown. Drain and keep hot. Peel the potatoes and cut into ½-inch cubes. Heat the remaining oil in the skillet and sauté the potatoes until tender, crisp and well browned. Drain well.

Transfer the duck to a heated serving dish and pour over any juices remaining in the casserole. Surround with the eggplants, artichokes and potatoes and serve.

SQUABS WITH BACON

Serves 6

6 squabs
1 lb shallots
2 medium-sized carrots
1 lb tomatoes
2¼ lb small new potatoes

6 slices Canadian-style bacon
¾ cup olive oil
¾ cup water
1 tablespoon vinegar

Rinse the squabs under cold running water and dry well with absorbent paper. Peel the shallots. Peel the carrots and cut into rounds. Peel and chop the tomatoes. Scrape the potatoes and cover with cold water until required. Line the bottom of a casserole with the bacon slices.

Heat the oil in a skillet and sauté the squabs for 5 minutes, or until lightly browned. Place in the casserole with the shallots, carrots and the drained potatoes. Pour the oil remaining in the skillet into the casserole. Cover tightly and cook in a preheated moderate oven (350°) for 40 minutes. Add the tomatoes, water and vinegar and cook for a further 40–50 minutes, or until the squabs are tender. Serve hot in the casserole.

QUAIL IN BRANDY SAUCE

Serves 4

8 quail
1 medium-sized carrot
2 cloves garlic
4 oz *serrano* or mild-cure smoked
  ham

3 tablespoons olive oil
3 tablespoons lard
2 teaspoons chopped parsley
2 teaspoons salt
⅔ cup brandy

Wipe the quail with a damp cloth and place in a flameproof casserole or large saucepan. Peel and chop the carrot and garlic. Chop the ham. Add the oil, lard, carrot, garlic, ham, parsley and salt to the casserole. Place over moderate heat for 5 minutes. Add the brandy and enough water to cover the quail completely, cover tightly and simmer for about 15–20 minutes, or until the quail are tender and the liquid is reduced by half.

Lift the quail from the casserole and arrange in a heated serving dish, pour over the sauce remaining in the casserole and serve.

Fried chicken with melon salad

SPICED WILD RABBIT STEW

Serves 6–8

1 rabbit, about 4½ lb	1 lb fresh asparagus
1 cup olive oil	2 large onions
2 cups white wine	1 bulb garlic
2 chilies	6 oz *chorizo* or garlic sausage
1 tablespoon salt	4½ lb potatoes
1 sprig thyme	2 bay leaves
3½ lb fresh fava or lima beans	1 tablespoon chopped parsley
3½ lb fresh peas or 1 lb frozen peas	2½–4 pints water
	6 young, tender globe artichokes

Rinse the rabbit under cold running water and pat dry with absorbent paper. Cut into small portions.

Heat the olive oil in a large cast-iron saucepan or heavy-based saucepan and sauté the rabbit pieces until lightly browned. Add the white wine, chilies, salt and thyme and bring to a boil. Lower the heat, cover the pan tightly and simmer the rabbit for 1 hour.

Meanwhile, shell the beans and peas. Cut off the woody fibrous base from each asparagus spear and lightly scrape any coarse skin from the lower half of the stem. Cook the peas and asparagus separately in lightly salted boiling water until tender. Drain and set aside until required. Peel and chop the onions. Peel the garlic. Cut the *chorizo* sausage into thick rounds. Peel the potatoes and cut into 2-inch cubes. Add the potatoes, onions, garlic, *chorizo*, bay leaves and chopped parsley to the rabbit and simmer gently for 15 minutes, or until the potatoes are partially cooked.

Meanwhile, cut the tips off the artichoke leaves and cut off the stems. Cut the artichokes in half and remove the chokes. Add the artichoke halves to the ingredients in the pan with the beans and the water, which should be sufficient to cover the ingredients. Bring to a boil, then lower the heat and simmer, partly covered, for about 20 minutes, or until the artichokes are almost tender. Add the pre-cooked peas and asparagus and heat through for a further 10 minutes. Remove from the heat, transfer to a heated serving dish and serve.

HARE IN CHOCOLATE SAUCE

Serves 4

1 small hare or about 2¼ lb hare pieces	12 oz shallots
4 cloves garlic	¾ cup olive oil
2 small onions	3 large tomatoes
2 medium-sized carrots	6 tablespoons dry white wine
1 bay leaf	¼ cup pine nuts
6 tablespoons red wine	¼ cup grated unsweetened cooking chocolate

Divide the hare into 8 pieces and place in a bowl. Peel 2 cloves of the garlic. Peel and thinly slice 1 onion and the carrots. Add the onion, carrots, peeled garlic, bay leaf and red wine to the hare pieces. Set aside to marinate for 24 hours.

Peel the shallots and cook in lightly salted boiling water

for 15 minutes. Drain and set aside until required. Heat the oil in a skillet. Remove the hare from the marinade and sauté the pieces in the hot oil for about 10 minutes, or until well browned. Remove from the skillet and place in a casserole.

Peel and chop the tomatoes. Peel and slice the remaining onion and garlic and sauté in the oil remaining in the skillet until lightly browned. Add the tomatoes and sauté until reduced to a pulp. Stir in the white wine and cooked shallots and pour the mixture over the hare. Pound the pine nuts in a mortar and sprinkle the nuts and the grated chocolate over the hare. Cover and cook in a preheated moderately hot oven (375°) for 1–1¼ hours, or until the hare is tender. Transfer to a heated serving dish and serve.

PARTRIDGES IN SALMOREJO SAUCE

Serves 4

4 partridges	2 fresh red sweet peppers or canned red pimientos
1 medium-sized onion	
1 bay leaf	8 hard-cooked eggs
1 tablespoon salt	6 tablespoons olive oil
4½ pints water	dash pepper
for the salmorejo sauce:	1 tablespoon vinegar
1½ pints stock (see recipe)	

Rinse the partridges under cold running water, drain and place in a large saucepan. Peel the onion and add to the pan with the bay leaf, salt and water. Place over high heat and bring to a boil. Lower the heat, cover tightly and simmer for about 45 minutes–1 hour, or until tender. Remove the partridges from the pan with a perforated spoon and set aside to cool. Reserve the 1½ pints stock.

If using fresh sweet peppers, place in a preheated hot oven (425°) for about 15 minutes, or until the skins are charred. Peel the peppers, remove the seeds and shred the flesh finely. If using canned pimientos, drain and shred finely.

Separate the egg yolks from the whites. Finely chop the whites. Pound the yolks in a bowl. Add the olive oil gradually, beating well after each addition. Add the pepper, vinegar, egg whites, sweet peppers or pimientos and the reserved stock and mix the sauce thoroughly.

Divide each partridge into four and place in a deep casserole. Pour the sauce over the partridges and set aside for 1 hour so the flavors in the sauce are absorbed by the partridge flesh. Serve cold.

STUFFED ONIONS

Serves 4

1 clove garlic	1 tablespoon lemon juice
12 oz lean pork, ground	8 large Spanish onions
1 teaspoon salt	1 cup fine fresh breadcrumbs
¼ teaspoon pepper	all-purpose flour for coating
dash cinnamon	⅔ cup olive oil
2 teaspoons finely chopped parsley	¼ cup all-purpose flour
	3 tablespoons dry white wine
1 egg	¾ cup water
3 tablespoons milk	

Peel and finely chop the garlic. Place the pork in a bowl, add the garlic, salt, pepper, cinnamon, parsley, egg, milk and lemon juice and mix together thoroughly. Set aside for about 30 minutes.

Peel the onions and cut a thin slice off the top of each one. Scoop out the inside of each onion and set aside, leaving only the 2 outer layers completely intact. Fill the onions with the prepared meat mixture and press the breadcrumbs on top. Roll the onions in flour to coat thoroughly.

Heat the oil in a heavy skillet over low heat and fry the stuffed onions very gently for about 20 minutes, or until golden brown. Baste frequently. Remove the onions carefully and drain on absorbent paper. Place in a shallow casserole.

Finely chop the reserved onion and sauté in the oil remaining in the skillet until lightly browned and soft. Stir in the flour and cook for about 30 seconds. Remove from the heat and gradually stir in the wine and water, mixing well after each addition. Bring to a boil over moderate heat, stirring constantly until the mixture thickens. Spoon the mixture over the stuffed onions. Bake the onions in a preheated moderate oven (325°) for about 1 hour, or until tender. Serve hot.

SAUTÉED VEGETABLES WITH SCRAMBLED EGGS

Serves 4

1 green sweet pepper	1 large potato
8 oz zucchini	6 tablespoons olive oil
1 medium-sized eggplant	2 teaspoons salt
1 medium-sized onion	6 eggs
1 lb tomatoes	

Halve the pepper, remove the seeds and chop the flesh. Cut the zucchini and eggplant into ½-inch rounds. Peel and chop the onion and tomatoes. Peel the potato and cut into ½-inch rounds.

Heat the oil in a heavy skillet. Add the pepper, zucchini, eggplant, onion, potato and salt. Sauté the vegetables for 10–15 minutes, or until lightly browned. Add the tomatoes and cook the mixture very gently for a further 15–20 minutes, or until all the vegetables are soft.

Beat the eggs and pour into the vegetable mixture. Stir very gently until the egg begins to thicken; it should not be allowed to set on the bottom of the pan. Serve immediately with fresh, crusty bread.

Spiced wild rabbit stew

165

FLAMBÉED CARAMEL CUSTARDS

Serves 6

for the caramel:
¼ cup sugar
3 tablespoons water

for the custard:
3 eggs

½ cup sugar
2 cups milk
generous dash cinnamon
thinly pared rind of 1 lemon
¾ cup rum or brandy

To make the caramel, place the sugar and water in a small heavy saucepan. Place over low heat until the sugar dissolves, then raise the heat to moderate and boil the syrup until it begins to turn golden brown. Remove from the heat immediately and pour a little into 6 ramekins or custard cups.

To make the custard, lightly beat together the eggs and sugar in a bowl. Pour the milk into a saucepan and add the cinnamon and lemon rind. Place over moderate heat until simmering. Remove from the heat and stir into the egg mixture. Discard the lemon rind and pour an equal quantity of the custard into each ramekin. Place the ramekins in a large saucepan and add enough water to come about two-thirds of the way up the sides of the ramekins. Bring to a boil over moderate heat. Lower the heat, cover the pan tightly and cook the custards for 10–15 minutes, or until set. Alternatively, place the ramekins in a deep roasting pan and add the water. Bake in a preheated cool oven (300°) for about 1 hour, or until set.

While still hot, turn out the custards on to a serving dish. Heat the rum or brandy in a ladle or small saucepan over an open flame until simmering. Tilt the container and allow the flame to ignite the rum or brandy. Burn for about 10 seconds and then pour over the custards. Spoon the flaming rum or brandy over the custards until the flames are extinguished. Serve immediately.

TURRON (ALMOND BRITTLE)

Makes 2¼ lb

1 tablespoon water
½ teaspoon lemon juice
2 cups sugar

3 cups blanched almonds
4 oz miniature candies

Put the water, lemon juice and sugar into a heavy saucepan. Place over low heat until the sugar has completely dissolved. Raise the heat to moderate and boil the syrup until it becomes golden brown. Remove from the heat immediately and stir in the almonds. Pour the mixture on to a well-greased marble slab or baking sheet and decorate with the miniature candies. Set aside until cold. Break into small pieces for serving. *Turron* can be stored in an airtight container or glass jar.

Flambéed caramel custards

BAKED APPLES WITH SHERRY

Serves 6

6 large baking apples
2 hard-cooked eggs
1 teaspoon anisette

6 tablespoons medium sweet
  sherry
½ cup sugar
2 tablespoons melted butter

Rinse the apples under cold running water. Remove the cores, taking care not to cut too deeply into the flesh.

Separate the egg yolks from the whites and reserve the whites for another dish. Pound the yolks to a paste. Add the anisette and mix well. Add the sherry gradually, mixing well after each addition. Stir in the sugar and the melted butter. Stand the apples in a shallow baking dish and spoon some of the mixture into the center of each one. Bake in a preheated hot oven (425°) for about 30–40 minutes, or until tender. If the skins of the apples become too brown before they are cooked, lower the heat after 30 minutes to 375° and bake for an extra 10–15 minutes. Serve hot or cold.

EGG AND SUGAR CANDIES

Makes about 18

12 egg yolks
¼ cup water
1 cup sugar
thinly pared rind of 1 lemon

stick cinnamon, about
  1 inch long
¼ cup sugar for coating

Beat the egg yolks and strain through a sieve into a bowl. Pour the water into a heavy saucepan. Add the sugar, lemon rind and cinnamon. Place over low heat until the sugar has completely dissolved and a thin syrup has formed. Raise the heat and simmer, stirring constantly, until the syrup begins to thicken and form threads. To test, dip a spoon into the hot syrup, then touch the syrup coating quickly with a knife blade. Small threads should draw out as the knife is lifted away. Remove from the heat and discard the lemon rind and the cinnamon stick. Pour the egg yolks into the syrup in a continuous stream, beating constantly. Return the pan to low heat and cook very gently, still stirring constantly, until the mixture forms a thick paste in the center of the pan. This takes about 5 minutes.

Spread the mixture on to a plate or a wooden board and set aside until cool enough to handle. Sprinkle with half the sugar and divide into small pieces. Roll each piece into a ball about 1 inch in diameter. Toss the balls in the remaining sugar and place in paper or foil candy cases. Serve freshly made or store in an airtight container until required.

ORANGE OMELET

Serves 1

2 eggs	sugar for sprinkling
1 tablespoon sugar	dash cinnamon
dash salt	3 tablespoons rum
1 tablespoon butter	3 tablespoons brandy
¼ cup orange marmalade	

Beat the eggs with the sugar and salt. Melt the butter in an omelet pan or skillet over moderate heat. Pour the egg into the pan and cook gently until the egg sets. Spoon the marmalade over the center of the omelet, fold in half and transfer to a heated plate.

Sprinkle the sugar and cinnamon over the omelet and with a red-hot poker burn a crisscross pattern in the sugar. Warm the rum and brandy, pour over the omelet and flambé at the table. Serve immediately the flames are extinguished.

ICED MILK DESSERT

Serves 6

1 lemon	1 cup sugar
4¼ cups milk	3 egg whites
stick cinnamon	ground cinnamon

Thinly pare the rind from the lemon and place it in a saucepan with the milk, cinnamon stick and three-fourths of the sugar. Bring to a boil over moderate heat, then set aside until cold. Discard the lemon rind and the cinnamon stick.

Beat the egg whites until stiff and then beat in the remaining sugar. Fold the egg white mixture into the cold milk and pour into 6 individual glasses. Place in the freezing compartment of the refrigerator until beginning to set, then sprinkle with ground cinnamon and serve.

FILLED SPONGE FINGERS

Makes 24

for the sponge fingers:	½ cup sugar
4 eggs	6 egg yolks
generous ½ cup sugar	**for the syrup:**
generous cup all-purpose flour	⅔ cup water
for the filling:	3–4 drops lemon extract
6 tablespoons water	1¼ cups sugar

Beat together the eggs and sugar in a bowl over simmering water until thick and creamy. Add the flour and fold in very carefully, using a metal spoon. Using a pastry bag with a large fluted tip, pipe 3-inch lengths of the mixture on to a baking sheet lined with waxed paper. Bake in a preheated

Orange omelet

cool oven (300°) for 20–25 minutes, or until crisp and lightly browned. Leave the sponge fingers on the baking sheet until cool, then remove from the waxed paper and place on a wire rack until cold.

To make the filling, place the water and sugar in a heavy saucepan. Heat gently until the sugar has completely dissolved. Raise the heat and boil the syrup until it thickens very slightly and begins to form threads. Remove from the heat and cool for about 5 minutes. Beat the egg yolks and pour into the syrup in a thin continuous stream, beating constantly. Return the pan to low heat and cook the mixture until it becomes thick and smooth. While the filling is still warm, spread the mixture over the bottom of each sponge finger and sandwich them together in pairs.

To make the syrup, place the water, lemon extract and sugar in a heavy saucepan. Heat gently until the sugar has dissolved. Raise the heat and boil the syrup until it becomes slightly thick. Remove from the heat and set aside to cool. Dip the filled sponge fingers in the syrup and place on a wire rack until cold. Serve freshly made or store in an airtight container lined with waxed paper.

SWEET WINE CAKES

Makes 8–12

6 eggs	**for the syrup:**
6 tablespoons sugar	½ cup water
¼ teaspoon grated lemon rind	1¼ cups sugar
2 cups all-purpose flour	dash cinnamon
	6 tablespoons sweet white wine

Separate the egg whites from the egg yolks. Place the egg yolks, sugar and lemon rind in a mixing bowl and beat well until thick and creamy. Sift the flour and fold into the egg yolk mixture with a metal spoon. Beat the egg whites until stiff and fold into the mixture. Pour into a large greased and lined jelly roll pan and bake in a preheated moderately hot oven (400°) for 20–25 minutes, or until well risen and golden brown. When slightly cool, turn out of the pan and cut into 8 to 12 pieces.

Meanwhile, to make the syrup, heat the water, sugar and cinnamon in a small heavy saucepan over low heat until the sugar has completely dissolved. Raise the heat and boil the syrup until it becomes thick. Remove from the heat, stir in the wine and set aside to cool.

Place the pieces of cake on a tray and pour the syrup over. Sprinkle with cinnamon and set aside for about 3 hours before serving so the cakes are thoroughly saturated with the syrup. Serve when freshly made as a dessert or store in an airtight container lined with waxed paper.

Filled sponge fingers

169

HOLY WEEK FRIED CAKES

Makes about 36

3 eggs
6 tablespoons olive oil
6 tablespoons milk
3 tablespoons brandy

2 tablespoons sugar
about 4 cups all-purpose flour
oil for deep-frying
½ cup sugar for dusting

Beat together the eggs, olive oil, milk, brandy and sugar in a mixing bowl. Add the flour gradually, beating well after each addition. When the mixture becomes firm, knead in enough flour to make a firm smooth dough. Knead the dough lightly on a floured surface and roll out to ⅛ inch thick. Cut into 3-inch squares or 4- by 2-inch rectangles.

Deep-fry in hot oil for about 1 minute, or until well risen and golden brown. Drain well on absorbent paper and, while still warm, sprinkle with sugar. Serve freshly made.

FRIED LEMON PASTRIES

Makes about 60

½ cake compressed yeast or
  ½ envelope active dry yeast
1 tablespoon warm water
3 eggs
1 teaspoon grated lemon rind
6 tablespoons olive oil

1 cup sugar
2–3 drops oil of lemon or
  lemon extract
3½ cups all-purpose flour
oil for deep-frying
sugar for coating

If using compressed yeast, blend the yeast with the warm water in a large bowl. If using dry yeast, add 1 teaspoon of the sugar to the water, sprinkle in the dry yeast and set aside for 10 minutes until frothy. Add the eggs and beat until slightly frothy. Add the lemon rind, olive oil, sugar and oil of lemon or lemon extract. Beat the mixture until it becomes thick and creamy. Sift the flour gently into the egg mixture and fold in carefully with a metal spoon.

Drop small teaspoons of the mixture into hot oil and fry until crisp and golden brown. Drain well on absorbent paper and toss in sugar. Serve freshly made or store in an airtight container until required.

ALMOND CAKE

Serves 10

12 eggs
2 cups sugar
dash cinnamon
1 teaspoon grated lemon rind

4 cups finely ground almonds
½ cup fine cookie crumbs
sugar for dusting

Separate the egg yolks from the whites. Place the yolks in a bowl with the sugar and beat until thick and creamy. Stir in the cinnamon, lemon rind and ground almonds. Beat the egg whites until stiff and carefully stir into the almond mixture, using a metal spoon.

Grease a 10-inch spring-form pan and coat with the cookie crumbs. Spoon the prepared batter into the pan. Bake in a preheated moderate oven (350°) for 1 hour, or until firm and golden brown. While still warm, turn the cake out on to a wire rack and set aside to cool. Sprinkle with the sugar and cut into slices for serving.

ALMOND COOKIES

Makes 30–36

1 cup lard
¾ cup sugar
1 egg
½ teaspoon grated lemon rind

generous dash cinnamon
about 4 cups all-purpose flour
1 cup finely ground almonds
¼ cup confectioners' sugar

Cream the lard with the sugar in a mixing bowl until soft and creamy. Beat the egg and gradually whisk it into the creamed mixture with the grated lemon rind and the cinnamon. Knead in the flour gradually, forming a fairly soft dough. Knead in the ground almonds. Roll the dough out on a lightly floured surface to about ½ inch thick. Cut into circles with a 2-inch cutter and place on a baking sheet. Bake in a preheated moderate oven (325°) for 25–30 minutes, or until golden brown.

While still warm, lightly dust the cookies with the confectioners' sugar and place on a wire rack to cool. Serve freshly baked or store in an airtight container until required.

ANISE COOKIES

Makes 16–18

1 egg
½ cup olive oil
6 tablespoons sugar
1 tablespoon anisette

6 tablespoons dry white wine
½ teaspoon grated lemon rind
about 3 cups all-purpose flour

Place the egg, oil, sugar, anisette, wine and lemon rind in a bowl. Beat vigorously for 5 minutes until frothy and well blended. Gradually add the flour, stirring well after each addition until the mixture becomes a soft dough. Continue adding the flour, which should be kneaded in until the dough becomes smooth and fairly firm. It should not be sticky.

Roll the dough out on a lightly floured surface to about ¼ inch thick. Cut into circles with a 2½-inch cutter and place on a baking sheet. Bake in a preheated moderate oven (325°) for 20–30 minutes, or until crisp and golden brown. Cool on a wire rack and serve freshly baked or store in an airtight container until required.

Almond cake

ITALIAN

Luigi Veronelli

Photography by Eric Carter

Until quite recently, Italy was like a crazy paving of independent states. Although unification was finally achieved in 1861, the last century has failed to eradicate deep and basic differences between the Italian provinces, far greater than between provinces in most other countries of the world. But it is precisely because it rests on a dozen distinct traditions that the Italian cuisine is among the finest in the world. The concept of an *Italian* restaurant is as puzzling to the Italians as a *continental* restaurant is to continentals, but they would know what to expect in a restaurant offering Neapolitan, Genoese or Florentine specialties.

The stereotype of an Italian meal as understood outside Italy would lay heavy stress on spaghetti, olive oil and tomatoes. But spaghetti is only one of the many varieties of pasta prepared in innumerable ways – in broth, with shellfish, stuffed with meat and cheese. Nor is the pasta family, with all its ramifications, the only source of carbohydrate on the Italian table. In the northern provinces its place is usurped by rice, often served as a *risotto*, and corn meal pudding (*polenta*) which is served with almost everything and can be boiled, fried, broiled or baked. It can be eaten with butter and cheese and is the natural accompaniment to salt cod (*baccalà*). Bread is a staple food throughout the country.

As for olive oil, Italy produces great quantities of wonderful, fruity oil, basic to much of the cooking in the southernmost areas and the far north. But great quantities of good butter are used also. The Milanese cuisine is almost entirely dependent on it. In and around Rome, pork lard (*strutto*) is used.

Soup is rarely served with a meal that includes pasta or rice. Thick vegetable-and-pasta soups such as *minestrone* are really meals in themselves. Many Italian soups are thickened at the table with grated cheese.

Octopus, squid and cuttlefish are eaten by the million. Red mullet, anchovies and sardines, scampi and lobster, oysters and sea-urchins, fresh from the ocean, are a revelation to any palate.

Popular desserts include pastries and, of course, rich ice cream made of natural ingredients. And the cheeses, made of milk from cows, goats, ewes and buffalo, are varied and mouth-watering: Parmesan, the blue-veined Stracchino and Gorgonzola, Bel Paese, Fontina from Piedmont – the list is endless.

The islands of Sicily and Sardinia, with their own culinary contributions, should not be forgotten. Pasta, in fact, is said to have originated in Sicily in the thirteenth century. Macaroni with sardines and fennel is a famous Sicilian dish. Sicily has no great indigenous meat dishes. Sardinia has two, which are really rival ways of cooking a suckling pig.

Both islands have superb fish recipes and many good vegetable dishes. Oranges and lemons grow abundantly in Sicily and form the fruity basis of many ice creams. A favorite Sicilian dessert is Sicilian pastry horns, filled with sweetened Ricotta cheese mixed with pistachio nuts and candied peel. Among Sicilian wines the best known must be Marsala, a rich brown sweet wine used in the preparation of *zabaione*.

These recipes are designed to be within the scope of any non-Italian kitchen, and whether cooked at home or eaten abroad, these Italian dishes should provide great pleasure.

TRUFFLE FONDUE

Serves 4

⅔ cup milk	2 tablespoons butter
10 oz Fontina or Gruyère cheese, thinly sliced	1 large Alba truffle, thinly sliced
dash salt	4 slices toast
3 egg yolks	

Place 4 ramekins in the oven to warm. Pour half the milk into the top of a double boiler or into an ovenproof bowl, then add the cheese and salt. Place over hot, but not boiling, water and stir vigorously until the cheese begins to melt and absorb the milk. Continue heating and stirring until the cheese has completely melted and the mixture is soft and creamy. Remove the double boiler from the heat immediately, since prolonged heating makes the cheese stringy.

Meanwhile, heat the remaining milk in a small saucepan until warm, remove from the heat, add the egg yolks and stir until blended. Gradually add the egg mixture to the melted cheese, mixing thoroughly after each addition. Add the butter and beat until the mixture is smooth and glossy. Trim the crusts from the toast and cut each slice into 4 triangles. Arrange in the heated ramekins and pour the *fondue* over the toast. Garnish with the truffle and serve immediately.

SKEWERED SCAMPI WITH BRANDY SAUCE

Serves 6

24 large fresh or frozen uncooked scampi or jumbo shrimp	6 anchovy fillets
18 bay leaves	6 tablespoons butter
salt and freshly ground black pepper	⅓ cup brandy
1 tablespoon olive oil	few drops *Duca d'Urbino* sauce or Worcestershire sauce
for the sauce:	1 tablespoon French mustard
2 cloves garlic	2 teaspoons lemon juice

Using 6 skewers, thread 4 scampi on to each skewer alternating with the bay leaves. Season with the salt and pepper and sprinkle with the olive oil. Grease a roasting pan with the oil and place the skewers in it. Cook in a preheated moderately hot oven (375°) for 15 minutes, or until tender and golden brown, brushing occasionally with the pan juices and a little more olive oil, if necessary.

Meanwhile, make the sauce. Peel and crush the garlic. Pound the anchovy fillets with two-thirds of the butter to make a paste. Heat the remaining butter in a skillet over moderate heat, add the garlic and sauté until lightly browned. Add the brandy and *Duca d'Urbino* sauce and reduce by half over high heat. Add the anchovy paste, mustard and lemon juice. Pour the sauce on to an oval heated serving dish and arrange the skewers of scampi on top. Serve very hot.

MARINATED EEL

Serves 6

2 lb cleaned eel	salt
3 cloves garlic	$\frac{1}{4}$ fresh chili, chopped, or
all-purpose flour for coating	$\frac{1}{2}$ teaspoon dried chili powder
olive oil for deep-frying	$1\frac{1}{2}$ cups red wine vinegar
$\frac{1}{4}$ teaspoon oregano	

Rinse the eel under cold running water, dry well and cut into 2-inch pieces. Peel 1 clove of the garlic and cut in half. Rub the eel with the cut sides of the garlic and coat with flour.

Peel and slice the remaining garlic. Heat the olive oil until very hot, add the eel and sauté until brown. Drain well and place in an earthenware bowl, in layers, seasoning each layer with the garlic, oregano, salt and chili. Pour the vinegar into a saucepan and reduce by one-third over high heat. Remove the pan from the heat, mix in 3 tablespoons of the frying olive oil and pour over the eel. Set aside and marinate for at least 24 hours, but preferably 2–3 days to allow the maximum flavor to develop, before using.

SNAILS WITH TOMATO AND ANCHOVY SAUCE

Serves 6

36 canned snails, with shells	4–5 tablespoons olive oil
6 anchovy fillets	1 teaspoon chopped parsley
$\frac{1}{4}$ cup milk	$\frac{1}{2}$ chili
1 lb tomatoes	1 tablespoon chopped mint leaves
3 cloves garlic	salt

Drain the snails, wash and dry the shells and replace the snails. Set aside until required.

To make the sauce, soak the anchovy fillets in the milk for about 10 minutes to remove the excess salt, then drain. Peel the tomatoes and press through a sieve. Peel and crush the garlic. Heat the olive oil in a flameproof casserole or a saucepan over moderate heat. Add the anchovy fillets, garlic, parsley and the tomato purée. Remove the seeds from the chili, chop the flesh and add to the casserole with the mint leaves. Season with salt to taste. Simmer the sauce for 30 minutes, stirring occasionally. Add the snails in their shells and simmer in the sauce for 2–3 minutes. Serve in the casserole.

Marinated eel

PEPERONATA

Serves 6

1 large onion	½ cup olive oil
2–3 cloves garlic	6 small bay leaves
2 lb red or green sweet peppers	salt and pepper
1½ lb tomatoes	

Peel and coarsely chop the onion. Peel and slice the garlic. Discard the seeds from the sweet peppers and chop the flesh. Peel the tomatoes. Heat the olive oil in a saucepan over moderate heat. Add the onion, garlic and bay leaves and sauté until golden brown. Add the sweet peppers and season with salt and pepper. Cook over high heat for about 10 minutes, stirring constantly. Add the tomatoes, lower the heat and simmer gently for a further 15 minutes. Pour into a heated serving dish and serve as an appetizer.

Note: This dish may be reheated and therefore can be prepared in advance when entertaining.

CREAMED SALT COD

Serves 6

1¼ lb dried salt cod	¼ cup olive oil
3 cloves garlic	dash cinnamon
2½–3¾ cups milk	salt and pepper

Soak the fish for 24 hours in plenty of cold water, changing the water frequently. Drain, rinse under cold running water and dry with a cloth or absorbent paper. Discard any skin and bones and thinly slice the fish. Peel the garlic and rub over the inside of a flameproof casserole or a large saucepan.

Place the fish in the casserole and add enough of the milk to cover. Simmer over moderate heat until the mixture begins to darken in color. While the fish cooks, break it into small pieces with a wooden spoon. Heat the remaining milk and gradually stir it into the casserole with the olive oil to obtain a soft purée. It may not be necessary to use all the milk. Season with the cinnamon and salt and pepper to taste. Serve hot with warm slices of *polenta* (see page 197).

Peperonata

MINESTRONE ALLA MILANESE

Serves 6

¼ cup *borlotti* beans (see note) or pinto beans	1 leek
4 oz Canadian-style bacon, in 1 piece	1 small celery heart
1 medium-sized potato	½ cup butter
1 large carrot	*bouquet garni* (see recipe)
1 medium-sized eggplant	salt and freshly ground black pepper
12 oz fresh peas or 1 cup frozen peas	4½ pints chicken stock
8 oz tomatoes	1 cup long-grain rice
½ small onion	1 clove garlic
	1 cup grated Parmesan cheese

Soak the beans in cold water for 24 hours. Drain well and cook in lightly salted boiling water for about 1 hour, or until tender. Drain before using. Simmer the bacon in boiling water for 15–20 minutes. Drain well and cut into ¼-inch cubes.

Peel and dice the potato, carrot and eggplant. Shell the peas, if using fresh ones. Peel the tomatoes. Peel and chop the onion. Cut off the green part of the leek and trim away the root. Rinse the white part very thoroughly under cold running water and chop coarsely. Trim and thinly slice the celery heart. Heat one-third of the butter in a saucepan over moderate heat and add the bacon, onion, leek and the *bouquet garni* (few sprigs parsley, 1 sprig rosemary, ½ bay leaf, tied together). Cook together over moderate heat for 3–4 minutes, remove the herbs, add the tomatoes and season with salt and pepper to taste. Simmer gently.

Heat the remaining butter in a second saucepan over high heat and sauté the beans, potato, carrot, eggplant, peas and celery over moderate heat for 5–8 minutes. Add to the tomato mixture, simmer together for 2–3 minutes then pour in the stock. Simmer over moderate heat until the vegetables are tender. Increase the heat and, when the stock boils, add the rice and simmer for about 15 minutes, or until *al dente* (cooked but still firm). Peel and chop the garlic. A few moments before removing the soup from the heat, add the garlic. Pour into a heated soup tureen and serve with the cheese as an accompaniment.

Note: Borlotti beans are the speckled red and white variety.

FAVA BEAN MINESTRONE

Serves 6

3 lb unshelled fava or lima beans	**for the pasta:**
1 small onion	5 eggs
1 small carrot	1 tablespoon olive oil
½ stalk celery	4 cups all-purpose flour
½ cup butter	1 teaspoon salt
3¾ pints water	1 cup grated Pecorino or Parmesan cheese
4 teaspoons salt	

Shell the beans. Peel and chop the onion and carrot. Chop the celery. Heat the butter in a saucepan over moderate heat, add the onion, carrot and celery and sauté until browned.

Add the beans and the water. Season with salt and bring to a boil. Lower the heat and simmer the beans for 30–40 minutes, or until soft and very tender.

To make the pasta, lightly beat together the eggs and olive oil in a small bowl. Sift the flour and salt on to a marble slab or into a mixing bowl and make a well in the center. Pour in the eggs and oil, mix to a firm, smooth dough and knead well. Wrap in a damp cloth and set aside for about 30 minutes.

Roll the dough on a floured surface into sheets, about 8 inches wide, 12 inches long and 1/16 inch thick. Fold each sheet in half lengthwise, then in half lengthwise again several times. Cut the roll into ¼-inch ribbon noodles. Unfold the noodles, arrange them on a lightly floured surface and allow to dry for about 30 minutes.

Bring the soup to a boil and add the egg noodles. Cook for 7–8 minutes, or until the noodles are *al dente* (cooked but still firm). Pour the soup into a tureen and serve with the cheese as an accompaniment.

TOMATO AND PASTA SOUP

Serves 6

3 cloves garlic	salt and freshly ground black pepper
1 medium-sized tomato	
10 oz *bavette* (see note)	3 tablespoons finely chopped basil
¼ cup olive oil	1 cup grated Pecorino or Parmesan cheese
3 oz ham or bacon fat, ground	
4¼ cups cold water	

Peel and chop the garlic. Peel and slice the tomato. Break the *bavette* into 1- to 1½-inch pieces. Heat the olive oil in a saucepan over moderate heat, add the garlic and ham fat and sauté until lightly browned. Add the slices of tomato, stir for a few minutes and then add the water. Season with salt and pepper and bring to a boil. Add the *bavette* and cook for 10–12 minutes, or until *al dente* (cooked but still firm). Remove the pan from the heat and add the basil and 3 tablespoons of the cheese. Serve hot with the remaining cheese as an accompaniment.

Note: Bavette are rods of pasta, each with a central groove, like a pencil split longitudinally with the lead removed.

Fava bean minestrone

176

CHEESE-STUFFED CAPPELLETTI IN BROTH

Serves 6

for the pasta:

4 eggs

2 teaspoons olive oil

3 cups all-purpose flour

¾ teaspoon salt

for the filling:

1 cup Ricotta cheese or half
    Ricotta cheese and half Cacio
    cheese

1¼ cups grated Parmesan cheese

1 egg

1 egg yolk

¼ teaspoon grated lemon rind

dash mixed dried herbs

salt

5½ pints beef or chicken bouillon

To make the pasta, lightly beat together the eggs and olive oil in a small bowl. Sift the flour and salt on to a marble slab or into a mixing bowl and make a well in the center. Pour in the eggs and oil. Mix to a smooth dough and knead well. Wrap in a damp cloth and set aside for about 30 minutes.

To make the filling, mix together the Ricotta cheese, one-third of the Parmesan cheese, the egg, egg yolk, lemon rind and herbs. Season with salt to taste. Roll the mixture into balls about the size of a small walnut and place on a floured surface until required.

Knead the dough lightly and roll out into sheets, $\frac{1}{16}$ inch thick. Using a 2-inch floured cutter, cut out circles of dough. Alternatively, cut 2-inch squares, using a floured sharp knife. Place one ball of filling in the center of each piece of dough. Fold in half and firmly press the edges together to form the *cappelletti*. Press the leftover dough into a ball and repeat the process until all the pasta and filling are used. Bring the bouillon to a boil. Add the *cappelletti* and simmer for 5–10 minutes, or until they rise to the surface. Serve immediately in heated soup dishes with the remaining cheese as an accompaniment.

Note: Cappelletti means 'little hats' and these ravioli appear throughout northern Italy with a variety of fillings.

RICE AND CHICKEN LIVER SOUP

Serves 6

4½ pints chicken stock

6 oz chicken livers

1 cup long-grain rice

1 tablespoon chopped parsley

1 cup grated Parmesan cheese

Bring the stock to a boil in a large saucepan. Clean the chicken livers and chop coarsely. Pour ¼ cup of the boiling stock over the livers to scald them. Add the rice to the pan and simmer for about 15 minutes, or until *al dente* (cooked but still firm). Add the chicken livers with the stock in which they were scalded and the parsley. Simmer for 2–3 minutes, then serve in heated soup bowls, sprinkled with the cheese.

Cheese-stuffed cappelletti in broth

MUSSEL HOT-POT

Serves 6

2 quarts mussels	4 medium-sized potatoes
3 tablespoons olive oil	4 oz bacon fat, ground
¼ teaspoon freshly ground black pepper	4½ pints cold water
	salt
1 small onion	1¾ cups long-grain rice
1 clove garlic	

Scrub the mussels very thoroughly under running water. Remove the beards. Heat half the olive oil in a saucepan over moderate heat. Add the mussels and pepper and sauté until the mussels open. Shake the pan frequently to prevent the mussels from sticking. Drain in a colander over a large bowl and cool. Discard any mussels that have not opened. Strain and reserve the liquid. Remove and discard the mussel shells. Set the mussels aside until required.

Peel and finely chop the onion and garlic. Peel and slice the potatoes. Heat the bacon fat and the remaining olive oil in a flameproof casserole or a saucepan over low heat. Add the onion and garlic and sauté until lightly browned. Add the water and the potatoes, season with salt and bring to a boil. After 10 minutes, add the rice and cook over high heat for about 15 minutes. Add the mussels and the reserved liquid 2–3 minutes before the end of the cooking time. Pour into a heated serving dish and serve immediately.

ANCHOVY OMELET

Serves 6

6 anchovy fillets	¼ cup olive oil
¼ cup milk	1 small chili
1 tablespoon chopped parsley	salt
1 clove garlic	10 eggs
12 oz tomatoes	pepper

Soak the anchovies in the milk for about 10 minutes to remove the excess salt. Drain and pound to a paste with the parsley. Peel and crush the garlic. Peel and chop the tomatoes. Heat one-third of the olive oil in a skillet over moderate heat, add the garlic and sauté until lightly browned. Discard the garlic and add the anchovy mixture to the skillet, then add the tomatoes and chili and season with a little salt. Continue cooking for 8 minutes, pour the mixture into a bowl and let stand until cool.

Discard the chili. Beat the eggs well and stir into the cooled anchovy mixture. Season with salt and pepper. Heat half the remaining oil in the skillet over moderate heat and pour in the egg mixture. Stir for a few seconds until the bottom of the omelet is golden brown. Continue cooking for 1–2 minutes until the mixture begins to set. Remove the skillet from the heat and invert the omelet on to a large round plate. Heat the remaining oil in the skillet and slide the omelet into the skillet with the browned side up. Cook until golden brown, then slide the omelet on to a heated serving plate and serve immediately.

SARDINES WITH CAPER AND OLIVE STUFFING

Serves 6

24 large fresh sardines	½ cup finely chopped parsley
1 large clove garlic	½ cup fine fresh breadcrumbs
⅓ cup pitted ripe olives	salt and pepper
½ cup capers	olive oil (see recipe)

Cut off the heads and tails of the fish, clean them and remove the backbones. Rinse thoroughly under cold running water and dry well with a cloth or absorbent paper. Place skin-side down on a flat surface. Peel and chop the garlic. Coarsely chop the olives and capers. Mix the garlic, olives, capers, parsley, breadcrumbs and salt and pepper together in a bowl. Add enough olive oil to bind the mixture together.

Spread a little of the mixture on the flesh, fold the fish over the filling and place in a greased casserole. Lightly sprinkle with olive oil, season with a little more salt and cook in a preheated moderately hot oven (400°) for about 20 minutes. Serve hot or cold.

BAKED SEA BASS

Serves 6

1 sea bass, about 3 lb	1 tablespoon olive oil
salt and pepper	1 medium-sized onion
¼ cup butter	2 lemons

Scale and clean the bass. Rinse under cold running water and dry with a cloth or absorbent paper. Make a diagonal slit on each side of the fish to help the heat to penetrate while cooking. Season with salt and pepper. Place the fish in a casserole with the butter and olive oil. Peel and slice the onion and arrange over the fish. Bake in a preheated moderately hot oven (375°) for 45–50 minutes, or until the flesh of the fish is firm and white. During cooking, baste occasionally with the juices in the casserole.

Carefully remove the fish from the casserole and place on a heated serving plate. Slice the lemons and arrange around the fish. Strain the juices left in the casserole, pour a little over the fish and serve immediately.

Sardines with caper and olive stuffing

OCTOPUS IN SPICY TOMATO SAUCE

Serves 6

2 rock octopus, 1 lb each
6 oz tomatoes
salt
1 chili

1 tablespoon chopped parsley
½ cup olive oil
1 lemon

Clean and skin each octopus. Remove the eyes, mouth (beak) and the small bladder. Rinse well under cold running water and pound lightly with a meat mallet to tenderize. Place the octopus in a large flameproof casserole. Peel and slice the tomatoes and place on top. Add the salt, chili, parsley and olive oil. Place waxed paper over the top of the casserole, secure with string and cover tightly. Simmer over low heat for about 2 hours.

Remove the casserole from the heat and set aside for 2–3 minutes. Remove the waxed paper and the chilli. Cut the lemon into wedges. Cut the octopus into pieces in the casserole and garnish with the lemon. This dish is excellent served either hot or cold.

RICE AND SHELLFISH SALAD

Serves 6

1 pint clams
1 pint mussels
1 pint cockles
¼ cup dry white wine
4 oz fresh or frozen uncooked
  scampi or jumbo shrimp
2¼ cups long-grain rice

3 hard-cooked eggs
about ¼ cup olive oil
dash saffron powder
few drops *Duca d'Urbino* sauce or
  Worcestershire sauce
salt and pepper
1 tablespoon chopped parsley

Scrub the clams, mussels and cockles and rinse well under cold running water. Place in a large saucepan with the wine. Cover tightly and cook over high heat. Shake the saucepan gently until the shellfish open. Drain and set aside to cool. Remove the fish from their shells and discard the shells. Shell the scampi and simmer in lightly salted boiling water for 4–5 minutes. Drain well and dice. Cook the rice in plenty of lightly salted boiling water for about 15 minutes, or until *al dente* (cooked but still firm). Drain and set aside to cool.

Pound the eggs to a paste, using a pestle and mortar or a blender. Add the oil gradually, beating constantly. Add the saffron powder and *Duca d'Urbino* sauce. Season with salt and pepper to taste. Mix the rice with the shellfish, place in a glass dish and cover with the sauce. Sprinkle with the parsley. Toss the salad at the table just before serving.

BAKED STUFFED SQUID

Serves 6

3 lb fairly large squid
2 cloves garlic
1 tablespoon chopped parsley
3 tablespoons fine fresh
  breadcrumbs

3 tablespoons olive oil
salt and pepper
¼ cup dry white wine

To clean the squid, carefully remove the transparent bone, the small bladder containing the black ink and the pouch containing the yellow colored deposit. Rinse the squid thoroughly in plenty of cold water and pat dry with a cloth or absorbent paper. Remove the tentacles and chop coarsely. Peel and finely chop the garlic. Mix together the squid tentacles, garlic, parsley, breadcrumbs, half the olive oil and salt and pepper. Fill the body of each squid with the stuffing.

Sew up the body or secure with wooden toothpicks to completely enclose the filling. Place the stuffed squid in a greased casserole and sprinkle with the remaining olive oil, a little salt and pepper and the wine. Place the casserole in a preheated moderately hot oven (375°) and bake for 45–50 minutes, or until tender. Remove the thread or toothpicks and serve.

CUTTLEFISH AND NAVY BEAN SALAD

Serves 6

2 cups navy beans
2¼ lb cuttlefish or squid
1 large onion
1 large carrot
1 stalk celery
4¼ cups water
salt and pepper

for the dressing:
⅓ cup olive oil
¼ cup lemon juice
3–4 tablespoons cuttlefish stock
  (see recipe)
salt
6 hard-cooked eggs

Soak the beans overnight in plenty of cold water. Drain and cook in plenty of lightly salted boiling water for about 45–50 minutes, or until tender. Drain well and set aside until required.

Meanwhile, clean the cuttlefish as for squid (see Baked Stuffed Squid, above), rinse under cold running water and slice quite thickly. Peel the onion and carrot and place in a large saucepan with the celery, water and salt and pepper. Place the pan over moderate heat and bring to a boil. Lower the heat and simmer for 5 minutes. Add the cuttlefish and simmer for about 1 hour, or until the fish is tender. Drain and set aside to cool. Discard the vegetables but reserve the required amount of stock for the dressing.

To make the dressing, mix together the olive oil, lemon juice and cuttlefish stock. Season with salt to taste. Shell the hard-cooked eggs and cut into quarters. Place the beans and cuttlefish in a salad bowl and pour over the dressing. Garnish with the eggs. Mix together at the table before serving.

TOMATO AND ANCHOVY PIZZA

Serves 6

for the pasta:	for the topping:
1 cake compressed yeast or 1 package active dry yeast	12 anchovy fillets
1¼ cups lukewarm water	¼ cup milk
4 cups all-purpose flour	12 oz tomatoes
1 teaspoon salt	2 cloves garlic
1 tablespoon olive oil	6 tablespoons lard
	½ teaspoon dried oregano (see recipe)
	salt and pepper

To make the pasta, dissolve the yeast in the water. Sift the flour and salt on to a marble slab or into a mixing bowl and make a well in the center. Pour in the yeast mixture and the olive oil. Gradually knead the flour into the liquid to make a smooth, soft dough. Form into a ball and put into a floured bowl. Cover and let stand in a warm place for 1½–2 hours, or until doubled in bulk.

To make the topping, soak the anchovy fillets in the milk for 10–15 minutes to remove the excess salt. Drain before using. Peel and slice the tomatoes and garlic. Sprinkle the table with a little flour and knead the risen dough for 2–3 minutes. Roll out the dough to ⅛ inch thick. Cut into 6 circles, each 6 inches in diameter. Melt the lard and brush a little over each circle. Arrange the anchovy fillets, tomatoes and garlic over the surface. Sprinkle with the oregano and the remaining melted lard and season with the salt and pepper. Place on a baking sheet and bake in a preheated hot oven (450°) for about 15–20 minutes. Serve hot.

MACARONI WITH SARDINES AND FENNEL

Serves 6

4 oz anchovy fillets	⅓ cup water
⅔ cup milk	small dash saffron powder
1 lb fresh sardines	salt and pepper
3 cloves garlic	1 tablespoon chopped parsley
¼ onion	¼ cup seedless white raisins
1 head fennel, about 12 oz	⅓ cup pine nut kernels
⅓ cup olive oil	1¾ lb macaroni

Soak the anchovy fillets in the milk for 10–15 minutes to remove the excess salt, then drain. Cut off the heads and tails of the sardines, clean them and remove the backbones. Rinse thoroughly under cold running water and dry well with a cloth or absorbent paper.

Peel the garlic. Peel and finely chop the onion. Trim and wash the fennel and cut into 8 pieces. Heat half the olive oil in a saucepan over moderate heat and add 2 cloves of the garlic, the water, saffron and 1 piece of fennel. Season with salt and pepper. Sauté together until golden brown, then add the sardines and cook for 2–3 minutes. Remove the pan from the heat and set aside until required. Discard the garlic.

Place the remaining fennel in a second saucepan with boiling salted water, simmer for 15 minutes, drain, chop and set aside. Reserve the cooking water.

Pound the anchovies to a paste with the parsley. Place the remaining olive oil in a saucepan over moderate heat, add the remaining clove of garlic with the onion and sauté until brown. Add the fennel, the anchovy mixture diluted with ½ cup of the cooking water from the fennel, the raisins and the pine nut kernels. Simmer over moderate heat for 2–3 minutes.

Place the remaining cooking water from the fennel in a third saucepan and bring to a boil. Add the macaroni and enough lightly salted boiling water to cover. Simmer until the macaroni is *al dente* (cooked but still firm), adding more boiling water if necessary. Drain well and place the macaroni in layers in a heated casserole, alternating with layers of the sardine mixture and the anchovy mixture, and beginning and ending with a layer of macaroni. Cook in a preheated moderate oven (350°) for 20 minutes. Serve very hot.

SPAGHETTI WITH CHEESE AND BACON

Serves 6

1¼ lb spaghetti	2 tablespoons lard
1 small onion	¼ chili
1 clove garlic	dash salt
10 slices bacon	1 cup grated Pecorino or Parmesan cheese
3 tablespoons olive oil	

Cook the spaghetti in plenty of salted boiling water for about 10–12 minutes, or until *al dente* (cooked but still firm). Drain, turn into a deep heated serving dish and keep hot. Meanwhile, peel and chop the onion and garlic and cut the bacon into ¼-inch pieces.

Heat the olive oil with the lard in a skillet over moderate heat and add the bacon and chili. When the bacon begins to brown, remove it from the skillet and set aside. Add the onion, garlic and salt to the skillet, stir together and remove from the heat when lightly colored. Discard the chili and add the bacon. Sprinkle the spaghetti with the bacon mixture and the cheese. Mix at the table and serve.

FETTUCCINE WITH RICOTTA CHEESE

Serves 6

for the pasta:	for the topping:
5 eggs	2 cups Ricotta cheese
1 tablespoon olive oil	4–5 tablespoons olive oil
4 cups all-purpose flour	salt and freshly ground pepper
1 teaspoon salt	

To make the pasta, lightly beat together the eggs and olive oil in a small bowl. Sift the flour and salt on to a marble slab or into a mixing bowl and make a well in the center. Pour in the eggs and the oil, mix to a firm, smooth dough and knead well. Wrap in a damp cloth and set aside for about 30 minutes.

Roll out the dough on a floured surface into sheets, about 8 inches wide, 12 inches long and 1/16 inch thick. Fold each sheet in half lengthwise, then in half lengthwise again, several times. Cut the roll into $\frac{1}{4}$-inch ribbon noodles. Unfold the noodles, arrange on a floured surface and allow to dry for about 30 minutes. Place the noodles in a large saucepan half filled with lightly salted boiling water and simmer for about 8 minutes, or until *al dente* (cooked but still firm). Drain and place on a heated serving plate. Reserve the cooking water.

Press the Ricotta cheese through a sieve over the noodles and sprinkle with olive oil, salt and pepper and, if necessary, a little of the water in which the noodles were cooked, to help melt and blend the cheese. Mix together and serve.

POTATO GNOCCHI WITH MEAT SAUCE

Serves 6

8 large potatoes	2 cups meat sauce (see page 198)
about $3\frac{1}{2}$ cups all-purpose flour	$\frac{1}{2}$ cup butter
2 teaspoons salt	$1\frac{1}{2}$ cups grated Parmesan cheese

Scrub the potatoes under cold running water and boil in lightly salted water to cover until barely tender. Drain, peel

and press through a sieve on to a marble slab or into a mixing bowl. While still warm, make a well in the center and add the flour and salt. Mix to form a soft dough, adding a little more flour if necessary. Knead lightly until smooth. Divide the dough into pieces and, with floured hands, form into long rolls, about 1 inch in diameter. Cut the rolls into $1\frac{1}{2}$-inch pieces and make a lengthwise groove on either side of each piece by pressing between the index and second fingers. Arrange the *gnocchi* on a lightly floured surface, making sure they do not touch. Set aside for 10–15 minutes to dry.

Place a few *gnocchi* at a time in a large saucepan half filled with lightly salted boiling water. As soon as they come to the surface, remove them with a perforated spoon, drain well and place on a large heated serving dish. Heat the meat sauce and pour half of it over the *gnocchi*. Dot the surface with pieces of butter and sprinkle with one-third of the cheese. Serve very hot, accompanied by the remaining sauce and cheese.

Tomato and anchovy pizza

Pansôti with walnut sauce

PANSÔTI WITH WALNUT SAUCE

Serves 6

for the filling:
2 oz lamb brains
2 oz lamb sweetbreads
12 oz spinach
8 oz beet leaves
8 oz fresh borage
8 oz watercress
5 tablespoons butter
1 cup Ricotta cheese
2 eggs
1 clove garlic
dash nutmeg
salt

for the pasta:
4 eggs
3 tablespoons warm water
6 cups all-purpose flour
1 teaspoon salt
1 beaten egg

for the sauce:
1 clove garlic
1 cup shelled walnuts
½ cup pine nut kernels
about ⅔ cup olive oil
1 cup grated Parmesan cheese

To make the filling, soak the brains and sweetbreads in cold water for 1 hour. Blanch in boiling water, drain well and remove any skin, blood vessels and coarse tissue. Rinse the spinach, beet leaves, borage and watercress under cold running water. Remove any tough stems and veins and shred all the leaves. Cook the leaves in lightly salted boiling water until tender. Drain thoroughly and press through a sieve into a large bowl. Heat the butter in a skillet over moderate heat and sauté the brains and sweetbreads for 5–6 minutes, stirring frequently. Press through a sieve into the bowl with the sieved greens.

Sieve the Ricotta cheese, beat the eggs, peel and crush the garlic and stir them all into the brain mixture. Add the nutmeg and season with salt to taste. Mix to a stiff paste. With floured hands, roll the paste into small balls, about the size of a walnut, and set aside while making the pasta.

To make the pasta, lightly beat together the eggs and water in a small bowl. Sift the flour and salt on to a marble slab or into a mixing bowl and make a well in the center. Pour in the eggs and water, mix to a firm smooth dough and knead well. Wrap the dough in a damp cloth and set aside for about 30 minutes.

Roll the dough into 2 sheets, about $\frac{1}{16}$ inch thick, and brush the first sheet with beaten egg. Place the balls of filling about 2 inches apart on the first sheet of dough. Cover with the second sheet and press firmly between the rounds of filling to seal together the two layers. Using a fluted pastry wheel or a sharp knife, cut the *pansôti* into 2-inch squares. Place on a floured surface until required.

To make the sauce, peel the garlic and grind with the walnuts and pine nut kernels. Press the mixture through a sieve into a bowl. Add the olive oil, drop by drop, beating constantly as if making a mayonnaise, until a thick coating mixture is formed. Add more oil, if necessary. Place a few *pansôti* at a time in a large saucepan half filled with lightly salted boiling water. Simmer for about 15 minutes. Remove with a perforated spoon and drain well. Place in a heated serving dish, sprinkle with the Parmesan cheese and cover with walnut sauce. Mix well and place in a preheated moderately hot oven (400°) for 3–4 minutes. Serve immediately.

Note: Pansôti are small squares of ravioli. The literal translation of *pansôti* is 'pot-bellied', implying that the ravioli should be well filled.

LASAGNE VERDE WITH MEAT SAUCE

Serves 6

8 oz spinach
2 eggs
1 tablespoon olive oil
4 cups all-purpose flour
1 teaspoon salt
2 cups meat sauce (see page 198)
¾ cup white sauce
1½ cups grated Parmesan cheese
½–¾ cup melted butter
1 truffle (optional)

Rinse the spinach under cold running water and drain well. Cook in a very little boiling salted water for 10 minutes. Drain thoroughly. Chop finely, press through a sieve and set aside until cold. Lightly beat together the eggs and olive oil in a small bowl. Sift the flour and salt on to a marble slab or into a mixing bowl and make a well in the center. Pour in the eggs and olive oil and add the spinach. Mix to a smooth firm dough and knead well until the mixture is evenly colored. Wrap in a damp cloth and set aside for about 30 minutes.

Roll the dough into 3 sheets, about $\frac{1}{16}$ inch thick, and cut into 3-inch squares. Cook 6 to 8 of the squares at a time in a shallow saucepan half filled with lightly salted boiling water for 3–4 minutes. Remove with a perforated spoon, drain well and set aside to cool on a damp cloth. Butter a 2-quart casserole and arrange the pasta in layers, covering each layer with ¼ cup of the meat sauce and a little white sauce, grated cheese and butter. Sprinkle the top with cheese and butter only. Bake in a preheated moderate oven (350°) for 20–30 minutes, or until the surface is well browned. Slice the truffle, if used. Garnish with the truffle and serve with any remaining cheese.

TAGLIATELLE WITH PESTO

Serves 6

5 eggs
1 tablespoon olive oil
4 cups all-purpose flour
1 teaspoon salt
12 oz potatoes
½ cup grated Pecorino Sardo or Parmesan cheese
pesto (see page 198)

Make the pasta as for Fettuccine, page 182. Wrap in a damp cloth and set aside for about 30 minutes.

Roll the dough into sheets, about $\frac{1}{16}$ inch thick. Fold each sheet in half lengthwise, then fold in half lengthwise again, several times. With a sharp knife, cut the dough into noodles, 1 inch wide. Unfold the noodles and place on a floured surface. Cover with a lightly floured cloth and set aside for 10–15 minutes, or until required.

Peel and thickly slice the potatoes and simmer in lightly salted boiling water until almost cooked. Add the noodles and continue simmering until *al dente* (cooked but still firm). Drain the noodles and potatoes and reserve 3 tablespoons of the liquid. Place the noodles and potatoes on an oval heated serving dish, sprinkle with the cheese and the reserved cooking liquid and mix lightly. Pour the *pesto* over and bring to the table. Mix together until the potatoes and noodles are well coated and serve.

GENOESE GNOCCHI WITH PESTO

Serves 6

4½ lb potatoes	2 tablespoons butter
about 3 cups all-purpose flour	1 teaspoon salt
1 tablespoon grated Pecorino or Parmesan cheese	4 egg yolks (optional)
3 tablespoons fine fresh breadcrumbs	*pesto* (see page 198)

Scrub the potatoes under cold running water and boil in lightly salted water to cover until barely tender. Meanwhile, mix together the flour, cheese, breadcrumbs, butter and salt. Drain and peel the potatoes and press through a sieve on to a marble slab or into a mixing bowl.

While the potato is still warm, make a well in the center and add the flour mixture and egg yolks. Mix to a soft dough, adding a little more flour if necessary. Mix lightly, handling the dough as little as possible. Divide the dough into pieces and, with floured hands, form into long rolls, about 1 inch in diameter. Cut the rolls into 1½-inch pieces and make a lengthwise groove on either side of each piece by pressing between the index and second fingers. Arrange on a lightly floured surface, making sure they do not touch. Set aside for 10–15 minutes to dry.

Place a few of the *gnocchi* at a time into a large saucepan half filled with lightly salted boiling water. As they come to the surface, remove with a perforated spoon, drain well and place on a large heated serving plate. Heat the *pesto* diluted with 3 tablespoons of the cooking liquid from the *gnocchi*. Pour over the *gnocchi*, mix and serve.

BEEF-STUFFED PASTA WITH HERB BUTTER

Serves 6

for the pasta:	1 tablespoon grated Parmesan cheese
5 eggs	dash nutmeg
1 tablespoon melted butter	salt and pepper
4 cups all-purpose flour	1–2 eggs
1 teaspoon salt	**for the serving:**
for the filling:	¾ cup butter
2 tablespoons butter	fresh sage leaves, chopped (see recipe)
2 cloves garlic	1 cup grated Parmesan cheese
1 tablespoon chopped parsley	
8 oz beef, ground	
3 tablespoons fine fresh breadcrumbs	

To make the pasta, lightly beat the eggs and butter in a small bowl. Sift the flour and salt on to a marble slab or into a mixing bowl and make a well in the center. Pour in the egg mixture, mix to a firm dough and knead well. Wrap in a damp cloth and set aside for about 30 minutes.

To make the filling, heat the butter in a skillet over moderate heat. Peel and finely chop the garlic. Add the garlic and parsley and sauté until they begin to brown, then add the beef and sauté for about 10 minutes, stirring frequently. Remove the skillet from the heat, add the breadcrumbs and

cheese and set aside in a bowl to cool. Season with the nutmeg and salt and pepper to taste and blend to a paste with the eggs.

Roll out the dough into sheets, about $\frac{1}{16}$ inch thick, on a lightly floured surface. Cut 3½-inch squares of dough and put 1 tablespoon of the filling on half of each square. Brush the edges of the square with the water. Fold the uncovered half of the square over the filling and press the edges together to completely enclose the filling. Place on a lightly floured tray until required.

Cook the pasta squares, a few at a time, in a large saucepan half filled with lightly salted boiling water for about 5 minutes. Remove with a perforated spoon as they come to the surface. Drain well and place on a heated serving dish. Heat the butter until golden brown, sprinkle in chopped sage leaves to taste and pour over the pasta. Sprinkle with the cheese and serve.

BONE MARROW-STUFFED PASTA

Serves 6

for the pasta:	salt and pepper
5 eggs	dash nutmeg
1 tablespoon olive oil	2 egg yolks
4 cups all-purpose flour	2–3 tablespoons beef stock
1 teaspoon salt	1 beaten egg
for the filling:	**for serving:**
5 cups dry breadcrumbs	¾ cup melted butter
1½ cups grated Parmesan cheese	1 cup grated Parmesan cheese
½ cup melted bone marrow	

Make the pasta as for Fettuccine, page 182. Wrap in a damp cloth and set aside for about 30 minutes.

To make the filling, mix together the breadcrumbs, cheese, bone marrow, salt and pepper and nutmeg. Add the egg yolks and mix to a soft dough, adding the stock if necessary. Roll the dough into two thin sheets, about $\frac{1}{16}$ inch thick. Brush the surface of the first sheet of pasta with beaten egg and, using a pastry bag and a ½-inch tip, pipe small amounts of filling on to the sheet about 2 inches apart. Cover with the second sheet of pasta, brush with the egg and seal the layers together by pressing the spaces between the filling with the fingertips. Cut into squares, using a pastry wheel or a sharp knife, and place on a lightly floured board until required.

Cook the pasta squares, a few at a time, in a large saucepan half filled with lightly salted boiling water, for 8–10 minutes, or until they rise to the surface. Remove with a perforated spoon and drain well.

Heat the butter in a saucepan over moderate heat until lightly browned. Arrange the pasta squares in layers in an ovenproof serving dish alternating with the butter and half the cheese. Heat through in a preheated moderate oven (350°) for about 15 minutes. Serve with the remaining cheese.

Noodles in hare sauce

NOODLES IN HARE SAUCE

Serves 6

3 lb hare pieces	1 teaspoon salt
for the marinade:	**for the sauce:**
½ small onion	½ onion
½ stalk celery	½ carrot
1 bay leaf	2 slices Canadian-style bacon
2 cups full-bodied red wine	1 tablespoon olive oil
2 peppercorns	salt
for the pasta:	dash nutmeg
4 eggs	chicken stock (see recipe)
1 tablespoon olive oil	¼ cup butter
4 cups all-purpose flour	

Rinse the hare pieces under cold running water and dry with a cloth or absorbent paper.

To make the marinade, peel the onion, slice the celery and crumble the bay leaf. Place in a bowl with the wine and peppercorns. Add the hare and set aside to marinate for several hours, turning occasionally.

Make the pasta as for Fettuccine, page 182. Wrap in a damp cloth and set aside for about 30 minutes.

Roll the dough on a floured surface to about $\frac{1}{16}$ inch thick. With a sharp knife, cut the dough into noodles about $\frac{1}{4}$ inch wide. Set aside on a floured surface to dry until required.

To make the sauce, peel and chop the onion and carrot. Chop the bacon. Heat the oil in a skillet over moderate heat, add the onion, carrot and bacon and sauté until lightly browned. Drain the pieces of hare, season with salt and nutmeg, add to the skillet and sauté until browned. Lower the heat and cook gently for about 1 hour, or until tender, occasionally adding 1 tablespoon of the marinade and 1 tablespoon of the stock to form a thin sauce. Remove the pieces of hare and strain the sauce through a fine sieve. Keep both hot.

Place the noodles in a large saucepan half filled with lightly salted boiling water. Simmer for 8–12 minutes, or until *al dente* (cooked but still firm). Drain and pour into a deep heated serving dish. Cover with the sauce and place small pieces of the butter on the surface. Bring to the table and mix thoroughly before serving.

Serve the hare as a separate course, accompanied by seasonal vegetables.

MIXED BOILED MEATS WITH GREEN SAUCE

Serves 8

8 oz *cotechino* sausage (see note)
1 lb Canadian-style bacon, in
   1 piece (optional)
1 capon, about 4 lb
2 lb lamb rib chops
1 veal foreshank
8 oz Italian pork sausage

1 small carrot
2 stalks celery
2 cloves
1 onion
coarse salt
green sauce (see page 198)

Prick the *cotechino* and place in a very large saucepan with the bacon, if used. Add just enough water to cover and bring to a boil over moderate heat. Lower the heat and simmer the meats for about 1 hour. Add the capon, lamb, veal and sausage and enough water to cover completely. Bring to a boil and skim the surface of the liquid. Peel the carrot, wash the celery and add to the pan. Stick the cloves into the onion and add to the pan with the salt. Cover the pan and simmer for 1½–2 hours. Remove the different meats when tender, drain and keep hot.

Meanwhile, make the green sauce following the instructions on page 198, and pour into a sauceboat. Serve the cooked meats as hot as possible on a wooden meat platter, with pickles, radishes, grated fresh horseradish root, a variety of seasonal green vegetables, boiled potatoes and *mostarda*, an Italian relish of candied fruits in a spicy mustard syrup.

Note: Cotechino is a large, round pork sausage, highly spiced and seasoned with garlic.

FRICASSÉE OF LAMB

Serves 6

2 lb rolled leg or shoulder of lamb
1 very small onion
3 tablespoons olive oil
2 oz lean and fat ham, ground
dash nutmeg
salt and pepper
¾ cup dry white wine

2 tablespoons all-purpose flour
2 cloves garlic
few sprigs parsley
4 egg yolks
3 tablespoons lemon juice

Cut the lamb into 1½-inch cubes. Peel and chop the onion. Heat the olive oil in a flameproof casserole or a saucepan over moderate heat. Add the lamb, onion, ham, nutmeg and salt and pepper and stir constantly. When the meat begins to brown, add the wine and reduce it to 1 tablespoon. Sprinkle in the flour and mix thoroughly. Stir in enough water barely to cover the lamb. Simmer over low heat for 50 minutes–1 hour, or until the lamb is tender. During the cooking add a few tablespoons of water to prevent the meat from sticking, if necessary.

Peel the garlic and chop with the parsley. Stir in the garlic and parsley 2–3 minutes before the end of the cooking time. Remove the casserole from the heat. Lightly beat the egg yolks with the lemon juice, blend into the liquid in the casserole and replace over the heat until the mixture is hot and the sauce thickens (see note). Remove the casserole from the heat immediately, pour the fricassée into a deep heated serving dish and serve.

Note: Special care should be taken to prevent the fricassée from reaching the boiling point since the egg will curdle and ruin the appearance and smooth texture of the sauce.

ITALIAN LAMB STEW

Serves 6

2 lb shoulder of lamb
½ small carrot
½ onion
1 clove garlic
1 stalk celery
1 tablespoon olive oil
4 oz bacon fat, ground

⅔ cup dry white wine
¾ cup tomato sauce
   (see page 197)
¾ cup water
salt
¼ teaspoon chili powder
3 medium-sized potatoes

Cut the lamb into 1½-inch cubes. Peel and finely chop the carrot, onion and garlic. Finely chop the celery. Heat the olive oil in a flameproof casserole or a saucepan over high heat, add the lamb and sauté until browned. Remove the lamb and set aside until required.

Add the bacon fat, carrot, onion, garlic and celery to the casserole. Sauté until browned, then pour in the wine and reduce to ¼ cup over high heat. Add the tomato sauce diluted with the water, season lightly with salt and chili powder and simmer gently over moderate heat for 15 minutes. Return the lamb to the casserole and simmer for a further 20–30 minutes, stirring frequently, until the lamb is tender. Meanwhile, peel the potatoes and cut into small pieces. Place in a saucepan, cover with water, bring to a boil and simmer until three-fourths cooked. Drain well and add to the lamb about 10 minutes before the end of the cooking time.

STEAK WITH TOMATO AND GARLIC SAUCE

Serves 4

2 medium-sized tomatoes
3 cloves garlic
3 tablespoons olive oil

4 porterhouse steaks, ¾ inch thick
salt and pepper
dash oregano

Peel and slice the tomatoes. Peel and crush the garlic. Heat the olive oil in a heavy skillet over high heat. Add the steaks and sauté on each side until well browned, then lower the heat and cook for a further 2–3 minutes. Remove the steaks from the skillet and place on a heated plate, sprinkle with salt and pepper and keep hot.

Add the garlic to the same skillet and sauté over moderate heat until lightly browned. Add the tomatoes and oregano, season with salt and simmer for about 8 minutes, stirring frequently. Return the steaks and any juices that have drained from them to the skillet and simmer for 3–4 minutes. Place the steaks on heated plates, pour a little of the sauce over each and serve.

Italian lamb stew

188

VEAL WITH HAM AND SAGE IN WHITE WINE

Serves 6

12 thin veal escalopes	12 thin slices *prosciutto*
salt and freshly ground black	all-purpose flour for coating
pepper	½ cup butter
12 fresh sage leaves	6 tablespoons dry white wine

Flatten the veal with a meat mallet or a wooden rolling pin. Season with the salt and pepper, then place 1 sage leaf and 1 slice of ham on each piece of veal. Roll the veal, or fold in half, and secure with a wooden toothpick. Coat lightly with flour.

Heat three-fourths of the butter in a skillet over moderate heat and fry the veal until evenly browned and tender. Remove the toothpicks, place the veal on a heated serving plate and keep hot.

Pour the wine into the skillet and reduce to 1 tablespoon over high heat. Loosen the residue on the bottom of the skillet and stir in the remaining butter. Simmer for a few seconds, then pour over the veal rolls and serve.

STUFFED VEAL

Serves 6

2 lb rolled breast of veal	8 oz shelled peas or roughly
for the stuffing:	chopped beet leaves
4 oz lamb or calf sweetbreads	½ cup pistachio nuts
½ lemon	4 eggs
8 oz white bread	dash nutmeg
1 cup milk	salt and pepper
1 lb pork or veal tenderloin,	**for cooking the veal:**
ground	1 medium-sized onion
4 oz bacon fat, ground	1 small carrot
3 tablespoons chopped fresh	½ bay leaf
marjoram or 3 teaspoons dried	2 peppercorns
marjoram	salt
6 tablespoons grated Parmesan	
cheese	

Cut a slit at one end of the veal, insert a long sharp knife through the slit and cut the inside of the veal, making a 'pocket' to hold the stuffing. Set aside until required.

To make the stuffing, soak the sweetbreads in cold water for 1 hour. Drain well and dry with a cloth or absorbent paper. Rub the surface of the sweetbreads with the cut side of the lemon, then replace in cold water and soak for about 30 minutes, or until they become very white. Drain the sweetbreads and rinse under cold running water. Dry thoroughly and cut into ¼-inch cubes. Cut off the bread crusts. Soak the bread in the milk, then squeeze out the excess moisture. Place the sweetbreads, bread, pork tenderloin, bacon fat, marjoram, cheese, peas, pistachio nuts, eggs, nutmeg and salt and pepper in a bowl. Mix to form a paste.

Press the stuffing into the 'pocket' in the veal and sew up the opening with white thread. Loosely tie the veal with thin string so that it maintains its shape when cooking. Place in a flameproof casserole or large saucepan and cover with plenty of cold water.

Peel and slice the onion and carrot and add to the casserole. Add the bay leaf, peppercorns and salt. Place over moderate heat and bring to a boil. Lower the heat and simmer, partially covered, for 2 hours, or until the veal is tender.

Remove the veal from the liquid and place on a firm flat surface (reserve the liquid for soup stock, if desired). Place a wooden board on top of the veal and press the meat, using heavy weights, for about 2 hours. Serve cold.

VEAL WITH TUNA FISH SAUCE

Serves 6

8 anchovy fillets	**for the sauce:**
¼ cup milk	1 (8-oz) can tuna fish
1 medium-sized onion	2 anchovy fillets
2 medium-sized carrots	¼ cup veal stock
6 sweet dill pickles	(see recipe)
1 stalk celery	4 egg yolks
½ lemon	2 cups olive oil
1 rolled breast of veal,	¼ cup lemon juice
about 2¼ lb	salt
⅔ cup dry white wine	**for the garnish:**
¼ cup olive oil	3 tablespoons capers
1¼ cups cold water	3 pickled onions

Soak the anchovy fillets in the milk for 10–15 minutes to remove the excess salt. Drain and discard the milk. Peel and slice the onion and one of the carrots. Peel the remaining carrot and cut into thick strips. Cut the dill pickles in half lengthwise. Slice the celery. Thinly pare the rind from the lemon and squeeze the lemon to extract the juice.

Using a sharp knife, make small incisions in the veal and insert the anchovy fillets. Tie the strips of carrot and the dill pickles on to the veal with thin string. Place the veal in a flameproof casserole or large saucepan with the sliced onion, carrot and celery. Add the lemon rind, lemon juice, wine, olive oil and water. Cover the casserole and simmer over moderate heat for about 2 hours, or until tender. Remove the casserole from the heat, take out the veal and remove the string. Place the veal in a bowl. Discard all the vegetables in the casserole, strain the stock over the veal and set aside to cool. When cold, pour the stock into a small saucepan and boil rapidly over high heat until reduced to about ⅓ cup. Remove from the heat and set aside until required.

To make the sauce, drain the tuna fish and pound with the anchovy fillets to form a paste. Dilute the paste with ¼ cup of the reserved veal stock and press through a fine sieve. Place the egg yolks in a mixing bowl or blender. Add the olive oil drop by drop, beating constantly until a thick mayonnaise is formed. Add the lemon juice and gradually stir in the tuna fish paste. The sauce should be of a thick pouring consistency. If it is too thick, add the remaining veal stock. Season with salt to taste.

Thinly slice the veal and place on a serving dish. Coat with some of the tuna fish sauce and garnish with the capers and the pickled onions. Serve cold, accompanied by the remaining sauce.

OSSOBUCO ALLA MILANESE

Serves 6

2 veal foreshanks, cut into 6
   pieces
all-purpose flour for coating
1 small onion
2 cloves garlic
1 medium-sized carrot
2 ripe tomatoes
1 stalk celery
few sprigs marjoram

small strip thinly peeled lemon
   rind
½ cup butter
salt and pepper
⅔ cup dry white wine
about 3–4 tablespoons vegetable
   stock
grated rind of ½ lemon
risotto alla milanese (see page 196)

Wipe the pieces of veal with a damp cloth or absorbent paper and coat with flour. Peel and finely chop the onion, 1 clove of garlic, the carrot and tomatoes. Finely chop the celery, marjoram and strip of lemon rind. Melt three-fourths of the butter in a large saucepan over high heat, add the pieces of veal and sauté until browned. Add the onion, garlic, carrot, celery, marjoram and strip of lemon rind and season with salt and pepper. When the mixture is lightly browned, add the wine and simmer until reduced to 1 tablespoon. Add the tomatoes and the stock. Lower the heat, cover the pan tightly and simmer for 1 hour or more, adding a little additional stock, if necessary, to prevent the sauce from sticking.

Meanwhile, prepare the *risotto alla milanese* following the instructions on page 196. Peel and chop the remaining clove of garlic. Add the garlic, grated lemon rind and remaining butter to the veal. Stir and simmer for 2–3 minutes over moderate heat. Arrange the veal in a crown shape on a round heated serving dish and cover with the sauce. Serve with the *risotto alla milanese*.

Veal with tuna fish sauce

SKEWERED MEATS WITH POLENTA

Serves 6

6 chicken livers	1½ lb veal tenderloin
salt and pepper	6 sage leaves
½ cup butter	6 slices cold *polenta* (see page 197)
1 lb Canadian-style bacon	3 tablespoons olive oil
4 oz calf sweetbreads	

Cut each chicken liver in half. Season with salt and pepper. Heat half the butter in a skillet, add the livers and sauté until firm but still soft in the center. Drain and cool. Cut the bacon into 24 pieces, each about ½ inch by 2 inches. Simmer the bacon in boiling water for 5 minutes. Drain and dry well on absorbent paper. Remove and discard any membrane from the sweetbreads. Cut the sweetbreads into 6 slices and each slice into quarters. Cut the veal tenderloin into 24 pieces.

Thread the liver, bacon, sweetbreads and veal alternately on to 6 skewers, adding 1 sage leaf to each skewer. Season with salt and pepper and arrange on a baking sheet greased with the remaining butter. Cook in a preheated moderately hot oven (400°) for 15–20 minutes.

Meanwhile, sauté the *polenta* slices in the oil until golden brown and arrange on a heated serving plate. Place the skewers of meat on top and serve.

SWEETBREADS IN MUSHROOM AND MEAT SAUCE

Serves 6

1 lb lamb sweetbreads	salt and pepper
1 lb fresh mushrooms	6 tablespoons Marsala
½ cup butter	⅔ cup meat sauce
1 tablespoon finely chopped onion	(see page 198)

Soak the sweetbreads in cold water for 30 minutes. Drain and rinse. Place in a saucepan and cover with cold water. Bring to a boil over moderate heat. Boil for 1 minute, then drain and rinse again under cold running water. Discard any skin and coarse tissue and dry the sweetbreads thoroughly with a cloth or absorbent paper. Rinse the mushrooms under cold running water and slice thickly.

Heat three-fourths of the butter in a skillet over moderate heat. Add the sweetbreads, onion and salt and pepper and sauté until golden brown. Remove the contents of the skillet, drain and keep hot. Add the mushrooms and a dash of salt to the skillet, sauté over moderate heat until soft, remove, drain and keep hot with the sweetbreads.

Pour the Marsala into the juices remaining in the skillet and reduce by half over high heat. Stir in the meat sauce and simmer to reduce and thicken. Stir in the sweetbreads, onion and mushrooms and add the remaining butter. Cook for a few seconds before serving in a heated serving dish.

OXTAIL IN WINE SAUCE

Serves 6

3–4 lb oxtail joints	½ teaspoon chopped fresh
1 small carrot	marjoram or ¼ teaspoon dried
1 leek	marjoram
6½ pints cold water	¾ cup dry white wine
2–3 teaspoons coarse salt	dash nutmeg
1 stalk celery	salt and pepper
½ bay leaf	3 lb celery hearts
1 small onion	dash cinnamon
2 lb tomatoes	1 tablespoon pine nut kernels
5 slices Canadian-style bacon	1 tablespoon seedless white raisins
3 tablespoons olive oil	

Soak the oxtail joints for 1 hour in cold water, or let stand for 30 minutes under slowly running water. Place in a large saucepan with plenty of cold water and bring to a boil. Simmer for about 10 minutes, drain well and dry with a cloth or absorbent paper. Peel the carrot. Trim the leek and wash thoroughly. Trim and wash the celery. Return the oxtail to the pan and add the measured cold water and the salt. Place over high heat and bring to a boil. Lower the heat and skim carefully. Add the carrot, leek, celery and bay leaf and simmer gently for 3 hours.

Remove the oxtail, drain and dry with a cloth or absorbent paper. Discard the vegetables and bay leaf and reserve the stock. Peel and finely chop the onion. Peel and chop the tomatoes and press through a sieve. Grind the bacon. Heat the olive oil in a saucepan over moderate heat, add the bacon, onion and marjoram and sauté until lightly browned. Add the oxtail. Simmer for 2–3 minutes, then pour in the wine and reduce to 1 tablespoon. Stir in the tomatoes, season with the nutmeg and salt and pepper and continue cooking for about 1 hour, or until the meat comes away from the bone. If the sauce begins to thicken too much, add a little of the reserved oxtail stock.

Meanwhile, cook the celery hearts in lightly salted boiling water until barely tender. Drain and add to the oxtail with the cinnamon about 10 minutes before the end of the cooking time. Just before serving, stir in the pine nut kernels and raisins. Pour into a deep heated serving dish and serve.

EASTER PIE

Serves 6

8 cups all-purpose flour	2 cups Ricotta cheese
1½ teaspoons salt	2 tablespoons all-purpose flour
1 tablespoon olive oil	¼ cup light cream
2½ cups water	salt and freshly ground black
for the filling:	pepper
4 oz young, small-veined beet	3 tablespoons olive oil
leaves or very young artichokes	6 eggs
¼ cup grated Parmesan cheese	¼ cup melted butter
1½ teaspoons chopped fresh	
marjoram and parsley or	
1 teaspoon dried marjoram	
and parsley	

Sift the flour and salt on to a marble slab or into a mixing bowl and make a well in the center. Pour in the olive oil and water and mix to a very soft dough. Knead well and divide into 20 pieces. Place the pieces on a floured cloth and cover with a damp cloth.

Rinse the beet leaves under cold running water. Drain well and shred finely. Cook in lightly salted boiling water for 8–10 minutes. Drain the beet leaves, squeeze to remove the excess moisture and spread on a large plate. Sprinkle with half the Parmesan cheese and the marjoram and parsley. If using artichokes, discard the coarse outer leaves, clean the remaining leaves thoroughly, cut into fine strips and cook in lightly salted boiling water. Drain well and continue as above.

Blend the Ricotta cheese with the remaining flour and press through a sieve into a bowl. Add the cream and the salt and pepper. Roll out 10 pieces of the dough into very thin round sheets, each about 14 inches in diameter. Place in layers in a greased 12-inch deep spring-form pan, brushing each layer except the last with olive oil. Carefully press them firmly against the bottom and sides of the pan. Spread the beet leaves evenly over the top layer of dough. Sprinkle with olive oil and cover with the Ricotta mixture. With the back of a spoon, make 6 hollows in the cheese mixture and carefully crack 1 egg into each one, without breaking the yolks. Pour a little of the melted butter over each egg. Season with salt and pepper to taste and sprinkle with the remaining Parmesan cheese.

Roll out the remaining pieces of dough to the same size as the previous pieces. Place in layers over the mixture, brushing each one with oil. Trim the surplus dough overlapping the edge of the pan. Make a braid with these trimmings and place it around the edge of the pie. Brush the surface of the dough with oil and lightly prick with a fork, without breaking the egg yolks, to allow the steam to escape during cooking. Bake in a preheated moderately hot oven (375°) for 50 minutes–1 hour. Serve hot or cold.

Easter pie

STUFFED CAPON

Serves 6

1 capon, about 4 lb	3–4 tablespoons chicken stock
salt and pepper	cold water (see recipe)
1 cup grated Stravecchio cheese	1 small carrot
(matured Parmesan)	1 small onion
6 tablespoons butter	1 clove
2 eggs	1 stalk celery
1 cup fine fresh breadcrumbs	

Using a sharp knife, remove the breast bone from the capon. Season the cavity of the capon with salt and pepper. Mix together the cheese, butter, eggs, breadcrumbs and salt and pepper to taste, adding enough stock to make a soft stuffing. Stuff the bird, sew up the opening and truss the bird with fine string. Place in a flameproof casserole or a large saucepan and cover with lightly salted cold water. Bring to a boil over moderate heat and skim the surface carefully.

Meanwhile, peel the carrot and onion. Stick the clove into the onion and add with the carrot and the celery to the casserole. Lower the heat, cover tightly and simmer for about 1½ hours, or until the capon is tender.

Remove the capon, drain well and remove the string. Carve and arrange on a heated serving plate. Surround with boiled seasonal vegetables or vegetables fried in butter. Serve with green sauce (see page 198).

STEWED GOOSE

Serves 6

1 goose, about 6 lb	2 tablespoons all-purpose flour
salt and pepper	vegetable stock (see recipe)
1 large onion	⅔ cup tomato sauce (see page 197)
1 large carrot	dash mixed spice
1 clove garlic	4 slices Canadian-style bacon
4 oz goose fat	1 lb *luganeghe* or pure pork
⅓ cup dry red wine	sausage

Cut the goose into pieces and season with salt and pepper. Peel and thinly slice the onion and carrot. Peel and crush the garlic. Heat half the goose fat in a saucepan. Add the goose, onion and carrot and sauté until browned. Add the wine and reduce it over moderate heat until evaporated almost completely, then sprinkle in the flour, a little at a time. Cook until golden brown, stirring constantly. Pour in enough stock to cover the goose completely. Add the garlic, tomato sauce and mixed spice. Bring to a boil, cover tightly and simmer for about 1½ hours, or until tender.

Meanwhile, dice the bacon and cut the sausage into 2-inch pieces. Heat the remaining goose fat in a second saucepan, add the bacon and sausage and sauté for 5–10 minutes.

Drain the goose, place in a clean saucepan and add the sautéed bacon and sausage. Strain the sauce over the goose through a fine sieve, place over low heat and bring to a boil. Cover the pan tightly and simmer for 1 hour. Serve very hot.

Stuffed capon; green sauce (see page 198)

ROAST WOODCOCK

Serves 2

1 woodcock, hung but not	1½ teaspoons chopped bacon fat
dressed	1 teaspoon brandy
salt and pepper	¼ cup chicken stock
3–4 thin slices bacon fat	1 teaspoon butter
½ cup butter	1 teaspoon lemon juice
2 slices bread	

Pluck the woodcock and remove and discard the feet, eyes and gizzard, but do not draw the bird. Singe, then wipe thoroughly with a clean cloth or absorbent paper. Truss the legs together. Bend the head toward the tail and push the long beak like a skewer through the nearest leg, the body, then the second leg, to hold the bird in position. Season with salt and pepper. Wrap the woodcock in the bacon fat and secure with fine string. Melt half the butter in a saucepan over high heat, add the woodcock and sauté until brown. Lower the heat and continue cooking for about 20 minutes.

Meanwhile, melt the remaining butter in a skillet over moderate heat. Cut off the bread crusts and sauté the bread until golden brown on each side. Remove from the skillet and drain.

Remove the woodcock from the saucepan, discard the string and slices of bacon fat, cut the bird in half lengthwise and scoop the intestines into a bowl. Add the chopped bacon fat, brandy and salt and pepper. Blend thoroughly with a fork and spread the mixture on the sautéed bread slices. Place in a preheated moderately hot oven (400°) for 2 minutes to set the mixture.

Add the stock to the juices remaining in the saucepan and reduce to ¼ cup over moderate heat. Remove the pan from the heat and add the butter and the lemon juice. Place the bread slices on 2 heated plates with half a woodcock on each. Pour over the gravy and serve.

SPIT-ROASTED WOOD PIGEONS WITH OLIVES AND WINE

Serves 6

3 wood pigeons	¼ cup dry white wine
12 green olives, pitted	¼ cup lemon juice
2–3 fresh or dried sage leaves,	salt and pepper
chopped	fried croutons
⅓ cup olive oil	

Clean, wash and dry the pigeons. Pound the olives with a pestle in a mortar or with a wooden rolling pin in a bowl. Add the sage to the olives with the olive oil, wine, lemon juice and salt and pepper. Thread the pigeons on to a spit rod and brush with the olive mixture, reserving a little for basting. Place over wood embers and charcoal or in a rôtisserie with a pan beneath to collect the juices. Cook for about 1 hour, brushing the pigeons occasionally with the remaining olive mixture.

Cut the pigeons in half lengthwise and arrange on a heated serving plate. Pour the juices from the drippings pan over them and garnish with fried croutons. Serve immediately.

Beans in a flask

RISOTTO ALLA MILANESE

Serves 6

¼ onion	2¼ cups long-grain rice
1 cup butter	salt
3 tablespoons bone marrow	dash saffron powder
dash pepper	about 4¼ cups vegetable stock
⅔ cup dry white wine	1 cup grated Parmesan cheese

Finely chop the onion. Melt about one-third of the butter in a saucepan over low heat and add the onion, bone marrow and pepper. Sauté the onion until soft, but not browned, then add the wine and reduce by half. Add the rice and salt and cook for 2–3 minutes, stirring constantly. Add the saffron powder and stock and bring to a boil, still stirring. Simmer for about 15 minutes, stirring constantly and adding a little additional hot stock, if necessary, to prevent the rice from sticking to the pan. Remove the pan from the heat when the rice is *al dente* (cooked but still firm). Add the remaining butter and 3–4 tablespoons of the cheese. Set aside for 2–3 minutes in a warm place, then transfer to a heated serving dish. Serve with the remaining cheese.

BEANS IN A FLASK

Serves 6

2 cups dried *toscanelli* beans or navy beans	6 tablespoons olive oil
2 cloves garlic	few fresh or dried sage leaves
	salt and freshly ground pepper

Clean the beans and soak in plenty of cold water for at least 12 hours. Drain and place in a chianti flask from which the straw has been removed. The flask should be about three-fourths full so that the beans can swell. Peel and crush the garlic. Add the garlic, olive oil and sage and cover with water. Plug the flask loosely with straw or cotton so the steam can escape during cooking and help the beans absorb the oil.

Place the flask over the glowing embers of a charcoal fire or in a preheated moderately hot oven (375°) and cook for 3 hours. Pour the beans into a heated serving bowl and season with a little more olive oil and salt and pepper to taste. Serve hot.

POLENTA (CORN MEAL PUDDING)

Serves 6

4¼ cups water

1 teaspoon salt

2 cups yellow corn meal

3–4 tablespoons boiling water

Boil the water with the salt in a large heavy saucepan. Sprinkle in one-third of the corn meal, a little at a time. Using a wooden spoon, stir the mixture constantly. As the mixture thickens, add the 3–4 tablespoons boiling water. After 15 minutes, sprinkle in another third of the corn meal, stirring constantly. Gradually add the remaining corn meal and continue stirring until the mixture is well blended. The *polenta* is perfectly cooked when it comes away easily from the side of the pan. This takes 30–45 minutes, but to make the corn meal easier to digest, and to remove its slightly bitter taste, it is advisable to extend the cooking period to at least 1 hour, stirring frequently.

The *polenta* may be eaten very hot with various sauces and garnishes, or cold, sliced in the classic way using strong fine thread or cheese wire rather than a knife, and served with butter and freshly grated Parmesan cheese. It may also be cut into thick slices and fried. Sliced cold *polenta* is a good substitute for bread, especially with a beef stew.

POLENTA WITH SALAMI AND TOMATO SAUCE

Serves 6

polenta (see preceding recipe)

1 lb *codeghì* salami (see note)

2 slices bacon

1½ lb tomatoes

¾ cup butter

dash nutmeg

salt and pepper

1½ cups grated Parmesan cheese

Prepare the *polenta* following the instructions in the preceding recipe. Turn it out of the saucepan on to a slightly dampened marble slab and, using the flat side of a knife dipped frequently in boiling water, spread it out to ½ inch thick. Let stand until cold. Slice the *codeghì*. Chop the bacon slices. Peel the tomatoes and press through a sieve into a small bowl. Melt two-thirds of the butter in a skillet over moderate heat. Add the *codeghì* and the bacon and sauté until well browned. Add the tomatoes and season with the nutmeg and salt and pepper to taste. Cook over moderate heat for about 1 hour, adding 3–4 tablespoons of water if the sauce becomes too thick.

Grease a 1½-quart casserole or pie dish with half the remaining butter and line with 2 or 3 layers of sliced *polenta*, laid crisscross, sprinkling each layer with a few tablespoons of sauce and cheese, leaving half the cheese for serving. Dot the remaining butter in small pieces on the surface. Cook in a preheated moderately hot oven (400°) until golden brown. Serve with the remaining cheese.

Note: Codeghì is salami with a high percentage of lean meat.

BOLOGNESE SAUCE

Makes approximately 2½ cups

½ small onion

½ small carrot

1 small clove garlic

1 small stalk celery

3 dried mushrooms, soaked and drained, or 3 fresh mushrooms

2 tablespoons butter

3 tablespoons olive oil

2 oz lean and fat ham or Canadian-style bacon, chopped

8 oz beef, coarsely ground

6 tablespoons dry red wine

sprig parsley

sprig marjoram

salt and pepper

2 teaspoons all-purpose flour

8 oz tomatoes

Peel and chop the onion, carrot and garlic. Chop the celery and mushrooms. Melt the butter in a skillet over moderate heat, add the onion, carrot, garlic and celery and sauté until lightly browned. Remove the skillet from the heat and set aside.

Heat the olive oil in a saucepan over moderate heat, add the ham and sauté until lightly browned. Add the onion mixture, mushrooms and beef. Cook for 10–15 minutes over moderate heat, then pour the wine over the ingredients. Chop the parsley and marjoram together, add to the pan and season with salt and pepper.

When the wine is almost completely reduced, remove the pan from the heat and stir in the flour. Mix thoroughly, then return to the heat and cook the mixture very gently for 10–15 minutes, stirring constantly. Peel and chop the tomatoes and add to the sauce. Add 1 tablespoon of water occasionally to prevent the sauce from sticking. Remove the pan from the heat as soon as the sauce is well blended and slightly thickened. Use as required.

TOMATO SAUCE

Makes approximately 2½ cups

2 lb tomatoes

1 medium-sized onion

1 small carrot

1 stalk celery

1 clove garlic

¼ cup lard

2 oz ham or bacon fat, finely ground

few sprigs parsley

few sprigs marjoram

1 clove

paprika

⅔ cup dry white wine

salt

Peel and slice the tomatoes, onion and carrot. Wash and slice the celery. Peel and crush the garlic. Heat the lard and ham fat in a saucepan over moderate heat, add the garlic and sauté until lightly browned. Add the onion, carrot, celery, parsley, marjoram, clove and paprika to taste. Stir together until lightly browned, then pour in the wine and reduce almost completely. Add the tomatoes and season with salt. Cover the pan tightly and simmer over moderate heat for about 1 hour, stirring occasionally. Add a little hot water occasionally, if necessary, to prevent the sauce from becoming too thick. Remove the pan from the heat and strain through a fine sieve. Use as required.

GREEN SAUCE

Makes approximately 1¼ cups

large bunch parsley	1 tablespoon chopped onion
2–3 anchovy fillets	dash salt
3–4 pickled onions	6 tablespoons olive oil
1 small potato, cooked	1 tablespoon vinegar
1 clove garlic	

Remove the parsley leaves from the stems and place with the anchovy fillets, pickled onions and cold potato in a mortar or a mixing bowl. Peel the garlic and chop finely. Add with the onion and salt to the mortar. Pound the ingredients with a pestle or wooden rolling pin to form a soft paste. Place the mixture in a bowl and gradually add the oil, drop by drop, beating well after each addition until it resembles thick mayonnaise. Stir in the vinegar. Serve with cold fish and egg dishes and with salads.

MEAT SAUCE

Makes approximately 3 cups

4 oz pork or ham rind	1½ oz ham, ground
4 oz Canadian-style bacon, in 1 piece	3 dried mushrooms, soaked and drained, or 3 fresh mushrooms
1 lb rolled rump of beef	1 clove
2 teaspoons salt	*bouquet garni* (see recipe)
¼ teaspoon pepper	⅓ cup dry red wine
2 medium-sized carrots	1 large tomato
1 medium-sized onion	¼ cup all-purpose flour
1 clove garlic	3¾ cups hot water
1 stalk celery	

Simmer the pork rind in boiling water for 5 minutes. Drain well and chop coarsely. Cut the bacon into ½-inch cubes. Make small incisions in the beef and press a cube of bacon into each incision. Sprinkle the beef with the salt and pepper. Peel and slice the carrots, onion and garlic. Clean and chop the celery.

Place the pork rind and ham in a flameproof casserole. Sauté very gently over low heat until the fat on the rind begins to melt. Place the beef in the casserole with the carrots, onion, garlic, celery, mushrooms and clove. Increase the heat to moderate and sauté the ingredients until the beef begins to brown. Add the *bouquet garni* (1 bay leaf, 1 sprig thyme, 1 sprig marjoram, tied together) and the wine. Increase the heat to high and boil rapidly until the wine is almost completely reduced. Peel and chop the tomato. Remove the casserole from the heat and stir in the flour. Return to moderate heat and simmer for 2–3 minutes, stirring constantly. Stir in the tomato and the water and bring to a boil. Cover tightly and cook in a preheated cool oven (300°) for 4 hours.

Remove the beef from the casserole and use in another dish. Remove the *bouquet garni* and press the sauce through a sieve into a saucepan. Simmer gently over moderate heat until reduced to a consistency thick enough to coat the back of a spoon. Adjust the seasoning and skim the surface to remove any fat. Pour the sauce into a bowl and set aside to cool. Use as required. This meat sauce will keep for several days in the refrigerator.

HOT GARLIC AND ANCHOVY SAUCE

Serves 6

5 cloves garlic	1 cup olive oil
1¼ cups milk	¼ cup butter
4 oz anchovy fillets	

Peel and finely chop the garlic and soak in half the milk for 2 hours. Soak the anchovy fillets in the remaining milk for 10–15 minutes to remove the excess salt.

Drain the garlic. Drain the anchovy fillets and pound to form a paste. Heat the olive oil and butter in a small saucepan over very low heat, add the anchovy paste and mix well. Add the garlic and continue cooking very gently for 20 minutes, stirring occasionally. Pour the sauce into a chafing dish, place over low heat and serve as a dip with raw vegetables such as celery, carrots, fennel stems, cauliflower florets and radishes.

PESTO (BASIL, GARLIC AND CHEESE SAUCE)

Serves 6

large bunch fresh basil	dash coarse salt
few spinach leaves (optional)	¾–1 cup grated Pecorino Sardo or Parmesan cheese
few sprigs parsley (optional)	
few sprigs marjoram (optional)	6 tablespoons olive oil
3 cloves garlic	2–3 tablespoons liquid (see recipe)

Remove the stems and thoroughly clean the basil in a cloth without washing. Clean the spinach, parsley and marjoram, if used, in a similar manner. Peel the garlic. Place the basil, spinach, parsley, marjoram, garlic and the salt in a large mortar or a bowl. Pound the mixture carefully, stirring occasionally, until reduced to a smooth pulp. Add the cheese and pound to a well-blended paste.

Add the oil drop by drop, beating constantly, as if making a mayonnaise. Blend liquid into the paste until smooth (preferably use water in which pasta has been cooked or, alternatively, cold water).

Note: If *pesto* is made in a large quantity, it may be poured into jars, covered with a layer of olive oil and stored for use as required.

Sicilian pastry horns

SICILIAN PASTRY HORNS

Serves 6

for the pastry:
3 cups all-purpose flour
dash salt
¾ cup Marsala
dash sugar
olive oil for deep-frying

for the filling:
¼ cup pistachio nuts
¼ cup chopped mixed candied peel
2½ cups Ricotta cheese
1 cup sugar
for the decoration:
sifted confectioners' sugar

Sift the flour and salt on to a marble slab or into a mixing bowl and make a well in the center. Pour in the Marsala, add the sugar and mix to a firm dough. Knead lightly until smooth, cover with a damp cloth and set aside for about 2 hours.

Roll the pastry into sheets, about ⅛ inch thick, and cut into 4-inch squares. Roll each square around a cream horn tin or a metal cone-shaped mold about 4 inches long, and set aside for about 30 minutes.

Heat the olive oil in a deep saucepan and add the pastry-covered tins. Remove them when the pastry is golden brown and drain well. Place on a cloth to cool slightly. Slide the pastry horns carefully off the tins and let stand until cold.

To make the filling, finely chop the pistachio nuts and the candied peel. Blend thoroughly with the cheese and the sugar. Place the filling in a pastry bag with a large plain tip. Fill the pastry horns and dust with confectioners' sugar.

ZABAIONE

Serves 4

4 egg yolks
½ cup sugar

1 tablespoon cold water
½ cup sweet white wine or
  Marsala

Stir together the egg yolks, sugar and cold water in the top of a double boiler or in a large ovenproof bowl over simmering water. When the mixture is smooth and slightly thickened, pour in the wine gradually. Beat vigorously until thick and foamy.

Remove the double boiler from the heat and continue beating for a few moments off the heat. Pour into 4 large serving glasses and serve immediately.

ZUPPA INGLESE (TRIFLE)

Serves 6

sponge cake (see below)
¼ cup Alkermes liqueur (see note)
   or fruit or flower liqueur
¼ cup rum
1 tablespoon cold water
for the custard:
2 cups milk
6 tablespoons sugar
½ cup all-purpose flour

3 egg yolks
1 tablespoon finely chopped
   mixed candied peel
for the meringue:
3 egg whites
½ cup sugar
for the decoration:
strips candied orange peel
sugar for dusting

Make the sponge cake following the instructions given below, cut into thin pieces and place on two plates. Sprinkle the Alkermes over the cake on one plate, and the rum, diluted with the water, over the remaining cake. Set aside for 20–30 minutes.

To make the custard, scald the milk in a small saucepan. Mix the sugar and flour together in a second saucepan. Lightly beat the egg yolks and blend into the sugar mixture. Gradually stir in the hot milk. Place over low heat and cook for about 5 minutes, or until the mixture thickens, stirring constantly with a wooden spoon or whisk. It should be a thick pouring consistency. Spread ¼ cup of the custard on a round ovenproof serving plate, about 12 inches in diameter. Arrange the cake soaked in Alkermes on top. Add the candied peel to the remaining custard, stir and spoon over the cake. Arrange the sponge slices soaked in rum on top in a dome shape.

To make the meringue, beat the egg whites until stiff and fold in the sugar. Spread the meringue smoothly over the surface of the trifle with a spatula. Decorate with the orange peel and lightly dust with sugar. Bake in a preheated moderate oven (325°) for about 15 minutes, or until the meringue is lightly colored. Remove from the oven and set aside to cool before serving.

Note: Alkermes is a cordial or liqueur flavored with various herbs and spices mixed with sugar.

SPONGE CAKE

Serves 6

1¼ cups sugar
6 eggs
dash salt
1 cup all-purpose flour

⅔ cup potato flour or
   cornstarch
2 tablespoons melted butter

Place the sugar, eggs and salt in a bowl, preferably copper, over a saucepan of simmering water. Beat lightly until the mixture begins to thicken, then remove from the heat and continue to beat until the mixture is very thick and almost white in color. Sift the flour with the potato flour, then sift it into the egg mixture and fold in very gently, using a metal spoon. Fold in the butter.

Pour the mixture into 2 lined, buttered and floured 9-inch round layer cake pans and bake in a preheated moderate oven (350°) for 35–40 minutes. Let stand in the pans to cool for 5 minutes, then turn on to a rack and set aside to cool completely. Use as required.

ST. JOSEPH'S SUGAR PUFFS

Serves 6

6 tablespoons butter
dash salt
1 cup cold water
1½ cups all-purpose flour
4 eggs
2 egg yolks

1 teaspoon sugar
2 teaspoons grated lemon rind
olive oil and lard for deep-frying
vanilla sugar for dusting (see
   Yeoman's Snuff, page 81)

Place the butter and salt in a saucepan and add the water. Bring to a boil over moderate heat, then remove from the heat and add the flour all at once. Blend together thoroughly with a wooden spoon, replace over the heat and stir until the paste comes away from the side of the pan to form a ball. Remove from the heat, allow to cool very slightly and then beat in the eggs and egg yolks one at a time, beating thoroughly after each addition.

When tiny bubbles appear, add the sugar and lemon rind and mix until thoroughly blended. Form into a ball, remove from the pan, wrap in a cloth and let stand in a cool place for about 30 minutes.

Roll pieces of the dough into walnut-sized balls. Heat the olive oil and lard in a large saucepan over moderate heat and drop in a few of the balls. The puffs will turn over automatically in the hot oil. When they begin to swell, increase the heat. Fry for about 5–10 minutes, or until golden brown. Remove and drain. Let the oil cool slightly, then repeat the procedure with a few more balls. Dust with vanilla sugar and serve very hot on a plate lined with a paper napkin.

CRISP FLORENTINE PASTRIES

Serves 6

3 cups all-purpose flour
¼ cup butter
3 eggs
dash sugar

dash salt
oil for deep-frying
vanilla sugar for dusting (see
   Yeoman's Snuff, page 81)

Sift the flour on to a marble or wooden surface or into a mixing bowl and make a well in the center. Cream the butter until soft, then place the butter, eggs, sugar and the salt in the well, mix to a dough and knead until all the flour has been absorbed. Continue kneading until the pastry is smooth and firm. Wrap in a lightly floured cloth and set aside in a cool place for about 1 hour.

Place the dough on a floured surface and cut into 2 or 3 pieces. Roll each piece into a sheet, about ⅛ inch thick, and cut into circles, rectangles and strips.

Heat the oil in a deep saucepan until very hot and fry the pastries, a few at a time, until golden brown. Drain well and sprinkle with vanilla sugar. Serve on a plate lined with a paper napkin.

Crisp Florentine pastries

EASTERN MEDITERRANEAN

Bulent Rauf

Photography by John Lee

The Byzantine-Ottoman, or Eastern Mediterranean, cuisine ranks among the most famous in the world. The area termed 'Eastern Mediterranean' comprises the geographic crescent of land that lies on the eastern shores of the Mediterranean, from Greece, east through Turkey and south to Lebanon. Further south is Israel which has a *kosher* cuisine. Since this is quite a different type of cooking, it has its own section in this book. Then comes Egypt which, again, falls under the influence of Eastern Mediterranean cooking.

Vegetables have a place to themselves as in no other cuisine. They constitute dishes in their own right, not as a mere side dish or garnish for meat and fish. The variety and taste are exceptional: they are considered to be at their best when still very young and tender. Most vegetables are cooked *mijote* (cooked very slowly in a covered container) with a plate, fitting loosely into the cooking pot, placed upside down on the vegetables before the lid is put on.

Istanbul, the focal point for Eastern Mediterranean cooking, is renowned for its vegetables and fish. The fish spawn in the Black Sea and the young ones are caught as they swim down the Bosporus on their way to the Mediterranean. Their taste is superb.

The Turkish province of Ismir is a region rich in mineral resources and the fertile soil yields many important crops such as chestnuts, olives, raisins, figs, sesame, wheat, barley and beans. Ismir is famous for its seedless raisins and delicious dried figs. When fresh, the green grapes from which the raisins are made are small, extremely thin-skinned and brown speckled. The figs are also small and some of them are left to ripen on the tree until they are entirely sun-soaked, half dried and the taste is concentrated.

The soft fruits of the Lebanon are among the best in the world. The queen of all apricots grows in the region around the city of Baalbek. It is a white, translucent fruit, with the pit visible through the flesh if held up to the light. These apricots do not travel well and consequently are never exported. Superb cherries are grown in the village of Hammana, and the purple plums from the sun-drenched slopes of the Lebanon Mountains are probably unequaled in size and juiciness.

Egypt, because of its climate, can produce three annual crops of each vegetable, and with such an abundance it was natural that the Egyptians should have favored the Eastern Mediterranean methods of preparing and cooking vegetables, since these are among the finest in the world. One dish that is so utterly 'ancient Egypt' it cannot be prepared elsewhere is *faseekh*. This is a fish which has to be cured buried in sun-soaked sands. When it is unearthed after 40–50 days' burial, its smell and taste are quite distinctive!

Greece has developed a style of cooking which is peculiar to its more limited natural resources. Lack of pasture land, and as a result, of butter, has resulted in a greater use of oil and a strong dependence on the sea for food. Fish is the staple diet along the coasts.

Yet, with all its differences, Greek cooking remains a part of the rich extensive school of Eastern Mediterranean cooking which links the Balkan States with Asia, the Black Sea with the Aegean, and reaches from the eastern shores of the Mediterranean down to the northern tip of Africa.

EGGPLANT IN TAHINA SAUCE

Serves 4

2 large eggplants	cold water (see recipe)
few drops lemon juice	2 tablespoons lemon juice
salt and pepper	salt and pepper
1 teaspoon chopped fresh parsley	1 teaspoon olive oil
for the sauce:	
3 tablespoons *tahina* (sesame paste, see note)	

Rinse the eggplants under cold running water. Place in a preheated moderately hot oven (400°) for 15–20 minutes, or until the skins are charred and the eggplants are limp. Remove from the oven and, when cool enough to handle, cut in half lengthwise and remove the pulpy flesh. Discard the skins. Mash the flesh in a bowl with a few drops of lemon juice, salt and pepper to taste and the parsley.

To make the sauce, mix the *tahina* in a bowl with enough cold water to give a soft, creamy consistency. Stir in the lemon juice, a little salt and pepper to taste and the olive oil. Mix the eggplant into the *tahina* sauce and serve cold.

Note: Prepare the *tahina* as for *Houmous v' tehina*, page 246. It may also be purchased in an oriental food store or in a health food shop.

CRACKED WHEAT PILAV

Serves 6

1¼ cups cracked wheat	salt and pepper
8 oz lamb, cut from the leg	1 Italian red pepper pod
1 large onion	(see note)
¼ cup butter	

Wash the cracked wheat in a sieve under cold running water and soak in cold water for 1 hour. Cut the lamb into 1-inch cubes. Peel and finely chop the onion. Melt the butter in a saucepan over moderate heat and sauté the onion until golden brown. Add the lamb and cook until it begins to brown. Add salt and pepper to taste and just enough water to cover the meat. Tightly cover the pan and boil the meat rapidly for 15 minutes. Reduce the heat to a minimum and simmer for a further 30–35 minutes, or until all the liquid has been absorbed.

Drain the cracked wheat and add to the meat with the red pepper pod. Cook very slowly, adding warm water at frequent intervals, until the cracked wheat bursts and all the liquid has been absorbed. This takes about 20–30 minutes.

Heap the *pilav* in a mound on a heated serving dish and place the red pepper pod on top. Serve the hot *pilav*, without accompaniment, to begin a meal.

Note: The Italian species of long, red pepper pods, less hot than chili pepper but more aromatic, is largely used in this region. A small dried red chili may be substituted.

SOUR LEEKS

Serves 4

12 large leeks	1 teaspoon sugar
¼ cup olive oil	salt and pepper
1 tablespoon vinegar	1 teaspoon chopped fresh parsley

Cut off the green upper part of the leeks and about ¼ inch from the root end. Reserve the tender green leaves for another dish. Cut the white part of the leeks in half lengthwise and rinse thoroughly under cold running water to remove any sand. Slice the leeks lengthwise very finely.

Heat the oil in a heavy saucepan over high heat, add the sliced leeks and sauté until golden brown, stirring constantly. Lower the heat, add just enough water to cover the leeks and stir in the vinegar, sugar and salt and pepper to taste. Simmer over fairly low heat for 30 minutes. Place the leeks in a serving dish and set aside until cold. Serve sprinkled with the parsley.

CUCUMBER IN YOGURT

Serves 4

1 cucumber	2 cups unflavored yogurt
1 teaspoon finely chopped fresh	salt and pepper
mint	olive oil

Peel and finely chop the cucumber, place in a bowl and add half the mint. Beat the yogurt with salt and pepper to taste and mix with the cucumber. Adjust the seasoning, if necessary, and trickle olive oil over the surface. Sprinkle with the remaining mint and serve well chilled with a bowl of olives and brown bread.

YOGURT SOUP

Serves 4

½ cup all-purpose flour	salt and pepper
cold water (see recipe)	½ teaspoon paprika
3¾ cups meat broth	2 teaspoons chopped fresh mint
1 cup unflavored yogurt	

Blend the flour with a little cold water to form a a smooth soft paste. Pour the broth into a large saucepan and bring to a boil. Remove the pan from the heat and stir in the flour and water paste. Return the pan to the heat and bring back to a boil, stirring constantly until the liquid thickens. Remove the pan from the heat.

Beat the yogurt with salt and pepper to taste, most of the paprika and the mint. Stir the mixture into the thickened broth. Serve in a heated soup tureen with a sprinkling of the remaining paprika. A spoonful of yogurt may also be added to each bowl.

FRIED MUSSELS

Serves 4–6

3 pints mussels	1 cup all-purpose flour
⅔ cup water	⅔ cup lager or pale ale
for the batter:	oil for deep-frying
2 eggs	1 lemon, sliced
salt and pepper	few sprigs parsley

Discarding any that are open, scrub the mussels well under cold water and remove the beards. Place the mussels in a large saucepan and add the water. Tightly cover the pan and place over high heat for 8–10 minutes, or until the mussels open. Remove the pan from the heat and, when cool enough to handle, remove each mussel from its shell. Discard the shells and any unopened mussels and set the mussels aside until required.

To make the batter, beat the eggs until frothy. Add the salt and pepper to taste. Sift the flour into a bowl and add the beaten eggs gradually, beating thoroughly after each addition, until the mixture is smooth. Beat in the lager. Let the batter stand for 40 minutes. Heat the oil in a deep-fat fryer. Dip each mussel into the batter and deep-fry until crisp and golden brown. Drain on absorbent paper. Serve the hot mussels garnished with the lemon slices and parsley.

FISH SOUP WITH TOMATOES

Serves 4

1½ lb cod, haddock or halibut	1 fish head
1 teaspoon salt	3–4 large sprigs fresh parsley
2 large onions	4 pints water
2 medium-sized carrots	salt and pepper
4 medium-sized tomatoes	½ cup olive oil
2 stalks celery	¼ cup short-grain rice

Discard the bones and skin from the fish. Rinse the flesh under cold running water and then cut into 2-inch pieces. Sprinkle the fish pieces with the salt and drain in a colander. Peel and thinly slice the onions and carrots. Peel the tomatoes. Chop the celery. Place the vegetables in a large saucepan with the fish head and parsley sprigs. Add the water and salt and pepper to taste. Place the pan over moderate heat, bring to a boil, then lower the heat and simmer for 45 minutes. Remove the fish head and parsley sprigs. Add the pieces of fish to the simmering stock and poach for 20–25 minutes, or until the fish is cooked but still firm.

Remove the fish from the pan and keep hot in a covered dish. Gently stir the olive oil into the soup and add the rice. Increase the heat to moderate and cook for 30 minutes, or until the rice is tender. The liquid will reduce in quantity during this cooking time. Replace the fish in the soup. Reheat gently and serve hot.

Fish soup with tomatoes

GREEK EASTER SOUP

Serves 8

3 lb lamb tripe, kidney, liver
   and heart
½ cup all-purpose flour
1 cup cold water
4 pints lukewarm water
6 scallions
¼ cup butter
3 tablespoons chopped fresh
   parsley

3 tablespoons chopped fresh dill
½ cup short-grain rice
for the avgolemono:
2 egg yolks
3 tablespoons lemon juice
½ cup soup (see recipe)
3 tablespoons milk

Clean the tripe thoroughly and rinse under cold running water. Discard any membrane and gristly parts from the kidney, liver and heart. Rinse the meat thoroughly under cold running water and drain for 2–3 minutes. Boil the tripe in salted water for 10 minutes, then drain and discard the liquid. When cool, cut the tripe into very small pieces and place in a large saucepan. Blend the flour to a very soft, smooth paste with the cold water and pour the paste over the tripe. Add the lukewarm water and bring to a boil over moderate heat, stirring constantly, until the liquid thickens slightly. Partially cover the pan, lower the heat and simmer gently for 20 minutes.

Cut the kidney, liver and heart into fairly small pieces, and boil in salted water to cover for 5–10 minutes. Drain off and discard the liquid. When cool, cut the meat into very small pieces. Chop the scallions.

Melt the butter in a skillet over moderate heat. Add the kidney, liver, heart, scallions, parsley and dill, and sauté the ingredients for 5–10 minutes, stirring frequently. Add the mixture to the simmering tripe and continue to simmer for 20–25 minutes, or until the offal is tender. Strain the liquid into a third saucepan and keep the offal warm. Add the rice to the strained liquid and bring to a boil over moderate heat. Tightly cover the pan and continue to boil for 30 minutes, or until the rice is cooked. Remove the pan from the heat.

To make the *avgolemono*, beat the egg yolks and lemon juice in a small bowl. Gradually add the ½ cup of soup, stirring constantly. Pour the egg yolk mixture back into the hot soup, add the offal and, if necessary, reheat the soup to the simmering point, but do not boil. Just before serving, add the milk.

Note: The Eastern Mediterranean sauce made from egg yolks and lemon juice is called *avgolemono* in Greece and *terbiye* in Turkey. It is blended with either soup or stock according to the individual recipe.

BROILED FISH WITH OLIVES

Serves 4

4 trout, mackerel or herring
for the sauce:
1 medium-sized onion
5 medium-sized tomatoes
12 stuffed green olives

⅓ cup olive oil
¼ cup lager or pale ale
salt and pepper
1 lemon, quartered
few sprigs parsley

Clean the fish and discard the fins and eyes. Rinse under cold running water and drain in a colander until required.

To make the sauce, peel and thinly slice the onion and the tomatoes. Slice the olives. Heat three-fourths of the oil in a skillet over moderate heat and sauté the onion until golden brown. Add the tomatoes, olives, lager and salt and pepper to taste. Lower the heat and simmer very gently for 20–30 minutes, stirring frequently.

Meanwhile, brush the prepared fish with the remaining oil and broil under moderate heat for 5–6 minutes on each side, or until the flesh becomes firm and white. Place the fish on a heated serving dish and spoon the sauce over and around them. Garnish with the lemon quarters and the parsley.

ALEXANDRIAN BAKED FISH

Serves 4

4 mackerel, trout or herring
salt and pepper
4 large onions
8 medium-sized tomatoes

1 tablespoon chopped fresh basil
   or 2 teaspoons dried basil
¼ cup olive oil

Clean the fish and discard the heads. Place the opened underside of each fish on a board and press firmly along the backbone to loosen the flesh from the bone. Turn the fish over and ease out the backbone. Rinse the fish under cold running water and dry with a cloth or absorbent paper. Sprinkle with salt and pepper to taste.

Peel and thinly slice the onions and tomatoes. Place half the onion and tomato slices in the bottom of a roasting pan or casserole and sprinkle with half the basil. Place the fish on top, cover with the remaining onion and tomato slices and sprinkle with the remaining basil and salt and pepper to taste. Sprinkle the olive oil over the top and bake the fish in a preheated moderate oven (325°) for 40–45 minutes, or until the fish is firm and white and the onions are soft.

Place the fish on a heated serving dish, arrange the onions and tomatoes over and around it, and serve hot with boiled potatoes.

Broiled fish with olives

COLD POACHED SEA BASS

Serves 4

1 sea bass, about 3 lb	4 bay leaves
for the broth:	salt and pepper
1 medium-sized onion	2 tablespoons lemon juice
1 large carrot	small strip lemon rind
small bunch celery leaves	2½ pints water

Clean the fish and wash under cold running water. Set aside while preparing the broth. Peel the onion and leave whole. Peel and thickly slice the carrot and place both in a large saucepan, with the celery leaves, bay leaves, salt and pepper to taste, lemon juice, lemon rind and water. Place the pan over high heat and bring to a boil. Lower the heat and simmer for about 25–30 minutes, or until the onion and carrot are cooked. Strain through a sieve and reserve the liquid, carrot and bay leaves. Discard the remaining ingredients.

Place the fish in the saucepan, if necessary cutting it in half. Add the reserved broth and poach slowly for 20–30 minutes, or until the flesh is firm and can be removed easily from the bones. Carefully lift the fish out of the stock. Remove the skin and bones and arrange the fish in a long shallow china serving dish. Garnish with the reserved carrot and bay leaves. Return the skin and bones to the pan and boil the broth rapidly until reduced to about one-third of the original quantity. Strain the liquid through a sieve and pour over the fish. Leave overnight in a cold place, preferably in the refrigerator, until well chilled. Serve cold in the serving dish, with boiled potatoes and lemon wedges as accompaniments.

SWORDFISH KEBAB

Serves 4

for the marinade:	**for the kebab:**
1 onion	1½ lb swordfish steaks or middle
2 dried bay leaves	cut of salmon
3 tablespoons olive oil	32 bay leaves
	1 lemon, quartered

To make the marinade, peel and chop the onion, crush the bay leaves and mix both with the olive oil.

To make the kebabs, carefully remove the skin and bones from the fish. Cut the fish into 1-inch cubes. Place about 8 fish cubes and 8 bay leaves alternately on each of 4 skewers, pushing the fish to the center of the skewer. Place the skewers in the marinade for 1 hour. If preferred, the kebabs may be cooked immediately instead of being marinated beforehand.

Cook the kebabs on each side for 3–4 minutes over a charcoal broiler, or under a hot electric broiler. If an electric broiler is used, the kebabs must be well marinated so that they are soaked in oil. Serve the kebabs hot, garnished with the lemon quarters.

FISH WITH GARLIC SAUCE

Serves 4

for the sauce:	lemon juice (see recipe)
1 large potato	**for the fish:**
4 cloves garlic, peeled	4 steaks of cod, haddock or
1 teaspoons salt	halibut, about 4–6 oz each
1 cup finely ground almonds	salt and pepper
½ cup olive oil	all-purpose flour for coating
¼ cup vinegar	oil for deep-frying
⅓ cup water	

To make the garlic sauce, peel and quarter the potato and cook in lightly salted water to cover until tender. Drain and set aside. Pound the garlic and salt in a mortar or bowl until it is a smooth paste. Add the almonds and potato and continue pounding until a smooth paste is formed. Add the olive oil very gradually, beating well after each addition. Stir in the vinegar and water and mix thoroughly. The mixture should be the consistency of thick mayonnaise. If necessary, add lemon juice until the correct consistency is achieved.

Wipe the fish with a damp cloth or absorbent paper. Sprinkle with salt and pepper to taste and coat the pieces with flour. Deep-fry in hot oil until crisp and golden brown. Drain on absorbent paper. Serve hot with the garlic sauce.

Note: When less garlic is used, this is an excellent sauce to accompany vegetables.

WHITEBAIT BIRDS

Serves 4

1 lb whitebait or sprats	salt and pepper
¾ cup all-purpose flour	bunch parsley
½ cup olive oil	1 lemon, quartered

Wash the whitebait under cold running water. Drain well. Put the flour into a large paper bag and toss the whitebait in the flour until the fish are well coated. Place the floured fish on a tray or a large plate. Take 4 or 5 whitebait at a time and press the heads together, the bodies radiating out like the spokes of a wheel or the wing of a bird. Heat the oil in a skillet over moderate heat and fry the whitebait 'birds' until crisp and brown. Drain on absorbent paper and sprinkle with salt and pepper to taste. Arrange the 'birds' on a heated flat plate and keep warm. Sauté the parsley in the oil until crisp and arrange around the fish like a nest. Garnish with the lemon quarters and serve hot.

Whitebait birds

left: *baklava (see page 228);* right: *stuffed vegetables (see page 220);*
in the background: *skewered lamb fillets*

STUFFED MACKEREL

Serves 4

4 mackerel

for the stuffing:

4 small onions
½ cup olive oil
3 tablespoons finely chopped fresh
   parsley
2 tablespoons currants
4 teaspoons chopped fresh dill or
   2 teaspoons dried dill weed

1 teaspoon cinnamon
salt and pepper
1 tablespoon pine nut kernels
½ cup water
all-purpose flour for coating
1 lemon, sliced

Remove the fins from the mackerel without breaking the
skin. With a sharp knife or scissors, make a cut along the
underside of the fish to within about 1 inch of the head and
tail. Clean the fish. Snip the backbone at each end from the
inside and very gently ease out the bone, removing as little of
the flesh as possible. To help loosen the backbone, carefully
press lightly along the bone on the outside of the fish,
without breaking the skin. Wash the fish inside and out and
dry with absorbent paper. Set aside until required.

To make the stuffing, peel and finely chop the onions.
Heat half the oil in a large skillet, add the onions and sauté
gently until soft. Add the parsley, currants, dill or dried dill
weed, cinnamon, salt and pepper and pine nut kernels. Sauté
for a further 5–10 minutes, stirring frequently until the
mixture begins to brown. Add the water and simmer for a
further 5–10 minutes until all the liquid has evaporated.
Remove the skillet from the heat and cool slightly. Spoon the
stuffing into the fish and loosely sew up the openings with
thread, or insert several small skewers and lace closed. Coat
the fish with flour.

Heat the remaining oil in the skillet over very moderate
heat and cook the mackerel for about 8–10 minutes on each
side. Remove from the skillet, drain on absorbent paper and
remove the thread or skewers. Serve the fish hot or cold,
garnished with the lemon slices.

Note: Traditionally mackerel are cleaned and boned
through the gills, leaving the fish whole and free from knife
cuts. The backbone is snapped at the head and tail end
without breaking the skin. The fish is then rolled gently but
firmly between the palms of the hands, after which the
backbone is removed through the gills.

IRONMONGERS' SALAD

Serves 4

4 large ripe tomatoes	½ teaspoon finely chopped fresh
2 long green sweet peppers	mint
1 large onion	2 tablespoons lemon juice
salt	1 teaspoon vinegar
1 tablespoon water	2–3 tablespoons olive oil
freshly ground black pepper	8–10 ripe olives
½ teaspoon finely chopped fresh	
parsley	

Peel the tomatoes and scoop out the seeds into a fine sieve placed over a bowl. Discard the seeds and reserve the juice. Trim the peppers, remove the seeds and cut the flesh into rings. Peel the onion and cut in half lengthwise. Slice each half lengthwise into very thin slices. Place the onion in a wire sieve and sprinkle liberally with salt. Press the onion and salt together until the salt has dissolved and the juice runs from the onion. Rinse the onion thoroughly under cold running water and set aside to drain.

Put half a teaspoon of salt in a salad bowl, add the water and stir well to dissolve the salt. Add the reserved tomato juice, pepper, parsley, mint, lemon juice and vinegar. Mix well and add the olive oil. The oil should be sufficient to completely cover the surface of the liquid already in the bowl. Add the tomatoes, green peppers, onion and olives and mix the ingredients. Let stand for about 30 minutes before serving.

SKEWERED LAMB FILLETS

Serves 4

1 large onion	3 tablespoons olive oil
4 fillets of lamb, about	salt and pepper
1–1½ lb (see note)	small bunch parsley

Peel and thinly slice the onion. Place in a bowl with the lamb. Add the olive oil and salt and pepper to taste. Turn the lamb over several times until the meat is well coated with oil and seasonings. Marinate overnight.

Thread each piece of meat on to a skewer in the shape of an S. Cook over a charcoal broiler, or under a moderately hot electric broiler, for about 10–12 minutes. Turn the skewers frequently so that the lamb is evenly cooked. Serve on a bed of parsley with rice.

Note: The lamb for this dish is usually cut from the narrow flat end of the neck fillet. Each piece of lamb should be no longer than 5–6 inches. If neck fillets are not available, thin, tapering fillets cut from the leg are a suitable alternative.

ONION SALAD

Serves 4

3–4 large Bermuda onions	1½ teaspoons cold water
⅓ cup salt	salt and pepper
1 teaspoon tarragon or other	¼ cup olive oil
vinegar	1 tablespoon coarsely chopped
2 tablespoons lemon juice	fresh parsley

Peel the onions and cut in half. Place cut side down on a chopping board and slice lengthwise very thinly. Place the sliced onions in a large wire sieve and sprinkle with the salt. Press the onions and salt together until all the salt has dissolved, then rinse the onions thoroughly under cold running water. Drain well.

Mix together the vinegar, lemon juice and water in a salad bowl and season with salt and pepper to taste. Beat in the olive oil gradually. Add the onion slices and parsley and mix thoroughly before serving.

LAMB SMOTHERED IN EGGPLANT

Serves 4

1½ lb lamb, cut from the leg	pepper
or shoulder	1 teaspoon chopped fresh parsley
4 eggplants	1 cup water
salt	½ cup olive oil
2 large onions	1 large tomato
¼ cup butter	

Cut the lamb into 3-inch pieces. Discard the stems from the eggplants and slice the eggplants lengthwise into the same number of slices as there are pieces of lamb. Sprinkle the slices very lightly with salt and set aside until required. Peel and coarsely chop the onions. Melt the butter in a saucepan over moderate heat and sauté the onions until golden brown. Add the pieces of meat and sauté until browned, turning frequently. Add salt and pepper to taste, the parsley and the water. Cover the pan and simmer for 35–40 minutes. Remove from the heat and let stand until cool.

Rinse the eggplant slices under cold running water and dry thoroughly with a cloth or absorbent paper. Heat the oil in a skillet over moderate heat and sauté the eggplants until lightly browned on both sides. Drain well on absorbent paper.

Remove the meat from the saucepan, wrap one slice of eggplant around each piece of lamb and place the wrapped pieces in a flameproof casserole. Pour over the liquid remaining in the saucepan.

Thinly slice the tomato, cut the slices in half and garnish each wrapped piece of lamb with one half slice. Cover the casserole, place over moderate heat and simmer for 30–40 minutes. Serve hot in the casserole. Alternatively, transfer to a heated serving dish, being careful to disturb the eggplants as little as possible, and pour over the sauce.

LITTLE DOMES

Serves 4

8 oz lamb, cut from the leg	¼ cup butter
¼ teaspoon dried thyme	1 teaspoon pine nut kernels
¼ teaspoon dried marjoram	salt and pepper
1⅓ cups cracked wheat	oil for deep-frying
1 large onion	few sprigs parsley

Finely grind the lamb and pound it very thoroughly to a smooth pulp in a mortar or a bowl with one end of a wooden rolling pin. Remove any sinews or gristle. Add half the thyme and marjoram, continue pounding for 1–2 minutes and then set aside until the mixture is required. Pound the cracked wheat in the same way to a fine gritty consistency. Set aside until required.

Peel and finely chop the onion. Heat the butter in a skillet over moderate heat. Add the onion, sauté until soft, and when the onion is just beginning to brown, add the pine nut kernels. Continue to sauté until both the onion and nuts are well browned. Remove the skillet from the heat, stir in the remaining thyme and marjoram and add salt and pepper to taste. Set aside until required.

Mix together the lamb and cracked wheat and squeeze the mixture together with the hands until the ingredients are thoroughly mixed. Divide into 24 small portions. Shape each one into a ball and make a hollow in the center. Place a little less than 1 teaspoon of the onion and nut mixture into the hollow. Seal up the opening, completely enclosing the filling, and shape into a dome. Continue until the meat and onion mixtures are used. Heat the oil in a deep-fat fryer and fry the domes. Drain the domes on absorbent paper, arrange on a serving dish and garnish with sprigs of parsley. Serve either hot or cold.

İSKENDER'S KEBAB

Serves 4

1 lb lamb, cut from the leg	1 *pide* (see note)
1 onion	2 cups unflavored yogurt
3 tablespoons olive oil	¼ cup butter
salt and pepper	

Cut the lamb into 1-inch cubes. Peel and thinly slice the onion. Place the lamb and onion in a bowl and add the olive oil and salt and pepper to taste. Mix thoroughly and set aside to marinate overnight.

Cut the *pide* into small cubes and place in 4 heat-resistant soup bowls. Place in a warm oven while preparing the kebabs. Beat the yogurt with salt and pepper to taste and set aside to come to room temperature. Thread the marinated lamb on to 4 skewers and cook over a charcoal broiler or under a hot electric broiler for 5–6 minutes, turning the skewers frequently to brown the lamb evenly. Melt the butter until it sizzles.

When the kebabs are cooked, slide the meat off the skewers on to the warmed *pide*. Cover with the beaten yogurt and pour a little hot butter over each serving. Serve immediately.

Note: Pide in Turkey is a special flat bread which is traditionally present on every table during the fasting month of Ramadan. It is very much like the Syrian bread, though whiter, larger and with quilt-like markings. If *pide* cannot be obtained, a Syrian bread, plain baked *pizza* dough (see page 182) or *pita* bread (see page 245) may be substituted.

BEEF STEW WITH QUINCES

Serves 6

1½ lb beef flank steak or	1¼ cups hot water
round steak	salt and pepper
1 medium-sized onion	1½ lb quinces
½ cup butter	2 teaspoons sugar

Cut the beef into small cubes. Peel and chop the onion. Melt the butter in a saucepan over moderate heat. Add the onion and sauté until transparent and soft. Add the beef and continue to sauté, stirring frequently, until the meat is well browned. Add the hot water and salt and pepper to taste, and bring slowly to a boil.

Meanwhile, peel, core and thickly slice the quinces. Place the quinces on top of the beef, sprinkle with the sugar and cook for 30–40 minutes, or until the beef and the quinces are tender. Transfer to a heated serving dish and serve immediately.

TRAY KIBBA (MEAT LOAF)

Serves 4

8 oz lean lamb, finely ground	½ cup butter
1⅓ cups cracked wheat	1 teaspoon fresh thyme
salt and pepper	or ½ teaspoon dried thyme
for the filling:	1 teaspoon pine nut kernels
1 large onion	

Pound the lamb to a fine pulp in a mortar or in a bowl with one end of a wooden rolling pin. Remove any sinews or gristle. Pound the cracked wheat in the same way to a fine gritty consistency. Mix the lamb and wheat together and add salt and pepper to taste. Set aside until required.

To prepare the filling, peel and finely chop the onion. Melt half the butter in a small saucepan over moderate heat. Add the onion and sauté until soft and golden brown. Remove the pan from the heat and stir in the thyme and pine nut kernels.

Spread half the lamb mixture in a small roasting pan. Cover with the filling, then spread the remaining lamb mixture over the filling. Cut the remaining butter into small cubes and place on top. Bake in a preheated moderately hot oven (375°) for 40 minutes. Cut the *kibba* into squares in the pan and serve hot as a main dish with a green salad or vegetables.

İskender's kebab

LAMB WITH OKRA

Serves 4

1½–2 lb lamb, cut from the leg	1 teaspoon chopped fresh parsley
2 large onions	1½ teaspoons chopped fresh
1 lb fresh okra or 2 (10-oz)	marjoram or 1 teaspoon dried
packages frozen okra	marjoram
2 tablespoons lemon juice	salt and pepper
¼ cup butter	1 cup water

Cut the lamb into 3-inch pieces. Peel and thickly slice the onions. If using fresh okra, wash them and trim the stems, shaping the ends into cones and taking care not to cut through the flesh. Cover with water and add the lemon juice to prevent the okra from discoloring. If using frozen okra, defrost in the packages.

Melt the butter in a saucepan over moderate heat. Add the onions and sauté gently until soft but not browned. Add the pieces of lamb, increase the heat slightly and sauté the lamb with the onions until the meat is lightly browned. Add the parsley, marjoram, salt and pepper to taste and the water. Tightly cover the pan and cook for 30 minutes. Add the okra, replace the lid and cook for a further 20 minutes. Check the amount of liquid in the pan 10 minutes before the end of the cooking time. If there is a lot, remove the lid and allow the liquid to evaporate. Serve in a heated serving dish.

LAMB LIVER IN SHARP SAUCE

Serves 4

1 lb lamb liver	3 tablespoons vinegar
½ cup all-purpose flour	⅔ cup water
½ teaspoon salt	1 teaspoon tomato paste
dash pepper	dash fresh or dried rosemary
½ cup olive oil	salt and pepper

Cut the liver into slices, about ½ inch thick, and remove any membrane or skin. Mix a third of the flour with the salt and pepper. Coat the slices of liver with the seasoned flour. Heat half the oil in a skillet over moderate heat and sauté the liver slices until browned on both sides. Remove from the skillet and place in a fairly deep serving dish.

Add the remaining oil to the oil and residue in the skillet. Stir in the remaining flour and cook over moderate heat, stirring constantly, until the mixture is golden brown. Gradually stir in the vinegar to form a smooth paste. Add the water, tomato paste and rosemary and mix well. Bring to the simmering point, adjust the seasoning, if necessary, and simmer for about 5 minutes. Pour the sauce over the liver, making sure that the liver is completely covered. Set aside until cold. Serve with a fresh green salad.

213

Paper-wrapped lamb

PAPER-WRAPPED LAMB

Serves 4

1 lb fillets of lamb, cut from the leg
1 medium-sized onion
2 tablespoons butter
½ teaspoon chopped fresh thyme or ¼ teaspoon dried thyme
½ teaspoon chopped fresh marjoram or ¼ teaspoon dried marjoram
½ teaspoon chopped fresh basil or ¼ teaspoon dried basil
½ teaspoon chopped fresh rosemary or ¼ teaspoon dried rosemary
½ teaspoon chopped fresh parsley or ¼ teaspoon dried parsley
½ teaspoon chopped fresh dill or ¼ teaspoon dried dill weed
½ dried bay leaf, crushed
salt and pepper

Cut the meat into 1-inch cubes. Peel and slice the onion very thinly. Spread equal amounts of butter on to the center of 4 12-inch squares of parchment or aluminum foil. Place equal quantities of meat, onion and herbs on each square. Sprinkle with salt and pepper to taste. Fold the paper or foil around the filling like an envelope and twist the ends firmly together, completely enclosing the filling. Cook the parcels in the center of a preheated moderately hot oven (375°) for 1–1¼ hours.

Serve the *kebabi* unopened, accompanied by zucchini or white *pilav* (see page 220).

KEFTEDES IN SAUCE

Serves 4

2 cloves garlic
4 slices bread
1 lb lean lamb, ground
½ teaspoon dried marjoram
2 eggs
3 tablespoons all-purpose flour
½ teaspoon salt
dash pepper
for the sauce:
1 medium-sized onion
2 tablespoons butter
2 tablespoons all-purpose flour
1 tablespoon tomato paste
2 cups water
salt and pepper
dash sugar
1 teaspoon chopped fresh parsley
½ teaspoon dried marjoram

Peel and crush the garlic. Cut off the crusts from the bread and discard them. Soak the bread in a little cold water for 2 minutes. Squeeze out as much water as possible. Place the lamb in a bowl. Add the bread, garlic, marjoram and eggs, and mix thoroughly to a fairly stiff paste. Roll the mixture into finger shapes, about 1 inch thick and 3 inches long. Mix the flour with the salt and pepper. Coat the meat fingers well with the seasoned flour and set aside until required.

To make the sauce, peel and finely chop the onion. Melt the butter in a saucepan over moderate heat and sauté the onion until golden brown. Stir in the flour and continue cooking for 1–2 minutes. Stir in the tomato paste. Add the

214

water gradually, mixing thoroughly after each addition. Add the salt and pepper to taste, sugar, parsley and marjoram, and bring the sauce to a boil, stirring constantly. Lower the heat to a minimum and simmer the sauce for 5 minutes.

Place the meat fingers, one by one, into the sauce, and simmer for 10–12 minutes. Transfer the meat fingers and sauce to a heated serving dish and serve hot with white *pilav* (see page 220).

CEPHALONIAN MEAT PIE

Serves 4–6

for the filling:
1 lb lamb, cut from the leg
1 large potato
1 large onion
2 cloves garlic
4 medium-sized tomatoes
3 tablespoons short-grain rice
$\frac{1}{4}$ teaspoon grated orange rind
$\frac{1}{4}$ cup grated hard cheese
1 tablespoon chopped fresh parsley

1 teaspoon chopped fresh mint
2 tablespoons melted butter
1 tablespoon olive oil
2 hard-cooked eggs
$\frac{1}{2}$ cup vegetable stock

for the basic pie dough:
4 cups all-purpose flour
dash salt
1 cup margarine or shortening
about $\frac{1}{2}$ cup water
1 tablespoon melted butter for glazing

Cut the lamb into $\frac{1}{2}$-inch cubes. Peel and finely dice the potato. Peel and finely chop the onion and garlic. Peel and chop the tomatoes, removing the seeds. Mix together the lamb, potato, onion, garlic, tomatoes, rice, orange rind, cheese, parsley, mint, butter and oil in a large bowl. Prepare the pastry as for Mince Pies, page 53.

Roll out half the pastry on a floured board into a circle, $\frac{1}{4}$ inch thick and about $1\frac{1}{2}$ inches larger than a 9-inch pie pan. Line the pie pan with the pastry and place the filling in the center. Shell and slice the hard-cooked eggs and place the slices on top of the filling. Moisten the edges of the pastry with a little of the stock and pour the remainder over the filling. Roll out the remaining pastry into a circle, slightly larger than the pie pan, and place it over the pie filling. Press the layers of pastry firmly together and trim off any excess pastry. Brush the top with the melted butter and bake in a preheated moderately hot oven (375°) for 1–$1\frac{1}{4}$ hours.

NAVY BEANS WITH LAMB

Serves 4–6

1 cup navy beans (see note)
8 oz lamb, cut from the leg
3 large onions

6 tablespoons butter
salt and pepper
dash sugar

Soak the beans overnight in plenty of cold water. Drain and put in a saucepan with just enough fresh water to cover. Place the pan over high heat and bring to a boil. Lower the heat to moderate and continue boiling the beans for 30 minutes, or until half cooked. Drain well.

Meanwhile, cut the lamb into 2-inch pieces. Peel and coarsely chop the onions. Melt the butter in a saucepan over moderate heat, add the onions and sauté until soft and golden brown. Add the lamb and cook until it is browned. Add the beans, salt and pepper to taste, sugar and enough water to cover. Cover tightly and simmer for $1\frac{1}{2}$ hours. If the lamb is not tender after this time, add a little warm water, replace the lid and continue to simmer for a further 30 minutes, stirring occasionally. Place in a heated serving dish and serve hot with white *pilav* (see page 220).

Note: Canned beans may be substituted for dried beans in this recipe, in which case the lamb should be previously cooked. The simmering time will need to be reduced accordingly.

MEAT BALLS WITH TERBIYE

Serves 4

$\frac{1}{4}$ cup short-grain rice
1 lb lean lamb or beef, ground
salt and pepper
all-purpose flour (see recipe)

$2\frac{1}{2}$ cups beef stock or bouillon
for the terbiye:
2 egg yolks
2 tablespoons lemon juice

Cook the rice in lightly salted boiling water for 10 minutes. Drain and cool. Place the rice and meat in a bowl. Season with salt and pepper. Knead and squeeze the ingredients to make a soft paste. Roll into $1\frac{1}{2}$-inch balls with floured hands. Measure the beef stock into a saucepan and bring to a boil over high heat. Drop the meat balls into the stock, reduce the heat and simmer until they rise to the surface. Remove the meat balls with a perforated spoon and keep hot in a heated covered serving dish.

Raise the heat and rapidly boil the stock until it is reduced to about half the original quantity. Remove the pan from the heat and make the *terbiye* as for Greek Easter Soup, page 207. Stir the *terbiye* into the remaining hot stock and, if necessary, reheat to simmering point, but do not boil. Pour the *terbiye* over the meat balls and serve immediately with boiled potatoes.

LAMB WITH PRUNES AND ALMONDS

Serves 6

1 lb pitted prunes	2 tablespoons all-purpose flour
2½ lb boned lamb, cut from the leg or shoulder	vegetable stock or water (see recipe)
1 large onion	salt and pepper
¼ cup lemon juice	1¾ cups blanched almonds
¼ cup butter	2 tablespoons sugar

Soak the prunes overnight in plenty of cold water. Cut the lamb into ½-inch cubes. Peel and thinly slice the onion. Mix the lamb, onion and half the lemon juice in a large bowl and marinate for at least 1 hour.

Remove the lamb from the marinade and dry with a cloth or absorbent paper. Heat the butter in a saucepan over moderate heat. Add the lamb and sauté gently for 5 minutes. Stir in the flour and continue cooking until the lamb and flour become lightly browned. Stir in enough stock or water to cover the meat completely. Add salt and pepper to taste. Bring to a boil, stirring constantly. When the mixture thickens, reduce the heat and simmer, partially covered, for 45 minutes.

Drain the prunes and add with the almonds to the meat in the pan. Continue to simmer for about 20–30 minutes, or until the prunes are cooked. Stir in the sugar and the remaining lemon juice, increase the heat and bring to the boiling point. Pour into a heated serving dish and serve immediately.

CIRCASSIAN CHICKEN

Serves 4

1 chicken, about 3 lb	1¼ cups chicken broth (see recipe)
1 large onion	3 cups ground walnuts
1 large carrot	1 small red chili or 1 Italian red pepper pod
1 large bay leaf	
1 teaspoon salt	salt and pepper

Wipe the chicken inside and out with a damp cloth or absorbent paper. Peel the onion and carrot. Place the chicken, onion, carrot, bay leaf and salt in a large saucepan. Add enough water to barely cover the chicken. Bring to a boil over high heat. Lower the heat and simmer the chicken for about 1½ hours, or until tender.

Meanwhile, place in a mortar the walnuts, red pepper and a seasoning of salt and pepper, and pound to a very fine paste. Take portions of the paste and place these in a clean fine cloth. Twist the ends in opposite directions and squeeze the paste to extract the oil from the walnuts. It is essential to do this, otherwise the texture of the dish may be too heavy. Retain the oil, which will be tinted with the red color from the chili, in a bowl and reserve the walnut paste.

When the chicken is cooked, remove the pan from the heat. Lift out the chicken, strain the broth and reserve the required amount to make the sauce. When the chicken is cool enough to handle, remove the skin and separate the chicken into joints. Discard the breastbone, the backbone and any other small bones except those in the wings and legs. Blend the walnut paste with sufficient of the reserved chicken

broth to make a thick sauce, adding the broth a little at a time. Pour the sauce over the chicken pieces. Pour over the red oil from the walnuts. Traditionally this dish is served on a platter surrounded with a border of boiled short-grain rice.

Note: A stainless steel knife should be used for cutting through the chicken since the combination of the chicken juices and the walnut oil causes discoloration.

ELBASAN CHICKEN SOUFFLÉ

Serves 4

1 chicken, about 3 lb	⅔ cup chicken broth (see recipe)
1 medium-sized carrot	¼ cup butter
1 medium-sized onion	¼ cup all-purpose flour
1 clove	2 eggs
1 bay leaf	½ cup unflavored yogurt
1 teaspoon salt	salt and pepper

Wipe the chicken inside and out with a damp cloth or absorbent paper. Place in a saucepan and add just enough water to cover. Peel the carrot and onion and add to the pan with the clove, bay leaf and salt. Bring to a boil then lower the heat and simmer the chicken for about 1½ hours, or until tender. Remove the chicken from the broth and set aside to drain and cool. Strain the broth and discard the vegetables, clove and bay leaf. Reserve the amount of chicken broth required in the recipe.

Butter a 1-quart soufflé dish or casserole. Cut the chicken into pieces. Remove the breast from the ribs and discard the bones. Place the pieces in the prepared dish and keep warm.

Melt the butter in a saucepan, stir in the flour and cook for 2–3 minutes. Remove the pan from the heat and add the chicken broth gradually, stirring well after each addition. Return the pan to moderate heat and bring the liquid to a boil, stirring constantly until the sauce is smooth and thick. Remove the pan from the heat. Separate the eggs. Beat a few tablespoons of the hot sauce into the egg yolks. Add the yogurt and salt and pepper to taste and beat the mixture thoroughly. Stir the egg yolk mixture into the sauce in the pan. Stiffly beat the egg whites, fold them into the sauce and pour the mixture over the chicken. Place the dish in a preheated moderately hot oven (375°) for 30–35 minutes until the soufflé is well risen and golden brown. Serve immediately.

CHICK PEA AND CHICKEN CASSEROLE

Serves 6

1 cup chick peas
1 chicken, about 3 lb
8 oz shallots
¼ cup butter
1 teaspoon chopped fresh parsley
¼ teaspoon dried thyme
½ teaspoon chopped fresh rosemary or ¼ teaspoon dried rosemary
dash sugar
salt and pepper

Soak the chick peas overnight in plenty of cold water. Drain well, remove the membranes and split the peas before using. Cut the chicken into 6 portions and discard the carcass. Peel the shallots and leave whole.

Melt the butter in a flameproof casserole over moderate heat and add the shallots and chicken. Sauté until the shallots just begin to soften. Add the drained chick peas, parsley, thyme, rosemary, sugar, salt and pepper to taste and just enough water to cover the ingredients. Cover the casserole and cook in a preheated moderately hot oven (400°) for 50 minutes–1 hour. Check the water from time to time, adding a little more if necessary. Serve hot.

PIGEONS WITH OLIVES

Serves 4

4 plump young pigeons or 6 squabs
¼ cup butter
1 bay leaf
salt and pepper
about 1¼ cups red wine
12 green olives
1 teaspoon all-purpose flour
1 teaspoon soft butter

Clean the pigeons, rinse under cold running water and dry with a cloth or absorbent paper. Cut each pigeon in half. Melt the butter in a heavy saucepan over low heat and sauté the pigeons until evenly browned. Add the bay leaf, salt and pepper to taste and enough red wine to cover the pigeons. Place the pan over moderate heat and bring to a boil. Reduce the heat and simmer very slowly, partially covered, for 1–1½ hours, or until the pigeons are tender.

Place the olives in a colander, rinse with boiling water and add to the pigeons for the last 2–3 minutes of cooking time. Blend the flour to a smooth paste with the soft butter and a little of the stock from the pan. Stir the paste into the wine stock and simmer for a further 10 minutes. Remove the pigeons and olives from the pan and arrange in a fairly deep serving dish. Strain the sauce, pour it over the pigeons and serve hot with boiled potatoes.

Lamb with prunes and almonds

QUAIL LOAF

Serves 6

1 round crusty white loaf, about	salt and pepper
8 inches in diameter	1 large onion
½ cup butter	6 tomatoes
6 plump quail	3 large eggplants

Cut a circular lid from the top of the loaf. Remove the soft bread from the inside. This may be set aside and used as required. Spread the inside of the loaf and lid very generously with half the butter. Open the quail along the back and remove the backbone, ribs and breastbone. Rinse the quail under cold running water, dry well with a cloth or absorbent paper and sprinkle with salt and pepper to taste. Peel the onion and slice thinly into rings. Thinly slice the tomatoes and eggplants.

Fill the inside of the loaf with alternate layers of tomato, eggplants, quail and onion rings. Sprinkle lightly with salt and pepper to taste between the layers. Repeat until all the ingredients have been used, finishing with a layer of tomato. Cover with the lid and spread the outside of the loaf with the remaining butter. Wrap the bread tightly in a large sheet of aluminum foil. Bake in a preheated moderate oven (350°) for about 2½ hours. Remove the foil and place the quail loaf on a decorative serving plate. Cut it into wedges for serving.

Note: The oven temperature must be steady so that the slow penetration of heat is constant. If in doubt, prolong the cooking time for another 30 minutes, or increase the heat to 400° for the last 20 minutes of the cooking time.

LAMB LIVER PILAV

Serves 4

4 oz lamb liver	1 tablespoon chopped fresh
¼ cup butter	parsley
1 teaspoon pine nut kernels	½ teaspoon cinnamon
1 teaspoon currants	salt and pepper
1 tablespoon chopped fresh dill or	1 cup long-grain rice
2 teaspoons dried dill weed	1¾ cups water

Wash the liver under cold running water and dry with a cloth or absorbent paper. Cut it into ¼-inch cubes. Melt the butter in a medium-sized saucepan over moderate heat and sauté the liver until it just begins to brown. Add the pine nut kernels and continue cooking, stirring frequently, for 4–5 minutes. Add the currants, dill, parsley, cinnamon, salt and pepper to taste and the rice. Continue to cook following the instructions on the next page for white *pilav*.

This *pilav* may also be served with lamb, roasted or cooked on the spit, or used as a stuffing for roast lamb.

Pigeons with olives (see page 217); quail loaf

WHITE PILAV

Serves 6

½ cup butter
2 cups long-grain rice

2–2½ pints water
salt and pepper

Heat the butter in a large heavy saucepan. Stir in the rice and cook gently until most of the grains become opaque. Remove the pan from the heat and gradually stir in the water. After each addition, push the spoon across the bottom of the pan from the near side toward the opposite side. When enough water has been added, the rice will form a peak just above the surface of the liquid, about three-fourths of the way across the pan. Add salt and pepper to taste.

Place the pan over high heat and bring to a boil. Lower the heat, tightly cover the pan and cook for 25 minutes. Stir the rice gently with a wooden spoon, starting from the edges and heaping the rice into a cone in the center. Replace the lid and leave the pan over low heat for a further 5 minutes. Remove from the heat, uncover and let the rice stand for 3 minutes. Use the rice as required or serve by itself, heaped into a cone shape, on a heated plate. If white *pilav* is served on its own, a bowl of unflavored yogurt should accompany it, and the yogurt may be spooned over the *pilav*.

Variations

Red pilav: This variation of *pilav* is usually eaten unaccompanied or occasionally with meat. It is never mixed with other ingredients or served with yogurt. Proceed as above, but before adding the water, add ¼ cup tomato paste. Add the water and continue as above.

Pilav with barley vermicelli: Proceed as above, but before adding the rice to the butter, sauté 1 oz barley-shaped vermicelli or fine noodles in the butter until dark brown. Add the rice and continue as above.

Pilav with thyme: Proceed as above, but before adding the water, add 2 teaspoons chopped fresh thyme or 1 teaspoon dried thyme. Add the water and continue as above.

EGGPLANT BÖREĞI

Serves 4

4 eggplants (see note)
1–2 teaspoons salt
½ cup curd or cottage cheese
¼ teaspoon finely chopped fresh mint
¼ teaspoon finely chopped fresh parsley

salt and pepper
2 eggs
1 tablespoon cold water
½ cup olive oil
all-purpose flour (see recipe)
few sprigs parsley

Pare the eggplants lengthwise at intervals of ¾ inch, to give a striped effect. Cut them crosswise into slices, about 1½ inches thick. Place the slices on a large plate or wooden board and sprinkle with the salt. Let stand for 15–20 minutes then rinse under cold running water and dry thoroughly with a cloth or absorbent paper. Using a sharp pointed knife, make a horizontal incision, about 1½ inches long, in the side of each slice of eggplant. Move the knife in both directions, making a pouch or a pocket inside the slice. Be careful not to cut the outside except where the knife enters.

Mix together the cheese, mint, parsley and salt and pepper to taste, and carefully press about 1 teaspoon of the mixture into the pouch in each slice. Beat the eggs with the cold water.

Heat the oil in a heavy shallow skillet over moderate heat. Coat the eggplant slices with flour, then dip them into the beaten egg. Place immediately in the hot oil and sauté on each side until golden brown. (The egg should run off the eggplant slices when they are first placed in the skillet, forming thin threads all round each slice.) Remove from the pan and drain on absorbent paper. Garnish with parsley and serve hot.

Note: Usually the round, flat type of eggplants are used for this dish, but long ones may be substituted, making smaller sized *böreği*.

STUFFED VEGETABLES

Serves 6

6 small eggplants
6 zucchini, not less than 1 inch thick
6 green sweet peppers
6 medium-sized tomatoes

for the stuffing:
3–4 large onions
1 cup olive oil
¼ cup pine nut kernels
¼ cup currants
¼ cup chopped fresh dill or 3 tablespoons dried dill weed

1½ teaspoons finely chopped fresh mint
3 tablespoons finely chopped fresh parsley
1 tablespoon cinnamon
salt and pepper
1 cup long-grain rice
2 tablespoons lemon juice
1¼ cups water
3 lemons
few sprigs parsley

Cut off the stems of the eggplants with a sharp knife. Using a teaspoon, hollow out the inside without piercing the skin, leaving a shell with a ¼-inch thick wall around the sides and the base. Prepare the zucchini in the same way. Cut off and reserve the tops of the green peppers. Scoop out and discard both the seeds and the coarse white portions. Cut a lid from the top of each tomato without detaching it and scoop out the seeds and center pulp. Press the pulp through a wire sieve, reserve the juice and discard the seeds.

To make the stuffing, peel and coarsely chop the onions. Heat about three-fourths of the oil in a large saucepan over moderate heat. Add the onions and sauté them, stirring frequently, until soft and golden brown. Add the pine nut kernels and sauté for 3–4 minutes, then add the currants, dill, mint, parsley, cinnamon, salt and pepper to taste and the rice. Continue cooking, stirring frequently, until the rice becomes opaque. Stir in the reserved tomato juice, the lemon juice and the water. Simmer gently for about 10 minutes, or until the water has been absorbed. It is not necessary, however, for the rice to be completely cooked at this stage.

Remove the pan from the heat and lightly pack the mixture into the prepared vegetables, starting with the peppers, then the eggplants, zucchini, and lastly the tomatoes. Stand the stuffed vegetables, open ends upward, in a large saucepan, with the peppers in the center. Replace the lids on the peppers. Add the remaining oil and enough water to come half-way up the tomatoes. Place a small plate upside down in the pan so that it rests on the vegetables. Cover the pan, place it over moderate heat and simmer for 1 hour.

Eggplant böreği

Remove the lid and plate and leave the vegetables in the pan until cold.

Thinly slice 2 of the lemons. Using two spoons, carefully remove the stuffed vegetables from the pan and arrange on a shallow serving dish. Pour over the juice remaining in the pan and garnish with sprigs of parsley and lemon slices. Let stand in a cool place until the following day. Cut the remaining lemon into wedges and serve with the stuffed vegetables.

Note: Cabbage and vine leaves may also be stuffed and cooked in a similar way to the above vegetables. Before stuffing they should be blanched in boiling water for 5–10 minutes until they are pliable. Remove any thick veins and stems. When cooking, line the bottom of the saucepan with several whole cabbage or vine leaves to prevent the stuffed leaves from sticking to the bottom of the pan.

FRIED ARTICHOKES

Serves 4

4 globe artichokes	$\frac{1}{2}$ teaspoon salt
1 lemon	1 tablespoon olive oil
for the batter:	$\frac{1}{2}$ cup water
1 egg	oil for deep-frying
1 cup all-purpose flour	

Wash each artichoke and discard the coarse outer leaves and the soft inner leaves. Discard the hairy choke and retain only the heart. Cut the lemon in half. Cut each heart into quarters and rub these with one of the lemon halves. Place the artichoke hearts in a bowl and add cold water to cover. Squeeze the juice from the remaining lemon half and add it to the water. Set the bowl aside while making the batter.

Beat the egg thoroughly in a small bowl. Sift the flour and salt into a large bowl and add the olive oil very gradually, beating well with a wooden spoon after each addition. Add the water gradually and beat until the batter is quite smooth. Stir in the beaten egg.

Drain the artichokes in a colander or sieve and dry them with a cloth or absorbent paper. Heat the oil in a deep-fat fryer. Coat each artichoke quarter with the batter and deep-fry until crisp and golden brown. Drain on absorbent paper and serve hot with broiled meat.

Note: The lemon and water prevents the artichokes from discoloring and also gives a slightly sour flavor to counteract the heaviness of the oil.

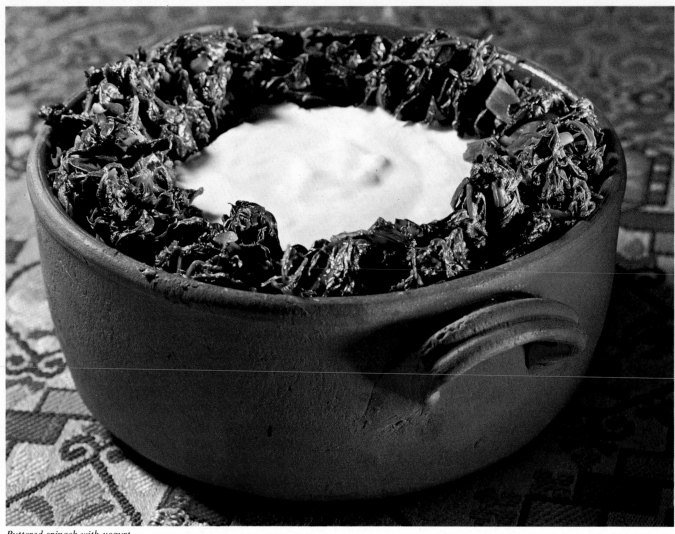

Buttered spinach with yogurt

STUFFED VINE LEAVES WITH CALF'S FOOT

Serves 6

1 calf's foot	½ cup butter
2 medium-sized onions	1 lb lean lamb, finely ground
3 celery leaves, about	generous ½ cup long-grain rice
3 inches long	1 tablespoon finely chopped fresh
1 sprig fresh dill	parsley
2 bay leaves	1 tablespoon finely chopped fresh
salt and pepper	mint
for the stuffed vine leaves:	1 tablespoon finely chopped fresh
12–14 oz fresh or canned vine	dill
leaves	salt and pepper
1 large onion	2 tablespoons lemon juice

Wash the calf's foot and rinse it well under cold running water. Peel the onions and leave whole. Place the calf's foot and onions in a large saucepan. Add the celery leaves, dill, bay leaves, salt and pepper to taste and cold water to cover. Bring to a boil over moderate heat. Lower the heat and simmer, partially covered, for about 2 hours. Remove the calf's foot from the pan and set aside to cool. Strain, reserve the stock and discard the onions and herbs.

If using fresh vine leaves, rinse well under cold running water and blanch in boiling water for 5–10 minutes, until soft and pliable. Drain well. Preserved leaves should be rinsed thoroughly with boiling water and drained well.

Peel and finely chop the onion. Melt the butter in a saucepan over low heat and sauté the onion until soft and transparent, but not browned. Add the lamb, rice, parsley, mint, dill, salt and pepper to taste and the lemon juice. Mix the ingredients thoroughly and remove the pan from the heat.

Line the bottom and sides of a large heavy saucepan with several vine leaves. Place the remaining vine leaves, dull side upward, on a flat working surface. Place a teaspoon of the rice mixture on each leaf. Roll up the leaf, tucking in the ends and completely enclosing the filling to make a neat roll, about 1½ inches long and 1 inch thick. Place the stuffed vine leaves very close together in the pan, starting around the outside and working toward the center. Make several layers, if necessary. Thinly slice the meat from the calf's foot and sprinkle the slices over the stuffed vine leaves. Cover with the stock from the calf's foot and place a small plate over the leaves and meat. Tightly cover the pan and simmer over low heat for 1–1¼ hours. Drain off the stock and arrange the stuffed vine leaves on a plate. Serve hot with unflavored yogurt.

BUTTERED SPINACH WITH YOGURT

Serves 4

2 lb fresh spinach	salt and pepper
1 large onion	1½ cups unflavored yogurt
¼ cup butter	salt and pepper

Wash the spinach thoroughly under cold running water. Discard the thick stems. Tear the spinach into shreds and drain it in a colander. Peel and finely chop the onion.

Melt the butter in a saucepan over moderate heat. Add the onion and sauté until transparent but not browned, stirring occasionally. Add the spinach, a little at a time, stirring constantly. Add salt and pepper to taste and cook gently until all the liquid has evaporated and the spinach is dark green. Place the spinach in a serving dish and make a well in the center. Beat the yogurt with a little salt and pepper to taste and pour into the well. Serve immediately.

ARTICHOKES IN OLIVE OIL

Serves 4

4 artichokes (see note)	salt and pepper
1 lemon	1 tablespoon chopped fresh dill or
8 oz fresh fava or lima beans	2 teaspoons dried dill weed
2 large potatoes	½ teaspoon chopped fresh parsley
4 oz shallots	few sprigs parsley
¼ cup olive oil	

Peel off and discard the coarse outer leaves of the artichokes until you reach the soft, blue-tinted inner leaves. Cut the artichokes horizontally with a sharp knife. Remove and discard the soft leaves and the choke (the hairy core in the center.) This will leave a semicircle with the stem as a handle. Trim the stem of each artichoke until it is flat-sided and about ¼ inch square. Cut the lemon in half. Rub the artichokes with one half of the lemon and squeeze the juice from the remaining half into a bowl of water. Add the prepared artichokes and set aside to soak until required. Shell the beans. Peel the potatoes and cut into quarters lengthwise. Peel the shallots and leave whole.

Heat the olive oil in a saucepan over moderate heat. Add the shallots and sauté until almost soft, but not browned. Add the beans, salt and pepper to taste, dill, chopped parsley and enough water to just cover the vegetables. Simmer very gently for about 5 minutes, or until the shallots are fully cooked. Drain the artichokes, add to the vegetables in the pan and simmer for 20 minutes, adding more water if necessary. Add the potatoes and simmer for a further 20 minutes, or until all the vegetables are tender. Remove the pan from the heat and set aside to cool.

Stand the artichokes, stems upward, on a china dish. Spoon the other vegetables and the juice around them. Garnish with the parsley sprigs and serve cold.

Note: Great care should be taken to choose artichokes that are large and fully grown, yet still young enough to be tender. Their stems should be about 2 inches long.

ZUCCHINI WITH MINT

Serves 4

6 large zucchini	2 teaspoons chopped fresh mint
2 large onions	salt and pepper
¼ cup butter	½ teaspoon sugar

Rinse the zucchini under cold running water and dry thoroughly with a cloth or absorbent paper. Scrape the zucchini, removing only the outer green skin, and cut crosswise into slices. Peel the onions and slice thinly into rings.

Melt the butter in a saucepan over moderate heat and add the zucchini, onion, mint, salt and pepper to taste and the sugar. Tightly cover the pan and cook gently for about 40 minutes.

Shake the pan from time to time and check that the ingredients are not sticking to the bottom. If necessary, add 1–2 tablespoons of cold water. When cooked, the ingredients should be tender, with just a suggestion of juice. Serve hot.

EGYPTIAN BROWN BEANS

Serves 4

1 cup dried brown Egyptian beans	2½ cups water
	½ teaspoon salt
1 medium-sized onion	butter or olive oil (see recipe)

Soak the beans overnight in plenty of cold water. Drain well before using. Peel the onion and leave whole. Place in a saucepan with the drained beans, water and salt. Bring to a boil over high heat. Lower the heat, tightly cover the pan and simmer for 2 hours, or until the beans are very soft and the liquid is thick. Discard the onion.

Serve hot with butter or cold with olive oil. The butter or oil is usually added by each diner, according to taste.

COTTAGE CHEESE BÖREĞI AND ZUCCHINI BÖREĞI

Makes 36 of each filling

for the pastry (see note):
4 cups all-purpose flour
1 teaspoon baking powder
1 teaspoon salt in 1¼ cups
  lukewarm water

for the first filling:
½ cup cottage or curd cheese
1 teaspoon finely chopped fresh
  parsley

1 teaspoon finely chopped fresh
  mint
salt and pepper

for the second filling:
6 oz zucchini
1 teaspoon chopped fresh mint
salt and pepper

for frying:
2 tablespoons butter

To prepare the pastry, sift together the flour and baking powder. Place about three-fourths of the flour mixture on a pastry board, reserving the remainder. Make a well in the center and gradually add the salted water, working the flour and salted water together to make a smooth elastic dough. Knead the dough on the board for 15–20 minutes. Wrap the dough in a cloth or waxed paper and set aside in a cool place for about 1 hour.

Sprinkle the remaining flour over a board. Cut the dough in half. Roll out each half until it is paper-thin and almost transparent. Use it immediately, or, if the dough is to be stored, cut it into strips, about 4 by 12 inches, and pile the strips, one on top of the other, with a thin coating of flour between to prevent them from sticking together. Wrap in a cloth, foil or waxed paper.

To make the first filling, mix together the cottage cheese, parsley, mint and salt and pepper to taste in a small bowl. To make the second filling, wash the zucchini and cut off the stems. Chop the zucchini coarsely and cook in boiling salted water for about 10 minutes, or until just tender. Drain well. Stir in the mint and salt and pepper to taste, and set aside until the mixture is cool.

To make the *muska* (triangular) *böreği*, cut half the amount of pastry into strips, 6 by 2 inches. Place a teaspoon of the cheese on the pastry and fold (see photograph). Tuck in the remaining flap. Repeat until all the pastry and filling have been used.

To make the *cigara* (cigar-shaped) *böreği*, cut the pastry into strips, 6 by 2 inches. Place a teaspoon of the zucchini on the pastry, and fold the shorter sides over the filling (see photograph). Roll the pastry around the filling, making *cigara böreği* of about 4 inches long. Repeat until the pastry and filling have been used.

Heat the butter in a skillet. Shallow-fry the *böreği*, a few at a time, until golden brown all over. Drain on absorbent paper and serve hot with *raki*, the Turkish national drink, or as an accompaniment to cocktails.

Note: Yufka pastry may be bought already prepared in Greek and Cypriot food shops under the name of *phylo* pastry.

GREEK EASTER BREAD

Serves 8–10

1 tablespoon anise seeds
6 tablespoons water
2 cakes compressed yeast or
  2 packages active dry yeast
½ cup lukewarm milk
6 cups all-purpose flour
½ teaspoon salt

1½ teaspoons grated orange rind
4 eggs
¾ cup melted butter
1 cup sugar
1 egg yolk
¾ cup chopped blanched
  almonds

Simmer the anise seeds in the water for 5 minutes. Strain through a sieve, reserve the liquid and discard the seeds. Place the yeast in a small bowl and add the lukewarm milk, a little at a time, stirring well after each addition until the mixture is smooth. Let stand for about 5 minutes, or until the mixture is frothy. Add ½ cup of the flour and mix to a smooth batter. Cover the bowl with a cloth and let stand in a warm place until large bubbles begin to form on the surface of the batter. Meanwhile, sift the remaining flour and the salt into a large bowl. Make a well in the center and add the anise seed water, yeast mixture, orange rind, eggs, melted butter and sugar. Mix thoroughly and knead to a smooth dough. Cover the bowl with a damp cloth and let stand in a warm place for 2–3 hours, or until the dough has doubled in bulk.

Turn the dough on to a well-floured board, and knead until smooth and elastic. Cut the dough into 3 portions and roll each portion into a rope about 12 inches long. Braid the three ropes together to make one large loaf. Tuck the ends under to prevent the braids from coming undone as the dough rises. Place on a greased baking sheet and cover lightly with a damp cloth. Let stand in a warm place until the dough has doubled in bulk. Beat the egg yolk with a little cold water and brush it over the dough, just before baking. Sprinkle with the chopped almonds and bake in a preheated moderately hot oven (400°) for 30–35 minutes, or until firm and golden brown. Cool the loaf on a wire rack.

Note: This delicious bread is sent to friends at Easter, surrounded by Easter eggs, dyed red. These eggs are often buried in the dough before the bread is baked.

GROUND ALMOND, LEMON AND CREAM DESSERT

Serves 4

1¼ cups heavy cream
2 teaspoons grated lemon rind
¼ cup finely ground almonds
¼ cup lemon juice

¼ cup sugar
4 small pieces candied lemon
  peel

Measure the cream into a bowl and add the lemon rind, ground almonds, lemon juice and sugar. Beat until the mixture is thick and light. Pour the mixture into 4 serving glasses and decorate each one with a piece of candied lemon peel. Chill for several hours before serving.

Cottage cheese böreği and zucchini böreği

VIZIER'S FINGERS

Serves 4

⅔ cup semolina flour
1 cup milk
1 egg
½ cup sugar
1 cup water

2 tablespoons lemon juice
few drops almond extract
¼ cup butter
rose water (optional)

Place the semolina flour in a saucepan and stir in the milk. Place the pan over moderate heat and bring to a boil, stirring constantly until the mixture becomes very stiff. Remove the pan from the heat and beat in the egg. Turn out the mixture on to a buttered plate or foil and let stand until cool.

Meanwhile, put the sugar, water and lemon juice into a heavy saucepan over low heat. Stir until the sugar dissolves, add the almond extract, and bring the liquid to a boil. Continue boiling until a thick syrup is formed. At this stage, the syrup will begin to turn to a pale golden brown and the pan should be removed from the heat immediately. Set aside in a warm place until the syrup is required.

Shape the cooled semolina mixture into finger shapes about 2½ inches long. Melt the butter in a heavy skillet and sauté the fingers until browned on both sides. A lighter band should be visible on either side along the length of each finger. Remove from the skillet and drain on absorbent paper. Arrange on a serving dish and pour over the warm syrup. Alternatively, a few drops of rose water may be sprinkled over the fingers, just before pouring over the warm syrup. Serve cold.

ALI'S MOTHER

Serves 4–6

for the layered pastry:
2 cups all-purpose flour
1 teaspoon salt
⅔ cup water
½ cup butter

for the sweetened milk:
1¼ cups milk
¼ cup sugar
2 teaspoons cinnamon

To make the pastry, sift the flour and salt into a bowl. Add the water and mix to a soft dough. Knead the dough for 20 minutes on a lightly floured surface. Cover with a damp cloth and set aside for 1 hour. Knead for a further 20 minutes, cover again with the damp cloth and set aside overnight in the refrigerator or a cold place.

The next day, shape the dough into a long rope, about 2 inches in diameter, and cut into 12 equal-sized portions. Roll all the portions of dough into 12 very thin circles of equal size, approximately 8 inches in diameter. Melt the butter in a heavy skillet over fairly low heat and sauté each pastry circle separately until golden brown. Stack the circles in a shallow ovenproof baking dish.

To make the sweetened milk, heat the milk, sugar and cinnamon together until the sugar has dissolved, and then pour the mixture over the pastry. Bake in a preheated moderately hot oven (400°) for about 30 minutes, or until the top layer is golden brown. Cut into wedges and serve warm in the dish in which it was cooked.

CHESTNUT BALLS

Serves 4–6

2 lb chestnuts or 2 (1-lb) cans
  unsweetened chestnut purée
1¼ cups milk
stick cinnamon
¾ cup sugar
⅓ cup chopped candied cherries
½ cup mixed chopped candied peel

2 eggs
1 cup fine dry breadcrumbs
oil for deep-frying
sugar for coating
ground cinnamon
light cream (optional)

If using fresh chestnuts, make a deep slit in the outer skin of each chestnut with a sharp knife. Place the chestnuts in a large saucepan and cover with water. Bring to a boil over moderate heat and simmer for 20 minutes. Drain the chestnuts into a colander and let stand until cool. Discard the outer and inner skins. Return the peeled chestnuts to the pan and add the milk, cinnamon stick and one-fourth of the sugar. Simmer gently over low heat until all the liquid has been absorbed. Discard the cinnamon stick. Press the chestnuts through a wire sieve, making a thick purée. If using canned chestnut purée, follow the recipe from this stage.

Mix the remaining sugar with the chestnut purée. Add the candied cherries and mixed candied peel and mix well. Roll the mixture into balls, about 1½ inches in diameter. Beat the eggs. Coat the balls with egg, roll them in the breadcrumbs and deep-fry in hot oil until crisp and golden brown. Drain the balls on absorbent paper and roll them several times in a mixture of sugar and cinnamon. Serve hot with cream, or leave until cold and serve with coffee.

PUMPKIN DESSERT

Serves 4

1 lb fresh pumpkin
1 tablespoon water
1¼ cups pumpkin liquid (see
  recipe)

¼ cup sugar
2 tablespoons lemon juice
1 cup finely chopped walnuts

Remove the seeds and the soft stringy pulp from the pumpkin flesh, but leave the pumpkin unpeeled. Cut it into 4 pieces, each piece about 2 by 3 inches. Place the pumpkin pieces, skin side up, in a saucepan. Add the water and tightly cover the pan. Cook gently over very low heat until the pumpkin is tender. Drain off the juice that forms during cooking into a measuring cup, and add water to make the amount of liquid required. Add the sugar and lemon juice and pour the mixture into a small saucepan. Place the pan over low heat to dissolve the sugar, then increase the heat and boil the liquid rapidly until reduced to about half the original quantity.

Place the pumpkin in a serving dish, with the skin side underneath. Pour over the juice and sprinkle with chopped walnuts. Serve warm or cold.

Chestnut balls

DOUGHNUTS IN SCENTED SYRUP

Serves 6

for the dough:

½ cake compressed yeast or
   ½ package active dry yeast
1 teaspoon sugar
1¼ cups lukewarm water
4 cups all-purpose flour
1¼ cups milk

for the syrup:

1¼ cups water
3 tablespoons lemon juice
3½ cups sugar
3 tablespoons rose water
3 tablespoons orange flower water
oil for deep-frying
¼–⅓ cup sugar for coating
ground cinnamon (optional)

If using compressed yeast, blend the yeast with the sugar and the water. If using dry yeast, set aside for 10–15 minutes, or until the liquid becomes frothy.

Sift the flour into a mixing bowl and make a well in the center. Lightly beat the milk into the yeast mixture and pour the mixture into the flour. Beat well to form a very soft batter. Cover the bowl and set aside in a warm place for 1 hour. Beat well, cover the bowl again and set aside to rise again for a further hour. Repeat this process once or twice. Thorough beating at regular intervals helps to make the dough elastic and the doughnuts a perfectly round shape.

Meanwhile, to make the syrup, pour the water and lemon juice into a heavy saucepan and add the sugar. Bring to a boil over moderate heat, taking care that the sugar dissolves before the boiling point is reached. Lower the heat and simmer the liquid until the syrup is thick enough to coat the back of a spoon. Add the rose water and orange flower water and simmer for a further 2–3 minutes. Remove the pan from the heat and set aside until cold. The syrup should be well chilled when used.

Heat the oil in a heavy saucepan. Beat the dough well and, using a wet teaspoon or a forcing bag and large plain tip, drop small amounts of the batter into the hot oil. The doughnuts will rise to the surface quickly. Turn them over and fry them for a further 2–3 minutes, or until crisp and golden brown.

Drain the doughnuts well on absorbent paper and, while still hot, dip them into the syrup. Serve hot or cold, with a sprinkling of sugar. A little cinnamon may also be sprinkled over the sugar-coated doughnuts.

FRESH PLUM COMPOTE

Serves 4

12 ripe plums
1¼ cups water
½ cup sugar
1 tablespoon whole blanched
   almonds

2 tablespoons lemon juice
cinnamon stick, about 1 inch
4 cloves

The plums should be ripe but firm. Make a small slit in the side of each plum. Place the water, sugar, almonds, lemon juice, cinnamon stick and cloves in a small heavy saucepan. Bring to a boil over moderate heat, making sure that the sugar has dissolved before the liquid boils. Simmer until the liquid becomes slightly thick and syrupy. Add the plums and cook gently until the skins begin to curl up along the slits. Remove the pan from the heat and chill the compote well before serving.

BAKLAVA

Makes 12

1 lb *yufka (phylo)* pastry (see
    Cottage Cheese Böreği,
    page 225)
1½ cups blanched almonds
1 cup butter

for the syrup:
scant 2 cups water
2 teaspoons lemon juice
1¾ cups sugar
stick cinnamon, about 2 inches

Prepare the *yufka* pastry, wrap and set aside in a cool place for 1 hour. Meanwhile, toast the almonds until lightly browned and chop coarsely. Melt the butter. Roll out the pastry until it is as thin as paper and cut into as many 9-inch squares as possible.

Using a little of the melted butter, grease a deep baking tray or meat pan, place a square of pastry in the bottom. Brush the pastry layer with a little of the melted butter and sprinkle with chopped almonds. Cover with a second layer of pastry. Continue in this way until all the pastry and almonds and most of the butter have been used. Brush the top layer of pastry well with melted butter. With a sharp knife, mark the top of the *baklava* into 12 oblong pieces. Place the tray in a preheated moderate oven (350°) for approximately 45 minutes, or until the *baklava* is golden brown.

Remove the tray from the oven and set aside until the *baklava* is cold.

Meanwhile, place the water, lemon juice, sugar and cinnamon stick in a small heavy saucepan. Heat slowly until the sugar has completely dissolved. Bring to a boil, lower the heat and simmer for 5 minutes.

Pour the hot syrup over the cold *baklava* and set aside until the syrup is cold. Cut along the marks that were made before baking and serve as required.

HALVA

Makes 16–20 portions

½ cup butter
1 cup sugar
4 eggs
1 cup finely ground almonds
1 teaspoon cinnamon

1⅓ cups semolina flour
for the syrup:
1 cup sugar
1¼ cups water
¼ cup lemon juice

Cream together the butter and sugar until the mixture is soft and creamy. Lightly beat the eggs and beat them into the mixture with the ground almonds, cinnamon and semolina flour.

Line a large jelly roll pan with waxed paper, allowing the paper to stand about 1 inch higher than the pan. Grease the paper lightly. Spread the mixture into the prepared pan. Bake in the center of a preheated moderate oven (350°) for about 40 minutes. Remove the pan from the oven and prepare the syrup.

Measure the sugar and water into a saucepan. Stir over low heat until the sugar has dissolved. Add the lemon juice and bring to a boil. Simmer for 5 minutes until the syrup is dissolved slightly. Remove the pan from the heat, let it cool a little, then pour the hot syrup over the *halva*. Leave to soak until the *halva* is cool. Cut into squares to serve.

TURKISH DELIGHT

Makes 1½ lb

¾ cup water
¼ cup orange juice
¼ cup lemon juice
3½ cups sugar

2 tablespoons gelatin
⅔ cup cornstarch
3–4 drops coloring (optional)
confectioners' sugar (see recipe)

Combine the water, the orange and lemon juice and the sugar in a heavy saucepan. Bring to a boil over low heat, taking care that the sugar has dissolved before the boiling point is reached. Lower the heat and boil the liquid very gently until it reaches a temperature of 230° on a candy thermometer – the long thread stage. Meanwhile, dissolve the gelatin in a little hot water. Blend the cornstarch with enough cold water to make a thin paste and add the paste to the hot syrup, stirring constantly. Stir in the gelatin and boil the mixture until clear, stirring occasionally. Add the coloring, if used, and pour the mixture into an 8-inch square cake pan. Set aside for at least 24 hours.

Loosen the Turkish delight in the pan and turn out on to a thick layer of confectioners' sugar. Sprinkle the top with confectioners' sugar and cut into 1-inch squares with a sharp knife. Coat each square with confectioners' sugar immediately. Serve as required.

Note: Alternatively, rose water may be substituted for the orange and lemon juice.

STUFFED APRICOT MERINGUE

Serves 6

9 fresh ripe apricots or peaches
1 tablespoon lemon juice
1 cup light brown sugar
1 cup pine nut kernels
2 cups finely ground almonds

3 tablespoons rose water
for the meringue:
4 egg whites
6 tablespoons sugar

Wash and halve the apricots and remove the pits. Place the apricots in a saucepan with the lemon juice. Simmer gently over low heat until some of the fruit juice has been extracted from the fruit. Add half the sugar and continue to simmer for about 15 minutes, or until the apricots are tender. Remove the pan from the heat and set aside to cool.

Finely chop the pine nut kernels. Mix together half the ground almonds, the remaining sugar and the pine nut kernels in a bowl. Add the rose water, blending the mixture to a soft paste. Drain the apricots and reserve the syrup. Place teaspoons of the mixture in the center of each of the apricot halves. Arrange the filled apricots in a well-buttered baking dish. Pour the syrup over and sprinkle with the remainder of the ground almonds. Beat the egg whites until stiff, add the sugar and beat again until the mixture is glossy. Spoon the meringue over the apricots, taking care that the meringue completely covers the apricots and is spread to the sides of the dish. Bake in a preheated cool oven (300°) for about 30 minutes, or until the meringue is golden brown and firm. Serve immediately with whipped cream.

Turkish delight

JEWISH

Molly Lyons Bar-David

Photography by John Miller

Jewish cooking has evolved from the adoption of culinary ideas from many nations, altered to keep within the traditional laws.

The laws of *kosher* cooking may have had their origins in hygiene as well as moral teachings. The ritually permitted meats are classified as *kosher* (clean). Animals must have cloven hooves and chew the cud. Beef, lamb and meat from the goat and deer families come within this category. The slaughtering must be done ritually and the animal carefully checked to make certain there is no infection. The meat is then salted and soaked to comply with the injunction against consuming blood. Liver must be salted and then broiled to extract the blood. If poultry flesh is broiled it does not require salting or soaking. It is also one of the traditional practices of Jewish religious life not to mix meat and dairy products.

Fish with fins and scales are the only permitted variety; shellfish are forbidden. Birds of prey, scavengers and all winged creeping creatures are not allowed in Jewish cooking. Poultry may not be cooked in milk or cream, as dressed veal or lamb could be mistaken for poultry.

These rules, then, have formed the core of all Jewish cookery throughout the ages and throughout the world. Cooking has been made easier today by the introduction of new *kosher* products, such as butter-tasting margarine which can be eaten with meat, *pareve* which is a non-meat and non-dairy vegetarian milk or cream product and *kosher* gelatins and aspics made of vegetable colloids.

Many Biblical and symbolic foods have retained their importance in Jewish cooking. Chief among these, perhaps, are the many breads using the Biblical grains of wheat, barley, spelt (rye) and millet. The symbolic *challah* loaves vary in shape depending on the festival. The Sabbath loaves are braided. The Rosh Hashana loaves are circular symbolizing happiness all the year round. Cakes using olive oil and honey recorded in the Bible are still made, and unleavened wafers 'anointed with oil' result in very rich cookies akin to Western shortbread.

Salted herring and other fish are popular in most Jewish communities since, until recent times, fish had to be salted or sun-dried or smoked to make it saleable throughout Israel. Today, fresh or frozen fish is more readily available. The use of fat is still high on the list of Jewish cooking in the Middle East, stemming from Biblical days when it was used in feasts. Its popularity is dwindling today in other Jewish communities because of the modern approach to diet. The vegetables listed in the Bible are the most-used in Israel, and the fruits, from the date to the grape, are symbolically served at many festivals. Unusual flavorings are still outstanding. Cassia is frequently used in baking. Cinnamon even goes into meat, lamb and poultry dishes. Mint is popular in local salads and coriander is still used to symbolize the ancient *manna* flavor. Dill and mustard – wild herbs in Israel – appear in many main dishes, and capers, which also grow wild, are invariably used in salads.

The Biblical foods are still a part of the Jewish cuisine because of ancient lore and prolific native crops, but there are many other dishes for the various festivals which have evolved from the Jewish communities throughout the world.

CHOPPED LIVER

Serves 6

4 eggs	¾ teaspoon salt
1 lb chicken or beef liver	dash pepper
3 onions	1 tomato
¼ cup chicken fat	lettuce leaves (see recipe)

Hard-cook the eggs, shell, cut in halves and separate the yolks and whites. Dip the liver in salted iced water and then broil until cooked according to taste. Peel and chop the onions. Melt the chicken fat in a skillet and sauté the onions until tender but not browned. Remove from the skillet. Put the liver, onions and egg yolks through a grinder and mix together. Add the salt and pepper and any fat left in the skillet after cooking the onions and mix well. Chop the egg whites and slice the tomato.

Wash and dry several lettuce leaves and either arrange on a serving dish or on individual plates. Place the liver mixture on the lettuce leaves and serve garnished with the egg whites and sliced tomato.

CHOPPED HERRING

Serves 6

2 salted herrings	¼ teaspoon freshly ground black
2 eggs	pepper
1 slice white bread	2 tablespoons oil
1 onion	3 tablespoons wine vinegar
1 dessert apple	few scallions
1 teaspoon sugar	few ripe olives
dash celery salt, mace or allspice	
(optional)	

Soak the herrings overnight in cold water. Drain and pat dry. Clean the fish and remove the skin and bones. Hard-cook the eggs and shell them. Soak the bread for a few minutes in cold water and squeeze out the excess moisture. Peel and quarter the onion. Peel, quarter and core the apple.

Put the fish, eggs, bread, onion and apple through a grinder. Add the sugar, celery salt, pepper, oil and vinegar and mix well. Wash and trim the scallions. Serve the chopped herrings garnished with the scallions and ripe olives.

FENNEL WITH OLIVES AND CAPERS

Serves 6

2 large or 3 small fennel bulbs	1 tablespoon chopped green
12 ripe olives	fennel tops
12 green olives	3 tablespoons olive oil
2 tablespoons pickled capers	salt

Wash, trim and drain the fennel and cut into thin slices across the grain. Arrange the slices on a serving dish and garnish with the ripe and green olives (pitted, if preferred). Sprinkle with the pickled capers and the chopped fennel tops. Pour over the olive oil and sprinkle with salt to taste.

AVOCADO MOLDS

Serves 6

1½ envelopes plain gelatin
2 tablespoons lemon juice
½ cup hot water
1 cup fruit juice (apple, cider,
  pineapple or citrus juices)
2 avocados
2–3 scallion stems
1 tablespoon finely chopped fresh
  herbs (mint, parsley or dill)

2 drops hot sauce (Worcestershire
  or Tabasco) or ¼ teaspoon
  prepared mustard
½ teaspoon salt
⅔ cup mayonnaise
for the garnish:
lettuce leaves
tomato slices
few ripe olives (optional)

Mix the gelatin and lemon juice with the hot water in a bowl. Set the bowl in a pan of boiling water and stir until the gelatin is dissolved. Remove the bowl from the heat. Add the fruit juice and stir well. Set aside until the mixture begins to thicken, stirring occasionally. At this stage, peel the avocados, remove the seeds and mash the flesh to a pulp.

Chop the scallion stems. Add the chopped herbs and scallion stems, hot sauce, salt and mayonnaise to the avocado pulp, and beat together until well blended. Stir in the slightly thickened fruit juice and pour the mixture into 6 individual molds or 1 large mold. Chill for several hours until firm.

To unmold, dip the molds in warm, but not hot water. Loosen the edges with a sharp knife. Place a plate over each mold and quickly invert. Shake gently and slowly lift off the mold. Slide each mold carefully on to a bed of lettuce and garnish each with slice of tomato. If desired, add ripe olives as an additional garnish.

Note: If using 1 large mold, an alternative method of unmolding is to place a serving plate over the mold, invert and press a warm, dampened cloth around the mold, shaking gently to loosen the contents. Repeat several times with a fresh warm cloth if necessary.

CARROT-FILLED AVOCADOS

Serves 6

3 oranges
juice of ½ lemon
5–6 medium-sized carrots
1 cup pineapple cubes
  (fresh or canned)

dash ginger or cloves
salt
sugar (see recipe)
2 avocados

Add the juice from 2 of the oranges to the lemon juice. Peel the carrots, grate coarsely and soak in the orange and lemon juice for about 2 hours. Peel the remaining orange and remove the white skin. Cut the flesh into small cubes, taking care to remove any seeds. Mix the carrot mixture with the orange and pineapple cubes; add the spice and salt and sugar to taste. Drain off the excess juices and reserve.

Cut the avocados lengthwise into three sections and discard the seeds. Rub the avocado flesh lightly with lemon juice to prevent discoloration. Fill each portion with the drained carrot mixture. Alternatively, remove the skins from the avocados using a sharp knife. Cut the flesh into thin slices and sprinkle with lemon juice. Place the carrot mixture in a serving dish and arrange the avocado slices around the outside.

Sprinkle the avocados with some of the reserved fruit juice before serving.

Note: If the avocados require ripening before they are used, set them aside in a dark place for several days, until the flesh is slightly soft. If the avocado flesh is prepared in advance, placing the seeds in the bowl with the slices will also act as a deterrent to discoloration.

CHICKEN COCKTAIL

Serves 6

for the cocktail:
2 cooked chicken breasts,
  about 8 oz
3 canned pineapple rings
2 oranges
1 small grapefruit
6 oz cooked cherries

for the sauce:
1 cup mayonnaise
½ cup tomato ketchup
1 tablespoon tomato paste
1 teaspoon grated horseradish
1 tablespoon brandy

Dice the chicken and pineapple rings. Peel the oranges and grapefruit, removing as much of the white inner skin as possible, and cut into cubes. Discard the seeds. Pit the cherries. Mix together the prepared chicken, pineapple, oranges, grapefruit and cherries and divide equally into 6 glasses.

To make the sauce, place the mayonnaise, tomato ketchup, tomato paste, grated horseradish and brandy in a bowl and mix thoroughly. Spoon over the chicken and fruit mixture. Chill well before serving.

HARD ROE WITH SMOKED SALMON

Serves 6

8 oz hard fish roe
1 cup oil (see recipe)
salt and pepper
2 slices white bread

½ cup lemon juice
lettuce leaves
6 thin slices smoked salmon

Put the raw roe into a bowl. Cover with oil and refrigerate for about 24 hours.

Remove the membrane from the roe. Replace the roe in the oil and beat until soft. Add salt and pepper to taste. Soak the bread in water for 2–3 minutes and squeeze well to remove the excess moisture before crumbling and adding to the roe.

Beat the mixture well to blend the ingredients together. Add the lemon juice slowly and continue to beat. If the mixture does not emulsify sufficiently (the consistency should be like mayonnaise), beat in more oil. Serve on lettuce leaves and garnish with smoked salmon slices.

Note: Ikre (fish eggs) is basically a Rumanian Jewish appetizer, just as *lox* (smoked salmon) is an American Jewish specialty. *Lox* is often eaten for breakfast with cream cheese and *bagels* (small doughnut-shaped rolls).

Carrot-filled avocados

ISRAELI FRESH FRUIT SOUP

Serves 6

2 dessert apples
6 bananas
1 lb fresh or frozen strawberries
12 oz fresh or canned loquats
4 cups orange juice
½ lemon

1 cup grapefruit juice
½ cup clear honey
for decorating:
sprigs of fresh mint
6 strawberries
whipped cream (optional)

Peel, quarter and core the apples. Peel and slice the bananas. Place all the fruits in a blender with a little of the orange juice and reduce to a purée. Squeeze the lemon and add the juice to the blender with the remaining orange juice, the grapefruit juice and honey. Place in the refrigerator and chill well.

Pour the fruit soup into 6 bowls and decorate each one with sprigs of mint, whole or sliced strawberries and a little whipped cream.

Note: A mixture of dried fruits may be used when fresh fruit is not readily available. Other fruit flavors which blend nicely in this soup are quince, apricot, mulberry, fig, cherry, grape, guava, melon, peach, pear and plum.

BORSCHT

Serves 6

4 beets
1 lb stewing beef
4 tomatoes
4½ pints water
2–3 cabbage leaves
2 teaspoons salt

½ bay leaf (optional)
3 peppercorns
6 tablespoons vinegar
3 tablespoons sugar
6 small potatoes
2 egg yolks (optional)

Cook the beets in boiling water to cover for about 30 minutes. Rinse under cold running water, drain and cool. Remove the skins and grate the beets into a large saucepan. Cut the beef into 3 or 4 large pieces. Peel and chop the tomatoes. Place the beef and tomatoes in the pan and add the water.

Coarse shred the cabbage leaves and add to the pan with the salt, bay leaf, peppercorns, vinegar and sugar. Place over high heat and bring to a boil. Lower the heat, cover the pan and simmer gently for about 1½ hours, or until the beef is tender.

Remove the beef and reserve for another dish. Peel the potatoes and drop them into the soup. Continue simmering until the potatoes are tender but still firm. Take the soup off the heat and mix 2–3 tablespoons of the soup with the egg yolks, if used. Stir this mixture back into the soup and serve

Yemenite Rosh Hashana soup

234

without reheating. Serve the soup with a potato in each soup bowl. Borscht may also be served chilled.

Note: There are several ways to garnish this soup. Slices of hard-cooked egg may be added or a little chopped dill sprinkled in the center of each bowl. Alternatively, crush or finely chop a cucumber and a few scallions with a small amount of salt. Add 1 teaspoon of the cucumber mixture to each bowl of soup.

YEMENITE ROSH HASHANA SOUP

Serves 6

1 oxtail or 2½ lb beef bones	2 teaspoons salt
2 onions	1 teaspoon curry powder
4 leeks	dash chili powder
4½ pints water	dash coriander
2 cloves garlic	dash cumin
½ cup tomato paste	dash cardamom

Chop the oxtail or beef bones into pieces of a manageable size. Peel and chop the onions and wash, trim and chop the leeks. Place all these ingredients in a large saucepan with the water. Bring to a boil. Lower the heat and simmer, partly covered, for 2½ hours. Remove the oxtail or beef bones from the soup. Peel and crush the garlic and add to the soup with the tomato paste, salt and all the spices, and cook for a further 5 minutes. Serve the soup poured over *pita* bread (see page 245) or with croutons.

ATONEMENT SOUP WITH KREPLACH (STUFFED DUMPLINGS)

Serves 6

1 chicken or chicken pieces, about 3 lb	salt
	5 pints water
1 carrot	**for the kreplach:**
1 celeriac (celery root) or bunch of celery	1 cup all-purpose flour
	salt and pepper
1 parsley root or small bunch fresh parsley sprigs	1 egg
	2 teaspoons water
1 onion	1 small onion
1 kohlrabi or turnip	3 tablespoons oil
1 small sweet potato or yam	4 oz cooked beef, ground
4 whole allspice or dash ground allspice	

To make the soup, cut the chicken into 6 portions. Peel or scrape the carrot, celeriac and parsley root (or chop the parsley sprigs). Peel the onion, kohlrabi or turnip and sweet potato. Chop the vegetables coarsely. Place the chicken, vegetables, allspice and water in a large saucepan, season to taste and simmer until the chicken is tender, about 2 hours.

Meanwhile, make the *kreplach*. Sift the flour with a dash of salt into a bowl. Beat together the egg and water. Add to the flour and salt and knead lightly. Roll out thinly and cut into 2-inch squares. Peel and chop the onion and sauté in the

oil. Add the beef and mix well. Season to taste. Put a spoonful of this mixture on each square of dough. Dampen the edges with water, fold into triangles and pinch the edges together.

Fasten together two corners of each triangle to make heart-shaped pockets.

Remove the chicken and vegetables, strain the broth but do not remove the surface fat. Reserve the chicken for another meal and return the broth to the pan. Bring to a boil, add the *kreplach* and simmer for 20 minutes before serving.

CHICKEN BROTH WITH MATZO-MEAL DUMPLINGS

Serves 6

for the broth:	pepper
2 onions	6 pints water
1 celeriac (celery root)	**for the dumplings:**
1 carrot	2 eggs
1 stewing chicken (including the neck, feet and gizzard)	1 cup fine matzo meal
	½ cup water or broth
1 chicken bouillon cube (optional)	1 teaspoon salt
	dash nutmeg, allspice or ginger
2 teaspoons salt	¼ cup oil

To make the broth, peel and chop the onions, celeriac and carrot. Place the vegetables, the chicken, chicken bouillon cube (if used), salt, pepper to taste and the water in a large saucepan and simmer over low heat for about 1½–2 hours, or until the chicken is tender. Strain off the broth and keep hot. The surface fat may be left on for this traditional soup. Reserve the chicken and vegetables for another meal.

To make the dumplings, beat the eggs well and mix in the matzo meal, water or broth, salt, nutmeg, allspice or ginger and the oil. Set aside for at least 4 hours before cooking. Roll into balls with moistened hands and drop gently into boiling water or the boiling broth. Simmer for 30 minutes. Serve in the hot broth.

GALILEAN FISH –
SEPHARDIC STYLE

Serves 6

1 large fish, about 3 lb (St. Peter's or other fish – see note)
salt and pepper
3 onions
1 clove garlic
⅓ cup olive oil
6 sprigs fresh parsley
4 tomatoes
½ lemon
dash powdered saffron or safflower
3 tablespoons pine nut kernels
white wine (see recipe)

Clean the fish, wash and pat dry and place in a greased casserole. Season with salt and pepper to taste. Peel and finely chop the onions and garlic and lightly sauté in half the oil in a skillet. Chop the parsley. Remove the onions and garlic from the skillet and mix with the parsley.

Chop the tomatoes and cook lightly in the remaining oil. Squeeze the juice from the half lemon and mix with the powdered saffron or safflower.

Cover the fish with the onions, garlic, tomato and parsley, and sprinkle with the lemon juice mixture and pine nut kernels. Add sufficient water to reach halfway up the fish. Bake in a preheated moderately hot oven (375°) for 35–40 minutes. Pour a little white wine over the fish, if desired, and bake for a further 5 minutes. Serve hot.

Note: St. Peter's fish thrives only in the Sea of Galilee. It is very popular whether broiled, roasted and served with *tehina* (sesame seed) sauce or prepared in this Sephardic way. Carp or bass make an excellent substitute.

GEFILTE FISH

Serves 6–8

1 whole carp or other freshwater fish, about 4 lb
for the stuffing:
1 large onion
1 small carrot or piece of celeriac (celery root)
2 teaspoons salt
½ teaspoon pepper
1 tablespoon sugar
2 eggs
slice of *challah* or other white bread, about 1 inch thick
for the base:
2 large carrots
2 large onions
1 parsnip or piece of celeriac (celery root)

Leaving the head attached to the skin, carefully remove the skin from the fish and reserve. Fillet the fish, discarding the bones (see Planked Lake Superior Whitefish, page 14).

To make the stuffing, peel the onion and carrot or celeriac and chop finely. Grind the fillets of fish and mix with the prepared vegetables. Add the salt, pepper, sugar and eggs. Soak the bread in a little water. Then squeeze dry and mix into the stuffing. Pack the stuffing into the fish skin and head to reshape the fish. Then sew up the opening.

Peel and slice the carrots, onions and parsnip or celeriac for the base. Place in a large oval pan or flameproof casserole and put the fish on top. Add water to cover the fish. Cover the pan and bring to a boil over high heat. Lower the heat and continue to simmer for 2 hours, or transfer to a preheated moderate oven (325°) and cook for the same length of time. When cooked, lift the fish out on to a serving plate. Reserve the vegetables.

Boil the cooking liquid until reduced to about half and strain over the fish. Set aside to cool and set. Garnish with some of the reserved carrot slices and serve with the remaining vegetables.

Note: Alternatively, the stuffing mixture may be formed into balls using slightly moistened hands. Place the balls, and the fish skin and head to provide additional flavoring, on top of the vegetable base. Proceed as above, but reduce the simmering time to 1 hour. Discard the fish skin and head at the end of the cooking time.

SWEET CARP

Serves 6

2 large onions
2 lb carp
1 teaspoon salt
2 tablespoons vinegar
1 tablespoon sugar
½ cup gingersnap crumbs
¼ cup white wine
⅓ cup brown sugar
3 tablespoons seedless raisins
juice of 1 lemon

Peel and finely slice the onions and place in a large skillet. Cut the carp into thick slices and arrange the pieces on top of the onions. Add the salt, vinegar and enough water to barely cover the fish. Simmer, uncovered, over low heat for 20–25 minutes, or until the fish is just cooked. Transfer the fish and onions to a serving dish and retain 1 cup of the liquid.

Mix the fish liquid with the crumbs, white wine, brown sugar and raisins. Add the lemon juice. Bring to a boil, stirring constantly, and pour over the fish. Serve hot, or leave in a cool place to set and serve cold.

PICKLED SOLE

Serves 6

2½ lb filleted sole
oil for deep-frying
1 lemon
2 tablespoons curry powder (optional)
1 tablespoon oil (optional)
2 cloves garlic
1 cup mild vinegar
1 teaspoon salt
½ cup water
3 bay leaves
6 black peppercorns
4 whole allspice
3 tablespoons sugar

Cut the fish into 12 pieces and deep-fry in very hot oil. Drain well and, when cool, arrange in a serving dish. Thinly slice the lemon and put half a lemon slice on each piece of fish.

If using curry powder, place in a saucepan with the 1 tablespoon of oil and heat gently until bubbling. Remove from the heat. Peel and crush the garlic and add to the pan with the vinegar, salt, water, bay leaves, peppercorns, whole allspice and sugar. Bring to a boil over moderate heat. Remove from the heat and, when cold, pour over the fish. Marinate the fish for 2 days in the refrigerator. It keeps very well for up to 1 week.

Pickled sole

Orange, onion and olive salad

MINT-FLAVORED SALAD

Serves 8

5 tomatoes	small bunch fresh mint
3 small cucumbers	1 tablespoon pickled capers
4 red radishes	⅓ cup olive oil
1 green sweet pepper	3 tablespoons lemon juice
1 red sweet pepper	salt and pepper
4 scallions	**for the garnish:**
1 clove garlic	few mint leaves
1 small mild chili	8 ripe olives
2 sprigs fresh parsley	

This salad will be most attractive if the vegetables are diced into cubes of the same size. Wash and dice the tomatoes. Dice the cucumbers, peeling them first if preferred. Trim, wash and dice the radishes. Trim the sweet peppers, remove the seeds and dice. Trim, peel and chop the scallions. Peel and very finely chop the garlic. Trim the chili, remove the seeds and chop very finely. Remove the stems from the parsley and mint and chop the leaves.

Place the olive oil, lemon juice, salt and pepper in a small jar and shake it vigorously to combine the ingredients. Alternatively, use a blender. Pour the salad dressing over the vegetables and toss well. Garnish the salad with the mint leaves and the olives.

ORANGE, ONION AND OLIVE SALAD

Serves 6

4 oranges	olive oil (see recipe)
2 onions	lemon juice (see recipe)
18 ripe olives	

Peel and thinly slice the oranges and onions. Remove the pits from the olives, if desired. Arrange the orange slices on a serving dish with the onions on top. Garnish with the olives. Sprinkle with olive oil and lemon juice to taste. Serve as an appetizer or a garnish.

RADISH CRACKLING SALAD

Serves 6

1 medium-sized onion	6 oz black or red radishes
3 tablespoons chicken fat or oil	salt and pepper
3 large poultry cracklings	3 small red radishes for garnishing
(see recipe)	

Peel and finely chop the onion and sauté in the chicken fat or oil until golden. Remove from the saucepan and drain. Chop the cracklings (crisply fried poultry skins). Coarsely grate the black or red radishes and mix with the onion and cracklings. Add salt and pepper to taste.

Before serving, garnish the salad with the remaining red radishes cut into thin slices or 'roses'.

Note: To make radish 'roses', see Danish Blue Cheese and Radish open sandwich, page 80.

FRUITED CABBAGE SALAD

Serves 6–8

1 kohlrabi or turnip	3 celery stalks
2 shallots or 6 scallions	1 cup pineapple cubes
1 green sweet pepper	mayonnaise or any other salad
1 grapefruit or pomelo	dressing
½ cup hazelnuts (see recipe)	salt
½ medium-sized head red cabbage	

Peel the outer layer from the kohlrabi or turnip and grate the flesh coarsely. Peel and chop the shallots or scallions. Trim the pepper, remove the seeds and shred the flesh finely. Remove the peel and white inner skin from the grapefruit or pomelo and cut the flesh into cubes. Chop the hazelnuts coarsely. (Other nuts may be used, if preferred. If walnuts are used add just before serving to avoid any discoloration of the salad.) Shred the red cabbage. Mix together all the prepared vegetables, fruits and nuts and add mayonnaise or salad dressing and salt to taste. Arrange on lettuce or cabbage leaves, or in a hollowed-out head of cabbage.

MARINATED BEAN AND PEPPER SALAD

Serves 6

1 lb fresh wax beans	2 tablespoons lemon juice
(see note)	3 tablespoons oil
1¼ cups water	dash garlic salt
¼ cup vinegar	dash pepper
2 green sweet peppers	dash paprika
1 red sweet pepper	½ teaspoon salt
1 small scallion	1 tablespoon honey or corn syrup
1 teaspoon chopped fresh dill or	lettuce leaves or tomato slices
chopped fresh parsley	

Remove the strings from the beans and cut the beans into 1-inch pieces. Place in a saucepan and add the water and vinegar. Bring to a boil, lower the heat and simmer for about 15 minutes.

While the beans are cooking, trim and remove the seeds from the peppers, and broil under high heat until the skins blister. Remove the charred skins under cold water. Cut the peppers into thin strips and simmer with the beans for the last 2–3 minutes. Chop the scallion. Drain the liquid from the beans and peppers and mix them with the scallion, dill or parsley, lemon juice, oil, seasonings and honey. Set aside until cold. Serve garnished with lettuce leaves or sliced tomatoes.

Note: If wax beans are not available, green beans may be substituted.

BAKED BEEF BRISKET

Serves 6

3 tablespoons plain flour	1 small celeriac (celery root)
1 teaspoon salt	1 parsnip
dash black pepper	1 clove garlic
dash paprika	1 bay leaf
1 tablespoon brown sugar	4 whole allspice
3 lb beef brisket	6 peppercorns
3 onions	½ cup water
2 carrots	

Mix together the flour, salt, pepper, paprika and sugar. Rub the meat with this mixture. Peel and chop the onions, carrots, celeriac, parsnip and garlic and place in a casserole with the meat on top. Add the bay leaf, spices and water. Place the casserole, uncovered, in a preheated moderately hot oven (400°) for 10 minutes. Lower the heat to 350° and continue cooking for about 1½–2 hours, or until the meat is tender. Baste the meat during cooking with the liquid in the casserole. About 20 minutes before the end of cooking, turn the meat over to brown evenly. Serve hot.

CHOLENT WITH DRIED FRUITS

Serves 6

1 lb yellow turnips or carrots	1 tablespoon salt
2 large potatoes	½ teaspoon pepper
2 lb beef brisket	⅓ cup honey
1 lb prunes	juice of 1 lemon

Peel the turnips or carrots and the potatoes and cut into even-sized pieces. Place the meat in a heavy saucepan, along with the prepared vegetables and prunes. Combine the salt, pepper, honey and lemon juice and pour over the meat and vegetables. Add enough water to cover. Place over moderate heat and bring to a boil. Lower the heat, cover the pan and simmer for at least 3 hours. Traditionally, *cholent* is cooked over very low heat or in a preheated very cool oven (225°) overnight. Most of the sauce evaporates or is absorbed during cooking. Transfer to a serving dish and serve hot.

KNAIDEL (DUMPLING)

Serves 6

1½ cups all-purpose flour sifted with 1½ teaspoons baking powder	dash nutmeg
	¾ cup chopped suet
2 tablespoons semolina flour	1 egg
salt and pepper	⅓ cup water

Mix the flour, semolina flour, seasonings and chopped suet in a bowl. Beat the egg well, then beat in the water and mix into the dry ingredients. Knead lightly on a floured board and form into a ball. Add to the *cholent* (see above) when the liquid is boiling. Cook for at least 1 hour, or as long as you cook the *cholent*.

KISHKE (STUFFED BEEF DERMA)

Serves 6

beef sausage casing (intestines), 18 inches if thin, 12 inches if thick	1½ cups sifted all-purpose flour
½ cup suet (see recipe)	1 teaspoon salt
2 large onions	¼ teaspoon pepper
	liquid to cover (see recipe)

Remove most of the suet from the outside of the casing and chop. Measure the amount required for the recipe and reserve the rest for another dish. Thoroughly clean the inside of the casing. Peel and grate the onions. Mix the grated onion with the suet, flour, salt and pepper.

Sew up one end of the casing and push the sewn end down the center of the casing to form a bag. Start filling the bag with the stuffing, pushing the sewn end through so the shiny inside becomes the outside. Do not fill the casing more than two-thirds full to allow for expansion. Sew the end closed.

Cook with a *cholent* or with a pot roast, or on a bed of sliced onions in a flameproof casserole. Cover with liquid (stock, gravy or water) and cook over low heat for 2 hours or in a preheated very cool oven (225°) overnight.

STUFFED ARTICHOKE HEARTS

Serves 6

6 large globe artichokes or 12 small artichokes	3 tablespoons breadcrumbs
	salt and pepper
1 tablespoon vinegar	2 eggs
1 teaspoon salt	all-purpose flour for coating
8 oz beef, ground	oil for deep-frying
2 tablespoons pine nut kernels (optional)	½ chicken bouillon cube (optional)
	juice of 1 lemon (see recipe)

Wash the artichokes thoroughly and cut off the stems. Place the artichokes in a saucepan with the vinegar, salt and enough water to cover. Bring to a boil and cook for about 30 minutes, or until tender, when a leaf may be easily removed. Lift the artichokes from the pan and drain them upside down for a few minutes. Remove the leaves and reserve for soup or stock. Discard the hairy choke from each artichoke, leaving the hearts intact. Mix the beef, nuts and breadcrumbs and season with salt and pepper according to taste. Pack the mixture into the center of the artichoke hearts. Beat the eggs. Dip the filled hearts into the beaten egg. Coat with flour. Dip again into the beaten egg. Deep-fry in hot oil for 3–4 minutes to seal the filling. Drain and place the artichokes in a saucepan, meat side upward. Add enough water to partially cover and add the chicken bouillon cube and lemon juice. If preferred, add more lemon juice for a sharp flavor. Simmer over low heat for about 1 hour. Drain well and serve hot or cold as a side dish or appetizer.

Note: The large artichokes may be cooked in a pressure cooker for 15 minutes at 15 lb or the small ones for 8 minutes at 15 lb rather than boiling them. Cool the pressure cooker under cold running water, remove the artichokes, drain and continue as above.

MEAT-FILLED QUINCES

Serves 6

6 large quinces
1 small onion
2 tablespoons oil
1 lb beef, ground
1 teaspoon salt

dash allspice, pepper or cinnamon
⅓ cup vinegar
½ cup black or red cherry jam or
  ½ cup sugar and 1 tablespoon
  rose water

Peel the quinces, slice off the pointed ends and scoop out and discard the core. With a small teaspoon remove the insides of the quinces, leaving them hollow. Take care not to break the sides or bases. Peel and chop the onion and lightly sauté in the oil. Then add the meat and sauté until browned. Add the salt and spices. Pack the mixture into the quinces. Place the filled quinces in a casserole or roasting pan and half cover with water. Cook in a preheated moderately hot oven (400°) for about 1½ hours, or until tender. Baste frequently during cooking and add more water, if necessary. About 30 minutes before the end of cooking, mix the vinegar with the jam (or sugar and rose water) and pour a little over each filled quince. Serve hot.

STUFFED CABBAGE ROLLS

Serves 6

12 large cabbage leaves
2 onions
1 celeriac (celery root) or 2–3
  parsnips
2 lb beef, ground
½ cup long-grain rice
1 egg
salt and pepper
dash nutmeg

1 clove garlic
¼ cup oil
1 cup tomato paste
3 tablespoons seedless raisins
  (optional)
¼ cup wine vinegar
½ cup brown sugar
½ cup rosé or white wine

Blanch the cabbage leaves in boiling water for 4–5 minutes to make them pliable. Peel and chop the onions and peel and grate the celeriac or parsnips. Mix with the ground beef, rice, egg, salt and pepper to taste and nutmeg. Place an equal quantity of the mixture into the center of each cabbage leaf. Fold over and tuck in the edges. Roll up the filled leaves, completely enclosing the stuffing. Place in a casserole. Peel and crush the garlic, mix together with the oil, tomato paste, raisins, wine vinegar, sugar and wine and pour over the stuffed cabbage leaves. Add a small quantity of water, if necessary, to cover the rolls. Cook, uncovered, in a preheated hot oven (425°) for 30 minutes.

Lower the heat to 350° and cook for about a further 30 minutes, by which time most of the liquid will have been absorbed. Serve hot.

Meat-filled quinces

ROLLED VEAL WITH CHICKEN LIVERS

Serves 6–8

4 lb boned veal ribs or
  breast of veal
2 lb zucchini
6 chicken livers
6 eggs
2 tablespoons olive oil
dash chili powder

dash garlic salt
dash sweet basil
salt and pepper
½ cup margarine
½ cup water or *Sharir*
  (sherry) wine

Beat the veal with a meat mallet to flatten it and to make it easier to roll. It should measure about 12 by 18 inches. Trim and wash the zucchini and slice into thin circles. Broil the chicken livers and thickly slice them. Beat the eggs. Heat the olive oil in a saucepan, add the eggs and stir over low heat to scramble. Remove from the heat. Spread the scrambled eggs on the veal and cover with the sliced chicken livers and sliced zucchini. Sprinkle on the chili powder, garlic salt, sweet basil and salt and pepper to taste. Roll up the meat, completely enclosing the filling. Secure with string or skewers.

Put the rolled veal into a large saucepan with the margarine and the water or *Sharir*. Use as little liquid as possible. Place the pan over medium heat and bring to the simmering point. Cover the pan and simmer the meat for 1¼–1½ hours until tender. Turn the meat over occasionally and if necessary replenish the liquid by adding extra water or *Sharir* from time to time. When cooked, cut the meat into slices and serve hot or cold.

MOCK VENISON

Serves 6

1 cup water
1 cup wine vinegar
2 teaspoons sugar
6 peppercorns
1 tablespoon salt
1 teaspoon caraway seeds
2 bay leaves

1 clove garlic
2 onions
3 lb rolled loin roast or
  rolled shoulder of lamb
1 tablespoon oil (optional)
½ cup sweet red wine
3 tablespoons plum jam

Place the water, vinegar, sugar, peppercorns, salt, caraway seeds and bay leaves in a saucepan. Bring to a boil. Remove from the heat and set aside until cold. Peel and chop the garlic and onions and add to the cooled liquid. Pour this liquid over the lamb and marinate for 24 hours, turning the lamb over occasionally.

Remove the meat from the marinade and wipe dry with absorbent paper. If the meat is lean, brush with the oil. Place in a roasting pan and roast in a preheated hot oven (450°) for 30 minutes, or until browned.

Meanwhile, strain the marinade. Discard the spices, onions and garlic. Combine the liquid with the wine and jam and pour over the browned meat. Return the pan to the oven, lower the temperature to 300° and cook for a further 1½ hours, basting from time to time.

When cooked, the meat may be sliced and served hot with any remaining liquid, or drained and left until cold.

BOKHARIAN RICE

Serves 4

6 cooked chicken drumsticks or
  broiled chicken livers
½ cup chicken fat
2 large onions
2 medium-sized carrots
small bunch fresh parsley

1 cup long-grain rice
3 tablespoons seedless raisins
  (optional)
1 teaspoon turmeric
1 teaspoon salt
dash pepper

If using chicken drumsticks, remove the meat from the bone and cut into small pieces. Alternatively, slice the broiled chicken livers. Place the pieces of chicken or chicken livers in a flameproof casserole.

Slowly melt the chicken fat in a saucepan with 1 tablespoon of hot water. Peel and chop the onions. Peel and grate the carrots. Add the onions and carrots to the melted fat and sauté until soft but not browned. Drain and add to the casserole. Remove the coarse stems and chop the parsley. Sprinkle over the meat mixture. Mix the rice with the raisins (if used), turmeric, salt and pepper and sprinkle over the vegetables. Add any remaining melted fat and water (the level must be 1 inch above the top of the rice).

Bring the rice to a boil. Cover the casserole and cook in a preheated moderate oven (350°) for about 30 minutes, or until the rice is tender and all the liquid has been absorbed. Transfer to a heated serving dish and serve immediately.

LAMB WITH LEMON

Serves 6

½ cup cooking oil
1 cup water
3 tablespoons rosé or white wine
dash powdered saffron
dash cinnamon

dash rosemary (optional)
salt and pepper
6 lamb chops, about 8 oz each
1 lemon

Place the oil, water, wine, saffron, cinnamon, rosemary (if used) and salt and pepper according to taste in a saucepan. Bring to a boil and then remove from the heat. Place the lamb chops in a flameproof casserole. Thinly slice the lemon and place one slice on each lamb chop. Pour over the hot liquid. Cover the casserole and place over low heat. Simmer for about 1 hour. Serve hot or cold.

GROUND COLD TURKEY BREAST

Serves 6

1 raw turkey breast (with skin but no bone)
½ cup margarine
4 oz sweet potatoes, cooked
½ cup fine fresh breadcrumbs
dash nutmeg
3 eggs
salt and pepper
3¾ cups chicken stock

Place the turkey breast flat on a working surface, skin side down. Leaving a thin layer, carefully remove most of the flesh from the skin. Melt the margarine. Grind the turkey flesh and mix with the margarine, sweet potatoes, breadcrumbs, nutmeg and eggs. Season with salt and pepper to taste and beat well until thoroughly mixed. Place the stuffing in the center of the turkey skin, draw the edges of the skin together and sew up securely. Do not over-fill or the skin will burst during cooking. As an extra precaution, puncture the skin in several places with a needle. Place the stuffed turkey breast in a saucepan with the stock and bring to a boil. Lower the heat to a minimum and simmer very gently for 1½ hours. Remove from the stock and cool before serving. The broth may be reserved for soup.

MATHILDE ALKILAY'S CHICKEN

Serves 5

1 chicken or chicken pieces, about 3 lb
¼ cup cooking oil
3 tomatoes
7 small cloves garlic
½ bunch celery
4 celery leaves
6 tablespoons cognac
2½ cups dry white wine
1 teaspoon salt
4 bay leaves
5 black peppercorns
dash ginger
12 green olives
2 oranges

Joint the chicken if using a whole bird. Heat the oil in a large skillet over moderate heat, add the chicken pieces and sauté until evenly browned on all sides. Peel and chop the tomatoes and 2 cloves of the garlic and add to the skillet. Cover and cook over low heat for 30 minutes.

Peel and chop the remaining garlic. Chop the celery and leaves and add to the skillet with the garlic, cognac, wine, salt, bay leaves, peppercorns, ginger and olives. Cover and cook over low heat for a further 30 minutes, or until the chicken is tender.

Slice the whole oranges thinly without removing the rind. Discard the seeds. When the chicken is tender, add the orange slices to the skillet and heat in the liquid with the chicken pieces for 2–3 minutes before serving.

Ground cold turkey breast

243

Duck with sweet rice filling

CHICKEN WITH ORANGE SAUCE AND STUFFED DATES

Serves 6

1 young chicken, about 5 lb	1 tablespoon lemon juice
½ chicken bouillon cube or	1 tablespoon prepared mustard
¼ teaspoon monosodium	**for the stuffed dates:**
glutamate	12 dates
salt and pepper	2 tablespoons cooked ground meat
¼ cup margarine	dash nutmeg
rind of 1 orange	salt
3 cups orange juice	3 tablespoons curaçao (optional)
3 tablespoons honey or ⅓ cup	1 tablespoon cornstarch
light brown sugar	3 tablespoons cold water

Rub the chicken inside and out with the chicken bouillon cube or monosodium glutamate and season with salt and pepper according to taste. Melt the margarine and brush the chicken with it. Finely shred the orange rind. Place the chicken in a roasting pan with the orange juice, shredded rind, honey or sugar, lemon juice and mustard. Cover to prevent the chicken from browning too quickly. Cook in a preheated moderate oven (350°) for 30 minutes. Uncover and continue cooking for a further 1¾ hours, or until tender. Baste from time to time with the pan juices.

Pit the dates. Season the ground meat with the nutmeg and salt. Stuff a little into each date. About 20 minutes before the chicken is cooked, drop the stuffed dates into the pan.

When the chicken is cooked, remove to a heated serving platter and surround with the dates. Stir the curaçao, if used, and the cornstarch blended with the cold water into the pan. Simmer gently until the sauce thickens. Serve the sauce separately in a sauceboat.

DUCK WITH SWEET RICE FILLING

Serves 6

1 duck, about 5 lb	¾ cup long-grain rice
1 chicken bouillon cube or	2 cups orange juice
½ teaspoon monosodium	1 large onion
glutamate	1 baking apple
salt and pepper	grated rind of ½ lemon
¼ cup margarine (see recipe)	½ cup seedless raisins
for the stuffing:	3 tablespoons sugar
3 tablespoons oil	dash nutmeg

Rub the duck inside and out with the crushed bouillon cube or monosodium glutamate and season with salt and pepper to taste. If the duck is lean, melt the margarine and brush the duck with it.

To make the stuffing, heat the oil in a saucepan and sauté the rice until it just begins to color. Add the orange juice and bring to a boil. Cover tightly and cook over low heat for about 15 minutes, until the rice is tender and all the liquid has been absorbed. Remove from the heat.

Peel and chop the onion. Peel, core and chop the apple. Mix the cooked rice with the onion, apple, lemon rind, raisins, sugar and nutmeg. Season to taste. Stuff the duck with this mixture and sew up each end or secure with small skewers. Place on a wire rack in a roasting pan. Cook in a preheated moderate oven (325°) for about 2 hours, until the duck is tender and golden brown. Baste from time to time during cooking with the excess fat in the pan. Serve hot.

PITA (PANCAKE BREAD)

Makes 18

1 cake compressed yeast or	¼ cup cooking oil
1 package active dry yeast	4 cups all-purpose flour
1 teaspoon sugar	1 teaspoon salt
1¼ cups lukewarm water	

Measure the yeast and sugar into a mixing bowl, pour over the lukewarm water and stir until the yeast and sugar have dissolved. Add the oil. Stir in the flour and the salt and mix together until well blended. Knead until smooth and then divide the dough into 18 portions. Shape each portion into a ball. Roll out each ball on a floured board until the dough is about ⅛ inch thick. Lightly cover the *pita* with a cloth and set aside in a warm place to rise for 30 minutes, or until doubled in bulk. Roll out each piece once more, lightly cover with the cloth and let rise a second time for 30 minutes, or until doubled in bulk. Transfer the *pita* to a lightly floured baking sheet. Bake in a preheated hot oven (450°) until they puff, about 4–5 minutes. Cool on a wire rack.

The hollow *pita* may be cut horizontally and filled with *felafel* (see below), relishes or salad, or dipped into *houmous v'tehina* (see page 246) or other pastes.

FELAFEL (CHICK PEA BALLS)

Serves 6–8

1¼ cups chick peas	1 egg
¼ cup cracked wheat	½ teaspoon coriander
¼ teaspoon baking soda	½ teaspoon cumin
2 cloves garlic	dash turmeric
1 teaspoon salt	dash chili powder
3 tablespoons all-purpose flour	oil for deep-frying

Soak the chick peas and cracked wheat in plenty of water, to which the baking soda has been added, for about 8 hours. Rinse well and drain. Peel and finely chop the garlic. Grind the chick peas and cracked wheat and place in a mixing bowl. Add the garlic, salt, flour, egg and spices and mix well. Shape portions of the mixture into small balls about the size of a walnut.

Heat the oil in a deep-fat fryer until very hot. Place the balls, a few at a time, into a frying basket and lower into the oil. Fry until golden brown. Drain and serve hot. If necessary these may be reheated without spoiling.

Note: Besides being a favorite appetizer, *felafel* is often used as a filling for *pita* (see below) and garnished with *schoog* or *tehina* (see page 246).

Pita bread with felafel

HOUMOUS V'TEHINA (CHICK PEA AND SESAME PASTE)

Serves 6–8

for the houmous:
2½ cups chick peas
3 cloves garlic
juice of 1 large lemon
salt and pepper
cayenne pepper

for the tehina:
juice of 2 lemons
1 cup sesame seeds
1 cup water
2 cloves garlic

1 teaspoon salt
dash cayenne pepper

for the garnish:
3 tablespoons olive oil
chick peas (see recipe)
few olives
red and green sweet pepper slices
    or pickled chilies
few sprigs fresh parsley
dash paprika or cayenne pepper

To make the *houmous*, soak the chick peas overnight. Cook in boiling water to cover until the skins come off. Save a few for the garnish and make a purée with the remainder in a blender while still hot. Peel and crush the garlic. Stir into the purée with the lemon juice. If the consistency is too stiff, add a little boiling water until it resembles a thick mayonnaise. Add salt, pepper and cayenne pepper to taste.

To make the *tehina*, place all the ingredients in a blender and blend to a purée, or pound to a paste in a mortar. Mix together the *houmous* and *tehina*. Place on a flat plate. Pour the olive oil on top and swirl around to make circular grooves. Garnish the center with the reserved whole chick peas, olives, sweet green pepper slices or chilies. Finely chop the parsley and add a sprinkling of parsley and paprika or cayenne pepper.

Note: Tehina may be used separately as a salad dressing, as a cocktail dip, as a topping for *felafels* and in *pitas* (see page 245). It will keep for several months in an airtight container stored in the refrigerator.

SCHOOG (FIERY YEMENITE SAUCE)

Serves 6–8

4–6 large ripe tomatoes
3 cloves garlic
3 small hot chilies
⅓ cup chopped fresh coriander
    or dash ground coriander

2 cardamom seeds or dash
    ground cardamom
2 teaspoons cumin
1 teaspoon salt

Peel the tomatoes, halve them and remove the seeds. Peel the garlic. Remove the stems and seeds from the chilies. Put the tomatoes, garlic and chilies through a grinder, or briefly into a blender. Place the ground tomatoes, garlic and chilies in a saucepan with the coriander, cardamom, cumin and salt. Bring slowly to a boil, then remove from the heat. Cool and mix with *tehina* or *houmous v'tehina* (see above) to tone down the sauce according to taste before serving as a dip or garnish.

POTATO KUGEL (PUDDING)

Serves 6

8 medium-sized potatoes
1 celeriac (celery root) or large
    parsnip or 2–3 carrots
1 large onion
3 tablespoons chicken fat

1–2 sprigs fresh parsley
3 cracklings (see recipe)
6 eggs
1 teaspoon salt
dash pepper

Peel the potatoes and cook in lightly salted boiling water until tender. Drain and mash. Peel and finely grate the celeriac or alternative vegetable. Peel and chop the onion and lightly sauté in the chicken fat until tender. Chop the parsley. Mix the potato with the celeriac, onion and parsley. Chop the cracklings (crisply fried chicken skins). Separate the egg yolks from the whites. Add the yolks with the salt, pepper and cracklings to the potato mixture, and beat thoroughly.

Beat the egg whites until stiff and fold into the potato mixture. Pour into a greased casserole and bake in a preheated moderate oven (350°) for about 30 minutes, or until golden brown. Serve hot.

POTATO LATKES (PANCAKES)

Serves 6–8

6 medium-sized potatoes
½ teaspoon baking soda
1 onion
1 egg
dash nutmeg or allspice

dash pepper
1 teaspoon salt
¼ cup all-purpose flour
oil for frying

Peel and finely grate the potatoes and immediately mix with the baking soda. Peel and grate the onion. Squeeze the potatoes to remove any excess liquid. Beat the egg lightly and mix with the onion, potato, nutmeg or allspice, pepper, salt and flour. Heat a small quantity of oil in a skillet. Drop a large spoonful of the potato mixture into the hot oil. Flatten with the back of the spoon. Cook until crisp and golden brown, turn with a spatula and brown the other side. Drain and keep hot. Continue until all the mixture has been used. Alternatively, prepare in advance and reheat when required. Serve with applesauce or apple chutney.

Note: These pancakes are thin and crisp. If thicker pancakes are preferred, do not flatten the potato mixture with the back of a spoon.

Houmous v'tehina; schoog

BAKED MANGOLD TURNOVERS

Makes 20

for the pastry:
2¾ cups all-purpose flour
1 teaspoon salt
1 cup margarine or butter
cold water (see recipe)

for the filling:
8 oz mangold leaves or spinach
4 sprigs fresh parsley

4 oz liver sausage, chopped,
   or ½ cup grated hard cheese
3 egg yolks
salt and pepper

for the topping:
1 egg yolk
1 teaspoon water
½ cup sesame seeds

To make the pastry, sift the flour and salt into a bowl. Cut the margarine or butter into small pieces and add. Rub in the mixture lightly with the fingertips, lifting and allowing it to fall back into the bowl. When the margarine is evenly distributed and the mixture resembles fine breadcrumbs, add about 3 tablespoons water and mix to a firm dough. Knead lightly on a floured board and roll out to about ⅛ inch thick. Using a floured plain cutter, cut into 3-inch circles.

To make the filling, wash the mangold leaves or spinach thoroughly in cold water. Cook in a minimum amount of water over moderate heat until tender. Drain, squeeze out excess moisture and chop the greens. Remove the parsley stems and chop the leaves. Add the liver sausage or cheese and the egg yolks to the chopped greens and mix well. Season with salt and pepper to taste. Place a generous spoonful of the mixture on each pastry circle. Dampen the edges of the pastry and fold the circles in half, completely enclosing the filling. Press the edges firmly together. For the topping, beat the egg yolk with the water and brush over each pastry turnover. Sprinkle with the sesame seeds. Place on a well-greased baking sheet in a preheated moderately hot oven (375°) and bake for about 25 minutes until golden brown. Serve hot or cold.

POTATO KNISHES (PASTRIES)

Serves 6

for the pastry:
1½ cups all-purpose flour sifted
   with 1 teaspoon baking powder
dash salt
⅓ cup shortening
1 egg
1 tablespoon cold water

for the filling:
2 large onions
¼ cup oil
12 oz cooked potatoes, mashed
1 egg
dash nutmeg
salt and pepper
oil for glazing

To make the pastry, mix the flour and salt together in a bowl. Melt the shortening. Add the egg, water and shortening to the flour. Mix thoroughly, turn out and knead on a floured board until smooth. Roll out thinly. Cut into 3-inch circles.

For the filling, peel and chop the onions and sauté in the oil. Mix the onions and oil with the mashed potatoes. Add the egg, nutmeg and seasoning and mix well. Place a spoonful of the filling on each circle. Dampen the edges of the pastry and pinch them together across the top of the filling. Brush with oil. If you want the pastry more flaky, chill for a few minutes and brush with more oil.

Place on a baking sheet and bake in a preheated moderately hot oven (400°) for about 10 minutes. Reduce the heat to 375° and bake for about 20 minutes more, or until golden. Serve hot or cold.

Note: An alternative way to prepare *knishes* is to make them look similar to slices of jelly roll. Prepare the pastry as given above. Roll the dough as thinly as possible into a large rectangle, then brush with a little oil. Spread the filling over the pastry. Begin rolling from the long side, dampen a small strip at the opposite side and gently pinch the edge of the pastry to seal it. Cut the roll into 1½-inch slices. Lightly oil a baking sheet, place the slices on the sheet and flatten slightly with the bottom of a glass or your fingers. Bake in a preheated moderately hot oven (400°) for about 10 minutes, then lower the heat to 375° and bake for 20 minutes more, or until golden brown. Serve hot or cold.

CARROT BAKE

Serves 6–8

3 medium-sized carrots
1 cup margarine
½ cup brown sugar
1 egg
1 tablespoon water

1¼ cups all-purpose flour
½ teaspoon cinnamon
¼ teaspoon nutmeg
½ teaspoon salt
½ teaspoon baking soda

Wash, peel and coarsely grate the carrots. Cream the margarine and sugar in a bowl until soft. Lightly beat the egg and stir into the creamed mixture with the water. Mix well.

Sift together the flour, cinnamon, nutmeg, salt and baking soda. Stir the sifted dry ingredients into the creamed mixture and beat well. Add the grated carrots and stir until the mixture is well blended. Spoon the mixture into a greased 8-inch ring mold. If this is not available, use a greased 7-inch cake pan. Bake in a preheated moderate oven (350°) for 1 hour. Turn out on to a serving dish and serve hot or cold.

FAVA BEANS WITH DILL

Serves 6

1 lb fresh green fava beans
1 large onion
1 clove garlic
¼ cup oil

3 sprigs fresh dill
salt and pepper
¾ cup water

Remove the strings from the bean pods and slice the pods thinly, leaving the beans inside. Peel and finely chop the onion and garlic. Heat the oil in a heavy saucepan. Add the beans, onion and garlic and lightly sauté for 3–4 minutes. Chop the dill and add with salt and pepper to taste and the water. Place the pan over low heat. Cover and simmer for 15 minutes until the beans are tender. Drain off any excess liquid. Transfer the beans to a heated serving dish and serve hot.

Carrot bake

SWEETENED CARROTS

Serves 6

6 medium-sized carrots	3 tablespoons oil or chicken fat
orange juice (see recipe)	finely pared rind of 1 lemon
½ cup clear honey	½ teaspoon salt
¼ cup brown sugar	dash cinnamon, ginger or cloves

Peel and slice the carrots and place in a saucepan. Add enough orange juice to cover and cook for about 15 minutes over low heat. Add the honey, brown sugar, oil or chicken fat, pared lemon rind, salt and a dash of cinnamon, ginger or cloves (only a subtle hint) and simmer for about 25 minutes, until the liquid has been absorbed and the carrots are highly glazed. Remove the lemon rind. Transfer the carrots to a heated dish and serve hot.

Note: The cooked carrots may be placed in a shallow flameproof casserole and broiled for a few minutes until golden brown before serving.

ASPARAGUS WITH PISTACHIOS

Serves 6

2 lb asparagus	½ cup fine fresh breadcrumbs
1 cup blanched pistachio nuts or	6 tablespoons margarine
blanched slivered almonds	¼ teaspoon salt
(see note)	

Wash the asparagus in cold water, lightly scrape the stalks with a knife and cut off the tough fibrous base. If the asparagus stalk is white, remove the outer fibrous skin from below the green tip to prevent a bitter flavor. Tie the asparagus spears in small bundles with white string or thread. Stand in a deep saucepan with the tips upward. Add enough salted water to come just below the tender tips. Cover the pan and simmer over low heat for 20–25 minutes, or until tender. Drain thoroughly and keep hot in a serving dish.

Lightly sauté the pistachio nuts or slivered almonds with the breadcrumbs in the margarine until golden brown. Add the salt. Serve the asparagus spears sprinkled with the browned nuts and breadcrumbs.

Note: Salted peanuts may be substituted for the pistachio nuts or almonds.

BEETS WITH ORANGE

Serves 6

9 small fresh beets	1 tablespoon margarine
rind of 1 orange	1 tablespoon lemon juice
1 tablespoon cornstarch	salt
1 cup orange juice	1 teaspoon dried rosemary

Cook the beets in boiling water to cover for about 45 minutes, or until tender. Meanwhile, finely grate the rind of the orange. Drain the beets, remove the skins and slice thinly. Blend the cornstarch with the orange juice. Melt the margarine in a saucepan and add the lemon juice with the blended cornstarch. Bring to a boil, stirring constantly, until thick and clear. Add the sliced beets, salt to taste, grated orange rind and rosemary, and cook gently for 3–4 minutes. Pour into a heated dish and serve hot.

PEAS WITH MINT

Serves 6

2 lb shelled peas	3 sprigs fresh mint
1 teaspoon dehydrated chicken	3 sprigs fresh parsley
soup (optional)	½ teaspoon salt
¼ teaspoon sugar	1 tablespoon margarine

Place the peas, dehydrated soup, sugar, mint, parsley and salt in a saucepan with enough boiling water to just cover. Place the saucepan over low heat, cover and simmer the peas for 10–15 minutes, or until tender. Remove the sprigs of mint and parsley. Drain off the liquid and toss the peas in the pan with the margarine. Transfer to a warmed serving dish and serve hot.

LAYERED ONION MATZO BAKE

Serves 6

2 large potatoes	½ cup chopped green herbs
6 medium-sized onions or leeks	(parsley, dill, etc.)
1 cup oil	4 eggs
4 matzos	salt and pepper

Peel and cut the potatoes into small even-sized pieces. Cook in boiling, salted water to cover until tender. Drain well. Peel and slice the onions (or trim, wash and slice the leeks) and cook in boiling, salted water until just tender. Drain well. Heat the oil and pour into a casserole. Dip the matzos in water and place 2 in the bottom of the casserole. Cover with half the sliced onions. Mash the potatoes with the herbs and spread over the onions. Cover with the remaining onions. Place the 2 remaining matzos on top. Beat the eggs, add salt and pepper to taste and pour over the matzos. Place the casserole in a preheated moderately hot oven (400°). After 10 minutes, reheat the remaining oil and pour over the top of the matzo bake. Cook for 30 minutes, remove from the oven and immediately pour off the excess oil before serving.

LOKSHEN (SWEET NOODLE PUDDING) WITH APPLES

Serves 6

8 oz broad noodles (green, if available)	½ cup margarine or butter (see recipe)
2 cups milk or 6 cups water (see recipe)	3 apples
1 teaspoon salt	½ cup sugar
3 tablespoons oil	½ cup chopped nuts
3 eggs	1 cup jam (blueberry or dark plum or grape)

If served with a dairy meal, cook the noodles in the milk with the salt until the liquid is almost absorbed. For meat meals, bring the water to a boil, put in the noodles with the salt and cook until just tender. Drain and rinse, then drain again. Pour the oil over the noodles and mix well. Set aside about a third of the noodles to use as a lattice for the top.

Beat the eggs and melt the margarine (or butter if the dish is to be served with a dairy meal). Mix the remainder of the noodles with the eggs and margarine or butter and place in a casserole. Peel and slice the apples thinly and mix with the sugar. Spread over the noodles in the casserole.

Mix the chopped nuts with the jam. Spread over the apples. Lattice the top with the reserved noodles so that the jam filling shows through. Bake in a preheated moderately hot oven (375°) for 35 minutes. Serve hot.

COTTAGE CHEESE BLINTZES

Serves 6

for the batter:	1 egg
2 eggs	2 tablespoons sugar
2 tablespoons butter	¼ cup seedless raisins (optional)
dash salt	dash cinnamon
⅔ cup milk	**for the topping:**
⅔ cup all-purpose flour	1 cup cultured sour cream
cooking oil	⅓ cup honey
for the filling:	cooked cherries or fresh strawberries (optional)
2⅔ cups cottage cheese	

To make the batter, beat the eggs lightly. Melt the butter. Add the butter, salt, milk and flour to the eggs and beat well. Heat a little oil in a small skillet. Pour in 2 tablespoons of batter and swirl the skillet around to distribute the batter. Cook over medium heat until the top is firm. Do not turn the pancake over while cooking. Pile each pancake, fried side up, on a cloth. Repeat until all the batter has been used.

For the filling, mix together the cottage cheese, egg, sugar, raisins (if used) and cinnamon. Spread a little of the mixture on to half of the fried side of each pancake. Fold the pancakes over the filling and then in half again to make into triangles. Fry in a little hot oil for 1 minute on each side, or until golden. Transfer to a serving dish.

For the topping, mix the sour cream with the honey and spread over the top. Decorate with the cherries or strawberries if desired. Serve slightly warm, allowing 2 per person.

Layered onion matzo bake

COCONUT KISSES

Makes about 24

4 egg whites

2 cups sifted confectioners' sugar

2½ cups shredded coconut

Beat the egg whites until stiff. Beat the confectioners' sugar into the egg whites a spoonful at a time. Fold in the coconut with a metal spoon. Drop heaped teaspoonfuls of the mixture on to a baking sheet lined with greased and floured foil. Bake in a preheated very cool oven (250°) for 45 minutes, or until they begin to color. Leave on the baking sheet until cold.

WINE FLUFF

Serves 6

2 envelopes plain gelatin

½ cup cold water

1½ cups sweet red wine

rind of 1 lemon or orange

2 teaspoons lemon juice

4 egg yolks

dash salt

¾ cup sugar

4 egg whites

shredded coconut

Soak the gelatin in the cold water for a few minutes. Heat the wine with the lemon or orange rind and lemon juice, but do not boil. Discard the rind. Beat the egg yolks with the salt and sugar until light in color. Pour the wine mixture into the beaten egg yolks, then place the mixture in a double boiler. Heat gently, stirring constantly, until the mixture is thick enough to coat the back of the spoon. Add the soaked gelatin and stir until dissolved. Remove from the heat and pour the mixture into a bowl.

Stand the bowl in cold water, or over ice, and continue stirring until the mixture begins to thicken. Beat the egg whites until stiff and carefully fold into the wine mixture. Pour into 6 glasses and, when almost set, sprinkle with the coconut.

NECTAR AND AMBROSIA

Serves 6

1 large orange

1 large grapefruit

3 tablespoons chopped candied
   citrus peel

⅓ cup shredded coconut

⅓ cup clear honey mixed with
   2 teaspoons rose water

6 dates

6 blanched almonds

6 red rose petals (optional)

Peel the orange and grapefruit and remove all the white inner skin. Cut each fruit horizontally into 6 slices. Place an orange slice and a grapefruit slice on each of 6 plates.

Heat the honey with the rose water in a small heavy saucepan and pour a little over the fruit slices on each plate. Sprinkle with the candied peel and coconut. Pit the dates and insert a blanched almond in each cavity. Place one date and one rose petal (if used) on each plate.

CANDIED CITRUS PEEL

Makes 1¼ lb

6 large oranges (see note)   1½ cups water

3 cups sugar   sugar for coating

Wash and dry the fruit and remove the peel in sections. Use the fruit for another purpose or for juice. Cut the sections of peel lengthwise into strips about ⅓ inch wide.

Place in a saucepan and cover with water. Bring to a boil over high heat and then drain. Repeat this process 6 times, using fresh water each time. Drain thoroughly. Add the sugar and water and place over very low heat until the sugar is dissolved. Increase the heat slightly and simmer until the syrup is absorbed. Dip each piece of citrus peel in sugar to coat and set aside on a tray for about 2 days to dry completely before storing in an airtight container. Serve as a confection or use as required for desserts.

Note: Although any kind of citrus fruit, such as lemon, lime, grapefruit or orange may be used, for this quantity of sugar and water the amount of peel should be equal to that of 6 large oranges (approximately 9½ oz).

FRITTERS IN WINE SAUCE

Serves 6

for the batter:

½ cup water

¼ cup oil

3 cups fine matzo meal

¼ cup sugar

3 eggs

½ teaspoon salt

dash cinnamon or grated rind
   of ½ lemon

for the filling:

½ cup chopped nuts

1 cup jam (any kind)

2 tablespoons fine matzo meal

oil for deep-frying

for the sauce:

1 cup white wine

½ cup clear honey

2 tablespoons potato flour

2 tablespoons water

2 egg yolks

To make the batter, heat together the water and oil until boiling. Mix the matzo meal and sugar in a bowl. Pour the water and oil over the matzo meal mixture and set aside until the liquid has been absorbed. Beat the eggs well and add, with the salt and cinnamon or grated lemon rind, to the matzo meal mixture. Knead to a soft dough and form into 12 flat circles.

To make the filling, mix together the chopped nuts, jam and matzo meal. Place 1 teaspoon of the mixture in the center of half the circles. Dampen the edges, cover with the remaining circles and pinch firmly together. Deep-fry in hot oil. Drain and keep warm.

To make the sauce, heat the wine and honey in a saucepan. Mix the potato flour with the water and stir into the hot wine and honey mixture. Bring slowly to a boil, stirring constantly until thick and clear. Beat the egg yolks and add a little of the hot sauce to them. Stir the yolk mixture back into the remaining sauce. Serve with the fritters.

Nectar and ambrosia

CHEESE PIE WITH FRUIT TOPPING

Serves 6–8

for the crust:
4 tablespoons butter
1 cup cookie crumbs
for the filling:
2 cups cottage cheese
1 cup cultured sour
  cream
½ cup sugar
2 eggs
1 teaspoon vanilla extract
2 tablespoons all-purpose flour
for the topping:
1 cup cultured sour
  cream
2 tablespoons sugar
1 teaspoon vanilla extract
canned or fresh peach slices
fresh sugared strawberries

To make the crust, melt the butter and mix with the crumbs. Press the mixture into a 9-inch pie dish. Chill well.

For the filling, blend the cottage cheese, sour cream, sugar, eggs, vanilla and flour together and pour into the crust. Bake in a preheated moderate oven (350°) for 20 minutes. Remove from the oven and increase the heat to 450°. For the topping, mix together the sour cream, sugar and vanilla. Spoon on to the partially cooked pie. Place in the oven for 5 minutes, or until set. Remove from the oven and cool. Decorate with the peach slices and strawberries.

PASSOVER PIE

Serves 6–8

for the crust:
1 cup fine matzo meal
2 tablespoons ground almonds
1 tablespoon sugar
¼ cup margarine
for the filling:
6 bananas
2 tablespoons lemon juice
1 cup cranberry sauce
for the topping:
2 egg whites
dash salt
¼ cup sugar
¼ clear honey
grated rind of 1 lemon

To make the crust, place the matzo meal, ground almonds, sugar and margarine in a bowl and mix thoroughly. Press the mixture over the bottom and sides of a 7-inch pie dish and chill for 10 minutes. Bake in a preheated moderately hot oven (400°) for 10 minutes, until golden brown. Set aside to cool.

For the filling, peel the bananas and mash with the lemon juice. Beat in the cranberry sauce and pour the mixture into the prepared crust.

For the topping, beat the egg whites with the salt until stiff. Beat in the sugar, then the honey and finally the lemon rind. Spoon over the filling and serve.

Cheese pie with fruit topping

254

MULLED WINE IN MELONS

Serves 6

3 tablespoons sugar	2 whole cloves
1 thin strip orange	½ cup water
and/or lemon rind	1 cup sweet red wine
cinnamon stick, about 1 inch	3 small cantaloupes or other sweet
dash allspice	melons

In a heavy pan simmer the sugar, rind, cinnamon, allspice and cloves in the water for about 10 minutes. Add a little water if the syrup evaporates too much. Add the wine and heat but do not allow the mixture to boil. Meanwhile, cut the melons horizontally in half and carefully remove the seeds. Remove the rind and spices from the syrup.

In summer, the wine mixture should be cooled and chilled in the refrigerator and then spooned into the chilled melons. On cool days, the hot wine mixture may be spooned into the unchilled melon halves.

Note: The flesh of some of the larger varieties of melon, such as a watermelon, may be cut into balls and placed in serving bowls with the wine mixture. A combination of several types of melons is also delicious and very attractive.

LAYERED FRUIT BAKE

Serves 12–14

for the pastry:	2 cups chopped dates
4 cups all-purpose flour	⅔ cup water
⅔ cup ground almonds	½ cup chopped nuts
1 cup sugar	1 cup cookie crumbs (gingersnaps,
1 cup shortening (see recipe)	preferably)
1 egg	**for the second filling:**
¾ cup water	8 pears or apples
for the first filling:	¼ cup sugar
1 cup brown sugar	½ cup seedless raisins

To make the pastry, mix together the flour, ground almonds and sugar in a bowl. Cut in the shortening (traditionally, chicken fat is used). Mix together the egg and water, add to the flour mixture and, using a knife, mix to a soft dough. Knead lightly on a floured board until smooth. Divide the pastry into 5 portions and roll each one into an 8-inch circle.

To make the first filling, gently heat the brown sugar, dates and water in a heavy saucepan until the sugar is dissolved. Beat in the nuts and cookie crumbs and set aside to cool.

To make the second filling, peel, core and thinly slice the pears or apples. Mix with the sugar and raisins.

Place the pastry circles and both fillings in alternate layers in an 8-inch round cake pan, starting and finishing with a layer of pastry. Bake in a preheated cool oven (300°) for 2 hours. Leave in the pan for about 10 minutes before turning out. Serve either warm or cold.

Note: If you wish to bake a more shallow *fladen*, divide the pastry into 3 portions and roll each one into a 10-inch circle. Place one circle of pastry in the bottom of a 10-inch cake pan. Alternate the layers of filling with the remaining pastry circles, ending with a layer of pastry. Bake in a preheated cool oven (300°) for 1½ hours. Cool in the pan for 10 minutes before turning out. Serve warm or cold.

APRICOT-MATZO PUDDING

Serves 6

3 lb fresh apricots or 2 large	⅔ cup margarine
(20-oz) cans apricots	3 eggs
2 cups water and 1½ cups sugar or	**for decoration:**
2 cups syrup from the apricots	12 fresh cherries or strawberries
(see recipe)	2 tablespoons castor sugar
6 matzos	

Halve the fresh apricots and remove the pits. Place in a saucepan with the water and sugar. Simmer gently over low heat for 2–3 minutes. Drain and retain the syrup. Alternatively, drain the syrup from the canned apricots (if these are used) and retain the amount required in the recipe. Dip the matzos into the syrup and place in alternate layers with the apricots in a greased casserole, finishing with a layer of apricots. Melt the margarine, beat in the eggs and the remaining syrup and pour the mixture over the apricots and matzos.

Decorate with the fresh cherries or strawberries rolled in sugar. Bake in a preheated cool oven (300°) for 30 minutes, or until the egg mixture is fairly firm and golden brown. Serve warm or cold.

POPPY SEED CAKE

Makes 8–10 portions

1⅓ cups poppy seeds	2 tablespoons brandy
¾ cup margarine	or vermouth
1 cup sugar	3 egg whites
3 egg yolks	**for the topping:**
¼ cup all-purpose flour	3 tablespoons dark plum jam
¼ cup cornstarch	1 cup sifted confectioners' sugar
2 tablespoons water	

Grind the poppy seeds in a mortar or electric grinder. Cream the margarine and sugar together until soft. Beat in the egg yolks, one at a time. Add the poppy seeds to the mixture and beat well. Sift the flour with the cornstarch. Mix the water with the brandy or vermouth. Fold the dry ingredients and liquid alternately into the creamed mixture.

Beat the egg whites until stiff and fold into the mixture carefully. Pour into a greased and lined 9-inch layer cake pan. Bake in a preheated moderate oven (350°) for about 50 minutes–1 hour. Turn out on to a wire rack and cool. Serve the cake topped with the dark plum jam mixed with the confectioners' sugar.

SESAME SEED CANDY

Makes about 36

1 cup clear honey	½ cup blanched slivered almonds
1 cup sugar	2 cups sesame seeds
½ cup water	

Boil the honey, sugar and water in a heavy saucepan until a little of the mixture dropped into a saucer of cold water forms a ball. Stir in the nuts and seeds and cook gently for about 5 minutes, or until the seeds are 'gilded'. Pour on to a wet board or marble slab and cut into diamond shaped pieces. When the candy has hardened it can be stored for a long time in an airtight container.

Note: Special care should be taken when making candy using honey. Make the candy on a dry day. Rainy or hot and humid weather is unsuitable since the honey absorbs moisture from the air and prevents the candy from hardening sufficiently. To prevent the pieces from sticking together, they may be individually wrapped in rice paper or saran wrap.

MARZIPAN MORDECAI

Makes about 18 cookies

1 cup margarine	1 tablespoon lemon juice
1 cup powdered sugar	1 tablespoon water
2 cups finely ground almonds	powdered sugar for dusting
2 cups all-purpose flour	

Cream the margarine with the sugar until soft. Mix together the ground almonds and flour and stir into the cream mixture. Add the lemon juice and water and mix to form a soft dough. If necessary, add a little more water. Knead on a floured board until smooth. Roll to ¼ inch thick and cut out with a 5-inch gingerbread-man cutter. Place on a baking sheet and bake in a preheated cool oven (300°) for about 30–40 minutes. While still hot, sprinkle with the sugar. Cool on a wire rack until completely cold, then store in an airtight container.

SPIRALED PASTRIES

Serves 6

3 cups all-purpose flour	oil for deep-frying
dash salt	juice of 1 lemon
1 egg	1 cup clear honey
1¾ cups water or milk	dash cinnamon
2 tablespoons oil	

Mix the flour and salt together in a bowl. Beat the egg and add with the water and the oil to the flour. Beat thoroughly until a thick batter is formed.

In a deep-fat fryer, heat the oil for deep-frying. Using a pastry bag and a ¼-inch tip, pipe 2- to 3-inch lengths of the mixture into the hot oil. The mixture will automatically fall into uneven circular shapes. Do not try to fry too many at one time as the pastries cook very quickly. When the pastries are golden, remove from the oil and drain. Continue until all the mixture has been used.

Heat the lemon juice, honey and cinnamon in a saucepan until almost boiling. Remove the pan from the heat and drop the drained spiraled pastries into the syrup, a few at a time. Remove and drain on a wire rack with a plate underneath, so that the honey syrup may be collected, reheated and used again to coat the pastries.

ROUND CHALLAH BREAD

Makes 2 loaves

1½ cups hot water	¼ cup lukewarm water
1 tablespoon salt	3 eggs
3 tablespoons castor sugar	8 cups all-purpose flour
3 tablespoons vegetable oil	½ cup seedless raisins (optional)
2 cakes compressed yeast or	1 egg yolk
2 packages active dry yeast	3 tablespoons poppy seeds

Mix the hot water with the salt, sugar and oil in a mixing bowl and set aside until lukewarm. Dissolve the yeast in the lukewarm water. Stir the yeast mixture into the mixing bowl. Beat in the eggs. Mix the raisins with the flour and stir into the liquid. Mix well to a rough dough. Turn on to a lightly floured board and knead until smooth and elastic.

Replace the dough in the bowl, cover with a damp cloth and set aside in a warm place to rise for about 1 hour, or until doubled in bulk. Do not let the cloth touch the dough.

Divide the dough in half. Roll each half into a long rope, about 1 inch in diameter, and place on a baking sheet in a circular cone shape. To do this, form the 'rope' of dough into a circle about 8 inches in diameter, and then fill the circle in, making each subsequent circle smaller and higher, until you have a cone shape. The loaf may be braided if preferred. Set aside for about 30 minutes, or until doubled in bulk.

Beat the egg yolk and brush it on the dough. Sprinkle on the poppy seeds. Bake in a preheated moderately hot oven (375°) for about 1 hour. When cooked, cool on a wire rack.

Note: At every Jewish festival two sweet loaves, usually braided, are placed on the table for benediction. On *Rosh Hashana* these loaves are round. Traditionally at *Rosh Hashana* and *Yom Kippur*, the loaves are decorated with a dove or a ladder, made from the dough, to represent the hope that prayers ascend heavenward.

Round challah bread; spiraled pastries

CHINESE

Kenneth Lo

Photography by John Miller

In China, for over 20 centuries a Confucian country which practised ancestral worship and reverence for the old, eating was by far the most important form of social entertainment available. The pinnacle of lavishness in Chinese cooking and eating was reached in the Mandarin and inter-Mandarin banquets and entertainments, when the important government officials and bureaucrats entertained one another.

To make a comprehensive survey of ordinary Chinese cooking and eating as enjoyed by the average Chinese today, many sections of the Chinese culinary scene would have to be studied. One would need to look at the food prepared and sold by the restaurants (very different from many of the chop suey houses which have grown up in the West), by housewives, snack specialists, tea-houses, outdoor markets and finally street vendors, who sell food cooked on the spot and move from street corner to street corner all day and night.

Writing about Chinese cooking for the Western public, one is immediately aware of the need for clarification and explanation so that the reader may have a proper grasp of the form and concept of a Chinese meal, without which any attempt at Chinese cooking is bound to be unsuccessful. First of all, a Chinese meal is essentially a communal one, and for this reason the aim is not to produce a certain number of portions for a given number of people: a dish is simply produced for a table of diners, which may be any number from four to a dozen people. Dishes of food may be large or small, but how large or small is usually determined by the number of diners likely to be present.

As a rule, there are a good many more dishes at a Chinese meal than at a corresponding Western one. For example, an ordinary Chinese dinner at home would consist of about four dishes, with one or two soups. The dishes are brought to the table at the same time, and the diners help themselves as they please. At a dinner party, there may be a dozen dishes or more, served in courses one after another with an interval of a few minutes between each. One could well have two or three soups, two or three fish or seafood dishes, several mixed quick-fried dishes, as many stews, casseroles and poultry dishes, two or three meats and several vegetables. This system gives an almost unlimited number of combinations when choosing and planning a Chinese menu. The scope of Chinese dishes is roughly divided into rice-accompanying dishes (*Fan Tsai*) – plain, home-cooked dishes; wine-accompanying dishes (*Ch'iu Tsai*) – quick-fried, highly seasoned, crispy-crunchy dishes; and 'big dishes' (*Ta Tsai*) – the larger casseroles and roasts. At a Chinese dinner, which invariably begins with some wine-accompanying dishes, rice is often not served at all, or else it is used for the purpose of 'settling the stomach'. Rice is usually served with those dishes which follow the 'big dishes'. The soups simply act as punctuations between the courses. There is no precise rule for the choice of ingredients, but the different divisions provide a framework on which the variation of texture, taste, flavor and substance may be built.

However, there are a few basic ingredients with which one has to get acquainted before attempting Chinese regional cooking – the glossary on the following page gives details of a few of them. You are advised to read this first and certainly before beginning to cook any of the recipes in this section.

CHINESE COOKING METHODS

Deep-frying : The Chinese use a pan which slopes toward the center, creating a well for the oil. The advantage of this pan is that when the food is pushed on to the sloping sides, the oil will drain off. In a Western kitchen, where the pan is equipped with a wire basket, deep-frying is much simpler. The ingredients are immersed in hot oil until pale golden in color, then removed while the oil is reheated. They are then immersed again and cooked until crisp and golden on the outside and tender inside. If the ingredients are returned to the pan once, the method is known as double-frying; if returned twice it is called triple-frying.

The oil itself should be heated to different degrees. If cooking fish, kidneys or chicken, heat until it just begins to bubble; if cooking beef or pork, heat until the oil smokes.

Steaming : This method is used more frequently in Chinese cooking than in Western cooking, probably because either boiling or steaming rice produces large quantities of steam. This steam is utilized to cook other dishes by placing layers of steamers (which are basket-work trays) on top of the rice. When the rice is ready a whole series of dishes will also be ready at the same time. If a steamer is not available, an ovenproof dish or plate may be inverted in a large saucepan, which is filled with water until the bowl holding the food is a third underwater. The food to be steamed should be placed in an ovenproof bowl and set on top of the inverted plate. When the water boils, the steaming will start. In short-steaming, the bowl containing the food can be left open, as in the cooking of fish; in long-steaming (steaming over 30 minutes), the food is usually cooked covered. This can be done with a lid or by covering the top of the bowl with aluminum foil. The large saucepan should be covered tightly in both instances.

Stir-frying (quick-frying) : The Chinese invented stir-frying (quick-frying), a cooking method similar to sautéing but needing only a few minutes of intense heat. The pan used for stir-frying is important – the thinner the metal, the faster it will conduct the heat. The process consists primarily of cooking one, or a number of foods, sliced into thin or matchstick-thin strips, in one or a few tablespoons of oil or fat. The ingredients in the pan are stirred with a metal spoon, spatula or a pair of bamboo chopsticks, while the ingredients cook. Seasonings and sauces are added and adjusted from time to time. Often the foods to be cooked together are stir-fried separately first, and then finally combined together in one big crescendo of cooking. This is sometimes necessary since the different foods combined in the dishes may require different lengths of cooking time. Another reason for separate cooking is the need to keep the flavors quite distinct until the final assembly. As a rule the oil used in stir-frying is corn oil or peanut oil; however, chicken fat is often employed in delicate cooking, for instance, to sauté vegetables. Although stir-frying may seem difficult at first, practice will make it increasingly easy.

An average Chinese family meal usually consists of 4 or 5 dishes, with an accompaniment of rice, to be eaten by 4 or 5 persons. Extra dishes would be prepared for a party meal for more persons. The recipes in this section can be selected and combined according to taste, taking these servings as a guide.

GLOSSARY

from left to right:
Bean-curd; water chestnuts; dried tangerine (or orange) peel; red bean-curd cheese; fermented brown beans; dried Chinese mushrooms; winter bamboo shoots; wood-ears; fermented black beans; brown rock sugar; bamboo shoots; ginger root; lichees; lotus root; chilies; bêche-de-mer (sea cucumber); Chinese salted cabbage; bean sprouts; egg noodles; Chinese cabbage; Chinese ham; transparent pea-starch noodles; rice stick noodles; wheat-flour noodles.

Bamboo Shoots
Probably eaten more for their crunchy texture than for their taste, which is extremely subtle. Winter bamboo shoots are somewhat more tender and smaller than ordinary bamboo shoots and are used by the Chinese for special dishes. Bamboo shoots are usually available canned, either whole or in large pieces. Rinse well with cold water before using.

Bean-curd
Soy bean purée is set in cake form (about 3 inches square and 1 inch thick) to make bean-curd. It is an unusual soft spongy custard, creamy in color and available either dried or fresh.

Bean-curd Cheese, Red (Chinese Red Cheese)
A fermented derivative of bean-curd that has no Western equivalent in flavor. It may be bought canned in a red sauce. Mash the cubes before using.

Bean Sprouts
The sprouts or shoots of Mung peas which are tiny whitish-green shoots, crunchy in texture. They should be cooked only briefly so that their crunchy quality is retained. They may be bought fresh, in cans, or in packages.

Beans, Fermented Black (Black Bean Sauce)
These small, preserved soy beans are very salty and have a strong flavor. If unavailable, add extra salt to the recipe. They usually come dried and must be soaked and often mashed before using.

Cabbage
Chinese Celery Cabbage (Chinese Lettuce): crisp vegetable resembling Romaine, with firm, tightly packed vertical leaves which are pale yellow with a light green color at the tips. As a substitute use young celery. Swiss chard or Savoy cabbage.
Chinese Cabbage (Chinese Chard): an extremely versatile and popular vegetable with long smooth whitish stems and large dark-green crinkly leaves. It requires little cooking and has a delicate flavor.
Chinese Salted Cabbage: generally salted and dried in the sun. Sometimes hot pepper is added. Salted cabbage is used with meat as a flavoring agent. It must be soaked for 15 minutes in warm water, then rinsed in several changes of cold water.
Mustard Cabbage: similar in taste to broccoli, this dark-green vegetable has tightly packed scalloped leaves. It is similar in both size and texture to a small head of cabbage.

Chilies
These small red peppers are extremely hot in taste (probably the hottest vegetable in existence). The white seeds inside are usually discarded. Chilies often come dried in which case they are even hotter. When dried chilies are fried in oil, they give it a red color and impregnate the oil with their hotness. This chili oil is used to cook meat and vegetables and is sometimes mixed with soy sauce to use as a dip at the table. Green and yellow chilies are occasionally available.

Chinese Ham
The two best known hams in China are the *Yunnan* ham and the *Ching Hua* ham. They are usually available sliced in cans. A country-cured ham is a good substitute – the redder its color the more similar it is to the Chinese variety.

Chinese Noodles
Chinese noodles come in four varieties:
Egg Noodles: more yellow in color than the following varieties, egg noodles are often precooked in 'pads' (like a small ball of wool but flattened). Precooked they require only a short period of simmering in boiling water to loosen up before they are stir-fried, cooked in sauce or added to soups.
Rice Stick Noodles (Rice-flour Noodles): usually whiter in color than the wheat-flour noodles, these come in straight fine strands, about 8 inches in

260

length. They are often cooked with wood-ears, mushrooms, meats or various seafoods such as oysters.

Transparent Pea-starch Noodles: made from ground Mung peas. Although the noodles are somewhat white and opaque when raw, they become transparent after a period of soaking or simmering in water. Soak in warm water for a few minutes before using to prevent absorbing excessive liquid from the prepared dish. Vermicelli may be substituted.

Wheat-flour Noodles: These noodles look like spaghetti and are made largely from the same ingredients. When cooked, they should be soft outside but still firm inside.

Doilies for Peking Duck
Very similar in appearance to ordinary pancakes, except that they are thinner and feel drier, these are made without eggs and heated without the use of fat (see recipe, page 279). Very thin ordinary pancakes may be substituted.

Dried Chinese Mushrooms
Fresh mushrooms are seldom used in Chinese cooking. The dried ones are brownish-black in color and have a much stronger flavor and firmer texture than ordinary mushrooms. Clean them by rinsing in cold water, then soak in warm water for 20–30 minutes before using.

Dried Tangerine or Orange Peel (Mandarin Orange Peel)
The dried peel of citrus fruits has a stronger flavor than fresh peel; therefore, it is used only in small quantities. If commercially unavailable, prepare it by drying fresh peel in a very cool oven (250°) for 3 hours. Turn the heat off and let stand in the oven overnight. Dried peel is usually soaked for 30–45 minutes before using.

Five-spice Powder
This very strong, fragrant mixed-spice powder consists of star anise, anise pepper, fennel, cloves and cinnamon. It is extremely pungent and should be used sparingly. Allspice may be used as a substitute.

Ginger Root
It has a coarse yellow skin and is green inside with a white core. Scrape the root before using. Thin slices (about ⅛ inch thick) are cut from the root as required. The unused portion may be wrapped in foil and stored for weeks in a cool, dry place or in the refrigerator.

Ginger Water
Prepare ginger water by placing 1 tablespoon chopped fresh ginger root into a pan with ⅓ cup of water. Simmer over low heat for 3 minutes, strain and use as required.

Haisein Sauce or Hoisin Sauce (Red Vegetable Sauce)
Very similar in appearance to plum sauce – thick and viscous, brownish-red in color, with a pungent sweet spiciness – this sauce is made from soy beans, garlic, chilies, sugar and vinegar.

Lotus Leaves (Water Lily Leaves)
These come in large sheets, often more than 18 inches across. In Chinese cooking, they are frequently used for wrapping together various foods and flavoring ingredients before steaming them. Since lotus leaves are not easily obtainable in the West, large cabbage leaves may be used as a substitute.

Monosodium Glutamate
This is a white, powdery substance, which enhances or accentuates the taste of foods. When increasing quantities of a recipe, the amount of the monosodium glutamate should remain unaltered. Used extensively in Japanese and Chinese cooking. Sold in jars and cans under a variety of brand names.

Oyster Sauce
A thick grayish-brown liquid, this concentrate of oysters, soy sauce and brine is usually sold in bottles or cans. Used as a flavoring agent for cooking with meat, poultry and seafood.

Plum Sauce
This is a thick amber-red sauce made from plums, apricots, sugar, chilies and vinegar. It is generally used as a table condiment for roast duck, pork and spare ribs. Available in jars and cans.

Rock Sugar, Brown (Rock Candy)
The Chinese use large grains or lumps of crystalized sugar in cooking. Light brown sugar may be substituted.

261

Secondary Broth
Bones are the only ingredients used in the preparation of secondary broth: chicken bones, fresh pork bones and smoked pork bones in the ratio of 2:2:1. Place the bones in a large saucepan and cover with cold water three times the depth of the bones. Bring to a boil, then reduce the heat immediately and skim the surface. Simmer for 4 hours, skimming at hourly intervals.

Sesame Jam (Sesame Paste)
Also called *tehina* (see *Houmous v' tehina*, page 246). A good substitute may be obtained by adding 1 teaspoon of sesame oil to about 6–8 teaspoons of peanut butter.

Sesame Oil
Similar to corn oil with a strong nutty taste and fragrance. Sesame oil is used sparingly as a flavoring agent (usually less than 1 teaspoon at a time). It is made from toasted sesame seeds.

Soy Jam (Soy Paste, Soy-bean Paste)
This thick, viscous, almost black paste is made from fermented soy beans. It is similar in flavor to soy sauce and may be interchanged with it. Soy jam is usually used where a thicker sauce is required – in the quick-frying of diced meat, for example. It may be obtained in cans or jars.

Soy Sauce
This is a fermented sauce made from soy beans, wheat, yeast and salt. The sediment which forms is soy jam.

Light-colored Soy Sauce: this is very delicate and is used where flavor is desired without excessive color.
Dark Soy Sauce: this is rich, full-bodied and has caramel added. Used where richer flavor and color are desired.

Superior Broth
This broth is richer, purer and more concentrated than secondary broth. It calls for a maximum of meat and a minimum of liquid. Use a 2 lb chicken and 2 lb shoulder of pork to 5 pints water. Prepare as for secondary broth. Canned consommé may be substituted.

Water Chestnuts
A root vegetable, round and somewhat flat in shape. They have a sweet, sugary juice and a crunchy texture. Only available in cans.

Wine-sediment Paste
This is a thick paste, often maroon although it may be purple or cream-colored. It is made from wine sediment and fermented rice. Wine-sediment paste is used in cooking meats, poultry and seafood, and especially snails.

Wood-ears
These are a species of lichen. The type most often used in Chinese cooking is black in color and dried. Before using the fungi, soak for about 1 hour and clean in several changes of water. Like bamboo shoots, they are used more for their texture (crunchy and slippery) than for their taste, which again is bland. Button mushrooms may be used as a substitute.

Hot and sour soup

HOT AND SOUR SOUP

3 tablespoons cornstarch
⅓ cup water
3 tablespoons soy sauce
¼ cup vinegar
½ teaspoon black pepper
1 oz bean curd (optional)
1 egg
2 dried Chinese mushrooms,
   soaked and drained

½ small chicken breast
1½ teaspoons lard
3 tablespoons chopped onion
3¾ cups beef bouillon
1 teaspoon monosodium
   glutamate (optional)
1 teaspoon sesame oil
½ teaspoon salt

Blend the cornstarch with the water. Add the soy sauce, vinegar and pepper and mix together. Cut the bean curd into ¼-inch squares. Beat the egg with a fork. Cut the mushrooms and chicken flesh into matchstick-thin strips.

Heat the lard in a saucepan. Add the onion and sauté for 2 minutes. Add the bouillon, then the bean curd, mushrooms and chicken. Bring to a boil and simmer for 15 minutes. Add the cornstarch mixture and monosodium glutamate. Stir the soup until it begins to thicken; then, as the soup is swirling around in the pan, pour in the beaten egg along the tines of a fork steadily and slowly so that it separates into threads. Add the sesame oil and salt.

Give the soup an additional stir so that the 'egg-flower' (as the Chinese call it) will mix evenly with the rich brown soup. Pour into a heated tureen and serve immediately.

CRISPY RAVIOLI SOUP WITH BAMBOO SHOOTS

for the Hun Tun skin :
1½ cups all-purpose flour
dash salt
⅓ cup boiling water
½ teaspoon lard
for the filling :
½ small onion
2 water chestnuts
1 teaspoon sesame oil
2 oz pork, finely ground
for the soup :
½ oz wood-ears, soaked for
   1 hour, or button mushrooms

1½ oz heart cabbage
3 tablespoons chopped leek
2 slices fresh ginger root
1¼ cups water
3¾ cups superior broth
   (see page 262)
2 tablespoons soy sauce
1½ oz bamboo shoots
½ teaspoon sesame oil
1 teaspoon monosodium
   glutamate (optional)
salt and pepper
vegetable oil for deep-frying

Prepare the *Hun Tun* skin as for Chinese swallow-skin ravioli (see Chinese Ravioli with Shrimp-Pork Filling, page 281). After kneading, cut into 24 portions and roll each portion into a very thin dough.

For the filling, peel and chop the onion and chop the water chestnuts. Heat the sesame oil in a small skillet and sauté the onion, water chestnuts and pork for 2 minutes. Remove from the heat and cool. Divide into 24 portions. Wrap a portion of filling in each dough skin.

For the soup, boil the wood-ears with the cabbage in water to cover for 5 minutes. Discard the water. Boil the leek and ginger in the 1¼ cups water for 10 minutes. Add the wood-ears, cabbage, one-third of the superior broth, the soy sauce and bamboo shoots to the leek and ginger. Simmer for 10 minutes.

Pour the soup into a large ovenproof tureen. Add the sesame oil, remaining superior broth, the monosodium glutamate and seasoning to taste.

Steam for 15 minutes. Simultaneously, deep-fry the ravioli in hot oil for 4 minutes, or until golden.

Place the fried ravioli at the bottom of a large, heated tureen and pour over the soup. Bring to the table quickly, while the crackling ravioli is 'singing' in the tureen.

CHICKEN VELVET AND SWEET CORN SOUP

1 chicken breast
2 egg whites
3¾ cups chicken bouillon
1 (7-oz) can whole kernel
   corn
1 tablespoon cornstarch
¼ cup water

3 tablespoons fresh green peas
1 teaspoon salt
½ teaspoon monosodium
   glutamate (optional)
1 thin slice smoked
   cooked ham

Finely chop the chicken flesh and mix thoroughly in a bowl with the egg whites. Bring the chicken bouillon to a boil in a saucepan. Add the corn and then stir in the cornstarch mixed with the water. When the contents reboil, stir in the chicken mixture. Stirring gently, add the peas, salt and monosodium glutamate. Simmer for 5–6 minutes over low heat. Chop the ham finely. Pour the soup into a heated tureen and garnish with the chopped ham before serving.

CUCUMBER SOUP

1 lb pork bone
2½ pints water
2 slim cucumbers
vegetable oil for deep-frying
3 tablespoons dried shrimp

1 teaspoon salt
1 slice fresh ginger root
½ teaspoon monosodium
   glutamate (optional)

Boil the pork bone in the water for 15 minutes. Skim and continue to simmer for another 40 minutes. Cut each cucumber across into 3 sections. Deep-fry in very hot oil for 30 seconds. Drain the cucumber and add to the pork bone broth. Add the dried shrimp, salt and ginger and simmer for 20 minutes. Add the monosodium glutamate.

Remove the pork bone. The soup should now be quite clear and the pieces of cucumber will appear like floating green logs. Pour into a heated soup tureen and serve.

Fish-broth chrysanthemum hot pot

FISH-BROTH CHRYSANTHEMUM HOT POT

1½ oz transparent pea-starch noodles	4 oz chicken livers
vegetable oil for deep-frying	4 oz pork liver
½ cup peanuts	fish bones, head and tail
½ small Chinese celery cabbage heart	3½ pints chicken bouillon
4 oz spinach	3 slices fresh ginger root
3 oz bean sprouts	few sprigs fresh parsley
½ bunch watercress	1½ teaspoons salt
2 scallions	1 large chrysanthemum blossom
8 oz fish fillets (sole, bream, carp, cod or halibut)	pepper
1 large chicken breast	1 tablespoon lard
	½ teaspoon monosodium glutamate (optional)

Deep-fry the noodles in the hot oil just until they puff up. Then drain. Deep-fry the peanuts quickly until brown and crispy. Transfer the noodles and peanuts to 2 plates and place on the dining table. Wash and trim the cabbage, spinach, bean sprouts and watercress and place them neatly on 4 other plates on the dining table. Cut the scallions into ½-inch lengths. Clean the fish and cut into very thin slices 2 by

1½ inches. Slice the chicken breast, chicken livers and pork liver into bite-sized pieces.

Prepare a fish broth by boiling the fish bones, head and tail for 5 minutes in the chicken bouillon, with the scallions, ginger, parsley and salt. Strain and reserve the broth.

Loosen and remove the petals of the chrysanthemum blossom and arrange on a small dish, imitating as nearly as possible the shape of the original bloom.

Heat the reserved broth and pour into the hot pot (see note), which is then placed in the center of the table in front of the diners. Light the spirit stove and when the broth boils, drop in all the chrysanthemum petals. Add the fish, chicken and livers. When the contents boil, add the noodles, peanuts, cabbage and watercress, then the spinach and bean sprouts. Add pepper to taste, the lard and monosodium glutamate. When the contents reboil, wait for 25 seconds. Pick the various ingredients out of the pot with a pair of bamboo chopsticks and place in each diner's rice bowl.

The items from the pot may also be dipped in various mixes and dips such as salt-pepper, soy sauce-vinegar or haisein sauce, which are placed conveniently on the table. Not all the food needs to be cooked in the pot at the same time. Different quantities may be put in at various stages.

Although the chrysanthemum is the most common flower used in this form of hot pot, other flowers such as peach blossom may also be used (Peach Blossom hot pot).

Note: The Chrysanthemum hot pot is always fired with

methylated spirit, unlike the Peking hot pot, which is fired with charcoal in a hot pot-cum-stove, with a funnel running up the center of the pot. The chrysanthemum type is more like a Swiss fondue set in that it is simply a brass or copper pot with a spirit stove burning underneath.

GLISTENING CRYSTAL SHRIMP

1 lb cooked shrimp, shelled and deveined	1 clove garlic
2½ cups salted water (use 1 tablespoon salt)	1 tablespoon chopped scallion
	1½ teaspoons chopped fresh ginger root
2 teaspoons cornstarch	**for the sauce mixture :**
2 egg whites	2 tablespoons cornstarch
3 tablespoons superior broth (see page 262)	1 teaspoon monosodium glutamate (optional)
½ teaspoon salt	¼ cup water
2 tablespoons lard	

Soak the shrimp in the salted water and place in the refrigerator for 2 hours. Drain, rinse quickly and dry thoroughly. Mix the cornstarch with the egg whites, broth and salt and stir in the shrimp. Heat the lard in a skillet until the fat begins to smoke. Add the shrimp and scramble-fry for 30–40 seconds over high heat. Remove the shrimp and set aside. Peel and crush the garlic.

Reheat the skillet and add the garlic, scallions and ginger. Sauté in the remaining lard for 10 seconds. Return the shrimp to the skillet. Stir, mix and scramble-fry for 10 seconds. Blend together the cornstarch, monosodium gluta-

mate and water. Add to the skillet and stir gently until the shrimp take on a glistening, glossy look.

Serve immediately with quantities of rice.

PORK-SHRIMP LION'S HEAD WITH CRAB

1½ lb pork, fresh picnic shoulder or loin roast	3 tablespoons cornstarch
	1 teaspoon salt
4 oz crab meat	2 large heads cabbage
3 tablespoons chopped onion	2 tablespoons lard
1 tablespoon chopped fresh ginger root	2 oz cooked shrimp, shelled and deveined
3 tablespoons dry sherry	3 tablespoons chicken bouillon

Remove the pork skin and coarsely grind the flesh. Chop the crab meat. Add half the onion, half the ginger, the sherry, cornstarch and salt to the pork and crab. Mix well and form into large balls. Discard any coarse outer leaves of the cabbages and chop off the stalks. Shred the leaves. Heat two-thirds of the lard in a large saucepan. Fry the shrimp for 1 minute. Then add the cabbage and fry for 3 minutes.

Heat the remaining lard and the bouillon in a large casserole. When the lard melts, line the bottom and sides of the dish with half the shrimp mixture. Arrange the meat balls on top. Sprinkle with the remaining onion and ginger. Finally, spoon the remaining shrimp mixture over the meat balls. Cover the dish and cook in a preheated moderate oven (350°) for 50 minutes.

Serve from the casserole. The host uses his chopsticks to remove the upper layer of shrimp and cabbage.

Glistening crystal shrimp

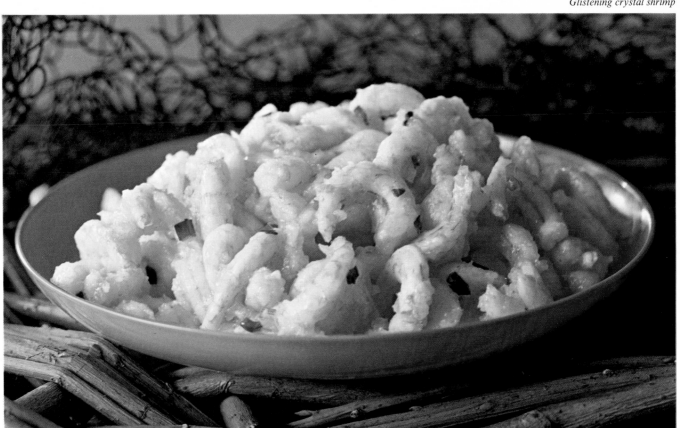

FRIED FISH STRIPS TOSSED IN CELERY

1 lb fish fillets (bass,
    haddock, pike or cod)
1 teaspoon salt
1 egg
2 tablespoons cornstarch
1 small bunch celery

1 tablespoon light-colored soy
    sauce
1 teaspoon sesame oil
½ teaspoon monosodium
    glutamate (optional)
1 oz cooked smoked ham
vegetable oil for deep-frying

Cut the fish first into thin slices, then cut again into matchstick-thin strips about 2 inches long. Add the salt to the egg and beat well. Coat the fish with this mixture and dredge with the cornstarch. Wash the celery and cut into matchstick-thin strips. Plunge into boiling water for 30 seconds, then drain. Add the soy sauce, sesame oil and monosodium glutamate to the celery. Toss and mix well. Cut the ham into matchstick-thin strips.

Place the fish in a wire basket and spread the pieces out evenly with a pair of bamboo chopsticks. Lower into very hot oil and deep-fry for 3–4 minutes, after which time the strips of fish will float to the surface. Remove and drain them. Place the celery mixture in a large heated serving dish. Arrange the fried fish on top. Mix gently. Garnish with the ham. This dish may be accompanied by a chili-soy dip (1 part chili sauce to 6 parts soy sauce).

DEEP-FRIED FISH IN RED WINE-SEDIMENT PASTE

2 lb fish fillets (haddock, cod,
    halibut or bass)
1 teaspoon salt
¼ dry sherry
¼ cup red wine-sediment
    paste
2 scallions
vegetable oil for deep-frying
1 tablespoon lard

1 tablespoon chopped fresh
    ginger root
1 tablespoon chopped onion
1 teaspoon sugar
1 teaspoon soy sauce
3 tablespoons chicken bouillon or
    superior broth (see page 262)
½ teaspoon monosodium
    glutamate (optional)

Cut the fish into thick pieces 2 inches by 1 inch by 1½ inches. Rub with the salt and marinate in a mixture of half the sherry and half the red wine-sediment paste for 1 hour. Cut the scallions into 1½-inch segments.

Heat the oil until very hot and deep-fry the fish for 3–4 minutes. Drain on absorbent paper then arrange the fish pieces on a large flat plate.

Heat the lard in a small skillet. Add the ginger and onion and sauté over high heat for 1 minute. Add the remaining sherry, remaining wine-sediment paste, the sugar, soy sauce, bouillon or superior broth and monosodium glutamate. Continue to stir-fry for 30 seconds. Pour the sauce over the fish and garnish with the scallions.

QUICK-FRIED SLICED FISH

8 oz fish fillets (sea bass,
    cod, haddock or sole)
6 tablespoons cornstarch
2½ cups vegetable oil for semi-
    deep-frying
for the sauce :
1 tablespoon soy sauce
1 tablespoon sugar
1 tablespoon dry sherry

2 teaspoons vinegar
½ teaspoon monosodium
    glutamate (optional)
2 teaspoons cornstarch
1 tablespoon water
2 tablespoons lard
1 tablespoon chopped shallot
1 teaspoon chopped fresh
    ginger root

Slice the fillets into strips 1½ inches by ¾ inch by ¼ inch. Dredge in the cornstarch. Fry the pieces of fish in vegetable oil to cover in a large skillet, adding each piece of fish separately (so they can be handled gently and do not stick to each other). The frying should be gentle, over low to medium heat, and the fish should be removed after 2 minutes. Drain and set aside while preparing the sauce.

Mix together in a bowl the soy sauce, sugar, sherry, vinegar, monosodium glutamate and cornstarch blended with the water. Stir and mix well. Discard the oil in the skillet and add the lard. When hot, add the shallot and ginger and fry for 30 seconds. Pour in the mixture from the bowl and stir until the sauce thickens. Return the slices of fish to the skillet. Turn them over in the sauce a few times and then transfer to a heated dish. Serve immediately.

SOFT-FRIED CRAB MEAT

1 lb crab meat
3 tablespoons chopped onion
¼ cup dry sherry
1 tablespoon cornstarch
3 tablespoons water
2 tablespoons fat back

3 tablespoons lard
¼ teaspoon salt
1 tablespoon soy sauce
1½ teaspoons sugar
⅓ cup chicken bouillon
2 tablespoons ginger water

Mix the crab meat with half the onion and half the sherry. Blend the cornstarch with the water. Cut the fat back into small cubes. Heat two-thirds of the lard in a skillet. Add the remaining onion and fat back and sauté until golden. Add the crab mixture and stir-fry very gently without breaking it into pieces. After 30 seconds add the remaining sherry, salt, soy sauce, sugar, chicken bouillon and ginger water. Mix gently and simmer for 3 minutes. Add the cornstarch mixture and remaining lard. When it boils, the dish is ready. The usual dips for this dish are mixtures of chopped ginger root with vinegar, or chopped garlic with vinegar.

Quick-fried sliced fish

FRY-BRAISED FISH BALLS

2 lb fish fillets (carp, cod, haddock, bass or halibut)
1 egg
1½ teaspoons salt
½ teaspoon monosodium glutamate (optional)
2 teaspoons sesame oil
pepper
3 tablespoons water
½ small green sweet pepper
3 water chestnuts
8 dried Chinese mushrooms, soaked and drained
2 cloves garlic
vegetable oil for deep-frying
¼ cup vegetable oil
1 oz bean sprouts
3 slices fresh ginger root
1 tablespoon chutney
¼ cup superior broth (see page 262)
2 tablespoons cornstarch

Clean the fish and grind the flesh. Beat the egg and add to the fish with 1 teaspoon of the salt, the monosodium glutamate, half the sesame oil, pepper to taste and the water. Mix together thoroughly. Form into balls about ½ inch in diameter. Trim and thinly slice the green pepper and slice the water chestnuts. Discard the mushroom stems. Peel and slice the garlic. Heat the oil and deep-fry the fish balls for 2 minutes. Drain and simmer in boiling water for 2 minutes. Drain and set aside.

Heat the ¼ cup oil in a large skillet over high heat for 30 seconds. Add the remaining salt, the green pepper, water chestnuts, mushrooms, garlic, bean sprouts, ginger and chutney. Stir-fry quickly for 2 minutes. Add the fish balls and continue to stir-fry more slowly over lower heat for 1 minute. Add the broth and cornstarch blended with a little water. Stir for 10 seconds and sprinkle with the remaining sesame oil. Transfer to a heated serving dish and serve immediately.

SOY-BRAISED FISH

1½ lb fish fillets (bream, bass, carp, halibut or cod)
1 teaspoon salt
4 scallions
vegetable oil for deep-frying
2 tablespoons lard
4 slices fresh ginger root
1 teaspoon coarsely chopped dried chili
1 tablespoon soy sauce
3 tablespoons dry sherry
½ teaspoon monosodium glutamate (optional)
1 teaspoon sesame oil

Chop the fish into approximately 1-inch cubes. Rub evenly with the salt, using your fingers. Cut the scallions into 1-inch long pieces. Heat the vegetable oil and deep-fry the fish for 2 minutes. Drain. Heat the lard in a skillet and sauté the ginger and chili for 30 seconds. Add the fish and turn it over in the lard a couple of times. Pour in the soy sauce and sherry. Turn the fish over several times and cover the skillet. Simmer the contents over low heat for 3 minutes. Remove the lid and sprinkle the fish with the monosodium glutamate and sesame oil. Add the scallions. Simmer for 1 minute and transfer to a heated serving dish. Because the gravy is sufficiently strong, no sauces or dips are required.

GARNISHED STEAMED SOLE

2 soles, about 1 lb each
2 teaspoons salt
¼ cup dry sherry
3 tablespoons chicken bouillon
1½ teaspoons sugar
½ teaspoon monosodium glutamate (optional)
1 tablespoon lard
for the garnish :
1 tablespoon diced fat back
1½ teaspoons sugar
2 slices cooked smoked ham
1 oz bamboo shoots
2 scallions
12 small dried Chinese mushrooms, soaked and drained
8 slices fresh ginger root

Clean the fish, wash thoroughly and dry well. Rub both sides with the salt and half the sherry. Cut 3 slashes on each side of the soles, halfway through the flesh. Place them on an oval ovenproof dish. Heat the bouillon. Add the remaining sherry, the sugar, monosodium glutamate and lard and mix well. Sprinkle this mixture evenly over the fish. To make the garnish, pile the diced fat back and sugar in the middle of each fish as a 'hub'. Cut the ham and bamboo shoots into thin 2-inch strips and cut the scallions into 1-inch segments. Use the ham and bamboo shoots to form 2 lines at right angles to each other, meeting at the 'hub'. Put the scallions, mushrooms and ginger in the spaces. Cover and steam over high heat for 20 minutes. Wipe the edge of the dish with a cloth and serve immediately.

DOUBLE-FRIED EEL

3–4 lb skinned eel
3 tablespoons sherry
vegetable oil for deep-frying
4 scallions
3 tablespoons vegetable oil
1 tablespoon chopped fresh ginger root
3 tablespoons soy sauce
1 tablespoon sugar
¼ teaspoon five-spice powder or allspice
pepper

Blanch the eel in boiling water for 1 minute. Drain, dry and rub with half the sherry. Place in a wire basket and deep-fry in hot oil for 4 minutes. Drain, and cut the flesh of the eel neatly into 2- by 1-inch strips, discarding the head and tail. Cut the scallions into 1-inch pieces.

Place the strips of eel in a wire basket and deep-fry again for 3 minutes, or until golden. (By this time there will probably be no more than 1 lb eel flesh left). Drain. Heat the 3 tablespoons oil in a skillet. Add the remaining sherry, the scallions, ginger, soy sauce, sugar and five-spice powder. Cook over high heat for 1 minute, stirring constantly. Add the eel strips. Baste and mix them with the sauce in the skillet. Season with pepper to taste. Place on a heated dish and serve immediately.

Hot-braised sliced beef

HOT-BRAISED SLICED BEEF

1 lb beef tenderloin
1 egg
$\frac{1}{4}$ cup cornstarch
1 teaspoon salt
1 small green or red sweet pepper
4 teaspoons coarsely chopped
   dried chilies
$\frac{1}{3}$ cup vegetable oil
1 tablespoon fermented black
   beans, soaked for 1 hour
2 oz bamboo shoots

3 scallions
1 tablespoon chopped onion
1 tablespoon chopped fresh
   ginger root
1 tablespoon sliced leek
$\frac{1}{4}$ teaspoon black pepper
1 tablespoon dry sherry
3 tablespoons white wine
$\frac{2}{3}$ cup superior broth
   (see page 262)
1 teaspoon monosodium
   glutamate (optional)

Cut the beef into thin slices, $1\frac{1}{2}$ inches long by 1 inch wide. Break the egg into a bowl. Add the cornstarch and salt and blend to a smooth batter. Mix in the beef, using your fingers to coat the meat evenly with the batter.

Remove the seeds from the sweet pepper and chilies. Slice the sweet pepper into strips. Stir-fry in half the oil for $1\frac{1}{2}$ minutes and set aside. Mash the fermented beans. Cut the bamboo shoots and scallions into $1\frac{1}{2}$-inch segments.

Heat the remaining oil in a large skillet. Add the black beans, bamboo shoots, scallions, onion, ginger, leek and pepper. Stir-fry slowly over medium heat for 2 minutes. Add the sherry and wine, and after 10 seconds add the broth and monosodium glutamate. Turn the heat to high. When the contents reboil, add the coated beef. After 30 seconds of stir-braising, transfer to a deep serving dish. Meanwhile, reheat the sweet pepper and chilies and pour them, with the oil, over the beef.

269

SALTED BEEF WITH CABBAGE HEART

4 oz salted beef or pork	1 teaspoon salt
1 large head cabbage	$\frac{1}{2}$ teaspoon monosodium
3 tablespoons vegetable oil	glutamate (optional)
$\frac{1}{3}$ cup chicken bouillon	1 tablespoon lard

Cut the meat into paper-thin slices, $1\frac{1}{2}$ inches long and $\frac{1}{2}$ inch wide. Discard the outer leaves of the cabbage and trim the stem, leaving only the tender inside leaves. Cut these crisscross into 2-inch pieces.

Heat the oil in a skillet over high heat. When very hot, add the cabbage and scramble-fry for $1\frac{1}{2}$ minutes. Add the pork and bouillon. Sprinkle with the salt and monosodium glutamate. Stir-fry gently for 3 minutes. Add the lard and after a couple of stirs and tosses, transfer to a heated dish and serve.

PINE-FLOWER MEAT SOUFFLÉ OMELET

6 eggs	1 oz bamboo shoots
$\frac{1}{4}$ cup all-purpose flour	1 teaspoon sugar
1 teaspoon salt	1 tablespoon soy sauce
1 teaspoon monosodium	$\frac{1}{4}$ teaspoon five-spice powder or
glutamate (optional)	allspice (optional)
4 oz lean pork	6 tablespoons lard
2 scallions	3 tablespoons chopped fresh
1 oz dried Chinese	parsley
mushrooms, soaked and	1 tablespoon dry sherry
drained	

Separate the egg whites from the yolks. Beat the whites for 2 minutes or until nearly stiff. Fold in the yolks, salt and monosodium glutamate. Finely chop the pork and scallions. Slice the mushrooms and bamboo shoots into matchstick-thin strips. Place the pork, scallions, mushrooms, bamboo shoots, sugar, soy sauce and five-spice powder in a bowl. Mix well.

Heat 1 tablespoon of the lard in a small saucepan. Add the pork mixture and stir-fry for 3 minutes. Remove from the heat and set aside. Place half the remaining lard in a large skillet over very low heat. When the lard has melted, add half the egg mixture, which will spread into a circle about 6 inches in diameter. When the egg has just started to set, gently put the cooked pork mixture into the center.

After 1 minute of cooking over low heat, pour the remaining egg mixture over the filling. Heat the remaining lard in a small saucepan until very hot and pour it over the soft egg mixture. Sprinkle the parsley over the omelet, then, pour over the sherry. Cook for 30 seconds without stirring. Gently lift one side of the omelet to drain away the lard. Use a large spatula to lift the omelet on to a heated serving plate.

STEAMED BEEF IN RICE FLOUR

$1\frac{3}{4}$ lb beef tenderloin	$1\frac{1}{2}$ teaspoons sugar
1 tablespoon chopped fresh	1 teaspoon chili sauce
ginger root	$\frac{1}{2}$ cup rice flour
$\frac{1}{3}$ cup water	crushed coriander seeds
2 tablespoons vegetable oil	bay leaves
1 tablespoon dry sherry	chopped chives
2 tablespoons soy sauce	fresh thyme
1 tablespoon fermented black	
beans, soaked for 1 hour	

Cut the meat into pieces, $1\frac{1}{2}$ inches by $\frac{3}{4}$ inch by $\frac{1}{2}$ inch. Prepare the ginger water by boiling the ginger in the water over low heat for 3 minutes; then strain. Place the meat in a bowl and add the ginger water, oil, sherry, soy sauce, black beans, sugar and chili sauce. Work the mixture into the meat with your fingers. Finally, dry-fry the rice flour until it begins to turn brown. Coat the pieces of meat with the rice flour.

Divide the meat among 4 ovenproof bowls. To the first bowl, add a few coriander seeds, to the second, add a few bay leaves, to the third, a few chives, to the fourth, a little thyme. Place the bowls in a steamer, cover and steam for 30 minutes.

The beef in four flavors makes an excellent meal if served with rice and accompanied by a soup, a fish or egg dish and a vegetable dish.

SLICED STEAK IN OYSTER SAUCE

8 oz beef tenderloin	2 tablespoons oyster sauce
3 tablespoons dry sherry	$\frac{1}{4}$ cup superior broth
1 tablespoon soy sauce	(see page 262)
1 tablespoon cornstarch	4–6 scallions
1 tablespoon water	3 slices fresh ginger root
$\frac{1}{3}$ cup vegetable oil	

Cut the meat across the grain into thin slices $1\frac{1}{2}$ inches by 1 inch. Place in a bowl with half the sherry, the soy sauce and half the cornstarch blended with the water. Mix thoroughly. Add 1 tablespoon vegetable oil and work it into the meat with your fingers.

In another bowl, mix the remaining cornstarch, the oyster sauce and broth. Cut the scallions into 1-inch segments, using the white part only. Heat the remaining vegetable oil in a skillet over high heat. When very hot, add the beef. Stir-fry for 30 seconds. Remove the beef and drain off the excess oil. Replace the skillet over the heat and sauté the scallions and ginger for 20 seconds.

Replace the beef in the skillet and pour in the remaining sherry. Spread the beef evenly in the skillet. Quickly pour in the oyster sauce mixture. Stir-scramble for about 8–10 seconds over high heat and transfer to a heated plate before serving.

Steamed beef in rice flour

RED-SIMMERED PORK HOCKS

3–4 lb pork hocks	¼ cup sugar
4 pints water	½ cup dry sherry
3 scallions	4 slices fresh ginger root
½ cup soy sauce	2 tablespoons lard

Clean the pork hocks and slash the meat with a knife on either side to facilitate cooking. Place in a heavy saucepan and add the water. Bring to a boil and simmer for 10 minutes. Skim and simmer for another 15 minutes. Skim again; ladle out and discard one-third of the broth. Cut the scallions into 1-inch segments. Add the scallions, soy sauce, sugar, sherry, ginger and lard to the remaining broth. Cover and continue to simmer over low heat for 2 hours, uncovering once every 30 minutes to turn the hocks over during cooking.

By the end of 2 hours, the liquid in the pan should have reduced to 2 cups. Reduce it again by half by increasing the heat for a few minutes. The gravy will have become rich brown and glossy. Remove the hocks and place in a deep bowl. Pour the gravy over without any further thickening. Serve with plain cooked vegetables and rice.

STEAMED RICE-PORK 'PEARLS'

1 cup short-grain rice	3 eggs
1¼ lb lean pork, arm steak or fresh ham center slice	1 tablespoon dry sherry
	2 tablespoons cornstarch
12 oz fat back	6 tablespoons water
8 water chestnuts	4 scallions, chopped
2 teaspoons salt	2 teaspoons chopped fresh ginger root
¼ teaspoon pepper	
1 teaspoon monosodium glutamate (optional)	

Wash the rice 3 times and soak in cold water for 1 hour. Drain well and spread on a baking sheet or sheet of waxed paper. Trim off any fat and grind the lean pork. Boil the fat back in water for 5 minutes, drain and cut into pea-sized pieces. Cut the water chestnuts into pieces of the same size.

Place the pork in a bowl and add the salt, pepper, monosodium glutamate, eggs, sherry and cornstarch blended with the water. Mix well. Then add the fat back, scallions, water chestnuts and ginger. Form the mixture into meat balls, ½ inch in diameter. Roll them in the rice to pick up a covering of grains. When well-covered, use your hands to press the rice more firmly into the meat balls.

Arrange the rice-covered meat balls in not more than 2 layers in a large ovenproof dish. Cover with foil and steam vigorously for 20 minutes.

Steamed rice-pork 'pearls'

STEWED PORK WITH SHERRY AND GINGER

2 lb pork, loin roast	1 tablespoon sugar
or fresh ham	1 teaspoon chopped fresh
2 tablespoons vegetable oil	ginger root
3¾ cups water	1 tablespoon chopped shallot
3 tablespoons dry sherry	1 tablespoon soy jam (optional)
3 tablespoons soy sauce	

Cut the meat into 1- to 1½-inch cubes, preferably across the meat, fat and skin so that each piece will have all three. Heat the oil in a saucepan and sauté the meat for 4–5 minutes, or until it has turned white. Meanwhile, boil the water. Add the sherry, soy sauce, sugar, ginger, shallot and soy jam to the pan, and then pour in the boiling water. Boil for 2 minutes and skim the surface. Then lower the heat to a minimum, cover and simmer for 1½–1¾ hours. During the cooking, turn the meat over several times with a wooden spoon.

Transfer to a heated serving dish and serve with rice and plain cooked vegetables.

SWEET AND SOUR PORK

1 lb pork, fresh shoulder	¾ cup vegetable oil
or loin	**for the sweet and sour sauce :**
1 teaspoon salt	½ cup brown sugar
3 tablespoons dry sherry	3 tablespoons white vinegar
3 tablespoons cornstarch	1 tablespoon tangerine (or
1 egg	orange) juice
1 green or red sweet pepper	1 tablespoon tomato paste
1 leek	1 tablespoon soy sauce
½ small onion	1 tablespoon cornstarch
2 oz bamboo shoots	

Cut away the skin from the pork. Dice the flesh into ½-inch cubes. Add the salt and sherry and marinate for 30 minutes. Place the cornstarch in a mixing bowl, make a well in the center and break in the egg. Stir thoroughly to make a batter. Trim the pepper, remove the seeds and cut into thin strips. Cut the leek into ½-inch sections. Chop the onion and the bamboo shoots into slices ½ by ½ by ¼ inch. For the sauce, mix together the brown sugar, vinegar, tangerine juice, tomato paste and soy sauce. Heat the mixture in a small saucepan until the sugar completely dissolves. Remove the pan from the heat.

Coat the pork in the batter. Heat the oil in a skillet. Add the pork and stir-fry gently over high heat for 2½ minutes. Add the bamboo shoots and continue to stir-fry for 30 seconds. Remove the pork and bamboo shoots and set aside. Pour off the excess oil.

Replace the skillet over the heat and add the pepper, leek and onion. Stir-fry for 1 minute. Add the cornstarch to the sweet and sour sauce, blend well and pour it into the skillet. Stir gently until the contents reboil. Then add the partially cooked pork and bamboo shoots. After a few quick stirs and scrambles, transfer to a heated serving plate and serve.

RED-COOKED PORK WITH CHESTNUTS

2 lb pork, fresh shoulder	½ teaspoon salt
or loin roast	3 tablespoons soy sauce
1 small onion	2 cups secondary broth
1 lb chestnuts	(see page 262)
3 tablespoons vegetable oil	1 tablespoon sugar
3 slices ginger root	3 tablespoons dry sherry

Wash the pork in hot water and cut into 1-inch cubes so that each piece has lean and fat. Peel and quarter the onion. Slash the chestnuts and cook in boiling water for 20–25 minutes. Drain and remove the skins. Heat the oil in a heavy saucepan. Sauté the onion and ginger for 1 minute over medium heat. Add the pork and, raising the heat to high, stir-fry for 3 minutes. Add the salt and half the soy sauce. Stir-fry for 3 more minutes then pour in the broth. Bring to a boil, lower the heat to a minimum and simmer, covered, for 45 minutes, turning the meat over 3 or 4 times in the process.

Add the chestnuts, the remaining soy sauce, the sugar and sherry. Continue to slow-simmer for 30 minutes, mixing the chestnuts with the meat and turning the mixture over gently 3 or 4 times in the process. Serve with rice.

AMOY PORK ESCALOPE

2 lb pork, fresh shoulder or	6 radishes
loin roast (with good proportion	2 teaspoons salt
of lean to fat)	1 tablespoon sugar
3 tablespoons soy sauce	1 tablespoon vinegar
3 tablespoons dry sherry	1 teaspoon sesame oil
2 bay leaves	2 duck or hen eggs
1 tablespoon brown rock sugar or	1 cup breadcrumbs
light brown sugar	vegetable oil for deep-frying
2 medium-sized carrots	

Boil the pork in water to cover for 5 minutes. Drain and cut into thin slices containing both lean and fat. Place the pork in an ovenproof bowl and add the soy sauce, sherry, bay leaves and rock sugar. Marinate for 30 minutes. Place the bowl of marinated pork in a steamer. Cover and steam for 1 hour. Remove and cool in the refrigerator.

Coarsely grate the carrots and radishes into a colander, rub in the salt and let stand for 10 minutes. Rinse under cold water, drain and dry. Put the grated carrots and radishes in a bowl and mix in the sugar, vinegar and sesame oil.

When the pork is quite cold and solid, break the eggs into a bowl, beat lightly and dip each piece of pork in the egg. Roll the pieces of pork in the breadcrumbs until completely covered. Heat the vegetable oil and deep-fry the pork in a wire basket (6 pieces at a time) for 3 minutes, or until golden. Cut each slice of pork into 3 pieces.

Arrange the grated radishes and carrots in a mound in the middle of a serving plate. Place the pieces of pork around and serve.

PORK KIDNEYS IN SESAME JAM

4 pork kidneys
1½ teaspoons salt
3 tablespoons dry sherry
2 tablespoons sesame jam
1 teaspoon sugar

½ teaspoon monosodium
  glutamate (optional)
3 tablespoons water
1 head lettuce

Remove the skins and discard the cores from the kidneys. Cut each one in half and cut again into paper-thin slices. Place in a bowl and marinate for 30 minutes in half the salt and the sherry.

Mix together the remaining salt, sesame jam, sugar, monosodium glutamate and water. Place the sliced kidneys with the marinade in a large skillet and cover with boiling water. Separate the slices carefully. Simmer for 2–3 minutes. By this time the slices of kidney will curl up and should be just cooked.

Arrange the lettuce leaves on a large round serving plate. Place the sliced kidney on top of the lettuce and then pour the sesame jam mixture evenly over the kidney slices. Use prepared mustard as a dip.

KUNG-PO HOT-FRIED KIDNEYS

12 oz pork kidneys
2 tablespoons cornstarch
1 tablespoon water
2 tablespoons dry sherry
½ teaspoon salt
1 tablespoon sugar
1 tablespoon vinegar
1 tablespoon soy sauce
½ teaspoon monosodium
  glutamate (optional)

3 tablespoons superior broth
  (see page 262)
3 scallions
1 dried chili
1 small leek
⅓ cup vegetable oil
2 cloves garlic
3 slices fresh ginger root
¼ teaspoon chili powder
pepper

Remove the skins and discard the cores from the kidneys. Cut each one in half. Slash with crisscross cuts ¼ inch apart and two-thirds through the kidney. Cut into 1- by ¾-inch pieces. Blend half the cornstarch with the water, sherry and salt. Thoroughly coat the kidney pieces in this mixture. In a separate bowl, mix the sugar, vinegar, soy sauce, monosodium glutamate and broth. Set aside. Cut the scallions into ½-inch pieces. Remove the seeds from the dried chili. Cut the leek into ½-inch pieces.

Heat the oil in a skillet until very hot. Add the kidney, spreading the pieces evenly, sauté for 4–5 minutes and then drain. Drain off the excess oil. In the same skillet, sauté the dried chili for 1 minute and discard. Crush the garlic, then stir-fry the scallions, leek, garlic, ginger and chili powder for 20 seconds. Add the kidney pieces and stir-fry for 10 seconds. Then gradually add the vinegar mixture to the skillet. Stir-fry the kidneys gently for 15 seconds. Add pepper to taste and serve immediately.

SPARE RIBS BRAISED IN FRUIT JUICE

2 lb meaty pork spare ribs
3 tablespoons finely chopped leeks
1 teaspoon salt
2 teaspoons sugar
2 tablespoons light-colored soy
  sauce
½ teaspoon monosodium
  glutamate (optional)
1 tablespoon cornstarch

¼ cup vegetable oil
3 tablespoons chopped onion
1 tablespoon apple juice
1 tablespoon orange juice
1 tablespoon tomato paste
⅓ cup secondary broth
  (see page 262)
3 tablespoons dry sherry

Separate each rib and chop across the bone into 1-inch lengths or leave whole. Combine the leeks with the salt, sugar, soy sauce and monosodium glutamate in a bowl. Add the spare ribs and marinate for 30 minutes. Dust with cornstarch and mix well.

Heat the oil in a skillet, add the ribs and stir-fry gently for 25 minutes, or until golden. Drain off the excess oil and set the ribs aside.

Sauté the onion for 1 minute in the oil remaining in the skillet. Add the spare ribs. Pour in the apple juice, orange juice, tomato paste, broth and sherry. Stir-fry for 1 minute. Cover the skillet and cook for 5–6 minutes, or until the liquid has largely evaporated. Serve on a heated dish.

SCRAMBLE-FRIED SLICED LAMB

8 oz leg of lamb
1 tablespoon cornstarch
1 tablespoon water
10 scallions
3 cloves garlic
⅓ cup vegetable oil

1 tablespoon soy sauce
½ teaspoon salt
1 tablespoon dry sherry
½ teaspoon monosodium
  glutamate (optional)
1 teaspoon sesame oil

Cut the lamb across the grain into thin slices 2 inches by 1 inch. Blend the cornstarch with the water and mix evenly with the meat. Cut the scallions diagonally into 2-inch segments (using the green parts as well as the white). Peel and crush the garlic.

Heat half the oil in a large skillet over medium heat. When very hot, pour in the meat mixture and spread it evenly over the bottom of the skillet. Stir-fry gently for 2 minutes. Remove the meat and set aside. Add the remaining oil to the skillet and sauté the scallions and garlic for 2 minutes. Return the lamb to the skillet and add the soy sauce, salt, sherry and monosodium glutamate. Turn the heat to high and scramble-fry for 1 minute. Just before serving, add the sesame oil.

Since this is a mixed, scrambled dish, no garnishing is required. It should be carefully poured out on to a heated dish and served immediately.

BEAN SPROUTS WITH SHREDDED PORK

4 oz lean pork

1 clove garlic

6 scallions

3 tablespoons vegetable oil

1 tablespoon soy sauce

2 teaspoons sugar

1 tablespoon dry sherry

1½ lb bean sprouts

1 teaspoon salt

Cut the pork across the grain into matchstick-thin strips. Peel and crush the garlic and cut the scallions into 1½-inch segments. Heat the oil in a large skillet. Add the pork and sauté over high heat for 30 seconds. Add the soy sauce, sugar and sherry. Stir-fry for 1 minute. Remove the meat and set aside to drain.

Add the garlic and scallions to the skillet and stir-fry for 15 seconds. Add the bean sprouts and sprinkle with the salt. Stir-fry and scramble for 1 minute, keeping the skillet over high heat. Replace the pork in the skillet. After 1 minute of stir-frying, transfer to a heated dish and serve.

Note: Shredded meat dishes, when freshly and carefully served, rarely need any further garnish. The meat, sugar and soy sauce provide the necessary savoriness.

YELLOW 'FLOWER' MEAT

4 eggs

½ teaspoon salt

4 oz lean pork

8 dried Chinese mushrooms, soaked and drained

3 scallions

⅓ cup vegetable oil

1 tablespoon soy sauce

3 tablespoons broth (superior or secondary, see page 262)

½ teaspoon monosodium glutamate (optional)

1 teaspoon sugar

1 tablespoon dry sherry

1 tablespoon sesame oil

Beat the eggs in a bowl for a few seconds and add the salt. Shred the pork into matchstick-thin strips. Cut the mushrooms into thin strips or small pieces. Cut the scallions into very thin slices. Heat half the oil in a skillet and add the beaten egg. Lower the heat (so that none of the egg will burn) and just before the egg sets completely, scramble slightly, remove the egg from the skillet and set aside.

Add the remaining oil to the skillet and place over high heat. Add the pork, mushrooms and scallions. Sauté for 2 minutes, then add the soy sauce, broth, monosodium glutamate and sugar. Cook for a further 30–40 seconds. Add the scrambled egg, sherry and sesame oil. Stir gently to mix all the ingredients. Serve on a heated dish.

Bean sprouts with shredded pork

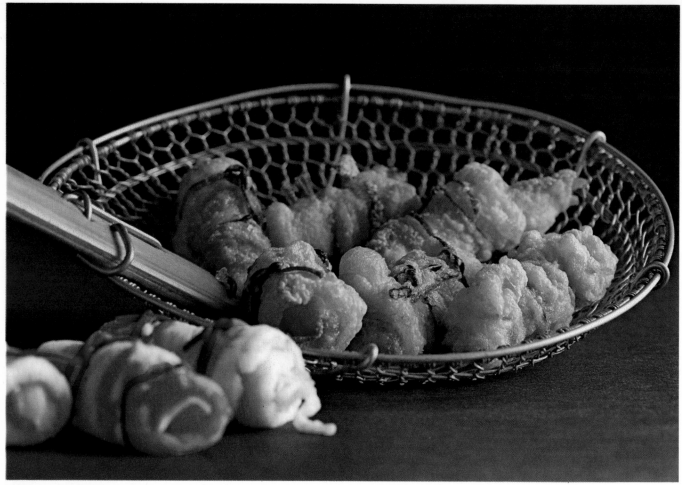

Cannon-cracker chicken

CANNON-CRACKER CHICKEN

1 chicken breast	1½ teaspoons chopped fresh
8 oz pork shoulder (fat part	ginger root
without skin)	2 slices cooked smoked ham
1 tablespoon soy sauce	1 bunch chives (see recipe)
½ teaspoon salt	2 eggs
1½ teaspoons sugar	1 tablespoon cornstarch
1 tablespoon chopped onion	vegetable oil for deep-frying
	1 teaspoon sesame oil

Cut the chicken into small thin slices. Cut the pork into thin slices about 3 by 2 inches. Lay the slices of pork on a large plate or tray. Brush with the soy sauce and sprinkle with the salt, sugar, onion and ginger. Lay a piece of chicken on top of each piece of pork. Cut the ham into strips and place a strip in the center of each piece of chicken. Roll up, wrapping the ham and chicken inside. Tie each roll securely with 2 of the chives (if unavailable, secure with a toothpick).

Beat the eggs and mix with the cornstarch to make a thin batter. Dip each pork-chicken roll lightly into the batter. Deep-fry the rolls in hot oil for 5–6 minutes. Drain, remove the toothpicks if used, and arrange on a heated dish in an attractive pattern. Sprinkle with the sesame oil and serve. A suitable dip for this dish is a salt-pepper mix.

SOOCHOW MELON CHICKEN

1 young chicken, about 1½ lb	4 slices fresh ginger root
2½ pints water	1½ teaspoons salt
1 oz cooked smoked ham	3 tablespoons dry sherry
1½ oz bamboo shoots	1 large honeydew melon
8 dried Chinese mushrooms.	1 teaspoon monosodium
soaked and drained	glutamate (optional)

Boil the chicken in the water for 2 minutes. Remove the chicken and rinse in fresh water. Skim the broth. Thinly slice the ham and bamboo shoots, cut the mushrooms into strips and marinate in one-third of the broth with the ginger, salt and sherry. Return the chicken to the remaining broth. Place in a steamer, cover and steam for 1 hour.

Cut a lid off the melon and set aside. Carefully scoop out the melon, leaving the wall at least ½ inch thick. Reserve half the scooped-out melon.

Place the melon shell in a large bowl and fit the steamed chicken inside it, breast upward. Arrange the ham, bamboo shoots and mushrooms on the chicken. Slip pieces of the melon flesh down the sides around the chicken. Add the monosodium glutamate to the marinade and carefully pour this into the melon. Replace the lid of the melon and secure it with 3 toothpicks. Place the bowl in a steamer, cover and steam for 20 minutes. Remove the bowl from the steamer and bring it to the table. Lift off the melon lid and serve the chicken from the melon shell.

PEPPERED CHICKEN

1 chicken, about 2–2¼ lb	1 teaspoon salt
6 scallions	2 tablespoons sesame oil
2 slices fresh ginger root	2 teaspoons coarsely chopped
1 tablespoon soy sauce	dried red chilies
1 tablespoon vinegar	

Plunge the chicken into boiling water to cover and simmer for 10 minutes. Chop into pieces about 1 by ½ inch, including the bones. Arrange the pieces in a large ovenproof bowl, skin-side down. Cut the scallions into ½-inch pieces. Add the scallions and ginger to the chicken. Mix the soy sauce, vinegar and salt in a bowl.

Heat the sesame oil in a small skillet and sauté the chilies in it for 2–3 minutes. Discard the chilies and pour the oil evenly over the chicken in the ovenproof bowl. Then pour the soy sauce mixture over the chicken. Place in a steamer, cover and steam for 30–35 minutes. Serve the chicken on a large heated serving dish.

RED-BRAISED CHICKEN

1 chicken, about 3 lb	1 tablespoon sugar
2½ oz winter bamboo shoots	3 tablespoons light-colored soy
2 scallions	sauce
3 tablespoons lard	3 tablespoons dry sherry
2 teaspoons chopped fresh	1 cup chicken bouillon
ginger root	1 teaspoon monosodium
3 tablespoons red wine-sediment	glutamate (optional)
paste	2 teaspoons sesame oil

Chop the chicken into pieces 1 inch by 1½ inches. Cut the bamboo shoots into similar-sized pieces and the white parts of the scallions into 1-inch segments. Heat the lard in a large skillet over high heat. Add the scallions, ginger and red wine-sediment paste and stir-fry for 1 minute. Add the chicken pieces and bamboo shoots and continue to stir-fry for 1 minute. Add the sugar, soy sauce and sherry and continue stir-frying for 1 minute. Finally, pour in the bouillon. Bring to a boil and reduce the heat to low. Simmer for 35 minutes.

Lift the bamboo shoots out first and place in the bottom of a heated deep serving dish. Arrange the pieces of chicken on top. Strain the liquid from the skillet and add the mono-sodium glutamate and sesame oil. Bring to a boil and pour over the chicken before serving.

QUICK-FRIED CHICKEN

2 large chicken breasts	¼ cup vegetable oil
1 small red sweet pepper	2 tablespoons lard
2 oz bamboo shoots	⅓ cup chicken bouillon
1 scallion	1 tablespoon dry sherry
1½ teaspoons coarsley chopped	½ teaspoon monosodium
dried chilies	glutamate (optional)
1 teaspoon salt	1 tablespoon light-colored soy
1 egg	sauce
1 tablespoon cornstarch	1 teaspoon sesame oil

Cut the chicken breasts into ¼-inch cubes. Trim the sweet pepper and remove the seeds. Cut the bamboo shoots and the sweet pepper into similar-sized pieces. Slice the scallion into ¼-inch pieces.

Place the diced chicken in a bowl. Add the salt and rub it into the chicken. Break the egg into the bowl and mix well. Then blend in the cornstarch. Heat the vegetable oil in a large skillet. When quite hot, add the chicken and stir-fry for 1½ minutes. Remove the chicken and drain off any remaining oil. Add the lard to the skillet. Stir-fry the bamboo shoots, sweet pepper, scallion and chilies over high heat for 2 minutes. Mix the chicken bouillon with the sherry and add with the monosodium glutamate, soy sauce and sesame oil. Stir-fry gently for 30 seconds. Add the pieces of chicken and continue to stir-fry for another 30 seconds. Transfer to a heated dish and serve.

STRANGE-FLAVOR CHICKEN

6–8 chicken drumsticks (about	2 teaspoons sugar
1½ lb)	1 tablespoon vinegar
3 tablespoons sesame seeds	1 teaspoon chili sauce
1½ teaspoons sesame oil	¼ teaspoon black pepper
2 tablespoons soy sauce	6–8 scallions

Cook the drumsticks in boiling water to cover for 20 minutes, allowing 5 minutes boiling and 15 minutes simmering time. Drain and cool for 10 minutes. Remove the bones from the drumsticks and slice each drumstick diagonally into 4 pieces.

Stir-fry the sesame seeds gently in a dry skillet over very low heat until they are just turning golden and beginning to crackle. Place a third of these seeds in a dry bowl and pound the remaining two-thirds to a powder in a mortar, adding the sesame oil to make a sesame paste. Mix this paste with the soy sauce, sugar, vinegar, chili sauce and pepper. Chop the white parts of the scallions (reserving the green parts for another dish) and pile them in the center of a heated serving dish. Arrange the pieces of chicken around the edge by overlapping them, skin-side out. Pour the sesame paste mixture evenly over the chicken and sprinkle the crispy, dry sesame seeds on top before serving.

CANTONESE CRYSTAL CHICKEN

1 chicken, about 2–3 lb
4 oz cooked smoked ham
2 envelopes powdered gelatin
1 teaspoon salt
1 teaspoon monosodium
   glutamate (optional)
¼ cup dry sherry
3¾ cups superior broth
   (see page 262)
red and green sweet peppers for
   garnishing

Clean the chicken thoroughly and dry. Place in a saucepan, cover with water, bring to a boil and simmer for 1 hour. Drain the chicken and, when cool, chop into 24 pieces. Cut the ham into similar sized pieces. Arrange the pieces of chicken and ham, interlaced in roof-tile fashion, in an oval dish.

Dissolve the gelatin in a little warm broth. Place the salt, monosodium glutamate, sherry, gelatin and broth in a saucepan and heat, stirring until the ingredients are well mixed. Cool for 15 minutes and then pour over the chicken. Place the dish in the refrigerator for 2 hours. After 2 hours, the jellied chicken and ham should have set. Turn out on to a plate. Trim the red and green sweet peppers, remove the seeds and cut into strips. Arrange around the jellied chicken as a colorful garnish.

HOT DICED CHICKEN IN CHOPPED PEANUTS

3 large chicken breasts
1 tablespoon cornstarch
1 egg
½ cup peanuts
2 scallions
1 tablespoon water
1½ teaspoons sugar
2 teaspoons vinegar
1½ teaspoons soy sauce
½ teaspoon salt
vegetable oil for deep-frying
4 teaspoons coarsely chopped
   dried chilies
2 tablespoons lard

Dice the chicken. Mix in a bowl half the cornstarch and the egg. Stir in the chicken. Chop the peanuts coarsely. Chop the scallions into ½-inch segments and combine with the remainder of the cornstarch blended with the water, sugar, vinegar, soy sauce and salt in a bowl. Deep-fry the diced chicken in the hot oil for 30 seconds. Drain and set aside. Discard the seeds from the chilies. Sauté in the lard for 30 seconds. Add the chicken and stir-fry for 10 seconds. Pour in the scallion mixture and continue to stir-fry for 20 seconds. Sprinkle in the peanuts. After a few stirs, pour on to a heated serving dish.

Cantonese crystal chicken

CANTONESE 'CRACKLING' CHICKEN

1 chicken, about 2–3 lb
3 tablespoons honey
1 tablespoon cornstarch

1 tablespoon soy sauce
vegetable oil for deep-frying

Clean the chicken thoroughly, then dip in boiling water for 2 seconds. Dry with a piece of cloth or absorbent paper. Dry for 5–6 hours (or overnight) in a cool, well-ventilated place.

Mix the honey, cornstarch and soy sauce in a bowl. Rub the chicken with the mixture. Heat the oil for deep-frying and suspend the chicken over the pan in a wire basket. Baste it evenly with a long-handled ladle until golden all over. The total time required for cooking in this manner is about 30–40 minutes. When well-cooked, the skin of the chicken should be crispy.

Chop the chicken into 10 to 12 pieces and serve on a heated flat plate. Accompany with dips of plum sauce or haisein sauce.

PEKING DUCK

1 duck, about 4–6 lb
3 tablespoons sugar
1 tablespoon dry sherry
3 tablespoons water
dash salt
30 doilies (see below)
15 scallions or 1 cucumber

for the garlic-vinegar dip :
6 cloves garlic
½ cup vinegar
for the mustard-soy sauce dip :
1 teaspoon dry mustard
3 tablespoons soy sauce
for the chili-soy sauce dip :
1 tablespoon chili sauce
¼ cup soy sauce

Clean the duck thoroughly and lower it momentarily into a pan of boiling water to scald. Dry immediately with absorbent paper and hang by the feet to dry overnight in a cool, airy place.

Mix together the sugar, sherry and water, adding the salt to help the sugar dissolve. Rub the outside of the duck with this sweetened water several hours before roasting. Hang to dry again. When dry, rub the duck a second time with the sweetened water.

Place the duck in a preheated moderately hot oven (375°) on a rack with a pan underneath to catch the drips. Roast for 20 minutes, then lower the temperature to 300° for 1 hour. Finally, raise the temperature to 400° for 20 minutes. The duck should then be well cooked and the skin very crispy.

While the duck is cooking, prepare the doilies according to the instructions given below, using double the quantities listed. Chop the scallions into segments 2 inches long. If using the cucumber, peel and cut into thin strips about 2 inches long. For the garlic-vinegar dip, peel and crush the cloves of garlic and mix with the vinegar.

For the mustard-soy sauce dip, combine the dry mustard with the soy sauce.

For the chili-soy sauce dip, combine the chili sauce with the soy sauce. Plum sauce and haisein sauce are also traditionally served with the dish.

The duck is carved at the dining table. At the first carving, only the skin is sliced off. To eat, dip 1 or 2 pieces of the skin in a sauce and place in the middle of a doily. Top with a piece of scallion or a strip of cucumber, fold over one end of the doily and roll up. Eat with the fingers while the duck skin is still crackling and warm.

Repeat the process until all the sliceable meat has been carved from the duck and each person has packed and eaten 3–6 doily rolls of duck skin and duck meat.

DOILIES (THIN CAKES)

Makes about 18
1½ cups all-purpose flour
⅔ cup boiling water

3 tablespoons sesame oil

Place the flour in a bowl. Pour in the boiling water very slowly and gradually work to a warm dough. Knead gently for 1–2 minutes, then let stand for 10 minutes. Shape the dough into a roll 2 inches in diameter. Cut the roll into ½-inch thick slices. Brush one side of each slice with sesame oil and lay another slice on top of it with the oiled surfaces together like a sandwich. Roll the double piece out from the center on a lightly floured working surface until it spreads out to a pancake with a diameter of about 5 inches. Make as many pancakes as the dough allows. Heat a large, flat, heavy, ungreased skillet or omelet pan over low heat. When quite hot, place a pancake in the skillet. Rotate the skillet above the heat every so often so the cooking is even. When the pancake starts to bubble, turn it over. After 2–3 minutes of heating on each side, pull each double piece of dough apart into separate slices. Fold each piece into a half circle on the side brushed with sesame oil. Pile the doilies on a plate and place in a steamer for 10 minutes. Bring to the table immediately for wrapping up pieces of duck.

QUICK-FRIED RIBBON OF DUCK

12 oz cooked or smoked duck
2–3 stalks celery
1 small leek
1 red sweet pepper
2 teaspoons coarsely chopped dried
  chilies
2 cloves garlic

¼ cup lard
1 tablespoon fermented black
  beans, soaked for 1 hour
1½ teaspoons sugar
1 tablespoon soy sauce
1 tablespoon vinegar

Slice the duck into matchstick-thin strips. Trim the celery and leek and cut into similar-sized strips. Remove the seeds from the red pepper and chilies. Cut the red pepper into thin strips. Peel and crush the garlic. Heat the lard in a skillet. Sauté the chilies for 1 minute to flavor the lard then discard the chilies. Add the celery, leek, garlic, sweet pepper and black beans. Stir-fry over high heat for 1 minute. Add the duck, sugar and soy sauce. Continue to stir-fry for 1 minute. Finally, add the vinegar and stir-fry quickly for 10 seconds.

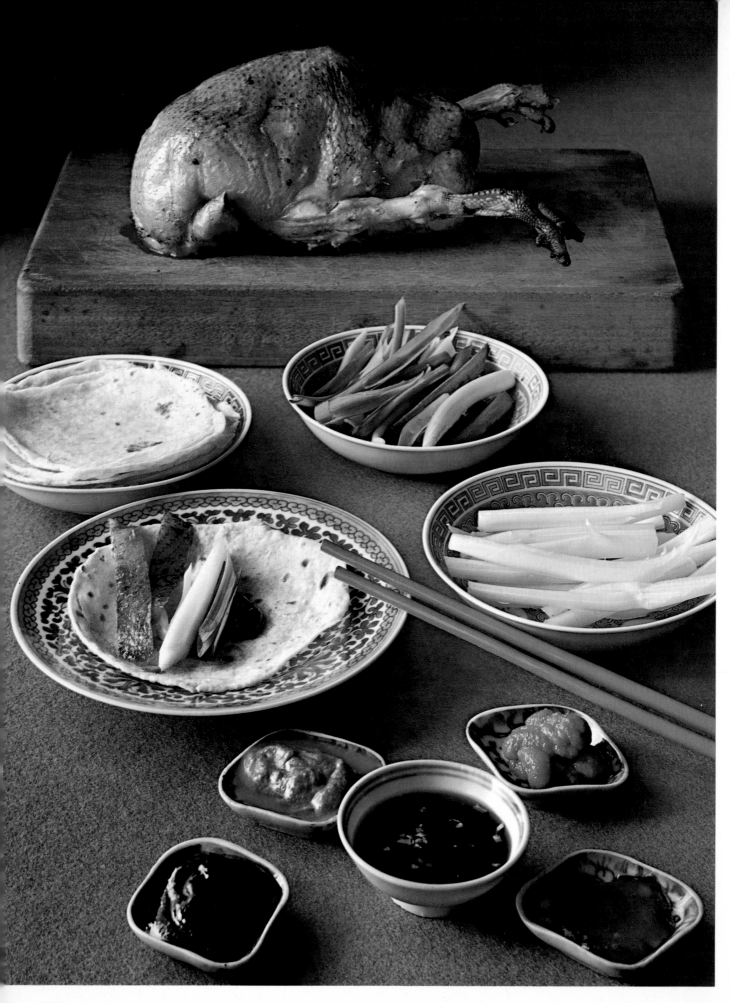

CHINESE RAVIOLI WITH SHRIMP-PORK FILLING

for the Chinese swallow-skin ravioli :
8 cups all-purpose flour
½ teaspoon salt
3¾ cups boiling water
2 tablespoons lard
for the filling :
8 oz cooked shrimp, shelled and deveined
1 oz fatty pork

2 oz lean pork
4 oz bamboo shoots
1 teaspoon salt
1½ teaspoons soy sauce
1 tablespoon dry sherry
½ teaspoon dry mustard
1½ teaspoons sesame oil
1 teaspoon sugar
pepper

To make the swallow-skin dough, sift the flour into a bowl. Add the salt to the boiling water and pour into the flour. Stir quickly with a wooden spoon. Add the lard and knead well on a board. Divide the dough into 2 portions and shape each into a long roll. Cut each roll into 12 pieces. Form each piece into a ball and roll out to 2 inches in diameter.

For the filling, finely chop the shrimp. Boil all the pork for 5 minutes, then chop finely. Cut the bamboo shoots into matchstick-thin strips and add to the shrimp and pork in a bowl. Add the salt, soy sauce, sherry, mustard, oil, sugar and pepper to taste. Place in the refrigerator for 30 minutes.

Divide the filling into 24 portions. Place the filling on one side of the dough skin and fold the other side over. Pinch the round sides together in the shape of a cock's comb. Place the 24 pieces on a greased ovenproof plate in a steamer. Cover and steam for 7 minutes. Serve immediately. Mix equal portions of vinegar and soy sauce as a dip.

T'UNG CHING VEGETARIAN NOODLES

¼ cup sesame paste
1 tablespoon sesame oil
3 tablespoons wine vinegar
1 teaspoon monosodium glutamate (optional)
1 tablespoon sugar
3 tablespoons soy sauce

1 teaspoon chili sauce
pepper
1 lb Chinese noodles or spaghetti
3 tablespoons finely chopped scallion stems
1 tablespoon finely chopped garlic

Mix together the sesame paste, sesame oil, vinegar, monosodium glutamate, sugar, soy sauce, chili sauce and pepper to taste. Divide the mixture among 5 separate bowls.

Boil the noodles or spaghetti for 15–20 minutes. Drain, and while steaming hot divide into equal portions and place on top of the mixture in the 5 bowls. Sprinkle the noodles with the scallion stems and garlic. Each diner may then toss and mix the noodles or spaghetti with the ingredients and seasonings according to taste.

TOSS-FRIED RICE NOODLES

1½ lb rice stick noodles
8 oz lean pork
1½ oz dried Chinese mushrooms, soaked and drained
2 oz bamboo shoots
½ stalk celery
1 small leek

2 cloves garlic
¼ cup lard
3 tablespoons soy sauce
¾ cup chicken bouillon or superior broth (see page 262)
1 teaspoon monosodium glutamate (optional)

Place the noodles in a saucepan of boiling water and boil gently for 5–10 minutes, or until soft and cooked. Drain and cool under cold running water and set aside.

Slice the pork, mushrooms, bamboo shoots, celery and leek into matchstick-thin strips. Peel and crush the garlic.

Heat three-fourths of the lard in a skillet over high heat. Add the pork and bamboo shoots and stir-fry for 30 seconds. Then add the mushrooms, leek and garlic. Fry for 1 minute. Add the celery, soy sauce, bouillon and monosodium glutamate. Simmer for 2 minutes. Remove from the heat and pour the contents of the skillet into a bowl.

Add the remaining lard to the skillet. Place over medium heat for 30 seconds then add the cooked noodles. Stir-fry gently for 3 minutes. Add half the pork mixture and all its liquid. Continue to stir-fry for 2 minutes. By this time, the noodles should have absorbed all the liquid. Turn the contents on to a large, flat, heated serving dish. Heat the remaining pork mixture in the skillet over high heat for 1 minute and use as a hot garnish or topping for the noodles.

MEAT-FILLED MUSHROOMS

30 large Chinese dried mushrooms
4 oz lean pork
1 oz cooked smoked ham
1 egg
1 tablespoon chopped onion
1 tablespoon ground dried shrimp
1 tablespoon cornstarch

1 tablespoon soy sauce
½ teaspoon salt
for the sauce :
⅔ cup chicken bouillon
2 teaspoons cornstarch
½ teaspoon monosodium glutamate (optional)
1 tablespoon lard

Remove the stems from the mushrooms. Soak the mushroom caps in warm water for 30 minutes. Grind the pork and ham and mix in a bowl with the egg, onion, shrimp, cornstarch, half the soy sauce and half the salt. Spread the mixture over the inside of 15 of the mushroom caps and cover each one with a second mushroom cap. Put a board over them and press gently to flatten, keeping the insides of the caps together sandwich-style. Arrange these 'sandwiches' on a large plate. Place in a steamer, cover and steam for 20 minutes.

Meanwhile, prepare a sauce by mixing the remaining soy sauce, salt and chicken bouillon with the cornstarch and monosodium glutamate. Bring to a boil and add the lard. Pour the sauce over the mushrooms and serve immediately.

Peking duck—a world-famous dish
(see page 279)

SPINACH BALLS

4 oz cooked fatty pork
8 oz cooked lean pork
3 eggs
1 teaspoon chopped fresh
  ginger root
2 tablespoons chopped onion
½ cup water
1 tablespoon cornstarch
½ teaspoon monosodium
  glutamate (optional)
1 teaspoon salt

pepper
2 lb spinach
1 oz dried Chinese
  mushrooms, soaked and
  drained
2 oz bamboo shoots
1 oz cooked ham
1¼ cups superior broth
  (see page 262)
1 teaspoon sesame oil

Finely grind the fatty and lean pork and mix together in a bowl. Beat the eggs for 1 minute and then mix well into the pork. Boil the ginger, onion and water in a saucepan. Remove from the heat and let stand for 6 minutes. Strain, discard the ginger and onion and pour the water into the pork mixture. Add the cornstarch, half the monosodium glutamate, half the salt and pepper to taste. Beat the mixture for 1 minute. Form into small meat balls.

Wash the spinach, remove the stems and add to a large saucepan of boiling water for a 10-second dip. Drain well and slice into matchstick-thin strips. Slice the mushrooms, bamboo shoots and ham into similar sized strips, mix together with the spinach strips and spread on a tray. Roll the meat balls over this to pick up the various colored strips. Place on an ovenproof plate, cover and steam for 8 minutes.

Arrange the remaining spinach, mushrooms, bamboo shoots and ham in the bottom of a heated deep casserole. Place the meat balls on top. Meanwhile, make a sauce with the broth by adding the remaining monosodium glutamate, remaining salt and pepper to taste. Heat and pour over the meat balls. Sprinkle with sesame oil and serve.

VEGETABLE RICE

3½ cups long-grained rice
1 medium-sized head cabbage
2 tablespoons lard

2 teaspoons salt
2½ cups cold water
⅔ cup boiling water

Wash the rice and let it soak in cold water for 3 hours. Wash the cabbage and discard the coarser outer leaves and stems. Cut the leaves into 1-inch squares.

Heat the lard in a large heavy saucepan. When very hot, add the cabbage. Reduce the heat and stir-fry gently for 3 minutes, then add the salt and the cold water. Turn the heat to high. When the water starts to boil, add the rice. Continue to stir gently with a wooden spoon until the water reboils. Then lower the heat and cover tightly. When the water has nearly all been absorbed by the rice (after about 10–12 minutes), pour in the boiling water. Poke 4 holes through the rice to the bottom of the pan to facilitate steaming. Cover firmly and insert an asbestos mat underneath the pan. After 5 minutes, remove the pan from the heat. Allow the rice to

Spinach balls

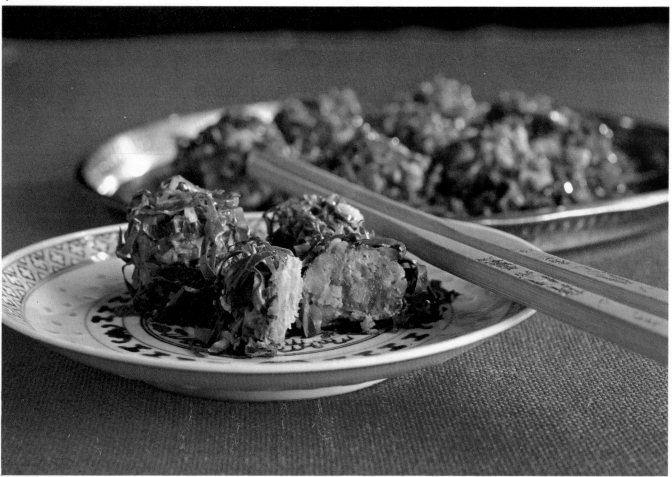

steam in its own heat for 10 minutes. The vegetable rice should then be ready.

LOTUS LEAF-WRAPPED RICE

2 cups short-grain rice
2 teaspoons soy sauce
1½ teaspoons salt
1 teaspoon monosodium
  glutamate (optional)
2½ cups water
6 tablespoons lard
4 oz roast pork
2 oz dried Chinese
  mushrooms, soaked and
  drained

1 egg
4 oz shelled cooked shrimp
  or crab
1 teaspoon sugar
2 teaspoons oyster sauce
⅔ cup secondary broth
  (see page 262)
1 tablespoon cornstarch
3 tablespoons water
2 teaspoons dry sherry
6 large lotus leaves

Wash the rice and place in a metal or ovenproof dish. Add the soy sauce, 1 teaspoon salt, half the monosodium glutamate and the water. Place in a steamer, cover and steam for 20–25 minutes until the rice is cooked. Stir in one-third of the lard. Set aside.

For the filling, cut the roast pork into ¼-inch cubes and dice the soaked mushrooms. Beat the egg and make a thin omelet by cooking the egg in another third of the lard. Cut into ½-inch squares.

Heat the remaining lard in a skillet. Add the remaining salt, pork, mushrooms, egg squares and shrimp. Stir-fry for 20 seconds. Add the remaining monosodium glutamate, the sugar, oyster sauce and broth. When the mixture boils, stir in the cornstarch blended with the water. Stir and cook for 2 minutes. Then add the sherry. Pour half of this mixture into the rice and stir. Set aside the remaining filling.

After blanching the lotus leaves quickly in boiling water, spread them out on the table. Divide the filling and the rice into 6 equal portions. One one side of the center of each leaf place a portion of filling and over it a portion of rice. Wrap the leaf in envelope fashion and make it into a 'parcel', about 2 by 2½ inches. Place in a steamer, cover and steam for 15–18 minutes. Pile the steaming 'parcels' on a heated plate and serve.

Vegetable rice

283

SOUR AND SWEET CHINESE CABBAGE

2–3 lb Chinese cabbage (or use a crinkly leaf type of Savoy cabbage)
1 tablespoon cornstarch
1 tablespoon water
¼ cup vinegar
1 tablespoon soy sauce
1 tablespoon sugar
1 tablespoon dry sherry
2 dried chilies
¼ cup vegetable oil
1 teaspoon salt
¼ cup secondary broth (see page 262)
½ teaspoon monosodium glutamate (optional)

Discard the coarse outer leaves of the cabbage. Cut off the bottom and cut the heart and inner leaves diagonally into 1½-inch long strips. In a bowl, mix the cornstarch, water, vinegar, soy sauce, sugar and sherry.

Sauté the chilies in the oil in a large skillet for 1 minute then discard the chilies. Add the cabbage and stir-fry over high heat for 3 minutes. Add the salt, broth and monosodium glutamate. Continue to stir-fry for 5 more minutes over medium heat. Add the cornstarch mixture and mix well with the cabbage. Stir-fry gently for 1 minute. Serve in a heated dish.

RIOT OF SPRING

3 medium-sized heads cabbage (compact, with firm hearts)
1 chicken breast
1 thin slice cooked ham
¼ cup winter bamboo shoots
8 dried Chinese mushrooms, soaked and drained
1 egg white
1 teaspoon cornstarch
2 cups chicken bouillon
1 teaspoon salt
1 teaspoon monosodium glutamate (optional)
1 tablespoon chicken fat
vegetable oil for deep-frying
1 tablespoon dry sherry

Cut off the stalks of the cabbages. Remove and discard the outer leaves until each heart stands out like an upstanding, firm green bud. Cut the chicken breast into thin slices 1 by ½ inch. Slice the ham and bamboo shoots in the same manner. Cut the mushrooms into ¼-inch wide strips. Mix the egg white and cornstarch in a bowl and dip the sliced chicken in it.

Bring the chicken bouillon to a boil in a large saucepan. Add half the salt, half the monosodium glutamate and half the chicken fat. Place the cabbages in this mixture and boil for about 1–1½ minutes.

Remove the cabbages and arrange the leaves to line the sides of a deep casserole, reserving the hearts. Use these to pack the middle with 3 or 4 layers of tender leaves. Deep-fry the chicken slices for 45 seconds. Arrange the chicken, ham, bamboo shoots and mushrooms in concentric rings on top of the layers of green leaves. Pour in the bouillon and dot with the remaining chicken fat. Sprinkle with the remaining salt and monosodium glutamate and the sherry. Place in a steamer, cover and steam for 25 minutes. Serve in the casserole.

DRAWN-THREAD HONEYED APPLES

2 lb apples
1 egg
3 tablespoons all-purpose flour
vegetable oil for deep-frying
⅓ cup sugar
3 tablespoons vegetable oil
¼ cup water
¼ cup corn syrup

Peel and core the apples. Cut into French-fry-shaped pieces, 1½ inches by ½ inch. Beat the egg. Dip the apple pieces in the egg and dredge with flour. Deep-fry in hot oil for 2½ minutes, then drain. Heat the sugar and 3 tablespoons of oil in a flameproof dish. When the sugar has melted, add the water and then the corn syrup. Continue to stir gently over the heat until the liquid has become golden. Add the apple pieces to the hot syrup, turning the pieces over so they are well coated, and bring to the table in the cooking dish.

Each diner should be provided with a bowl of water with ice floating in it. Using chopsticks, a piece of apple should be taken from the dish and plunged into the water. The coating syrup will instantly cool into a brittle hardness. After the dipping, the apple should be placed in a saucer to cool for a few moments before eating. In the process of dipping, the apple should not be left for any length of time in the water or it will become sodden.

Note: This recipe can be applied with equal success to bananas, pears, oranges, pineapple or other fruit.

ICE-MOUNTAIN FRUIT SALAD

1 lb apples
1 lb pears
1 lb peaches
1 honeydew melon
1 lb cherries
1 lb strawberries
1 lb grapes
8 oz water chestnuts
1 small pineapple
crushed ice (see recipe)

Peel the apples, pears and peaches. Cut into quarters and place in iced water (to prevent browning) while preparing the other fruits. Halve the melon, remove the seeds and cut the flesh into similar-sized pieces. Rinse and pit the cherries and hull the strawberries. Peel and halve the grapes and remove the seeds. Slice the water chestnuts. Peel and slice the pineapple, removing the woody center core.

Make a bed of crushed ice on a very large serving plate. Arrange the pieces of fruit on top in an artistic pattern, interspersing the fruits with larger chunks of ice. Alternatively, a raised mound of ice may be piled in the middle of the large serving plate to give the effect of a miniature ice-mountain. Decorate the ice-mountain with the fruit.

Note: Small saucers of sugar, or a mixture of sugar and ground ginger, may be used as dips.

Drawn-thread honeyed apples

FAR EASTERN

Nina Froud

Photography by John Lee

All good cooking in the Far East originated in China and India. But although the influence of these two countries continues to dominate oriental cookery, individual countries have succeeded in developing their own characteristic styles of food preparation and presentation.

The staple food of the Indian sub-continent is a cereal crop of one sort or another. In the north, wheat is made into excellent bread; in the south the people are rice-eating and to a great extent vegetarian. But it is difficult to define the differences between Indian, Pakistani and Kashmiri food. Eating habits throughout the sub-continent are dictated by many factors, not least by religion and economics. Religious influence and foreign occupations have also left their mark on the cooking of Sri Lanka – 'The Isle of Spices'. The staple diet is rice with curried vegetables, fish or meat, and *sambals* (called *sambols* in Sri Lanka) as accompaniments to the various main dishes.

Rice is the staple food of Burma and vegetables, salads, fish and shellfish are very popular. A fish dish is served at all main meals. A delightful feature of Burmese cooking is their lavish use of fragrant flowers in soups, salads and other dishes.

Thailand is perhaps the most exotic of the Far Eastern countries. Colorful boats poled along the network of canals bring to Bangkok markets the vast variety of Thailand's superb vegetables, herbs, spices and fruit. In Thailand, as in Japan, the same meticulous care is taken with the presentation as with the preparation of food.

Malaysia has vast areas of dense forest and jungle, inhabited by primitive peoples. Singapore is a complete contrast . . . it is the great melting pot of South East Asia. The Chinese form the biggest community, followed by the Malays, Indians, Pakistanis and Singhalese. All have contributed to the cuisine, but a Malay cook interprets a dish in his own way, such as adding red chilies and *blachan* to accompany Chinese fried rice or serving a hot *sambal* with a bland noodle dish.

Indonesia is made up of thousands of beautiful islands, the principal ones being Java, Bali, Sumatra, Borneo and Celebes. A reminder of the lengthy occupation of Java by the Dutch is the famous Indonesian specialty, *rijstafel*. It consists of a basic rice dish accompanied by up to 40 side dishes, including satays, *sambals,* pickles and chutneys.

As befits the inhabitants of a rugged highland country, the Koreans are hearty eaters. Not for them the dainty Japanese morsels or the sophistication of Chinese *haute cuisine.* Three essentials of a Korean menu are rice, soup and *keem chee* (pickles), with fresh fruit to end a meal.

Filipino cooking is subject to many influences. Restaurant menus may offer you at one and the same time a noodle or rice dish of unmistakable Chinese origin, a Spanish specialty and a typically American dessert. Fresh fruit is abundant and the coconut palm plays an important part in the cuisine.

Japanese food is a fascinating reflection of the Japanese approach to life and talent for artistic expression. The use of seasonings is restrained in order to preserve the natural flavor of the original ingredients. Their predilection for purity of taste accounts for their simplicity of garnishing. Another characteristic is the smallness of the servings.

All the countries of the Far East share one talent – the ability to transform familiar fish, meat, fowl and vegetables into exquisite and exotic dishes.

GLOSSARY

Blachan or Balachaung
A salted fermented paste made of shrimp, spices and chilies, much used in Burmese and Malaysian cooking. Anchovy paste may be used as a substitute.

Bombay Duck
A dried fish, served as a side dish to curries and particularly popular in southern India. It is available in cans. Bombay duck should be baked or fried until crisp and then crumbled.

Cinnamon Bark
Or cinnamon stick. Both are the dried bark of the cinnamon tree. Cinnamon bark is rougher and more uneven in appearance than the smooth curls or sticks of cinnamon that come from the inner bark of the tree. Either can be used where called for in a recipe. Remove from the dish before serving.

Coconut Cream or Milk
Coconut milk of a thick consistency is usually referred to as coconut cream. The cream is the result of the first extraction of liquid from the coconut flesh. If the process is repeated and water added, the slightly thinner liquid is referred to as coconut milk. To prepare coconut cream, proceed as follows: Have the top sawn off the coconut. Discard the natural liquid found in the coconut – this should not be confused with coconut milk. Remove the flesh and grate coarsely. (About 3 oz desiccated coconut may be substituted for freshly grated coconut.) Pour over boiling milk or water to cover and leave to soak for 1½–2 hours. Squeeze out through a fine strainer two or three times to get as much thick cream as you can. To obtain the thinner coconut milk, repeat the process. Coconut cream is also available in packages or cans. When using this dissolve 2 oz coconut cream in ¾ cup hot milk. This makes a thick mixture which may be diluted according to taste. Dishes containing coconut milk should not be allowed to boil after the addition of the coconut milk.

Coconut Palm Heart
The tender inner heart of the coconut palm, white and cylindrical in shape. It is available in cans.

Curry Leaves
The aromatic leaves of a small tree or shrub of the orange family, used in India and Ceylon for flavoring curries, hence the name. Both fresh and dried leaves are used.

Dhal
Several kinds of split peas, described according to their color. The commonest *dhal* is the lentil or red *dhal*. Some *dhals*, particularly white *dhal*, are ground into flour. *Dhal* is widely used in the East, particularly in India. Various kinds are obtainable from Indian food shops.

Fenugreek
An aromatic herb used in many oriental dishes to impart flavor, but mainly used to thicken gravies. If not available, the best substitutes are cashew nuts or peanuts, lightly roasted and ground to a paste.

Garam-masala
Indian mixture of curry spices and an essential ingredient of curries. For 6 oz, grind together in a mortar or coffee grinder: 2 oz coriander seeds, 2 oz black peppercorns, 1½ oz caraway seeds, ½ oz whole cloves, 20 peeled cardamom seeds and ½ oz ground cinnamon. The powder may be used immediately or stored in an airtight container.

Ghee
Clarified butter which is available in cans. To make *ghee*, melt butter over very low heat until it begins to look like olive oil and a whitish deposit begins to form on the bottom of the pan. Strain into a clean jar, removing the deposit.

Gingko Nuts
Used as a garnish in many Japanese dishes. The canned variety is ready for use. The dried nuts must be shelled and blanched first.

Gula Malacca
Unrefined palm sugar, also known as 'Malacca sweet' and 'jaggery'. Usually sold moulded into round cakes. It can be grated, shredded or chopped as required in a recipe. Maple sugar or soft dark brown sugar may be used as a substitute.

Harusame
Japanese noodles made from soya bean powder.

Jalebi Powder
A yellow powder used in India for colouring and in particular for making *jalebis*. Readily available in Indian shops. If unobtainable, saffron or turmeric may be substituted.

Kamaboko
A fish paste or steamed loaf made of fish for forcemeat. Sold in Japanese shops in the form of small flat cakes.

Lemon Grass or Lemon Leaf
The aromatic stems and leaves of a plant cultivated in most tropical countries and used as a flavouring. Lemon balm may be used as a substitute.

Mien Chiang
Chinese bean paste, used widely in Chinese and Korean cooking. Available from Chinese food shops.

Mirin
A Japanese sweet wine fortified with *sake*, used for flavouring soups and sauces. Sweet white wine or sherry may be used as a substitute.

Nam Pla
Thai fish paste, with a piquant fishy flavour. Available in shops specialising in oriental produce. For a substitute blend equal proportions of anchovy paste and soya sauce, and use as directed in the recipe.

Nori
An edible species of marine algae. Sold in Japanese food shops in dried sheets or square pieces. It should be heated, then crushed, and the crumbs sprinkled over prepared dishes. Particularly good with fish recipes.

Poppadum
Poppadums are crisp 'breads' made of red lentil flour flavoured with black pepper, assafoetida and various spices, and served as an accompaniment to curry. Before serving, they should be fried very quickly in hot fat, one at a time. Poppadums are sold ready-made in Indian food shops.

Sake
A Japanese rice wine for drinking and for use as a flavouring. As a drink it is usually served hot. In recipes, dry sherry, and in certain cases brandy, may be used instead.

Shoyu
This is the Japanese name for soya bean sauce. A universal flavouring agent for which there is no substitute. It is made from wheat and soya beans, mixed with malt seed and allowed to ferment; then pressed and filtered. Both salt and monosodium glutamate enter into its composition.

Shrimp Paste
A preparation similar to dried shrimp powder.

Shrimp Powder
Dried shrimps ground into powder.

Tamarind
The fruit of the tamarind tree. The pods are filled with an acid pulp which is used in many Asian countries in preference to lemon juice or vinegar. For cooking purposes use dry tamarind which should be soaked long enough to make it pliable. Remove the fibres before using. To make tamarind juice proceed as follows: Soak the tamarind in water, using 1 oz (25 g) dried tamarind for every 4 tablespoons water. Remove the fibres and strain the juice through a muslin cloth. Use the juice as directed in the recipe. Tamarind should be used for dishes to be eaten the same day. As a substitute, fresh lime or lemon juice may be used.

Tiger Lily Bulbs
Available in Japanese food shops. Shallots could be used instead but they are not really a substitute.

India, Pakistan, Kashmir, Sri Lanka

MULLIGATAWNY

Serves 4

6 oz red *dhal*	1 tablespoon *garam-masala*
2 large onions	3½ pints stock (meat,
1 bay leaf	chicken, fish or vegetable)
2½ cups water	salt and pepper
1 clove garlic	6 tablespoons coconut cream
2 tablespoons *ghee*	1 lemon

Rinse the *dhal* under cold running water and place in a bowl. Cover with cold water and set aside to soak for 1½–2 hours. Peel and slice one of the onions. Drain the *dhal* and place in a saucepan with the onion, bay leaf and water. Bring to a boil over moderate heat. Reduce the heat and simmer for about 1 hour, or until the *dhal* is soft. Press the mixture through a sieve, or reduce to a purée in a blender.

Peel and chop the garlic and remaining onion. Heat the *ghee* in a saucepan and sauté the onion and garlic until soft but not browned. Add the *garam-masala* and cook for 2–3 minutes. Add the *dhal* purée and mix well. Stir in the stock and season to taste with salt and pepper. Increase the heat and bring the soup to a boil. Boil for 2–3 minutes. Remove from the heat and stir in the coconut cream. Pour the soup into a heated tureen and garnish with thin slices of lemon.

FISH PILAU

Serves 6

1½ lb cod fillet	1 teaspoon *garam-masala*
1¾ cups long-grain rice	1 teaspoon salt
1 large onion	1 tablespoon lemon juice
¼ cup *ghee*	3¾ cups hot water
1 teaspoon turmeric	8 oz fresh or frozen cooked
½ teaspoon coriander	jumbo shrimp, shelled
dash chili powder	and deveined

Rinse the fish under cold running water and pat dry with absorbent paper. Cut into pieces about 2 inches by 1 inch. Rinse the rice in a sieve, then cover with cold water in a bowl and set aside until required. Peel and chop the onion.

Heat half the *ghee* in a saucepan. Add the turmeric, coriander, chili powder, *garam-masala* and salt. Cook for 2 minutes. Add the lemon juice and continue cooking over high heat, stirring constantly, until the excess liquid has evaporated. Add the fish and cook on both sides for 3 minutes, taking care not to break the pieces. Remove the fish from the pan and reserve. Drain the rice.

Heat the remaining *ghee* in the saucepan. Add the onion and sauté until soft. Add the rice and sauté for 2 minutes. Add the hot water and bring to a boil. Reduce the heat, cover and simmer for 20 minutes. Stir lightly and place the fish on top of the rice. Cover and simmer for 10 minutes. Garnish with the shrimp, cover and leave over very low heat for 2–3 minutes. Serve immediately.

Mulligatawny

COD IN ALMOND AND YOGURT SAUCE

Serves 4

2 lb cod fillet	1 piece cinnamon bark, about
1 teaspoon turmeric	2 inches long
1 teaspoon salt	2 cups milk
dash white pepper	2 cups finely ground
4 medium-sized onions	almonds
$\frac{1}{4}$ cup butter	1$\frac{1}{4}$ cups unflavored yogurt

Rinse the fish under cold running water and pat dry with absorbent paper. Cut into 2-inch pieces and sprinkle with the turmeric, salt and pepper.

Peel and chop the onions. Heat the butter in a skillet and add the onions and cinnamon. Sauté until the onions are soft but not browned. Add the fish and sauté until lightly browned. Pour in the milk and bring to a boil. Lower the heat and simmer for 15 minutes.

Blend the ground almonds to a paste with the yogurt and pour over the fish. Cover and simmer gently for 10 minutes. Transfer to a heated serving dish and serve hot with boiled rice.

SHRIMP DOHPIAZA (DRY CURRY)

Serves 4

1 lb fresh or frozen	1 green sweet pepper
uncooked jumbo shrimp,	1 teaspoon turmeric
shelled and deveined	small dash cayenne pepper
1 tablespoon coriander	1 teaspoon cumin seeds
6 medium-sized onions	1$\frac{1}{2}$ teaspoons salt
$\frac{1}{3}$ cup *ghee*	1 lemon
2 cloves garlic	

Rinse the shrimp thoroughly under cold running water and place in a saucepan with just enough water to cover. Add the coriander and bring to a boil. Lower the heat and simmer the prawns for 2–3 minutes (overcooking will toughen them). Remove with a perforated spoon and set aside until required. Reserve the cooking liquid.

Peel 4 of the onions. Make two crosswise cuts two-thirds of the way through each onion so it is quartered but remains joined at the bottom. Heat the *ghee* in a skillet and sauté the onions for about 5 minutes, or until lightly browned on the outside but uncooked in the center. Remove the onions from the skillet and set aside until required.

Peel and chop the garlic and remaining onions. Remove the seeds from the sweet pepper and shred the flesh. Heat the *ghee* remaining in the skillet and sauté the chopped garlic and onion until soft but not browned. Stir in the turmeric, cayenne pepper and cumin seeds. Sauté for 2 minutes. Add the pepper and sauté for 3–4 minutes. Add the salt, the quartered onions and the reserved liquid. Simmer until the quartered onions are tender. Add the shrimp and simmer until the excess liquid has evaporated.

Transfer the mixture to a heated serving dish and arrange the quartered onions on top. Garnish with slices of lemon and serve immediately with *puri* (see below).

SAMOSAS (DEEP-FRIED PASTRIES)

Makes 24–30

for the dough :	3 large cooked potatoes
2$\frac{1}{2}$ cups all-purpose flour	1 tablespoon *ghee*
dash salt	1$\frac{1}{2}$ teaspoons chopped fresh
$\frac{2}{3}$ cup unflavored yogurt or	ginger root
curds (see note)	1 tablespoon coriander
$\frac{1}{3}$ cup melted *ghee*	1 teaspoon chili powder
for the filling :	2 tablespoons sieved mango
1 medium-sized onion	1–1$\frac{1}{2}$ teaspoons *garam-masala*
2 teaspoons dried pomegranate	1$\frac{1}{2}$ teaspoons salt
seeds (optional)	oil for deep-frying

Sift the flour and salt into a bowl and make a well in the center. Add the curds or yogurt and the *ghee*. Mix to a dough and knead well until smooth. Cover and set aside for 25–30 minutes.

To make the filling, peel and chop the onion. Pound the pomegranate seeds to a powder. Mash the potatoes. Heat the *ghee* in a skillet and sauté the onion until soft but not browned. Add the ginger, coriander and chili powder and cook for 2–3 minutes. Stir in the pounded pomegranate seeds, mashed potato, mango pulp, *garam-masala* and salt. Mix well. Continue cooking over low heat until the moisture evaporates and the mixture is quite dry and firm.

Roll out the dough to $\frac{1}{16}$-inch thickness. Cut into 3-inch squares and place 1 teaspoon of the prepared filling on each square. Brush the edges of the squares with milk and fold in half to make a triangle. Press the edges firmly together to seal in the filling.

Deep-fry the *samosas* in hot oil until golden brown. Drain on absorbent paper and keep hot. Transfer to a heated serving dish and serve hot with a chutney.

Note: Traditionally, curds are used in this recipe. They are obtained when milk becomes sour, either naturally or by the addition of an acid such as lemon juice. Unflavored yogurt makes an excellent substitute for the curds.

PURI (INDIAN DEEP-FRIED BREAD)

Makes about 20

2 cups whole-wheat flour	about $\frac{2}{3}$ cup warm water
1 teaspoon salt	oil for deep-frying
1 tablespoon slightly softened	
ghee	

Sift the flour and salt into a bowl and rub the *ghee* into the flour. Make a well in the center. Add the water gradually and mix to a fairly stiff dough. Knead well until the dough becomes smooth and soft. Divide into about 20 pieces. Shape each piece into a ball and roll out each ball into a circle about 5–6 inches in diameter. Deep-fry in hot oil until risen and golden brown. Drain well on absorbent paper and serve hot.

Samosas (deep-fried pastries)

ROGHAN JOSH (SPICY LAMB IN CREAM SAUCE)

Serves 6

2½ lb lean lamb, cut from the leg
½ teaspoon finely chopped fresh
  ginger root
6 tablespoons *ghee*
2 teaspoons coriander
1½ teaspoons *garam-masala*
salt

dash chili powder
2½ cups water
¼ cup finely ground almonds
⅓ cup heavy cream
¼ cup chopped pistachio nuts
¼ cup chopped blanched almonds

Wipe the meat with a cloth and cut into 1-inch cubes. Place on a shallow dish and sprinkle with the ginger. Heat the *ghee* in a skillet and sauté the lamb until evenly browned. Add the coriander, *garam-masala,* salt and chili powder, then gradually stir in the water. Bring to a boil, reduce the heat and simmer for 30–40 minutes, or until the lamb is tender and the water has evaporated.

Mix the ground almonds with a little cold water to make a thick, smooth paste. Blend with the cream and stir into the lamb mixture. Cook very gently for 5 minutes. Transfer to a heated serving dish. Sprinkle with the chopped nuts and serve immediately with rice.

LAMB QORMA

Serves 4

1½ lb lean lamb, cut from the leg
1 tablespoon chopped mint
2 medium-sized onions
2 cloves garlic
¼ cup *ghee*
1 tablespoon coriander
1 teaspoon chopped fresh
  ginger root

¼ teaspoon freshly ground black
  pepper
1¼ cups unflavored yogurt
few saffron strands
3 tablespoons lemon juice
3 tablespoons blanched almonds
3 tablespoons raisins
salt and pepper

Wipe the meat with a damp cloth and cut into 1-inch cubes. Place in a bowl, sprinkle with the mint and set aside for 1–2 hours.

Peel and thinly slice the onions. Peel and chop the garlic. Heat three-fourths of the *ghee* in a saucepan and sauté the onions until soft and golden brown. Add the garlic, coriander, ginger and pepper and sauté for 5 minutes. Add the meat and sauté until well browned. Stir in the yogurt. Cover the pan, lower the heat and cook the meat for 45–50 minutes, or until tender.

Meanwhile, soak the saffron in the lemon juice. Soak the almonds in hot water for 2–3 minutes. Drain well and cut into thin slices. Heat the remaining *ghee* in a skillet and sauté the almonds and raisins for 2–3 minutes. Drain on absorbent paper and add to the lamb with the saffron and lemon juice. Season to taste with salt and pepper. Transfer the *qorma* to a heated serving dish and serve hot with boiled rice.

291

Kashmiri kebab

KASHMIRI KEBAB

Serves 6–8

2 lb lean lamb, cut from the leg	1 teaspoon chopped fresh
1 medium-sized onion	ginger root
dash saffron powder	dash ground cloves
3 tablespoons lime or lemon juice	dash pepper
1–2 cloves garlic	1¼ cups unflavored yogurt

Cut the lamb into thin slices, about ¼–½ inch thick. Peel the onion, cut in half and rub the cut sides over the slices of meat. Pound the slices flat with a meat mallet. Cut each slice into strips ½–¾ inch wide and beat again to make thin flat ribbons with slightly ragged, very thin edges. Blend the saffron with the lime juice. Peel and chop the garlic. Mix together the garlic, ginger, cloves, pepper, yogurt and saffron mixture. Pour over the lamb and set aside to marinate for 4–5 hours.

Wind the meat on to 6 to 8 skewers. Each strip should be wound round so that it overlaps, making a fat sausage shape (see photograph). The thin edges will make the meat stick to itself so there is no need to pierce it with the skewer. Press each sausage gently with the fingers into a lozenge shape. Cook under a hot broiler until well browned and serve hot on the skewers accompanied by onion salad (see below).

ONION SALAD

Serves 4

4 medium-sized onions	salt
3 large tomatoes	chili powder
1 teaspoon coriander	⅔ cup white vinegar

Peel and thinly slice the onions and tomatoes. Arrange on a plate and sprinkle with the coriander. Season with salt and chili powder to taste. Add the vinegar and mix well. Set aside for at least 1 hour before serving.

SINGHALESE CHICKEN CURRY

Serves 4

1 chicken, about 4 lb, with	1–4 red chilies, according
giblets (see note)	to taste
10 cardamom seeds	3 tablespoons coconut oil
10 peppercorns	or peanut oil
4–5 cloves	2 pieces cinnamon bark, each
2 tablespoons coriander	about 2 inches long
1 teaspoon cumin	2 cups coconut milk
dash dried fennel	1 teaspoon salt
½ teaspoon turmeric	⅔ cup coconut cream
small dash fenugreek	2–3 tablespoons fresh lime or
12 shallots	lemon juice

Rinse the giblets well under cold running water. Dry with absorbent paper and reserve. Divide the chicken into 8 portions.

Lightly crush the cardamom seeds and peppercorns to release the flavors, and place in a skillet with the cloves, coriander, cumin, fennel, turmeric and fenugreek. Heat gently over moderate heat for 2–3 minutes, stirring constantly to prevent the mixture from burning. Remove from the heat and set aside.

Peel and thinly slice the shallots. Remove the seeds from the chilies and chop the flesh finely. Heat the oil in a skillet and sauté the shallots and chilies until lightly browned. Add the chicken, the giblets, the heated spices and the cinnamon bark. Sauté for about 10 minutes, or until the chicken changes color. Add the coconut milk and salt. Cook very gently for 15–20 minutes, or until the chicken is tender. Add the coconut cream and simmer for a further 12–15 minutes, or until the excess liquid has evaporated. Remove and discard the cinnamon bark. Transfer the mixture to a heated serving dish, sprinkle with the lime juice and serve hot with rice, onion or cucumber *sambol* (see page 295), Singhalese chutney (see below) and hot sautéed cashew nuts.

Note: Beef or pork may be substituted for the chicken.

SINGHALESE CHUTNEY

Makes 3 lb

¾ cup pitted prunes	4–6 cloves garlic
¾ cup dried peaches	¾ cup dried chilies (see note)
¾ cup dried apricots	1 teaspoon salt
1⅓ cups dried apple rings	2¼ cups sugar
2½ cups vinegar	½ cup seedless white raisins
1 piece green ginger root, about	½ cup sliced cashew nuts
1 inch long	

Place the prunes, peaches, apricots and apple rings in a bowl. Add a fourth of the vinegar and set aside for 45–50 minutes. Strain off the vinegar and reserve.

Cut the fruit into ¼-inch pieces. Peel and chop the ginger and garlic. Pound the garlic, ginger and chilies in a mortar and add 3 tablespoons of the vinegar. Pour the remaining vinegar and the reserved vinegar into a saucepan. Add the garlic mixture, the salt and sugar. Bring to a boil over low heat. When the sugar has dissolved, add the soaked fruit, the raisins and the cashew nuts. Lower the heat and simmer for about 1 hour, or until the excess liquid has evaporated and the mixture has become fairly thick. Remove from the heat and set aside to cool. Pour into jars and seal. Store in a cool dry place until required.

Note: This is a very hot chutney and the quantity of chilies may be reduced by half, if preferred.

CHICKEN BIRIANI

Serves 4–6

1 chicken, about 4 lb	3 cloves
1 tablespoon lime or lemon juice	1 piece cinnamon bark, about
1 teaspoon finely chopped fresh	2 inches long
ginger root	dash freshly grated nutmeg
2 large onions	2½ cups sour milk
⅓ cup *ghee*	2 cups long-grain rice
1 tablespoon coriander	2½ cups water
1 teaspoon cumin	1 teaspoon chopped chives
½ teaspoon ground fennel seed	**for the garnish :**
2–3 tablespoons poppy seeds	8 shallots
2 teaspoons salt	½ cucumber
¼ teaspoon freshly ground white	1½ lb tomatoes
pepper	1 green sweet pepper
¼ cup finely ground almonds	6 slices pineapple

Wipe the chicken with a damp cloth and chop into 2½-inch pieces. Sprinkle the chicken with the lime juice and ginger. Peel and thinly slice the onions. Heat three-fourths of the *ghee* in a saucepan and sauté the onions until soft but not browned. Stir in the coriander, cumin, fennel, poppy seeds, salt, pepper and half the ground almonds. Add the chicken, cloves, cinnamon, nutmeg and sour milk. Bring to the simmering point. Lower the heat, cover the pan and cook for 30 minutes. Meanwhile, rinse the rice very thoroughly under cold running water. Place in a saucepan with the remaining ground almonds and the water. Bring to a boil and cook for 5 minutes. Drain well.

Take half of the rice out of the pan and pour the chicken stew on top of the remaining rice. Sprinkle with the chives. Replace the rice that was removed from the saucepan. Cover with a tight-fitting lid and cook over low heat for 10–15 minutes, or until the rice is tender.

Meanwhile, peel and slice the shallots and sauté in the remaining *ghee* until crisp and brown. Slice the cucumber and tomatoes. Remove the seeds from the sweet pepper and slice the flesh. Stir the rice and chicken mixture and transfer it to a heated serving dish. Garnish with the cucumber, tomato, sweet pepper and pineapple. Sprinkle with the shallots and serve immediately.

TANDOORI CHICKEN

Serves 4

2 chickens, about 2½ lb each	1 teaspoon cumin
1 medium-sized onion	1 teaspoon chili powder
6 cloves garlic	1 teaspoon coriander
1 piece fresh ginger root, about	1–1½ teaspoons salt
1 inch long, or	⅓ cup lime or lemon juice
¼ teaspoon ground ginger	1 teaspoon *garam-masala*
½ cup unflavored yogurt or	melted *ghee* (see recipe)
curds (see *Samosas*, page 290)	

Skin the chickens and prick all over with the point of a knife. Peel and chop the onion, garlic and ginger and press through a sieve. Add the yogurt, cumin, chili powder, coriander and salt and blend to a thin paste. Spread this mixture over the chickens and set aside to macerate for 5–6 hours, then sprinkle with the lime juice and half the *garam-masala* and set aside for 1 hour.

Cook the chickens for 1–1½ hours, or until tender (see note). If roasting, the oven should be moderately hot (400°). Baste the chickens occasionally with melted *ghee* during the cooking.

When the chickens are cooked, remove from the oven, pour 1 teaspoon melted *ghee* over each one and set alight. Once the flames are extinguished, sprinkle with the remaining *garam-masala* and transfer to a heated serving dish. Serve with a green salad, onion salad (see page 293) and lemon wedges.

Note: This famous dish takes its name from *tandour*, the utensil in which it is cooked. Ideally this should be a clay oven, thus permitting heat to be applied from both below and above. The best Western alternatives are the barbecue and the spit rotisserie, but the chicken may also be roasted.

DUCK VINDALOO

Serves 4

1 duck, about 5 lb (see note)	3 tablespoons *vindaloo* paste
2 medium-sized onions	(see recipe below)
3 cloves garlic	3 tablespoons lime or lemon juice
¼ cup butter	⅔ cup water
	salt

Divide the duck into 8 pieces. Peel and chop the onions and garlic. Heat the butter in a saucepan and sauté the onion and garlic until soft but not browned. Add the *vindaloo* paste and lime juice. Simmer very gently for 5 minutes.

Place the pieces of duck in the saucepan. Add the water and salt. Cover tightly and simmer for 45–50 minutes, or until the duck is tender. If necessary, add a little extra water during cooking to prevent the mixture from sticking or burning. Adjust the seasoning and arrange the duck in a heated serving dish. Serve hot with rice.

Note: Pork or goose may be substituted for the duck.

VINDALOO PASTE

1–2 cloves garlic	1½ teaspoons coriander
6 red chilies (see note)	1 teaspoon cumin
½ teaspoon chopped green	¼ teaspoon turmeric
ginger root	

Peel and chop the garlic. Remove the seeds from the chilies and chop the flesh finely. Place the garlic and chilies in a mortar with the ginger, coriander, cumin and turmeric. Pound until reduced to a smooth paste. Alternatively, this may be done in a blender.

Store in an airtight container and use as required.

Note: The amount of chilies in this recipe may be increased or decreased, according to how hot the curry is preferred.

ONION SAMBOL

Serves 4

2 large onions
3 tablespoons *ghee* or peanut oil
1–2 teaspoons fresh shrimp paste
1 teaspoon chili powder
¼–½ teaspoon turmeric

1 teaspoon salt
3–4 curry leaves
dash cinnamon
3 tablespoons lime or lemon juice

Peel the onions and cut lengthwise into very thin slices. Heat the *ghee* in a skillet and sauté the onions for 5 minutes, or until slightly softened. Add the shrimp paste, chili powder, turmeric, salt, curry leaves and cinnamon and sauté for 3–4 minutes. Sprinkle with the lime juice. Transfer to a heated serving dish and serve as an accompaniment to rice, as a side dish to curries or as a filling for *bouchées, vol-au-vents* or stuffed vegetables such as green sweet peppers.

CUCUMBER SAMBOL

Serves 4

2 cucumbers
1 tablespoon salt
3 scallions
1 green sweet pepper

3 tablespoons shrimp powder
3 tablespoons lime or lemon juice
¼ cup coconut cream or
    unflavored yogurt

Peel the cucumbers and cut in half lengthwise. Remove the seeds. Cut into thin slices and then into very fine strips; or grate coarsely. Place on a dry cloth, sprinkle with salt and set aside for 30 minutes. Trim and chop the scallions. Remove the seeds from the sweet pepper and cut the flesh into thin strips.

Wrap the cloth around the cucumber and squeeze lightly to remove the excess liquid. Place it in a bowl and add the scallions, green pepper and shrimp powder. Mix lightly. Add more salt, if necessary, and sprinkle with the lime juice. Just before serving dress with the coconut cream or yogurt. Serve as an accompaniment to a hot curry.

Cucumber sambol

EGGPLANT RELISH

Makes 2 cups

2 large eggplants	1 tablespoon coriander seeds
salt (see recipe)	12 dried red chilies
¼ teaspoon turmeric	1 teaspoon mustard seeds
1 bulb garlic	1 teaspoon cumin
4 oz shallots	¼ cup vinegar
12 green chilies	2 teaspoons shrimp powder
3 tablespoons oil	1 teaspoon sugar

Cut off the stems and rinse the eggplants under cold running water. Cut into ½-inch slices and arrange on a large plate in a single layer. Sprinkle liberally with salt and set aside for about 30 minutes to extract the juices. Drain and dry the eggplant slices and sprinkle with turmeric.

Meanwhile, peel the garlic and shallots. Remove the seeds from the green chilies and slice the flesh. Heat the oil in a skillet and sauté the eggplant slices for 2 minutes on either side without browning. Add the green chilies, shallots and garlic and sauté for 3 minutes. Lower the heat to a minimum and cook for 10 minutes.

Meanwhile, place the coriander seeds, red chilies, mustard seeds and cumin in a mortar. Pound to a paste. Stir this paste into the eggplant mixture with the vinegar and shrimp powder. Cook for 15 minutes. Add the sugar and adjust the seasoning, if necessary. Set aside to cool. Pour into preserving jars, cover tightly and store until required.

CHAPATTIES (UNLEAVENED INDIAN PANCAKES)

Makes 16

2½ cups whole-wheat flour	¾ cup warm water
1 teaspoon salt	3 tablespoons slightly
¼ cup vegetable oil	warmed *ghee*

Sift the flour and salt into a bowl. Make a well in the center and add the oil and water. Mix to a fairly stiff dough and knead well. Wrap in a slightly dampened cloth and set aside for 1 hour.

Knead the dough and divide into 16 portions. Knead each portion lightly on a floured surface; then roll out to a round about 5 inches in diameter. Pat the *chapatties* between the hands to make them thin.

Heat a griddle, or a heavy skillet, over moderate heat and brush very lightly with *ghee*. Cook the *chapatties* for 1 minute on each side, or until very pale brown (overcooking will toughen them). Brush the griddle or skillet with more *ghee* when necessary. Serve hot with curries.

EGGPLANT FOOGATH

Serves 6

4 large eggplants	¼ cup *ghee* or
salt	vegetable oil
3 medium-sized onions	1 tablespoon *garam-masala*
2 cloves garlic	⅔ cup coconut milk
1–2 dried chilies (optional)	dash dry mustard
2 green sweet peppers	

Cut off the stems and rinse the eggplants under cold running water. Cut into 1-inch thick slices, then cut each slice into quarters. Place on a large, flat plate and sprinkle liberally with salt. Set aside for 15 minutes, or until the bitter juices of the eggplants have been extracted.

Peel and thinly slice the onions. Peel and chop the garlic. Remove the seeds of the chilies and pound the flesh. Remove the seeds of the green sweet peppers and dice the flesh. Heat the *ghee* in a skillet and sauté the onion and garlic until soft but not browned. Stir in the *garam-masala*. Drain the eggplants thoroughly and add to the cooked onion and garlic. Sauté for 1 minute, stirring gently. Add the chilies, sweet peppers, coconut milk and mustard. Cover and simmer for 30 minutes. Do not let the mixture boil. Add more salt, if necessary, and serve hot.

Note: Foogaths are curried vegetable dishes, usually fried with spices and often cooked with fresh shredded coconut. These dishes are acceptable to all Indian communities irrespective of religious taboos. They may be served independently or as accompaniments to other curry dishes.

PARATHAS (FLAKY INDIAN PANCAKES)

Makes 10

2 cups whole-wheat flour	⅔ cup warm water
½ teaspoon salt	½ cup *ghee*

Sift the flour and salt into a bowl. Make a well in the center and add the water. Mix to a fairly stiff dough and knead well. Wrap in a slightly dampened cloth and set aside for 1 hour.

Knead the dough and divide into 10 portions. Knead each portion on a lightly floured board and roll into a 5-inch round. Spread the *paratha* thinly with *ghee*. Fold into quarters, roll out again, and repeat the process once more.

Heat a griddle, or a heavy skillet, over moderate heat and brush well with *ghee*. Cook the parathas for 2 minutes, brush with *ghee* and turn over. Cook for a further 2 minutes, or until golden brown on both sides. Serve very hot.

Parathas may also be stuffed with *dahl* or a lightly curried vegetable. The filling is placed in the center of a rolled out circle of dough. This is folded to enclose the filling and carefully flattened out into a circle.

Eggplant relish

COCONUT ICE CREAM

Serves 6

2½ cups coconut cream   ½ cup vanilla sugar (see note)
3 eggs   ½ cup cashew nuts

Heat the coconut cream in a heavy saucepan over low heat, but do not allow it to boil. Beat the eggs and sugar until frothy and stir into the coconut cream. Remove from the heat and set aside to cool. Stir in the cashew nuts and pour into a shallow container. Place in the freezing compartment of the refrigerator until half frozen. Beat well, then return to the freezing compartment until frozen. Serve alone, or with fruit.

Note: If vanilla sugar is not available use ½ cup granulated sugar and ½ teaspoon vanilla extract.

MANGO ICE CREAM

Serves 6–8

3 egg yolks   ½ cup sugar
1½ cups milk   8 oz fresh or canned mangoes
1 teaspoon vanilla extract   1¼ cups whipped cream
¼ teaspoon salt

Blend the egg yolks with ⅓ cup of the milk. Pour the remaining milk into a saucepan and add the vanilla extract, salt and sugar. Heat gently until the sugar has dissolved, then stir into the egg yolks. Pour into the top of a double boiler, or into a bowl placed over hot water. Heat gently, stirring constantly, until the mixture is thick enough to coat the back of the spoon. Remove from the heat and stir until cool. Strain into a bowl and place in the freezing compartment of a refrigerator until thick but not completely frozen.

Peel and slice the fresh mangoes or thoroughly drain the canned mangoes and fold into the semi-solid ice cream. Chill well and serve with the whipped cream.

RICE DESSERT WITH CANDIED FRUITS AND NUTS

Serves 6

2½ cups milk   ⅓ cup shredded fresh coconut
6 tablespoons short-grain rice   ½ teaspoon orange flower water
3 tablespoons sugar   ¼ cup chopped candied fruit
¼ teaspoon salt   (cherries, apricots, pears,
¼ teaspoon cinnamon   greengages)
⅓ cup chopped, blanched   coconut cream or *gula-malacca*
   pistachio nuts   syrup (see page 306)
¾ cup finely ground almonds

Pour the milk into a saucepan and add the rice, sugar, salt and cinnamon. Bring to the simmering point over moderate heat and simmer for 7–8 minutes. Add the pistachio nuts, ground almonds, coconut, orange flower water and candied fruit. Mix well, cover and cook very gently until the rice is soft and the milk has been absorbed. Pour into a serving dish

and chill. Serve the rice with the coconut cream or *gula-malacca* syrup. For festive occasions decorate with gold and silver leaf, silver balls or silver sprinkles.

JALEBIS (DEEP-FRIED SWEETMEATS IN SYRUP)

Serves 4

for the batter :   **for the syrup :**
1½ cups all-purpose flour   1¼ cups water
¾ tablespoon baking powder   2¼ cups sugar
1 cup water   1 teaspoon *jalebi* powder
¼ cup unflavored yogurt or   few drops rose water
   curds (see *Samosas*, page 290)   *ghee* or oil for deep-frying

Sift the flour and baking powder into a bowl and make a well in the center. Gradually stir in the water and yogurt to form a batter. Set aside overnight in a warm place to ferment.

To make the syrup, pour the water into a small heavy saucepan and add the sugar. Heat gently until the sugar has dissolved. Add the *jalebi* powder and rose water. Simmer the syrup until it thickens. Keep warm.

Beat the batter well. Heat the oil. Pour the batter through a funnel into the hot oil to form rings about 3 inches in diameter. Fry the *jalebis* a few at a time to prevent them from sticking to each other. When crisp and golden brown, remove from the hot oil and drain well on absorbent paper.

Place the *jalebis* in the hot syrup and set aside for 15 minutes. Drain and arrange in a heated shallow serving dish. Serve freshly made.

CASHEW CANDY

Serves 4

2½ cups milk   1 cup cashew nuts
1½ cups sugar   2 tablespoons butter

Heat the milk in a saucepan until boiling. Add the sugar. Lower the heat and simmer very gently until the liquid becomes thick and syrupy. Add the cashew nuts, then stir in the butter, a little at a time. Continue simmering until a candy thermometer registers a temperature of 230–240°. If a candy thermometer is not available, drop a little of the mixture into cold water; when the correct temperature has been reached it should mold into a soft ball. Remove from the heat and beat until thick. Pour into a 7-inch square pan and cool slightly.

While still warm, divide into small squares or diamond shapes and set aside until cold. Store wrapped in waxed paper and serve as required.

Burma, Thailand, Malaysia and Singapore, Indonesia

FRESH GINGER AND NUTS

Serves 4–6

6 oz fresh ginger root	¾ cup cashew nuts
½ teaspoon salt	¾ cup peanuts
¼ cup lime or lemon juice	1 cup shrimp powder
¼ cup white sesame seeds	1⅓ cups roasted shredded
dash sugar	coconut

Peel and finely shred the ginger. Sprinkle with salt and set aside for 10 minutes. Rinse well under cold running water and squeeze dry. Place in a bowl and cover with the lime juice–this turns the ginger pink. Set aside until required.

Heat the sesame seeds in a skillet until they begin to 'jump' and turn brown. Remove from the heat and cool. Drain the ginger and sprinkle with the sugar. Arrange the ginger, sesame seeds, cashew nuts, peanuts, shrimp powder and coconut in separate piles on a serving tray.

LETH-OH (BURMESE MIXED VEGETABLES)

Serves 4

8 oz green beans	2 medium-sized onions
6 scallions	1 lb spinach
4 oz okra	⅓ cup vegetable oil
4 oz bamboo shoots	salt and pepper
¼ cup sesame seeds	

Trim the beans and scallions and cut into 1-inch lengths. Pare the stems from the okra and slice the bamboo shoots. Cook the prepared vegetables separately in lightly salted boiling water for 5 minutes. Drain well and keep hot.

Meanwhile, heat the sesame seeds in an ungreased skillet until they begin to 'jump' and turn brown. Remove from the skillet and reserve. Peel and slice the onions. Rinse the spinach and dry well with absorbent paper. Heat half the oil in a skillet and sauté the onions until soft and lightly browned. remove from the skillet and keep hot.

Heat the remaining oil in the skillet. Add the scallions and spinach and sauté for 2–3 minutes. Arrange the beans, okra, bamboo shoots and spinach mixture on a heated serving dish. Season with salt and pepper, garnish with the onions and sesame seeds and serve hot as an appetizer or a luncheon dish.

Leth-oh (Burmese mixed vegetables)

Burmese fish soup

CHICKEN AND MUSHROOM SOUP

Serves 6

1 chicken, about 4 lb, with giblets	½ teaspoon chili powder
1 medium-sized onion	3 tablespoons chicken fat
5 pints water	2 teaspoons *nam pla*
6 oz button mushrooms	1 tablespoon *gula malacca*
2–3 cloves garlic	salt
1 teaspoon coriander	1 teaspoon soy sauce
	1 tablespoon chopped parsley

Rinse the chicken and giblets under cold running water. Peel the onion. Place the chicken and onion in a saucepan and add the water. Bring to a boil over high heat. Cover, lower the heat and simmer for 45 minutes–1 hour, or until the chicken is tender. Remove the chicken from the stock and set aside to cool. Strip the chicken flesh from the bones and return the bones to the stock. Continue to simmer the stock until reduced to half the quantity. Remove the bones.

Meanwhile, slice the chicken flesh and giblets. Rinse the mushrooms under cold running water and simmer in lightly salted boiling water for 2 minutes. Drain before using. Peel the garlic and pound to a paste with the coriander and chili powder.

Heat the chicken fat in a skillet. Add the pounded mixture and the *nam pla*. Fry for 3 minutes, stirring constantly. Add the chicken and sauté for 2 minutes. Transfer the chicken mixture to the stock. Add the *gula malacca* and salt to taste.

Bring to a boil and add the mushrooms and soy sauce. Simmer for 5 minutes. Pour into a heated soup tureen, sprinkle with chopped parsley and serve hot.

BURMESE FISH SOUP

Serves 4

1 lb mackerel or sea bass	2 tablespoons long-grain rice
2 tablespoons soy sauce	2 stalks celery
dash black pepper	4 oz white cabbage, finely shredded
1 onion	1 teaspoon *balachaung*
1 teaspoon salt	
2½ pints water	

Scale and clean the fish. Cut off and reserve the head. Bone the fish and reserve the bones. Rinse the fish under cold running water and dry with absorbent paper. Cut into 1½-inch pieces and place in a dish. Sprinkle with the soy sauce and pepper and set aside while preparing the stock. Peel the onion. Place in a saucepan with the fish head and bones, salt and water. Bring to a boil over moderate heat. Lower the heat and simmer, uncovered, for 50 minutes.

Rinse the rice well under cold running water. Strain the stock into a clean pan and bring to a boil. Add the rice and simmer for 12 minutes. Add the fish and reboil. Lower the heat and simmer for 5–6 minutes. Chop the celery. Add to the soup with the cabbage and *balachaung* and simmer for 5–6 minutes. Transfer to a heated soup tureen and serve.

LOBSTER IN COCONUT

Serves 4

4 fresh coconuts	6 tablespoons butter
2½ cups water	1 teaspoon salt
12 oz lobster meat	dash pepper
1 large onion	½ teaspoon flour
1 clove garlic	**for the flour and water paste :**
2 green sweet peppers	2 cups all-purpose flour
1 large tomato	⅔ cup water
1¼ cups coconut milk	rum for serving
(see recipe)	

Pierce the 'eyes' in each coconut and pour away the liquid. Saw the pierced end off each coconut and reserve to use as a lid. Remove the coconut flesh from each shell, without breaking the shell, and place in a large bowl. Add the water and set aside to soften for 2–3 hours.

Meanwhile, flake the lobster meat. Peel and chop the onion and garlic. Remove the seeds from the peppers and slice the flesh thinly. Peel and slice the tomato. Drain the soaked coconut, squeezing it well to extract as much thick milk as possible. Measure the required amount of milk. Shred, or coarsely grate, the coconut flesh.

Heat half the butter in a skillet and sauté the onion and garlic until soft. Add the lobster and peppers and sauté for a further 5 minutes. Add the tomato, salt, pepper and coconut milk. Cover and simmer for 20 minutes. Blend the remaining butter with the flour and stir into the lobster mixture. Simmer for 2–3 minutes, then remove from the heat.

Stand the coconut shells upright in a deep cake pan or casserole. Fill the coconut shells just over half full with the lobster mixture. Fill to the top with grated coconut. Place the lids on top. Blend the flour and water together to make a thick paste. Press enough paste over each coconut to cover the holes and seal the lid. Add sufficient water to the baking pan to come a fourth of the way up the height of the coconuts. Bake in a preheated cool oven (300°) for 1–1¼ hours. Spoon a little water over the sealed coconuts from time to time to prevent them from burning.

When ready, remove from the pan and dry with a cloth. Place in a serving dish. Remove the lids, pour a tablespoon of rum over each coconut, flambé and serve.

SPICED FISH FILLETS

Serves 4

1 lb mullet or herring fillets	½ teaspoon finely chopped chili (optional)
1 small piece tamarind	1 tablespoon soy sauce
2 medium-sized onions	3 tablespoons water
2 cloves garlic	1 teaspoon light brown sugar
⅓ cup peanut oil	3 tablespoons lime or lemon juice

Rinse the fish under cold running water and dry well with absorbent paper. Rub the fish with the tamarind. Peel and chop the onions and garlic. Heat the oil in a skillet and fry the fish for 2–3 minutes on each side, or until lightly browned. Reduce the heat and add the onions and garlic. Cook for 3–4 minutes. Add the chilies, if used, and fry lightly for 1 minute.

Mix together the soy sauce, water, sugar and lime juice and pour over the fish. Bring to a boil and cook for 3–4 seconds only. Transfer to a heated serving dish and serve hot.

FISH WITH RICE NOODLES IN SPICY COCONUT SAUCE

Serves 4

1 lb white-fleshed fish (cod, haddock, halibut)	3 cloves garlic
	4 large onions
⅔ cup Burmese fish sauce (see note)	⅔ cup peanut oil
	4¼ cups water
2 blades lemon grass, each 1 inch long, or ½ teaspoon dried lemon balm (see note)	1¼ cups coconut cream
	2–3 tablespoons rice flour (see note)
2 chilies	2–3 tablespoons *dhal* flour
¼ teaspoon turmeric	2 hard-cooked duck or hen eggs
1½ teaspoons chopped fresh ginger root	2 lb rice noodles

Clean the fish and wash thoroughly. Place in a saucepan. Add the Burmese fish sauce, one of the blades of lemon grass, one of the chilies, the turmeric and enough water to cover. Bring to a boil. Lower the heat and simmer for about 10 minutes, or until the fish is just cooked but still firm. Remove with a perforated spoon. Strain and reserve the stock. Remove and discard the fish skin and bones. Flake the fish into large pieces and set aside until required.

Peel and chop the ginger and garlic. Remove the seeds from the remaining chili. Place the ginger, garlic, chili and remaining blade of lemon grass in a mortar and pound to a paste. Peel and slice two of the onions. Peel and quarter the remaining onions and reserve. Heat the oil in a skillet and sauté the sliced onions until soft. Add the pounded ginger mixture and cook gently for 2–3 minutes, stirring constantly. Add the fish and cook for 2 minutes. Remove from the heat and set aside until required.

Add the water and coconut cream to the reserved fish stock and bring to a boil. Blend the rice flour and *dhal* flour with a little of the boiling stock to make a thin paste. Pour the paste into the stock and bring to a boil. Cook, stirring constantly, until a thick sauce is formed. Lower the heat, add the quartered onions and simmer for 20 minutes.

Shell the eggs and cut into quarters. Add to the *dhal* sauce with the fish mixture. Heat gently for 2–3 minutes.

Meanwhile, plunge the rice noodles into lightly salted boiling water and boil for 1 minute. Drain thoroughly and transfer to a heated dish. Pour the fish mixture into a heated deep serving dish and serve immediately with the noodles. The traditional accompaniments are fried onions, lime wedges and chili powder, served in separate dishes.

Note: Burmese fish sauce, lemon grass and rice flour can be obtained from oriental food shops.

CURRIED EGGS IN COCONUT SAUCE

Serves 4

4 eggs

for the sauce :

2 small onions

2 cloves garlic

1 piece fresh ginger root, about
  1 inch long

3 red chilies

3 tablespoons coconut oil

5–6 curry leaves or 1 tablespoon
  garam-masala

1½ teaspoons turmeric

1¼ cups coconut milk

6 tablespoons tamarind juice
  (see note) or ½ cup
  lemon juice

⅔ cup coconut cream

Boil the eggs for 10 minutes. Plunge into cold water, shell and set aside in warm water until required.

To make the sauce, peel and thinly slice the onions, garlic and ginger. Remove the seeds from the chilies. Heat the oil in a skillet and sauté the onions, garlic, chilies, ginger and curry leaves or *garam-masala* for 3 minutes. Add the turmeric and sauté for 1 minute. Lower the heat and gradually stir in the coconut milk. Simmer for 30 seconds and add the tamarind juice.

Drain the eggs and place in the sauce. Spoon the sauce over the eggs and heat gently for 4–5 minutes. The sauce should not be allowed to boil. Stir in the coconut cream and heat for 1 minute. Transfer to a heated serving dish and serve immediately.

Note: It is the tamarind juice that gives Malay curries their distinctive sour flavor.

NASI GORENG (INDONESIAN FRIED RICE)

Serves 4

1 cup long-grain rice

2 cups water

8 oz cooked meat or fish

2 oz dried shrimp

2 medium-sized onions

1 clove garlic

1 chili or ½ teaspoon chili
  powder

¾ cup peanut oil

3 eggs

salt and pepper

1 tablespoon vegetable oil

Rinse the rice in a sieve under cold running water. Place in a saucepan and add the water. Bring to a boil over moderate heat, then lower the heat and simmer for 10 minutes. Drain well. Spread on a large plate and set aside to dry.

Finely slice the meat or fish. Place the dried shrimp in a bowl with enough water to cover and soak for 10–15 minutes. Peel and chop the onions and garlic. Remove the seeds from the chili and chop the flesh. Heat the oil in a skillet and sauté the onions until soft but not browned. Add the garlic and sauté for 1 minute. Add the chili and sauté for 3 minutes. Add the meat or fish and sauté for 2 minutes. Drain the shrimp and add to the skillet with the rice. Sauté for 5–6 minutes, or until the rice is lightly browned.

Meanwhile, lightly beat the eggs with a dash of salt and pepper. Heat the vegetable oil in a large skillet. Add the beaten eggs and cook gently to make a thin omelet.

Season the rice mixture to taste and transfer to a heated serving plate. Cover with the omelet and serve immediately with *atjar* (Indonesian mixed vegetable pickle, see page 305).

Nasi goreng (Indonesian fried rice)

THAI NOODLES

1 lb Chinese rice noodles
   or fine egg noodles
1 medium-sized onion
4 cloves garlic
6 oz pork tenderloin or lean pork
   cut from the leg
8 oz boned chicken
4 oz crab meat
8 oz fresh or frozen raw
   shrimp, shelled and
   deveined
4 oz bean curd

4–5 oz bean sprouts
4 scallions
1¼ cups vegetable oil
1 tablespoon soy sauce
1 tablespoon vinegar
1 tablespoon *nam pla*
1 tablespoon sugar
salt
4 eggs
dash coriander
red chilies for garnishing
   (optional)

Break the noodles into 2½-inch pieces and drop into lightly salted boiling water. Simmer for 1 minute. Drain well and spread on a board. Set aside to dry for 30 minutes.

Peel and chop the onion and garlic. Thinly slice the pork and chicken. Flake the crab meat and chop the shrimp. Cut the bean curd into ½-inch cubes. Rinse the bean sprouts under cold running water and drain well. Trim and chop the scallions.

Heat three-fourths of the oil in a deep saucepan and fry the noodles, a few at a time, until crisp and golden brown. Drain on absorbent paper and set aside until required. Heat the remaining oil in a skillet and sauté the onion and garlic for 3–4 minutes. Add the pork and sauté for 8–10 minutes, stirring frequently. Add the chicken and cook for 3 minutes. Add the crab meat, shrimp and bean curd, and cook until the chicken and shrimp change color. Stir in the soy sauce, vinegar, *nam pla,* sugar and salt to taste. Beat the eggs and stir into the meat mixture. When the egg begins to set, add the bean sprouts and noodles and cook for about 5 minutes, stirring frequently. Transfer to a heated serving dish, sprinkle with the scallions and coriander and garnish with the chilies, if used. Serve immediately.

BEEF OR VEAL SATAY

Serves 4

1 tablespoon finely ground almonds
1 slice fresh ginger root
1 teaspoon coriander
1 teaspoon turmeric
1¼ cups coconut milk

1 lb beef round or
   veal tenderloin
salt and pepper
1 teaspoon light brown sugar

Place the almonds, ginger, coriander and turmeric in a mortar and pound to a paste. Gradually add the coconut milk. Cut the meat into 1-inch cubes. Place in a bowl and sprinkle with salt and pepper. Add the flavored coconut milk and set aside to marinate for 2 hours.

Drain the milk from the meat and reserve. Thread the meat on to 4 metal skewers and sprinkle with the sugar. Cook under a moderately hot broiler for 4–5 minutes, turning frequently and basting with the reserved coconut milk. Serve hot, on the skewers, with satay sauce (see following recipe).

SATAY SAUCE WITH OIL

Makes 1¼ cups

2 large onions
¾ cup roasted peanuts
½ teaspoon chili powder
3 tablespoons peanut oil
⅔ cup warm water

1 teaspoon light brown sugar
1 tablespoon soy sauce
2 tablespoons lime or lemon juice
½ teaspoon salt

Peel the onions. Thinly slice one onion and finely chop the other. Pound the chopped onion, peanuts and chili powder in a mortar.

Heat the oil in a skillet and sauté the sliced onion until soft but not browned. Add the pounded mixture and sauté for about 3 minutes, stirring constantly. Stir in the water and sugar and cook the mixture for 3 minutes. Add the soy sauce, lime juice and salt. Serve hot with satay dishes.

BURMESE MUTTON CURRY

Serves 4

1 lb lean mutton, cut
   from the leg
2 large onions
3 thin slices fresh ginger root
2 cloves garlic

½ teaspoon salt
¼ teaspoon turmeric
¼ teaspoon chili powder
¼ cup peanut oil
1 tablespoon soy sauce

Cut the mutton into 1-inch strips. Peel and finely chop the onions, ginger and garlic. Mix together in a bowl and sprinkle with the salt, turmeric and chili powder. Heat the oil in a skillet and fry the onion mixture for 2–3 minutes. Add the meat and sauté until lightly browned. Add the soy sauce and enough water just to cover the meat. Simmer for 25–30 minutes, or until the meat is tender. Serve hot with rice.

Note: Beef or pork may be substituted for the mutton, if preferred.

INDONESIAN BRAISED PORK

Serves 4

1 lb pork tenderloin or lean
   pork cut from the shoulder
1 medium-sized onion
1 clove garlic
3 tablespoons peanut oil

6 tablespoons soy sauce
3 tablespoons water
1 teaspoon lemon juice
1 teaspoon light brown sugar

Cut the pork into 1-inch cubes. Peel and chop the onion and garlic. Heat the oil in a skillet and sauté the meat until well browned. Add the onion and garlic and sauté for 3 minutes.

Mix together the soy sauce, water, lemon juice and sugar. Pour this mixture over the meat and simmer uncovered for 12–15 minutes. Transfer to a heated serving dish and serve hot.

PORK IN ORANGES

Serves 4

1 clove garlic	1 teaspoon *nam pla*
¼ cup peanuts	dash coriander
1 tablespoon peanut oil	¼ teaspoon chili powder
12 oz pork tenderloin or lean pork cut from the leg, ground	1 teaspoon salt
	4 large oranges

Peel and finely chop the garlic. Chop the peanuts. Heat the oil in a skillet and sauté the garlic for 1–2 minutes. Add the pork and sauté for 5 minutes, stirring frequently. Add the peanuts, *nam pla,* coriander, chili powder and salt. Reduce the heat and simmer for 10 minutes, stirring frequently.

Cut the oranges into quarters without cutting right through and open out to form a tulip shape. Place the oranges in a casserole and spoon the pork mixture into each one. Bake in a preheated moderate oven (350°) for 10–12 minutes. Serve hot with boiled rice.

COCONUT CHICKEN

Serves 4

2 chicken breasts	1 teaspoon grated lemon rind
1 small onion	dash sugar
1 clove garlic	dash salt
1 dried chili	¼ cup butter
¼ cup ground peanuts	1¼ cups coconut cream
½ teaspoon coriander	1½ teaspoons soy sauce

Remove and discard the skin from the chicken breasts and slice each breast horizontally into 2 thin pieces. Pound the slices lightly to flatten. Peel and chop the onion and garlic. Remove the seeds from the chili and chop the flesh. Place the onion, garlic, chili, peanuts, coriander, lemon rind, sugar and salt in a mortar and pound to a paste. Spread this mixture over the chicken slices.

Heat the butter in a skillet and fry the chicken for 2–3 minutes on each side. Reduce the heat, then add the coconut cream and soy sauce. Simmer for 25 minutes, or until the chicken is tender. Serve hot with boiled or fried rice.

Pork in oranges

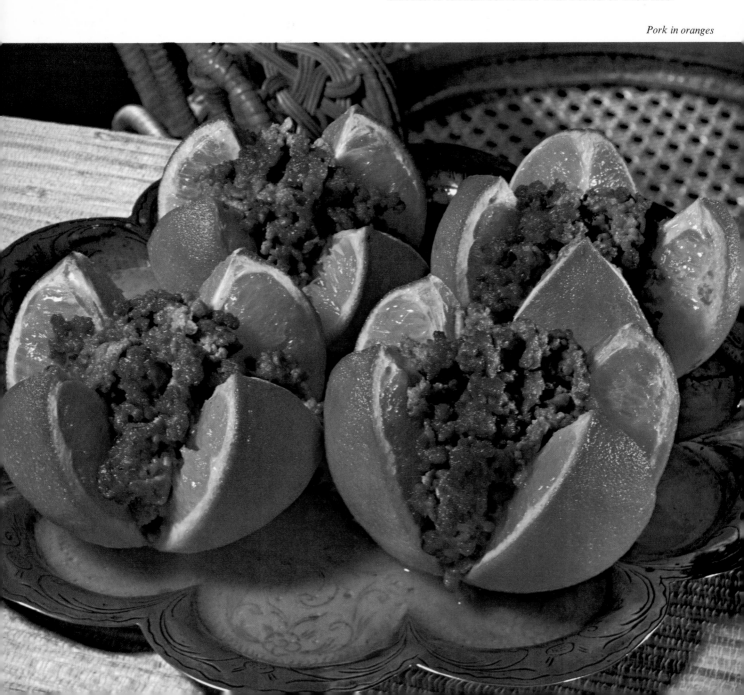

BURMESE COCONUT RICE

Serves 4

1 small onion	3¾ cups coconut milk
⅓ cup *ghee*	dash sugar
1 cup long-grain rice	dash salt

Peel and chop the onion. Heat the *ghee* in a saucepan and sauté the onion until soft but not browned. Add the rice and fry for 2 minutes, stirring constantly. Add the coconut milk, sugar and salt and bring to a boil. Lower the heat and simmer until all the milk has been absorbed and the rice is dry and fluffy. Serve hot as required.

SHRIMP SAMBAL

Serves 4

2 chilies	1 lb fresh or frozen raw
1 medium-sized onion	jumbo shrimp, shelled and
1 clove garlic	deveined
1 teaspoon crushed tamarind	½ teaspoon ginger
½ bay leaf	1 teaspoon sugar
3 tablespoons coconut oil	1¼ cups coconut milk

Remove the seeds from the chilies and chop the flesh. Peel and chop the onion and garlic. Place the chilies, onion, garlic, tamarind and bay leaf in a mortar and pound to a paste.

Heat the oil in a skillet and fry the pounded mixture for 3–4 minutes. Add the shrimp, ginger and sugar and sauté for 3–4 minutes. Add the coconut milk. Cook for a further 4–5 minutes, without boiling, until the mixture thickens. Pour into a heated serving dish and serve hot.

TOMATO SAMBAL

Serves 4

3 cloves garlic	¼ cup peanut oil
1 small onion	1½ teaspoons salt
1 small piece tamarind	1 tablespoon light brown sugar
2 red chilies	⅔ cup coconut milk
6 large tomatoes	3 tablespoons shrimp *sambal*
2 leeks	(see preceding recipe)

Peel and crush the garlic. Peel and chop the onion. Crush the tamarind. Remove the seeds from the chilies and shred the flesh. Peel and slice the tomatoes. Trim the leeks, rinse thoroughly under cold running water and slice thinly.

Heat the oil in a skillet and sauté the garlic, onion and tamarind for 3–4 minutes. Add the chilies and tomatoes and sauté for 2 minutes. Add the leeks and sauté for 2 minutes. Sprinkle with the salt and sugar, then gradually stir in the coconut milk and shrimp *sambal*. Simmer gently for 10 minutes and serve hot.

ATJAR (INDONESIAN VEGETABLE PICKLE)

Makes 3 pints

2 green sweet peppers	½ teaspoon chopped fresh
1 small carrot	ginger root
1 cucumber	5 cashew nuts or blanched almonds
4 oz green beans	1 teaspoon turmeric
8 oz shallots	2½ cups malt vinegar
2 cloves garlic	⅔ cup water
3 teaspoons salt	2 tablespoons light brown
	sugar

Trim the peppers, remove the seeds and shred the flesh. Peel and thinly slice the carrot and cucumber. String and slice the beans. Peel the shallots and garlic. Place the peppers, carrot, cucumber, beans, shallots and 2 teaspoons salt in a saucepan and add enough boiling water to cover. Bring to a boil over high heat. Boil for 5 minutes, then drain well.

Meanwhile, place the garlic, ginger, nuts and turmeric in a mortar and pound to a paste. Add the vinegar, water, sugar and remaining salt. Pour into a large heavy saucepan and bring to a boil. Add the vegetables and boil for 10 minutes. Remove from the heat and set aside to cool. Transfer to jars, seal tightly and use as required.

BURMESE CABBAGE SALAD

Serves 4

2 large onions	1 white cabbage, about 1 lb
2 cloves garlic	3–4 tablespoons sesame or peanut
2–3 thin slices fresh ginger root	oil

Peel the onions and slice into thin rings. Peel and chop the garlic. Chop the ginger. Remove the hard core and outer leaves from the cabbage. Wash and finely shred the rest.

Heat the oil in a skillet and sauté the onions and garlic until transparent. Add the ginger and sauté for 2 minutes. Add the cabbage and heat gently for 2 minutes, or until coated with the mixture. Serve hot or cold as required.

TOMATO FONDUE

Serves 4

6 large tomatoes	dash turmeric
2 oz dried shrimp	dash salt
4 medium-sized onions	¼ cup vegetable oil
2 cloves garlic	¼ cup water

Peel and quarter the tomatoes. Pound the shrimp to a powder in a mortar. Peel and slice the onions. Peel and chop the garlic. Place the tomatoes, shrimp, onions, garlic, turmeric, salt, oil and water in a saucepan. Heat very gently for about 45 minutes, or until the tomatoes and onions are very soft and the excess liquid has evaporated. Pour into a heated dish and serve as a relish with boiled rice or noodles.

Burmese coconut cake

BURMESE COCONUT CAKE

Serves 8

½ cup all-purpose flour	4 egg yolks
¾ cup semolina flour	1⅓ cups finely grated fresh coconut
dash salt	4 egg whites
1 teaspoon baking powder	**for decoration :**
½ cup butter	⅔ cup heavy cream
1 cup vanilla sugar	¼ cup shredded fresh coconut
(see note)	

Sift together the flour, semolina flour, salt and baking powder. Cream the butter and sugar in a bowl until soft and white. Add the egg yolks one at a time, beating well after each addition. Add the sifted ingredients and mix well. Stir in the grated coconut. Beat the egg whites until stiff and fold into the cake mixture. Divide the mixture between 2 greased 8-inch layer cake pans. Bake in a preheated moderate oven (350°) for 25 minutes, or until firm and golden brown. Turn out on to a wire tray and set aside to cool.

Whip the cream until thick and spread one of the cakes with it. Sprinkle with the coconut and place the second cake on top to make one deep cake. Alternatively, pipe half the cream and sprinkle half the coconut on each, and leave as 2 separate cakes.

Note: If vanilla sugar is not available add 1 teaspoon vanilla extract to 1 cup granulated sugar.

SAGO WITH COCONUT CREAM AND PALM SUGAR SYRUP

Serves 6

2½ cups water	**for the gula malacca syrup :**
1½ cups sago	⅓ cup *gula malacca* or soft
for the coconut cream sauce :	dark brown sugar
1¼ cups thick coconut milk	⅔ cup boiling water
dash salt	

Measure the water into a saucepan and bring to a boil. Add the sago and stir until the mixture forms a thick paste. Remove from the heat and pour into 6 individual molds rinsed out with cold water. Set aside to cool.

To make the sauces, gently heat the coconut milk. Add the salt and simmer until the mixture thickens. Remove from the heat, pour into a jug and set aside to cool.

For the second sauce, cut the palm sugar into pieces and place in a saucepan. Add the boiling water. Bring to a boil, stirring to dissolve the sugar. Simmer, stirring all the time, until the mixture thickens slightly. Remove from the heat and set aside to cool.

Unmold the sago desserts on to individual serving dishes. Pour a little of each sauce over them and serve.

CHRYSANTHEMUM SHRIMP WITH TEMPURA SAUCE

Serves 4

4 oz fresh or frozen cooked
   jumbo shrimp, shelled
   and deveined
2 egg whites
dash salt
1 tablespoon cornstarch
dash monosodium glutamate
½ oz *harusame* noodles

oil for deep-frying
for the tempura sauce :
1¼ cups *dashi*
   (see page 313)
⅓ cup soy sauce
⅓ cup *sake* or dry sherry
dash monosodium glutamate

Finely chop the shrimp, then pound in a mortar until reduced to a paste. Add the egg whites, salt, cornstarch and monosodium glutamate. Mix well. Shape the mixture into 8 patties. Cut the noodles into pieces about 2 inches long and press one side of each patty on to the noodles. The patties should retain their shape and pick up as many 'petals' as possible. Deep-fry the patties until golden brown. Drain on absorbent paper and keep hot.

To make the *tempura* sauce, place the *dashi,* soy sauce and *sake* in a saucepan. Bring to a boil over moderate heat. Season with monosodium glutamate to taste.

Arrange the chrysanthemum shrimp on a flat serving dish (a straw dish is ideal) and serve with the *tempura* sauce.

Note: The traditional garnish for this dish is edible chrysanthemum leaves.

CRAB WITH HAM AND WALNUTS

Serves 4

1 medium-sized onion
6 oz lean cooked ham
1 small piece fresh ginger root
¼ cup shelled walnuts
2 eggs
2 tablespoons vegetable oil
2 teaspoons cornstarch

⅓ cup cold water
3 tablespoons soy sauce
1 teaspoon salt
¼ teaspoon freshly ground white
   pepper
6 oz white crab meat

Peel and chop the onion. Grind the ham. Peel and chop the ginger. Chop the walnuts. Beat the eggs. Heat the oil in a skillet and sauté the onion and ham for 7–8 minutes. Blend the cornstarch with the water and soy sauce and stir into the ham mixture. Add the eggs, ginger, walnuts, salt and pepper. Cook gently for 5–6 minutes, stirring constantly. Add the crab meat and cook gently for 4–5 minutes, or until the crab is heated through. Pour into a heated serving dish and serve with boiled rice and a salad.

STUFFED PANCAKE ROLLS WITH SWEET SOY SAUCE

Serves 4–6

for the filling :
2 tablespoons chick peas
   (optional)
4 oz pork tenderloin or lean pork
   cut from the leg
2 slices cooked ham
1 clove garlic
1 medium-sized onion
2 oz fresh or frozen cooked
   jumbo shrimp, shelled
   and deveined
6 oz green beans
1 large carrot
12 oz cabbage
8 oz coconut palm heart
   (see note)
3 tablespoons vegetable oil

1 teaspoon salt
dash pepper
12 crisp lettuce leaves
for the pancake batter :
2 eggs (duck eggs, if available)
⅔ cup cornstarch
1¼ cups water
peanut oil
for the sauce :
¾ cup chicken stock
¼ cup sugar
3 tablespoons dark soy sauce
1 teaspoon salt
1 tablespoon cornstarch
¼ cup water
1–2 cloves garlic

To make the filling, soak the chick peas in cold water overnight. Simmer in lightly salted boiling water until tender and drain well. If using canned chick peas, drain well. Cut the pork into ½-inch cubes. Cut the ham into matchstick-thin strips. Peel and chop the garlic. Peel the onion and slice very thinly. Chop the shrimp. Trim the green beans and slice thinly. Peel and grate the carrot. Finely shred the cabbage. Drain and shred the coconut palm heart.

Place the pork in boiling water and simmer for 5 minutes. Drain well. Heat the oil in a skillet and sauté the garlic for 2–3 minutes. Add the pork and ham and sauté for 2 minutes. Add the shrimp and chick peas and sauté for 2 minutes. Add the beans, carrot, cabbage, coconut palm heart, salt and pepper. Cook gently for 6–8 minutes, or until the vegetables are tender but still firm and crisp. Remove from the heat, drain off any liquid and set aside to cool. Wash and dry the lettuce leaves.

To make the pancake batter, separate the egg yolks from the whites. Beat the egg whites until stiff. Add the yolks and beat lightly. Blend the cornstarch with the water and stir into the egg mixture to make a thin batter. Brush a 6-inch skillet lightly with oil. Add 3 tablespoons of the pancake batter and tilt the skillet until the mixture covers the bottom. As soon as the pancake is set, but not browned, remove from the skillet and keep warm. Continue until all the mixture has been used.

Divide the filling into 12 portions. Wrap each portion in a lettuce leaf and then in a pancake. Arrange on a wooden serving dish and keep hot.

To make the sauce, pour the stock into a saucepan. Add the sugar, soy sauce and salt and bring to a boil. Blend the cornstarch with the water and stir into the boiling stock. Simmer for 2–3 minutes, stirring constantly until the mixture thickens.

Pour the sauce into a heated bowl. Peel and chop the garlic and sprinkle on top. Serve the stuffed pancakes hot with the sauce.

Note: A combination of bean sprouts and scallions may be substituted for the coconut palm heart.

CHICKEN BUNDLES

Serves 6

6 oz boned chicken
1 tablespoon *shoyu*
1 tablespoon *sake* or
   dry sherry

½ sheet *nori* seaweed
1 beaten egg white
vegetable oil for frying

Remove and discard the skin of the chicken. Cut the chicken into strips about 2 inches long and ¼ inch thick. Place in a bowl and sprinkle with the *shoyu* and *sake*. Set aside to marinate for 1 hour.

Cut the seaweed into ½-inch strips and brush with egg white. Divide the chicken into bundles of 4 to 5 pieces and bind with the seaweed. Fry in shallow oil for 5-6 minutes, or until the chicken is tender and golden brown. Drain on absorbent paper and serve hot as an appetizer.

RICE BALL SHRIMP ZUSHI

Makes 24

4 teaspoons grated horseradish
4 teaspoons water
2 cups cooked *zushi* rice (see below)

24 fresh or frozen cooked jumbo
   shrimp, shelled and deveined

Pound the grated horseradish to a paste, then blend with the water. Take a spoonful of the rice and press gently to form a shape similar to a shrimp. Brush the top with a little of the horseradish mixture, then press a shrimp gently into the rice. Mold the rice to the exact shape of the shrimp. Place on a serving dish. Repeat until all the ingredients have been used.

RICE FOR ZUSHI

Makes about 4 cups

1 cup long-grain rice
1¼ cups water
1½ tablespoons vinegar

dash monosodium glutamate
1 teaspoon salt
1 teaspoon sugar

About 3 hours before cooking, rinse the rice thoroughly under cold running water and set aside to drain. Pour the water into a heavy saucepan and bring to a boil. Add the rice. Return to a boil, lower the heat and simmer for 10 minutes, or until the water has been completely absorbed and the rice is cooked but still firm. Transfer to a shallow dish and set aside to cool. Divide the rice in half. Mix one half with the vinegar, monosodium glutamate and three-fourths of the salt, and the other half with the sugar and remaining salt. Serve the two mixtures separately or together, depending how sweet or sharp you like your *zushi*.

Sashimi (raw fish hors d'oeuvre)

SEA BREAM SASHIMI

Serves 4

1 lb sea bream or porgy	⅓ cup *shoyu*
2 teaspoons grated horseradish	1 bunch watercress

Sashimi is a famous Japanese specialty, justly considered an exquisite delicacy and completely free of any 'fishy' taste or smell. It usually consists of slices of raw fish but chicken can also be used. To render it more digestible, and to add flavor, it is usually served with grated *wasabi* (Japanese horseradish) and invariably with *shoyu*. Garnish and presentation are of great importance.

Scale and clean the fish and cut off and discard the head, tail and fins. Rinse well under cold running water, then soak in cold water for 30 minutes. Blend the horseradish with the *shoyu*. Fillet the fish (see Planked Lake Superior Whitefish, page 14) and remove the skin. Cut the fillets obliquely into 1½-inch wide slices. Place the slices, slightly overlapping each other, on a long narrow dish (see note). Garnish with watercress and serve with the horseradish mixture.

Note: If possible the fish should be arranged in the shape of a whole fish. The watercress garnish should give the impression of the fish seen through a growth of seaweed. For a variation of this recipe make fresh tuna fish *sashimi*, using parsley for 'seaweed'. Serve with a dressing made of 2 teaspoons freshly grated ginger and ⅓ cup *shoyu*.

SOLE IN CHRYSANTHEMUM WREATHS

Serves 6

6 sole fillets	1 tablespoon distilled malt vinegar
¼ cup soy sauce	dash sugar
1 cucumber	6 tablespoons *mirin* or sweet
salt	white wine
1 tablespoon *sake* or	1 red sweet pepper
dry sherry	

Rinse the fish fillets under cold running water and pat dry with absorbent paper. Place in a shallow dish and add the soy sauce. Set aside to marinate for 3 hours.

Peel the cucumber and cut lengthwise into slices about ¼ inch thick. Cut the long cucumber slices on one side at brief intervals without cutting right through. At this stage each strip looks rather like a comb. Sprinkle with salt and leave to soften for 10–15 minutes, then moisten with the *sake* and vinegar and sprinkle with the sugar. Set aside for 1 hour.

Drain the fish fillets, reserving the soy sauce. Sprinkle with salt on both sides and thread them on to 6 skewers. Mix the reserved soy sauce with the *mirin* and dip the skewered fish in the mixture. Broil under a preheated hot broiler for 5–10 minutes, dipping the fish in the sauce 2 or 3 times during the broiling. Arrange the fillets on a serving dish. Roll up the cucumber strips and arrange cut side up on the fish. Using a chopstick or similar implement, open out the petals of each cucumber 'flower'. Cut small discs of sweet pepper and put one in the center of each 'flower'. Decorate the dish with chrysanthemum flowers.

Beef sukiyaki

BEEF SUKIYAKI

Serves 4

1 lb beef round	8 oz spinach
1¼ cups *dashi* (see page 313)	1 head crisp lettuce
⅔ cup *shoyu*	1 lb bean curd
3 tablespoons *sake* or	16 button mushrooms
dry sherry	1 tablespoon lard or suet
6 tablespoons sugar	4 eggs
2 small onions	

Sukiyaki is an excellent dish for a party because it offers the hostess an opportunity to serve a delicious, festive-looking meal with very little cooking. All the cooking, in fact, is done in batches at the table in front of the guests.

Cut the meat across the grain into slices about 5 inches by 1½ inches by ⅛ inch. Mix together the *dashi, shoyu, sake* and sugar. Peel and quarter the onions. Rinse the spinach and lettuce under cold running water and dry well. Shred the lettuce by hand, not with a knife, into fairly thick strips. Cut the bean curd into squares about 1 inch by 1 inch by ¼ inch. Cut off the mushroom stems, rinse the mushrooms under cold running water and drain. Arrange the vegetables and meat attractively on a large plate in separate groups and place on the dining table.

Melt half the lard or suet in a large heavy chafing dish over moderate heat. Add half the strips of meat and brown lightly on both sides. Place the meat to one side of the dish and moisten with 3–4 tablespoons of the *dashi* mixture. Add half the onions, spinach, lettuce, bean curd and mushrooms to the dish, but keep separate. Cook gently for 3–4 minutes, turning all the ingredients carefully to avoid mixing them. Moisten and season with the *dashi* mixture to taste. Serve immediately. Cook the remaining ingredients in exactly the same way.

The *sukiyaki* is accompanied by rice and raw egg, both served in individual bowls. Each diner helps himself to an ingredient and dips it into the beaten egg which cools it and serves as a dressing.

Note: To make chicken *sukiyaki,* substitute chicken for the beef and use chicken fat for greasing the chafing dish.

KOREAN FIERY MEAT WITH SESAME SEED DIP

Serves 4

	for the dip :
12 oz beef tenderloin	3 tablespoons sesame seeds
4 shallots	¼ teaspoon salt
1 clove garlic	1 clove garlic
1 leek	3 scallions
5 scallions	¼ teaspoon sugar
¼ teaspoon sugar	1 teaspoon *mien chiang*
½ teaspoon salt	¼ teaspoon cayenne pepper
⅓ cup light soy sauce	⅓ cup light soy sauce
1 tablespoon sesame oil	3 tablespoons vinegar
dash chili powder or 3–4 drops Tabasco	
⅔ cup peanut oil	

Cut the meat into thin slices about 3 inches by 1 inch by ¼ inch. Pound lightly to flatten and place on a plate.

Peel and chop the shallots and garlic. Trim the leek and scallions and rinse thoroughly under cold running water. Drain well and chop finely. Mix together the shallots, garlic, leek, scallions, sugar, salt, soy sauce, sesame oil and chili powder or Tabasco and pour over the meat. Mix well and set aside for 3–4 hours.

To make the dip, heat the sesame seeds in an ungreased skillet until they begin to 'jump' and turn brown, then pound with the salt in a mortar. Peel and chop the garlic. Trim and chop the scallions. Mix together the sesame seed mixture, garlic, scallions, sugar, *mien chiang,* cayenne pepper, soy sauce and vinegar.

Heat the peanut oil in a saucepan until hot. Dip the slices of meat into the oil for a few seconds, then drain on absorbent paper. Dip each slice into sesame seed dip and serve immediately with the remaining sesame seed dip, or vinegar and soy sauce dip (see page 313).

KOREAN STEAMED DUMPLINGS

Serves 6

for the filling :	
1 lb boned chicken	dash monosodium glutamate
6 oz bean sprouts	dash freshly ground black pepper
6 cubes bean curd	1 tablespoon light soy sauce
2–3 oz fresh or frozen cooked shrimp, shelled and deveined	1 tablespoon sesame oil
	for the dough :
2 tablespoons lard	2 cups all-purpose flour
dash chili powder	¾ cup boiling water

Grind the chicken. Rinse the bean sprouts under cold running water, then place in a saucepan with just enough water to cover. Bring to a boil and cook for 2 minutes. Drain well and chop finely. Simmer the bean curd in a little water for 2 minutes. Drain well and cut into ½-inch cubes. Finely chop the shrimp.

Heat the lard in a skillet and sauté the chicken, bean sprouts and bean curd for 5 minutes, or until the mixture begins to change color. Add the shrimp, chili powder, monosodium glutamate, pepper, soy sauce and sesame oil. Cook for 1 minute. Remove from the heat and set aside until required.

To make the dough, sift the flour into a bowl, Add the water, a little at a time, and mix to a soft dough. Knead well on a lightly floured surface. Divide the dough into 24 pieces and roll each piece into a 3-inch round. Gently press out a hollow in the center of each.

Place a teaspoonful of the prepared filling in each hollow and moisten the edges of the dough with water. Fold in half to form a semi-circular dumpling. Steam the dumplings for 10 minutes. Serve hot with sesame seed dip (see Korean Fiery Meat With Sesame Seed Dip, above) or vinegar and soy sauce dip (see page 313).

311

CHICKEN WITH SPICED PINEAPPLE SAUCE

Serves 4

4 Cornish hens, about 1 lb each	¾ cup chicken stock
5 pints water	(see recipe)
¼ cup finely chopped fresh	oil for deep-frying
ginger root	½ cup peanut butter
2 teaspoons sugar	1 teaspoon Worcestershire sauce
2½ pints pineapple juice	few drops Tabasco
1 tablespoon salt	salt

Rinse the Cornish hens under cold running water and dry with absorbent paper. Truss with fine string. Pour the water into a large saucepan and add the ginger, sugar, pineapple juice and salt. Bring to a boil and add the hens. Simmer for 10–15 minutes, or until tender. Remove the hens with a perforated spoon and set aside to drain and cool. Measure and reserve the required amount of stock. Deep-fry the hens in the oil for 4–5 minutes, or until crisp and golden brown. Drain on absorbent paper and keep hot.

Heat the peanut butter in a saucepan. Add the chicken stock. Worcestershire sauce, Tabasco and salt to taste. Heat until simmering. Pour into a small bowl and serve as a dip with the Cornish hens.

YAKITORI (BROILED CHICKEN ON SKEWERS)

Serves 4

6 oz boned chicken	2 tablespoons sugar
4 oz chicken giblets	1 cup grated Japanese radish or red
2 medium-sized onions	radishes
1 large sweet potato	1 teaspoon ground ginger
3 tablespoons *shoyu*	dash freshly ground white pepper
3 tablespoons *sake* or dry sherry	

Cut the chicken and giblets into 1-inch cubes. Peel and thickly slice the onions and sweet potato. Thread the chicken, giblets, onion and sweet potato on to 4 bamboo or metal skewers.

Mix together the *shoyu, sake* and sugar. Brush this mixture over the skewered ingredients. Place the skewers over a charcoal brazier or under a hot broiler and cook until golden brown, brushing frequently with the remaining *shoyu* mixture during cooking. Mix together the radish, ginger and pepper.

Serve the *yakitori* accompanied by the radish mixture as a dip.

Yakitori (broiled chicken on skewers)

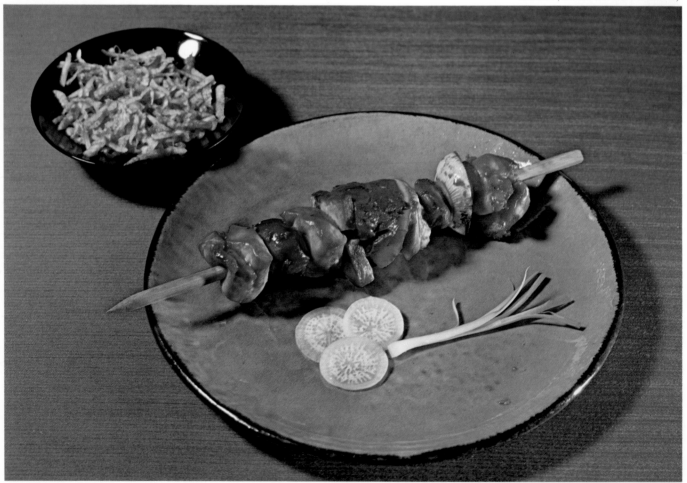

312

SPICED PORK AND CHICKEN

Serves 6

1 chicken, about 3 lb
1 lb pork tenderloin or lean pork
   cut from the leg
3 cloves garlic
3 small bay leaves
6 tablespoons vinegar

1 tablespoon salt
¼ teaspoon freshly ground white
   pepper
3 tablespoons melted butter or oil
1¼ cups coconut cream

Chop the chicken flesh into 2½-inch pieces. Cut the pork into 1-inch cubes. Peel and finely chop the garlic. Place the chicken, pork, garlic, bay leaves, vinegar, salt and pepper in a flameproof casserole. Set aside for about 15 minutes, stirring frequently to coat the meat with the seasonings.

Add enough boiling water just to cover the meat and bring to a boil over moderate heat. Lower the heat, partly cover and simmer until the meat is almost tender and the liquid has evaporated. Add the butter or oil and continue cooking until the meat is evenly browned and tender.

Heat the coconut cream gently and stir into the meat. Pour into a heated serving dish and serve with plain boiled rice.

ROAST SUCKLING PIG

Serves 8

1 suckling pig, including
   the liver
salt and pepper
12 tamarind leaves or 6 thin,
   unpeeled lemon slices
½ cup melted lard

1¼ cups boiling water
5–6 cloves garlic
3 medium-sized onions
¼ cup lime or lemon juice
2–3 tablespoons sugar

Have the suckling pig ready for roasting with the head on. Reserve the liver, which is to be used for the sauce. Rub the inside of the pig with a mixture of salt and pepper. Put the tamarind leaves or lemon slices inside and brush the outside of the pig with 3–4 tablespoons of the melted lard. Protect the ears with oiled foil or waxed paper and roast in a preheated moderately hot oven (375°) for 2–2½ hours. Baste frequently with the meat juices. Meanwhile, slice the liver and brown lightly in 1 tablespoon of the remaining lard. Drain, then chop or grind. Add the water and rub the mixture through a fine sieve, or reduce to a purée in a blender. Keep hot in a bowl over simmering water.

Peel and finely chop the garlic, and peel and slice the onions. Heat the remaining lard in a saucepan. Add the garlic and fry for a few moments to brown. Remove the garlic and reserve. Add the onions to the hot fat remaining in the pan and fry gently until soft but not brown. Add the liver purée and stir to blend. Sprinkle with the lime juice, season to taste and add the sugar. Simmer for 10 minutes over low heat, stirring frequently. Pour the sauce into a heated sauceboat and sprinkle with the reserved garlic. Serve with the roast suckling pig.

VINEGAR AND SOY SAUCE DIP

Serves 6

½ cup vinegar
2 tablespoons sugar
½ cup soy sauce

1–2 tablespoons chopped pine
   nuts

Heat the vinegar and sugar gently until the sugar has dissolved. Add the soy sauce and pour the mixture into 6 small individual dishes. Sprinkle some chopped pine nuts into each dish. Serve with Korean steamed dumplings (see page 311) or as an accompaniment to broiled and fried foods.

DASHI (JAPANESE STOCK)

Makes 5 cups

¼ oz *konbu* seaweed (see note)
2½ pints water
1½ oz *katsuobushi* (see note)

¼ teaspoon monosodium
   glutamate

Put the *konbu* seaweed in a saucepan with the water. Place over moderate heat and bring to a boil. Remove from the heat and add the *katsuobushi*. Return to the heat and bring just to a boil. Remove from the heat immediately. Add the monosodium glutamate and set aside for 10 minutes. Strain and use as required.

Note: Dashi is the foundation of Japanese cooking. Both *konbu* seaweed and *katsuobushi* (dried bonito shavings) are available from Japanese food shops.

KEEM CHEE (KOREAN PICKLES)

Makes 3 pints

2 lb small cucumbers
   (see note)
3 tablespoons salt
6 scallions
3 cloves garlic
1 tablespoon chopped fresh
   ginger root

1 teaspoon Korean red pepper or
   chili powder
1 tablespoon light soy sauce
1 teaspoon monosodium
   glutamate
1¼ cups water

Scrub the cucumbers gently under cold running water and drain well. Cut in half lengthwise, then into ½-inch pieces. Place on a tray or a large plate and sprinkle with half the salt. Set aside for 30 minutes.

Trim and chop the scallions. Peel and chop the garlic. Rinse the cucumber under cold running water, drain well and place in a bowl. Sprinkle the cucumber with the scallions, garlic, ginger, red pepper, remaining salt, soy sauce and monosodium glutamate. Add the water and mix well. Cover tightly and set aside for 4–5 days. Chill well and serve as required.

Note: The cucumbers may be replaced by cabbage, baby turnips, carrots or other vegetables.

INDEX

319